WriteNow

Second Edition

Karin Russell
Keiser University

McGraw Hill Education

WRITE NOW: ANNOTATED INSTRUCTOR'S EDITION, SECOND EDITION

Published by McGraw-Hill Education, 2 Penn Plaza, New York, NY 10121. Copyright 2016 by McGraw-Hill Education. All rights reserved. Printed in the United States of America. Previous editions © 2012. No part of this publication may be reproduced or distributed in any form or by any means, or stored in a database or retrieval system, without the prior written consent of McGraw-Hill Education, including, but not limited to, in any network or other electronic storage or transmission, or broadcast for distance learning.

Some ancillaries, including electronic and print components, may not be available to customers outside the United States.

This book is printed on acid-free paper.

1 2 3 4 5 6 7 8 9 0 RMN/RMN 1 0 9 8 7 6 5

ISBN 978-0-07-339713-9
MHID 0-07-339713-X

Senior Vice President, Products & Markets: *Kurt L. Strand*
Vice President, General Manager, Products & Markets: *Michael Ryan*
Vice President, Content Design & Delivery: *Kimberly Meriwether David*
Managing Director: *David Patterson*
Director: *Susan Gouijnstook*
Senior Brand Manager: *Nancy Huebner*
Executive Brand Manager: *Claire Brantley*
Director, Product Development: *Meghan Campbell*
Senior Product Developer: *Carla Samodulski*
Executive Market Development Manager: *Nanette Giles*
Marketing Manager: *Brigeth Rivera*
Director of Development: *Lisa Pinto*
Senior Digital Product Developer: *Scott Harris*
Director, Content Design & Delivery: *Terri Schiesl*
Program Manager: *Jennifer Gehl*
Content Project Manager: *Mary E. Powers*
Buyer: *Susan K. Culbertson*
Design: *Debra Kubiak*
Content Licensing Specialists: *John Leland, Ann Marie Jannette*
Cover Image: *Cadence Design Studio*
Compositor: *Laserwords Private Limited*
Printer: *R. R. Donnelley*

All credits appearing on page or at the end of the book are considered to be an extension of the copyright page.

The Internet addresses listed in the text were accurate at the time of publication. The inclusion of a website does not indicate an endorsement by the authors or McGraw-Hill Education, and McGraw-Hill Education does not guarantee the accuracy of the information presented at these sites.

www.mhhe.com

WriteNow

BRIEF CONTENTS

Table of Contents

11 > Evaluating: Film and the Arts 256

Preface

WHY *WRITE NOW*?

Now available in the innovative SmartBook format as well as customizable chapters within McGraw-Hill's CREATE, the second edition of *Write Now* guides students through the process of writing, revising, and editing their work and gives them greater confidence as they approach writing for college, for their careers, or for their everyday lives. The SmartBook version provides students with an adaptive reading experience, assists them in long-term knowledge retention, and prepares them for active in-class participation and writing assignments.

The second edition offers students plenty of practical, hands-on advice for exploring ideas, drafting, revising, and editing for any writing situation they might encounter.

FEATURES OF *WRITE NOW*

An Adaptive Learning Experience—The SmartBook version of *Write Now* reinforces key writing concepts for students in an engaging, interactive learning environment.

Rhetorical Star—Unique to *Write Now,* the Rhetorical Star is used throughout the text to keep students focused on their writing situation as they draft, revise, edit, and design their work.

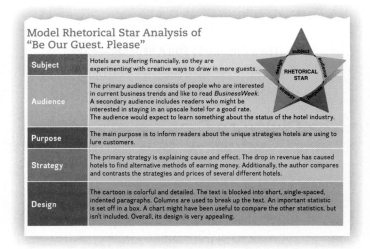

Model Rhetorical Star Analysis of "Be Our Guest. Please"

Subject	Hotels are suffering financially, so they are experimenting with creative ways to draw in more guests.
Audience	The primary audience consists of people who are interested in current business trends and like to read *BusinessWeek*. A secondary audience includes readers who might be interested in staying in an upscale hotel for a good rate. The audience would expect to learn something about the status of the hotel industry.
Purpose	The main purpose is to inform readers about the unique strategies hotels are using to lure customers.
Strategy	The primary strategy is explaining cause and effect. The drop in revenue has caused hotels to find alternative methods of earning money. Additionally, the author compares and contrasts the strategies and prices of several different hotels.
Design	The cartoon is colorful and detailed. The text is blocked into short, single-spaced, indented paragraphs. Columns are used to break up the text. An important statistic is set off in a box. A chart might have been useful to compare the other statistics, but isn't included. Overall, its design is very appealing.

Spotlights—**Graduate Spotlights** provide testimonials from real college graduates who emphasize the importance of writing skills in their careers. New to this edition, **Employer Spotlights** give students additional insight into the importance of writing in the work world.

Graduate SPOTLIGHT

Tawana Campbell, Occupational Therapy Assistant

Tawana Campbell earned a degree in occupational therapy assisting. She currently works as an occupational therapy assistant for a pediatric outpatient facility. Here's what Tawana has to say about the importance of writing in her career:

" I take careful notes about each session I have with a patient and write a case study. I document everything that happens because the philosophy where I work is, 'If it isn't written down, it didn't happen.' When I meet with a patient, I write out an evaluation of his or her condition and needs, and I determine ways to get effective treatment. Written proof of my evaluation is necessary to persuade the insurance company that special adaptive equipment, such as a wheelchair, splint, or orthotic insert, is necessary.

Because I work with children, I have to be very creative with how I go about treatment. For example, one child had a deficiency in communication skills, so I showed him a movie and asked him to retell the plot. Another child was having problems with sensorimotor skills, so I taught her to dance using her favorite songs from *High School Musical*. Also, I frequently use arts and crafts with children because something as simple as gluing a bead on a piece of construction paper is a useful

Career-Based Writing Examples— Each chapter in Part 2 includes at least one career-based writing example, as well as a section explaining how students will apply each writing strategy in school, in their careers, and in their personal lives.

Career-Based DESCRIPTIVE WRITING

[preview] **THE FOLLOWING** is a description of exercise-induced asthma from **mayoclinic .com.** Have you had trouble breathing? What kinds of symptoms did you experience?

Exercise-Induced Asthma

Description

If you cough, wheeze, or feel out of breath during or after exercise, it may be more than exertion causing your symptoms. You might have exercise-induced asthma. As with asthma triggered by other things, exercise-induced asthma symptoms occur when your airways tighten and produce extra mucus.

Feeling a little short of breath or fatigued when you work out is normal, especially if you aren't in great shape. But with exercise-induced asthma, these symptoms can be more severe.

For many people, exercise is just one of a few asthma triggers. Others can include pollen, pet dander, and other airborne allergens.

STUDENT WRITING

Mursing
by Thomas James "TJ" Pinkerton

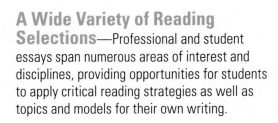

Not many people are used to seeing a male nurse or "murse" walk into their room in the hospital due to the fact that there are not many males in the nursing profession. However, nursing is a great profession for men to get into, and men can make significant contributions to the nursing field. The physical strength of being a man and the power of male camaraderie are both factors in making nursing a logical career choice for men.

One reason for men to get into the nursing field is the physical requirements of a nursing position. For instance, a nurse might have to move patients who cannot move themselves. One example of this would be if a patient needed to use the restroom but could not find the strength to get out of bed. A male nurse would have the strength to lift most patients off of a bed without needing to call for additional help. Furthermore, during a patient's hospital stay, he or she will often need to be moved from one room to another for testing. In that case a nurse needs to be able to lift the patient out of bed, place him or her into a wheelchair, push the wheelchair to the test site, lift the patient out of the wheelchair, and place him or her on one of the numerous machines used for testing. When the testing is complete, the nurse must repeat this whole process in reverse to return the

are in the hospital, especially if it is for a male-related problem. While the preference for a male nurse may be discriminatory toward women, the hospital is not the place to fix this type of ailment. Getting the patient healthy enough to return to everyday life should always be the first goal of the hospital, and the comfort of the patient while in the care of the hospital should be a close second. No matter how silly the reason for the patient's request for a male nurse is, his or her needs should be met.

Overall, many career fields that have traditionally been reserved mainly for women, including nursing, are opening their doors to men. While in the past it may have seemed a little awkward for a man to pursue a career as a nurse, today the need for men in the nursing field is evident. Men can provide beneficial services for the nursing industry such as physical strength and male companionship for

A Wide Variety of Reading Selections—Professional and student essays span numerous areas of interest and disciplines, providing opportunities for students to apply critical reading strategies as well as topics and models for their own writing.

Custom Options for Using
MH CREATE

With MH CREATE, instructors can easily arrange chapters to align with their syllabus, eliminating chapters they do not wish to assign and adding any of the content available only from McGraw-Hill's CREATE platform to build one or more print or eBook texts—including Connect Composition access codes—for their program. Instructors can also add their own material, such as the course syllabus, course rubric, course standards, or specific instruction, from which they want their students to benefit. Instructors may also add their own Graduate and Employer Spotlights, using templates provided by McGraw-Hill Education.

ExpressBooks within CREATE provide a simple solution for instructors, enabling them to order alternative tables of contents for two course sequences, rather than for a single text.

With CREATE you can

- **Choose which chapters you want from McGraw-Hill texts**

    - including *The McGraw-Hill Reader, The Short Prose Reader,* and *75 Readings*

- **Choose which resources you want**

    - from other McGraw-Hill collections, such as *The Ideal Reader* (800 readings by genre, mode, theme, discipline, and author); *Annual Editions* (5,500 articles from journals and periodicals); *Traditions* (readings in the humanities); *Sustainability* (readings with an environment focus); and *American History and World Civilization Documents* (primary sources including maps, charters, letters, memoirs, and essays)

    - from your own works, such as syllabi, institutional information, study guides, assignments, diagrams, and artwork; and student writing, art, and photos

- **Choose a McGraw-Hill ExpressBook in CREATE as a starting point to build your custom text**

- **Choose which format you want**

    - print

    - electronic

Once you have built a CREATE book, you will receive a complimentary print review copy in 3 to 5 business days or a complimentary electronic review copy (eComp) via email in about one hour. Go to **mcgrawhillcreate.com** and register today.

Teaching Resources

Karin Russell has over twenty-five years' experience teaching composition, literature, developmental English, and business writing for various Florida schools. She currently oversees curriculum development for a variety of writing, literature, and communication courses. Drawing on her extensive teaching and administrative background, she has prepared the instructor notes for the Annotated Instructor's Edition of *Write Now* as well as the Instructor's Manual, with Karen Durand of Delta Career Education Corporation.

ANNOTATED INSTRUCTOR'S EDITION: ON-PAGE TEACHING TIPS

The Annotated Instructor's Edition includes classroom tips, tips for using SmartBook and LearnSmart, and answers to activities and Grammar Window exercises.

INSTRUCTOR'S MANUAL

The Instructor's Manual provides a wealth of material to draw on, including the following:

- **Chapter outlines**
- **Lecture notes**
- **Class activities**
- **Sample assignments and writing topics**
- **Connect resources**
- **Discussion questions for online/hybrid classes**
- **Graphic organizers that can be used as handouts**
- **Grading rubrics for each type of writing covered**
- **Peer review worksheets**

Grammar Window
POINT OF VIEW

First person: I, me, my, mine, we, our, ours
Second person: you, yours
Third person: he, she, they, their, theirs

The point of view needs to be consistent within a sentence or paragraph or readers will become confused. Watch for sentences where the point of view shifts for no reason.

Exercise

Correct the shifts in point of view in the following sentences:

1. I looked at the spider and you got really scared.
2. You were driving along and they saw something furry cross the road.

Grammar Window: Possible Responses

1. I looked at the spider and got really scared.
2. As they were driving along, they saw something furry cross the road.

Teaching Tip

Have students work in pairs to review and discuss each other's paragraphs from the Shifting Viewpoints activity.

A Word from Karin Russell

For more than twenty-five years, I have taught college-level writing courses and observed students and how they learn to become better writers. I chose to create Write Now *because I felt there was a need for a complete yet concise four-in-one (rhetoric, reader, research guide, and handbook) textbook that incorporates sound pedagogical theory, appeals to students' interests, and demonstrates the relevance of being able to write clear, effective documents.* Write Now *emphasizes a process-oriented approach to writing that focuses on revision and the recursive nature of writing. One of the unique features of* Write Now *is the Rhetorical Star, which I developed to help students analyze their rhetorical situation. Building on Aristotle's rhetorical triangle, the Rhetorical Star guides students through each writing assignment by encouraging them to consider their subject, audience, purpose, strategy, and design.*

In addition to providing students with a variety of engaging readings, images, and activities to stimulate critical thinking and writing skills, I have included Graduate Spotlights, Employer Spotlights, and Career-Based Writing examples to emphasize to students just how important writing is, not only during their college experience but also in their careers and personal lives. Above all, Write Now *sends students the message that being able to write effectively is essential for achieving success and that writing well can be a worthwhile and satisfying experience.*

Acknowledgments

The second edition of *Write Now* would not be possible without the tremendous effort put forth by the McGraw-Hill team. First of all, my thanks go to Mike Ryan, vice president and general manager, and David Patterson, managing director for the skills group, for their leadership. I'm very grateful to Nancy Huebner, senior brand manager for composition, for her wisdom and guidance in shaping this edition through our lively phone conversations. I'm also grateful to Claire Brantley, executive brand manager for composition, for her expert advice and guidance as we finalized the text. Thanks as well go to Carla Samodulski, senior product developer, for her vast knowledge, attention to detail, high standards, and insightful suggestions for improving every aspect of the text. Lisa Pinto, lead product developer, provided her expertise throughout the development of this edition. I'd also like to thank Brigeth Rivera, senior marketing manager for composition; Nanette Giles, executive market development manager; and Ray Kelley, senior field publisher for expertly marketing the second edition. Mary Powers, lead content project manager, has attended to the many details necessary to get this edition ready. My thanks also go to John Leland, senior content licensing specialist, for overseeing the photo research, and to Ira Roberts, photo researcher, for giving me amazing options for the new images that appear in this edition. I am grateful as well to Ann Marie Jannette, content licensing specialist, for overseeing the text permissions and especially for dealing so adroitly with the last-minute surprise changes. I'd also like to thank Debra Kubiak, senior designer, for overseeing the design and cover of the text. She has done wonders with the visual appeal of *Write Now*.

I am grateful to Karen Durand of Delta Education Corporation for updating the Instructor's Manual and adding the sections on the resources available on Connect.

My thanks also go to the following reviewers, who have provided helpful comments and suggestions as we developed the second edition of *Write Now*:

Arkansas State University, Beebe
Sheila Chase

Blue Ridge Community College
Jennifer Parrack-Rogers
Mary Katherine Winkler

Bryant & Stratton College
Molly M. McKnight

Bryant & Stratton College, Downtown Campus, Cleveland
Katie Wallace

Bryant & Stratton College, Eastlake Campus
Marcia R. Backos

Bryant & Stratton College, Milwaukee Campus
Melodie Fox

Bryant & Stratton College, Syracuse North Campus
Charles Herbert Jerred

Columbia Southern University
Tamrala Swafford

Craven Community College
Pamela Flannery

Crowder College
Debra J. Brown

Davenport University, Grand Rapids Campus
Joseph LaMontagne

East Central College
Susan T. Henderson

Elizabeth City State University
Stephen March
Peter H. Porosky
Eric A. Weil

Fisher College, Boston Campus
Susan Jordan

Florence-Darlington Technical College
Laura J. Floyd
Mark T. Rooze
Alan Michael Trusky

Florida State College at Jacksonville
Sally Nielsen
Daniel Powell

Fortis Institute, Erie Campus
Robert Karney

Genesee Community College
Marie Iglesias-Cardinale

Jackson State University
Monica L. Granderson
Kathi R. Griffin
Stephen G. McLeod

Kaplan University, Maine Campuses
Kevin Kelly

Keiser University, eCampus
Anne Marie Fowler

Keiser University, Fort Lauderdale Campus
Hayley Sogren

Keiser University, Fort Myers Campus
Paula Porter

Keiser University, Lakeland Campus
Terry Don

Keiser University, Tallahassee Campus
Sheryl Davis
Hal Shows

Macomb Community College, South Campus
Cynthia Bily
Linda Brender
Nancy McGee

Mississippi Gulf Coast Community College, Perkinston Campus
Robin Lyons
Gaye Winter

Mississippi Gulf Coast Community College, Jackson County
April Lawson
Shana Nero
Jordan Tyler Sanderson
Lydia McCalop Steele

Murray State University
Gina Smith Claywell

Northeast Alabama Community College
Joan Reeves

Potomac State College
Richard Hunt

Rose State College
Sandra K. Keneda
Dianne Krob
Sherri Mussatto

Shawnee College
Susan Barry

Shelton State Community College
Janice Filer
Danielle Griffin
Wynora W. Freeman

South University, Columbia Campus
Philip Wayne Corbett

St. Johns River State College
Paul Robert Andrews
Jeannine Morgan
Roger Vaccaro

St. Johns River State College, Orange Park Campus
Melody Hargraves

Tri-County Technical College, Anderson Campus
Mary Smith Green

Tri-County Technical College, Pendleton Campus
Jennifer Beattie

Tyler Junior College
Jim Richey

Western Piedmont Community College
Rani Burd

West Kentucky Community and Technical College
Kimberly G. Russell

West Shore Community College
Sean Henne
John B. Wolff

Many thanks as well to the following instructors who reviewed probes for the SmartBook version of the text and provided many useful suggestions:

Delta Career Education Corporation
Karen Durand

Goodwin College
Diane Sperger

Ultimate Medical Academy
Michelle Frankich

University of Northwestern Ohio
Holly Norton
Mark Putnam
Christine Cavallaro

New to the Second Edition of *Write Now*:

Part 1: Introduction to Writing

- An Employer or a Graduate Spotlight has been added to each chapter.
- Tone and formality are now discussed as aspects of audience analysis in Chapter 1.
- A Grammar Window on parallel structure has been added to Chapter 2.
- More help on developing a thesis is provided in Chapters 2 and 3.
- The sample Writing Attitude Survey has been expanded in Chapter 3.
- A new advertisement and analysis for "Interpreting an Ad" appears in Chapter 4.

Part 2: Writing Strategies

- An improved design makes the chapter structure easier to follow. For example, "Writing Assignment Options," "Interpreting an Advertisement," "Writing about an Image," and "Media Connection" writing suggestions have been gathered together under the title "Options for Writing a Narrative Essay" in Chapter 5 (and other chapters have the same design for these elements).
- "Considering the Rhetorical Star" questions have been added after each "Reading and Reflection" selection.
- New career-based reading selections have been added: "Case Narrative" by Kris Bishop (Chapter 5); "Steps in Venipuncture" by Rose Farhat-Goodson (Chapter 7); "The Evolving Workplace" and "Characteristics of the Social Age" by Peter Cardon (Chapter 8); "Career Choice: Easy for Superheroes, Hard for Us" by Bryan Dik (Chapter 10).
- New "Reading and Reflection" selections have been added: "The Workers" by Richard Rodriguez and "Even Anthropologists Get Culture Shock" by Conrad Kottak (Chapter 5); "High Street: Hip-Hop's Boldest Choreographer" by Joan Acocella and "We Real Cool" by Gwendolyn Brooks (Chapter 6); "Bringing Out the Flirt in You" by Christine Ng and "Take Me Out to the Ballgame" by Jack Norworth (Chapter 7); "Love, Internet Style" by David Brooks and "My Flamboyant Grandson" by George Saunders (Chapter 8); "Dietary Recommendations for Carbohydrates" by Charles B. Corbin and Sonnet 147: "My Love Is As a Fever Longing Still" by William Shakespeare (Chapter 9); "Facebook Relationship Problems: How Social Networking and Jealousy Affect Your Love Life" by Katherine Bindley and "The Appeal of the Androgynous Man" by Amy Gross (Chapter 10); Reviews of *Harry Potter and the Deathly Hallows—Part 2* by Kenneth Turan and *The Hunger Games* by Peter Travers (Chapter 11); "Facebook 'Likes' Not Protected Speech, Says Virginia Court" by Lee E. Berlik and "Why Should Thousands of Prisoners Die Behind Bars for Nonviolent Crimes?" by Liliana Segura (Chapter 12).
- "Media Connection" topic suggestions have been expanded in each chapter.

Part 3: Research Guide

- Graduate Spotlights have been added to all three chapters.
- Works-cited (MLA) and references list (APA) models for citing an eBook have been added.
- A new sample title page and copyright page for a source have been added for the MLA (Figures 14.1 and 14.2) and APA (Figures 14.6 and 14.7) styles.
- Research Paper Formatting Guides have been added for both the MLA and APA styles.

Part 4: Editing Guide

- Marginal definitions for key terms have been added throughout the Editing Guide.
- Coverage of pronoun agreement problems with collective nouns has been added.
- Coverage of linking verbs has been added to the section on verbs.

ABOUT THE AUTHOR

Karin Russell is a college English teacher whose experience in helping students achieve success has spanned more than twenty-five years. Russell earned her undergraduate degree in elementary education at Stetson University and her master's degree in reading and language arts education at Florida State University. She continued her education in the English field by earning thirty-six graduate credit hours beyond the master's degree. She has taught composition, literature, developmental English, and business writing courses for various Florida schools, including Eastern Florida State College (formerly Brevard Community College), Nova Southeastern University, and several career colleges.

KARIN L. RUSSELL

For more than twenty years, Russell has been a full-time English instructor for Keiser University, where she is the university department chair for English, humanities, and communications. She oversees curriculum development for a variety of writing, literature, and communications courses. She also serves as a member of the Keiser Writes leadership team and as a faculty advisor to the Student Government Association and Phi Theta Kappa. Russell is especially interested in enabling students to develop their writing skills through a process-oriented approach and showing students how writing is applicable to their future careers. She passionately believes that nearly anyone can become a good writer with the right instruction and enough practice.

On a personal note, Karin Russell loves spending time with her husband, Todd, and their wonderful rescue dogs and cats. She also enjoys creating stained glass art pieces, riding her scooter, traveling around the country in her family's RV, and reading multicultural novels.

The author would like to extend a special thank you to Sally Hudson, Lisa Lawrence, and Rhonda Wetherington for their insights.

PART 1

Introduction to Writing

Why Writing Is Important for Success

Writing effectively is an important skill, one that you can take with you and use for the rest of your life. To be successful in college, in your career, and in your life, you will need to be able to communicate effectively through writing. Whether you are composing a report for your boss, a paper for an instructor, or a letter to resolve a personal matter, being able to write well is essential. The good news is that you don't have to be naturally gifted to learn to become a strong writer. You can develop your writing skills by studying and practicing writing. Whether you are 17 or 77, you have something worthwhile to say that others will be interested in reading. As you read this second edition of *Write Now*, you will learn and practice many valuable techniques that will help you to become a better reader, critical thinker, and writer so that you are able to interpret and communicate messages in an effective manner. Those skills will help you to accomplish your educational, career, and personal goals.

OVERVIEW of Part 1

Chapter 1
You will have an opportunity to create a writing environment that best suits your personality. You will also learn how to assess your rhetorical (or writing) situation.

Chapter 2
You will discover some strategies that work for you as you participate in the steps of the writing process to produce a final, polished document. You will also see how a student writer went through the entire writing process.

Chapter 3
You will learn some methods for writing well-organized sentences, paragraphs, and essays.

Chapter 4
You will gain a better understanding of the connection between critical thinking, reading, and writing, and you will learn some strategies for applying critical thinking skills to analyze written and visual texts as well as websites.

CHAPTER 1

GETTING STARTED WITH WRITING

1.1 CREATE AN IDEAL WRITING ENVIRONMENT

Even if you haven't had much success with writing in the past, you can become a good writer at school, on the job, and in your personal life. Your academic history doesn't define your future as a writer. Through this course, you will learn and apply many strategies that will strengthen your writing skills so you can say something worthwhile in a way that readers will find interesting. Instead of feeling overwhelmed by writing assignments, you will learn to break them into manageable tasks. Take a moment to visualize yourself writing a strong paper, one that you can proudly submit to your instructor or boss.

One way to help you achieve success is to create a comfortable writing atmosphere that contains everything you need to accomplish your task. Whether you are taking your class on campus or online, here are some steps to help you find your writing groove.

1. Find a Good Place to Write

Try writing in different places to discover where you experience the most success. Do you work better at home, in a library, in an empty classroom, outside, or in a café? Choose a place that won't be too distracting, whether at home or away from home. If you can't find a peaceful place, try listening to something soothing on your iPod to reduce outside interference.

2. Plan Your Time to Write

What time of day are you the sharpest? Do you like to compose first thing in the morning, or does your brain get fired up in the middle of the night? Try to schedule your writing time when you are likely to develop your best work. If your busy life prevents you from writing at the opportune time, then learn to adapt your writing habits to your schedule. Though it may not be ideal, you can write a little bit at a time if necessary. For example, you might be able to write during your commute (if you're not driving) or even while waiting at the dentist's office. With the right attitude, you can be productive in nearly any environment at any time. Instead of making excuses for not having time to write, use the time that you do have wisely. Consider using a paper or digital calendar to plan time to write. Look for gaps in your schedule. If your writing time is on your calendar, you are less likely to fill that time with other, less productive tasks such as hanging out with friends or watching television.

SmartBook Tip

Students receive an overview of the learning outcomes and topics in Chapter 1 in the "Preview" phase of SmartBook.

Teaching Tip

Emphasize to students that they don't have to be naturally gifted writers. They can develop their writing skills through study and practice.

3. Select Your Materials

Before you begin writing, assemble the materials you will need. Some writers like to brainstorm ideas on paper. If that's your style, do you prefer a legal pad, spiral notebook, or fancy journal? Do you have a favorite pencil or pen? Also, you should have a dictionary and thesaurus nearby. *Dictionary.com* and *Thesaurus .com* are excellent Web-based resources.

Other writers are comfortable starting right in with a computer. Make sure you have enough battery strength or a power supply so you won't lose momentum by having to stop writing. Choose a font style, color, and size that make you comfortable during the composing process. You can always change them before you submit your work.

4. Establish a Method for Saving Your Work

What happens if you lose the folder or notebook that has your assignment in it? Whether you are writing on paper or on a computer, you'll need a backup system for situations like this one. Make a copy of written assignments. If you compose your assignment on a computer, then don't just trust your hard drive. Save a copy to a CD, a flash drive, or another data-storage device. You can even e-mail your assignment to yourself as an extra precaution so that it is stored safely in cyberspace.

For an online class, compose your assignments in a word processing program (such as Microsoft Word or Pages). Then copy and paste them into the online course platform. That way if you lose your Internet connection, or if the course system goes down while you are trying to post your assignment, you won't lose your work.

5. Create an Inviting Atmosphere

Determine what kind of environment most inspires you to write. Do you prefer order or chaos? Do you like bright or soft lighting? Do you prefer complete silence, or does listening to music help you to think clearly? Are you most comfortable sitting at a desk, or are you more creative on the sofa? Try different scenarios to see what kind of ambience helps you produce your best work.

6. Minimize Distractions

If you live with other people, ask them to give you some time for writing without interruptions. If you have children, arrange to have someone else watch them while you write. Turn off your TV and cell phone. Try to focus all of your energy on what you are writing so that you can concentrate and do your best work.

Sometimes you won't have an opportunity to choose your writing environment, such as when you're writing an in-class essay or when you're at work. If that's the case, do what you can to minimize distractions. Try to distance yourself from people with annoying habits, such as pen clicking or humming. Sit away from the door if noises from the hallway are likely to bother you. As you develop your writing skills, also work on learning how to tune out distractions so that you are able to write in a variety of circumstances.

> ▶ *Activity* **Imagining Your Ideal Writing Environment**
>
> Make a collage that represents your ideal writing environment. Include what you would see, where you would write, the materials you would use, and anything else you would need to create the right atmosphere for you. Write a brief description explaining the collage. You may be asked to share your ideal writing environment with a few classmates.

Imagining Your Ideal Writing Environment Activity:

Answers will vary.

1.2 ANALYZE THE RHETORICAL SITUATION: THE STAR APPROACH

The term *rhetoric* simply refers to the art of communicating effectively through writing or speaking. Whether you are writing an essay for school, a report for your boss, or an e-mail to your friend, your goal is to convey a message to the reader. You want to be sure that your reader understands the intent of your message. Therefore, every time you sit down to write, you need to consider five points of the rhetorical situation: subject, audience, purpose, strategy, and design.

These five points make up the "rhetorical star" (Figure 1.1). Each point of the star is an essential component of your final written product. Using the rhetorical star will help to ensure that you communicate effectively.

Subject

For some writing projects, you will need to determine what **subject** to cover. A subject is a general concept, such as health, technology, or crime. Choose an appropriate subject that fits within the parameters of your assignment (Figure 1.2). After you have selected a broad subject, you will need to narrow it to a specific topic, such as nutritional shakes, tablet features, or home security systems. Make sure your topic is narrow enough that you can adequately cover it in your document. For example, you wouldn't be able to cover the entire subject of "staying fit" in a short paper, but you could adequately cover a few specific fitness techniques.

As you consider what you want to say and how much detail you want to include, keep your purpose and audience in mind. You might think about what your readers will already know about your subject and what they might want to learn. Also, consider whether research is necessary for you to adequately cover your topic. See Chapter 2 for more details about discovering and narrowing a topic for your paper.

Audience

Consider the readers who make up your **audience** (Figure 1.3). Are you writing for a particular *discourse community* (a group of people who share common interests, knowledge, and values related to a particular subject)? Each of us belongs to a number of discourse communities such as school clubs, social or

FIGURE 1.1
The Rhetorical Star

FIGURE 1.2 Subject

FIGURE 1.3 Audience

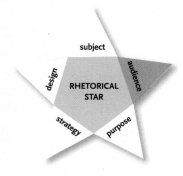

SmartBook Tip

Key concepts in Chapter 1 are highlighted for students during the "Read" phase. As students demonstrate understanding of these concepts during the "Practice" phase by responding to probes, the highlighting adapts to the individual student's learning by changing color.

religious groups, and professional organizations. Each group has its own vocabulary and conventions of communication, called *jargon*. For example, if you are writing a software review for members of the computer club, you can probably safely assume that they will understand terms that are specific to the computer world, such as *bits* and *bytes*. Similarly, if you are writing a letter to members of a certain professional field, such as health care or homeland security, you won't need to explain concepts related to that field.

Keep in mind the needs and interests of your primary audience, but realize that others (your secondary audience) might also read your document. See Table 1.1 for audience characteristics to consider when you are writing.

Some audience characteristics will matter more than others depending on your subject and purpose. For example, if you are writing an article about a work-related topic that will be published in your company's newsletter, your readers' interests and knowledge of the subject would be more important than their gender and cultural background. If most of the readers are employees, then you can use the vocabulary that is specific to your career field. If, on the other

Employer SPOTLIGHT

Tracy Wetrich, Director of Human Resources for the National Aeronautics and Space Administration at Kennedy Space Center

Tracy Wetrich has a BS degree in industrial organizational sociology with a minor in human resources. As a human resources director, one of Wetrich's responsibilities is to find the best people for the available positions. She reviews résumés and cover letters and provides hiring managers with quality candidates to interview. Here's what Wetrich has to say about the qualities she looks for in a job applicant:

66 The résumé is the first opportunity for a candidate to make a good impression. If it clearly and effectively communicates the applicant's education, skills, experience, and knowledge, he or she is likely to fare well in the job search process. If an applicant doesn't write well, then he or she probably doesn't speak well, and the ability to communicate is critical in most aspects of the jobs. For example, written communication is important in everything from e-mail to writing formal proposals, project summaries, performance plans, and evaluations. Written communication also serves as a foundation for preparing materials for presentation. Individuals who are proficient in oral and written communication are often well suited for advancement to lead and supervisory positions, where these skills become even more critical. A candidate who has completed formal college classes in writing, oral communication, and literature is more likely to be able to communicate effectively, have a broad vocabulary, read and interpret materials with critical comprehension, and influence people and decisions. Candidates who possess good communication skills have a strong foundation that will prepare them for many opportunities. 99

TABLE 1.1

Audience Characteristics		
Age	Experience	Opinions
Beliefs	Gender	Political views
Cultural background	Interests	Reading ability
Education level	Knowledge of the subject	Religion
Ethnicity	Occupation	Socioeconomic status

hand, the newsletter is geared more for your organization's clients, then you may need to explain specialized terms in more detail and consider other audience characteristics.

After you have determined who your audience will be, you will need to consider your tone and level of formality.

- **Tone:** *Tone* is the mood or feeling you are trying to create through your writing. Your tone can be businesslike (serious), academic, humorous, or opinionated. Choose a tone that is appropriate for your purpose and audience.

- **Level of formality:** Your writing style can be *formal* or *informal.* Formal writing tends to be more serious than informal writing. The use of contractions (such as *I'm* and *doesn't*) is usually limited. In formal writing you generally need to spell out complete words and choose your words carefully. On the other hand, informal writing, such as the writing in this book, tends to be fairly casual. Contractions are acceptable and can help the writing not to sound too stuffy. You would likely use a more formal approach in a report for your boss than you would in an e-mail to a co-worker. In school, a research essay would be much more formal than a journal entry.

Purpose

Determine your reason, or **purpose,** for writing (Figure 1.4). Why are you writing? What are you hoping to accomplish? What effect do you wish to have on your audience? Whether you are composing a class assignment, workplace document, or personal letter, your writing will have at least one of five main purposes: to inform, to interpret, to persuade, to entertain, and to express feelings.

1. **Writing to Inform** Most writing is informative in some way. When you write to inform, your goal is to provide readers with useful information about your subject or teach them how to do something. For example, you might write an essay summarizing an article or a story you have read, a set of instructions explaining how to perform a workplace procedure, or a recipe for making your grandmother's special chili.

2. **Writing to Interpret** Sometimes writing can help you or your audience better understand something. For example, you might write an essay interpreting (analyzing) a poem for a literature class, or you may write a comparison of two software

Teaching Tip

Have students brainstorm and share additional audience characteristics that may be relevant to their writing.

FIGURE 1.4 Purpose

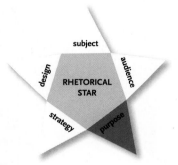

>> Netiquette

You should always use proper *netiquette* (Internet etiquette) when communicating with your instructor via e-mail.

1. Use an appropriate screen name (e-mail address) that includes your name.
2. Write a clear subject heading.
3. Address your instructor professionally.
4. Write your message clearly and concisely. If you have questions, make them specific.
5. Use standard grammar, capitalization, and punctuation.
6. Avoid using all capital letters. This can be considered shouting.
7. Maintain a professional tone.
8. End with a polite closing and your name.

Poor Netiquette

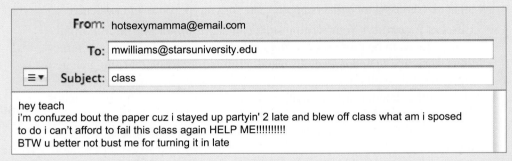

From: hotsexymamma@email.com
To: mwilliams@starsuniversity.edu
Subject: class

hey teach
i'm confuzed bout the paper cuz i stayed up partyin' 2 late and blew off class what am i sposed to do i can't afford to fail this class again HELP ME!!!!!!!!!!
BTW u better not bust me for turning it in late

Good Netiquette

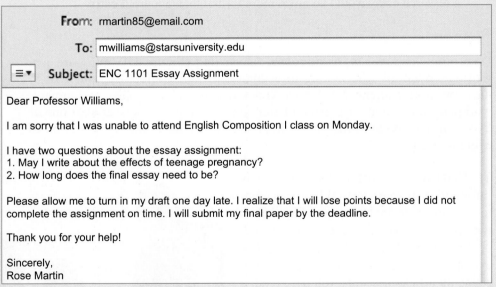

From: rmartin85@email.com
To: mwilliams@starsuniversity.edu
Subject: ENC 1101 Essay Assignment

Dear Professor Williams,

I am sorry that I was unable to attend English Composition I class on Monday.

I have two questions about the essay assignment:
1. May I write about the effects of teenage pregnancy?
2. How long does the final essay need to be?

Please allow me to turn in my draft one day late. I realize that I will lose points because I did not complete the assignment on time. I will submit my final paper by the deadline.

Thank you for your help!

Sincerely,
Rose Martin

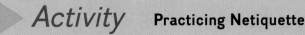

Activity — Practicing Netiquette

In pairs or small groups, write a short e-mail to an instructor using poor netiquette. Trade papers with another pair or group, and revise the other paper using proper netiquette.

Practicing Netiquette Activity:
Answers will vary.

packages that your boss is considering implementing. When you write interpretatively, you are giving your opinions about the subject rather than just reporting information. Sometimes your interpretation may include an evaluation of your subject. For instance, you might write an evaluation of an employee or a review of a movie you have seen.

3. Writing to Persuade Although almost any type of writing needs to be convincing, sometimes your main purpose is to argue a point. For example, you might write an essay arguing for or against a proposed law, or you might submit a letter to your boss convincing him or her why you deserve a raise. Other times you may want to persuade your readers to actually do something. For instance, you might challenge your readers to do more than just recycle bottles, cans, and paper products to help preserve the environment for future generations.

4. Writing to Entertain Some types of writing are primarily intended to entertain readers. You might choose to write a story, a poem, a cartoon, or song lyrics to move your readers or make them laugh. Often you can entertain your readers at the same time that you address another purpose. You might want to use humor in an informative or a persuasive paper to help engage your readers in the material being covered.

5. Writing to Express Feelings You can use personal expression in many ways. You might write a note to someone special, an essay about an exciting or a scary event you experienced, a reaction to a magazine or newspaper article, or a letter to your apartment manager expressing your dissatisfaction with the length of time it is taking to get your leaky faucet repaired.

Combined Purposes The five purposes for writing are not mutually exclusive; they overlap. For instance, if you are writing an essay as part of an application for a scholarship, you may address three purposes by informing the readers about your background and situation, expressing your feelings about how much you need the scholarship and how grateful you would be to receive it, and persuading your readers that you are a worthy recipient of the scholarship.

Strategy

You'll need to choose an approach, or **strategy,** that best serves your purpose and audience (Figure 1.5). In this textbook you will learn about eight major writing strategies: narrating, describing, explaining a process, comparing and contrasting, explaining causes and effects, persuading, evaluating, and solving a problem. You may be able to combine writing strategies as well. Table 1.2 offers a quick overview of the different strategies.

Design

Finally, think about how you are going to **design** your document (Figure 1.6). Consider the design expectations of your instructor or boss and the discourse community for which you are writing. Determine the genre, format, length, appearance, and visual aids that are appropriate for your document.

- **Genre:** What type of document do you need to write? Determine the genre that is most appropriate for your task: story, essay, research paper, letter, e-mail, memo, advertisement, flyer, website, blog, and so on. Most of the writing you do in college will be in essay form.
- **Format:** How should you structure your writing? Some instructors may allow you to turn in handwritten informal assignments, but

FIGURE 1.5 Strategy

FIGURE 1.6 Design

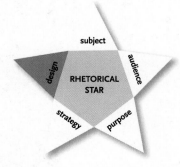

TABLE 1.2

Writing Strategies	
Narrating	Tell a story about something that happened. Usually you will present the details of the event in chronological order, but occasionally a flashback can be useful. Be sure to cover *who*, *what*, *where*, *when*, *why*, and *how*.
Describing	Use words to paint a picture of an object, scene, or event for your audience, incorporating as many senses as are appropriate for your subject: sight, sound, taste, smell, touch. Include colorful adjectives to give your reader a clear impression of the subject.
Explaining a Process	Tell how something works or what something does. You may give step-by-step instructions so your reader can perform the task, or you can write an explanation so that your audience is able to understand your subject.
Comparing and Contrasting	Show how two people, places, or objects are similar and/or different. Be sure to make a worthwhile point while using this strategy.
Explaining Causes and Effects	Examine how one event or situation caused another to occur, or determine the effects of an event or situation. Be careful to apply sound logic as you analyze causes and effects.
Persuading	Take a stand about an important or controversial issue, and convince your reader that your position is valid. You may use personal experience or research to support your main idea.
Evaluating	Make a judgment about your subject by determining how well it meets specific standards that you feel are important for that subject.
Solving a Problem	Explain a problem to your reader and offer several solutions. You may evaluate each possible solution before persuading your reader that one specific solution is best.

Teaching Tip
Individually or in groups, students can list topics illustrating how each writing strategy might be employed.

Teaching Tip
Give students examples of types of writing they may use in their future careers and ask them to explain what design features they might choose for each example.

others will require that you use a computer to write all assignments. Be sure to follow your instructor's guidelines very closely. Also, you may need to adhere to guidelines provided by the Modern Language Association (MLA) or the American Psychological Association (APA), especially if you are writing a paper based on research. See Chapters 13 and 14 for more information about writing and documenting research papers.

- **Length:** How long should your document be? Is there a word or page minimum (or limit)? If your instructor does not specify a length, then let the topic guide you. Be sure to fully develop each point that you want to make.

- **Appearance:** How should your document look? Find out if you need to single-space or double-space your papers. Typically, if you single-space a paper, you will begin each paragraph at the left margin. However, if you double-space a paper, you will need to indent each paragraph. Choose a font size, style, and color that are appropriate for your writing situation. Also, determine if you can use headings, bullets, columns, or boxes to emphasize your main points.

- **Visual aids:** Would adding visual aids enhance your paper? Often pictures, diagrams, charts, or graphs will help get your ideas across to your audience. For example, if you are including a variety of statistics in a research paper, then you may decide to include a chart or graph to help the reader visualize the impact of the concept you are discussing.

Applying the Rhetorical Star Analysis

You can apply the rhetorical star analysis to all types of writing. Whether you are composing a paper for school, writing an e-mail message to your boss, or creating a flyer for an item you are selling, you will benefit from considering the five points of your rhetorical star: subject, audience, purpose, strategy, and design. Also, being aware of how other writers apply the rhetorical star can help you understand your own rhetorical star as you write. Whether you are reading a textbook for school, a professional journal for work, or a magazine or newspaper for pleasure, understanding the writer's rhetorical star can help you to interpret the material and comprehend it on a deeper level.

> ### ▶ *Activity*   Analyzing Writing Situations Using the Rhetorical Star
>
> Choose three specific hypothetical writing situations that you could encounter (currently or in the future): one for school, one at work, and one in your personal life. For each scenario, determine your rhetorical star:
>
> 1. What is your subject?
> 2. Who is your primary audience? Is there a secondary audience? If so, who? What does your audience expect from your document?
> 3. What is your primary purpose? Do you intend to inform, to interpret, to persuade, to entertain, or to express feelings? Would you use a combination of purposes? If so, which ones?
> 4. What primary writing strategy would you use: narrating, describing, explaining a process, comparing and contrasting, explaining causes and effects, persuading, evaluating, or solving a problem? Would you combine strategies? If so, which ones?
> 5. How would you design your document? What specific design features related to format, appearance, and visual aids would be appropriate for your document?

Analyzing Writing Situations
Using the Rhetorical Star
Activity:

Answers will vary.

article
"BE OUR GUEST. PLEASE"

Preview

"Be Our Guest. Please" appeared in the May 25, 2009, issue of *BusinessWeek*. As you read, notice the five points of the rhetorical star: subject, audience, purpose, strategy, and design. After you finish reading the article, look at the rhetorical star analysis that follows it.

BE OUR GUEST. PLEASE

Pool passes for locals, contests for upgrades, free food, even rooms set aside for post-op patients. Hotel operators, desperate for business, are turning to all sorts of tricks. "Every guest has become important, every niche segment has become important," says hospitality researcher Bjorn Hanson at New York University.

U.S. hoteliers are suffering from the sharpest slide since the September 11, 2001, attacks. Industrywide, revenue per available room is down 20% from last spring—down 30% for luxury hotels, Hanson says. And occupancy rates are likely to slip to under 56% this year, from about 60% last year and 63% in 2007, according to Atlanta-based PKF Hospitality Research.

55.7%

Predicted 2009 occupancy rate for the U.S. hotel industry, down from 60% last year and 63% in 2007
Data PKF Hospital Research

Thus the aggressive promotions. Dozens of Ritz-Carlton hotels are offering guests up to $200 worth of free food and spa services, depending on length of stay. The Four Seasons Hotel in Houston is appealing to locals, selling $20 weekend and holiday "daycation" passes to its outdoor pool, where attendants spritz patrons hourly with Evian water. Starwood Hotels & Resorts Worldwide, parent of the Westin and Sheraton brands, is charging guests based on their birth year for second and third night stays at some locations. (Customers born in 1960, for example, pay $60.) The Kimpton Hotel & Restaurant Group is advertising free room upgrades at check-in this summer for guests who can hulahoop for 20 seconds or win a game of rock, paper, scissors.

And perhaps taking a cue from Los Angeles hotels that cater to plastic surgery patients, the Fairmont Chicago is offering post-operative recuperation rooms in partnership with the Neurologic & Orthopedic Hospital of Chicago. Post-surgical guests can bring their own nurses, physical therapists, and doctors to their rooms. The Fairmont's owner, Strategic Hotels & Resorts, has been publicizing a recent stay by Phyllis Coors, a member of the brewing family, who was a post-op guest for

10 days after traveling from Colorado for a double knee replacement. The company plans similar hospital partnerships in California–at its Loews Santa Monica, for instance. Industry experts say wooing such patients is risky, since hotel guests want to feel they're at a getaway, not a convalescent home. But Strategic Hotels CEO Laurence Geller isn't anticipating problems. "It's such a small but profitable population," he says. –*Joseph Weber and Christopher Palmeri*

MICHAEL WITTE

SOURCE: J. Weber and C. Palmeri, "Be Our Guest. Please," *BusinessWeek*, May 25, 2009, p. 11.

Model Rhetorical Star Analysis of "Be Our Guest. Please"

Subject	Hotels are suffering financially, so they are experimenting with creative ways to draw in more guests.
Audience	The primary audience consists of people who are interested in current business trends and like to read *BusinessWeek*. A secondary audience includes readers who might be interested in staying in an upscale hotel for a good rate. The audience would expect to learn something about the status of the hotel industry.
Purpose	The main purpose is to inform readers about the unique strategies hotels are using to lure customers.
Strategy	The primary strategy is explaining cause and effect. The drop in revenue has caused hotels to find alternative methods of earning money. Additionally, the author compares and contrasts the strategies and prices of several different hotels.
Design	The cartoon is colorful and detailed. The text is blocked into short, single-spaced, indented paragraphs. Columns are used to break up the text. An important statistic is set off in a box. A chart might have been useful to compare the other statistics, but isn't included. Overall, its design is very appealing.

subject

design | audience

RHETORICAL STAR

strategy | purpose

Choose an article or essay in a popular print or online newspaper, magazine, or professional journal. Determine the five points of the rhetorical star by answering the following questions:

1. What is the subject?

2. Who is the primary audience? Is there a secondary audience? If so, who? What does the audience expect from the document?

3. What is the primary purpose? Does the author wish to inform, interpret, persuade, entertain, or express feelings? Has the author combined purposes? If so, which ones?

4. What strategy does the author use? Is the author narrating, describing, explaining a process, comparing and contrasting, explaining causes and effects, persuading, evaluating, or solving a problem? Is more than one strategy used? If so, what are they?

5. How is the article designed? Are headings, bullets, or visual aids included? How effective is the design?

Rhetorical Star Analysis Activity:

Answers will vary.

Teaching Tip

Have students work in groups to complete the Rhetorical Star Analysis Activity and share their results with the class.

[CHAPTER SUMMARY]

1. Increase your chances for success by creating an ideal atmosphere for writing.

2. Every time you write, consider the five points of the rhetorical star: subject, audience, purpose, strategy, and design.

3. Choose an interesting and useful subject for your paper.

4. Consider your audience's needs and expectations as you write your document.

5. The five purposes for writing are to inform, interpret, persuade, entertain, and express feelings.

6. Choose a writing strategy that best suits your purpose and audience. Narrating, describing, explaining a process, comparing and contrasting, explaining causes and effects, persuading, evaluating, and solving a problem are all popular writing strategies.

7. Use an effective and appealing design for your document.

SmartBook Tip

During the "Recharge" phase, students can return to Chapter 1 and practice concepts that they need to work on.

[WHAT I KNOW NOW]

Use this checklist to determine what you need to work on to feel comfortable with your understanding of the material in this chapter. Check off each item as you master it. Review the material for any unchecked items.

❏ 1. I am ready to create my own **ideal writing environment.**

❏ 2. I know the five points of the **rhetorical star.**

❏ 3. I can choose an interesting and useful **subject.**

❏ 4. I am aware of important **audience** characteristics to consider.

❏ 5. I understand the five **purposes** for writing.

❏ 6. I know what the eight **writing strategies** are.

❏ 7. I am aware that I need to choose an effective document **design.**

[FURTHER READING ON THE WEB]

- Explore Writing: **www.explorewriting.co.uk/CreatingAWritingEnvironment.html**
- The Rhetorical Situation: **http://owl.english.purdue.edu/owl/resource/625/01/**
- Audience Analysis: **http://owl.english.purdue.edu/owl/resource/629/01/**
- Rhetorical Strategies for Essay Writing: **www.nvcc.edu/home/lshulman/rhetoric.htm**
- College Writing Info: **www.tc.umn.edu/~jewel001/CollegeWriting/home.htm**

2

THE WRITING PROCESS

learning outcomes

In this chapter you will learn techniques for achieving these learning outcomes:

2.1 DISCOVER IDEAS ABOUT A TOPIC.

2.2 PLAN AND ORGANIZE A DOCUMENT.

2.3 COMPOSE A DOCUMENT.

2.4 GET APPROPRIATE FEEDBACK ON A DOCUMENT.

2.5 REVISE A DOCUMENT.

2.6 EDIT A DOCUMENT.

2.7 PROOFREAD A DOCUMENT.

FOLLOWING THE WRITING PROCESS

SmartBook Tip

Students receive an overview of the learning outcomes and topics in Chapter 2 in the "Preview" phase of SmartBook.

After you have analyzed your rhetorical star to get a good sense of what you need to do (see Chapter 1), it's time to start writing. Just like you need to find your own ideal writing environment, you will need to find the writing process that works well for you. The seven steps of the writing process are (1) discovering, (2) planning, (3) composing, (4) getting feedback, (5) revising, (6) editing, and (7) proofreading (see Figure 2.1). Learning to apply these seven steps will help you find the methods that work best for your writing process.

Writing can be a messy process, so you won't always follow all of the steps in sequence. Sometimes you might get to the composing step and decide you need more supporting points, which will take you back to the discovering step. Also, the steps are flexible. Some writers are comfortable beginning with the planning or even composing step while others prefer to try a number of discovering techniques before writing. Try different strategies to learn what works well for you. Continue working through the steps of the writing process until you are satisfied with your paper—or at least until your deadline arrives.

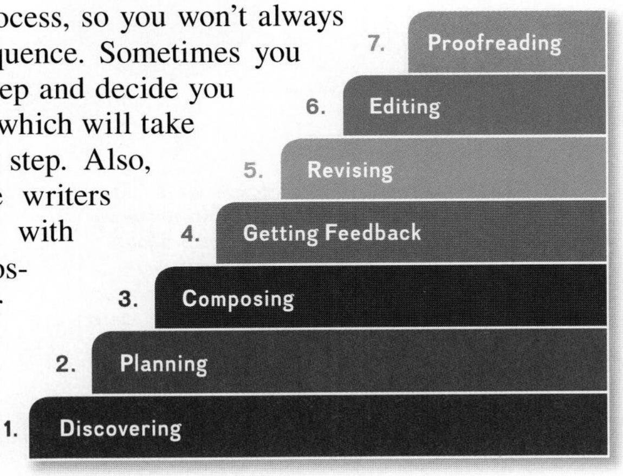

FIGURE 2.1 The Seven Steps of the Writing Process

7. Proofreading
6. Editing
5. Revising
4. Getting Feedback
3. Composing
2. Planning
1. Discovering

Teaching Tip

Emphasize the recursive nature of the writing process.

2.1 DISCOVERING

During this step you will explore your topic. You have several options for going about the discovery process. Your goal is to generate ideas about the topic you have selected. Have you ever experienced writer's block? The following strategies can help you overcome that ominous blank piece of paper or computer screen.

Brainstorming When you **brainstorm,** you write whatever comes to mind about your topic. If you don't have a topic, then use this approach to generate one. You can write all over the page if you like. Use arrows, boxes, question marks, circles, doodles, or whatever you can think of to explore ideas. Don't worry about writing in complete sentences or organizing your ideas. Just let your creativity spill onto the page.

Amanda Laudato chose to write an essay for her English composition class about the influential musician Eminem. Figure 2.2 shows her brainstorming notes.

FIGURE 2.2
Brainstorming Notes

Teaching Tip

Explain to students how a brainstorming session can help them to overcome writer's block.

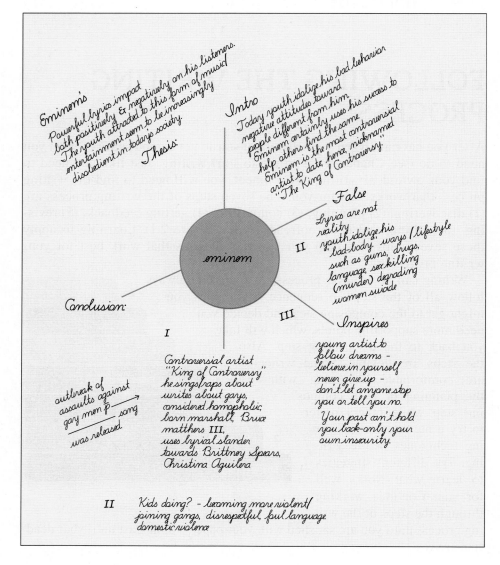

Listing List all the ideas that you can think of that relate to your topic. **Listing** is different from brainstorming because it's focused on a specific topic. There are no wrong ideas at this point. Keep writing for about 10 minutes. You should then review your list to see which ideas you like and which you want to eliminate. Put an "X" next to items you think won't be useful, but don't cross them out because you may change your mind. Some items on your list may stand out as potential main ideas, whereas others would make good supporting points. If that's the case, your list will also be helpful during the planning stage.

Here's a sample list on the subject of having a career rather than just a job:

greater financial reward

higher interest level

greater self-esteem

better potential for development

more required skills and training

more advancement opportunities

higher level of competence required

long term instead of short term

larger contribution to the community

greater sense of satisfaction

using talents to do something well

professionalism necessary

higher education required

Freewriting Take 10 or 15 minutes to write everything that comes to mind about your topic. This discovery method is like brainstorming and listing except that you are more likely to use complete sentences when you **freewrite.** Don't worry about grammar or punctuation; just keep writing. When finished, look at what you have written to see if you have stumbled upon any ideas that you would like to develop further. You might try a second freewriting session using one of the ideas you came up with during the first one.

Here's a sample freewriting exercise that Roberto Gonzales completed on his laptop computer in about 12 minutes during his English composition class:

Freewriting Unstructured writing for a set amount of time.

Teaching Tip

Ask students to freewrite about a topic, such as "why I enrolled in college," and have volunteers share their responses.

Job vs Career
by Roberto Gonzales

A job is something you have to do. You need money to pay your bills and to eat and a job usually gets you there. A job is usually a way to get your foot in the door or to experiment with what you really like or don't like. Something might be fun for a few hours, but eight hours of such work might cause a change in your perspective.

A career is a ladder. You know where you want to be and you know you have to climb to get there. A career is more than a paycheck, but where you choose to make your contribution to society. In a career small things matter more . . . who you work for, what people think, how well you are doing compared to someone else trying to climb that same ladder.

For most, their work experience starts with jobs. Not many people want to make a fast food joint or supermarket a career. You make a little cash, meet people, and start learning to develop a work ethic. Once you have finished school and obtained an appropriate certification or degree, then the focus shifts unto a career. Some place you will end up working for a long time; that will provide you with the means to have a family and fund the American dream. A career is that security blanket that allows you to not worry so much about a job, but gives you the assurance that you're going places and that each step of that ladder equals a better life for you and your family.

Questioning Consider the journalist's questions as you try to discover ideas about your topic. Who? What? When? Where? Why? How? (See Figure 2.3.) Write everything you can think of for each question. Afterward, you can decide which ideas you would like to investigate further. Use your answers as a starting point for your essay. This technique works especially well for informative pieces, narrative writing (storytelling), and problem solving.

Journaling Begin keeping a daily writer's **journal** (paper or electronic) where you jot down ideas that pop into your head. These ideas can be related to an assignment you are pondering, or they can be just general thoughts that you might like to explore later. You can use your journal to reflect on your feelings about yourself and your surroundings.

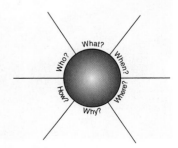

FIGURE 2.3
Journalist's Questions

Journal A place to keep track of thoughts and feelings.

You might write about events from your past and consider how these events have affected you or others. You may even want to predict what could happen in the future. When journaling, don't worry about grammar or sentence structure; just let your ideas flow and see where they lead you. Reread your journal entries in search of ideas to expand on for your assignments.

Sketching Even if you don't have an artistic side, you may find that doodling or drawing will help you generate ideas about your topic, especially if you are a visual person. A simple stick figure sketch might help you visualize your subject and give you material you can write about later. You might write captions for your drawings so that when you review them later you'll remember what you had in mind when you were creating them.

Teaching Tip
Tell students about the discovering techniques you employ when writing.

Talking You may find it useful to bounce your ideas off classmates, friends, co-workers, or family members. Tell them about your assignment and the ideas you have about approaching the task. You may come up with a brilliant idea while you are talking about your assignment, or someone else may say something that sparks your interest. Either way, just hearing the ideas being spoken can stimulate your creativity. Additionally, you might seek out someone who is familiar with the topic of your paper. Ask the person questions to learn more about your subject. He or she might be able to help you focus your topic.

Reading Sometimes you may find it helpful to read what others have written about your topic. Printed or online books, magazines, newspapers, or professional journals can serve as great resources for an assignment, especially a research essay. Seeing the approach that others have taken can enable you to formulate your own ideas. If you do decide to use someone else's words or ideas in your paper, be sure to cite your sources appropriately to avoid plagiarism. (See Part 3 to learn more about documenting sources.)

What ideas come to mind when you look at this image?

Viewing Often you'll find that looking at a photograph, painting, advertisement, television show, film, or website will stir your emotions and inspire you to write. If you are having trouble coming up with a topic for a writing assignment, you might think about something you have seen recently that caught your attention. Or you could surf the Web to look for an intriguing topic. You might also watch the History Channel or Discovery Channel to get ideas for papers. As with printed sources, you will need to document visual sources if you use specific details from them in your writing (see Part 3).

▶ Activity Discovering

Choose one of the following topics:

education	music	computers	television
health	movies	celebrities	video games
pets	commercials	fashion	nature
vacations	sports	musicians	
crime	cuisine	medicine	

Try one or more of the discovery techniques, such as brainstorming, listing, freewriting, questioning, or sketching, to see how many ideas you can come up with in 5 to 10 minutes that relate to your topic. Be prepared to share your findings.

Discovering Activity:
Answers will vary.

Employer SPOTLIGHT

Murielle Pamphile, Director of Student Services

Murielle Pamphile is the director of student services for a private university that offers degrees in a wide variety of majors that prepare students for specific careers. She has a **BS** in biology, an **MS** in health management, and a **PhD** in educational leadership. Here's what Pamphile has to say about the skills graduates need when they enter the workforce in a new career:

❝I work with students to ensure they have good employability skills. To determine exactly what skills graduates need to land a good job, I meet with employers in the fields related to students' majors and review comments from advisory board meetings and employer surveys. Employers frequently tell me that, in addition to developing skills related to a specific career field, students need to possess good résumé writing and job interviewing skills. Those skills are important for obtaining a job because employees will need to have good communication skills in the workplace. Also, students need to tailor their résumés to showcase the exact skills, qualifications, and certifications (if applicable) they have to demonstrate that they are a good fit for an employer. For example, a graduate looking for a job in the radiology field needs to include key terminology from that field on his or her résumé. Furthermore, employers often contact me to ask for a list of candidates who are qualified for a specific position. The graduates I recommend are those who have the appropriate job skills as well as strong communication skills. While students are in school, I encourage them to take their composition courses seriously and to visit the writing center so that they will develop the skills they need to be successful in their careers.❞

LearnSmart Achieve Tip

The Writing Process unit of LearnSmart Achieve determines what students do and do not know about the writing process. Learning outcomes within the Writing Process unit cover generating ideas, planning and organizing, drafting, revising, and proofreading. Learning resources and questions automatically adapt to each student's individual needs and help students thoroughly master this content. See the Instructor's Manual for *Write Now* for a list of learning outcomes as well as additional information on how to use LearnSmart Achieve with your students.

2.2 PLANNING

After you have discovered your topic and some supporting ideas, you will want to plan your essay. Having a plan will help you write a better finished product. Begin to organize what you came up with during the discovering stage. Also, remember to keep your rhetorical star (subject, audience, purpose, strategy, and design) in mind. Here are some planning techniques to try.

Narrowing Your Focus Often the ideas that writers generate during the discovery stage of the writing process are too broad to develop fully in a short paper. For example, "cooking" is too broad to write about in a short paper; however, you could focus an essay on "tips for healthy cooking."

▶ *Activity* **Narrowing Your Focus**

When you generate potential topics for essays, you will find that many are too broad to adequately cover in a short essay. When that happens, it's time to narrow your focus. When you narrow a topic, you get more specific. You may need to narrow your topic several times before it is narrow enough to cover in your paper.

EXAMPLE
Broad Topic: Computers
Narrower Topic: Computers and writing
Fully Narrowed Topic: How computers influence the writing process

Narrow the focus of several of the following topics to make them suitable for a short essay:

careers	fitness
music	student organizations
entertainment	drugs
sports	business
natural disasters	terrorist events
laws	movies
college	children

Narrowing Your Focus Activity: Answers will vary.

Thesis A statement that identifies the main idea of an essay.

Writing a Preliminary Thesis A **thesis** is a statement that identifies your topic and your opinion about that topic. Here's an example: *Joining the Student Government Association (SGA) has many benefits.* Keep your tentative thesis in mind when you are planning your essay. You can revise your thesis later if you change your opinion as you discover more about the topic. See Chapter 3 for more details on thesis statements.

Determining Main Points After your focus is clear and you have a tentative thesis, decide what main points you want to cover in your document. You will need enough main points to fully support your thesis. While there is no "correct" number of main points, having three to five of them in an essay often works well. Choose your main points carefully. The next planning technique can help you determine your main points.

Clustering Write your topic in the center of the page and draw a circle around it. Draw several lines out from your topic. At the end of each line, write a main idea and circle it. Then draw lines radiating out from each main idea. At the end of each line, write supporting ideas that relate to the circled word it connects to. One clustering exercise might lead to another. For instance, you may find that you have a lot to say about one of your main points and decide to shift your focus to just that main point. Then you may cluster again, this time putting the new idea in the center of the page. Clustering is a great way to begin to organize your ideas because it helps you to see the relationships among them. For example, if you are writing an essay about why your trip to the Bahamas was the best vacation you ever went on, your cluster might look like the one shown in Figure 2.4.

FIGURE 2.4
Sample Cluster

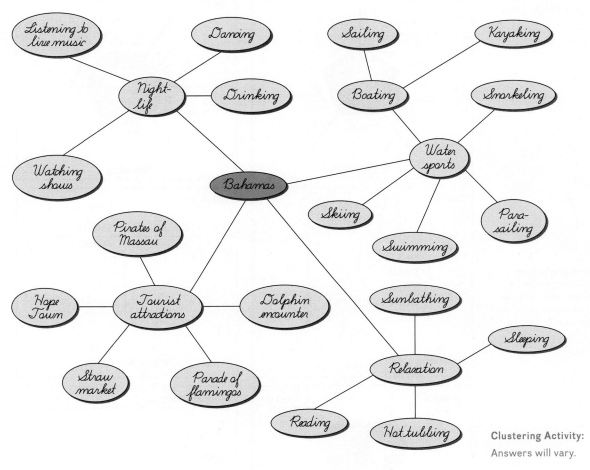

Clustering Activity:
Answers will vary.

▶ ## *Activity* **Clustering**

Choose one of the following topics, or one that you used in a previous activity, and narrow it down to a more focused topic. For example, if you chose "exercise" as your topic, your subtopic might be "winter sports."

television shows	music artists
recreational activities	hobbies
exercise	magazines
tablets	video games
transportation	computers

Create a cluster diagram for your topic. Make sure that you have at least three or four headings radiating out from your main topic. If you find that you have a lot of ideas for one heading but not the others, you may want to begin again using that one as your main topic.

Creating a Graphic Organizer Developing a graphic organizer can help you plan and organize your document. It can enable you to see the relationships among your ideas so that you can put them into a logical order before composing your first draft.

Figure 2.5 shows examples of graphic organizers you can use for the various writing strategies covered in this textbook. You may modify them as needed to fit your specific writing assignments and preferences.

FIGURE 2.5
Sample Graphic Organizers

Teaching Tip

Assign individual students or groups a graphic organizer to complete. You may select topics or ask your students to generate them. Have students share their results.

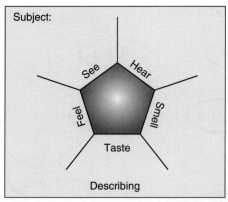

Describing

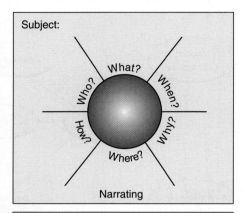

Narrating

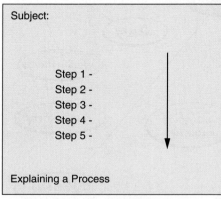

Step 1 -
Step 2 -
Step 3 -
Step 4 -
Step 5 -

Explaining a Process

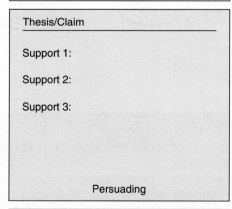

Explaining Causes and Effects

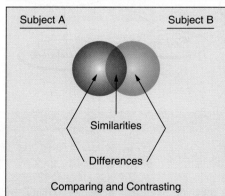

Comparing and Contrasting

Thesis/Claim

Support 1:

Support 2:

Support 3:

Persuading

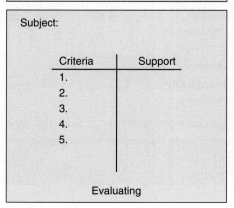

Evaluating

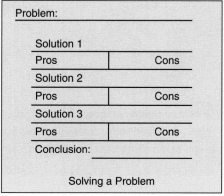

Solving a Problem

Here are some tips for using each type of graphic organizer.

1. **Describing:** When writing a description you need to appeal to the senses. Write what you can see, hear, smell, taste, and feel. Some senses will be more appropriate than others.

2. **Narrating:** When writing a narrative, answer the journalist's questions about a particular event.
   - *Who* was involved?
   - *What* happened?
   - *When* did the event take place?
   - *Where* did it occur?
   - *Why* did the event happen?
   - *How* did it occur?

3. **Explaining a Process:** When writing a "how-to" paper, explain each step of the process in chronological order.

4. **Explaining Causes and Effects:** Make a list of the causes (reasons) and the effects (results) related to your topic.

5. **Comparing and Contrasting:** When comparing and contrasting two subjects, write ideas that are unique to the first subject in the left-hand side of the first circle, and write ideas that are unique to the second subject in the right-hand side of the second circle. Place ideas that are common to both in the center, where both circles intersect. This is called a *Venn diagram.*

6. **Persuading:** When writing a persuasive document, write your thesis (claim) at the top of the page, and then list relevant details for each supporting point.

7. **Evaluating:** When writing an evaluation, make a list of criteria you will use to judge the topic and support for each judgment.

8. **Solving a Problem:** When proposing a solution to a problem, write out the pros and cons for several possible solutions before coming to a final conclusion.

Ordering Ideas After you've completed a cluster or rough graphic organizer, you will need to decide how to arrange your main points logically in your paper. Some writers find that simply listing the main points works best for them. Others prefer to create an informal or a formal outline (see the next section). For example, in the informal outline on page 26, it makes sense to cover tourist attractions, water sports, and relaxation before nightlife because that is the order in which the events would likely occur.

Outlining One purpose for creating an **outline** is to help you organize your writing. An outline is a blueprint of the divisions and subdivisions in your paper that illustrates the relationships among the ideas you present. Outlines can be formal or informal. To develop an informal outline, note each main point that you plan to cover in your essay, and then list the supporting ideas that you want to include with each point. An informal outline can help you see the structure of your paper, but it is less detailed than a formal outline. Although you don't necessarily need to include the introduction or conclusion in your outline, you will need them for your final essay. (See Chapter 3 for more details about essay structure.)

SmartBook Tip

Key concepts in Chapter 2 are highlighted for students during the "Read" phase. As students demonstrate understanding of these concepts during the "Practice" phase by responding to probes, the highlighting adapts to the individual student's learning by changing color.

Outline A blueprint of the divisions and subdivisions in a paper.

Sample Informal Outline

Attention-Getter: As soon as I stepped into my hotel room and looked out the sliding glass doors that opened right onto the white sand beach and turquoise ocean, I knew this was going to be a trip to remember.

Thesis Statement: My vacation to the Bahamas was the best experience of my life.

    Tourist Attractions
        Pirates of Nassau
        Hope Town
        Straw market
        Dolphin encounter
        Parade of flamingos
    Water Sports
        Boating: sailing and kayaking
        Parasailing
        Snorkeling
        Skiing
    Relaxation
        Reading books about local culture
        Sunbathing
        Sleeping
        Hot tubbing
    Nightlife
        Listening to live music
        Watching shows
        Dancing

Some writers prefer to use a formal topic or sentence outline, and some instructors require students to write one. A formal outline has more structure than an informal one. To develop a formal outline, assign each main point in your essay a Roman numeral: I, II, III, and so on. Then break down each idea into at least two parts (supporting points) and label those A, B, C, and so on.

Continue breaking down points as needed (see the basic outline structure), but remember that you always need to have at least two points when you subdivide your ideas. In other words, an "A" must be followed by a "B," and a "1" must be followed by a "2." Capitalize the first word of each line and all proper nouns.

Basic Outline Structure

I. First main point
  A. First supporting point
    1. Major detail or example
      a. Minor detail or example
      b. Minor detail or example
    2. Major detail or example
    3. Major detail or example
  B. Second supporting point
    1. Major detail or example
    2. Major detail or example
II. Second main point (and so on)

Although you do not need to have the same number of supporting points under each heading, your outline should be somewhat balanced. If most of your ideas fit beneath one main point, then you may want to narrow your focus to just that point and break it down further.

Also, be sure to keep like ideas parallel by stating similar ideas in a similar way. (See Part 4 for more on parallel structure.)

Not Parallel: Parasailing, snorkeling, and to water ski are fun activities.
Parallel: <u>Parasailing</u>, <u>snorkeling</u>, and <u>water skiing</u> are fun activities.
Discussion: The second sentence includes a series of words that end with "ing." Lists of nouns, verbs, adjectives, or adverbs should all be in the same form.

Sample Formal Topic Outline

Attention-Getter: As soon as I stepped into my hotel room and looked out the sliding glass doors that opened right onto the white sand beach and turquoise ocean, I knew this was going to be a trip to remember.

Thesis Statement: My vacation to the Bahamas was the best experience of my life.

  I. Tourist Attractions
   A. Pirates of Nassau
     1. Brief history
     2. Museum
   B. Hope Town
   C. Straw market
     1. People
     2. Merchandise
   D. Dolphin encounter
   E. Parade of flamingos
 II. Water Sports
   A. Boating
     1. Sailing
     2. Kayaking
   B. Parasailing
   C. Snorkeling
   D. Skiing
III. Relaxation
   A. Reading books about local culture
   B. Sunbathing
   C. Hot tubbing
IV. Nightlife
   A. Listening to live music
   B. Watching shows
   C. Dancing

Partial Sample of a Formal Sentence Outline

IV. The nightlife in the Bahamas is amazing.
   A. Many restaurants offer live music featuring Goombay drums that reflect the local culture.
   B. Live shows are abundant, especially during the Junkanoo festival, when costumed people parade through the streets dancing to music played on drums, cowbells, and whistles.
   C. For those who like more active entertainment, dancing is quite popular at the local bars and restaurants.

Grammar Window
PARALLEL STRUCTURE

Revise the following sentences to give them parallel structure:

1. This school encourages students to have good attendance, to turn in assignments on time, and displaying a positive attitude.

2. Ray says that when he graduates he will get a great job, purchase a newer car, and he doesn't like his current apartment.

Grammar Window: Possible Responses

1. School encourages students to have good attendance, to turn in assignments on time, and to display a positive attitude.

2. Ray says that when he graduates he will get a great job, purchase a newer car, and move to a nicer apartment.

Teaching Tip

Suggest that students write a topic sentence for each main point in their outline to help them with the next step of the writing process, composing.

▶ *Activity* Outlining

Based on the clustering activity that you completed, write an informal outline or a formal topic or sentence outline. Be sure to organize your ideas logically. You may need to write a draft first and then rework it to make the ideas flow logically.

2.3 COMPOSING

Once you have narrowed your topic and have a plan for organizing your ideas, you are ready to begin composing your essay. Use the ideas that you generated during the discovering and planning stages to help you develop your rough draft. Let your cluster or outline serve as your guide. Also, be sure to focus on the first four points of the rhetorical star: subject, audience, purpose, and strategy. You can determine the design of your document later. As you begin to write, focus more on getting your ideas on the computer screen (or on paper) than on how you present your ideas. Go easy on yourself. You are not aiming for perfection, especially with the first draft.

You may want to write the easiest parts first to help build your confidence. In a short essay, you might write a paragraph about each main point. In a longer assignment, you might need several paragraphs to fully develop each main point. (See Chapter 3 for more details about thesis statements and essay development.)

Keep writing until you feel that you have covered all, or most, of the main points you had planned to address in your paper. Be sure to save your rough draft or put it in a safe place. Now take a well-deserved break! If you have time, let your ideas gel a bit before you continue to the next step of the writing process. If you give yourself a little time off, then you'll be able to review your work from a fresh perspective.

▶ *Activity* Composing

Write a paper on the topic you have chosen, using the informal or formal outline you developed in the previous activity to guide its organization. Don't worry about grammar and punctuation for your first draft.

2.4 GETTING FEEDBACK

After you have written your first draft, you will find that it is helpful to get someone else's advice about your paper. Unless you are writing an essay for an in-class assignment, you should have an opportunity to get feedback from someone who can give you useful tips for revising your paper. Having a conference with your instructor, participating in a peer review activity with a classmate, or working with a campus-based or online writing tutor are all excellent ways to help you improve your writing.

Conferences One technique you can use to get feedback on your assignment is to have a conference with your instructor, if possible. He or she should be able to provide you with insightful suggestions for revision. If you're taking an online course, you may be able to e-mail your assignment to your instructor and wait for feedback. Many instructors are willing to provide students with general suggestions for improving their papers. However, don't expect your instructor to correct your paper for you. Your job is to learn how to revise and edit your own papers. You may also have a conference with a peer review partner or a writing lab tutor.

Peer Review Participating in a peer review exercise is a great way to improve your writing. Your instructor may give you an opportunity to complete a peer review activity in class. Usually you will pair up with another student (or a group of students) and provide constructive criticism (ideas for improvement) about each other's drafts. You can also use this method in an online class via e-mail.

You will receive valuable suggestions for revising your paper, and you will be able to offer your peer review partner helpful feedback as well. Additionally, you'll have an opportunity to see how someone else has approached the assignment. Even after you finish your writing course, you can continue to use these peer review strategies. Outside of college, co-workers, family members, and friends often review each other's writing before it reaches its intended audience.

Tips for Peer Reviewers

- **Consider the writer's feelings.** Begin by pointing out something positive in the paper. What do you like best about the paper? Is there a particular part that you find especially interesting or insightful? What details and examples are most useful?

- **Provide constructive criticism.** Even if you are not the strongest writer, you know good writing when you see it. Are there specific areas that could be clearer or that need more explanation? Focus mostly on the larger issues, such as content, organization, and development. Avoid marking every error in grammar, punctuation, or spelling unless the writer has specifically asked you to do so. Be tactful with the comments you make, but don't just say you like everything if there are areas that need improvement.

  Additionally, be sure to give the writer concrete suggestions for how to improve the paper. For example, maybe the paper needs more specific examples to fully support the thesis statement, or perhaps some areas could be clearer.

Tips for Writers

- **Communicate with the reviewer.** Tell your peer review partner what you would like him or her to review. Depending on how rough your draft is, you might not be ready for help with grammar, punctuation, and mechanics. Maybe there are particular parts of your paper that you're not sure about or that seem awkward or undeveloped to you. Ask the reviewer to focus on those areas.

- **Take the suggestions in stride.** Remember that your peer review partner is trying to offer you constructive suggestions for making your paper better. Also, keep in mind that there are many ways (not just a right way and a wrong way) to approach a writing assignment. Thank the reviewer for the feedback, and then make your own decision about what to change . . . or not. In the end, you are the author, so the choices you make about your paper are up to you.

Teaching Tip

Encourage students to have someone else look at their work before submitting it whenever possible. Mention that even professional writers need to get feedback before submitting important documents for publication.

SAMPLE PEER REVIEW QUESTIONS

1. Which sentence states the main idea (thesis) of the essay? Is it clear? Is its placement appropriate? Why or why not?
2. Are there any additional details that could be included to help you better understand the essay? What is missing or unclear?
3. Are the details covered in a logical sequence? Which ones, if any, seem out of place?
4. What part of the essay is most memorable? Why?
5. Are transitions, such as "furthermore," "for example," and "next," used to help the ideas in the paper flow logically? If not, which ones would be useful?
6. Does the author provide the reader with a sense of completion at the end? If so, how?
7. What kinds of grammatical errors, if any, are evident in the essay?
8. What final suggestions do you have for the author?

Writing Centers and Online Writing Labs Some schools offer an avenue for getting feedback on your papers from a qualified professional through a writing center or online writing lab (OWL). These resources are designed for writers of all ability levels. If you have access to a writing center on campus, find out what kinds of services it provides and when it is open. At the writing center, you may have an opportunity to sit down with a person who can read your rough draft and provide suggestions for revising and editing. Additionally, writing centers often have a wide variety of print and computerized materials to help you with every aspect of the writing process.

If your campus doesn't have a writing center, or if the timing doesn't work with your schedule, you might have an OWL you can utilize. When you use an OWL, you typically submit your draft electronically via e-mail and then receive feedback from a qualified professional, often within a day or two.

Tips for Working with Writing Tutors Regardless of whether you use a writing center or an OWL, here are some tips that will help you make the most of it:

- **Have a rough draft ready.** If you haven't put any thought into your assignment, a writing tutor will have difficulty helping you. Even if your draft is extremely rough, you need to have something the writing tutor can read so that you can receive useful feedback.

- **Have your instructor's directions handy.** Often a writing tutor will ask you about the assignment's specifications. That way he or she can help determine if you have met your instructor's requirements or if you have gotten off track. Also, if your instructor provides you with grading criteria (in the form of a rubric or grid), be sure to share that information with your writing tutor.

- **Have specific questions in mind.** Asking a writing tutor simply to tell you what is wrong with your paper isn't the best approach. What specific areas would you like him or her to review? Are you concerned about the organization or development of your paper? Do you need help with any grammar issues? Also, don't expect to have your paper corrected for you. A writing tutor may point out a few errors so that you can see what kinds of issues you need to work on, but it is your responsibility to proofread and correct your paper.

- **Keep an open mind and a positive attitude.** Remember that the writing tutor, like a peer reviewer, wants to help you become a better writer by providing you with constructive criticism. Try not to be too sensitive about your work. Consider the feedback you receive, and make the changes you feel are necessary. Keep in mind that it is your paper. If you disagree with some of the feedback, or if you have additional questions, you can always get a second opinion. Ultimately, you have to decide what strategies work best for your paper.

2.5 REVISING

Many writers are tempted to take that first draft, correct the "mistakes," and then turn it in. If you do that, you will be skipping one of the most important steps of the writing process. Good writers typically spend more time revising than working on any other step. The term *revision* literally means to see again. You'll need to read back over your work and make improvements. Here are some higher-order concerns to consider as you revise your paper:

Adding and Deleting Ideas

- Have you included all of the main points you had hoped to cover?
- Will including more ideas strengthen your essay?
- Are any of the points irrelevant?
- Are any points repetitious?
- Have you included any points that you could delete without weakening your paper?

Developing

- Have you included enough details and examples to support your main points?
- Can you expand on some points to provide greater clarity for your audience?

If you feel your paper needs more development, you can try additional discovery techniques to come up with more details and examples. You want to make sure to have enough support for your paper to convince your audience that the opinion in your thesis is accurate.

Arranging

- Does the order of your main points make sense?
- Can you rearrange main points and details to help your readers better understand the point you are making?

As you are revising your paper, move sentences and paragraphs around to see what flows better and makes more sense. If you are revising on a computer, the cutting and pasting features in your word processing program will simplify this procedure. Be sure to save different versions of your drafts so that you can go back to previous versions if you need to. If you are revising on paper, you can literally cut and paste (or tape or staple) sentences and paragraphs. You may want to make multiple copies of your draft before revising so that you can remember how you originally wrote it. Continue cutting and pasting until you find the arrangement that best fits with your rhetorical star.

Activity   Getting Feedback

Have someone else (such as a classmate, writing tutor, friend, or family member) read the rough draft you composed in your last activity. Read the reviewer's feedback and decide which suggestions you want to accept, ignore, or modify. If you are working with another classmate, then you will need to provide him or her with constructive feedback as well.

Getting Feedback Activity:
Answers will vary.

2.6 EDITING

Once you are satisfied with the large-scale revisions you have made to your paper, you will want to examine it more closely. When you edit a paper, you are looking for lower-order concerns, such as errors in words, sentence structure, grammar, punctuation, spelling, and mechanics. You can use your computer's spell checker as well as a print or digital thesaurus and dictionary to help you edit your paper. Read your paper aloud (to yourself or an audience). Listen to the flow of ideas. Consider the following questions as you edit your paper and make changes accordingly. (See Part 4 for more details about editing.)

Word Choice (Diction)

- Have you chosen precise words that will create a specific picture in your readers' minds?
- Do any important words have a common meaning that readers might think of instead of the meaning you intend?
- Are there any words that could be more interesting or lively?

ESOL Tip >

Use a standard American dictionary as well as a dictionary written for nonnative speakers to help you with diction.

Teaching Tip

Draw students' attention to the editing marks listed on the inside back cover of the book. Tell students about the editing marks you use most frequently when grading.

Teaching Tip

Explain that although it is tempting to edit and proofread while composing, writers should determine what ideas they are keeping, revising, or deleting first so as not to waste time.

Sentence Structure

- Do any sentences sound awkward?
- Do the sentences vary in length and style?
- Are any sentences too short and choppy?
- Are any sentences long enough to create confusion for your readers?

Grammar

- Are there any problems with subject-verb agreement?
- Do all of the pronouns make sense?
- Are there enough adjectives to fully describe the nouns?
- Are all of the adverbs used correctly? For example, is *well* used to modify verbs instead of *good*, which is an adjective?
- Do all of the modifiers make sense?

Punctuation

- Do all sentences end with an appropriate punctuation mark?
- Are quotation marks used correctly?

- Are commas, semicolons, and colons used effectively? Are any of them unnecessary or misplaced?
- Do special punctuation marks, such as dashes and ellipses, fit with the writing?

Spelling

- Are there any spelling errors that the spell checker might overlook, such as *they're* instead of *their* or *you're* instead of *your?*
- Does the spelling of each word, such as *affect* or *effect,* reflect the intended meaning?

Mechanics

- Are the correct words capitalized?
- Are abbreviations appropriate, or do they need to be spelled out?
- Are numerals and spelled-out numbers used correctly?

2.7 PROOFREADING

After you have finished revising and editing, be sure to proofread your final paper. As you read your paper this time, you are looking for the really nit-picky details, such as repeated words and typographical errors, that you may have overlooked previously. You might want to read your paper aloud again. Another strategy is to read your paper backward, from the last sentence to the first sentence. That way you can focus on every word. Most writers have difficulty finding all of the errors in their own papers. Therefore, you may want to have another person review your paper again. The more feedback you receive the better.

After you have proofread for the last time, be sure to submit your essay in the correct format. Is your paper supposed to be double-spaced? Are you expected to turn in a hard copy, an electronic version, or both? Have you followed all of the directions for the assignment? Following your instructor's guidelines is an important part of the assignment. Once you submit your final paper, you'll have the satisfaction of having completed an original piece of writing.

ONE STUDENT'S JOURNEY THROUGH THE WRITING PROCESS

Thomas Ryan Gorsuch followed the steps of the writing process (Figure 2.6) as he wrote his first essay for English Composition 1. He began by completing an analysis based on the rhetorical star (Figure 2.7), and then proceeded with the stages shown here.

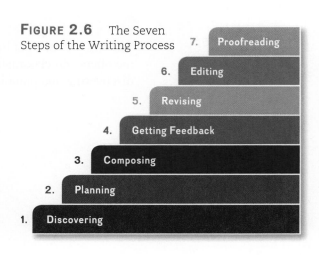

FIGURE 2.6 The Seven Steps of the Writing Process

7. Proofreading
6. Editing
5. Revising
4. Getting Feedback
3. Composing
2. Planning
1. Discovering

Rhetorical Star Analysis Worksheet

Subject	Gaming media's influence of "Rock Band" and "Rock Band 2." How the gaming media have encouraged people to buy and play Rock Band.
Audience	People who might read this paper would range from young teens to late 40's. Might appeal to musicians and males or females.
Purpose	To inform the reader how the media have influenced people to think or feel that purchasing Rock Band they will have a more exciting, healthy happy family life.
Strategy	Cause How we're blinded by the truth about what the media have to say. Appreciation for musicians. Effects Wanting to pursue musical arts, fun family togetherness, and a more fulfilling life
Design	APA format, 750-word essay, 12 pt font, double spaced, Times New Roman, indented paragraphs, page #s in header header and title

FIGURE 2.7 Rhetorical Star Analysis Worksheet

1. Discovering

Thomas did much of his discovery work in his head. He also talked with family members and classmates about his topic. He used a clustering exercise for both discovering and planning purposes.

2. Planning

Thomas created a cluster to begin to generate and organize his ideas for his essay about the impact of Rock Band (Figure 2.8).

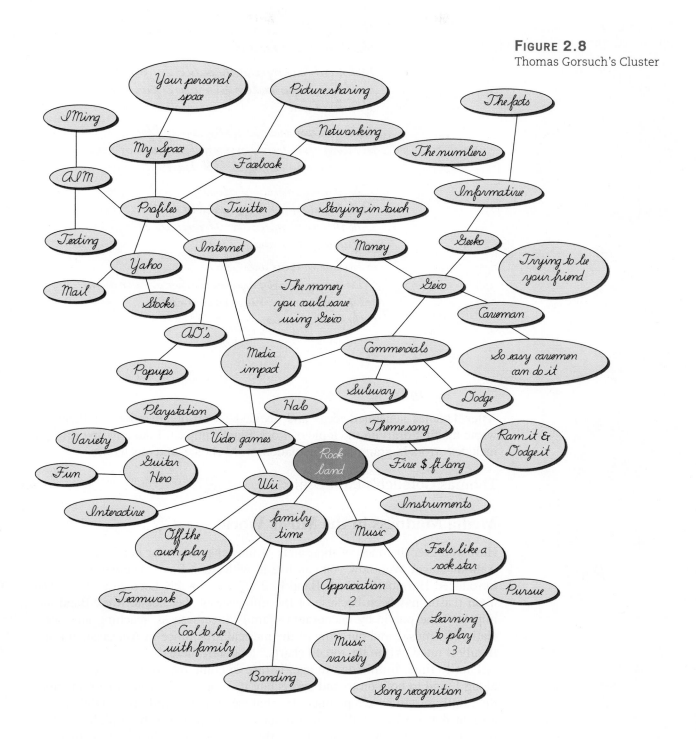

FIGURE 2.8
Thomas Gorsuch's Cluster

Teaching Tip

Discuss the value of using some kind of organizational strategy when planning an essay.

Informal Outline Thomas chose not to write a formal outline, but many students do benefit from creating one. Instead, he organized his ideas into the informal outline shown in Figure 2.9.

FIGURE 2.9 Thomas's Informal Outline

The impact of Rock Band or the impact that Rock Band has had.

Thesis — Rock band has impacted the public by family togetherness, appreciation for music & pursuing of musical arts.

Hook — Have you ever dreamed of thousands of fans chanting your band's name as you walk on stage? Well now you can with Rock Band.

Intro — The gaming media introduced Rock Band in 2007 and quickly became a "hit". The main reason has been through the influence of the media.

Body —
• Pursue musical arts
• Bringing family together, for family fun night
• Appreciation for music and interest in the form of media

3. Composing

After Thomas generated ideas and decided on an organization for them, he wrote his first draft on the topic of Rock Band's impact. Like any first draft, it includes errors in grammar, punctuation, word choice, and mechanics.

Thomas Gorsuch's First Draft

Media Madness in the Music World

Have you ever dreamed of thousands of fans chanting your band name as you walk on stage? Well now you can live it, with Rock Band. The gaming media introduced Harmonix's Rock Band in 2007 and quickly became a "Hit". The main reason has been because of the influence of the media. Rock Band has impacted the public by encouraging family togetherness, teaching an appreciation for music, and pursuing of the musical arts. Since in American culture, family is rated "#1 on the top 40 charts," let's start there.

Family time, in this day in age, is rare to come by, so when it does come along I tend to hold on to and appreciate it. When I was younger I remember my family use to have a planned day that we called "family fun night". It was a night that we would all enjoy dinner together followed by a night of playing games. Sadly this is an activity that is rarely seen in family gatherings today. Through the media, this new game of Rock Band has made this picture more appealing and possible. Since this game reached stores everywhere I have heard many of my friends and family talk of how this game has brought them closer together. Since this game succeeds only when everyone works together, or in this case, plays together, this creates an attitude of team work and cooperation. Together, my family, friends and I each play a different instrument making up one Rock Band! Even if I'm not playing an instrument I feel included and involved by being part of the concert, cheering the band on, and becoming like one of the groupies. This new age of technology gaming has now replaced rolling dice on a flat game board to picking up an instrument or microphone, moving along as if really standing on stage. This get's my heart pumping, whether from trying to keep up with the beat, listening to cheering fans, or just from making a fool of myself. My family has so much fun, enjoying a wonderful experience that will bond us and probably be talked and laughed about for a long time. If you thought keeping the rhythm was hard, try singing on tune.

In this game, almost without my knowledge of it, it gave me an appreciation for music. Music is hard, and takes a lot of practice to perfect. When playing Rock Band the success of my band and the score shown is based on accuracy of hitting the right notes and the right time. This does not come naturally to everyone and definitely not to me. Although I know the song, listened to it in the car, or have scene it performed live, it is a completely different story to have to play it myself. Another point of music appreciation I learned is through the different styles of music. Rock Band has a variety of genres, of course starting out with Classic Rock turning to Alternative Rock and Country. When I play this game I learn about the different styles of music, how to play it, recognize it, and distinguish it apart from other styles. Suddenly I found that I had a new or renewed interest in music itself which lead to my interest in music lessons.

Now that I have been playing Rock Band, I, and many of my friends and family I have talked to, have wanted to learn to play an instrument for real. Rock Band gave me a taste of what performing music would be like and gave me a beginning level feel for each instrument that makes up a rock band. Thanks to the media, Rock Band slowly pushed to the top of the gaming list, making it a hit with everyone I know, including me. As Rock Band continues to add things making it even better and more difficult, it made me appreciate musicians and in turn, made me want to become one, at least for fun. I am not the only one, the media's influence in making Rock Band so popular has impacted the world in a way that many others have also taken up or started to pursue either a career or hobby in musical arts. I would say that the media has a pretty powerful influence.

As you can see, the media has influenced viewers like me, through TV, radio, and online advertisement that by purchasing Rock Band I will have a more exciting and fun life. It tells me that I will have fun with my family for a change, learn about music and its different genres, and also will help me to become a better musician, if I chose to pick up an instrument for real. So now let Rock Band bring you together, so you can have your own "family fun night!"

4. Getting Feedback

Peer Review Before revising his essay, Thomas submitted it to two classmates for peer review. The feedback he received from Elizabeth Robson and Lana Darby is shown in Figures 2.10 and 2.11.

FIGURE 2.10
Elizabeth's Peer Review

Author: Thomas Gorsuch
Reviewer: Elizabeth Robson

Peer Review Questions

1. Which sentence states the main idea (thesis) of the essay? Is it clear? Is its placement appropriate? Why or why not?

"Rock Band has impacted the public by encouraging family togetherness, teaching an appreciation..."

2. Are there any additional details that could be included to help you better understand the essay? What is missing or unclear?

Source for quote "#1 on top 40 charts"

3. Are the details covered in a logical sequence? Which ones, if any, seem out of place?

Yes, they are starting with family ending w/pursuing of the musical arts.

4. What part of the essay is most memorable? Why?

"My family has so much fun...talked and laughed about for a long time"

5. Are transitions, such as "furthermore," "for example," and "next," used to help the ideas in the paper flow logically? If not, which ones would be useful?

*Could use some transitions.
I only found couple, maybe use "As a Result" in the 4th paragraph instead of "now that"*

6. Does the author provide the reader with a sense of completion at the end? If so, how?

Yes, he states thesis again and leaves me w a memorable statement

7. What kinds of grammatical errors, if any, are evident in the essay?

*A few words should be replaced.
"now that" changed to "since" (4th paragraph)
take "it" out of sum sentence "... it, and many of ... family have ... ."*

8. What final suggestions do you have for the author?

Use the 3rd person point of view.

FIGURE 2.11
Lana's Peer Review

Author: Thomas Gorsuch
Reviewer: Lana Darby

Peer Review Questions

1. Which sentence states the main idea (thesis) of the essay? Is it clear? Is its placement appropriate? Why or why not?

The 3rd sentence states the main idea. "The gaming media introduced Harmonic's Rock Band in 2007 and quickly became a "Hit" It is clear and is placed well following the opening "attention getter" line

2. Are there any additional details that could be included to help you better understand the essay? What is missing or unclear?

Explain gaming media. Explain to reader that this is a game that hooks up to XBox or Playstation. Therefore you and your family get interaction versus your son or daughter sitting in their room alone playing a war/or violent video game for hours while the parent watches it

3. Are the details covered in a logical sequence? Which ones, if any, seem out of place?

Details are O.K.

4. What part of the essay is most memorable? Why?

Parts that emphasize family time and once you spend time as a family you realize what you may have been missing.

5. Are transitions, such as "furthermore," "for example," and "next," used to help the ideas in the paper flow logically? If not, which ones would be useful?

"Since" is used a lot. Find different word.

6. Does the author provide the reader with a sense of completion at the end? If so, how?

Yes. The author recaps ideas in the summary and ends with a positive suggestion.

7. What kinds of grammatical errors, if any, are evident in the essay?

Possible commas missing.

8. What final suggestions do you have for the author?

Detail more the options or features of the game. Also, suggest that he hopes his children will remember the time as he remembered his family tradition.
Also, go in depth about how you can change levels in the singing and instrument. Start on easy move up to beginner then to harder levels. That makes you want to focus and try harder to achieve the goal From personal experience, I know how hard it is to sing on key with the game.

Teaching Tip

Emphasize the value of having more than one peer reviewer when possible.

NetTutor Feedback Some schools provide students with online writing tutoring services through a third party, such as SmarThinking or NetTutor. Thomas was fortunate to have this opportunity. The NetTutor writing expert's response is shown in Figure 2.12.

Paper Meta Information and Summary

FIGURE 2.12
NetTutor Sample

Your Name:	Thomas Gorsuch
Student ID:	XXXXXXXXXXXXXXX
Email:	XXXXXXXXXXXXXXX
Campus:	MELBOURNE
Course Title and #:	ENC1101 ENGLISH COMPOSITION I
Professor's Name:	RUSSELL, KARIN
Course Section:	Day: Mon., Tues., Thurs.
Due Date:	12-15-14
English as a second language?	No
Taken ENC 1101?	No
Describe Assignment:	Write a cause-and-effect essay about the effect the media have on the public, in this case it's the gaming media.
Required Length:	700 words
Two Areas for Feedback:	Grammar, Word Usage/Spelling

Proofing Summary:
Hi Thomas! Thank you for submitting your paper. I think you made the right choice of topic because this is something that you are familiar with and interested in. I really enjoyed reading about how a video game brought your family together where most people would guess that it would cause you to drift further apart. Your spelling was good for the most part but there are a couple instances where you have used the wrong word. Those are easily revised, however. Any other issues with the essay were small and sporadic. Look over your proofed paper for further feedback. Thanks again for your submission and good luck with your revisions!

5. Revising

Thomas made some revisions to his paper based on the NetTutor and peer review feedback he received. He focused mainly on higher-order concerns, such as adding, deleting, and rearranging ideas, as he revised his first draft. For example, he switched the third and fourth paragraphs because he decided that it made more sense to discuss specific instruments before mentioning music appreciation in general. He also strengthened his topic sentences and added more transitions. (See Chapter 3 for more details about topic sentences and transitions.)

Thomas Gorsuch's Second Draft
In the second draft shown below, all of Thomas's changes appear in angle brackets and red type. Since Thomas was concentrating on higher-order concerns, this draft includes errors in grammar, punctuation, word choice, and mechanics.

Media Madness in the Music World

Have you ever dreamed of thousands of fans chanting your band name as you walk on stage? Well now you can live it, with <<*Rock Band, Rock Band II, or even Rock Band III*>>. <<In 2007>> the gaming media introduced Harmonix's Rock Band, which quickly became a "Hit". The main reason has been because of the influence of the media.<<The *Rock* Band video games have been wildly popular among gamers of all ages throughout the United States.>> <<*Rock Band*>> has <<affected>> the public by encouraging family togetherness, <<influencing people to pursue>> the musical arts, and teaching an appreciation for music.

<<One way *Rock Band* has influenced families is by giving them an opportunity to spend time together. Today,>> family time is rare to come by, so families should hold on to and appreciate it. When I was younger I remember my family use to have a planned day that we called "family fun night". It was a night that we would all enjoy dinner together followed by a night of playing games. Sadly this is an activity that is rarely seen in family gatherings today. <<The new *Rock Band* game has>> made this picture more appealing and possible. Since this game reached stores everywhere I have heard many of my friends and family talk of how this game has brought them closer together. This new age of technology gaming has now replaced rolling dice on a flat game board to picking up an instrument or microphone, moving along as if really standing on stage. Since this game is successful only when everyone plays together, this creates an attitude of team work and cooperation. Together, my family, friends, and I play a different instrument, making up one Rock Band! Even if I'm not playing an instrument I feel included and involved by being part of the concert, cheering the band on like groupies. <<*Rock Band* get's the players' hearts>> pumping, whether from trying to keep up with the beat, listening to cheering fans, or just from making a fool of myself. My family has so much fun <<playing *Rock Band* and>> enjoying a wonderful experience that we will probably <<talk and laugh>> about for a long time. If you thought keeping the rhythm was hard, try singing on tune.

<<Another effect of the *Rock Band* game is that it has caused many players to want to play a real instrument. *Rock Band*>> gave me a taste of what performing music <<as a singer, guitar player or drummer>> would be like and a beginning level feel for each instrument that makes up a rock band. As <<players progress through Rock Band, the game>> continues to add <<new levels, songs, and venues, causing the game to be>> even better and more difficult. <<These advancements>> make me appreciate musicians and in turn, want to become one, at least for fun. The media's influence in making Rock Band so popular has <<affected>> the world in a way that <<has likely caused>> many <<people>> to pursue either a career or hobby in musical arts.

<<Furthermore, the Rock Band game has helped people to develop a stronger>> appreciation for music. Music <<can be difficult to perform>>, and takes a lot of practice to perfect. When playing Rock Band the success of <<the>> band and the score shown is based on accuracy of hitting the right notes and the right time. This does not come naturally to everyone. Although I know the song <<from listening>> to it in the car or <<hearing>> it performed live, it is a completely different story to have to play it myself. <<*Rock Band* also helps gamers to appreciate>> music is through <<introducing them to>> different styles of music. Rock Band has a variety of <<musical>> genres, <<such as>> Classic Rock, turning to Alternative Rock, and Country. When I learn about the different styles of music, how to play it, recognize it, and distinguish it apart from other styles. Suddenly I found that I had a new or renewed interest in music itself which lead to my interest in music lessons.

Note: Thomas took the advice from Lana, one of his peer reviewers, and added more details about how the game works to his third paragraph.

As you can see, the media has influenced viewers like me, through TV, radio, and online advertisement that by purchasing <<*Rock Band* they>> will have a more exciting and fun life. <<Players>> will have fun with <<their families>> for a change, become <<better musicians, if they choose to pick up an instrument for real>>, and learn <<more>> about music and its different genres, So now let <<*Rock Band*>> bring you together <<with your family and friends>>, so you can have your own "family fun night!"

6. Editing

After Thomas completed his second draft, he used the paper proof that he received from his NetTutor feedback to help him edit his paper. During this step, he focused mostly on lower-order concerns, such as correcting his grammar, punctuation, and sentence structure. Thomas knew not to rely completely on the paper proof, but he did find it useful for catching some aspects of his paper that needed attention.

Additionally, he took his classmate's peer review suggestion and switched from the first-person to the third-person point of view, which uses *he, she,* and *they* instead of *I, me,* and *my.*

Thomas Gorsuch's Third Draft All of Thomas's changes appear in angle brackets and red type.

Media Madness in the Music World

Have you ever dreamed of thousands of fans chanting your band name as you walk on stage? Well now you can live it, with *Rock Band* or *Rock Band II.* <<In 2007>> the gaming media introduced Harmonix's *Rock Band,* which quickly became a "Hit". <<The *Rock Band* video games have been wildly popular among gamers of all ages throughout the United States.>> *Rock Band* has <<affected>> the public by encouraging family togetherness, <<influencing people to pursue>> the musical arts, and teaching an appreciation for music.

<<One way *Rock Band* has influenced families is by giving them an opportunity to spend time together. Today,>> family time is rare to come by, so families should hold on to and appreciate it. <<In the past, some families uses to have planned nights when they>> would all enjoy dinner together followed by a night of playing games. Sadly this is an activity that is rarely seen in family gatherings today. <<The new *Rock Band* game has>> made this picture more appealing and possible. Since this game reached stores, it has brought <<families>> closer together. This new age of technology gaming has now replaced rolling dice on a flat game board to picking up an instrument or microphone, moving along as if really standing on stage. Since this game is successful only when everyone plays together, this creates an attitude of team work and cooperation. <<Each participant plays>> a different instrument making up one Rock Band! Even <<the people who are not>> playing an instrument feel included and involved by being part of the concert. <<They cheer>> the band on like groupies. <<*Rock Band* get's the players' hearts>> pumping, whether from trying to keep up with the beat, listening to cheering fans, or just from making fools of <<themselves>>. <<Families have>> so much fun <<playing *Rock Band* and>> enjoying a wonderful experience that <<they>> probably <<will talk and laugh>> about for a long time. If you thought keeping the rhythm was hard, try singing on tune.

<<Another effect of the *Rock Band* game is that it has caused many players to want to play a real instrument.>> Rock Band <<gives players>> a taste of what performing music <<as a singer, guitar player or drummer>> would be

Note: Thomas took the advice of Elizabeth, one of his peer reviewers, and changed his point of view from the first person to the third person beginning in his second paragraph.

like and a beginning level feel for each instrument that makes up a rock band. As <<players progress through Rock Band, the game>> continues to add <<new levels, songs, and venues, causing the game to be>> even better and more difficult. <<These advancements help players to>> appreciate musicians and, in turn, want to become one, at least for fun. The media's influence in making Rock Band so popular has <<affected>> the world in a way that <<has likely caused>> many <<people>> to pursue either a career or hobby in musical arts.

    <<Furthermore, the *Rock Band* game has helped people to develop a stronger>> appreciation for music. Music <<can be difficult to perform>>, and takes a lot of practice to perfect. When playing <<*Rock Band*>> the success of <<the>> band and the score shown is based on accuracy of hitting the right notes and the right time. This does not come naturally to everyone. <<Even if players are familiar with a>> song <<from listening>> to it in the car or <<hearing>> it performed live, it is a completely different story to have to play it <<themselves>>. <<*Rock Band* also helps gamers to appreciate>> music is through <<introducing them to>> different styles of music. Rock Band has a variety of <<musical>> genres, <<such as>> Classic Rock, Alternative Rock, and Country. <<Players>> learn about the different styles of music, how to play it, recognize it, and distinguish it apart from other styles.

    As you can see, the media has influenced viewers through TV, radio, and online advertisement that by purchasing Rock Band <<they>> will have a more exciting and fun life. <<Players>> will have fun with <<their families>> for a change, become <<better musicians, if they choose to pick up an instrument for real>>, and learn <<more>> about music and its different genres, So now let *Rock Band* bring you together <<with your family and friends>>, so you can have your own "family fun night!"

Rock Band Jam Session

7. Proofreading

Thomas read through his paper one more time, proofreading for errors, awkward sentences, and word choice. He also took out the word *media* in the title because his emphasis shifted from the media to just the Rock Band game.

NetTutor Paper Proof As noted earlier, Thomas received some proofreader suggestions in addition to the narrative explanation with suggestions from the writing tutor from NetTutor (Figure 2.13).

Media Madness in the Music World

Have you ever dreamed of thousands of fans chanting your ~~band~~ [band's] name as you walk on stage? Well now you can live it, with Rock Band. The gaming media introduced Harmonix's Rock Band in 2007 and quickly became a ▪Hit▪ [lc]. The main reason has been because of the influence of the media. Rock Band has impacted the public by encouraging family togetherness, teaching an appreciation for music, and pursuing of the musical arts. Since in American culture, family is rated "#1 on the top 40 charts," let's start there. [Is this an actual quote? If it isn't, you don't need to put it in quotations.]

Family time, in this day in age, is rare to come by so [cap] when it does come along I tend to hold on to and appreciate it. When I was younger, I remember my family use to have a planned day that we called "family fun night." It was a night that we would all enjoy dinner together, followed by a night of playing games. Sadly this is an activity that is rarely seen in family gatherings today¶ Through the media, this new game of Rock Band has made this picture more appealing and possible. Since this game reached stores everywhere, I have heard many of my friends and family talk of how this game has brought them closer together. Since this game succeeds only when everyone works together, or in this case, plays together, this creates an attitude of team work and cooperation. Together, my family, friends and I each play a different instrument making up one Rock Band! Even if I'm not playing an instrument I feel included and involved by being part of the concert, cheering the band on, and becoming like one of the ~~groupies~~ [fans]. This new age of technology gaming has now replaced rolling dice on a flat game board to picking up an instrument or microphone, [and] moving along as if really standing on stage. This get's my heart pumping, whether from trying to keep up with the beat, listening to cheering fans, or just from making a fool of myself. My family has so much fun, enjoying a wonderful experience that will bond us and probably be talked and laughed about for a long time. If you thought keeping the rhythm was hard, try singing on tune. [This doesn't fit here. If you want to include it, you should move it to the section that discusses the game.]

In this game, almost without my knowledge of it, it gave me an appreciation for music. Music is hard, and takes a lot of practice to perfect. When playing Rock Band, the success of my band and the score shown is based on accuracy of hitting the right notes and the right time. This does not come naturally to everyone and definitely not to me. Althought I know the song, [have] listened to it in the car, or have scene [ww] it performed live, it is a completely different story to have to play it myself. Another point of music appreciation I learned is through the different styles of music. Rock Band has a variety of genres, of course starting out with Classic Rock turning to Alternative Rock, and now coming out with Country in July. When I play this game, I learn about the different styles of music, how to play it, recognize it, and distinguish it apart from other styles. Suddenly, I found that I had a new or renewed interest in music itself which, [led] ~~lead~~ to my interest in music lessons.

Now that I have been playing Rock Band, I, and many of my friends and family I have talked to, have wanted to learn to play an [actual] instrument ~~for real~~. Rock Band gave me a taste of what performing music would be like and gave me a beginning level feel for each instrument that makes up a rock band. Thanks to the media, Rock Band slowly pushed to the top of the gaming list, making it a hit with everyone I know, including me. As Rock Band continues to add things, making it even better and more difficult, it made me appreciate musicians and, in turn, made me want to become one, at least for fun. I am not the only one [cap] the media's influence in making Rock Band so popular has impacted the world in a way that many others have also taken up or started to pursue either a career or hobby in [awk] musical arts. I would say that the media has a pretty powerful influence.

As you can see, the media has influenced viewers like me, through TV, radio, and online advertisement [You may want to mention this in your opening paragraph. It doesn't fit here if you are mentioning it for the first time.] that by purchasing Rock Band I will have a more exciting and fun life. It tells me that I will have fun with my family for a change, learn about music and its different genres, and also will help me to become a better musician, if I chose to pickup an instrument for real. So now [cap] let Rock Band bring you together, so you can have your own "family fun night"

FIGURE 2.13 NetTutor Paper Proof

Thomas Gorsuch's Final Draft Thomas's final corrections appear in angle brackets and red type.

Madness in the Music World

Have you ever dreamed of thousands of fans chanting your band <<'s>> name as you walk on stage? Well now you can live it, with *Rock Band* or *Rock Band II.* In 2007 the gaming media introduced Harmonix's <<*Rock Band*>>, which quickly became a <<hit>>. <<Since then>> the *Rock Band* video games have been wildly popular among gamers of all ages throughout the United States. *Rock Band* has affected the public by encouraging family togetherness, influencing people to pursue the musical arts, and teaching an appreciation for music.

One way *Rock Band* has influenced families is by giving them an opportunity to spend time together <<and become closer.>> Today, family time is rare to come by, so families should appreciate <<the time they have together by doing something engaging>>. In the past, some families use<<d>> to have planned nights when they would all enjoy dinner together followed by a night of playing games. Sadly this is an activity that is rarely seen in family gatherings today. The new *Rock Band* game has made this picture more appealing and possible. This new age of technology gaming has now replaced rolling dice on a flat game board <<with>> picking up an instrument or microphone <<and playing songs>> as if <<the players are>> really <<performing>> on stage. Since this game is successful only when everyone plays together, <<it>> creates an attitude of <<teamwork>> and cooperation. Each participant plays a different instrument making up one <<r>>ock <<b>>and<<.>> *Rock Band* <<gets>> the players' hearts pumping, whether from trying to keep up with the beat, listening to cheering fans, or just making fools of themselves. Even the people who are not playing an instrument feel included and involved by being part of the concert. <<The observers>> cheer the band on like groupies. Families have so much fun playing *Rock Band* and enjoying a wonderful experience that they probably will talk and laugh about <<it>> for a long time.

Another effect of the *Rock Band* game is that <<it encourages>> many players to want to play a real instrument. *Rock Band* gives players a taste of what performing music <<would be like>> as a singer, guitar player, or drummer and a beginning level feel for each instrument that makes up a rock band. As players progress through *Rock Band,* <<new levels, songs, and venues continue to open>>, causing the game to be even better and more <<challenging>>. These advancements help players to appreciate musicians and, in turn, want to become <<like them>>, at least for fun. The media's influence in making *Rock Band* so popular has affected the world <<by influencing>> many people to pursue either a career or hobby in <<the>> musical arts.

Furthermore, the *Rock Band* game has helped people to develop a stronger appreciation for music. Music can be difficult to perform and takes a lot of practice to perfect. When playing *Rock Band* <<,>> the success of the band and the score shown <<are>> based on accuracy of hitting the right notes and the right time. This does not come naturally to everyone. Even if players are familiar with a song from listening to it in the car or hearing it performed live, <<they find>> it completely different to have to play <<the song>> themselves. *Rock Band* also helps gamers to appreciate music through introducing them to different styles of music. *Rock Band* has a variety of musical genres, such as <<classic rock, alternative rock, and country.>> Players <<can>> learn about the different styles of music, how to play <<them>>, recognize <<them>>, and distinguish <<them>> from other styles.

<<*Rock Band* has revolutionized family fun time.>> Players will have <<a great time>> with their families for a change, become better musicians, if they choose to pick up an instrument for real, and learn more about music and its different genres<<.>> So now let *Rock Band* bring you <<and your family together,>> so you can have your own "family fun night!"

Madness in the Music World

Have you ever dreamed of thousands of fans chanting your band's name as you walk on stage? Well now you can live it, with *Rock Band* or *Rock Band II.* In 2007 the gaming media introduced Harmonix's *Rock Band,* which quickly became a hit. Since then the *Rock Band* video games have been wildly popular among gamers of all ages throughout the United States. *Rock Band* has affected the public by encouraging family togetherness, influencing people to pursue the musical arts, and teaching an appreciation for music.

One way *Rock Band* has influenced families is by giving them an opportunity to spend time together and become closer. Today, family time is rare to come by, so families should appreciate the time they have together by doing something engaging. In the past, some families used to have planned nights when they would all enjoy dinner together followed by a night of playing games. Sadly this is an activity that is rarely seen in family gatherings today. The new *Rock Band* game has made this picture more appealing and possible. This new age of technology gaming has now replaced rolling dice on a flat game board with picking up an instrument or microphone and playing songs as if the players are really performing on stage. Since this game is successful only when everyone plays together, it creates an attitude of teamwork and cooperation. Each participant plays a different instrument making up one rock band. *Rock Band* gets the players' hearts pumping, whether from trying to keep up with the beat, listening to cheering fans, or just making fools of themselves. Even the people who are not playing an instrument feel included and involved by being part of the concert. The observers cheer the band on like groupies. Families have so much fun playing *Rock Band* and enjoying a wonderful experience that they probably will talk and laugh about it for a long time.

Another effect of the *Rock Band* game is that it encourages many players to want to play a real instrument. *Rock Band* gives players a taste of what performing music would be like as a singer, guitar player, or drummer and a beginning level feel for each instrument that makes up a rock band. As players progress through *Rock Band,* new levels, songs, and venues continue to open, causing the game to be even better and more challenging. These advancements help players to appreciate musicians and in turn, want to become like them, at least for fun. The media's influence in making *Rock Band* so popular has affected the world by influencing many people to pursue either a career or hobby in the musical arts.

Furthermore, the *Rock Band* game has helped people to develop a stronger appreciation for music. Music can be difficult to perform and takes a lot of practice to perfect. When playing *Rock Band,* the success of the band and the score shown are based on accuracy of hitting the right notes at the right time. This does not come naturally to everyone. Even if players are familiar with a song from listening to it in the car or hearing it performed live, they find it completely different to have to play the song themselves. *Rock Band* also helps gamers to appreciate music through introducing them to different styles of music. *Rock Band* has a variety of musical genres, such as classic rock, alternative rock, and country. Players can learn about the different styles of music, how to play them, recognize them, and distinguish them from other styles.

Rock Band has revolutionized family fun time. Players will have a great time with their families for a change, become better musicians, if they choose to pick up an instrument for real, and learn more about music and its different genres. So now let *Rock Band* bring you and your family together, so you can have your own "family fun night!"

1. Read the first sentence. Does it capture your attention? Why or why not?
2. Based on the introduction, what do you expect from the rest of the essay?
3. Does the essay deliver what Thomas promised in the introduction? Explain.
4. Which supporting details seemed the most helpful? Why?
5. Would you want to play Rock Band based on this essay? Why or why not?

SmartBook Tip

During the "Recharge" phase, students can return to Chapter 2 and practice concepts that they need to work on.

[CHAPTER SUMMARY]

1. Follow the seven stages of the **writing process** to write effective documents.
2. Use different **discovery** methods to help you choose and narrow your subject.
3. Create a cluster or outline to help you **plan** and organize your document.
4. **Compose** your rough draft without worrying too much about grammar and punctuation.
5. **Get feedback** on your paper from someone who can give you suggestions for revision.
6. When **revising** a document, you may add and delete ideas, further develop your concepts, or rearrange your points to make your writing more effective.
7. **Edit** your paper carefully for diction, sentence structure, grammar, punctuation, spelling, and mechanics.
8. **Proofread** your paper and make corrections before submitting your final draft.

[WHAT I KNOW NOW]

Use this checklist to determine what you need to work on to feel comfortable with your understanding of the material in this chapter. Check off each item as you master it. Review the checklist periodically for any unchecked items.

❏ 1. I have found several **discovery methods** I can use to find and explore topics.

❏ 2. I am familiar with how to develop a cluster or outline to **plan** my paper.

❏ 3. I won't be too hard on myself as I **compose** my first draft.

❏ 4. I understand the importance of **getting feedback** from a classmate, a tutor, or an online writing service to help me improve my paper.

❏ 5. I am aware that I will need to **revise** my paper by adding, deleting, rearranging, and further developing my ideas.

❏ 6. I know that I need to carefully **edit** my paper for diction, sentence structure, grammar, punctuation, spelling, and mechanics.

❏ 7. I'll leave time to **proofread** my final paper before turning it in to my instructor.

[FURTHER READING ON THE WEB]

- Journal Writing Prompts: **www.creative-writing-now.com/journal-writing-prompts.html**
- Developing an Outline: **http://owl.english.purdue.edu/owl/resource/544/01/**
- Starting the Writing Process: **http://owl.english.purdue.edu/owl/resource/587/01/**
- The Writing Process: **www.csuohio.edu/academic/writingcenter/writproc.html**
- Editing and Proofreading: **www.bestessaytips.com/writing_steps_edit.php**

3

WRITING SENTENCES, PARAGRAPHS, AND ESSAYS

3.1 WRITE COMPLETE SENTENCES, INCLUDING TOPIC SENTENCES AND THESIS STATEMENTS.

3.2 WRITE AND DEVELOP EFFECTIVE PARAGRAPHS USING TRANSITIONAL WORDS AND PHRASES TO CREATE BETTER FLOW.

3.3 WRITE EFFECTIVE MULTI-PARAGRAPH ESSAYS THAT INCLUDE AN INTRODUCTION, A BODY, AND A CONCLUSION.

3.1 WRITING A SENTENCE

Sentence Components

Writing an effective sentence requires careful thought. Basically, every sentence needs to have three elements. It needs to have a subject and a verb, and it needs to express a complete thought. The subject is the topic of your sentence; the verb is the action in the sentence; and the complete thought allows the sentence to stand on its own.

Incomplete sentence: While I was driving to work today.

Complete sentence: While I was driving to work today, I saw a bobcat near the road.

Discussion: The first sentence has a subject (I) and a verb (was driving), but the word *while* causes it to be incomplete.

For more on complete and incomplete sentences, see pages 400–404 in Part 4.

Writing Complete Sentences Activity: Possible Responses

1. While I was enrolling in college, I discovered that I was interested in helping patients.

2. Some of the most popular majors are allied health, computers, criminal justice, and business.

3. Dr. Coggins is the best instructor I have had so far.

4. Joining a social or professional organization helps students to develop leadership skills.

5. The best way to achieve success in college is to follow all of the instructors' directions.

▶ *Activity* **Writing Complete Sentences**

Revise each incomplete sentence below so that it contains a subject and a verb and expresses a complete thought:

1. While I was enrolling in college.
2. Some of the most popular college majors are.
3. Is the best instructor I have had so far.
4. Joining a social or professional organization.
5. The best way to achieve success in college.

Parts of Speech

Reviewing the eight *parts of speech* can strengthen your sentence-writing skills. Table 3.1 lists the parts of speech and describes their functions. Basically, every word in a sentence serves a particular function. Although a complete sentence

Teaching Tip

You may want to introduce students to the term "independent clause" at this point.

TABLE 3.1

The Eight Parts of Speech		
Parts of Speech	**Descriptions**	**Examples**
Nouns	Name a person, place, or thing	Dr. Oz, New York, book
Pronouns	Replace a noun	me, them, herself, it, that, who
Verbs	Show action or a state of being	jump, surfed, has been running, will be swimming, is, was
Adjectives	Modify or describe a noun	cute, sweetest, green, playful, funny, Asian
Adverbs	Modify or describe a verb, an adjective, or another adverb	slowly, carefully, completely, sooner
Prepositions	Link a noun to another word	to, before, on, over, with, beyond
Conjunctions	Join clauses, sentences, or words	for, and, nor, but, or, yet, so, although, unless, because
Interjections	Express a strong feeling	Oh! Cool! Ouch! Wow!

▶ ## Activity   Parts of Speech

Identify the part of speech of each highlighted word in the sentences below:

1. The friends assembled food, drinks, and fishing gear for the outing.
2. It was a sunny day, and the water was perfectly calm.
3. Sophie said, "Wow! Look at the size of that fish."
4. She tried to get the fish into the boat, but it got away too quickly.
5. The boat rapidly approached the shore.

Parts of Speech Activity: Answers

1. noun, noun
2. verb, adjective, adverb
3. verb, interjection
4. preposition, conjunction, adverb
5. adverb, verb

ESOL Tip >

When writing in standard American English, place an adjective before, not after, a noun. For example, write "the blue car" instead of "the car blue."

needs to include only a noun and a verb and express a complete thought, you may use other words, such as adjectives and prepositions, to provide more details for your readers.

Sentence Variety

Whether you are writing a short paragraph or an entire essay, you will need to vary your sentence length and style. If all of your sentences are similar, then your writing style will probably seem dull to your readers. A short, simple sentence can help you to emphasize a key point, whereas a longer, more complex sentence may enable you to illustrate the relationships among the ideas you are presenting. Varying your sentence lengths and patterns creates greater interest for the reader. Read the following passages:

▶ # Draft

Some forms of body art have been around for centuries. Body art is growing in popularity. Many men and women are getting tattoos. Some people are also getting a variety of body piercings. Other people are getting implants to change their appearance. Many people who try body art want to make a bold statement.

Read the previous passage aloud. How does it sound? Is it exciting or boring? You probably noticed that the ideas are presented in a short, choppy manner and that some words are repeated unnecessarily. Basically, the sentences are similar in structure and lack variety.

SmartBook Tip

Students receive an overview of the learning outcomes and topics in Chapter 3 in the "Preview" phase of SmartBook.

 ## *Revised* for Better Sentence Variety

Although various forms of body art have been around for centuries, today it is growing in popularity. Many men and women are using tattoos, body piercings, and implants to change their appearance and make a bold statement.

The revised passage sounds much better when read aloud because the sentences vary in length and structure, and the ideas flow better together. Notice that some ideas were combined to create more variety in sentence structure and to eliminate repeated words such as *body art* and *people*.

Sentence Variety Activity: Answers will vary.

 ## *Activity* Sentence Variety

Revise the following paragraph by varying the structure of the sentences to make the ideas flow more smoothly. You may reword, reorganize, and combine sentences, but be sure to keep all of the ideas present in the original paragraph. To be effective, your final paragraph will need to have fewer sentences and words without losing any of the details.

Vacationing in Key West

Key West, Florida, is a fun-filled vacation destination. It is an island situated at the southernmost point of the United States. First of all, there are many activities to enjoy in Key West. Some people enjoy water sports in Key West. The fishing is first-class. The dolphin encounters are wonderful for nature lovers. Diving and snorkeling are popular sports in Key West. Additionally, the nightlife in Key West is exceptional and makes it a fun place to visit. Duval Street has great bars. There are numerous bars with live music. Sloppy Joe's is a famous bar. Ernest Hemingway loved to go to Sloppy Joe's. Hog's Breath Saloon is a popular nightspot. Two Friends Bar is a popular evening destination. There is karaoke at Two Friends Bar. Key West provides tourists with opportunities for several other activities as well. There are quaint shops to visit. Visitors can see a live performance at the Tennessee Williams Theatre. Travelers can tour Ernest

Key West, Florida

Hemingway's house. There is so much to do in Key West. As a result, many people enjoy traveling to Key West every year.

Paragraph A group of sentences related to one idea.

Topic sentence A sentence that states the main idea of a paragraph.

3.2 WRITING A PARAGRAPH

A **paragraph** is a group of sentences that all relate to one idea. Sometimes a paragraph can stand on its own, and other times a paragraph is part of a larger essay or document. Typically, a stand-alone paragraph consists of three main parts: a topic sentence, several main points with supporting sentences, and a concluding sentence (see Figure 3.1).

FIGURE 3.1 Basic Paragraph Structure

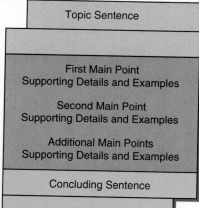

Topic Sentence

First Main Point
Supporting Details and Examples

Second Main Point
Supporting Details and Examples

Additional Main Points
Supporting Details and Examples

Concluding Sentence

Topic Sentence

A **topic sentence** states the main idea of a paragraph.

A good topic sentence has two main components—a topic and an opinion about the topic. It also has to be a complete sentence. Remember, a complete sentence contains a subject and a verb and expresses a complete thought. For example, the following includes all of the necessary components of a good topic sentence: "Even though working and going to school full time can be challenging at times, the advantages far outweigh the disadvantages."

Poor topic sentence: Reasons to learn to write.

Revised topic sentence: Learning to become a better writer can help you to be more successful in achieving your educational, career, and personal goals.

Discussion: The poor sentence lacks a verb, an opinion, and a complete thought. The revised sentence has all of the required components.

▶ *Activity* **Writing Topic Sentences**

Brainstorm a list of at least five topics to which most college students can relate. The topics can be about music, television, movies, current events, school, careers, or other areas of interest. From that list, choose the two that you like best. Write a topic sentence for each topic you choose. Be sure each topic sentence includes the topic and an opinion and is a complete sentence.

Writing Topic Sentences Activity:

Answers will vary.

Supporting Sentences

The body of your paragraph will include supporting points and examples that support the opinion in your topic sentence. While there is no magic number of supporting sentences, you will usually need at least three to five sentences to support each topic sentence in an academic paper. You will want to have enough supporting sentences to fully develop your topic. Keep in mind that college writers are more likely to have too few supporting sentences than too many. Also, make sure that your paragraph is unified. In other words, every idea you include must help support the opinion in your topic sentence.

Choose one of the topic sentences that you created in the Writing Topic Sentences activity. Write four to five supporting sentences to go along with your topic. Be sure that all sentences clearly relate to the opinion expressed in the topic sentence.

Transitions

Use transitional words and phrases throughout your paragraphs to help signal your reader when you are changing direction or moving to a new point. (See examples of transitions in Table 3.2.) Transitions make your writing more coherent for the audience because they serve to bridge ideas. Without transitions, your readers might not understand the connection you are trying to make between two ideas.

Writing Supporting Sentences Activity:

Answers will vary.

TABLE 3.2

Transitions	
Types of Transitions	**Examples**
To give examples	for example, for instance, such as, that is
To show time or order	about, after, afterward, as soon as, at, before, beforehand, during, finally, first, immediately, in the meantime, later, meanwhile, next, presently, second, soon, subsequently, then, third, today, tomorrow, until, when, without delay, yesterday
To show location	above, across, against, along, alongside, among, around, away from, behind, below, beneath, beside, between, beyond, by, down, in back of, in front of, inside, into, near, nearby, off, on top of, onto, outside, over, throughout, to the left, under, underneath
To compare (show similarities)	also, as, as though, in the same way, like, likewise, neither, both, similarly
To contrast (show differences)	although, but, even though, however, in contrast, in spite of, on the other hand, otherwise, still, yet
To show a cause	another reason, because, one reason, since
To show an effect	as a result, consequently, hence, therefore, thus
To add information	additionally, again, along with, also, and, another, as well, besides, equally important, finally, furthermore, in addition, moreover, next
To show emphasis or repetition	again, even, certainly, emphatically, in other words, in particular, in fact, in the same way, more importantly, more specifically, obviously, of course, to emphasize, truly
To conclude or summarize	all in all, as a result, consequently, finally, for this reason, hence, last, to conclude, to summarize

Teaching Tip

Give students sample paragraphs or ask students to bring in print or digital articles to use to identify transitions and discuss their usage and effectiveness.

LearnSmart Achieve Tip

The Writing Process unit of LearnSmart Achieve determines what students do and do not know about the writing process. Learning outcomes within the Writing Process unit cover drafting paragraphs; revising; and proofreading, formatting, and producing texts. Learning resources and questions automatically adapt to each student's individual needs and help students thoroughly master this content. See the Instructor's Manual for *Write Now* for a list of learning outcomes as well as additional information on how to use LearnSmart Achieve with your students.

Using the words below, fill in the blanks in the following paragraph by adding transitional words or phrases. Be sure that your transitions show the logical relationships among the ideas in the paragraph.

for example	all in all	first of all	also
in addition	another reason	as well	second

See You at the Movies

Going to see a movie at a theater is far superior to viewing one at home. _____, the technology is much better at the theater. _____, the screen is many times larger than home televisions. This causes the characters and events to appear much larger than in real life. The sound system is better _____. The Dolby surround sound and booming volume help viewers to feel as if they are actually on location with the actors. _____, sharing the experience with a large audience adds to the excitement of the movie. Audience members can laugh, gasp, or cheer together when important scenes occur. _____ why the theater is more enjoyable is the vast selection of snacks at the concession stand. _____ to the standard popcorn, chocolate, and cola products, many movie theaters _____ offer nachos with cheese, personal pizzas, cinnamon-glazed

nuts, and a variety of other options to satisfy the audience's hunger. _____, watching a movie at the theater beats viewing one at home every time.

Concluding Sentence

If you are writing a stand-alone paragraph, the last sentence should serve as your conclusion. Restate the main idea and opinion you introduced in your topic sentence. Be sure to use different words than you did the first time.

> **Topic sentence:** Learning to become a better writer can help you to be more successful in achieving your educational, career, and personal goals.

> **Reworded concluding sentence:** Strengthening your writing skills will enable you to become more accomplished in school, on the job, and in your personal life.

Depending on the length of your paragraph, you may want to add one more sentence after your reworded thesis. If so, you will want to include something that readers will remember. See the example in the model paragraph that follows. Notice that the transitional words are highlighted.

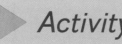

Activity   Concluding Sentences

Write a concluding sentence for the topic sentence and supporting sentences you created in the Writing Topic Sentences (page 52) and Writing Supporting Sentences (page 53) activities. Be sure your concluding sentence uses different words to remind your readers of the opinion in the topic sentence.

Model Paragraph

Internships

Topic Sentence — Working as an intern for a local medical facility is an excellent way to begin your career in the allied health field.

First Main Point — First of all, as an intern you will learn valuable skills that you may not learn in college.

Supporting Details — For example, you will have an opportunity to work with real patients and learn how to meet their needs while they are in the office. Also, you will gain a greater understanding of what doctors and other health professionals will expect from you while you are on the job.

Second Main Point — Another benefit to taking on an internship is that you will have a chance to prove that you are capable of handling the duties that you will be responsible for when you are on the job.

Supporting Details — For instance, you can demonstrate your competence in performing crucial administrative and clinical tasks.

Third Main Point — Finally, the greatest benefit to serving as an intern is that the experience may very well lead to a permanent position.

Supporting Details — If you work hard, know your stuff, and get along well with others, then you are likely to land a job at the intern site.

Reworded Thesis — Consequently, the skills, real-world experience, and job opportunities that an internship provides are extremely advantageous to your career in the allied health field.

Memorable Statement — Even though internships are usually not paid positions, they are well worth their time for the benefits you will receive.

Graduate SPOTLIGHT

MeiLynn D'Alessandro, Sales Representative

MeiLynn D'Alessandro has a degree in marketing and works as a sales representative for an educational consulting group. Here's what D'Alessandro has to say about the importance of written communication in her career:

" I do a tremendous amount of writing in my career. First, I write a summary of each school's needs to send to others in my company so they can understand how we can best serve the needs of teachers and students. My summaries have to be detailed and accurate, with specific suggestions that are appropriate because many people depend on the solutions my company develops. Also, every day I write dozens of e-mail messages to my customers to answer questions and explain technology in a clear and concise manner. Additionally, I develop digital sales flyers that I use to showcase our newest products. These flyers must be descriptive and persuasive. Finally, I write a monthly report summarizing the meetings I have had with customers to make the management team aware of my activity in my territory. Having strong writing skills is critical to my success as a sales representative. **"**

3.3 WRITING AN ESSAY

Essay A group of paragraphs related to a particular subject.

FIGURE 3.2 Basic Essay Structure

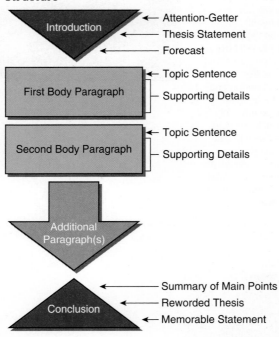

Introduction
← Attention-Getter
← Thesis Statement
← Forecast

First Body Paragraph
← Topic Sentence
← Supporting Details

Second Body Paragraph
← Topic Sentence
← Supporting Details

Additional Paragraph(s)

Conclusion
← Summary of Main Points
← Reworded Thesis
← Memorable Statement

An **essay** (also known as a *composition*) is a group of paragraphs related to a particular subject or theme. Essays are usually designed to achieve one of the five purposes for writing: to inform, to interpret, to persuade, to entertain, and to express feelings (see Chapter 1 for more details). An essay with a clear organizational structure is easier for your readers to understand. Like virtually every other type of document that you write, an essay needs to have a beginning, a middle, and an ending (introduction, body, and conclusion). Figure 3.2 illustrates the basic structure of an essay.

Introductory Paragraph

Your introduction should accomplish three tasks: capture the audience's attention, state your thesis, and provide an overview of the main points you will cover in the body of the essay. Avoid beginning a paper with dull statements such as, "This essay is going to be about . . ." or "I'm going to explain. . . ." Instead, start with something that will capture your audience's interest.

Attention-Getters The first sentence is one of the most important sentences in your entire essay. This is your one chance to convince the audience that your paper is worth reading. You will need to make the most of this opportunity. Whatever type of lead-in you choose to get your audience's attention, you will want to ensure that it effectively introduces your thesis statement. The idea is to entice your audience to continue reading your paper. Table 3.3 lists examples of attention-getting strategies for introductory paragraphs.

Thesis Identifies the main idea of an essay.

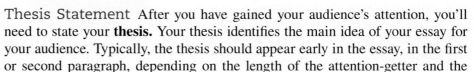

Thesis Statement After you have gained your audience's attention, you'll need to state your **thesis.** Your thesis identifies the main idea of your essay for your audience. Typically, the thesis should appear early in the essay, in the first or second paragraph, depending on the length of the attention-getter and the length of the essay. A thesis statement is just like a topic sentence except that it states the main idea for an entire essay instead of just one paragraph. A thesis has the same two components as a topic sentence: the topic and your opinion. (See Table 3.4 for some sample thesis statements.) A thesis, like any complete sentence, needs to have a subject and a verb and express a complete thought.

Poor thesis: Many people earn a college degree.

Poor thesis: The benefits of a college education.

Revised thesis: Obtaining a college education has several benefits.

Discussion: The first "poor thesis" example simply states a fact about the subject without offering an opinion. The second "poor thesis" example has a subject and an opinion, but it lacks a verb and doesn't express a complete thought. The revised thesis is a complete sentence with a subject, a verb, and an opinion.

TABLE 3.3

Sample Attention-Getters	
Brief description or story	Two trains were headed toward each other. One was traveling 70 mph, the other 45 mph. The trains collided, causing a loss of 14 lives and injuries to over 100 others. What the passengers didn't know when they boarded the train that fateful day was that one of the engineers had been smoking marijuana before work.
Comparison or contrast	Just as a tiger stalks its prey, serial killers often follow their victims before attacking them.
Dialogue	When Senator Joe Somebody was a young boy, his father said to him, "If you work hard, you're going to have a successful career someday." At the time Little Joey, as he was called then, had no idea of how true his father's words were.
Inspiring or intriguing quote	Samuel Johnson once stated, "Great works are performed, not by strength, but by perseverance."
List of relevant examples	Many public figures have used their celebrity status to help promote a worthy cause. Bono, the lead singer for the band U2, was nominated for the Nobel Peace Prize for his global humanitarian efforts. Talk show host Oprah Winfrey has inspired hundreds of thousands of people to read classic novels. Actress Angelina Jolie has encouraged people to consider the plight of children in Third World countries.
Relevant statistic	According to the United States Department of Labor, occupations and industries related to health care are expected to add the greatest number of jobs between now and 2022.
Short summary	On October 29, 2012, Hurricane Sandy ripped through the New Jersey shore, New York City, and Long Island, causing massive damage. It flooded subways, destroyed buildings, and left millions of people stranded without electricity.
Surprising statement	I looked into the woods beyond the rocky path and couldn't believe the grotesque creature I saw!
Thought-provoking question	Have you ever been in a situation that you knew would change your life forever?

Teaching Tip

Assign individual students or groups different types of attention-getters. Ask them to develop examples for the assigned types.

SmartBook Tip

Key concepts in Chapter 3 are highlighted for students during the "Read" phase. As students demonstrate understanding of these concepts during the "Practice" phase by responding to probes, the highlighting adapts to the individual student's learning by changing color.

Be sure your thesis statement makes a significant point that will engage your readers. Also, avoid including absolute terms such as *always* and *will definitely* in your thesis because readers will usually be able to think of exceptions to the point you are making.

Poor Thesis: People who exercise live longer than those who don't exercise.

Revised Thesis: People who exercise are likely to live longer than those who don't exercise.

Discussion: The qualifier "are likely" tempers the thesis and makes it easier to support.

Overview of Main Points Another function of an introduction is to give the reader an overview of the supporting ideas you will cover in the body of the paragraph. This is called a **forecast.** Similar to a forecast that predicts the

Forecast Helps the reader predict the main points.

Table 3.4

Sample Thesis Statements	
Strategy	**Example**
Narrating	What began as a casual camping trip to the Great Smoky Mountains turned into a near-tragic event for everyone involved.
Describing	Venice, Italy, is one of the most spectacular cities in the world.
Process writing	Landing the perfect job can be easy if you follow five simple steps.
Comparing and contrasting	Providing for the needs of a child is similar to maintaining a vehicle.
Analyzing causes and effects	Americans can help make the planet a greener place by changing a few simple habits at home, at work, and out in the community.
Persuading	The age at which adults can drink alcoholic beverages should be lowered to 18 throughout the United States.
Evaluating	The *Hunger Games* series by Suzanne Collins is an excellent read for teens and adults.
Solving a problem	The best strategy for finding a job in a tough economy is to earn a degree in a rapidly growing career field.

▶ *Activity*

Developing a Thesis Statement

Narrow the following topics and write a thesis statement for each one.

1. A reality television show
2. A career field
3. A celebrity
4. A sports figure
5. Professionalism

Developing a Thesis Statement Activity:

Answers will vary.

Unity Ensures every idea relates to the overall thesis of the essay.

weather, a forecast in an essay helps the reader to predict what the main points will be.

Thesis with forecast: Obtaining a college education is beneficial because it can lead to greater self-esteem, a higher-paying job, and a better style of living.

Discussion: This thesis statement suggests that the body paragraphs of the essay will explain each of the benefits mentioned: greater self-esteem, a higher-paying job, and a better style of living.

If the thesis does not contain an overview of the supporting points you will cover in the essay, then you can include another sentence, or a series of sentences, to give the reader an indication of what to expect. Remember, your forecast should not sound mechanical. You do not necessarily need to include a list of your main points; however, you owe it to your readers to give them some idea of what to expect in the body of the essay.

Body Paragraphs

Body paragraphs are similar to stand-alone paragraphs except that they are part of a larger essay. Often they begin with a topic sentence and include several supporting sentences. Be sure to include enough details and examples to fully support your topic sentence. You may develop your ideas by using one or more of the writing strategies covered in this text: narrating, describing, explaining a process, comparing and contrasting, analyzing causes and effects, persuading, evaluating, or solving a problem. Also, use transitions within the paragraph to help your ideas flow smoothly and at the end of the paragraph to lead the reader into the next body paragraph. To maintain **unity** in your essay, make sure every idea relates to the overall thesis of the essay.

Identify the sentences that do not support the opinion in the topic sentence of the following paragraph. Explain why those sentences should not be included in the paragraph.

Getting around on Two Wheels

Using a scooter for transportation has many benefits. First of all, riding a scooter saves gasoline. Scooters get anywhere from about 60 to 125 miles per gallon depending on the size of the motor. Riders can feel good about consuming less fuel and enjoy the reward of spending less money at the gas pump. Second, scooters are easy to park. They take up less space, giving riders more parking options. Some scooters have a center stand to use when parked that is difficult to operate. Also, many parking lots have spaces set aside for motorcycles and scooters. This can be extremely convenient, especially at places where parking lots tend to fill up. Finally, riding a scooter is fun. Commuting to work or school doesn't seem like a chore when riding a scooter. On a beautiful day riders can enjoy a great breeze and the soothing warmth of the sunshine. Riding in the rain

is a whole different story. There's nothing worse than arriving at your destination soaked or muddy, which is why many scooter riders also own a car.

Concluding Paragraph

The last paragraph of your essay should wrap up the entire document. Similar to the introduction, the conclusion should accomplish three tasks: reword your thesis statement, summarize your main points, and end with a memorable thought.

> **Thesis statement in introduction:** Earning a college degree has several benefits.

> **Reworded thesis in conclusion:** Once you have completed your college education, you will enjoy the rewards for the rest of your life.

Avoid introducing new ideas, changing your focus, or upsetting your readers in your conclusion. Also, even though you might be tempted to end with a cliché, such as "and that's the way the cookie crumbles," please resist. Instead, end with a powerful idea that will make a lasting impression on the readers. You may use techniques that are similar to attention-getters (see Table 3.3), such as quotes, surprising statements, or thought-provoking questions.

Achieving Unity Activity: Answers

These three sentences do not support the topic sentence: Some scooters have a center stand to use when parked that is difficult to operate. Riding in the rain is a whole different story. There's nothing worse than arriving at your destination soaked or muddy, which is why many scooter riders also own a car.

Model Essay

"The Art of Eating Spaghetti" from *Growing Up* by Russell Baker

Russell Baker, a graduate of Johns Hopkins University, is a two-time Pulitzer Prize winner who is known for his humor and satire. He has served as a journalist and newspaper columnist and has written several books. The following excerpt is from his autobiography *Growing Up*. As you read his essay, pay particular attention to the organizational strategies he uses as well as the ideas he presents.

The only thing that truly interested me was writing, and I knew that sixteen-year-olds did not come out of high school and become writers. I thought of writing as something to be done only by the rich. It was so obviously not real work, not a job at which you could earn a living. Still, I had begun to think of myself as a writer. It was the only thing for which I seemed to have the smallest talent, and, silly though it sounded when I told people I'd like to be a writer, it gave me a way of thinking about myself which satisfied my need to have an identity.

The notion of becoming a writer had flickered off and on in my head since the Belleville days, but it wasn't until my third year in high school that the possibility took hold. Until then I'd been bored by everything associated with English courses. I found English grammar dull and baffling. I hated the assignments to turn out "compositions," and went at them like heavy labor, turning out leaden, lackluster paragraphs that were agonies for teachers to read and for me to write. The classics thrust on me to read seemed as deadening as chloroform.

When our class was assigned to Mr. Fleagle for third-year English I anticipated another grim year in that dreariest of subjects. Mr. Fleagle was notorious among City students for dullness and inability to inspire. He was said to be stuffy, dull, and hopelessly out of date. To me he looked to be sixty or seventy and prim to a fault. He wore primly severe eyeglasses, his wavy hair was primly cut and primly combed. He wore prim vested suits with neckties blocked primly against the collar buttons of his primly starched white shirts. He had a primly pointed jaw, a primly straight nose, and a prim manner of speaking that was so correct, so gentlemanly, that he seemed a comic antique.

I anticipated a listless, unfruitful year with Mr. Fleagle and for a long time was not disappointed. We read *Macbeth*. Mr. Fleagle loved *Macbeth* and wanted us to love it too, but he lacked the gift of infecting others with his own passion. He tried to convey the murderous ferocity of Lady Macbeth one day by reading aloud the passage that concludes.

… I have given suck, and know
How tender 'tis to love the babe that milks me.
I would, while it was smiling in my face,
Have plucked my nipple from his boneless gums…

The idea of prim Mr. Fleagle plucking his nipple from boneless gums was too much for the class. We burst into gasps of irrepressible snickering. Mr. Fleagle stopped.

"There is nothing funny, boys, about giving suck to a babe. It is the—the very essence of motherhood, don't you see."

He constantly sprinkled his sentences with "don't you see." It wasn't a question but an exclamation of mild surprise at our ignorance. "Your pronoun needs an antecedent, don't you see," he would say, very primly. "The purpose of the Porter's scene, boys, is to provide comic relief from the horror, don't you see."

Late in the year we tackled the informal essay. "The essay, don't you see, is the…" My mind went numb. Of all forms of writing, none seemed so boring as the essay. Naturally we would have to write informal essays. Mr. Fleagle distributed a homework sheet offering us a choice of topics. None was quite so simple-minded as "What I Did on My Summer Vacation," but most seemed to be almost as dull. I took the list home and dawdled until the night before the essay was due. Sprawled on the sofa, I finally faced up to the grim task, took the list out of my notebook, and scanned it. The topic on which my eye stopped was "The Art of Eating Spaghetti."

This title produced an extraordinary sequence of mental images. Surging up out of the depths of memory came a vivid recollection of a night in Belleville when all of us were seated around the supper table—Uncle Allen, my mother, Uncle Charlie, Doris, Uncle Hal—and Aunt Pat served spaghetti for supper. Spaghetti was an exotic treat in those days. Neither Doris nor I had ever eaten spaghetti, and none of the adults had enough experience to be good at it. All the good humor of Uncle Allen's house reawoke in my mind as I recalled the laughing arguments we had that night about the socially respectable method for moving spaghetti from plate to mouth.

Suddenly I wanted to write about that, about the warmth and good feeling of it, but I wanted to put it down simply for my own joy, not for

Supporting Details —— Mr. Fleagle. It was a moment I wanted to recapture and hold for myself. I wanted to relive the pleasure of an evening at New Street. To write it as I wanted, however, would violate all the rules of formal composition I'd learned in school, and Mr. Fleagle would surely give it a failing grade. Never mind, I would write something else for Mr. Fleagle after I had written this thing for myself.

When I finished it the night was half gone and there was no time left to compose a proper, respectable essay for Mr. Fleagle. There was no choice next morning but to turn in my private reminiscence of Belleville. Two days passed before Mr. Fleagle returned the graded papers, and he returned everyone's but mine. I was bracing myself for a command to report to Mr. Fleagle immediately after school for discipline when I saw him lift my paper from his desk and rap for the class's attention.

"Now, boys," he said, "I want to read you an essay. This is titled 'The Art of Eating Spaghetti.'"

And he started to read. My words! He was reading *my words* out loud to the entire class. What's more, the entire class was listening. Listening attentively. Then somebody laughed, then the entire class was laughing, and not in contempt and ridicule, but with openhearted enjoyment. Even Mr. Fleagle stopped two or three times to repress a small prim smile.

Supporting Details —— I did my best to avoid showing pleasure, but what I was feeling was pure ecstasy at this startling demonstration that my words had the power to make people laugh. In the eleventh grade, at the eleventh hour as it were, I had discovered a calling. It was the happiest moment of my entire school career. When Mr. Fleagle finished he put the final seal on my happiness by saying, "Now that, boys, is an essay, don't you see. It's—don't you see—it's of the very essence of the essay, don't you see. Congratulations, Mr. Baker."

Conclusion ——
Reworded Thesis —— For the first time, light shone on a possibility. It wasn't a very heartening possibility, to be sure. Writing couldn't lead to a job after high school, and it was hardly honest work, but Mr. Fleagle had opened a door for me. After that I ranked Mr. Fleagle among the finest teachers in the school.
Memorable Statement ——

SOURCE: Russell Baker, "The Art of Eating Spaghetti" from pp. 186–189 of *Growing Up* by Russell Baker. Copyright © 1982 by Russell Baker. Published by Congdon and Weed/Contemporary Publishing. Reprinted by permission of Don Congdon Associates, Inc.

Labeling an Article Activity:
Answers will vary.

▶ *Activity*   Labeling an Article

Choose an interesting article from a printed or online magazine or professional journal. Make a copy of the article or print it out so that you can write on it. Label the essay parts or note any areas that are missing. Being aware of how professional writers organize their essays can help you to become a better writer.

Introduction: Attention-getter, thesis statement, overview of main points.
Body paragraphs: Topic sentences, supporting points, transitions.
Conclusion: Reworded thesis, summary of main points, memorable statement.

After you have labeled the document, determine the effectiveness, or lack thereof, of the article and its organization:

- How effective is the thesis? The introduction as a whole?

- Are the supporting details sufficient?

- Does the conclusion seem sufficient? Why or why not?

- What, if anything, would make the article better?

Teaching Tip

As an alternative to the Labeling an Article activity, you may choose an article for the class to review individually or together or post it online for students to review in a threaded discussion.

WRITING ATTITUDE SURVEY

How do you feel about writing? Do you find it to be painful, as Russell Baker once did? Or do you get excited about the prospect of creating a new written work? Take this attitude survey to explore your thoughts on writing. There are no right or wrong answers, but you may learn something about yourself as a writer when you review your answers. Figure 3.3 is an example of one student's writing attitude survey.

1. How do you feel about writing in general?
2. What are characteristics of good writing?
3. Why is effective writing important?
4. How confident are you in your writing abilities?
5. What are your strengths and weaknesses with writing?
6. What kinds of writing do you enjoy?
7. What kinds of writing do you dislike?
8. How much time do you spend writing each week for work, school, and yourself?
9. What joys or challenges have you faced as a writer?

USE SOME OF THE IDEAS from your responses to the writing attitude survey to write an essay about how you perceive yourself as a writer. Your thesis statement should state your overall view of how you see yourself as a writer. To support your main idea, be sure to include specific details about your past writing experiences.

For example, if writing is one of your favorite activities, you might include details about how you have always kept a journal or how you have received recognition for your excellent writing abilities. You may also choose to include what you like about writing and why it is important to you. If your feelings about writing aren't favorable, you might write about some of the experiences you have had that have led to your discomfort with or dislike for writing. You might also explore what it would take for you to become more confident in your writing abilities.

Another option is to focus on a pivotal experience that changed your perception of yourself as a writer (as Russell Baker did in his essay). Maybe you always hated (or loved) to write until you encountered a particular teacher, boss, or assignment. Exploring your perceptions of yourself as a writer will help you to make the most out of your composition class.

FIGURE 3.3   Student
Example of a Writing
Attitude Survey

Matthew Ruffell

Writing Attitude Survey

How do you feel about writing? Do you find it to be painful, as Russell Baker once did? Or do you get excited about the prospect of creating a new written work? Take this attitude survey to explore your thoughts on writing. There are no right or wrong answers, but you may learn something about yourself as a writer when you review your answers.

1. How do you feel about writing in general?

I feel that I spend too much time on wording my writing. I also put a lot of effort into writing, making it entertaining.

2. What are characteristics of good writing?

Good characteristics in writing:
- *Organization: Thoughts, not random babbling*
- *Flow: Is it easy to read, no reading twice*
- *Grammar: Is it written well, does it sound good read out loud?*

3. Why is effective writing important?

Effective writing is important to:
- *Convey information about a topic*
- *To catch the reader's interest*

4. How confident are you in your writing abilities?

I'm not as confident as I'd like to be. I haven't written a paper since 10th grade of high school. I'm challenged when it comes to choosing my words, using a better choice per se.

5. What are your strengths and weaknesses with writing?

I have the basics of writing down. I'm terrible with the flow of information and spelling.

6. What kinds of writing do you enjoy?

I enjoy poetry. It's kind of like writing lyrics to a song; plus it's easy to put my emotions behind it. I also like writing research papers because I learn a lot from them.

7. What kinds of writing do you dislike?

I don't like to write novels or short stories. I cannot keep the plot going, and I struggle to stay on topic.

8. How much time do you spend writing for work, school, and yourself?

I don't write much in my spare time. I do write for my classes. So far, I'm actually enjoying it, but I'm worried about writing in psychology class.

9. What joys or challenges have you faced as a writer?

Poetry is personal expression; I can do that pretty well☺ My challenges are working on patience, organization, and word choice.

Teaching Tip

Explain that often students who don't feel confident about their own writing are better than they think, as evidenced in Matthew Ruffell's essay.

STUDENT WRITING

Matthew Ruffell completed a writing attitude survey (see page 63) as part of his discovery process. The following is Matthew's final essay about how he perceives himself as a writer.

A Literary Genius I Am Not
by Matthew Ruffell

When it comes to writing, I'm about as dumb as a bag of hammers. In other words, English composition is not my strongest course of study. I have always dreaded tackling anything that had to do with demonstrating my writing skills. The reason for this is that there are a number of challenges I face when it comes to writing.

The first challenge I face when writing is having the patience to actually sit down and do the assignment. I don't typically write for any other purpose than an assignment for school or work. The truth is, I have never really had an interest in writing. I guess I have always thought of it as boring, just not for me. By nature, I'm more of a visual person. I prefer pictures and movies to written words. As a result, I always procrastinate when I have to write a paper, waiting until the day before the assignment is due to work on it. I always manage to get my assignments completed, but I find it difficult to be patient enough to write them.

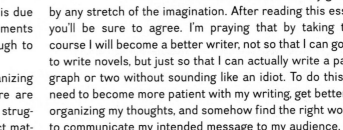

The next challenge I face when writing is organizing my thoughts. Finding a topic is easy for me. There are plenty of things that I can rant and rave about. The struggle is collecting my thoughts on a particular subject matter. I have so many thoughts pin-balling around my head at any one given moment. To collectively organize them would take a lifetime to achieve. When writing about a particular subject, I just can't seem to get my thoughts out on paper. They tend to be choppy and not flow well together. I find myself spending much of my time writing and rewriting my thoughts. I spend much of my time trying to get the wording right and making sure I don't go off on a tangent about something unrelated to the topic. The last thing I want to do is confuse the reader by having an unorganized train of thought. In the end, I will eventually end up with a nicely organized and flowing paper that makes sense to the reader although I nearly beat myself blind doing so.

Another obstacle I face when writing is choosing the right words to emphasize my thoughts on a particular topic. I tend to think that much of my writing is boring, not very exciting to read. One reason for this is I don't have a very large vocabulary. I spend so much time searching for words that will add a little pizzazz to my work, which can be somewhat challenging. I often find myself asking questions such as, "Does that sound right?" "Will the readers understand what I mean?" I want to keep the readers interested and not lull them off to sleep. Using the right word combinations and substitutions in order to emphasize the key points and cut down wordiness is essential. There is almost nothing worse than reading a wordy and boring piece of writing.

Overall, I am not a literary genius by any stretch of the imagination. After reading this essay, you'll be sure to agree. I'm praying that by taking this course I will become a better writer, not so that I can go on to write novels, but just so that I can actually write a paragraph or two without sounding like an idiot. To do this, I'll need to become more patient with my writing, get better at organizing my thoughts, and somehow find the right words to communicate my intended message to my audience.

[QUESTIONS FOR REFLECTION]

1. Which sentence or sentences best state Matthew's main idea?

2. What three points does Matthew make to support his main idea?

3. Are his supporting details effective? Why or why not?

4. What is your overall opinion of Matthew's writing? Is he as bad as he thinks he is? Why or why not?

5. How do your writing experiences compare with Matthew's?

[CHAPTER SUMMARY]

SmartBook Tip
During the "Recharge" phase, students can return to Chapter 3 and practice concepts that they need to work on.

1. An effective sentence has a subject and a verb and expresses a complete thought.

2. Vary sentence length and structure to add interest to your writing style.

3. A good paragraph contains a topic sentence, supporting sentences, transitions, and a concluding sentence.

4. An effective essay includes an introduction, a body, and a conclusion.

5. A good introduction captures your audience's attention, states your thesis, and lets the reader know what to expect from the rest of the essay.

6. Well-developed body paragraphs provide enough details and examples to fully support the opinion in your thesis.

7. A solid concluding paragraph restates the thesis in different words, summarizes the main points in the essay, and ends with a memorable thought.

[WHAT I KNOW NOW]

Use this checklist to determine what you need to work on to feel comfortable with your understanding of the material in this chapter. Check off each item as you master it. Review the checklist periodically for any unchecked items.

❑ 1. I understand the three requirements for a **complete sentence.**

❑ 2. I am able to **vary the structure** of my sentences.

❑ 3. I can write a suitable **topic sentence** and **concluding sentence** for a paragraph.

❑ 4. I understand how to develop a **paragraph** using specific **supporting details** and examples.

❑ 5. I know the three parts of an **essay.**

❑ 6. I understand how to write an **introductory paragraph** with a **clear thesis.**

❑ 7. I know how to develop **body paragraphs** in an essay.

❑ 8. I can write a solid **concluding paragraph** for an essay.

[FURTHER READING ON THE WEB]

- Paragraph Development and Topic Sentences: **http://grammar.ccc.commnet.edu/grammar/paragraphs.htm**
- Creating a Thesis Statement: **http://owl.english.purdue.edu/owl/resource/545/01/**
- How to Write an Essay: **http://howtowriteanessay.com**
- The Essay: **www.sabri.org/Elements-Essay.htm**
- Essay Structure: **www.fas.harvard.edu/~wricntr/documents/structure.html**

CHAPTER

4

THE **CRITICAL THINKING,**
READING, AND **WRITING**
CONNECTION

66

learning outcomes

In this chapter you will learn techniques for achieving these learning outcomes:

4.1 INTERPRET WRITTEN TEXTS USING CRITICAL THINKING SKILLS.

4.2 PARTICIPATE IN CLASS DISCUSSIONS ABOUT READINGS.

4.3 INTERPRET VISUAL TEXTS, INCLUDING PHOTOGRAPHS, GRAPHS, ADVERTISEMENTS, AND WEBSITES.

4.4 IDENTIFY LOGICAL FALLACIES.

SmartBook Tip

Students receive an overview of the learning outcomes and topics in Chapter 4 in the "Preview" phase of SmartBook.

THINKING CRITICALLY

You are surrounded by written and visual texts on a daily basis. Whether watching television, surfing the Web, reading an article, viewing a clip on *YouTube. com*, instant messaging with a friend, or studying a textbook, you are being bombarded by different kinds of messages and images. The messages that you encounter are often misleading or contradictory. Therefore, you have to be able to think critically about them to determine what ideas to accept or reject.

Critical thinking is similar to detective work. When you think critically, you interpret (analyze) ideas and reflect on them. You are going beyond your initial impression of a written or visual text to uncover the deeper, less obvious meanings within. To think critically you have to evaluate the credibility of written and visual texts and the logic presented through them to determine if you agree or disagree with the information you are receiving. Being able to think critically will help you to become a better reader, writer, and decision maker. One way to strengthen your critical thinking skills is by learning how to read and interpret written and visual texts.

Critical thinking Interpreting ideas and reflecting on them.

4.1 READING AND INTERPRETING WRITTEN TEXTS

Reading is one of the best ways to get inspiration for writing. In addition to providing stimulating ideas to respond to, reading helps you strengthen your vocabulary and see how others have approached writing tasks. Becoming a good analytical reader can help you become a good critical thinker and writer. These skills will help you to be successful in school, in your career, and in other areas of your life.

Reading critically is different from reading for pleasure. When you read with a critical eye, you are searching for clues, analyzing details, and making inferences to form your own opinions about the work. Different readers will likely have unique responses to a written text based on their own knowledge, experiences, and interests. While there may not be one "right" way to interpret a particular text, some interpretations are more informed than others. Use this three-step process for a close, critical reading: (1) pre-read and anticipate; (2) read and analyze; (3) reread and annotate.

1. Pre-read and Anticipate

Before reading, look over the work to get an idea of what to expect when you read it.

- **Publication information:** Where and when was the article originally published? Is the content relevant today, or does it provide a glimpse into the past?
- **Biographical information:** If you have access to it, consider the author's biographical information. What is the writer's occupation and education? Does he or she appear to be qualified to discuss the topic at hand? Does the writer seem to have any particular bias about the topic?
- **Title:** Contemplate the title. What do you expect from the work based on the title? Does the title entice you to want to read the material?
- **Overview:** Skim through the text. Look at the headings, visual images, and overall organization to help prepare you for a more careful reading. Read the introductory paragraph and the topic sentence in each supporting paragraph so you have an idea of what you will learn from the material.
- **Predictions:** Based on your preview, identify what you already know about the subject, and make predictions about what you will learn from the text. Keep in mind that your predictions may or may not be accurate.

2. Read and Analyze

After you have skimmed through the text and thought about what you know about the subject and hope to find out, it's time to read the text carefully and analyze it. The term *analyze* means to break something down into its parts. You can examine the parts of an essay to understand it better.

- **Main idea:** As you begin reading, find the author's thesis. What point is the author trying to convey to the reader? Is the thesis stated clearly and effectively?
- **Supporting points:** What specific details and examples does the author use to substantiate his or her thesis? How does the supporting material serve to extend or clarify the author's main point? Is the support sufficient and accurate?
- **Rhetorical star:** Determine the five points of the author's rhetorical star (Figure 4.1). What is the *subject*? What *audience* is the author trying to reach? What was the author's *purpose* in writing (to inform, persuade, analyze, express feelings, or entertain)? What writing *strategy* (or strategies) does the author use to achieve his or her purpose. Is the author narrating, describing, explaining a process, comparing and contrasting, explaining causes and effects, persuading, evaluating, or solving a problem? What is the *design* of the text? How is it organized? Are visuals included? (See Chapter 1 for more details about the rhetorical star.)

3. Reread and Annotate

After you have carefully read the text, you should read it again to annotate it by highlighting key ideas, making notes in the margins, and recording your

FIGURE 4.1
The Rhetorical Star

thoughts about what you are reading. Annotating the text will help you to process what you have read so that you can use the information later for a test, discussion, or writing assignment.

- **Define:** Note any words you come across that are unfamiliar to you. While you don't have to look up every new word you read, sometimes you may encounter a word that is critical to your understanding of the work. Determine if you need to look up the meanings of words you don't know or if you can figure them out well enough in context.

- **Summarize:** One of the best ways to understand and remember something that you have read is to summarize it in your own words. To write a **summary,** follow these three steps:

  1. Identify the thesis statement (main point) and rewrite it in your own words.

  2. Identify the supporting points and write one or two sentences explaining each supporting point.

  3. Write a one-sentence conclusion that summarizes the main point of the text.

  Be sure to place any exact wording you borrow from the original text in quotation marks so that you can distinguish your words from the author's when you read your summary later.

- **Visualize:** You may find it helpful to create some sort of visual representation of a text you have read, especially if you are a visual learner. Making charts, graphs, and other visual organizers might help you to comprehend the material more readily. This is especially true for textbook material. For example, you might read a chapter in a history book and then create a chart or graph that highlights key events, times, and locations.

  Summary A shortened version of an original work including only the main ideas.

- **Synthesize:** The term *synthesize* means to put together. After you have read and broken down the material, then you want to put the ideas together in a meaningful way. When you write a **synthesis,** you connect the ideas you are reading to what you already know about the subject based on other texts and personal experience. When you connect the new material to prior knowledge, you will be better able to comprehend and recall the new material.

  Synthesis A combination of ideas from different sources to form a new whole.

- **Question and evaluate:** After you have carefully read and reread the text, critique it by asking a variety of questions:

  » What is the author's tone? Is it straightforward, sarcastic, or pretentious?

  » Is the thesis fully supported?

  » Are the details and examples relevant?

  » Does the author seem biased? If so, how?

  » Which details are based on verifiable facts, opinionated statements, or personal values?

  » Has the author used any logical fallacies? (See the discussion of fallacies on pages 79–81.)

  » Is the text convincing and effective? Why or why not?

ESOL Tip >
Use contextual clues to determine the meaning of words instead of relying too heavily on dictionary definitions.

annotated essay

"ANIMATING A BLOCKBUSTER: INSIDE PIXAR'S CREATIVE MAGIC" BY JONAH LEHRER

Preview

Jonah Lehrer, a graduate of Columbia University, is the author of several books, including *How We Decide* (2010) and *Imagine* (2012). He has written articles for a number of periodicals, including *The New Yorker*, *The Washington Post*, and *The Boston Globe*. Currently he is a contributing editor for *Scientific American Mind* and *Wired*, where the following article about Pixar's creative process originally appeared in 2010. Go to *Pixar.com* for a complete list of movies and a more detailed explanation of how Pixar makes films. Have you ever seen a Pixar film, such as *Toy Story 3* (2010) or *The Good Dinosaur* (2014)? Did you enjoy it? Did you ever wonder how Pixar created its movies?

attention-getter

Screenwriter William Goldman once famously declared that the most important fact of life in Hollywood is that "nobody knows anything." It was his way of describing a reality that continues to haunt the movie business: Studio executives have no idea which pictures will make money.

bold quote

Unless, of course, those pictures are made by Pixar Animation Studios. Since 1995, when the first *Toy Story* was released, Pixar has made nine films, and every one has been a smashing success.

main idea

Pixar's secret? Its unusual creative process. Most of the time, a studio assembles a cast of freelance professionals to work on a single project and cuts them loose when the picture is done. At Pixar, a staff of writers, directors, animators, and technicians move from project to project. As a result, the studio has built a team of moviemakers who know and trust one another in ways unimaginable on most sets.

This explains Pixar's creative process

Which explains how they can handle constant critiques that are at the heart of Pixar's relentless process. Animation days at the studio all begin the same way: The animators and director gather in a small screening room filled with comfy couches. They eat Cap'n Crunch and drink coffee. Then the team begins analyzing the few seconds of film animated the day before, as they ruthlessly "shred" each frame. Even the most junior staffers are encouraged to join in.

Do the sugar and caffeine help with creativity?

rank or level of authority
interesting term

The upper echelons also subject themselves to megadoses of healthy criticism. Every few months, the director of each Pixar film meets with the brain trust, a group of senior creative staff. The purpose of the meeting is to offer comments on the work in progress, and that can lead to some major rivisions. "It's important that nobody gets mad at you for screwing up," says Lee Unkrich, director of *Toy Story 3*. "We know screwups are an essential part of making something good. That's why our goal is to screw up as fast as possible."

Nice idea— "screwups" are a welcome part of the creative process

The proof is in the product. The average international gross per Pixar film is more than $550 million, and the cartoons are critical darlings—the studio has collected 24 Academy Awards. Nobody in Hollywood knows anything. Pixar seems to know *everything*.

This brainstorming process works for medical teams, business leaders, and more.

Source: Jonah Lehrer. "Animating a Blockbuster: Inside Pixar's Creative Magic," *Wired*, June 2010, p. 141.

▶ *Activity* **Interpreting an Essay**

Choose an interesting article from a newspaper, magazine, or online source that relates to your major or a particular interest or hobby.

Pre-read and anticipate: Preview the article and make predictions about what it will cover.

Read and analyze: Read through the text and determine the main points, supporting points, and rhetorical star.

Reread and annotate: Go through the text more thoroughly and annotate it with your comments. You might circle vocabulary words, write questions, summarize material, create a visual organizer, and write a synthesis.

Note: You may want to choose a reading selection from later in this textbook or a chapter from a textbook for another class.

4.2 PARTICIPATING IN CLASS DISCUSSIONS ABOUT READINGS

Whether you are taking your composition course on campus or online, your instructor will likely have you discuss some of the readings for the course. Here are some tips to follow for live or virtual class discussions:

1. Read the selection carefully, and have your notes and annotations handy during the discussion.

2. Skim through the questions at the end of the selection in case your instructor asks you to discuss some of them in class or in a threaded discussion.

3. Listen to (or read) your classmates' comments with an open mind.

4. Share your opinions about the work, even if they contradict another classmate's opinion. However, be tactful with your responses. Also, you will need to support your opinions with specific details and examples from the text. Remember to use quotation marks for exact wording you use from the text.

5. Feel free to ask questions about areas of the text that are confusing or ambiguous (having more than one interpretation). If you have a question about a text, you are probably not the only one in the class who does.

6. Take notes during the discussion. You never know what might show up later on a test or writing assignment.

Interpreting an Essay Activity:
Answers will vary.

Teaching Tip
Remind students that quoting the text is an excellent way to help support their own opinions.

4.3 READING AND INTERPRETING VISUAL TEXTS

Visual literacy The ability to read and interpret a variety of visual texts.

Visual texts surround you on a daily basis. Sometimes visual texts accompany written texts, and other times they appear alone. You find them in e-mail messages, websites, magazines, television shows, films, billboards, textbooks, and newspapers. Similar to written texts, visual texts are designed to serve a particular purpose and convey a message to the reader. As a result, people who are visually literate are best able to make sense of them.

Visual literacy refers to the skill of being able to read and interpret a variety of visual texts. While visual texts may seem easier to understand than written texts, often they are not. For example, the message is frequently a little more challenging to discern. Understanding the hidden meanings in visual texts requires many of the critical thinking strategies that you use for written texts. You can make annotations to visual images next to the image itself or in the form of interpretation notes. The list that follows provides some ideas to consider when analyzing different images, such as photographs and paintings, charts and graphs, and advertisements.

Reading and Interpreting Visual Texts

1. **Subject:** Does the image focus on people, objects, numbers, a setting, or an event? How is the subject matter portrayed? What kind of action is taking place (if any)?

2. **Purpose:** Is the goal to evoke emotions, persuade the viewer to do something, provide an example of a concept, or visually represent ideas presented in a written text? What message is being conveyed?

3. **Audience:** Who is targeted by the image? Is it geared toward the general public, or is it aimed at people who represent a particular education level, age group, background, ethnicity, attitude, religious affiliation, hobby, or other group?

4. **Writing:** If written text is included, how is it integrated with the visual image? Does the text consist of just a caption, or are more details included? Do the written text and visual image complement each other, or are they contradictory? Which receives more emphasis, the written or the visual aspects of the text?

5. **Logic:** Is the image misleading in any way, or does it fairly and accurately represent the subject?

6. **Effectiveness:** Does the image or advertisement accomplish its purpose? Is it convincing? Why or why not?

Note: See Tables 4.1, 4.2, and 4.3 for examples of interpretation notes for a photograph, a graph, and an advertisement.

Visual texts surround us every day. They are designed to serve a particular purpose and convey a specific message.

INTERPRETING A PHOTOGRAPH

Fish Pedicures: Carp Rid Human Feet of Scaly Skin

Ready for the latest in spa pampering? Prepare to dunk your tootsies in a tank of water and let tiny carp nibble away.

Fish pedicures are creating something of a splash in the D.C. area, where a northern Virginia spa has been offering them for the past four months. John Ho, who runs the Yvonne Hair and Nails salon with his wife, Yvonne Le, said 5,000 people have taken the plunge so far.

"This is a good treatment for everyone who likes to have nice feet," Ho said.

He said he wanted to come up with something unique while finding a replacement for pedicures that use razors to scrape off dead skin. The razors have fallen out of favor with state regulators because of concerns about whether they're sanitary.

Ho was skeptical at first about the fish, which are called garra rufa but typically known as doctor fish. They were first used in Turkey and have become popular in some Asian countries.

But Ho doubted they would thrive in the warm water needed for a comfortable footbath. And he didn't know if customers would like the idea.

"I know people were a little intimidated at first," Ho said. "But I just said, 'Let's give it a shot.'"

Customers were quickly hooked.

Tracy Roberts, 33, of Rockville, Md., heard about it on a local radio show. She said it was "the best pedicure I ever had" and has spread the word to friends and co-workers.

"I'd been an athlete all my life, so I've always had calluses on my feet. This was the first time somebody got rid of my calluses completely," she said.

First time customer KaNin Reese, 32, of Washington, described the tingling sensation created by the toothless fish: "It kind of feels like your foot's asleep," she said.

Source: "Fish pedicures: Carp rid human feet of scaly skin," The Associated Press, July 21, 2008.

TABLE 4.1

Photograph Interpretation Notes	
Subject	Fish that give pedicures: The large photo is of a foot with red painted toenails that are submerged in water with fish that appear to be sucking on the toes. The small picture shows four women at a spa with their feet immersed in water that is filled with toe-sucking fish. From the looks on their faces, they seem to be intrigued by the fish.
Purpose	To illustrate a new trend that is beginning at spas.
Audience	Women primarily, and possibly men too, who go to spas and might be interested in a natural pedicure experience.
Writing	The title is very catchy. While the pictures stand out the most, the text does provide useful additional information, such as sanitation concerns and testimonials from spa patrons who have experienced a spa pedicure. The written text also explains that the fish are toothless, which would be impossible to tell just from the photo. The photos and writing complement each other well, and both are essential to the audience's understanding of the subject.
Logic	The story is presented clearly and effectively. There are no tricks or apparent flaws in logic.
Effectiveness	The article is very effective for anyone interested in the subject. The close-up photograph of the fish makes the viewer wonder what it would be like to have a fish pedicure, even if he or she doesn't regularly frequent spas.

INTERPRETING A GRAPH

Nearly Full Recovery: Health-care shares are approaching their two-year highs.

CUMULATIVE PERCENTAGE CHANGE
■ S&P 500 HEALTH-CARE INDEX
■ S&P 500 INDEX

Data: Bloomberg

2010 FORECAST FOR LARGE U.S. HEALTH-CARE COMPANIES

	EARNINGS GROWTH	PROFIT MARGIN
Pfizer	11%	31%
Merck	6%	31%
Abbott Laboratories	12%	22%
Amgen	2%	36%
Medtronic	10%	26%

Data: Bloomberg

NUMBERS

Yes, The Health-Care Business Is Recession-Proof

By Tara Kalwarski/Charts by David Foster

Health-care companies in the Standard & Poor's 500-stock index held up better than the overall market during the crash. In fact, many industry execs think the recession helped them. No wonder: Profit margins mostly rose, and the earnings outlook is good.

Source: "Numbers: Yes, The Health-Care Business Is Recession-Proof," *Bloomberg Businessweek*, February 2010, p. 9.

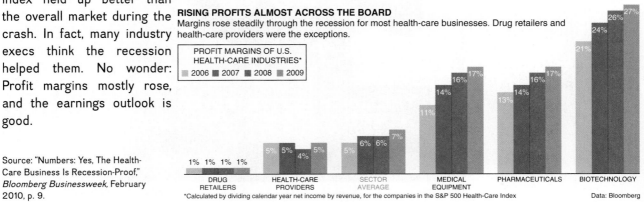

RISING PROFITS ALMOST ACROSS THE BOARD
Margins rose steadily through the recession for most health-care businesses. Drug retailers and health-care providers were the exceptions.

PROFIT MARGINS OF U.S. HEALTH-CARE INDUSTRIES*
■ 2006 ■ 2007 ■ 2008 ■ 2009

DRUG RETAILERS: 1% 1% 1% 1%
HEALTH-CARE PROVIDERS: 5% 5% 4% 5%
SECTOR AVERAGE: 5% 6% 6% 7%
MEDICAL EQUIPMENT: 11% 14% 16% 17%
PHARMACEUTICALS: 13% 14% 16% 17%
BIOTECHNOLOGY: 21% 24% 26% 27%

*Calculated by dividing calendar year net income by revenue, for the companies in the S&P 500 Health-Care Index

Data: Bloomberg

TABLE 4.2

Graph Interpretation Notes	
Subject	Health care: The graphs display various statistics related to the health care industry. The line graph illustrates that shares of stock for health care companies made a rebound in 2009. The table at the top shows the earnings growth and profit margins for several companies. The bar graph at the bottom clearly indicates that rising profits were nearly universal in the health care industry, with a couple of exceptions.
Purpose	The main purpose of the graphs is to inform the readers that the health care industry still thrives during a recession. A second purpose is to persuade the audience of the accuracy of the claim by including a variety of tables and graphs to help the audience visualize the positive growth.
Audience	The audience is the readership of *Bloomberg Businessweek,* which is probably a fairly educated group. Readers might include business owners, college students, people working in the health care industry, people considering an investment in health care stocks, and people who are considering going into the health care field.
Writing	The title of the article is simply "Numbers," which may cause the readers to look more closely to find out what kinds of numbers are being discussed. The sentences at the beginning introduce the graphs and make the claim that the health care industry is recession-proof. Additionally, each table or graph has a descriptive title to catch the audience's attention as well as a few clear labels and brief explanations.
Logic	The logic of the graphs seems fine, and the numbers do not appear to be skewed or misrepresented in any way. The statistics illustrated in the table and graphs come from reputable sources.
Effectiveness	The table seems to depict the findings accurately; however, only five large health care companies are included in the findings. Additional research might be necessary to determine if those numbers hold true for other, smaller companies. Overall, the article appears to be effective.

INTERPRETING AN AD

Source: This Burger King advertisement appeared in a British magazine in 2008.

TABLE **4.3**

Advertisement Interpretation Notes	
Subject	Burger King Angus Mini-Burgers: The ad contains an image of a woman wearing armor made of cooking utensils, pot lids, and other kitchen supplies. A small picture of the Burger King logo appears near the bottom of the ad along with more details about the burgers.
Purpose	To persuade the readers that they should go to Burger King and eat angus mini-burgers for lunch.
Audience	People who enjoy hamburgers and like to eat out for lunch.
Writing	The heading near the bottom of the ad states, "THE LUNCH BATTLE IS OVER." Below that, in slightly smaller letters appears the subheading, "NEW BK ANGUS MINI-BURGERS." The fine print at the bottom explains the benefits of the new angus burgers and points out that they are flame-grilled, high quality, and enjoyable.
Logic	The image gives the audience the impression that the burgers are made by a motherly person in a kitchen. The woman in armor catches the readers' attention because she looks like a combination of a medieval warrior and mom with a friendly smile.
Effectiveness	The ad is effective because the image of the woman is eye-catching and the Burger King logo is easily recognizable. Many people eat fast food during a break from work or school. Also, many people might like to try something new. Overall, the ad is fairly catchy and persuasive.

Choose a photograph, a graph, or an advertisement in a printed or an online textbook, magazine, or newspaper. Interpret the image based on its subject, purpose, audience, writing, logic, and effectiveness. You may want to share your chart with another classmate or group. See Tables 4.1, 4.2, and 4.3 for examples of interpretation notes for a photograph, graph, or advertisement.

Reading and Interpreting Websites

Critical thinking skills are especially important when it comes to analyzing websites. Unlike most books, magazines, television shows, and movies, some websites do not go through a review process. That means anyone with limited computer skills can post something on the Web, no matter how inaccurate it may be. While the Internet is an extremely valuable tool for obtaining information, you want to be sure that the ideas and images presented on a particular site are trustworthy. Use professional websites from reputable organizations. Here are some tips for making sure that the websites you use are useful and credible:

1. **Source:** Notice who posted the information on the Web. Is the author an expert in the field with the appropriate credentials? Is the organization reputable? If you have doubts about the author or organization, then you may want to investigate by searching for a biography of the author or the history of the organization. Also, check the uniform resource locator (URL). Look for clues that tell you about the identity of the website. For example, commercial sites end in "com," government sites end in "gov," educational sites end in "edu," and nonprofit organization sites end in "org."

2. **Date:** Check to see when the information was posted. In many cases you will want to have the most up-to-date information. If the information seems too old, then find a more current source.

3. **Logic:** If the claims seem too good to be true or highly improbable, then you will want to verify the information by consulting another source.

4. **References:** Notice if the website documents its sources. Many reputable sites will include a bibliography to back up the information they present. If there is a list of sources, look to see if they seem appropriate. If no sources are cited, then you should be wary of the information, unless an expert with good credentials provides the ideas.

5. **Visual images:** Use the strategies you read about earlier in this chapter to analyze the visual material included in the website. If you can hardly believe what you're looking at, then it's possible that a photograph has been altered and is intentionally misleading.

6. **Links:** See if the links work and if they lead to useful information. If they don't work or seem inappropriate, then you'll want to try another website.

7. **Effectiveness:** How useful is the content? Is it relevant? Is it presented clearly and logically? Does the material seem accurate? If a website you are viewing seems to be inaccurate, then you can always go to an *anti-hoax site* to check its validity. Two popular anti-hoax sites are **www.nonprofit.net/hoax** and **www.scambusters.org**. If the website you are viewing is listed, then find a new source.

Interpreting an Image Activity:
Answers will vary.

Teaching Tip
Show students a spoof website and discuss it with them before explaining that it is a fake. Go to www.philb.com/fakesites.htm for examples.

INTERPRETING A WEBSITE

Source: news.nationalgeographic.com/news/2008/09/photogalleries/animal-photosweek10/index.html.

TABLE **4.4**

Website Interpretation Notes	
Source	National Geographic: The URL ends in "com," but that's no guarantee of authenticity. National Geographic has a reputable magazine. John Roach is a regular writer for *National Geographic* and appears to be a credible author.
Date	The article was posted eight days after the event, so the material was current when it was posted.
Logic	The website presents factual information in a clear and effective manner. The title is intentionally misleading, but supported by the photograph of the pig "flying."
References	References are not included, but they are not necessary for this particular topic. The website is just reporting an event that took place in Melbourne, Australia.
Visual images	The "flying" pig photograph tells more than the words do. The picture really captures the essence of the event.
Links	All of the links work, and they lead to useful information from reputable sources.
Effectiveness	The website is quite effective. In addition to the pig story in the screen shot, the website covers a wide variety of other plant and animal subjects. This would be a useful Web source for a research project related to plants or animals.

Go to **www.malepregnancy.com**, or choose another website that interests you. You might consider a site on a topic that you would like to investigate further. Complete a chart, like the one in Table 4.4, giving your interpretation of the site. You may want to share your chart with another classmate or group.

4.4 LOGICAL FALLACIES

Logical reasoning uses sound judgment. **Logical fallacies**, on the other hand, occur when someone draws a conclusion without using sound reasoning. To identify logical fallacies, or flaws in reasoning, you have to think critically about the written and visual texts you read. Sometimes writers purposely employ logical fallacies to try to mislead the reader into seeing things a particular way. For instance, politicians and advertisers may use logical fallacies to try to fool their audiences into believing they are the best candidate or have the best product. Such tactics are not an ethical means of influencing an audience. Other times writers use logical fallacies inadvertently as they try to prove a point because they are not aware of the flawed reasoning they are presenting.

As you read written and visual texts, you need to be familiar with logical fallacies so that you can recognize them and take them into account in your analysis. Also, you will want to avoid using flawed logic in your own writing. Table 4.5 presents a few of the most common types of logical fallacies.

> **Logical fallacies** Occur when someone draws a conclusion not based on sound reasoning.

Interpreting a Website Activity:
Answers will vary.

Teaching Tip
Have students analyze several advertisements (of your choice or theirs) for logical fallacies.

False Authority or Testimonial Fallacy: James Bond wears an Omega Watch, so you should wear one too.

TABLE 4.5

Logical Fallacies			
Type	Definition	Example	Explanation
Band Wagon	Implying that an idea must be true if it is popular. Join the crowd.	Everyone knows that holistic medicine is better than traditional medicine.	Even if many people believe it, that doesn't provide scientific proof for the argument.
Card Stacking	Providing evidence for only one side of a case or deliberately omitting essential information that would change the reader's opinion.	Sunni should get a promotion because she has never missed a day at work and she completes all of her tasks in a timely manner.	Supervisors consider many factors when deciding whom to promote. Maybe Sunni often arrives late or does poor work.
Character Attack or *Ad Hominem* Attack	Attacking a person rather than an issue.	Candidate X should not become the next company president because he divorced his wife and married his assistant.	His private life has nothing to do with whether or not he would make a good company president.
Circular Reasoning or Begging the Question	Attempting to support a position by simply restating it in a different way.	Dr. Brilliant is a good instructor because he teaches his students well.	The idea is merely being repeated without offering any specific evidence as to what makes Dr. Brilliant an effective instructor.
Either/Or Reasoning	Suggesting there are only two possible solutions to a problem (one right and one wrong) when, in reality, there could be many potential options for resolving the issue.	Either the government needs to subsidize gas costs or our economy is going to collapse.	First of all, does the entire economy depend on the price of gas? Also, there are several ways to cut down on fuel costs other than having the government help to offset the price.
False Analogy	Comparing things that are not similar in the most important respects.	The governor hit the jackpot with the new property tax increase proposal.	The governor is not gambling, so the analogy doesn't make sense.
False Authority or Testimonial	Mentioning an authority figure or celebrity as support for arguing a point.	Eric Zane, who plays Dr. Mark Gnome on *Haye's Anatomy*, recommends taking "Cure It All" pills, so they must be effective.	Eric Zane is an actor playing a role, not a real doctor, so he is not qualified to recommend a specific type of treatment.
False Cause or *Post Hoc*	Suggesting that because one thing happened after another, the first event caused the second one.	I ate chocolate and my sore throat disappeared.	The sore throat could have gone away for another reason unrelated to the chocolate.
Glittering Generality	Using emotionally charged words, such as *love, truth, honor, democracy,* and *justice,* to gain the audience's approval.	If you are truly patriotic, you need to do the honorable thing and vote to increase your local sales tax.	The implication is that voting a particular way will determine if someone is (or is not) patriotic and honorable.
Hasty Generalization	Drawing a conclusion without having sufficient evidence.	A child comes home two days in a row without homework, so the parent assumes that the teacher has stopped assigning homework.	The child may have forgotten to bring home the work or may be intentionally misleading the parent.
Non Sequitur	The conclusion does not logically follow the evidence that is provided.	Fast-food chains are very popular in the United States. No wonder obesity is so common.	Many factors contribute to high obesity rate in the United States. One can't assume that there is only one cause or that fast-food chains are the cause of obesity.

Red Herring	Diverting the reader's attention from the main issue by introducing something irrelevant. It comes from the practice of dragging a stinky fish across the ground to distract tracking dogs away from a scent.	The idea of gay marriages is an important issue, but do gay people really want to deal with all of the pressures associated with marriage?	The second part is irrelevant because it has nothing to do with whether gay marriages should be legal or not.
Slippery Slope	Suggesting that if one change occurs, then other, unwanted, changes will inevitably occur as well. The analogy is that once someone starts sliding down a "slippery slope," he or she won't be able to stop.	If we allow dogs on the beach, then the next thing you know dogs will be sitting at tables in fine restaurants.	The two events are unrelated, so there's no reason to assume that one event will lead to the other.
Stereotyping	Attaching a trait to people who belong to a particular religious, ethnic, racial, age, or other group.	Old people make terrible drivers, so they shouldn't be allowed to drive.	This is an unfair claim because many senior citizens are fine drivers.
Tradition	If something has always been done a certain way, then it must be the correct way.	Our company has always bought cigars and champagne for our clients during the holidays. We don't need to change to something else.	Just because the tradition is long-standing doesn't mean that it's a good one. Some clients may not like cigars, and some might not be able to tolerate alcohol. Another gift might be more appropriate.

▶ *Activity*   **Identifying Logical Fallacies**

A. Identify and explain the fallacies in these statements. Note that some statements contain more than one fallacy:
   1. Amalie Dubois speaks English as a second language, so she will never be a good writer.
   2. People who ride motorcycles are all rebellious outlaws who should be locked up in prison.
   3. Dean Meanzie is incompetent because he doesn't know what he is doing.
   4. We should nominate Susie Saucer for president of the Student Government Association because she gets good grades in math class.

What logical fallacy appears in the Kia advertisement above?
Source: Advertisement from *Rolling Stone*, June 11, 2009, p. 42.

   5. Either the college will have to allow students to retake classes for free, or the enrollment is going to seriously decrease.
   6. Everyone eats at Princess Pizza after the game, so that restaurant must have the best pizza in town.
B. Choose five types of logical fallacies and write original examples for each of them. If possible, trade lists with another classmate or group. Identify the fallacies in each other's examples and explain why the reasoning is flawed.

Identifying Logical Fallacies
Activity A: Answers

1. Stereotyping, hasty generalization, *non sequitur* 2. Stereotyping, hasty generalization, character attack, *non sequitur*, false analogy 3. Circular reasoning 4. False cause, card stacking 5. Either/or reasoning 6. Band wagon, tradition, false cause, hasty generalization
Kia Ad: Non sequitur

Activity B:
Answers will vary.

STUDENT WRITING

Stacie Ross wrote the following essay in response to an advertisement for milk, sponsored by America's Milk Processors, that she came across in *Women's Health*. The image shown here contains the original advertisement used with the addition of a person comparing herself to Olympian Dara Torres.

The Body of an Olympian
by Stacie Ross

Would you like to have a lean, sculpted, and healthy body? Drinking milk could help you develop the body of an Olympian. Well, that is the message implied in the milk advertisement that appeared in the June 2009 issue of *Women's Health* magazine. It's summer, that time of year when people will wear fewer clothes and want to look their best doing it. Subscribers are reading this magazine in hopes of learning new ways to achieve a healthier lifestyle. The "got milk?" ad is convincing because the images and words inspire readers to want to add nutritious milk to their diets so they can experience the healthful benefits.

The purpose of the ad is to convince readers that they too should drink milk after exercising to obtain the same wellness as an Olympic swimmer. The ad never makes any claims that anyone who drinks milk three times a day can look as good as Dara Torres, yet viewers cannot help but wonder if their bodies would look like that. Nor does that ad imply that drinking milk gives Dara the stamina to train hard and achieve picture perfect results. However, when consumers see this ad, they might want to knock back a big cool glass of low-fat or fat-free milk.

Additionally, the images in the ad are quite appealing and serve to make the ad more persuasive. There is an ocean of calm, blue water that seems to go on forever. It just about makes the readers want to jump in and go for a swim. Then there are the huge, fluffy, milky white clouds that let the reader almost feel the cool, gentle wind. There stands forty-six-year-old, five-times Olympic swimmer, Dara "Dairy" Torres with all her rippling muscles, wearing a tiny bikini, and sporting a thick milk mustache. On a warm summer day, after a long, exhausting workout, athletes would want a cold, revitalizing drink to help them cool down.

Finally, Dara Torres's words in the "got milk?" advertisement add to its credibility. Dara states, "I'm a natural in water. But after a workout, my natural choice is milk." She also gives the readers a few facts about milk: "The protein helps build muscle, plus its unique mix of nutrients helps me refuel. Three glasses of lowfat or fat free milk a day. Lap it up." Her statements might convince the readers that milk is the logical choice of beverage they need to be strong and healthy. Many of the readers of *Women's Health* magazine are aware that the National Institutes of Health has been advising consumers to drink more milk for years. Furthermore, women have become more aware of the fact that they need to consume enough calcium daily to promote bone health and prevent osteoporosis. Savvy readers will react positively to the ad when they are reminded of these facts.

Most readers realize they will never attain the physique of Dara Torres. However, after viewing the "got milk?" advertisement in *Women's Health* magazine, many might just be persuaded to add a glass or two with their daily meals or after a workout. Why not drink milk if it could possibly help one to obtain the body of an Olympian?

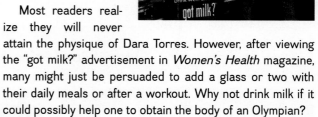

[QUESTIONS FOR REFLECTION]

1. What kind of attention-getter does Ross use? Is it effective? Why or why not?

2. Identify Ross's thesis. What is her overall opinion of the "got milk?" advertisement? Do you agree or disagree with her position? Why?

3. What are the main points in the essay? Are the body paragraphs in the essay organized effectively? Why or why not?

4. Find examples of transitions in the essay. Are they helpful? Are there enough transitions for Ross's essay to flow smoothly? Explain.

5. The advertisement uses the testimonial of a famous Olympian to help encourage consumers to buy milk. Is it logical for Dara Torres to sell milk? Is she a credible authority figure for this product? Why or why not?

USE THE CRITICAL THINKING SKILLS you have learned in this chapter to write a response to the Kia advertisement on page 81 or another visual image, website, or written text. For the subject you choose, fill in an interpretation chart like the one in this chapter for that type of subject (for example, if you are responding to a website, use the chart on page 78).

[CHAPTER SUMMARY]

1. Strengthening your critical thinking skills will help you to become a better reader, writer, and decision maker.

2. Learning to read written texts, visual texts, and websites with a critical eye will help you to strengthen your reading and writing skills.

3. Applying your critical thinking skills during a live or online class discussion will help you to strengthen your reading and writing skills.

4. Learning to recognize logical fallacies will help you to strengthen your critical thinking, reading, and writing skills.

[WHAT I KNOW NOW]

Use this checklist to determine what you need to work on in order to feel comfortable with your understanding of the material in this chapter. Check off each item as you master it. Review the material for any unchecked items.

SmartBook Tip

During the "Recharge" phase, students can return to Chapter 4 and practice concepts that they need to work on.

❏ 1. I know what **critical thinking** means.

❏ 2. I am familiar with the **three-step reading process.**

❏ 3. I know how to use an **interpretation chart** to evaluate a written text, image, or website.

❏ 4. I am aware of strategies I can use to communicate in **class discussions.**

❏ 5. I know how to recognize several different types of **logical fallacies.**

[FURTHER READING ON THE WEB]

- The Critical Thinking Community: **www.criticalthinking.org**
- Critical Thinking on the Web: **www.austhink.org/critical**
- SQ3R Reading Strategy: **www.studygs.net/texred2.htm**
- Picture This—Visual Literacy Activities: **http://museumca.org/picturethis/visual.html**
- Logical Fallacies: **www.logicalfallacies.info**

PART 2

Writing Strategies

Why Writing Strategies Can Be Combined

Each chapter in Part 2 is based on a writing strategy and a theme, so the readings and images are connected. The writing strategies are addressed one at a time so that you can master the specific skills that each type of writing requires. You may want to practice the strategies individually at first to become proficient with them. As you become more comfortable with each technique, then you may want to begin combining writing strategies as needed.

In many writing situations, writing methods are combined, depending on the circumstances of the writing task. For example, someone writing an article about yoga might begin by describing what yoga is. Then the author may explain the physical and mental benefits (effects) of participating in yoga to convince (persuade) the reader that learning to do yoga is worthwhile. Finally, the writer might explain the steps in the process so that the reader understands what to do. You will notice that many of the readings in this text reflect the common practice of mixing writing strategies. As you go about your writing assignments in Part 2, you will want to choose the writing methods that best suit your rhetorical star.

OVERVIEW of Part 2

Chapter 5
You will learn how to write a narrative essay and study this writing strategy in the context of memories.

Chapter 6
You will learn the skills needed to write a descriptive essay as you consider the theme of media and popular culture.

Chapter 7
You will learn techniques for explaining a process in writing while focusing on cultures and traditions.

Chapter 8
You will learn strategies for writing a comparison and contrast essay while concentrating on the theme of computers.

Chapter 9
You will learn methods for writing a cause-and-effect essay while studying health and medicine.

Chapter 10
You will learn how to write persuasively as you explore the theme of relationships.

Chapter 11
You will learn techniques for writing evaluations while you consider film and the arts.

Chapter 12
You will learn strategies for writing problem-solving essays related to the topic of crime and justice.

5

NARRATING: MEMORIES

learning outcomes

In this chapter you will learn techniques for achieving these learning outcomes:

5.1 IDENTIFY REAL-WORLD APPLICATIONS FOR WRITING A NARRATIVE.

5.2 UNDERSTAND THE QUALITIES OF AN EFFECTIVE NARRATIVE.

5.3 INTERPRET IMAGES AND NARRATIVE READINGS ABOUT MEMORIES.

5.4 ANALYZE THE RHETORICAL STAR FOR NARRATING.

5.5 APPLY THE QUALITIES OF NARRATIVE WRITING.

WRITING STRATEGY FOCUS: NARRATING

Narration is the art of storytelling. When we narrate a story, we retell the event or series of events, based on our memories, so that someone who wasn't there has a good idea of what happened. Although narratives can be fiction, this chapter focuses mostly on real, nonfiction narratives. While fictitious stories are fabricated, nonfiction narratives need to be based on events that really occurred.

We are constantly surrounded by stories in the news, documentaries, movies, television programs, commercials, and even Facebook posts. We find others' stories engaging because they allow us to peek into someone else's world. Sometimes we relate to the experiences of the storyteller, and other times we are surprised by the unique situations that others have faced. In this chapter you will have an opportunity to read about others' memories and to write about your own. Storytelling, however, is not limited to your personal life; you can also use narrative writing in college and in the workplace.

SmartBook Tip

Students receive an overview of the learning outcomes and topics in Chapter 5 in the "Preview" phase of SmartBook.

5.1 REAL-WORLD APPLICATIONS FOR NARRATING

Writing Narratives in College

You will have many opportunities to write narratives in college. You might need to retell what happened during an important historical event. Your humanities instructor may ask you to attend a cultural event, such as a concert or play, and write about the experience. If doing fieldwork is a requirement for your major, your instructor may ask that you keep a narrative journal to document what you observe and do while in the field.

Writing Narratives in Your Daily Life

Writing narratives can also be an important part of your personal life. You may choose to keep a travel journal to document some of the places you visit. You might want to write stories about special occasions and events on your Facebook page. If you have children, you may decide to keep a baby book where you record the details of their most memorable experiences so they can read about them when they're older. Additionally, if you have any special interests or hobbies, you may decide to participate in online forums and contribute to Weblogs (blogs) to retell stories related to your interest to fellow participants.

Writing Narratives in Your Career

Being able to write a good narrative can be critical to your career. Before interviewing for a job, you can benefit from writing a cover letter telling about some of your relevant work experiences to supplement your résumé. If you're applying for a promotion, you might write a report for your superiors, telling them about your past accomplishments and illustrating why you are a worthy candidate for the position. If you notice a problem with a procedure or an employee in your workplace, you may need to write a narrative retelling the exact details of what occurred so that the problem can be resolved. Including accurate details in a narrative can be crucial because a poorly written narrative can cost a company money, lead to a lawsuit, or cause injury or even death. Here are a few specific applications for writing narratives on the job:

Health care: patient history, patient care report, accident report, medical narratives.

Law: deposition, court report, letter explaining an event to a client or opposing party, police report.

Education: report card narratives, observations of students or other teachers, newsletters to parents.

Homeland security: recollection of a terrorist event, details about past or current safety plans.

Business: history of financial activities for the IRS, story about a grand opening, explanation of findings for an audit report.

Graduate SPOTLIGHT

Doug Tolliver, Ultrasound Technologist

Doug Tolliver has a degree in diagnostic medical sonography. He works as an ultrasound technologist in a hospital. Here's what Tolliver has to say about the importance of written communication to his career:

❝ Writing is really important to my work at the hospital. When a patient's image comes up on the screen, I have to annotate the image for the doctors. After that, I have to write a narrative explaining how I read each scan. For example, if I see a cancerous mass, an aneurysm, or a degenerative fetal condition, I must explain that in my notes. I also have to document in the patient's chart exactly what procedure I performed with the date and time. All of this documentation is important because the doctor will use the information I write to give a diagnosis to the patient. Therefore, writing an accurate narrative is critical to the patient's health and safety. ❞

Culinary arts: regional history for a menu, story of how your restaurant got started for a newspaper or a magazine article.

Computers: story to accompany a video game being designed, history of how a computer company or program was developed, explanation documenting how a particular program was created.

> **Activity** **Real-World Narrative Writing**

On your own, in pairs, or in small groups, brainstorm uses for writing narratives at school, in your daily life, and on the job. You may want to choose your own career field or the prospective career field(s) of the participants in your group. Be prepared to share your results.

5.2 QUALITIES OF AN EFFECTIVE NARRATIVE

Before reading professional or student examples of narrative writing, you will need to understand the qualities involved. Look for these characteristics when you read the selected essays in this chapter, and follow these suggestions when you write your own narrative essays.

1. Establish a Clear Purpose

Your introductory paragraph should include some kind of attention-getter to engage your readers in your narrative. For instance, you could begin your essay with an intriguing statement, such as, "As I stood at the edge of the hazy woods at dusk, I had the distinct sensation that I was not alone."

State or Imply the Thesis. When writing a narrative, typically you will want to state your thesis early so readers know what to expect as they continue reading. For example, your thesis might be "Surviving Hurricane Sandy helped me to fully appreciate how precious my family is to me." Occasionally, you might save your thesis for the ending of your narrative, as a lesson or moral to your story. This technique is particularly effective when you're trying to surprise your audience. Sometimes it may be appropriate to imply your thesis. When you leave the thesis unstated, you lead your reader to draw a conclusion about your narrative. In most types of essays, however, the thesis should appear in the introduction.

Develop a Title. Create a title for your narrative that will entice your readers. It can be fairly precise, such as "Backpacking on the Appalachian Trail," or a little more vague, such as "The Night When Terror Struck My Family's Home."

Even though your title and introduction will come first in your final essay, many writers find success in writing them later. If you use that technique, be sure to have a preliminary thesis in mind as you write the body of your essay.

2. Identify the Time and Place

Somewhere in the early part of your narrative you will need to mention when and where the event occurred. If you are writing about a really important event in your life, you may be able to give an exact date and time as well as a precise location of where the action took place. Keep in mind that an essay shouldn't read like a list of diary entries.

- **Time:** If you don't want to date yourself, you might just mention that the event occurred on the eve of your ninth birthday. Mentioning the time of year may also be relevant to your story. For example, hiking in the mountains in December is quite different from doing so in spring or summer.

- **Place:** Telling where the event took place will help readers better understand your story. Provide the readers with physical descriptions of the setting, including the natural environment, building, room, décor—whatever is necessary for your audience to visualize the events in your story.

3. Keep a Consistent Point of View

Although it is not appropriate in all types of academic and workplace writing, when you write about yourself it is typically best to use the first person point of view. Be careful not to begin too many sentences with *I*. Vary your sentence structure and approach. Also, generally it is better not to shift to the second person point of view; however, sometimes authors use *you* intentionally to make the readers feel as if they are right there in the story. If you do shift your point of view, make sure you are doing so for a reason. A sentence such as "*I* was so scared because *you* didn't know what was going to happen next" can confuse your readers. If you are writing a narrative about someone else, then you should write in the third person point of view, using pronouns such as *he, she,* and *they*.

▶ *Activity*   Shifting Viewpoints

Write a one-paragraph narrative about yourself in the first person point of view. Revise your narrative using the third person point of view. For example, your first version might start as follows: "When I was in 10th grade, I. . . ." Your second version might start this way: "When Danielle was in 10th grade, she. . . ." Be prepared to share your paragraphs and discuss how each version might affect the audience.

4. Keep the Verb Tense Consistent

You should also be consistent in the verb tense or tenses you use throughout your narrative. You will probably want to retell your story in the past tense to show that the event or events happened previously. For example, you might say, "I went to the edge of the murky river to get a better view and was alarmed when an alligator burst out of the water and looked me straight in the eyes." However, you may prefer to keep the action in the present tense for a more dramatic effect: "As I am standing at the edge of the water to get a better view, I am alarmed when an alligator bursts out of the water and looks me straight in the eyes." Either choice can work, but be careful not to shift verb tenses and write, "While I *stood* at the edge of the murky river an alligator *looks* me straight in the eyes." Whichever tense you choose, make sure that you use it consistently.

5. Include Plenty of Details and Sensory Appeal

When you are writing a story, be sure to consider all of the journalist's questions: *who, what, where, when, why,* and *how.* Also, include ample sensory details to fully engage your readers. What did you see, hear, feel, smell, and taste? You will need to include enough concrete sensory details so that your reader fully grasps what it was like for you during the experience. You want your readers to feel something when they read your essay.

For example, if you are writing a story about a family reunion, let the readers *hear* the loud music playing and the children gleefully laughing in the background; help them *see* the multigenerational family members gathered around picnic tables adorned with colorful arrays of homemade delicacies; make them *feel* the warm, loving embrace of your favorite relative, Grandma Martha. However, be sure to not get so carried away with your details that your narrative loses its focus. Every detail you include should help support the main point of your narrative.

6. Present the Details in a Logical Sequence

When you write a narrative, you will typically want to present the events in chronological order. Use a variety of transitions to help your reader follow your sequence of events. Transitional expressions, such as *first, next, then,* and *after that,* will help keep your readers on track. (See Chapter 3 for more on transitions.) Experiment with different transitions to see which ones help your narrative to flow smoothly. Your essay should not sound like a checklist, nor should it be one long paragraph. Instead, write fully developed paragraphs to get your point across to your audience.

You may even decide to include specific times or dates along the way to help make the flow of ideas clear for the reader. Sometimes it may be appropriate to include a flashback to illuminate an event that occurred before the action in your story. If you choose the flashback method, be sure to signal the change in sequence with a transition so you don't lose your readers. Also, don't overuse flashbacks. Your audience shouldn't have to read your narrative several times to figure out what happened when.

7. Use Dialogue Effectively

Often in a narrative you can use dialogue to help make your story more realistic. Including the exact words that someone says is often more effective than just summarizing that person's ideas. For example, it would be much more dramatic to quote your cousin saying "Help, I can't swim! Please save me!" than simply

Grammar Window:
Answers will vary.

Teaching Tip

Have students work in groups on the Verb Tenses Grammar Window activity. They can write the present tense verbs, trade papers with another group, and change them to past tense verbs. They can share their revisions with the class.

to state that Marisa said she couldn't swim and pleaded for someone to save her. If you do use dialogue, be sure to make the language appropriate for the speakers. Your four-year-old nephew shouldn't sound like a rocket scientist, and your great-grandmother shouldn't sound like a rap star.

8. Include Visual Aids If Appropriate

Pictures, diagrams, or other visual images can help your reader more fully comprehend the story you are retelling. For instance, if you are recalling an experience you had while white-water rafting, you might include a photograph of yourself on a raft. Make sure any images you include support, and don't overshadow, your writing. Your goal is to use your words to help the reader envision what happened.

9. End with a Thought-Provoking Conclusion

Your narrative needs to make a significant point about something that you learned or came to understand as a result of your experience. While the point doesn't have to be earth shattering, it should strike readers as relevant and interesting. However, don't make your ending sound mechanical by stating, "The point of this story is . . ." or "The lesson I learned is. . . ." Instead, wrap up your narrative in a natural way and end on a memorable note. For example, if your story is about the horrible calamities you suffered on a primitive camping trip in the wilderness, you might end by writing, "Although I am thrilled to have survived the challenges I faced in the Rocky Mountains, I've decided that my next vacation will be aboard a luxurious cruise ship. Grand Cayman, here I come!"

Career-Based NARRATIVE WRITING

[preview] **KRIS BISHOP** has an AA degree in rehabilitating assisting, which combines the fields of occupational and physical therapy, a BS degree in health services administration, and an MBA with a concentration in healthcare management. Her passion is working with older patients, and her career in occupational therapy has provided her with experience working with all age groups and in many practice settings including acute care, rehabilitation hospitals, skilled nursing facilities, and home care. Bishop wrote the following case narrative about a patient she treated, Mrs. Thompson, who was in declining health after the death of her husband and needed rehabilitation to increase her ability to manage several daily living skills.

Case Narrative by Kris Bishop, COTA/L

Each Wednesday the rehabilitation team members of the 120-bed skilled nursing and rehabilitation facility meet to discuss patients' progress and challenges on the sub-acute rehabilitation unit. Attending today's meeting was Mary, a Registered Nurse (RN); Sam, the Registered Physical Therapist (RPT); Renee, a Registered Occupational Therapist (OTR); Jeannie, the Discharge Planner; Betty, the Registered Dietician (RD); Terry, the Speech and Language Pathologist (SLP); and myself, a Certified Occupational Therapy Assistant (COTA). Facilitating the meeting was the Rehabilitation Director, Allison.

Patients who were admitted to this unit would be scheduled for daily therapies as prescribed by their Physiatrist, a physician who specializes in physical medicine and rehabilitation, or a Gerontologist, who specializes in aging adults. Most of the patients who were discussed were meeting goals as identified on their individual care plans. Patients' rehabilitative services and skilled nursing care are reimbursed under a prospective payment system which predetermines how much the facility will be paid based upon diagnosis and other factors. This system has a strong influence on when services are provided and the length of time a beneficiary can receive those services. Patients must make progress towards established goals, or they may not be eligible to continue with rehabilitation services such as occupational, speech, and physical therapies.

The patient who was being discussed was Mrs. Thompson, [3] a 75-year-old widow. Her husband of fifty years had passed away suddenly about a year ago. Prior level of function indicates Mrs. Thompson was in good health with some chronic issues such as high cholesterol, obesity, and hypertension, which were controlled by oral medication and diet. She was independent in her activities of daily living including eating, grooming, bathing, transfers, and mobility. Her instrumental activities of daily living (IADL), which are more complex activities such as driving, community mobility, health management, meal preparation, shopping, financial management, and safety, were all intact. Mrs. Thompson had social support from her married daughter and three grandchildren who live in the same town. Sabrina, Mrs. Thompson's daughter, started to notice her mother was not driving much and was declining visits from her family and friends. Sabrina scheduled a doctor's appointment, and no significant medical problems were noted. Global mental functions such as orientation and temperament were not problematic. Her specific mental functions, such as attention, memory and thought processes, were noted to be within normal ranges. Energy, drive, and sleep quality were the only areas that were described as not at her prior level.

Despite this assessment and medical monitoring by [4] her physician as well as the support of her family, Mrs. Thompson continued to decline. She no longer drove, and her daughter had to assist with managing the finances and homemaking. As the weeks passed, Mrs. Thompson rapidly lost her ability to ambulate, requiring the use of a cane, then a walker, and finally a wheelchair. She was unable to get in the shower without help and needed assistance with meals. Sabrina made arrangements for her mother to move in with her family and set up an area for her including a bedroom and bathroom. Mrs. Thompson continued to decline until she became bedridden. A mechanical lift was the only way that she could get out of her hospital bed. Sabrina's home was too small for all this necessary equipment, and her mother needed more care than she could provide. Mrs. Thompson was transported to the hospital for a full medical work up and, when stable, was discharged to the skilled nursing and rehabilitation unit in our skilled nursing facility.

When Mrs. Thompson arrived, she was completely bed- [5] bound. She was unable to raise her head off the pillow. She could not roll from side to side in the bed and was unable to tolerate the head of the bed being raised past 10 degrees. She was incontinent of bowel and bladder and needed total care for all of her activities of daily living such as bathing, grooming, and dressing. She was even unable to feed herself! The only thing she was able to do was watch television, and she was only able to use the remote control if it was positioned correctly in her hand. If she needed assistance, she required a light touch device to use her call system or she would yell for help. According to her medical history, there was no clear physical reason why the patient was unable to perform any activities. Her cognitive abilities were reassessed utilizing an Allen Cognitive Screening Assessment, and it was determined she would be able to learn new skills, her short term and long term memory were intact, and she verbalized motivation to return home and to her prior level of independence.

The rehabilitation team met previously, and it was [6] decided that physical therapy would work with the patient first, with a goal of improving her active range of motion, strength, and endurance. The team established an exercise program that nursing could follow through with to facilitate more rapid progress. The physician decided that occupational therapy was not indicated until Mrs. Thompson could tolerate a higher level of activity. Unfortunately, Sam from physical therapy did not have a lot of success with Mrs. Thompson. She did not like exercising and made many excuses not to participate. Other PT's tried to motivate her without progressing towards goals. The treatment team discussed different options: discharging the patient back to the hospital for an additional medical workup prescribing psychiatric care, or discharging her to long-term custodial care. The consensus of the team was that she was poorly motivated, she had poor rehabilitation potential, and she should be discharged from skilled services. As the case was being discussed, Renee, the OTR, and I decided to ask once again for orders for an evaluation to see if we could improve Mrs. Thompson's quality of life through adaptation of her environment and assistive devices. Occupational therapy was given an order to evaluate.

The occupational therapy evaluation measures many [7] skills that could be utilized to return a patient to more purposeful activity. Strength, endurance, and range of motion are assessed as it relates to a person's ability to participate in an occupation. Manual muscle testing of her bilateral upper extremities revealed poor strength, which is defined as being unable to move an extremity to overcome gravity. The 9 Hole Peg Test was performed to assess fine motor skills, which were determined to be below normal range for her age. Sensory functions such as vision, hearing, balance, sensitivity to touch, smell, taste, pain, and kinesthesia are assessed for their impact on engaging in activity. Cognitive ability and motivational factors are factored into the evaluation. One of the most important aspects of an evaluation is to determine the patient's goals and interests. The patient is the most important member of the treatment team!

Upon completion of the evaluation, goals were estab- [8] lished for environmental assessment and modifications to accommodate safe wheelchair mobility and use of a mechanical lift by the nursing staff. Development of a positioning program to prevent joint contractures and skin breakdown due to dependent mobility was also a goal. A restorative program was to be established to maintain passive range of motion. The long term goal was for the patient to be discharged to the Residential Care unit.

I was assigned to Mrs. Thompson for treatment to 9 address goals as established by the Occupational Therapy evaluation. Part of an initial intervention involves establishing a rapport with the patient. We talked about her family— her late husband, daughter, son-in-law, and grandchildren. We chatted about what she did for work, her leisure interests, and what she wanted to accomplish. She shared her feelings about living in a nursing home for the rest of her life. The longer we worked together the more she opened up. She seemed to be more comfortable with the idea of occupational therapy and what she might accomplish. I gave her the opportunity to decide when she wanted her therapy sessions and on which goals we would focus for the day. I found out two things—she loved the game of Scrabble, and she was embarrassed for her grandchildren to see her in a nursing home. I had a game board at home and brought it in to challenge her to a game. She stated that she played the game regularly with her late husband, and she always won. One of our goals was to change her position to take the pressure off areas that were prone to breakdown. I positioned her on her side with the use of wedges and a pillow for support. Since she was right-hand dominant, I put her on her left side so she could manage the tiles with her right hand. She was so excited to play she cried! The next session she was positioned on her right side to use her left arm. We put light weights on her arms to increase her strength during play. We were making progress. Discussion with the OTR resulted in upgrading our goals to address bed mobility and sitting tolerance. Next, we positioned the board on an over-bed table and increased upright sitting by 10 degrees. She progressed with her sitting tolerance to 30-minute durations at about 75 degrees. This was adequate for her to begin to feed herself meals due to improved sitting tolerance and increased upper extremity strength.

At this point the goals need to be upgraded once again. 10 Through occupation-based intervention, we were able to develop her ability to sit without the support of her hospital bed and progress to participation in bathing and grooming at the bedside. The next goal was transfers. Mrs. Thompson was so excited at her progress she agreed to work with Physical Therapy for lower-body strengthening and transfer training. The education on some basic adaptive equipment such as a long reacher, shoe horn, and leg lifter provided some additional motivation and help in regaining independence in lower body dressing.

Family education is important to help a patient in progress- 11 ing with goals and maintaining accomplishments achieved in Occupational Therapy. While Mrs. Thompson's family members were supportive and visited regularly, they had not been involved with her therapy sessions. With the patient's permission, I spoke with Sabrina and arranged a time she could meet with her mother and me. She was amazed at the progress her mother had made and what she was able to do. This facilitated a discussion with Mrs. Thompson about returning to live in her daughter's home. The patient was motivated to return home, and her family was excited to have her there. A home assessment session was scheduled to determine any environmental barriers to mobility and safety concerns and to provide recommendations.

It was determined that Mrs. Thompson would not have 12 much assistance during the day due to her daughter's and son-in-law's work schedules and the children being in school, so there were a few more goals to address. She needed to be able to prepare simple meals for herself. She wanted to walk to the mailbox to get the mail. Her family wanted peace of mind that Mrs. Thompson would be safe during the day. I taught her safety techniques in the kitchen. We recommended that she obtain a personal response system so she could press the panic button if she got in trouble. Home health occupational and physical therapy was ordered so she could transition her skills to her home environment.

The final team meeting was her discharge meeting. 13 Mrs. Thompson walked into and out of the meeting with her rolling walker without assistance. She returned home that week with her daughter, her grandchildren, and a profound sense of accomplishment. Her progress was a tribute to all the therapists who were part of her team and those who were able to think outside the box to help her achieve her goals. By the way, she never beat me in Scrabble, but she was clearly the winner.

Source: Courtesy of Kris Bishop.

[QUESTIONS FOR REFLECTION]

1. Bishop uses the first person point of view when she describes her treatment of Mrs. Thompson. How does this point of view affect the reader?

2. Which specific details from the narrative give you the clearest idea of what happened? Are the details presented in a logical sequence? Explain.

3. Bishop uses narration as her primary writing strategy, but she also uses comparison and contrast. Identify passages where she uses comparison and contrast and explain why those passages are significant to the narrative.

4. This narrative goes beyond the details of the events that Bishop observed and includes information about the patient's personal life. Why do you suppose an occupational therapist would want to include that in a narrative? Is it useful information? Why or why not?

5. How do you feel about the ending of the narrative? Is the conclusion effective? Why or why not?

[preview] **REINALDO IRIZZARY, SR., PhD,** wrote the following sample police report so that police officers would have an example to use for their own police report writing. He included a few blank lines where the victim's and perpetrator's names would be included in an authentic police report.

Sample Narrative of a Violent Domestic Incident Police Report by Reinaldo Irizzary, Sr., PhD

On July 10, 2014, at 9:00 PM, I, Officer John Doe, was dispatched to a Violent Domestic call at 125 NW 111 Street, Apt. #4A, South Pointe, Miami, Florida. Upon arrival, I met the (victim) White Female, _____, DOB, 02/07/1985. She was crying and had five large cuts on the right side of her face and was bleeding. I immediately requested rescue and an ID-Unit to respond for photos of the Victim's injuries. [1]

While waiting for rescue, I asked what had happened, if there were any witnesses, and how long ago had it occurred. She said that it had just happened, ten minutes before I had arrived. She said her husband White Male, _____ _____ , DOB, 06/19/1982, had come home drunk and because she did not have his food ready began to hit her on her face with his right fist causing many open cuts to her face. She said that there were no witnesses. I immediately requested a description and placed a (BOLO), BE ON THE LOOK OUT, to all units in the area. [2]

She described her husband as white male 6 feet tall, weighing about two-hundred pounds with a black mustache, short black hair. He had a two-inch (2") scar on the right cheek of his face. He had on a long sleeve white shirt and faded blue jeans. He was driving a 2006 black four (4)-door Chevy sedan with dark tinted windows with minor [3] damage to the right front passenger door; it had Florida tag #000000. He left the scene west on 111 Street and turned north on 2nd Avenue in an unknown direction.

Rescue Unit #25 arrived. Lt. Doe checked and treated the victim, and saw that her injuries needed stitches and more medical attention. He requested that she go with them to the hospital but she refused. He further advised her to seek medical attention as soon as possible before her injuries became infected. She agreed. ID Unit C-10 also arrived and took ten (10) photos of the victim's injuries. [4]

I advised the victim on the procedure to follow involving a Domestic Victim and to seek a restraining order against her husband for protection. I gave her a Domestic Victims Pamphlet with all the phone numbers she needed to call. I then called and placed her in contact with a Victims of Domestic Violence Advocate for further counseling. I then left and canvassed the area for the defendant with negative results. [5]

Detective John Smith, Unit-109 from the Violent Domestic section, was notified of the incident. A copy of the report has been forwarded to him for further investigative follow-up and final disposition of the case. [6]

Source: http://searchwarp.com/swa220385.htm.

[QUESTIONS FOR REFLECTION]

Considering Writing Strategies

1. Dr. Irizzary uses the first person point of view throughout the sample report. What effect does this have on the reader?

2. What are the time and place of the events in the narrative? Is it necessary for the author to be that specific in a police report? Why or why not?

3. Which details give you the clearest idea of what happened? Do you feel the narrative is complete? If not, what additional ideas might be included?

4. This narrative goes beyond the details of the events and includes advice the officer gave to the victim. Why do you suppose a police officer would want to include that information in the narrative? Is it useful? Why or why not?

5. If this woman were sent to the emergency room, a domestic abuse program, and a law office, what kinds of narratives would personnel in each one of these places need to write for an accurate and detailed medical report, victim file, and legal client profile?

5.3 NARRATING IN THE CONTEXT OF MEMORIES

Of all the resources we have as writers, our memories rank among the best. Without our memories, we would have little understanding of where we have been or where we are going. As human beings, we naturally look back over the past and recall experiences to help us make sense of our lives and our world. Some of our most poignant memories revolve around major life events, such as births and deaths, marriages and divorces, joyous occasions and tragedies. Before writing about your own memory, read one or more of the narratives that follow and answer the questions for reflection. Reading and interpreting the narratives of others can help you write your own narratives for your daily life, school, and career.

Reading and Reflection NARRATIVE WRITING

[preview] **AMY TAN** is a Chinese-American author who became famous when her first novel, *The Joy Luck Club* (1993), won multiple awards and was made into a major motion picture. Like millions of other children born in the United States to immigrant parents, Tan grew up speaking one language at home and another in public. In "Mother Tongue" Tan explores this dichotomy. To learn more about Amy Tan and her works, go to her Web site, **amytanauthor.com**. Before reading, consider your own language. Do you always speak the same way around your friends or at work as you do at home? What differences do you notice?

Mother Tongue by Amy Tan

I am not a scholar of English or literature. I cannot give 1 you much more than personal opinions on the English language and its variations in this country or others.

I am a writer. And by that definition, I am someone 2 who has always loved language. I am fascinated by language in daily life. I spend a great deal of my time thinking about the power of language—the way it can evoke an emotion, a visual image, a complex idea, or a simple truth. Language is the tool of my trade. And I use them all—all the Englishes I grew up with.

Recently, I was made keenly[1] aware of the different Englishes I do use. I was giving a talk to a large group of people, the same talk I had already given to half a dozen other groups. The nature of the talk was about my writing, my life, and my book, *The Joy Luck Club*. The talk was going along well enough, until I remembered one major difference that made the whole talk sound wrong. My mother was in the room. And it was perhaps the first time she had heard me give a lengthy speech, using the kind of English I have never used with her. I was saying things like, "The intersection of memory upon imagination" and "There is an aspect of my fiction that relates to thus-and-thus"—a speech filled with carefully wrought grammatical phrases, burdened, it suddenly seemed to me, with nominalized[2] forms, past perfect tenses, conditional phrases, all the forms of standard English that I had learned in school and through books, the forms of English I did not use at home with my mother.

Just last week, I was walking down the street with my mother, and I again found myself conscious of the English I was using, the English I do use with her. We were talking about the price of new and used furniture and I heard myself saying this: "Not waste money that way." My husband was with us as well, and he didn't notice any switch in my English. And then I realized why. It's because over the twenty years we've been together I've often used that same kind of English with him, and sometimes he even uses it with me. It has become our language of intimacy, a different sort of English that relates to family talk, the language I grew up with.

So you'll have some idea of what this family talk I heard sounds like, I'll quote what my mother said during a recent conversation which I videotaped and then transcribed.[3] During this conversation, my mother was talking about a political gangster in Shanghai who had the same last name as her family's, Du, and how the gangster in his early years wanted to be adopted by her family, which was rich by comparison. Later, the gangster became more powerful, far richer than my mother's family, and one day showed up at my mother's wedding to pay his respects. Here's what she said in part:

"Du Yusong having business like fruit stand. Like off the street kind. He is Du like Du Zong—but not Tsung-ming Island people. The local people call putong, the river east side, he belong to that side local people. That man want to ask Du Zong father take him in like become own family.

Du Zong father wasn't look down on him, but didn't take seriously, until that man big like become a mafia. Now important person, very hard to inviting him. Chinese way, came only to show respect, don't stay for dinner. Respect for making big celebration, he shows up. Mean gives lots of respect. Chinese custom. Chinese social life that way. If too important won't have to stay too long. He come to my wedding. I didn't see, I heard it. I gone to boy's side, they have YMCA dinner. Chinese age I was nineteen."

You should know that my mother's expressive command of English belies how much she actually understands. She reads the *Forbes* report, listens to *Wall Street Week*, converses daily with her stockbroker, reads all of Shirley MacLaine's books with ease—all kinds of things I can't begin to understand. Yet some of my friends tell me they understand 50 percent of what my mother says. Some say they understand 80 to 90 percent. Some say they understand none of it, as if she were speaking pure Chinese. But to me, my mother's English is perfectly clear, perfectly natural. It's my mother tongue. Her language, as I hear it, is vivid, direct, full of observation and imagery. That was the language that helped shape the way I saw things, expressed things, made sense of the world.

Lately, I've been giving more thought to the kind of English my mother speaks. Like others, I have described it to people as "broken" or "fractured" English. But I wince when I say that. It has always bothered me that I can think of no way to describe it other than "broken," as if it were damaged and needed to be fixed, as if it lacked a certain wholeness and soundness. I've heard other terms used, "limited English," for example. But they seem just as bad, as if everything is limited, including people's perceptions of the limited English speaker.

I know this for a fact, because when I was growing up, my mother's "limited" English limited *my* perception of her. I was ashamed of her English. I believed that her English reflected the quality of what she had to say. That is, because she expressed them imperfectly her thoughts were imperfect. And I had plenty of empirical evidence to support me: the fact that people in department stores, at banks, and at restaurants did not take her seriously, did not give her good service, pretended not to understand her, or even acted as if they did not hear her.

My mother has long realized the limitations of her English as well. When I was fifteen, she used to have me call people on the phone to pretend I was she. In this guise, I was forced to ask for information or even to complain and yell at people who had been rude to her. One time it was a call to her stockbroker in New York. She had cashed out her small portfolio and it just so happened we were going to go to New York the next week, our very first trip outside California. I had to get on the phone and say in an adolescent voice that was not very convincing, "This is Mrs. Tan."

---

[1] **Keenly** Sharply.

[2] **Nominalize** To convert a word or phrase to another part of speech.

[3] **Transcribe** To make a written copy of spoken words.

And my mother was standing in the back whispering [11] loudly, "Why he don't send me check, already two weeks late. So mad he lie to me, losing me money."

And then I said in perfect English, "Yes, I'm getting [12] rather concerned. You had agreed to send the check two weeks ago, but it hasn't arrived."

Then she began to talk more loudly. "What he want, I [13] come to New York tell him front of his boss, you cheating me?" And I was trying to calm her down, make her be quiet, while telling the stockbroker, "I can't tolerate any more excuses. If I don't receive the check immediately, I am going to have to speak to your manager when I'm in New York next week." And sure enough, the following week there we were in front of this astonished stockbroker, and I was sitting there red-faced and quiet, and my mother, the real Mrs. Tan, was shouting at his boss in her impeccable broken English.

We used a similar routine just five days ago, for a situ- [14] ation that was far less humorous. My mother had gone to the hospital for an appointment, to find out about a benign brain tumor a CAT scan had revealed a month ago. She said she had spoken very good English, her best English, no mistakes. Still, she said, the hospital did not apologize when they said they had lost the CAT scan and she had come for nothing. She said they did not seem to have any sympathy when she told them she was anxious to know the exact diagnosis, since her husband and son had both died of brain tumors. She said they would not give her any more information until the next time and she would have to make another appointment for that. So she said she would not leave until the doctor called her daughter. She wouldn't budge. And when the doctor finally called her daughter, me, who spoke in perfect English—lo and behold—we had assurances the CAT scan would be found, promises that a conference call on Monday would be held, and apologies for any suffering my mother had gone through for a most regrettable mistake.

I think my mother's English almost had an effect on limit- [15] ing my possibilities in life as well. Sociologists and linguists[4] probably will tell you that a person's developing language skills are more influenced by peers. But I do think that the language spoken in the family, especially in immigrant families which are more insular, plays a large role in shaping the language of the child. And I believe that it affected my results on achievement tests, IQ tests, and the SAT. While my English skills were never judged as poor, compared to math, English could not be considered my strong suit. In grade school I did moderately well, getting perhaps B's, sometimes B-pluses, in English and scoring perhaps in the sixtieth or seventieth percentile on achievement tests. But those scores were not good enough to override the opinion that my true abilities lay in math and science, because in those areas I achieved A's and scored in the ninetieth percentile or higher.

This was understandable. Math is precise; there is only [16] one correct answer. Whereas, for me at least, the answers on English tests were always a judgment call, a matter of opinion and personal experience. Those tests were constructed around items like fill-in-the-blank sentence completion, such as, "Even though Tom was _____, Mary thought he was _____." And the correct answer always seemed to be the most bland combinations of thoughts, for example, "Even though Tom was shy, Mary thought he was charming," with the grammatical structure "even though" limiting the correct answer to some sort of semantic opposites, so you wouldn't get answers like, "Even though Tom was foolish, Mary thought he was ridiculous." Well, according to my mother, there were very few limitations as to what Tom could have been and what Mary might have thought of him. So I never did well on tests like that.

The same was true with word analogies, pairs of words [17] in which you were supposed to find some sort of logical, semantic relationship—for example, "Sunset is to *nightfall* as _____ is to _____." And here you would be presented with a list of four possible pairs, one of which showed the same kind of relationship: *red* is to *stoplight*, *bus* is to *arrival*, *chills* is to *fever*, *yawn* is to *boring*. Well, I could never think that way. I knew what the tests were asking, but I could not block out of my mind the images already created by the first pair, "*sunset* is to *nightfall*"—and I would see a burst of colors against a darkening sky, the moon rising, the lowering of a curtain of stars. And all the other pairs of words—red, bus, stoplight, boring—just threw up a mass of confusing images, making it impossible for me to sort out something as logical as saying: "A sunset precedes nightfall" is the same as "a chill precedes a fever." The only way I would have gotten that answer right would have been to imagine an associative situation, for example, my being disobedient and staying out past sunset, catching a chill at night, which turns into feverish pneumonia as punishment, which indeed did happen to me.

I have been thinking about all this lately, about my [18] mother's English, about achievement tests. Because lately I've been asked, as a writer, why there are not more Asian Americans represented in American literature. Why are there few Asian Americans enrolled in creative writing programs? Why do so many Chinese students go into engineering? Well, these are broad sociological questions I can't begin to answer. But I have noticed in surveys—in fact, just last week—that Asian students, as a whole, always do significantly better on math achievement tests than in English. And this makes me think that there are other Asian-American students whose English spoken in the home might also be described as "broken" or "limited." And perhaps they also have teachers who are steering them away from writing and into math and science, which is what happened to me.

Fortunately, I happen to be rebellious in nature and [19] enjoy the challenge of disproving assumptions made about me. I became an English major my first year in

---

[4] **Linguists** People who study languages.

college, after being enrolled as pre-med. I started writing nonfiction as a freelancer the week after I was told by my former boss that writing was my worst skill and I should hone my talents toward account management.

But it wasn't until 1985 that I finally began to write [20] fiction. And at first I wrote using what I thought to be wittily crafted sentences, sentences that would finally prove I had mastery over the English language. Here's an example from the first draft of a story that later made its way into *The Joy Luck Club*, but without this line: "That was my mental quandary in its nascent state." A terrible line, which I can barely pronounce.

Fortunately, for reasons I won't get into today, I later [21] decided I should envision a reader for the stories I would write. And the reader I decided upon was my mother, because these were stories about mothers. So with this reader in mind—and in fact she did read my early drafts—I began to write stories using all the Englishes I grew up

with: the English I spoke to my mother, which for lack of a better term might be described as "simple"; the English she used with me, which for lack of a better term might be described as "broken"; my translation of her Chinese, which could certainly be described as "watered down"; and what I imagined to be her translation of her Chinese if she could speak in perfect English, her internal language, and for that I sought to preserve the essence, but neither an English nor a Chinese structure. I wanted to capture what language ability tests can never reveal: her intent, her passion, her imagery, the rhythms of her speech and the nature of her thoughts. [22]

Apart from what any critic had to say about my writing, I knew I had succeeded where it counted when my mother finished reading my book and gave me her verdict: "So easy to read."

Source: Amy Tan, "Mother Tongue," copyright © 1990 by Amy Tan. First appeared in *The Threepenny Review*. Reprinted by permission of the author.

[QUESTIONS FOR REFLECTION]

Considering Ideas

1. When Tan was a child, how did she feel about her mother's language? How has her perception changed as she has aged? What caused this change?

2. Why, even after all the success she has experienced as a writer, does Tan need her mother's approval?

3. Do you feel that standardized tests are equally fair to multilingual speakers? Do they accurately measure someone's potential to succeed? Why or why not?

Considering the Rhetorical Star

1. What is the main *subject* of Tan's narrative? Is the specific topic engaging? Why or why not?

2. Who is the intended *audience* for the story? How do you know?

3. What is the author's main *purpose* (to inform, to interpret, to persuade, to entertain, to express feelings) for the narrative? Does she use a combination of purposes? How effective is her approach? Explain.

4. The author uses narrating as the primary *strategy* for the story. Does she employ any other writing strategies? What are they, and how do they affect the piece?

5. What is the *design* of the narrative? Is it effective? Why or why not?

Considering Writing Strategies

1. What effect does Tan's use of dialogue have on her narrative? Give specific examples to illustrate your point. Would the story work as well without the dialogue? Why or why not?

2. Find examples of transitions that Tan uses to move from one idea to another. How do the transitions affect the flow of ideas in the narrative?

3. Tan uses both past and present verb tenses in her narrative. Does she shift between verb tenses purposely, or are the shifts awkward? Explain your answer using specific examples from the text.

Writing Suggestions

1. Recall a time when you made a conscious choice to vary your language based on your audience. What changes did you make? Why did you alter your speech? Write a narrative telling what happened. Be sure to include specific dialogue of conversations you had to illustrate how you used language differently.

2. When you were a child, did you ever feel embarrassed about something a family member did or said? Write a narrative telling about the situation. What did he or she do to make you feel this way? How did you deal with the situation? Have you changed your mind about what happened now that you're an adult, or do you still feel the same way you did at the time of the incident?

ESOL Tip >

Has a language barrier ever impeded opportunities you may have had? Write an essay about opportunities you lost because of your language barrier. What happened? What steps have you taken to change your circumstances?

[preview] **RICHARD RODRIGUEZ** was born in California into a Mexican immigrant family. He has a BA from Stanford University and an MA from Columbia University. He has served as a teacher and an international journalist. He has also appeared regularly on the PBS show *News Hour*. Rodriguez has written numerous books, including *Days of Obligation: An Argument with My Father* (1992), which was nominated for a Pulitzer Prize. His first book, a collection of auto-biographical essays titled *Hunger of Memory: The Education of Richard Rodriguez* (1982), caused him to be noticed as a prominent Hispanic essayist in America. His works have appeared in *Harper's Magazine*, *Mother Jones*, and *Time*. He writes primarily about the Mexican-American experience and the challenges of assimilation into the American culture. To learn more about Rodriguez, go to **www.scottlondon.com/interviews/rodriguez.html**. In the essay that follows, Rodriguez writes about the experience of doing manual labor. Have you ever had a job or chore to do that required physical labor? How did that experience affect you?

The Workers by Richard Rodriguez

It was at Stanford, one day near the end of my senior year, that a friend told me about a summer construction job he knew was available. I was quickly alert. Desire uncoiled within me. My friend said that he knew I had been looking for summer employment. He knew I needed some money. Almost apologetically he explained: It was something I probably wouldn't be interested in, but a friend of his, a contractor, needed someone for the summer to do menial jobs. There would be lots of shoveling and raking and sweeping. Nothing too hard. But nothing more interesting either. Still, the pay would be good. Did I want it? Or did I know someone who did? I did. Yes, I said, surprised to hear myself say it.

In the weeks following, friends cautioned that I had no idea how hard physical labor really is. ("You only *think* you know what it is like to shovel for eight hours straight.") Their objections seemed to me challenges. They resolved the issue. I became happy with my plan. I decided, however, not to tell my parents. I wouldn't tell my mother because I could guess her worried reaction. I would tell my father only after the summer was over, when I could announce that, after all, I did know what "real work" is like.

The day I met the contractor (a Princeton graduate, it turned out), he asked me whether I had done any physical labor before. "In high school, during the summer," I lied. And although he seemed to regard me with skepticism, he decided to give me a try. Several days later, expectant, I arrived at my first construction site. I would take off my shirt to the sun. And at last grasp desired sensation. No longer afraid. At last become like a *bracero*. "We need those tree stumps out of here by tomorrow," the contractor said. I started to work.

I labored with excitement that first morning—and all the days after. The work was harder than I could have expected. But it was never as tedious as my friends had warned me it would be. There was too much physical pleasure in the labor. Especially early in the day, I would be most alert to the sensations of movement and straining. Beginning around seven each morning (when the air was still damp but the scent of weeds and dry earth anticipated the heat of the sun), I would feel my body resist the first thrusts of the shovel. My arms, tightened by sleep, would gradually loosen; after only several minutes sweat would gather in beads on my forehead and then—a short while later—I would feel my chest silky with sweat in the breeze. I would return to my work. A nervous spark of pain would fly up to my arm and settle to burn like an ember in the thick of my shoulder. An hour, two passed. Three. My whole body would assume regular movements; my shoveling would be described by identical, even movements. Even later in the day, my enthusiasm for primitive sensation would survive the heat and the dust and the insects pricking my back. I would strain wildly for sensation as the day came to a close. At three-thirty, quitting time, I would stand upright and slowly let my head fall back, luxuriating in the feeling of tightness relieved.

Some of the men working nearby would watch me and laugh. Two or three of the older men took the trouble to teach me the right way to use a pick, the correct way to shovel. "You're doing it wrong, too f_____ hard," one man scolded. Then proceeded to show me—what persons who work with their bodies all their lives quickly learn—the most economical way to use one's body in labor.

"Don't make your back do so much work," he instructed. 6 I stood impatiently listening, half listening, vaguely watching, then noticed his work-thickened fingers clutching the shovel. I was annoyed. I wanted to tell him that I enjoyed shoveling the wrong way. And I didn't want to learn the right way. I wasn't afraid of back pain. I liked the way my body felt sore at the end of the day.

I was about to, but, as it turned out, I didn't say a thing. 7 Rather it was at that moment I realized that I was fooling myself if I expected a few weeks of labor to gain me admission to the world of the laborer. I would not learn in three months what my father had meant by "real work." I was not bound to this job; I could imagine its rapid conclusion. For me the sensations of exertion and fatigue could be savored. For my father or uncle, working at comparable jobs when they were my age, such sensations were to be feared. Fatigue took a different toll on their bodies—and minds.

It was, I know, a simple insight. But it was with this real- 8 ization that I took my first step that summer toward realizing something even more important about the "worker." In the company of carpenters, electricians, plumbers, and painters at lunch, I would often sit quietly, observant. I was not shy in such company. I felt easy, pleased by the knowledge that I was casually accepted, my presence taken for granted by men (exotics) who worked with their hands. Some days the younger men would talk and talk about sex, and they would howl at women who drove by in cars. Other days the talk at lunchtime was subdued; men gathered in separate groups. It depended on who was around. There were rough, good-natured workers. Others were quiet. The more I remember that summer, the more I realize that there was no single *type* of worker. I am embarrassed to say, I had not expected such diversity. I certainly had not expected to meet, for example, a plumber who was an abstract painter in his off hours and admired the work of Mark Rothko. Nor did I expect to meet so many workers with college diplomas. (They were the ones who were not surprised that I intended to enter graduate school in the fall.) I suppose what I really want to say here is painfully obvious, but I must say it nevertheless: The men of that summer were middle-class Americans. They certainly didn't constitute an oppressed society. Carefully completing their work sheets; talking about the fortunes of local football teams; planning Las Vegas vacations; comparing the gas mileage of various makes of campers—they were not *los pobres* my mother had spoken about.

On two occasions, the contractor hired a group of 9 Mexican aliens. They were employed to cut down some trees and haul off debris. In all, there were six men of varying age. The youngest in his late twenties; the oldest (his father?) perhaps sixty years old. They came and they left in a single old truck. Anonymous men. They were never introduced to the other men at the site. Immediately upon their arrival, they would follow the contractor's directions, start working—rarely resting—seemingly driven by a fatalistic sense that work which had to be done was best done as quickly as possible.

I watched them sometimes. Perhaps they watched 10 me. The only time I saw them pay me much notice was one day at lunchtime when I was laughing with the other men. The Mexicans sat apart when they ate, just as they worked by themselves. Quiet. I rarely heard them say much to each other. All I could hear were their voices calling out sharply to one another, giving directions. Otherwise, when they stood briefly resting, they talked among themselves in voices too hard to overhear.

The contractor knew enough Spanish, and the Mexicans— 11 or at least the oldest of them, their spokesman—seemed to know enough English to communicate. But because I was around, the contractor decided one day to make me his translator. (He assumed I could speak Spanish.) I did what I was told. Shyly I went over to tell the Mexicans that the *patrón* wanted them to do something else before they left for the day. As I started to speak, I was afraid with my old fear that I would be unable to pronounce the Spanish words. But it was a simple instruction I had to convey. I could say it in phrases.

The dark sweating faces turned toward me as I spoke. 12 They stopped their work to hear me. Each nodded in response. I stood there. I wanted to say something more. But what could I say in Spanish, even if I could have pronounced the words right? Perhaps I just wanted to engage them in small talk, to be assured of their confidence, our familiarity. I thought for a moment to ask them where in Mexico they were from. Something like that. And maybe I wanted to tell them (a lie, if need be) that my parents were from the same part of Mexico.

I stood there. 13

Their faces watched me. The eyes of the man directly 14 in front of me moved slowly over my shoulder, and I turned to follow his glance toward *el patrón* some distance away. For a moment I felt swept up by that glance into the Mexican's company. But then I heard one of them returning to work. And then the others went back to work. I left them without saying anything more.

When they had finished, the contractor went over 15 to pay them in cash. (He later told me that he paid them collectively—"for the job," though he wouldn't tell me their wages. He said something quickly about the good rate of exchange "in their own country." I can still hear the loudly confident voice he used with the Mexicans. It was the sound of the *gringo* I had heard as a very young boy. And I can still hear the quiet, indistinct sounds of the Mexican, the oldest who replied. At hearing that voice I was sad for the Mexicans. Depressed by their vulnerability. Angry at myself. The adventure of the summer seemed suddenly ludicrous. I would not shorten the distance I felt from *los pobres* with a few weeks of physical labor. I would not become like them. They were different from me.

After that summer, a great deal—and not very much really—changed in my life. The curse of physical shame was broken by the sun: I was no longer ashamed of my body. No longer would I deny myself the pleasing sensations of my maleness. During those years when middle-class black Americans began to assert with pride, "Black is beautiful," I was able to regard my complexion without shame. I am today darker than I ever was as a boy. I have taken up the middle-class sport of long-distance running. Nearly every day now I run ten or fifteen miles, barely clothed, my skin exposed to the California winter rain and wind or the summer sun of late afternoon. The torso, the soccer player's calves and thighs, the arms of the twenty-year-old I never was, I possess now in my thirties. I study the youthful parody shape in the mirror, the stomach lipped tight by muscle; the shoulders rounded by chinups; the arms veined strong. This man. A man. I meet him. He laughs to see me, what I have become. [16]

The dandy. I wear double-breasted Italian suits and custom made English shoes. I resemble no one so much as my father—the man pictured in those honeymoon photos. At that point in life when he abandoned the dandy's posture, I assume it. At the point when my parents would not consider going on a vacation, I register at the Hotel Carlyle in New York and the Plaza Athenée in Paris. I am as taken by the symbols of leisure and wealth as they were. For my parents, however, those symbols became taunts, reminders of all they could not achieve in one lifetime. For me those same symbols are reassuring reminders of public success. I tempt vulgarity to be reassured. I am filled with the gaudy delight, the monstrous grace of the nouveau riche. [17]

In recent years I have had occasion to lecture in ghetto high schools. There I see students of remarkable style and physical grace. (One can see more dandies in such schools than one ever will find in middle-class high schools.) There is not the look of casual assurance I saw students at Stanford display. Ghetto girls mimic high-fashion models. Their dresses are of bold, forceful color; their figures elegant, long; the stance theatrical. Boys wear shirts that grip at their overdeveloped muscular bodies. (Against a powerless future, they engage images of strength.) Bad nutrition does not yet tell. Great disappointment, fatal to youth, awaits them still. For the moment, movements in school hallways are dancelike, a procession of postures in a sexual masque. Watching them, I feel a kind of envy. I wonder how different my adolescence would have been had I been free. . . . But no, it is my parents I see—their optimism during those [18] years when they were entertained by Italian grand opera.

The registration clerk in London wonders if I have just been to Switzerland. And the man who carries my luggage in New York guesses the Caribbean. My complexion becomes a mark of my leisure. Yet no one would regard my complexion the same way if I entered such hotels through the service entrance. That is only to say that my complexion assumes its significance from the context of my life. My skin in itself, means nothing. I stress the point because I know there are people who would label me "disadvantaged" because of my color. They make the same mistake I made as a boy, when I thought a disadvantaged life was circumscribed by particular occupations. That summer I worked in the sun may have made me physically indistinguishable from the Mexicans working nearby. (My skin was actually darker because, unlike them, I worked without wearing a shirt. By late August my hands were probably as tough as theirs.) But I was not one of *los pobres*. What made me different from them was an attitude of *mind*, my imagination of myself. [19]

I do not blame my mother for warning me away from the sun when I was young. In a world where her brother had become an old man in his twenties because he was dark, my complexion was something to worry about. "Don't run in the sun," she warns me today. I run. In the end, my father was right—though perhaps he did not know how right or why—to say that I would never know what real work is. I will never know what he felt at his last factory job. If tomorrow I worked at some kind of factory, it would go differently for me. My long education would favor me. I could act as a public person—able to defend my interests, to unionize, to petition, to speak up—to challenge and demand. (I will never know what real work is.) I will never know what the Mexicans knew, gathering their shovels and ladders and saws. [20]

Their silence stays with me now. The wages those Mexicans received for their labor were only a measure of their disadvantaged condition. Their silence is more telling. They lack a public identity. They remain profoundly alien. Persons apart. People lacking a union obviously, people without grounds. They depend upon the relative good will or fairness of their employers each day. For such people, lacking a better alternative, it is not such an unreasonable risk. [21]

Their silence stays with me. I have taken these many words to describe its impact. Only: the quiet. Something uncanny about it. Its compliance. Vulnerability. Pathos. As I heard their truck rumbling away, I shuddered, my face mirrored with sweat. I had finally come face to face with *los pobres*. [22]

From *Hunger of Memory: The Education of Richard Rodriguez* by Richard Rodriguez. Reprinted by permission of David R. Godine, Publisher, inc. Copyright © 1982 by Richard Rodriguez.

Considering Ideas

1. How does the narrator of the story feel about manual labor? Is he ashamed to be a college student doing physical work? Explain his attitude toward the work and himself.

2. What details from the story are most memorable to you? Why did those details catch your attention?

3. Discuss the significance of the conclusion of the story and the narrator's comment about *los pobres* (the poor). How does he feel about his encounter with them? Does he relate to them? Explain.

Considering the Rhetorical Star

1. What is the main *subject* of Rodriguez's narrative? Is the specific topic engaging? Why or why not?

2. Who is the intended *audience* for the story? How do you know?

3. What is the author's main *purpose* (to inform, to interpret, to persuade, to entertain, to express feelings) for the narrative? Does he have a combination of purposes? How effective is his approach? Explain.

4. The author uses narrating as the primary *strategy* for the story. Does he employ any other writing strategies? What are they, and how do they affect the piece?

5. What is the *design* of the narrative? Is it effective? Why or why not?

Considering Writing Strategies

1. Rodriguez wrote the narrative in the first person point of view. How would the story have been different if the author had chosen the third person point of view? Would the story have been as powerful? Why or why not?

2. How does Rodriguez's use of dialogue affect the story? Which comments are particularly important to the narrative? Explain.

3. The author frequently uses sentence fragments instead of complete sentences. Why do you suppose he does that? How does this technique affect the narrative? Give several examples from the story to support your answer.

Writing Suggestions

1. Have you ever had a job or chore to do that required strenuous physical labor? What did you have to do? What was it like to work that hard? Did you learn anything? Write a narrative essay telling about your experience.

2. Write a narrative essay about an experience from your youth that has affected you as an adult. What happened? What, if anything, did you learn from the experience? How do you feel about the memory now?

ESOL Tip >

Write a narrative about moving from your homeland to a foreign land. From where did you move? How old were you? What was the reason for your move?

Reading and Reflection NARRATIVE WRITING

[preview] **CONRAD KOTTAK** is an anthropologist who has done field work in cultural anthropology in Brazil, Madagascar, and the United States. He has a PhD from Columbia University, and he is a professor and chair of the Department of Anthropology at Michigan State University. Kottak has received numerous awards for his teaching, including the Mayfield Award for Excellence in the Teaching of Under-graduate Anthropology, awarded by the American Anthropological Association. In the narrative that follows, which is an adaptation from one of his numerous publications on anthropology, Kottak tells about the culture shock he experienced on his first trip to Brazil. To learn more about Brazil, visit **www.visitbrasil.com**. Before reading, think about your own travels locally, out of state, or abroad. Have you ever felt out of place? Did you experience culture shock?

Even Anthropologists Get Culture Shock by Conrad Kottak

My first field experience in Arembepe (Brazil) took place [1] between my junior and senior years at New York City's Columbia College, where I was majoring in anthropology. I went to Arembepe as a participant in a now defunct program designed to provide undergraduates with experience doing ethnography—firsthand study of an alien society's culture and social life.

Brought up in one culture, intensely curious about others, anthropologists nevertheless experience culture shock, [2] particularly on their first field trip. *Culture shock* refers to the whole set of feelings about being in an alien setting, and the ensuing reactions. It is a chilly, creepy feeling of alienation, of being without some of the most ordinary, trivial (and therefore basic) cues of one's culture of origin.

As I planned my departure for Brazil that year, I could [3] not know just how naked I would feel without the cloak of my own language and culture. My sojourn in Arembepe would be my first trip outside the United States. I was an urban boy who had grown up in Atlanta, Georgia, and New York City. I had little experience with rural life in my own country, none with Latin America, and I had received only minimal training in the Portuguese language.

New York City direct to Salvador, Bahia, Brazil. Just a brief [4] stopover in Rio de Janeiro; a longer visit would be a reward at the end of fieldwork. As our prop jet approached tropical Salvador, I couldn't believe the whiteness of the sand. "That's not snow, is it?" I remarked to a fellow field team member. . . .

My first impressions of Bahia were of smells—alien [5] odors of ripe and decaying mangoes, bananas, and passion fruit—and of swatting the ubiquitous fruit flies I had never seen before, although I had read extensively about their reproductive behavior in genetics classes. There were strange concoctions of rice, black beans, and gelatinous gobs of unidentifiable meats and floating pieces of skin. Coffee was strong and sugar crude, and every tabletop had containers for toothpicks and for manioc (cassava) flour to sprinkle, like Parmesan cheese, on anything one might eat. I remember oatmeal soup and a slimy stew of beef tongue in tomatoes. At one meal a disintegrating fish head, eyes still attached, but barely, stared up at me as the rest of its body floated in a bowl of bright orange palm oil. . . .

I only vaguely remember my first day in Arembepe. [6] Unlike ethnographers who have studied remote tribes in the tropical forests of interior South America or the highlands of Papua New Guinea, I did not have to hike or ride a canoe for days to arrive at my field site. Arembepe was not isolated relative to such places, only relative to every other place I had ever been. . . .

I do recall what happened when we arrived. There was [7] no formal road into the village. Entering through southern Arembepe, vehicles simply threaded their way around coconut trees, following tracks left by automobiles that had passed previously. A crowd of children had heard us coming, and they pursued our car through the village streets until we parked in front of our house, near the central square. Our first few days in Arembepe were spent with children following us everywhere. For weeks we had few moments of privacy. Children watched our every move through our living room window. Occasionally one made an incomprehensible remark. Usually they just stood there. . . .

The sounds, sensations, sights, smells, and tastes [8] of life in northeastern Brazil, and in Arembepe, slowly grew familiar. . . . I grew accustomed to this world without Kleenex, in which globs of mucus habitually drooped from the noses of village children whenever a cold passed through Arembepe. A world where, seemingly without effort, women . . . carried 18-liter kerosene cans of water on their heads, where boys sailed kites and sported at catching houseflies in their bare hands, where old women smoked pipes, storekeepers offered cachaça (common rum) at nine in the morning, and men played dominoes on lazy afternoons when there was no fishing. I was visiting a world where human life was oriented toward water—the sea, where men fished, and the lagoon, where women communally washed clothing, dishes, and their own bodies.

In Arembepe, Brazil, I learned about fishing by sailing on [9] the Atlantic with local fishers. I gave Jeep rides to malnourished babies, to pregnant mothers, and once to a teenage girl possessed by a spirit. All those people needed to consult specialists outside the village. I danced on Arembepe's festive occasions, drank libations commemorating new births, and became a godfather to a village girl. Most anthropologists have similar field experiences. The common humanity of the student and the studied, the ethnographer and the research community, makes participant observation[1] inevitable.

Source: Conrad Kottak, "Even Anthropologists get Culture Shock" from *Assault on Paradise: The Globalization of a Little Community,* copyright © McGraw Hill Companies.

---

[1] Participant observation when an anthropologist or other social scientist is an active participant, not just an observer.

[QUESTIONS FOR REFLECTION]

Considering Ideas

1. Based on Kottak's story, how does Brazil compare to the United States? Explain some of the similarities and differences.

2. What details from the story are most memorable to you? Why did those details catch your attention?

3. How does Kottak define *culture shock*? Have you ever experienced it? Explain.

Considering the Rhetorical Star

1. What is the main *subject* of Kottak's narrative? Is the specific topic engaging? Why or why not?

2. Who is the intended *audience* for the story? How do you know?

3. What is the author's main *purpose* (to inform, to interpret, to persuade, to entertain, to express feelings) for the narrative? Does he have a combination of purposes? How effective is his approach? Explain.

4. The author uses narrating as the primary *strategy* for the story. Does he employ any other writing strategies? What are they, and how do they affect the piece?

5. What is the *design* of the narrative? Is it effective? Why or why not?

Considering Writing Strategies

1. What point of view does Kottak use for the narrative? Would the story be as effective if he had chosen a different point of view? Why or why not?

2. What kind of time sequence does the author use to recall his experiences? Are there any places in the narrative where you become confused about the sequence? Why or why not?

3. Does Kottak use a traditional approach to conclude his essay? What effect does the ending have on you? Why do you think the author chose to leave the readers with those final thoughts?

Writing Suggestions

1. Write a narrative essay telling about a trip you went on with family or friends. Where did you go? What happened while you were there? Why is this memory significant to you?

2. Have you ever been on a trip within the United States or abroad that caused you to experience culture shock (the feeling that everything is unfamiliar and "alien" compared to your own culture) as Kottak did on his first trip to Arambepe, Brazil? Where did you go? What caused you to feel culture shock? Was it a good trip? Why or why not? Did you learn anything from your travels? Write a narrative essay telling about your experience.

Reading and Reflection NARRATIVE WRITING

[preview] **LANGSTON HUGHES** (1902–1967) was an early twentieth-century writer known especially for his poetry. In the following poem, Hughes writes about a mother giving her son advice. He may be recalling an experience he had with his mother. Hughes has captured an endearing moment when a young boy learns about life's challenges. Before reading, think about what kind of advice your mother, or another significant role model, gave you when you were a child. How has the advice affected your life?

Mother to Son by Langston Hughes

Well, son, I'll tell you:
Life for me ain't been no crystal stair.
It's had tacks in it,
And splinters,
And boards torn up,
And places with no carpet on the floor—
Bare.
But all the time
I'se been a-climbin' on,
And reachin' landin's,
And turnin' corners,
And sometimes goin' in the dark
Where there ain't been no light.
So boy, don't you turn back.
Don't you set down on the steps
'Cause you find it's kinder hard.
Don't you fall now—
For I'se still goin', honey,
I'se still climbin',
And life for me ain't been no crystal stair.

[QUESTIONS FOR REFLECTION]

Considering Ideas

1. What advice is the mother passing along to her son?

2. Why do you think the mother has a need to share this information with her son?

3. What is the theme or overall point of the poem?

Considering the Rhetorical Star

1. What is the main *subject* of Hughes's poem? Is the specific topic engaging? Why or why not?

2. Who is the intended *audience* for the poem? How do you know?

3. What is the author's main *purpose* (to inform, to interpret, to persuade, to entertain, to express feelings) for the narrative? Does he use a combination of purposes? How effective is his approach? Explain.

4. The poet uses narrating as the primary *strategy* for the poem. Does he employ any other writing strategies? What are they, and how do they affect the poem?

5. What is the *design* of the poem? Is it effective? Why or why not?

Considering Writing Strategies

1. Notice the dialect and missing letters in the poem. Why does Hughes use this style of writing? What effect does he accomplish in doing so?

2. Identify several of the metaphors (comparisons that don't use *like* or *as*) that Hughes uses in the poem. What do these metaphors represent? How effective are they?

3. What aspects of narration does Hughes incorporate into the poem?

Writing Suggestions

1. Write an essay recalling a time when a parent or other role model gave you some advice. What did he or she say? Why has this memory stuck with you for so long? Was the advice useful to you? Has it changed your life in any way?

2. Write an essay to a younger sibling or child about something you have learned through your experiences. Tell a story to fully illustrate your point.

STUDENT WRITING

Adrenaline Rush
by Claudia Martinez

Skydiving is a wild and amazing experience. Jumping out of an airplane about 15,000 feet in the air and plunging towards the earth at a speed of 160 miles per hour would give anyone an adrenaline rush like no other. The entire skydiving experience takes no more than 30 minutes, but the memory lasts a lifetime. Skydiving is something I would recommend to everyone to try at least once in his or her life. My first and only skydiving experience had my emotions go all the way from fear, to excitement, to relief, making it the most unforgettable day of my life.

Now just because I agreed to jump out of a plane does not mean that I was not scared or nervous. From the moment I promised my friend, Calixto, that we would go skydiving for our birthdays, I would get that roller coaster feeling in my stomach just thinking about it. Once we arrived at the Sebastian Airport, my fear doubled! I could not believe I was actually there. I almost even backed out when I was filling out the 20-page packet filled with insurance waivers

and the words "POSSIBLE DEATH" on every other page I signed. After the paperwork was complete, the instructors prepared my friend and me with harnesses and goggles, and shortly afterwards we were loading the plane. The plane had a total of 15 people on it. The plane climbed up at such an angle that I had to put my feet firmly on the floor to keep from sliding off the bench on which I was sitting. It seemed like an eternity before we reached the appropriate height, and all I could see through the window was the Atlantic Ocean down below.

After I jumped out of the plane, the excitement I felt falling straight down made me scream at the top of my lungs. There was no way anyone could hear me though because all I could hear was the air rushing up against my body. My instructor and I fell for a minute straight; it was the most awesome feeling in the world. The air hitting my face made my cheeks flap around, and the air coming in my nose was overwhelming. I had difficulty moving my arms towards my face because of the intensity of the wind. When the parachute opened, we were pulled up suddenly. Then we just slowly cruised down to the ground. The view was absolutely gorgeous. I could see some land now and not just the ocean, which made me feel a little more at ease. We glided down for seven minutes, and, surprisingly, landed right where we had taken off.

When I was safe on the ground again, the relief I felt to have survived and enjoyed skydiving is indescribable. I was glad I had the courage to go through with it. My family and friends seemed to be just as relieved as I was once they saw me again all in one piece after I landed. When the crew took off my equipment, I did not have any particular thoughts in my head. I could not hear much either because of the change in altitude. Everything sounded distant. I was surprised at how different the actual experience was from how I had imagined it. As I walked over to my family and friends, I could see the relief on everyone's faces, especially my parents'. In the end, I think we were all just at ease once my feet were on the ground.

Skydiving is something that I plan on doing again in the near future. I do not think it is something that I will ever get tired of doing because it is a wonderful experience like no other. Although I had never considered doing it before Calixto suggested it, I do not regret it at all. All in all, skydiving is an out of this world experience, and I would recommend that anyone, adventurous or not, should try it.

[QUESTIONS FOR REFLECTION]

1. Identify Martinez's thesis statement. Is it effective? Why or why not?

2. Are the events narrated in a logical sequence? Why or why not?

3. What is the most memorable part of the essay? What makes it memorable?

4. List several transitions used in the essay. Are there enough to keep the essay flowing smoothly? Why or why not?

5. Would you ever want to go skydiving? Why or why not?

STUDENT WRITING

Ireland: A Country of Illumination
by Sally Wilson

Traveling in Europe has always been a wonderful experience for me. I have wandered through the lush green, sloping terrain of Scotland, journeyed within the colorful city streets of England, explored the beautiful yet biting cold areas of rural Estonia, and gorged myself on the whimsical history and illuminating country that is Ireland. The trip that made the deepest impression on me is the trip I took with my sister to our homeland of Ireland; we visited Donegal, Glendalough, and Dublin.

The first place we visited was Donegal, and both of us really appreciated our time there. After an eight-hour airplane ride and a four-hour car ride, my sister and I were plopped into a genuine Irish family home (complete with cows, goats, lambs, and a thatched roof) where many boisterous voices stained with Irish accents clamored for our dazed and dwindling attentions. We were staying within the county lines of Donegal, and after only two weeks, I felt like I must have met practically everyone in the county! I respected the families immensely and appreciated how they took my sister and me to a new location every day. One day they took us to a beach, where only the most zealous, extreme surfers would brave the bone-chilling ocean water to catch a beautifully proportioned wave. The beach in Donegal was a sight to behold: clear water reflecting the enormous clouds that decorated the sky and light golden grains of sand mixed with pieces of shiny and colorful shells; the environment was surprisingly virgin in comparison to the molested beaches that I was used to back home, in the United States. I was also lucky enough to explore the historic remains of priories, churches, castles, and other pieces of architecture throughout the country, including a beautiful priory built c. 1508, which was later adapted into a castle, in Rathmullan. Even the local pubs have deep roots in the community, some dating back hundreds of years ago.

The pubs in Donegal were filled with the same local people almost every night, and I found it highly enjoyable to sit with a mug of Guinness ale in my hand and my sister at my side, being entertained by their soon-to-be-all-too-familiar stories and songs; it indicated how close their community was, and has been for generations.

After my sister and I said our tearful goodbyes in Donegal, we were off to Glendalough, where we relished another exciting adventure! Glendalough is translated in English as "the glen of two lakes," and is located in the Wicklow Mountains. Glendalough is home to the remains of St. Kevin's Monastery, founded in the latter part of the 6th century. What I found so intriguing was a legendary cave in the mountains called "St. Kevin's Bed," where St. Kevin was said to have spent seven years in solitude with nothing but prayer and self-denial to keep him company. My sister and I got to see the round tower, where St. Kevin's Monastery once stood, but, due to pillaging throughout the ages, not much is left. The last historical site in Glendalough that left an everlasting impression in my mind is an old mining village. A thirty-minute hike through a mountainous forest of pine and oak separates St. Kevin's Monastery from the ruins of an ancient mining village. Boulders, ranging from smaller than my fist to ten times my size, blanket the steep terrain while shells of crudely made rock homes stand firm, mocking the tests of time. The journey and physical exertion from hiking, climbing, and swimming on the trip left me in a state of content euphoria, and I treasure that memory and the connection I felt with my sister while experiencing it.

The last place my sister and I visited in Ireland was the famous city of Dublin, where the experience was different, yet unbelievably wonderful, and a bit more personal than the other parts of the trip because I was without my sister at least half of the time. I say "personal" because during the time I had to myself I created my own experiences, ones I could separate from my sister's with more than just subjective reality. My sister found a job not far from the hostel in which we were staying. While she worked I wandered around the streets of Dublin. I saw Trinity College and its beautiful library/museum that houses "The Book of Kells," which is a historic book that tells a rough story of Celtic beliefs. I also got to stop by numerous shops, pubs, and nightclubs while in Dublin. Good food was hard to come by, but good alcohol was in vast supply!

The articulate mesh of culture, history, geography, romanticism, and beauty that blossoms within Europe manifests itself to me in its diverse people and ancient expressions of art. Although I have traveled to many places, the trip that made the deepest impression on me is the trip I took with my sister to our homeland of Ireland, where we visited Donegal, Glendalough, and Dublin. Ireland showed me that art does not have to be an old painting or piece of architecture—it is all around me, subtly begging to be recognized.

[QUESTIONS FOR REFLECTION]

1. Identify Wilson's thesis. What is her overall opinion about her trip to Ireland?

2. How has the student organized her essay? Is this essay structure logical? Why or why not?

3. Which parts of Wilson's narrative are especially descriptive? Which specific words help you to visualize her experience?

4. Are any areas unclear? Explain.

5. Do you have a favorite memory of a trip? Where did you go? What did you do?

▶ *Activity*   **Sharing a Memory**

In pairs or small groups, brainstorm a list of events that the members in your group have experienced. These events can be fun, scary, inspirational, exciting, exhilarating, horrifying, and so on. Briefly discuss the list to see which events seem most interesting to the group. Next, each participant will tell a brief story about one incident so the other students have a good idea what happened during the experience. A representative from each group may share a few of the highlights from the stories with the class. This activity may give you ideas for writing a narrative essay.

Teaching Tip

Online students can complete a modified version of the Sharing a Memory activity by using a blog or threaded discussion.

Sharing a Memory Activity:

Answers will vary.

Now that you have read one or more examples of narratives, it's time to write your own. You may choose to write about one of the writing options that follow, the advertisement, the image, or one of the media suggestions. Consider your rhetorical star and the qualities of an effective narrative as you begin to compose your assignment.

Writing Assignment Options

Use one of the following topics to write a narrative essay recalling a memory.

1. A memorable childhood experience
2. An entertaining pet story
3. A scary or dangerous event you witnessed or experienced
4. Your best (or worst) vacation
5. A lesson you learned as a member of a team or in a club
6. Resisting or succumbing to peer pressure
7. Your worst (or best) day on the job
8. An event that led to a significant decision in your life
9. Meeting someone new or losing someone special
10. A day that changed your life forever

Teaching Tip
Have students bring advertisements to class from print or digital sources. Students can discuss them in class and/or use them for narrative writing prompts.

Interpreting an Advertisement

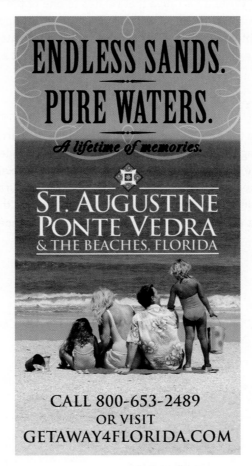

Source: Advertisement from *Arthur Frommer's Budget Travel*, June 2008, p. 134.

This advertisement appeared in *Budget Travel* magazine. Who is the intended audience for the ad? How do the picture and text interact? Why do you suppose the people are facing the other way? Is the advertisement persuasive? Why or why not? What story does it tell? Write a narrative essay that relates to the ad.

Writing about an Image

Look at several of the images in this chapter and consider these questions: What experience does the image represent? What story does it tell? What emotions do the people in the image portray? What ideas about your own memories does the image conjure? Write a narrative that relates to one of the images in this chapter. You can tell about the people in the photograph and what they are doing. Imagine what happened before or after the snapshot was taken. What other events might have occurred? Another option is to write about an experience of your own that the image reminds you of. For example, you might write a narrative about a time when you went on a camping trip or visited the beach.

Media Connection for Narration

You might watch, read, and/or listen to one or more of the suggested media narratives to discover additional examples of this type of writing. Exploring various media may help you to better understand methods for narration. You may also choose to write about one or more of the media suggestions. For example, you might listen to (or watch the music video of) Brad Paisley's song "Letter to Me" and write a letter to yourself in the past, offering advice you have learned as you have gotten older and wiser. Another option is to go to the *This I Believe* website and read others' essays before writing about a belief of your own and the life experiences that led you to this belief.

Television	A&E Biography	History Channel	Travel Channel	*Dateline*
Film	*Letters to Juliet* (2010)	*Moulin Rouge* (2001)	*The Joy Luck Club* (1993)	*The Secret Life of Walter Mitty* (2013)
Print/ E-Reading	*I Know Why the Caged Bird Sings* by Maya Angelou	*Reader's Digest*	*The Color Purple* by Alice Walker	*Life of Pi* by Yann Martel
Internet	*Adventure Blog* **www.adventureblog .org**	*This I Believe* **thisibelieve.org**	*Diaries & Journals* **www.worldimage.com/ diaries**	*Multimedia Storytelling* **www.interactivenarratives .org**
Music	"Letter to Me" by Brad Paisley	*Telling Stories* by Tracy Chapman	*Radio Diaries* (NPR)	"Angels" by The xx

5.4 ANALYZING THE RHETORICAL STAR FOR WRITING A NARRATIVE

FIGURE 5.1 The Rhetorical Star

As you prepare to write your narrative, consider the five points of the rhetorical star (Figure 5.1). You might use some of the questions in the chart as you conduct your rhetorical star analysis.

Subject	Have you had an experience that you have been eager to share with others? Maybe you often tell this story to new acquaintances. If so, that may be the perfect story for you to narrate. You will want to write about a personal experience that has significance for you. Your story could be exciting, humorous, shocking, or terrifying. Maybe you learned something from the experience, or perhaps the experience changed you in some way. If you don't feel like writing about something from your past, you might try going to a café, watching a sporting event, or attending a concert. You can document your experience in your narrative.
Audience	Who are your readers? What do they need to know about your experience? Will the readers relate to your narrative? What emotions do you want them to experience as they read your narrative? Will they be amused, surprised, or horrified by the details?
Purpose	What are you hoping to accomplish through your narrative? Is your main purpose to inform or entertain the reader? Or are you combining purposes? Are you writing objectively (sticking to just the facts), or are you writing subjectively (including your feelings and opinions)? Keep your purpose in mind as you begin narrating your story.
Strategy	Will you include other writing strategies in addition to narration to tell your story? For example, do you want to use description, process analysis, or cause and effect to enhance your narrative? If you are using other strategies, is narration your main organizational method, or are you using a brief narrative to introduce an essay that uses another strategy?
Design	How long should your narrative be? How many details do you need to include to fully explain your story? What other design elements, such as headings, photographs, or diagrams, might help your reader to better understand what happened?

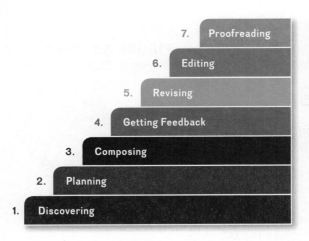

FIGURE 5.2 The Seven Steps of the Writing Process

5.5 APPLYING THE WRITING PROCESS FOR NARRATING

After you have completed your rhetorical star analysis, follow the steps of the writing process (Figure 5.2) to compose your paper.

1. **Discovering:** As you begin to explore your topic, you might freewrite everything that comes to mind about your topic, including why it is meaningful to you. Also, you can use the journalist's questions to help you generate ideas about your topic (Figure 5.3). After you have come up with some ideas, you might tell one of your stories to a classmate or friend to see if he or she becomes engaged in your narrative.

2. **Planning:** Once you have chosen an event or series of events to write about, try listing everything you can remember about your topic. Also, try numbering the events, creating a cluster, or developing an outline (informal or formal) to help you organize your ideas. Remember to follow a chronological sequence for your narrative. You may include flashbacks as well if they are appropriate for your topic.

3. **Composing:** Earlier in this chapter you learned about the nine qualities of an effective narrative (see pages 89–92). These characteristics are a key part of the writing process:

   1. Establish a clear purpose.
   2. Identify the time and place.
   3. Keep a consistent point of view.
   4. Keep the verb tense consistent.
   5. Include plenty of details and sensory appeal.
   6. Present the details in a logical sequence.
   7. Use dialogue effectively.
   8. Include visual aids if appropriate.
   9. End with a thought-provoking conclusion.

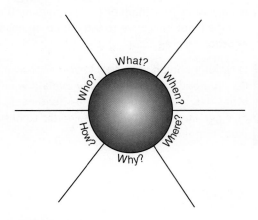

FIGURE 5.3
Journalist's Questions

Write a first draft of your narrative using these nine qualities. Don't worry too much about grammar and punctuation at this time. Keep focused on retelling the details related to the event. Be sure to keep your overall point in mind as you write.

4. **Getting feedback:** Have at least one classmate or other person read your rough draft and answer the peer review questions that follow. If you have access to a writing tutor or center, get another opinion about your paper as well.

5. **Revising:** Using all of the feedback available to you, revise your narrative. Make sure that your narrative is full of specific details and that you have used enough transitions for your reader to easily follow the flow of your ideas. Add, delete, and rearrange ideas as necessary.

6. **Editing:** Read your narrative again, this time looking for errors in grammar, punctuation, and mechanics. Pay particular attention to your consistency with verb tenses and point of view, as these areas can be tricky for narrative writing.

7. **Proofreading:** After you have thoroughly edited your essay, read it again. This time, look for typographical errors and any other issues that might interfere with the readers' understanding of your narrative.

PEER REVIEW QUESTIONS FOR NARRATING

Trade rough drafts with a classmate and answer the following questions about his or her paper. Then, in person or online, discuss your papers and suggestions with your peer. Finally, make the changes you feel would most benefit your paper.

1. Identify the thesis statement. Is its placement appropriate? Why or why not?

2. Could the author include additional details to help you better understand the story? What is missing or unclear?

3. Are the details covered in a logical sequence? If flashbacks are used, are they clear? Why or why not?

4. What part of the narrative is most memorable? Why?

5. Does the narrative include dialogue? If so, does the dialogue flow smoothly and seem appropriate for the speakers?

6. Does the author provide the reader with a sense of completion at the end? If so, how?

7. What kinds of grammatical errors, if any, are evident in the narrative?

8. What final suggestions do you have for the author?

WRITER'S CHECKLIST FOR WRITING A NARRATIVE

Use the checklist below to evaluate your own writing and help ensure that your narrative is complete. If you have any "no" answers, go back and work on those areas.

❑ 1. Are my title and introduction enticing?

❑ 2. Have I clearly stated or implied my thesis?

❑ 3. Have I included enough details so the reader can visualize my experience?

❑ 4. Are the events presented in a logical sequence?

❑ 5. Have I used transitions to help the sequence of events flow smoothly?

❑ 6. Have I used dialogue to enhance my story?

❑ 7. Have I used a consistent point of view and verb tense?

❑ 8. Have I ended the story satisfactorily?

❑ 9. Have I proofread thoroughly?

[CHAPTER SUMMARY]

1. Narrative writing is about retelling a story so that your readers understand what happened during an important event.

2. Narrative writing is an important part of your education, daily life, and career.

3. Interpreting narrative readings and images can help you to prepare to write a narrative.

4. Carefully analyze your rhetorical star before writing a narrative: subject, audience, purpose, strategy, and design.

5. Use these qualities when writing a narrative: establish a clear purpose; identify the time and place; keep a consistent point of view; keep the verb tense consistent; include plenty of details and sensory appeal; follow a logical sequence; use dialogue effectively; include visual aids if appropriate; and end with a thought-provoking conclusion.

[W H A T   I   K N O W   N O W]

Use this checklist to determine what you need to work on in order to feel comfortable with your understanding of the material in this chapter. Check off each item as you master it. Review the material for any unchecked items.

SmartBook Tip

During the "Recharge" phase, students can return to Chapter 5 and practice concepts that they need to work on.

❏ 1. I know what **narrative** writing is.

❏ 2. I can identify several **real-world applications** for writing narratives.

❏ 3. I can **evaluate** narrative readings and images.

❏ 4. I can analyze the **rhetorical star** for writing a narrative.

❏ 5. I understand the **writing process** for writing a narrative.

❏ 6. I can apply the **nine qualities** of narrative writing.

DESCRIBING: MEDIA AND POPULAR CULTURE

In this chapter you will learn techniques for achieving these learning outcomes:

6.1 IDENTIFY REAL-WORLD APPLICATIONS FOR WRITING A DESCRIPTION.

6.2 UNDERSTAND THE QUALITIES OF EFFECTIVE DESCRIPTION.

6.3 INTERPRET IMAGES AND DESCRIPTIVE READINGS ABOUT MEDIA AND POPULAR CULTURE.

6.4 ANALYZE THE RHETORICAL STAR FOR DESCRIPTION.

6.5 APPLY THE QUALITIES OF DESCRIPTIVE WRITING.

SmartBook Tip

Students receive an overview of the learning outcomes and topics in Chapter 6 in the "Preview" phase of SmartBook.

WRITING STRATEGY FOCUS: DESCRIBING

Writing a vivid description can help to evoke an image in your readers' minds. To be good at describing, you need to be a keen observer. While description can be used as a primary method of development for an essay, it is often combined with another writing strategy, such as narration. Whether you are describing people, places, objects, conditions, or events, you will need to appeal to your readers' senses. Show the readers what you observed by carefully selecting details to portray your observations accurately. In this chapter you will have an opportunity to interpret images and descriptive readings and to write your own descriptions. You may use descriptive writing in college, in your personal life, and in the workplace.

6.1 REAL-WORLD APPLICATIONS FOR DESCRIBING

Writing Descriptions in College

College courses will provide you with numerous opportunities for writing descriptions. You might need to describe what you see under a microscope in an anatomy or biology class. If you go on a field trip, your instructor may require that you keep a journal where you describe what you observe while out in the field. In a psychology class, you may need to describe someone's personality traits.

Writing Descriptions in Your Daily Life

Writing descriptions will also be useful in your personal life. If you decide to purchase a home, you will need to describe the features you desire to a real estate agent. If you have a car accident, you may need to describe what happened to the police or your insurance company. If you sustain an injury, you may need to describe your symptoms to your physician. Additionally, you might need to write a product description for an item you would like to sell on *eBay* or *Craigslist*.

Writing Descriptions in Your Career

Being able to write an effective description can be essential on the job. When applying for a job, you might describe some of your past achievements. You may need to write a case study or field observation or describe the features of a plan you are proposing. For marketing purposes, you may need to write a description of the products or services your company offers. Here are a few specific applications for writing descriptions in the workplace:

Health care: descriptions of symptoms, X-ray results, or treatment plans.

Law: descriptions of alleged criminals, crimes, and sentences.

Education: descriptions of a child's behavior, a classroom activity, or a lesson plan.

Computer-aided drafting: descriptions of buildings, architectural plans, or concepts for planned neighborhoods.

Business: descriptions of employee duties, business proposals, or marketing plans.

Culinary arts: descriptions of ingredients, menu items, cooking techniques, or buffet presentations.

Massage therapy: descriptions of massage techniques, essential materials, or the perfect ambience.

Graduate SPOTLIGHT

Lisa Fournier, President/Owner

Lisa Fournier has a degree in business administration. She is the president and owner of Southern Photo, a retail store that specializes in photo restoration, printing services, custom framing, and photography equipment. Here's what Fournier has to say about the importance of written communication in her field:

“ Writing is vital to my career. I have to use a variety of media to get my message across to my customers. I write letters, e-mails, blogs, television and newspaper advertisements, and employee training manuals. I have to understand the power of words to influence my customers as well as my employees. When I write an ad, I have to do much more than just say that Southern Photo provides quality printing. That statement will not motivate the customer to buy prints. Instead I give specific examples to illustrate how my prints are of a higher quality than the local drugstore's prints. I describe what can happen without quality printing, such as 'Aunt Jean turning green' and 'Uncle Fred's cut off head.' I explain that we actually look at the prints and correct the problems before the customer ever sees them so that the photos look natural and will become a treasured keepsake in a photo album.

Additionally, digital technology has caused some people to change their habits. They think that they don't need to print their photos. As a result, I have to remind them that a printed photo can bring back memories and feelings. I write descriptively to evoke the customers' emotions. I recently wrote a blog for my website where I described the best birthday gift I ever received, which is a photograph album my two sisters put together especially for me. It contains some of the most embarrassing, memorable, and great pictures of my life. Maybe the customers who read my blog will do the same for someone they love. ”

Teaching Tip
Ask students to tell how they anticipate using the descriptive writing strategy in their future careers.

> **Activity**   **Real-World Descriptive Writing**
>
> On your own, in pairs, or in small groups, brainstorm uses for descriptive writing at school, in your daily life, and on the job. You may want to choose your career field or the prospective career field(s) of the participants in your group. Be prepared to share your results with your instructor or the class.

Real-World Descriptive Writing Activity:

Answers will vary.

6.2 QUALITIES OF EFFECTIVE DESCRIPTION

1. Begin by Creating a Dominant Impression

As you begin composing your essay, think about the overall mood or feeling you want your readers to experience. Your thesis statement should portray this dominant impression. Every detail you include should support the dominant impression you are creating. For example, if your dominant impression captures the excitement of New York City, then you probably wouldn't want to mention anything about the woman sitting on a bench reading a novel, oblivious to all that is going on around her. Instead, focus on the details that illustrate what makes New York an exciting city. Keep your dominant impression consistent throughout your entire essay.

SmartBook Tip

Key concepts in Chapter 6 are highlighted for students during the "Read" phase. As students demonstrate understanding of these concepts during the "Practice" phase by responding to probes, the highlighting adapts to the individual student's learning by changing color.

2. Use an Objective or a Subjective Approach

Depending on your purpose for writing, you may choose to make your description objective or subjective. Objective descriptions stick to just the facts and don't include personal opinions or emotions, whereas subjective descriptions are sometimes more imaginative and do include the writer's interpretations and feelings. For example, a police report describing an incident at a concert might objectively state, "A 16-year-old Caucasian male sustained serious injuries at the arena after the performance ended at 11:55 P.M. last night."

On the other hand, a journalist who wants to give readers a better sense of what people experienced at the concert by making it more subjective might write, "Tragedy struck just before midnight last night when an innocent 16-year-old high school boy suffered life-threatening injuries as the panic-stricken, stampeding fans pummeled him on their way out of the overcrowded arena after the heavy metal band finished its wild, head-banging performance." Both accounts of the incident may be accurate, but they serve different purposes and are intended for different audiences. The subjective description, unlike the objective one, is designed to stir the reader's emotions.

Teaching Tip

Provide students with news articles (or ask students to bring them to class). Have students work in groups to identify objective and subjective language in the articles and discuss them with the class.

3. Appeal to the Senses

When you're writing a description, be sure to include enough sensory details to capture your readers' attention. What do you see, hear, smell, and so on? You'll want your readers to feel as if they are observing firsthand what you are describing.

For example, if you are describing an exciting scene you witnessed from a sidewalk café in New York City, let the readers *see* the young man covered in colorful tattoos sporting a purple mohawk and multiple body piercings; enable them to *hear* the honking horns and blasting music; help them to *smell* the delicious aromas emanating from the street vendors' food carts. Be sure to choose precise adjectives for your descriptions. Replace vague words such as *a lot, pretty,* and *great* with more precise terms that create vivid images for the readers.

4. Include Similes and Metaphors

Often you can enhance your descriptions by using figurative language, such as similes and metaphors. Similes are comparisons that use *like* or *as*. For instance, if you are describing a dragonfly, you might say, "The dragonfly looks like a mini helicopter hovering over the bow of the canoe." Metaphors are more direct comparisons that do not use *like* or *as*. For example, you could say, "The dragonfly is a fragile mini helicopter hovering over the bow of the canoe."

Similes and metaphors can help make your descriptions more vivid for the reader. However, be careful to use original similes and metaphors rather than clichés. You don't want to describe someone as being "as nervous as a two-tailed cat in a room full of rocking chairs" because that simile has been used many times and lacks an element of freshness and surprise.

5. Organize Your Description Logically

Use an organizational strategy that makes sense for your topic. If you're describing a panoramic view from a mountain, you might move from left to right. When describing your friend's crazy outfit, you might go from head to toe. If you want to describe your new car, moving from front to back would work well. Choose an organizational pattern that will help your reader to visualize your subject.

6. End on a Memorable Note

The conclusion is a good place to remind your reader of the dominant impression you created in the essay. Close with a lasting, vivid image for your readers to envision. Again, stay away from clichés in the conclusion.

▶ *Activity*   Objective and Subjective Descriptions

Observe a person, place, or object. First, write a one-paragraph, objective description of your subject. Next, revise your description, making it subjective. How do the paragraphs differ? When might one approach be more effective than the other?

Career-Based DESCRIPTIVE WRITING

[preview] **THE FOLLOWING** is a description of exercise-induced asthma from **mayoclinic .com.** Have you had trouble breathing? What kinds of symptoms did you experience?

Exercise-Induced Asthma

Description

If you cough, wheeze, or feel out of breath during or 1 after exercise, it may be more than exertion causing your symptoms. You might have exercise-induced asthma. As with asthma triggered by other things, exercise-induced asthma symptoms occur when your airways tighten and produce extra mucus.

Symptoms

Exercise-induced asthma symptoms can include:

- Coughing
- Wheezing
- Shortness of breath
- Chest tightness or pain
- Fatigue during exercise
- Poor athletic performance

2

Exercise-induced asthma symptoms may start a few 3 minutes after you begin exercising. Some people have symptoms 10 to 15 minutes after finishing a workout. It's possible to have symptoms both during and after exercise.

Feeling a little short of breath or fatigued when you 4 work out is normal, especially if you aren't in great shape. But with exercise-induced asthma, these symptoms can be more severe.

For many people, exercise is just one of a few asthma 5 triggers. Others can include pollen, pet dander, and other airborne allergens.

If you have exercise-induced asthma—also called 6 exercise-induced bronchospasm (BRONG-ko-spaz-um)— physical exertion may be the only thing that triggers your symptoms. Or, exercise may be just one of several things that trigger your asthma. But having exercise-induced asthma doesn't mean you shouldn't exercise. Proper treatment and precautions can keep you active— whether you're strolling through the park or competing for Olympic gold.

Source: Mayo Clinic, "Exercise-Induced Asthma," **www.mayoclinic.com/health/ exercise-induced-asthma/DS01040/DSECTION=symptoms.**

[QUESTIONS FOR REFLECTION]

1. What is the primary purpose of the article? Does the article achieve its purpose?

2. Which part of the article uses descriptive words? Does the article include vivid appeals to the senses? Explain.

3. Compare and contrast the design of this article to the design of a typical college essay. Which type of design is more effective for this type of writing? Why?

4. Why did the writer include headings? Are they useful? Why or why not?

5. What advice does the article give for people who suffer from this type of asthma?

[preview] **MOST OF THE TIME** everything goes smoothly in a junior high school classroom; however, occasionally a student needs help remembering his or her manners. When things go awry, the teacher usually has to describe the problem and the consequences on a discipline form to create a record for the school and the student's parent(s) or guardian(s). A junior high instructor completed the following discipline form when an incident occurred in his classroom. The names have been changed to protect the privacy of the individuals involved. Do you remember attending junior high school? What did some of the children do to get into trouble? How were those children punished?

School Discipline Form

Description of Infraction:

During today's science class Kenny was loud and unruly. [1] He entered the classroom at the beginning of the period by pushing through the other students who were lined up at the door and then slammed his books down hard on the table. During our opening bell activity, he was turned around in his seat pestering another student to give him a pencil. When asked to turn around, he rudely said, "If I need a dumb pencil, what am I supposed to do?" Finally, during a paired reading activity, Kenny pulled a book out from his partner's hands while she was reading her assigned paragraph and told her to go get another one.

Explanation of Teacher Actions:

After Kenny talked back when he was turned around [2] in his seat, I went to his desk and warned him that he needed to settle down and begin following the classroom procedures or he would need to go to the office. Taking his partner's book away from her was unacceptable and required disciplinary intervention.

Student Explanation:

Kenny did not provide further explanation, nor did he dispute Mr. Williams's account of the events. [3]

Additional Information:

I called and discussed this matter with Kenny's mother on [4] 11/12/2014. Kenny will be serving a 30-minute detention on 11/15/2014, and will write a letter of apology to his reading partner.

[QUESTIONS FOR REFLECTION]

1. Based on the teacher's description, can you envision what happened? Explain.

2. Which words in the description are objective? Which words are subjective?

3. Why did the teacher include dialogue from the student in the description? Is it helpful? Why or why not?

4. What other writing strategy has the teacher used in addition to description? Why did he combine approaches?

5. Was Kenny's punishment fair? Why or why not?

6.3 DESCRIBING IN THE CONTEXT OF MEDIA AND POPULAR CULTURE

Pop culture is all about the way we live, what we do, where we go, how we communicate, what we buy and wear, and what we believe. Various media reflect what is popular in our culture today. The articles and books we read, the movies and television programs we watch, the music and talk shows we listen to, the websites we surf, the video games we play, and the advertisements we observe all reveal our popular culture. The media and pop culture offer ample material for descriptive writing. Read one or more of the following descriptive essays. Reading and interpreting professional and student writing samples of descriptive writing can help you to write more descriptively for school, at work, or in your daily life.

[preview] **NEAL GABLER** has written several books, including *Walt Disney: The Triumph of American Imagination* (2006), and has contributed to numerous publications, including the *New York Times* and the *Los Angeles Times*. He also has reviewed movies for PBS on a program called *Sneak Previews* (originally hosted by Gene Siskel and Robert Ebert) and later became a panelist for *Fox News Watch*, a weekly media review program. In the following essay, which was originally published in the *Los Angeles Times*, Gabler examines our fascination with urban legends, which are modern stories that become widespread even though they have little or no basis in fact. Before reading, think about an urban myth that you have heard via e-mail or from another person. Was the story plausible? How did you react to it? Were you frightened in some way?

How Urban Myths Reveal Society's Fears by Neal Gabler

The story goes like this: During dinner at an opulent wedding reception, the groom rises from the head table and shushes the crowd. Everyone naturally assumes he is about to toast his bride and thank his guests. Instead, he solemnly announces that there has been a change of plan. He and his bride will be taking separate honeymoons and, when they return, the marriage will be annulled. The reason for this sudden turn of events, he says, is taped to the bottom of everyone's plate. The stunned guests quickly flip their dinnerware to discover a photo of the bride *in flagrante*[1] with the best man. 1

At least that is the story that has been recently making the rounds up and down the Eastern seaboard and as far west as Chicago. Did this really happen? A *Washington Post* reporter who tracked the story was told by one source that it happened at a New Hampshire hotel. But then another source swears it happened in Medford, Massachusetts. Then again another suggests a banquet hall outside Schenectady, New York. Meanwhile, a sophisticated couple in Manhattan has heard it happened at the Pierre. 2

In short, the whole thing appears to be another urban myth, one of those weird tales that periodically catch the public imagination. Alligators swarming the sewers 3

---
[1] **In flagrante** Caught in the act of being unfaithful.

after people have flushed the baby reptiles down the toilet. The babysitter who gets threatening phone calls that turn out to be coming from inside the house. The woman who turns out to have a nest of black-widow spiders in her beehive hairdo. The man who falls asleep and awakens to find his kidney has been removed. The rat that gets deep-fried and served by a fast-food outlet. Or, in a variation, the mouse that has somehow drowned in a closed Coca-Cola bottle.

These tales are preposterous, but in a mass society like ours, where stories are usually manufactured by Hollywood, they just may be the most genuine form of folklore we have. Like traditional folklore, they are narratives crafted by the collective consciousness. Like traditional folklore, they give expression to the national mind. And like traditional folklore, they blend the fantastic with the routine, if only to demonstrate, in the words of University of Utah folklorist Jan Harold Brunvand, the nation's leading expert on urban legends, "that the prosaic contemporary scene is capable of producing shocking or amazing occurrences." 4

Shocking and amazing, yes. But in these stories, anything can happen not because the world is a magical place rich with wonder—as in folktales of yore—but because our world is so utterly terrifying. Here, nothing is reliable and no laws of morality govern. The alligators 5 in the sewers present an image of an urban hell inhabited by beasts—an image that might have come directly from Hades and the River Styx in Greek mythology. The babysitter and the man upstairs exploits fears that we are not even safe in our own homes. The spider in the hairdo says that even on our own persons, dangers lurk. The man who loses his kidney plays to our fears of the night and the real bogymen who prowl them. The mouse in the soda warns us of the perils of an impersonal mass-production society.

As for the wedding reception tale, which one hacker on the Internet has dubbed "Wedding Revenge," it may address the greatest terror of all: that love and commitment are chimerical[2] and even friendship is meaningless. These are timeless issues, but the sudden promulgation[3] of the tale suggests its special relevance in the age of AIDS, when commitment means even more than it used to, and in the age of feminism, when some men are feeling increasingly threatened by women's freedom. Thus, the groom not only suffers betrayal and humiliation; his plight carries the hint of danger and emasculation, too. Surely, a legend for our time.

Of course, folklore and fairy tales have long subsisted on terror, and even the treacly[4] cartoons of Walt Disney are actually, when you parse them, dark and complex expressions of fear—from Snow White racing through the treacherous forest to Pinocchio gobbled by the whale to Dumbo being separated from his mother. But these crystallize the fears of childhood, the fears one must overcome to make the difficult transition to adulthood. Thus, the haunted forest of the fairy tales is a trope[5] for haunted adolescence; the witch or crone, a trope for the spent generation one must vanquish to claim one's place in the world, and the prince who comes to the rescue, a trope for the adult responsibilities that the heroine must now assume.

Though urban legends frequently originate with college students about to enter the real world, they are different from traditional fairy tales because their terrors are not really obstacles on the road to understanding, and they are different from folklore because they cannot even be interpreted as cautionary. In urban legends, obstacles aren't overcome, perhaps can't be overcome, and there is nothing we can do differently to avoid the consequences. The woman, not knowing any better, eats the fried rat. The babysitter is terrorized by the stranger hiding in the house. The black widow bites the woman with the beehive hairdo. The alligators prowl the sewers. The marriage in Wedding Revenge breaks up.

It is not just our fears, then, that these stories exploit. Like so much else in modern life—tabloids, exploitalk programs, real-life crime best sellers—urban legends testify to an overwhelming condition of fear and to a sense of our own impotence within it. That is why there is no accommodation in these stories, no lesson or wisdom imparted. What there is, is the stark impression that our world is anomic.[6] We live in a haunted forest of skyscrapers or of suburban lawns and ranch houses, but there is no one to exorcise the evil and no prince to break the spell.

Given the pressures of modern life, it isn't surprising that we have created myths to express our malaise. But what is surprising is how many people seem committed to these myths. The *Post* reporter found people insisting they personally knew someone who had attended the doomed wedding reception. Others went further: They maintained they had actually attended the reception—though no such reception ever took place. Yet even those who didn't claim to have been personally involved seemed to feel duty bound to assert the tale's plausibility.

Why this insistence? Perhaps the short answer is that people want to believe in a cosmology of dysfunction because it is the best way of explaining the inexplicable in our lives. A world in which alligators roam sewers and wedding receptions end in shock is at once terrifying and soothing—terrifying because these things happen, soothing because we are absolved of any responsibility for them. It is just the way it is.

But there may be an additional reason why some people seem so willing to suspend their disbelief in the face of logic. This one has less to do with the content of these tales than with their creation. However they start, urban legends rapidly enter a national conversation in which they are embellished, heightened, reconfigured. Everyone can participate—from the people who spread the tale on talk radio to the people who discuss it on the Internet to the people who tell it to their neighbors. In effect, these legends are the product of a giant campfire around which we trade tales of terror.

If this makes each of us a co-creator of the tales, it also provides us with a certain pride of authorship. Like all authors, we don't want to see the spell of our creation broken—especially when we have formed a little community around it. It doesn't matter whether these tales are true or not. What matters is that they plausibly reflect our world, that they have been generated from the grass roots and that we can pass them along.

In a way, then, these tales of powerlessness ultimately assert a kind of authority. Urban legends permit us to become our own Stephen Kings, terrorizing ourselves to confirm one of the few powers we still possess: the power to tell stories about our world.

Source: Neal Gabler, "How Urban Myths Reveal Society's Fears," *Los Angeles Times*, November 12, 1995. Reprinted by permission of the author.

---

[2]**Chimerical** Fanciful or mythical.
[3]**Promulgation** Publication or dissemination.
[4]**Treacly** Overly sentimental.

---

[5]**Trope** Figure of speech.
[6]**Anomic** Disoriented or alienated.

Considering Ideas

1. Before reading Gabler's essay, were you familiar with any of the urban legends he mentions? Which ones? What was your initial reaction to them?

2. Why do you think urban myths spread so fast? Why do we find some of them to be fascinating?

3. What fears does Gabler suggest urban myths address? Do you agree or disagree with the author? Why?

Considering the Rhetorical Star

1. What is the main *subject* of Gabler's descriptive essay? Is the specific topic engaging? Why or why not?

2. Who is the intended *audience* for the story? How do you know?

3. What is the author's main *purpose* (to inform, to interpret, to persuade, to entertain, to express feelings) for the essay? Does he use a combination of purposes? How effective is his approach? Explain.

4. The author uses description as the primary *strategy* for the story. Does he employ any other writing strategies? What are they, and how do they affect the piece?

5. What is the *design* of the work? Is it effective? Why or why not?

Considering Writing Strategies

1. Which specific passages in Gabler's essay appeal to the reader's senses? What do these passages add to the piece? Explain.

2. What dominant impression is Gabler trying to get across to the reader? How successful is he at making his point? Explain your answer.

3. What specific details caught your attention in the essay? Why are those particular ideas more memorable than others?

Writing Suggestions

1. Have you ever observed (or participated in) something that seems stranger than fiction? Write a descriptive essay about your experience. Make your description vivid by capturing the sensory details and emotions related to the incident.

2. What scares you? Write your own urban myth that addresses one of your fears. Be sure to include enough sensory appeal so that your readers are fully immersed in your creative story.

Reading and Reflection DESCRIPTIVE WRITING

[preview] **BILL WINE,** a native of San Francisco, California, is an award-winning writer and movie critic. He has achieved three Emmy Awards (and eight Emmy nominations) for "Individual Achievement" in the "Writer/Commentary and Review" category. He has contributed numerous articles to a variety of publications, including the *Philadelphia Daily News* and the *New Jersey Monthly.* He has also written several plays that have been published and produced. To learn more about Bill Wine, visit **http://philadelphia.cbslocal.com/personality/bill-wine/.**

Even in the age of home surround systems, 3-D, and high-definition television, going to the movie theater is still an extremely popular pastime. There's something special about seeing a flick with a captivated audience, but sometimes we are at the mercy of the individuals seated around us. In his essay "Rudeness at the Movies," Wine describes a less than perfect moviegoing experience. Before reading, consider your own experiences at the movie theater. Have you experienced rudeness at the movies? What did the other viewers do that annoyed you? Did you do anything about it?

Rudeness at the Movies by Bill Wine

Is this actually happening or am I dreaming? 1

I am at the movies, settling into my seat, eager with 2 anticipation at the prospect of seeing a long-awaited film of obvious quality. The theater is absolutely full for the late show on this weekend evening, as the reviews have been ecstatic for this cinema masterpiece.

Directly in front of me sits a man an inch or two taller 3 than the Jolly Green Giant. His wife, sitting on his left, sports the very latest in fashionable hairdos, a gathering of her locks into a shape that resembles a drawbridge when it's open.

On his right, a woman spritzes herself liberally with 4 perfume that her popcorn-munching husband got her for Valentine's Day, a scent that should be renamed "Essence of Elk."

The row in which I am sitting quickly fills up with mem- 5 bers of Cub Scout Troop 432, on an outing to the movies because rain has canceled their overnight hike. One of the boys, demonstrating the competitive spirit for which Scouts are renowned worldwide, announces to the rest of the troop the rules in the Best Sound Made from an Empty Good-n-Plenty's Box contest, about to begin.

Directly behind me, a man and his wife are ushering 6 three other couples into their seats. I hear the woman say to the couple next to her: "You'll love it. You'll just love it. This is our fourth time and we enjoy it more and more each time. Don't we, Harry? Tell them about the pie-fight scene, Harry. Wait'll you see it. It comes just before you find out that the daughter killed her boyfriend. It's great."

The woman has more to say—much more—but she 7 is drowned out at the moment by the wailing of a six-month-old infant in the row behind her. The baby is crying because his mother, who has brought her twins to the theater to save on babysitting costs, can change only one diaper at a time.

Suddenly, the lights dim. The music starts. The credits 8 roll. And I panic.

I plead with everyone around me to let me enjoy the 9 movie. All I ask, I wail, is to be able to see the images and hear the dialogue and not find out in advance what is about to happen. Is that so much to expect for six bucks, I ask, now engulfed by a cloud of self-pity. I begin weeping unashamedly.

Then, as if on cue, the Jolly Green Giant slumps down 10 in his seat, his wife removes her wig, the Elk lady changes her seat, the Scouts drop their candy boxes on the floor, the play-by-play commentator takes out her teeth, and the young mother takes her two bawling babies home.

Of course I am dreaming, I realize, as I gain a certain 11 but shaky consciousness. I notice that I am in a cold sweat. Not because the dream is scary, but from the shock of people being that cooperative.

I realize that I have awakened to protect my system 12 from having to handle a jolt like that. For never—NEVER—would that happen in real life. Not on this planet.

I used to wonder whether I was the only one who 13 feared bad audience behavior more than bad moviemaking. But I know now that I am not. Not by a long shot. The most frequent complaint I have heard in the last few months about the moviegoing experience has had nothing to do with the films themselves.

No. What folks have been complaining about is the 14 audience. Indeed, there seems to be an epidemic of galling inconsiderateness and outrageous rudeness.

It is not that difficult to forgive a person's excessive 15 height, or malodorous perfume, or perhaps even an inadvisable but understandable need to bring very young children to adult movies.

But the talking: that is not easy to forgive. It is inexcus- 16 able. Talking—loud, constant, and invariably superfluous—seems to be standard operating procedure on the part of many movie patrons these days.

It is true, I admit, that after a movie critic has seen 17 several hundred movies in the ideal setting of an almost-empty screening room with no one but other politely silent movie critics around him, it does tend to spoil him for the packed-theater experience.

And something is lost viewing a movie in almost total 18 isolation—a fact that movie distributors acknowledge with their reluctance to screen certain audience-pleasing movies for small groups of critics. Especially with comedies, the infectiousness of laughter is an important ingredient of movie-watching pleasure.

But it is a decidedly uphill battle to enjoy a movie— 19 no matter how suspenseful or hilarious or moving—with nonstop gabbers sitting within earshot. And they come in sizes, ages, sexes, colors, and motivations of every kind.

Some chat as if there is no movie playing. Some greet 20 friends as if at a picnic. Some alert those around them to what is going to happen, either because they have seen the film before, or because they are self-proclaimed experts on the predictability of plotting and want to be seen as prescient geniuses.

Some describe in graphic terms exactly what is hap- 21 pening as if they were doing the commentary for a sporting event on radio. ("Ooh, look, he's sitting down. Now he's looking at that green car. A banana—she's eating a banana.") Some audition for film critic Gene Shalit's job by waxing witty as they critique the movie right before your very ears.

And all act as if it is their constitutional or God-given 22 right. As if their admission price allows them to ruin the experience for anyone and everyone else in the building. But why?

Good question. I wish I knew. Maybe rock concerts 23 and ball games—both environments which condone or even encourage hootin' and hollerin'—have conditioned us to voice our approval and disapproval and just about anything else we can spit out of our mouths at the slightest provocation when we are part of an audience.

But my guess lies elsewhere. The villain, I'm afraid, is 24 the tube. We have seen the enemy and it is television.

We have gotten conditioned over the last few decades 25 to spending most of our screen-viewing time in front of a little box in our living rooms and bedrooms. And when we watch that piece of furniture, regardless of what is on it—be it commercial, Super Bowl, soap opera, funeral procession, prime-time sitcom, Shakespeare play—we chat. Boy, do we chat. Because TV viewing tends to be an informal, gregarious, friendly, casually interruptible experience, we talk whenever the spirit moves us. Which is often.

All of this is fine. But we have carried behavior that 26 is perfectly acceptable in the living room right to our neighborhood movie theater. And that isn't fine. In fact, it is turning lots of people off to what used to be a truly pleasurable experience: sitting in a jammed movie theater and watching a crowd-pleasing movie. And that's a first-class shame.

Nobody wants Fascist-like ushers, yet that may be 27 where we're headed of necessity. Let's hope not. But something's got to give.

Movies during this Age of Television may or may not 28 be better than ever. About audiences, however, there is no question.

They are worse. 29

Source: Bill Wine, "Rudeness at the Movies," copyright © 1989. Reprinted by permission of the author.

[QUESTIONS FOR REFLECTION]

Considering Ideas

1. What activities does Bill Wine find to be irritating at the movies? Do those behaviors bother you, or do you have other pet peeves?

2. Do you feel that Wine is reporting exactly what he has seen while at the movies, or is he exaggerating his examples to make a point? Explain your answer.

3. Why do you think some people behave in the movie theater as they might in their own living room? Do you think those people are aware of the effect they have on others? Why or why not?

Considering the Rhetorical Star

1. What is the main *subject* of Bill Wine's descriptive essay? Is the specific topic engaging? Why or why not?

2. Who is the intended *audience* for the essay? How do you know?

3. What is the author's main *purpose* (to inform, to interpret, to persuade, to entertain, to express feelings) for the essay? Does he use a combination of purposes? How effective is his approach? Explain.

4. The author uses description as the primary *strategy* for the story. Does he employ any other writing strategies? What are they, and how do they affect the piece?

5. What is the *design* of the work? Is it effective? Why or why not?

Considering Writing Strategies

1. Which parts of the essay seem to have a sarcastic tone? Refer to specific quotes from the essay to support your answer. What effect does Wine's sarcasm have on the reader?

2. Find examples of similes and metaphors in Wine's essay. Which ones do you find to be most interesting or humorous? How do they enhance the essay?

3. Which parts of the essay do you find to be most descriptive? What senses does Wine appeal to? Identify specific examples.

Writing Suggestions

1. Write a description of an event you observed, such as a concert or football game. You might capture what is happening on the stage or field as well as what the spectators are doing. Create a dominant impression for the reader, and use as many sensory details as are appropriate for your subject. Help your readers to feel as if they are attending the event.

2. Watch a television show or movie and choose one aspect of it to describe. You might write about a character, a scene, or an object that you find to be noteworthy. Use a multitude of adjectives in your description so that your readers can visualize your subject.

[preview] **STEPHEN KING,** born in Portland, Maine, is the master of horror fiction. He became a best-selling author with the publication of his first novel, *Carrie* (1974), which was transformed into a hit movie in 1976. Since then he has written numerous screenplays, short stories, essays, and more than 40 novels, many of which have been made into blockbuster movies. He wrote several popular novels under the pseudonym of Richard Bachman, proving his works would sell even without his famous name. For fun King plays guitar in a charitable band called The Rock Bottom Remainders with Amy Tan, Dave Barry, Matt Groening, and other famous writers. You can visit the band's website at **www.rockbottomremainders.com** and King's home page **www.stephenking.com** for more details. In the following essay, "My Creature from the Black Lagoon," King describes his first moviegoing experience and explores our fascination with the horror genre. Before reading, think about movies you saw as a child. Did any of them truly scare you? Why were you frightened?

My Creature from the Black Lagoon by Stephen King

The first movie I can remember seeing as a kid was *Creature from the Black Lagoon.* It was at the drive-in, and unless it was a second-run job I must have been about seven, because the film, which starred Richard Carlson and Richard Denning, was released in 1954. It was also originally released in 3-D, but I cannot remember wearing the glasses, so perhaps I did see a rerelease. [1]

I remember only one scene clearly from the movie, but it left a lasting impression. The hero (Carlson) and the heroine (Julia Adams, who looked absolutely spectacular in a one-piece white bathing suit) are on an expedition somewhere in the Amazon basin. They make their way up a swampy, narrow waterway and into a wide pond that seems an idyllic South American version of the Garden of Eden. [2]

But the creature is lurking—naturally. It's a scaly, batrachian[1] monster that is remarkably like Lovecraft's half-breed, degenerate aberrations—the crazed and blasphemous results of liaisons between gods and human women (It's difficult to get away from Lovecraft). This monster is slowly and patiently barricading the mouth of the stream with sticks and branches, irrevocably sealing the party of anthropologists in. [3]

I was barely old enough to read at that time, the discovery of my father's box of weird fiction still years away. I have a vague memory of boyfriends in my mom's life during that period—from 1952 until 1958 or so; enough of a memory to be sure she had a social life, not enough to even guess if she had a sex life. There was Norville, who smoked Luckies and kept three fans going in his two-room apartment during the summer; and there was Milt, who drove a Buick and wore gigantic [4]

blue shorts in the summertime; and another fellow, very small, who was, I believe, a cook in a French restaurant. So far as I know, my mother came close to marrying none of them. She'd gone that route once. Also, that was a time when a woman, once married, became a shadow figure in the process of decision-making and bread-winning. I think my mom, who could be stubborn, intractable, grimly persevering and nearly impossible to discourage, had gotten a taste for captaining her own life. And so she went out with guys, but none of them became permanent fixtures.

It was Milt we were out with that night, he of the Buick and the large blue shorts. He seemed to genuinely like my brother and me, and to genuinely not mind having us along in the back seat from time to time (it may be that when you have reached the calmer waters of your early forties, the idea of necking at the drive-in no longer appeals so strongly . . . even if you have a Buick as large as a cabin cruiser to do it in). By the time the Creature made his appearance, my brother had slithered down onto the floor of the back and had fallen asleep. My mother and Milt were talking, perhaps passing a Kool back and forth. They don't matter, at least not in this context; nothing matters except the big black-and-white images up on the screen, where the unspeakable Thing is walling the handsome hero and the sexy heroine into . . . into . . . the Black Lagoon! [5]

I knew, watching, that the Creature had become *my* Creature; I had bought it. Even to a seven-year-old, it was not a terribly convincing Creature. I did not know then it was good old Ricou Browning, the famed underwater stuntman, in a molded latex suit, but I surely knew it was some guy in some kind of a monster suit . . . just as I knew that, later on that night, he would visit me in the [6]

---
[1]**Batrachian** Amphibian or frog-like.

black lagoon of my dreams, looking much more realistic. He might be waiting in the closet when we got back; he might be standing slumped in the blackness of the bathroom at the end of the hall, stinking of algae and swamp rot, all ready for a post-midnight snack of small boy. Seven isn't old, but it is old enough to know that you get what you pay for. You own it, you just bought it, it's yours. It is old enough to feel the dowser suddenly come alive, grow heavy, and roll over in your hands, pointing at hidden water.

My reaction to the Creature on that night was per- 7 haps the perfect reaction, the one every writer of horror fiction or director who has worked in the field hopes for when he or she uncaps a pen or a lens: total emotional involvement, pretty much undiluted by any real thinking process—and you understand, don't you, that when it comes to horror movies, the only thought process really necessary to break the mood is for a friend to lean over and whisper, "See the zipper running down his back?"

I think that only people who have worked in the field 8 for some time truly understand how fragile this stuff really is, and what an amazing commitment it imposes on the reader or the viewer of intellect and maturity. When Coleridge spoke of "the suspension of disbelief" in his essay on imaginative poetry, I believe he knew that disbelief is not like a balloon, which may be suspended in air with a minimum of effort; it is like a lead weight, which has to be hoisted with a clean and a jerk and held up by main force. Disbelief isn't light; it's heavy. The difference in sales between Arthur Hailey and H.P. Lovecraft may exist because everyone believes in cars, and banks, but it takes a sophisticated and muscular intellectual act to believe, even for a little while, in Nyarlathotep, the Blind Faceless One, the Howler in the Night. And whenever I run into someone who expresses a feeling along the lines of, "I don't read fantasy or go to any of those movies; none of it's real," I feel a kind of sympathy. They simply can't lift the weight of fantasy. The muscles of the imagination have grown too weak.

In this sense, kids are the perfect audience for horror. 9 The paradox is this: Children, who are physically quite weak, lift the weight of unbelief with ease. They are the jugglers of the invisible world—a perfectly understandable phenomenon when you consider the perspective they must view things from. Children deftly manipulate the logistics of Santa Claus's entry on Christmas Eve (he can get down small chimneys by making himself small, and if there's no chimney there's the letter slot, and if there's no letter slot there's always the crack under the door), the Easter Bunny, God (big guy, sorta old, white beard, throne), Jesus ("How do you think he turned the water into wine?" I asked my son Joe when he—Joe, not Jesus—was five; Joe's idea was that he had something "kinda like magic Kool-Aid, you get what I mean?"), the devil (big guy, red skin, horse feet, tail with an arrow

on the end of it, Snidely Whiplash moustache), Ronald McDonald, the Burger King, the Keebler Elves, Dorothy and Toto, the Lone Ranger and Tonto, a thousand more.

Most parents think they understand this openness 10 better than, in many cases, they actually do, and try to keep their children away from anything that smacks too much of horror and terror—"Rated PG (or G in the case of *The Andromeda Strain*), but may be too intense for younger children," the ads for *Jaws* read—believing, I suppose, that to allow their kids to go to a real horror movie would be tantamount to rolling a live hand grenade into a nursery school.

But one of the odd Doppler effects that seems to 11 occur during the selective forgetting that is so much a part of "growing up" is the fact that almost *everything* has a scare potential for the child under eight. Children are literally afraid of their own shadows at the right time and place. There is the story of the four-year-old who refused to go to bed at night without a light on in his closet. His parents at last discovered he was frightened of a creature he had heard his father speak of often; this creature, which had grown large and dreadful in the child's imagination, was the "twi-night double-header."

Seen in this light, even Disney movies are minefields 12 of terror, and the animated cartoons, which will apparently be released and rereleased even unto the end of the world,[2] are usually the worst offenders. There are adults today, who, when questioned, will tell you that the most frightening thing they saw at the movies as children was Bambi's father shot by the hunter, or Bambi and his mother running before the forest fire. Other Disney memories which are right up there with the batrachian horror inhabiting the Black Lagoon include the marching brooms that have gone totally out of control in *Fantasia* (and for the small child, the real horror inherent in the situation is probably buried in the implied father-son relationship between Mickey Mouse and the old sorcerer; those brooms are making a terrible mess, and when the sorcerer/father gets home, there may be PUNISHMENT. . . . This sequence might well send the child of strict parents into an ecstasy of terror); the night on Bald Mountain from the same film; the witches in *Snow*

---

[2]In one of my favorite Arthur C. Clarke stories, this actually happens. In this vignette, aliens from space land on earth after the Big One has finally gone down. As the story closes, the best brains of this alien culture are trying to figure out the meaning of a film they have found and learned how to play back. The film ends with the words *A Walt Disney Production*. I have moments when I really believe that there would be no better epitaph for the human race, or for a world where the only sentient being absolutely guaranteed of immortality is not Hitler, Charlemagne, Albert Schweitzer, or even Jesus Christ—but is, instead, Richard M. Nixon, whose name is engraved on a plaque placed on the airless surface of the moon. [This note is the author's.]

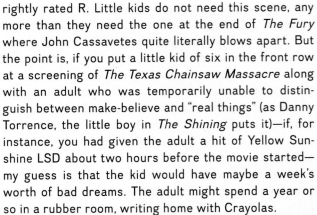

White and *Sleeping Beauty*, one with her enticingly red poisoned apple (and what small child is not taught early to fear the idea of POISON?), the other with her deadly spinning wheel; this holds all the way up to the relatively innocuous *One Hundred and One Dalmatians* which features the logical granddaughter of those Disney witches from the thirties and forties—the evil Cruella DeVille, with her scrawny, nasty face, her loud voice (grownups sometimes forget how terrified young children are of loud voices, which come from the giants of their world, the adults), and her plan to kill all the dalmatian puppies (read "children," if you're a little person) and turn them into dogskin coats.

Yet it is the parents, of course, who continue to underwrite the Disney procedure of release and rerelease, often discovering goosebumps on their own arms as they rediscover what terrified them as children . . . because what the good horror film (or horror sequence in what may be billed a "comedy" or an "animated cartoon") does above all else is to knock the adult props out from under us and tumble us back down the slide into childhood. And there our own shadow may once again become that of a mean dog, a gaping mouth, or a beckoning dark figure.

Perhaps the supreme realization of this return to childhood comes in David Cronenberg's marvelous horror film *The Brood*, where a disturbed woman is literally producing "children of rage" who go out and murder the members of her family, one by one. About halfway through the film, her father sits dispiritedly on the bed in an upstairs room, drinking and mourning his wife, who has been the first to feel the wrath of the brood. We cut to the bed itself . . . and clawed hands suddenly reach out from beneath it and dig into the carpeting near the doomed father's shoes. And so Cronenberg pushes us down the slide; we are four again, and all of our worst surmises about what might be lurking under the bed have turned out to be true.

The irony of all this is that children are better able to deal with fantasy and terror *on its own terms* than their elders are. You'll note I've italicized the phrase "on its own terms." An adult is able to deal with the cataclysmic terror of something like *The Texas Chain Saw Massacre* because he or she understands that it is all make-believe, and that when the take is done the dead people will simply get up and wash off the stage blood. The child is not so able to make this distinction, and *Chainsaw Massacre* is quite

rightly rated R. Little kids do not need this scene, any more than they need the one at the end of *The Fury* where John Cassavetes quite literally blows apart. But the point is, if you put a little kid of six in the front row at a screening of *The Texas Chainsaw Massacre* along with an adult who was temporarily unable to distinguish between make-believe and "real things" (as Danny Torrence, the little boy in *The Shining* puts it)—if, for instance, you had given the adult a hit of Yellow Sunshine LSD about two hours before the movie started—my guess is that the kid would have maybe a week's worth of bad dreams. The adult might spend a year or so in a rubber room, writing home with Crayolas.

A certain amount of fantasy and horror in a child's life seems to me a perfectly okay, useful sort of thing. Because of the size of their imaginative capacity, children are able to handle it, and because of their unique position in life, they are able to put such feelings to work. They understand their position very well, too. Even in such a relatively ordered society as our own, they understand that their survival is a matter almost totally out of their hands. Children are "dependents" up until the age of eight or so in every sense of the word; dependent on mother and father (or some reasonable facsimile thereof) not only for food, clothing, and shelter, but dependent on them not to crash the car into a bridge abutment, to meet the school bus on time, to walk them home from Cub Scouts or Brownies, to buy medicines with childproof caps, dependent on them to make sure they don't electrocute themselves while screwing around with the toaster or while trying to play with Barbie's Beauty Salon in the bathtub.

Running directly counter to this necessary dependence is the survival directive built into all of us. The child realizes his or her essential lack of control, and I suspect it is this very realization which makes the child uneasy. It is the same sort of free-floating anxiety that many air travelers feel. They are not afraid because they believe air travel to be unsafe; they are afraid because they have surrendered control, and if something goes wrong all they can do is sit there clutching airsick bags or the in-flight magazine. To surrender control runs counter to the survival directive. Conversely, while a thinking, informed person may understand intellectually that travel by car is much more dangerous than flying, he or she is still apt to feel much more comfortable behind the wheel, because she/he has control . . . or at least an illusion of it.

This hidden hostility and anxiety toward the airline pilots of their lives may be one explanation why, like the Disney pictures which are released during school vacations in perpetuity, the old fairy tales also seem to go on forever. A parent who would raise his or her hands in horror at the thought of taking his/her child to see *Dracula* or *The Changeling* (with its pervasive imagery of the drowning child) would be unlikely to object to the baby sitter reading "Hansel and Gretel" to the child before bedtime. But consider: the tale of Hansel and Gretel begins with deliberate abandonment (oh yes, the stepmother masterminds that one, but she is the symbolic mother all the same, and the father is a spaghetti-brained nurd who goes along with everything she suggests even though he knows it's wrong—thus we can see her as amoral, him as actively evil in the Biblical and Miltonian sense), it progresses to kidnapping (the witch in the candy house), enslavement, illegal detention, and finally justifiable homicide and cremation. Most mothers and fathers would never take their children to see *Survive,* that quickie Mexican exploitation flick about the rugby players who survived the aftermath of a plane crash in the Andes by eating their dead teammates, but these same parents find little to object to in "Hansel and Gretel," where the witch is fattening the children up so she can eat them. We give this stuff to the kids almost instinctively, understanding on a deeper level, perhaps, that such fairy stories are the perfect points of crystallization for those fears and hostilities.

Even anxiety-ridden air travelers have their own fairy tales—all those *Airport* movies, which, like "Hansel and Gretel" and all those Disney cartoons, show every sign of going on forever . . . but which should only be viewed on Thanksgivings, since all of them feature a large cast of turkeys. **19**

My gut reaction to *Creature from the Black Lagoon* on that long-ago night was a kind of terrible, waking swoon. The nightmare was happening right in front of me; every hideous possibility that human flesh is heir to was being played out on that drive-in screen. **20**

Approximately twenty-two years later, I had a chance to see *Creature from the Black Lagoon* again—not on TV, with any kind of dramatic build and mood broken up by adverts for used cars, K-Tel disco anthologies, and Underalls pantyhose, thank God, but intact, uncut . . . and even in 3-D. Guys like me who wear glasses have a hell of a time with 3-D, you know; ask anyone who wears specs how they like those nifty little cardboard glasses they give you when you walk in the door. If 3-D ever comes back in a big way, I'm going to take myself down to the local Pearle Vision Center and invest seventy bucks in a special pair of prescription lenses: one red, one blue. Annoying glasses aside, I should add that I took my son Joe with me—he was then five, about the age I had been myself, that night at the drive-in (and imagine my surprise—my *rueful* surprise—to discover that the movie which had so terrified me on that long-ago night had been rated G by the MPAA . . . just like the Disney pictures). **21**

As a result, I had a chance to experience that weird doubling back in time that I believe most parents only **22** experience at the Disney films with their children, or when reading them the Pooh books or perhaps taking them to the Shrine or the Barnum & Bailey circus. A popular record is apt to create a particular "set" in a listener's mind, precisely because of its brief life of six weeks to three months, and "golden oldies" continue to be played because they are the emotional equivalent of freeze-dried coffee. When the Beach Boys come on the radio singing "Help Me, Rhonda," there is always that wonderful second or two when I can re-experience the wonderful, guilty joy of copping my first feel (and if you do the mental subtraction from my present age of thirty-three, you'll see that I was a little backward in that respect). Movies and books do the same thing, although I would argue that the mental set, its depth and texture, tends to be a little richer, a little more complex, when re-experiencing films and a lot more complex when dealing with books.

With Joe that day I experienced *Creature from the Black Lagoon* from the other end of the telescope, but this particular theory of set identification still applied; in fact, it prevailed. Time and age and experience have all left their marks on me, just as they have on you; time is not a river, as Einstein theorized—it's a big . . . buffalo herd that runs us down and eventually mashes us into the ground, dead and bleeding, with a hearing-aid plugged into one ear and a colostomy bag instead of a .44 clapped on one leg. Twenty-two years later I knew that the Creature was really good old Ricou Browning, the famed underwater stuntman, in a molded latex suit, and the suspension of disbelief, that mental clean-and-jerk, had become a lot harder to accomplish. But I did it, which may mean nothing, or which may mean (I hope!) that the buffalo haven't got me yet. But when that weight of disbelief was finally up there, the old feelings came flooding in, as they flooded in some five years ago when I took Joe and my daughter Naomi to their first movie, a reissue of *Snow White and the Seven Dwarfs.* There is a scene in that film where, after Snow White has taken a bite from the poisoned apple, the dwarfs take her into the forest, weeping copiously. Half the audience of little kids was also in tears; the lower lips of the other half were trembling. The set identification in that case was strong enough so that I was also surprised into tears. I hated myself for being so blatantly manipulated, but manipulated I was, and there I sat, blubbering into my beard over a bunch of cartoon characters. But it wasn't Disney that manipulated me; I did it myself. It was the kid inside who wept, surprised out of dormancy and into schmaltzy tears . . . but at least awake for a while. **23**

During the final two reels of *Creature from the Black Lagoon,* the weight of disbelief is nicely balanced somewhere above my head, and once again director Jack Arnold places the symbols in front of me and produces **24** the old equation of the fairy tales, each symbol as big and as easy to handle as a child's alphabet block. Watching, the child awakes again and knows that this is what dying is like. Dying is when the Creature from the Black Lagoon dams up the exit. Dying is when the monster gets you.

In the end, of course, the hero and heroine, very much alive, not only survive but triumph—as Hansel and Gretel do. As the drive-in floodlights over the screen came on and the projector flashed its GOOD NIGHT, DRIVE SAFELY slide on that big white space (along with the virtuous suggestion that you ATTEND THE CHURCH OF YOUR CHOICE), there was a brief feeling of relief, almost of resurrection. But the feeling that stuck longest was the swooning sensation that good old Richard Carlson and Julia Adams were surely going down for the third time, and the image that remains forever after is of the creature slowly and patiently walling its victims into the Black Lagoon; even now I can see it peering over that growing wall of mud and sticks.

Its eyes. Its ancient eyes.

Source: Stephen King, "My Creature from the Black Lagoon." Copyright © Stephen King. Reprinted with permission. All rights reserved.

[QUESTIONS FOR REFLECTION]

Considering Ideas

1. Compare King's most recent viewing of *The Creature from the Black Lagoon* to his first viewing. What similarities and differences do you notice? How does seeing the movie as an adult make him feel?

2. King mentions a number of other movies besides *The Creature from the Black Lagoon*. Why do you think he includes these other movies in his essay? Have you ever seen any of the movies he discusses? What were you thinking, or visualizing, as he mentioned each movie?

3. Why does King think horror movies are so popular in today's culture? What does he feel they do for the viewer? Do you agree or disagree with King's position? Why?

Considering the Rhetorical Star

1. What is the main *subject* of King's descriptive essay? Is the specific topic engaging? Why or why not?

2. Who is the intended *audience* for the essay? How do you know?

3. What is the author's main *purpose* (to inform, to interpret, to persuade, to entertain, to express feelings) for the essay? Does he use a combination of purposes? How effective is his approach? Explain.

4. King uses description as the primary *strategy* for the story. Does he employ any other writing strategies? What are they, and how do they affect the piece?

5. What is the *design* of the work? Is it effective? Why or why not?

Considering Writing Strategies

1. After reading King's essay, how do you envision his "creature"? Find specific descriptive passages that help you to imagine what it looks like. How realistic is the creature? Does it seem scary to you? Why or why not?

2. Find several examples of similes (comparisons using *like* or *as*) that King uses to help the reader understand his thoughts on horror movies. Are these similes effective? Why or why not?

3. Would you describe King's writing style as being formal or informal? What specific words give you this impression? How does his style of writing affect you as the reader?

Writing Suggestions

1. Did you have a favorite movie when you were a child? Write an essay describing how you perceived it as a child. Have you seen the movie as an adult? How was your moviegoing experience similar to or different from your first viewing?

2. What is your favorite type of movie? Do you prefer horror, drama, comedy, romance, action adventure, or documentary? Write an essay telling why you prefer that particular genre. Be sure to include descriptions of some of the movies that have influenced your preference.

ESOL Tip >

If you choose a movie from your native country, translate the title for your English instructor.

[preview] **JOAN ACOCELLA** holds a PhD in comparative literature from Rutgers University. She is an award-winning author who has written about dance, literature, and other art forms for numerous publications including the *Times Literary Supplement* and *The New York Review of Books.* Additionally, Acocella has authored several books, including *Twenty-eight Artists and Two Saints* (2007), which is a collection of her essays. She is currently dance critic for *The New Yorker,* where the essay that follows originally appeared in 2014. In this essay, Acocella describes several hip-hop stage performances choreographed by Rennie Harris. Have you ever watched a hip-hip performance live or on television? What was your reaction?

High Street: Hip-Hop's Boldest Choreographer **by Joan Acocella**

Rennie Harris has said that he never really liked most of the work that he choreographed. That is a minority view. Harris, age fifty, is the most respected—and, to my knowledge, the most brilliant—hip-hop choreographer in America. Hip-hop dancing is very hard to transfer to the stage. As in other "street" forms, most of the dances are short, improvisational solos, and they don't travel much. They're meant to be done more or less in one spot. Also, because they have so short a time to make their point, they do not build gradually. They go from here to the moon in one shot. [1]

Yet Harris—and, in my experience, he alone—has created hip-hop productions that actually work as unified, evening-length shows. The first was "Rome & Jewels" (2000), a hip-hop adaptation of "Romeo and Juliet," with a d.j. and warring gangs. (The Caps do hip-hop; the Monster Q's do Africanist dancing.) In 2003 came "Facing Mekka," which included a bone-chilling solo, "Lorenzo's Oil," based on a memory of jogging beside the Schuylkill River and seeing a dead body float to the surface. In the solo, Harris jerked and trembled and crumpled, and then froze in those poses, making the picture even more frightening. (In the freeze-frames he was using Japanese Butoh, and proud of it.) His dreads smacked across his face. Sweat poured off him, onto the floor. Later, Harris combined "Lorenzo's Oil" with another solo, "Endangered Species," which he had made for himself after an experience he had while touring in Jamaica: for six hours he had been chased by a group of armed men trying to rob him. On the accompanying audio tape, you can hear him gasping for air, his heart pounding. [2]

Part of the glory of classic hip-hop dancing is its sheer punch: the locking and popping and flipping and spinning on your head. But this is also aggressive, or at least challenging, competitive. Harris grew up in a rough neighborhood in North Philadelphia. He met his father only once. As he told an audience in a post-performance talk one night, he was molested as a child. He saw people shot. Two of his brothers went to jail. [3]

So Harris's history, as well as his skill, fitted him to hip-hop's tough-guy-ism. But eventually, he has said, he tired of the emphasis on manliness. Like very many hip-hop artists, he resented the way that the form was represented on TV and in the movies, and he feels that this was partly where it acquired its testosterone surplus. Violence is much criticized in "Rome & Jewels." (When Rome hesitates to fight, one of his friends says to him, "You sit down when you piss?") But the distortion of hip-hop—and the general commercialization of it—seems to have left him discouraged. Several times, he has dispersed his dancers and then reassembled them, and he hasn't made much major work in the past decade. [4]

This week, at the Joyce, his company, Rennie Harris Puremovement, will have a six-day run, consisting of five pieces, including an excerpt from "Rome & Jewels." All this work is more than ten years old. Catch it while you can. [5]

Source: Joan Acocella, "High Street: Hip-Hop's Boldest Choreographer, at the Joyce," *The New Yorker,* February 3, 2014, **http://www.newyorker.com/arts/reviews/2014/02/03/140203goli_GOAT_dance_acocella.**

Considering Ideas

1. How does Acocella describe the strengths of Harris's hip-hop productions? Give specific examples from the essay to illustrate your answer.

2. Why do you think hip-hop is so popular? What effect does it have on its audience?

3. The author suggests that Harris resents the media's portrayal of hip-hop as being too manly and violent. Do you feel that the media's portrayal of hip-hop is too manly and/or too violent? Why or why not?

Considering the Rhetorical Star

1. What is the *subject* of Acocella's essay?

2. Who is the intended *audience* for the essay? How do you know?

3. What is Acocella's main *purpose* for the essay? Has she achieved her purpose? Why or why not?

4. In addition to description, what other *strategies* has the author employed? Give specific examples from the essay to support your answer.

5. As part of her *design,* Acocella uses dashes and parentheses, especially in the second paragraph. What effect do these features have on the reader. Explain your answer.

Considering Writing Strategies

1. What is Acocella's thesis? Does it effectively serve the essay? Why or why not?

2. Do you feel the essay is more objective or subjective? How do you know? What particular words does the author use to indicate her approach?

3. Identify several descriptive passages in the essay. Which ones have the strongest effect on you? Why?

Writing Suggestions

1. Acocella suggests that Harris feels hip-hop has become too "distorted" and "commercialized." Do you agree or disagree with Harris? Does modern-day hip-hop honor its roots, or has it evolved so far that it has lost its impact? Include examples of specific artists to subjectively or objectively support your opinion.

2. Choose a particular hip-hop or rap song and write a descriptive essay about the song. What is the tone (mood) of the music? What does it remind you of? How does it make you feel when you hear it? Describe it in such a way that your audience can almost hear it just from reading your words.

Reading and Reflection DESCRIPTIVE WRITING

[preview] **GWENDOLYN BROOKS** (1917-2000) was born in Topeka, Kansas, but she spent most of her life in Chicago, Illinois. She wrote more than twenty books of poetry, including *Children Coming Home* (1991) and *Annie Allen* (1949), for which she earned a Pulitzer Prize in 1950. Brooks served as a Consultant in Poetry to the Library of Congress from 1985-1986 and received an American Academy of Arts and Letters award, the Frost Medal, and two Guggenheim Foundation Fellowships. Go to **http://www.youtube.com/watch?v=JBpxJb2408A** to listen to the poet (and the actor Morgan Freeeman) recite the poem that follows. Before reading, consider your youth. Did you ever skip school or consider dropping out? Describe what happened.

We Real Cool by Gwendolyn Brooks

The Pool Players.
Seven at the Golden Shovel.

We real cool. We
Left school. We

Lurk late. We
Strike straight. We

Sing sin. We
Thin gin. We

Jazz June. We
Die soon.

Source: From *Blacks.* Copyright © 1991 Gwendolyn Brooks. Reprinted by permission of Brooks Permissions.

Considering Ideas

1. What is the Golden Shovel? Explain.

2. How do the pool players feel about themselves? Explain.

3. What point is Brooks making through her poem?

Considering the Rhetorical Star

1. What is the main *subject* of Brooks's poem? Is the specific topic engaging? Why or why not?

2. Who is the intended *audience* for the poem? How do you know?

3. What is the author's main *purpose* (to inform, to interpret, to persuade, to entertain, to express feelings) for the poem? Does she use a combination of purposes? How effective is her approach? Explain.

4. What writing *strategies* does Brooks use in the poem? How do these strategies affect the work?

5. What is the *design* of the poem? Is it effective? Why or why not?

Considering Writing Strategies

1. What is the tone (mood) of the poem? Which specific words from the poem indicate the tone?

2. What is the effect of including the word *we* at the ends of the lines instead of at the beginnings?

3. Alliteration occurs when an author repeats the initial consonant sound in words, such as in the words *sing* and *sin*. How does the poet's use of alliteration and rhyme affect the poem?

Writing Suggestions

1. Think about a place you are familiar with that people from somewhere else might find exciting or interesting to experience. Write an essay describing the place with as much vivid detail as you can. Help your readers to feel as if they have been there in person.

2. Write an essay describing an experience you had as a teenager when you rebelled against your parents' or society's expectations of you. What happened? Use as much sensory imagery as you can so that the reader can imagine what it would be like to have that experience.

STUDENT WRITING

The Ring
by Danielle Malico

People all over the world spend valuable time and cash to see championship fights. Whether it is for boxing, wrestling, or ultimate fighting, crowds gather in bars and around televisions to support their favorite fighters. Many know what it is like to be a spectator, but few know the fighter's experience. I, on the other hand, have first-hand knowledge of what it is like to be in the ring.

The first sound I hear is the familiar bell that brings me to reality. All around are my friends, family, and people who want to see women brawl. This is far from a quiet event. The onlookers are comparable to screeching howler monkeys with beer and snacks in their hands. My body feels heavy; I am covered in all the necessary places to prevent injury. The guard in my mouth causes excess fluid to run down my chin. The ring smells like rubber and sweat from previous battles. These conditions are not ideal for the average woman, but for me boxing is my place in the world, my sanctuary, my one talent.

I look over at my competition. She is shorter and thicker than I am, and her stance is impeccable. Immediately I realize that this will be a memorable occasion. I can tell everything about my opponent by her reaction to the first punch, whether she backs away or comes in closer. I always test the water with a three-punch combination: a jab, a strong right, and a left hook. With each strike I exhale, making the hits more effective. She moves in closer, mainly because of her height, partially because she is confident. This makes me hesitate, but I know I cannot let this stab of fear affect my performance.

I prance around on my tiptoes, and she follows me like a lost puppy. During the first two-minute round, she and

I do the well-known first round dance. This is how we figure each other out. Not much damage is done on either end, a couple of simple blows, and soon enough the bell rings signifying our thirty-second break. I stagger over to my corner of the ring. My coach gives me the usual pep talk as I spit my mouth guard into a bowl. He takes a bottle and pours cold water into my mouth, while simultaneously wiping beads of sweat off my head, neck, and chest. He reminds me of a father, very proud of his little girl.

Soon enough, before I am fully rejuvenated, it will be 5 time to go back to the fight for the second round. I am so prepared. Whether I win or lose the fight, I know that I will fight my best and make my coach and myself proud. I will relish every moment of my time in the boxing ring. There is no other place I would rather be.

[QUESTIONS FOR REFLECTION]

1. When you saw a picture of the author and read the title, what kind of ring did you expect to read about in the essay?

2. Identify several examples of sensory details in Malico's essay. What could you see, hear, smell, feel, and so on?

3. What comparison does the author make in the essay?

4. Is the description objective or subjective? Explain.

5. What is the point of Malico's essay? How do you know?

► *Activity*   **Sensory Showdown**

In pairs or small groups, share a few personal objects, drawings, or photographs that have special meaning or reveal something about you. The items should appeal to different senses. Take turns describing the items you chose and explaining why they are significant. As a team, come up with a dominant impression, original similes and/or metaphors, and a specific sensory appeal for each item. A representative from each group will share descriptive ideas about a couple of favorite items with the class. This activity may give you ideas for writing a descriptive essay.

Sensory Showdown Activity:
Answers will vary.

Now that you have read one or more examples of descriptive writing, it's time to write your own description. You may choose to write about one of the writing options that follow, the advertisement, the image, or one of the media suggestions. Consider your rhetorical star and the qualities of an effective narrative as you begin to compose your assignment.

Writing Assignment Options

Use one of the following topics to write a descriptive essay.

1. A natural setting, such as a beach, mountainside, woods, or lake
2. A work of art, such as a poster, photograph, painting, or sculpture
3. The music of a particular artist or band
4. A shopping mall, parking lot, sports stadium, or other crowded place
5. A ride at a theme park or an exhibit at a zoo or museum
6. The best or worst meal you have ever eaten (or pushed away)
7. A person you love, cherish, or admire
8. A souvenir or artifact from a place you have visited
9. A special photograph of a person, place, pet, or object
10. A restaurant, bakery, or other place that appeals to the senses

Interpreting an Advertisement

How would you describe this advertisement? Who is the intended audience for the ad? How do the image and text interact? What does the ad suggest about Suzuki cars? Based on this ad, would you consider buying one? Why or why not? What does the ad suggest about popular culture? Explain. Write a descriptive essay about the Suzuki advertisement. Remember to create a dominant impression and appeal to the senses.

Writing about an Image

Choose one image from this chapter and consider these questions: How would you describe the image? What aspect of popular culture does the image represent? Is the image mainstream or alternative? Do you personally relate to the image? If so, how? What does the image suggest about pop culture? Write a description that relates to one of the pictures or advertisements in this chapter. You may describe what you see in the photograph, or you might describe something that relates to one of the images. For example, you might describe the scene at a concert or café.

Media Connection for Describing

You might watch, read, and/or listen to one or more of the media products or outlets listed below to discover additional examples of descriptions. Exploring different media may help you to better understand methods for describing. You may also choose to write about one or more of the media suggestions. For example, you might watch a *Star Trek* movie and decide to describe some of the beings and destinations Captain Kirk and his crew encounter.

Television	*America's Funniest Home Videos*	MTV, VH1, or CMT	*Glee*	*Entertainment Tonight*
Film	*Across the Universe (2007)*	*Rent (2005)*	*Star Trek: Renegades (2014)*	*OZ: The Great and Powerful (2013)*
Print/E-Reading	*People*	*National Geographic*	*Vanity Fair*	*Scientific American*
Internet	**eBay.com**	**motherjones.com**	**youtube.com**	**culturalpolitics.net/ popular_culture**
Music	"Brown Skin Girl" by Santana	"Lucy in the Sky with Diamonds" by The Beatles	"Diamonds" by Rihanna	"Beam Me Up" by P!nk

6.4 ANALYZING THE RHETORICAL STAR FOR WRITING A DESCRIPTION

FIGURE 6.1
The Rhetorical Star

As you prepare to write your description, consider the five points of the rhetorical star (Figure 6.1). You might use some of the questions in the chart as you conduct your rhetorical star analysis.

Subject	Choose a topic that you can observe firsthand or one that you can experience through a photograph, television show, or other medium. You might describe an interesting place, an exciting event, a unique person or animal, or an unusual object. Write about something that catches your attention that you would like to capture and share with your readers.
Audience	Who will read your description? What will interest your readers about your subject? What do they already know about it? Are they reading to learn something or be entertained? Think about what kinds of details would be most appealing to your readers.
Purpose	Think about what you are trying to accomplish through your description. Are you using description to inform your reader of something you witnessed? Do you want to describe a scenario so that you can persuade your reader to believe or do something? Perhaps your purpose is to describe some of the graphics in a video game you are evaluating. Keep focused on your purpose as you write your description.
Strategy	Sometimes a description can stand alone, but more often it will be combined with other writing strategies. For example, you might include a description of a character in a television show you are evaluating, or you may describe two music groups you are comparing and contrasting. Choose the strategies that will best suit your purpose.
Design	How lengthy should you make your description? How many details do you need to convey your point to your audience? What other design elements, such as a photograph or drawing, might aid your readers? If you decide to include visuals in your description, be sure that they don't overshadow your words.

6.5 APPLYING THE WRITING PROCESS FOR DESCRIBING

After you have completed your rhetorical star analysis, follow the steps of the writing process (Figure 6.2) to compose your descriptive paper.

FIGURE 6.2 The Seven Steps of the Writing Process

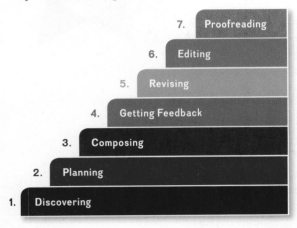

1. **Discovering:** As you begin to explore your topic, you might make a list of sensory details, freewrite everything that comes to mind about your topic, make a rough sketch of your subject, describe it to someone else, or complete a graphic organizer like the one shown in Figure 6.3.

2. **Planning:** Create a list of adjectives you might like to include. Decide what order you want to use to present the details. If you are describing a scene, you may want to describe it from left to right, top to bottom, or close to far. You might try creating a cluster or an outline to determine how you want to organize your description.

3. **Composing:** Write a first draft of your description using the six qualities of effective descriptive writing earlier in the chapter.

    1. Begin by creating a dominant impression.
    2. Use an objective or a subjective approach.
    3. Appeal to the senses.
    4. Include similes and metaphors.
    5. Organize your description logically.
    6. End on a memorable note.

Don't worry too much about grammar and punctuation at this time. Focus on concrete sensory details. Describe your subject so that your audience's senses are engaged. Be sure to keep your dominant impression in mind as you write.

Teaching Tip

Show students a vivid photo in a natural or urban setting and have students complete a "describing" graphic organizer for the photo. Have volunteer students share their results.

FIGURE 6.3 Describing

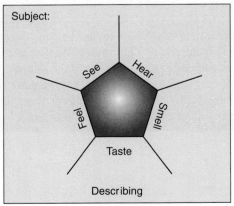

4. **Getting feedback:** Have at least one classmate or other person read your rough draft and answer the peer review questions that follow. If you have access to a writing tutor or center, get another opinion about your paper as well.

5. **Revising:** Using all of the feedback available to you, revise your description. Make sure that your description is full of specific sensory details to help your readers feel as if they are experiencing your subject. Check to see that your essay is unified. In other words, look for any details that don't fit with the dominant impression you are creating for your audience. Also, pay particular attention to using precise diction (word choice). Replace vague words with concrete words. Add, delete, and rearrange ideas as necessary.

6. **Editing:** Read your description again, this time looking for errors in grammar, punctuation, and mechanics. Look carefully for sentence fragments, which are common in rough drafts of descriptive writing. Writing in complete sentences will help you to communicate your ideas more clearly to your audience.

7. **Proofreading:** After you have edited your essay one or more times, read it again. This time, look for typographical errors and any other issues that might interfere with the readers' understanding of your description. Check it again to make sure you have written complete sentences rather than fragments.

PEER REVIEW QUESTIONS FOR DESCRIBING

Trade rough drafts with a classmate and answer the following questions about his or her paper. Then, in person or online, discuss your papers and suggestions with your peer. Finally, make the changes you feel would most benefit your paper.

1. What is the dominant impression in the essay? Do the ideas in the paper help to support this overall mood or feeling? Why or why not?

2. Which sensory details are most appealing to you? Could any additional sensory details be included to help you better imagine the subject? What is missing or unclear?

3. Are the ideas in the description organized logically? If not which parts could be rearranged?

4. Is the description primarily objective or subjective? Do you feel the author's approach is appropriate for the subject? Why or why not?

5. Does the description include similes and/or metaphors? How effective are they?

6. What part of the description is most memorable? Why?

7. What kinds of grammatical errors, if any, are evident in the description?

8. What final suggestions do you have for the author?

LearnSmart Achieve Tip

The Writing Process unit of LearnSmart Achieve determines what students do and do not know about the writing process. Learning outcomes within the Writing Process unit cover planning, organizing, drafting, and revising an informative text. Learning resources and questions automatically adapt to each student's individual needs and help students thoroughly master this content. See the Instructor's Manual for *Write Now* for a list of learning outcomes as well as additional information on how to use LearnSmart Achieve with your students.

WRITER'S CHECKLIST FOR DESCRIBING

Use the checklist below to evaluate your own writing and help ensure that your explanation of the process is complete. If you have any "no" answers, go back and work on those areas.

- ❏ 1. Is my dominant impression clear?
- ❏ 2. Is my description objective or subjective? Is this the best approach for my topic?
- ❏ 3. Have I included enough sensory details so the reader can imagine what I am describing?
- ❏ 4. Are the details organized logically?
- ❏ 5. Have I used similes and/or metaphors to enhance my description?
- ❏ 6. Are my adjectives precise?
- ❏ 7. Is my conclusion effective?
- ❏ 8. Have I proofread thoroughly?

[CHAPTER SUMMARY]

1. Descriptive writing is about appealing to the senses to evoke images in the minds of the audience.

2. Descriptive writing is an important part of your education, daily life, and career.

3. Interpreting descriptive readings and images can help you to prepare to write a description.

4. Carefully analyze the rhetorical star before writing a description: subject, audience, purpose, strategy, and design.

5. Use these qualities when writing a description: begin by creating a dominant impression; decide whether to use an objective or subjective approach; appeal to the senses; include similes or metaphors; organize your description logically; end on a memorable note.

[WHAT I KNOW NOW]

Use this checklist to determine what you need to work on in order to feel comfortable with your understanding of the material in this chapter. Check off each item as you master it. Review the material for any unchecked items.

❑ 1. I know what **descriptive writing** is.

❑ 2. I can identify several **real-world applications** for writing descriptions.

❑ 3. I can **interpret** descriptive readings and images.

❑ 4. I can analyze the **rhetorical star** for writing a description.

❑ 5. I understand the **writing process** for writing a description.

❑ 6. I can apply the **six qualities** of descriptive writing.

SmartBook Tip

During the "Recharge" phase, students can return to Chapter 6 and practice concepts that they need to work on.

CHAPTER **7**

EXPLAINING A PROCESS: CULTURES AND TRADITIONS

learning outcomes

In this chapter you will learn techniques for achieving these learning outcomes:

7.1 IDENTIFY REAL-WORLD APPLICATIONS FOR EXPLAINING A PROCESS IN WRITING.

7.2 UNDERSTAND THE QUALITIES OF EFFECTIVE PROCESS ANALYSIS WRITING.

7.3 INTERPRET IMAGES AND READINGS ABOUT PROCESSES RELATED TO CULTURES AND TRADITIONS.

7.4 ANALYZE THE RHETORICAL STAR

FOR EXPLAINING A PROCESS.

7.5 APPLY THE QUALITIES OF PROCESS ANALYSIS WRITING.

WRITING STRATEGY FOCUS: EXPLAINING A PROCESS

Process writing explains how to do something, how something works, what something does, or how something was done. Writing about a process, sometimes called *process analysis,* involves breaking a procedure into its component steps. Processes can be instructional or informative. If the readers need to be able to perform the process, then the writing is instructional. For example, a step-by-step explanation of how to conduct a business meeting with an executive from an Asian country would be instructional. If the readers just want to understand the basic sequence of steps or events, then the writing is informative. A news article explaining what happened during a recent event on campus or in your community would be informative. In that case, the readers would not try to replicate the process. Instead they would just want to understand what took place. You will have opportunities to write about processes in college, in your personal life, and in your career.

SmartBook Tip

Students receive an overview of the learning outcomes and topics in Chapter 7 in the "Preview" phase of SmartBook.

7.1 REAL-WORLD APPLICATIONS FOR EXPLAINING PROCESSES

Process Writing in College

You will have many opportunities for writing about processes in college. You might need to explain a process, such as mitosis or meiosis, on a biology exam or explain for a history paper what happened during a particular battle. For classes in your major, your instructor may ask you to write step-by-step instructions for performing a particular procedure to demonstrate your understanding of the process.

Process Writing in Your Daily Life

Writing about processes will also be a necessary part of your personal life. You may need to write instructions for someone taking care of your home, pets, or children while you are away. You might want to write out a dessert recipe to share

Teaching Tip

Ask students to tell how they anticipate using the process analysis writing strategy in their future careers.

LearnSmart Achieve Tip

The Writing Process unit of LearnSmart Achieve determines what students do and do not know about the writing process. Learning outcomes within the Writing Process unit cover planning, organizing, drafting, and revising an informative text. Learning resources and questions automatically adapt to each student's individual needs and help students thoroughly master this content. See the Instructor's Manual for *Write Now* for a list of learning outcomes as well as additional information on how to use LearnSmart Achieve with your students.

with a friend or family member. Maybe you'll need to explain a step-by-step process to the police or insurance company if you witnessed or experienced an accident or natural disaster.

Process Writing in Your Career

Every career field includes processes that need to be explained or performed. You might need to leave instructions for someone who will be filling in for you when you are on vacation or away at a seminar, or you may need to write an explanation of how to perform your job for the person replacing you because of your promotion. Here are a few specific applications for process writing on the job:

Health care: admitting a patient, drawing blood, dressing a wound, diagnosing an illness, recording medical exam findings, taking an X-ray.

Massage therapy: creating ambience, using Swedish techniques, working with hot stones.

Computers: installing a program, utilizing a new software application, designing a three-dimensional illustration.

Criminal justice: investigating a crime scene, handling evidence, documenting findings in a report.

Business: opening or closing for the day, keeping the books, tracking inventory, dealing with customer service issues.

Culinary arts: sharpening knives, baking a casserole, cleaning up the kitchen.

Graduate SPOTLIGHT

Deborah Buza, Caterer

Chef Deborah A. Buza is a caterer with an AS degree in culinary arts. She owns her own company, Buza's Catering, and is currently writing a cookbook. Here's what Buza has to say about the importance of writing in her career:

SmartBook Tip

Key concepts in Chapter 7 are highlighted for students during the "Read" phase. As students demonstrate understanding of these concepts during the "Practice" phase by responding to probes, the highlighting adapts to the individual student's learning by changing color.

" In the catering business, everything relies on possessing good communication skills. I have to be able to explain my menu to potential clients over the phone and in writing in order to get their business. I have to write in clear, complete sentences, or the client will think I am incompetent. Because my parents are from different cultures, Polish and Italian, I enjoy deconstructing recipes from each culture and then combining them to create something totally different. I have to be able to explain how to perform the procedures and techniques that each culture uses during the cooking process. Also, my grandmother always said to put in a pinch of this or a handful of that, but our culture today is much more technical. I have to be precise with the measurements and ingredients. Overall, writing is imperative to my career as a caterer. "

On your own, in pairs, or in small groups, brainstorm uses for process writing at school, in your daily life, and on the job. You may want to choose your own career field or the prospective career field(s) of the participants in your group. Be prepared to share the results with your instructor or the class.

Real-World Process Writing Activity:

Answers will vary.

Teaching Tip

Provide students with a fairly simple set of instructions, such as for a recipe or for assembling a toy, and ask individuals or groups of students to evaluate the instructions and share their analysis.

7.2 QUALITIES OF EFFECTIVE PROCESS ANALYSIS WRITING

1. Begin with a Clear Introduction

Your introduction should include some kind of attention-getter to engage your readers in the process. For instance, an essay could begin with a question, such as, "Have you ever dreaded having your in-laws come to stay with you for the holidays?" Of course the most important part of your introduction is your thesis statement. State your thesis clearly so readers know what to expect. For example, "If you are trying to throw the best birthday bash ever, then you need to plan a great menu, invite the right people, organize some fun activities, and decorate appropriately."

Create an informative title for your process. It can be straightforward, such as "How to Throw the Perfect Themed Party," or catchy, such as "Surviving a Week with the In-Laws."

2. Include a List of Materials

If your reader is going to perform the process you are explaining, you will need to list all of the materials (ingredients, tools, equipment) necessary to complete the process. Be sure to include specific details and amounts. For example, if you are explaining how to create a costume for a Mardi Gras parade, you would include the types, colors, and quantities of fabrics, sequins, beads, feathers, and makeup that are needed. You would need to mention useful tools for making and assembling the costume, such as scissors, a stapler, and a tape measure. You would also need to include types and quantities for materials needed to hold the costume together, such as staples, glue, elastic, and thread. Try to think of every essential detail.

3. Explain Each Step in Chronological Order

As you write your steps, keep in mind your main purpose, which is either to instruct or inform the audience. Include every necessary step, even if it seems insignificant, to ensure that your reader will be able to perform or understand the process. Make sure to place your steps in chronological order so as not to confuse the reader. At times, you may need to explain why

Parallel Structure Grammar
Window:

Answers will vary.

a particular step is performed, especially if you feel the reader may try to skip it. To help your reader understand the flow of steps in the process, use transitions, such as *first, next, then, after that,* and *meanwhile.* Also, be sure to use a variety of action words (verbs) to guide your reader through the process. For example, if you are instructing your readers on how to bake a traditional Mardi Gras king cake, you might use verbs such as *preheat, combine, decorate,* and *bake.* Finally, be sure you cover everything you promised the reader in the thesis.

4. Define Special Terms

If you are using a term that your reader may not know, then be sure to define the word the first time you mention it. Most of the time, you won't need to include a dictionary definition. Instead, explain the term in your own words based on your own experiences. For example, if you are writing about your family's Kwanzaa traditions, you might define *Kwanzaa* by saying it is a tradition celebrated from December 26 through January 1 in African communities around the world that has its origins in the ancient first fruit harvest ceremonies in Africa. You may include additional details about the significance of the holiday, such as the seven principles of Kwanzaa, in your explanation of your family's customs.

5. Give Helpful Tips and Warnings as Needed

You may find that you need to mention useful tips or safety warnings, especially if the process you are explaining is instructional. Include tips or warnings just before or right along with the step they relate to because many readers won't read all of the instructions before trying to complete the process (even if the directions tell them to do so). For example, if you are explaining how to make the most of an Independence Day celebration, you might need to include a cautionary note about handling the grill safely. You could use a symbol, such as a skull and crossbones, to indicate a potential danger.

6. Include Visual Aids as Needed

You may want to include pictures, diagrams, or other visual images to help your reader more fully comprehend the process you are explaining. For instance, if you are explaining how to make a Japanese origami lion, pictures illustrating each step would be of great value to the reader. You would likely want to include a picture of the finished product as well.

7. End with a Decisive Conclusion

Let the reader know when the process is complete. For example, if you are explaining the steps for making potatoes au gratin, you might mention that the dish is ready when the cheese on top turns golden brown. Finally, end with any additional suggestions you have for the readers. If you explain the steps for preparing a traditional Mexican dish, you might suggest serving it with margaritas or mojitos (or nonalcoholic versions of those beverages).

Career-Based PROCESS WRITING

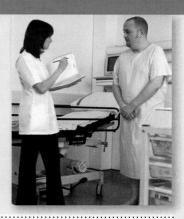

[preview] **WHILE THEY** are in college, most people learn the information and skills they need to be successful in their careers; however, sometimes they do not get training in how to be polite in the workplace. Calvin Sun designed the following poster to hang on a wall in the workplace to provide employees with some tips for being considerate of their colleagues. Have you ever had an annoying co-worker? What did he or she do to get on your nerves?

10 Ways to Improve Your Office Etiquette by Calvin Sun

We spend one-third of our working lives at the office. The people we work with can affect our productivity and our careers, and vice versa. Practicing office etiquette makes the place and the workday just a bit more bearable.

1 Watch the volume of your voice

Keep your voice at a reasonable level. Other people are trying to work, and your voice may distract them. Besides, do you really want them to overhear what you're saying? If you have something personal or otherwise sensitive to discuss, consider doing it in a private office or conference room.

2 Use speakerphones with care

If you're on hold and waiting for someone to pick up, then yes, a speakerphone can save you time. Just keep the volume as low as possible. On the other hand, if you're planning to have a regular conversation with the other person, do it behind closed doors. Your co-workers in the area will not appreciate your disturbing them with a conference call.

3 Be sensitive about what you bring for lunch

We're supposed to be inclusive and accepting of people from different backgrounds and cultures, I know. And those other people are supposed to behave likewise. Nonetheless, be aware of how others may react to the lunch you bring. If you think about it, any reaction it causes can't be good for you. They'll either hate the smell and complain about you, or they'll love the smell, assassinate you, and eat your lunch. Either way, you lose out. If you have food with a distinctive aroma, consider either eating it outside or in the lunchroom, rather than at your desk. And some foods probably shouldn't be brought in at all, even to the lunchroom, such as stinky tofu or durian.

4 Respect people's privacy

Because you're most likely in a cubicle or other open office area, you inevitably will overhear snippets of conversations other people are having. Maybe you'll hear something about a project you're involved with or a problem you've encountered before, and you believe you have something to contribute. Yes, if you go over and join the conversation, you could save the day or provide valuable insight. However, you might also be viewed as a busybody.

Think carefully before joining that conversation. One consideration might be the amount of desperation you sense in their voices. The more desperate, the more willing they might be to hear from others.

If you do choose to join them, I suggest you go to their office or cubicle, let them see you as you're listening to them. Then, at a break, casually mention that it sounds like there is a problem, and that if you can help, you'd be happy to. This approach is better than rushing over and telling them you overheard their conversation.

5 Fix, or attempt to fix, what you break

How many times have you gone to the photocopier to find that it was either out of toner, out of paper, or experiencing a paper jam? The problem was still around when you arrived because the previous person did nothing about it and simply left the copier in its problem condition.

Don't be that person. If you can clear the paper jam safely and according to procedure, try to do so. Most photocopiers have diagrams to show you how. If you can't fix the jam or the other problem, leave a signed dated note describing the issue and what you are doing to fix it or have it fixed. Those actions could be a call to the maintenance vendor or to an administrative department. Your co-workers will appreciate your efforts, and signing your name to the note demonstrates your willingness to take ownership.

6 Keep the lunchroom clean

Neither the refrigerator nor the microwave should resemble the Queens Botanical Garden. If you spilled something in either place, clean it up. If you forgot to eat something from the refrigerator, and it's starting to mold, throw it out yourself. Don't leave it for someone else.

7 Be punctual for meetings

If you're an attendee, be on time. If you can't make a meeting or you're going to be late, let someone know. Don't arrive late and ask for a recap. Doing so wastes everyone else's time. If you're the one who's running the meeting, start it on time and resume it on time after a break. To do otherwise (for example, to start late to accommodate latecomers) is unfair to those who showed up on time and only encourages more lateness in the future.

8 Be careful about solicitations

Even if your company has no strict prohibition against solicitations (for example, selling candy for a child's sports team fundraiser), be careful about doing so. Your co-workers may not appreciate being put on the spot. If you do anything at all, the best approach is to display the merchandise in a central location, with a notice about the reason, and an envelope to receive checks or cash.

9 Avoid borrowing or lending

The rich rule over the poor, and the borrower is servant to the lender.

We've heard, in the past few weeks, more than we want to about issues with borrowing and lending. Those issues still apply even at the office level, even between individuals. Any borrowing that occurs can jeopardize a relationship if the repayment is slow, late, less than expected, or nonexistent. No matter how small the amount, the lender may feel resentment. In fact, a small amount might cause resentment precisely because the lender feels embarrassed about asking about repayment.

Avoid borrowing or lending if you can. If you absolutely must borrow, write the lender an IOU with the amount and sign it. Then, pay it back as soon as you can.

10 Don't ask co-workers how to spell

Microsoft Word has a spell checker. Use it. Don't bother your co-workers with such questions. It hampers their productivity and lowers their opinion of you. Some probably won't even want to answer, because doing so makes them feel stupid. When I get such questions, my response is, "Wait a minute while I check the dictionary" or "Wait while I use the Word dictionary."

Source: Calvin Sun, "10 Ways to Improve Your Office Etiquette," http://www.scribd.com/doc/12589359/10-Things-for-Office-Etiquette.

[QUESTIONS FOR REFLECTION]

1. What is the purpose of the poster? Is the poster helpful? Why or why not?

2. Make a list of the action verbs in each heading. Which ones are most effective? Why?

3. Discuss the design of the poster. Is it appealing? Which features are the strongest? Do you think employees would take the time to read it? Why or why not?

4. Which office etiquette tips are the most important? Which are the least important? Why?

5. Have you ever violated any of the tips on the poster? Which ones? How did your co-workers react?

[preview] **ROSE FARHAT-GOODSON** is a registered medical assistant and a registered phlebotomy technician. She has served as an instructor at Keiser University for more than twenty years. Farhat-Goodson has taught medical assisting students many skills including how to draw blood, as the instructions that follow explain. As you are reading them, imagine that you are following the steps or that someone is drawing your blood.

Steps in Venipuncture by Rose Farhat-Goodson

There are many steps in the venipuncture process that must be followed to ensure the integrity of the results. Following these steps will also safeguard you as well as your patient from injury.

Step 1: Identify yourself. Patients have the right to know who is providing their care.

Step 2: Verify patient identification by asking the patient to state his or her full name and date of birth. If the patient is in an inpatient facility, check the ID band. If necessary, inquire if the patient is fasting and on any medications.

Step 3: Wash your hands using the proper medical aseptic procedure and put on non-latex gloves.

Step 4: Select and check your equipment ensuring that you have the correct tubes, needle size, and other necessary items to complete the draw successfully. Assemble your needle and syringe.

Step 5: Palpate for a viable vein. The most common vein used is the median cubital, which runs across the antecubital fossa.

Step 6: Clean the draw site in a circular motion from the inside out with alcohol. Allow to air dry for 30 seconds. Do not retouch the site.

Step 7: Apply the tourniquet two to four inches above the site. Enter the site quickly with the bevel of the needle facing up. You should feel a slight "give" into the vein.

Step 8: Complete your collection using the correct order of draw and invert the tubes as required within thirty seconds.

Step 9: Release the tourniquet, remove the needle, and apply pressure to the site with gauze. Immediately discard your needle.

Step 10: Label the tubes with the patient's name, date, time of the collection, and your initials. Always label the tubes in front of your patient.

Step 11: Recheck the patient's site for bleeding, apply a bandage, and discard your used equipment in the proper waste receptacles.

Step 12: Wash your hands using the proper medical aseptic procedure.

Step 13: Document the procedure accordingly.

In conclusion, following the proper steps will not always guarantee that you will "hit" the vein. However, following the proper steps will guarantee your safety, your patient's safety, and the integrity of your specimen results.

Source: "Steps in Venipuncture" by Rose Farhat-Goodson.

[QUESTIONS FOR REFLECTION]

1. Who is the audience for the instructions? Do the instructions effectively meet the needs of the audience? Why or why not?

2. Which steps are the clearest? Do any steps need further explanation? Elaborate on your answers.

3. Make a list of the major action verbs in each step. Which ones are the most effective? Why?

4. Would this set of instructions be as effective if it had been written in paragraph form instead of in numbered steps? Why or why not?

5. If you have never drawn blood before, would you be able to do so after simply reading these steps? Why or why not?

Career-Based PROCESS WRITING

[preview] **MARISSA SCOTT** worked in a nursing home while she was attending college. She wrote the following essay for her English Composition I course. Have you ever cared for someone who was ill? How does your experience compare to Scott's?

How to Feed a Nursing Home Resident by Marissa Scott

Working in a nursing home with different residents can be difficult at times, especially when it comes to feeding a resident who is in bed. While working in a nursing home, you will encounter people from different cultures, backgrounds, and languages. You will also have to deal with residents who are confused or suffering from dementia. There are a few important steps to remember that can help to simplify the feeding process.

The first step is to greet the resident. You should knock on the door to show the patient respect. As you enter the room, greet the resident and identify yourself. Next, explain to the resident that you are there for a feeding, and obtain his or her consent to continue. At this time if the patient is confused or speaks a different language, try to point or use gestures or pictures to help explain the procedure to him or her. If the resident just does not want to be bothered, you should encourage him or her and be supportive. Keep in mind that the patient may come from a culture or background that causes him or her to feel embarrassed that another person has to help with feeding. However, if the resident is confused or combative, just leave him or her alone for a few minutes, and then go back and try it again.

The second step, after the resident agrees to the feeding procedure, is to raise the head of the bed, making sure that the resident is sitting in an upright position. Adjust the bed to where you will be able to sit at the resident's eye level. While doing this, you should make sure the resident is aware that you are moving the bed to a different position; otherwise he or she might become frightened. Once you start adjusting the bed, make sure the patient is conscious of what you are about to do because, as previously stated, you need to respect the cultural background of the resident.

Once you have the bed adjusted, make the final preparations for feeding the patient. Be sure resident's hands are clean. Additionally, place the food tray over the bed table at a comfortable position for the resident to see the food on the tray. Next, ask the resident if he or she would like a clothing protector. Some people consider a clothing protector to be too similar to a child's bib and would not like to have one on while eating. You don't want to offend the patient and interrupt the feeding process. Next, tell the resident what foods are on the tray and ask what he or she would like to eat first. You shouldn't just choose for the resident. Now you are ready to feed the patient.

Begin feeding the resident with fairly small amounts of food on a fork or spoon. Give the patient time to chew and swallow before offering another bite. Look for cues from the resident to help you determine the pace. After every few bites, you should ask if the patient wants a sip of the drink. During the feeding, you should try to make conversation with the resident to help him or her feel more comfortable. Be sure to speak only English. For example, if another person walks into the room and you hold a conversation with that person in Spanish or another language that the resident does not speak, the resident may become offended, confused, or scared and think he or she is in a foreign country. Continue feeding until the patient says he or she is full or until the tray of food is empty. Then you can remove the tray and make sure the patient, the bed, and the tray are clean.

While working in a nursing home with residents or patients from different cultures and backgrounds, you need to make sure you give them respect during the feeding process because someone could easily get offended and feel like you are not being considerate of his or her feelings. As you greet the patients, get them ready for a meal, and feed them, always keep these steps in mind to help the nursing home residents feel as comfortable as possible.

[QUESTIONS FOR REFLECTION]

1. Which sentence in the first paragraph introduces the process that will be described? Is it clear? Why or why not?

2. Does the order of the steps make sense? Why or why not?

3. Which steps are explained the best? Why?

4. Which transitions seem to work best in the essay? What effect do they have on the explanation of the process?

5. Does Scott identify any special tips that the reader should consider before performing the process? If so, what are they?

7.3 PROCESS WRITING IN THE CONTEXT OF CULTURES AND TRADITIONS

In the readings that follow, you will have an opportunity to examine cultures from different perspectives. The term *culture* refers to the way people in a particular group behave based on their beliefs and values. Groups can have a multitude of cultural orientations. They can be based on social interests, attitudes, hobbies, values, ethnicity, educational goals, work endeavors, or a variety of other characteristics. People from various cultures all around the world have traditions that they like to uphold. Whether these traditions are for sports, holidays, birthdays, entertainment, religious ceremonies, work, or everyday life, they all have specific procedures that the participants or observers follow. For example, fans at a heavy metal concert behave very differently than the audience at a symphony orchestra concert.

As human beings we need to be aware of and sensitive to different cultures and traditions. One reason for this sensitivity is that we are likely to encounter people from many different cultures in the workplace. Additionally, each work environment has its own culture (beliefs, values, and guidelines). These principles guide the behavior of the employees. How employees dress, communicate, perform their tasks, and interact with their clients, customers, or patients all depends on the culture of the organization. The readings in this chapter relate to a variety of different types of cultures and include some of the processes that go along with membership in those cultures. Reading and interpreting what others have written can help you see the structure and style of a process analysis and learn how to write about processes for school, work, and your daily life.

Reading and Reflection PROCESS WRITING

[preview] **MARLO MORGAN,** a doctor from Kansas City, decided to sell her practice and travel to Australia to provide medical assistance for the people there. When she arrived in Australia, she imagined that she was being taken to a luncheon where she might receive an award. She even prepared a speech just in case. Instead, she found herself an unwilling participant in a 1,400-mile journey across the rugged Outback with a tribe of Aborigines. Visit **www.australia.com** to learn more about Australia and Aboriginal culture.

In her novel *Mutant Message Down Under,* Dr. Morgan describes some of the experiences she had on this "walkabout," as the Aborigines called it. In the following excerpt, she explains some of the traditions that the Aborigines celebrate and mentions some American traditions that she taught to the people she encountered on her adventure. The "Mutants" she refers to in the story are people who don't share the beliefs and practices of the Aborigines or "Real People." Even though Morgan did not volunteer for this journey, she made some unexpected discoveries about the unique people of Australia and about herself. Before reading, think about an adventure that you have gone on that has had a lasting impact on your life. How has that experience affected you?

Happy Unbirthday by Marlo Morgan

During our journey there were two occasions that we celebrated by honoring someone's talent. Everyone is recognized by a special party, but it has nothing to do with age or birthdate—it is in recognition of uniqueness and contribution to life. They [the Aborigines] believe that the purpose for the passage of time is to allow a person to become better, wiser, to express more and more of one's beingness. So if you are a better person this year than last, and only you know that for certain, then you call for the party. When you say you are ready, everyone honors that. 1

One of the celebrations we had was for a woman whose talent, or medicine, in life was being a listener. Her name was Secret Keeper. No matter what anyone wanted to talk about, get off their chest, confess, or vent, she was always available. She considered the conversations private, didn't really offer advice, nor did she judge. She held the person's hand or held their head in her lap and just listened. She seemed to have a way of encouraging people to find their own solutions, to follow what their hearts were directing them to do. 2

I thought of people at home in the United States: the number of young people who seemed to have no sense of direction or purpose, the homeless people who think they have nothing to offer society, the addicted individuals who want to function in some reality other than the one we are in. I wished I could bring them here, to witness how little it takes, sometimes, to be a benefit to your community, and how wonderful it is to know and experience a sense of self-worth. 3

This woman knew her strong points and so did everyone else. The party consisted of Secret Keeper, sitting slightly elevated, and the rest of us. She had requested that the universe provide bright foods, if that was in order. Sure enough, that evening we found ourselves walking in plants that held berries and grapes. 4

We had seen a rainfall in the distance some days before, and we found scores of tadpoles in small pools 5 of water. The tadpoles were laid upon the hot rocks and quickly dried into another form of food I had never dreamed possible. Our party menu also included some type of unattractive mud-hopping creature.

At the party we had music. I taught the Real People a Texas line dance, Cotton-Eyed Joe, which we modified to their drumbeat, and before long we were all laughing. Then I explained how Mutants like to dance with partners and asked Regal Black Swan to join me. He learned waltz steps immediately, but we couldn't get the beat just right. I started humming the tune and encouraged them to join me. Before long we had the group humming and waltzing under the Australian sky. I also showed them how to square dance. Ooota did a great job as the caller. That night they decided that perhaps I had already mastered the art of healing in my society and might wish to go into the music field! 6

It was the closest I ever got to receiving an Aborigine name. They felt I had more than one talent and were discovering that I could love them and their way of looking at life as well as remaining loyal to my own, so they nicknamed me Two Hearts. 7

At Secret Keeper's party, various people took turns telling what a comfort it was to have her in the community and how valuable her work was for everyone. She glowed humbly and took the praise in a dignified and royal manner. 8

It was a great night. As I was falling asleep, I said, "Thank you" to the universe for such a remarkable day. 9

I would not have agreed to come with these people had I been given the choice. I would not order tadpole to eat if it were on a menu; and yet I was remembering how meaningless some of our holidays have become and how wonderful these times were. 10

Source: M. Morgan, "Happy Unbirthday." In M. Morgan, *Mutant Message Down Under* (Thorndike, ME: Thorndike Press, 1994), pp. 218–21 (large print edition).

[QUESTIONS FOR REFLECTION]

Considering Ideas

1. What Aborigine customs does Morgan explain? Do any of these customs seem unusual to you? Which ones? Why?

2. What is the significance of an "unbirthday" in the Aborigine culture? How does this celebration compare to birthday celebrations in your culture?

3. Based on the last two paragraphs, how does Morgan feel about her "unbirthday" experience with the Aborigines?

Considering the Rhetorical Star

1. What is the main *subject* of Morgan's "Happy Unbirthday" chapter? Is the specific topic engaging? Why or why not?

2. Who is the intended *audience* for the explanation? How do you know?

3. Identify several paragraphs where Morgan explains processes. Is her *purpose* to be instructional or informative? How effective are her explanations? Explain.

4. What other writing *strategies*, besides process writing, does the author use?

5. How important is the photograph to the *design* of the work? Is it effective? Why or why not?

Considering Writing Strategies

1. Typically, writers use the second or third person point of view for process analysis writing, but Morgan uses the first person point of view here. Why does she use this point of view, and how does it affect the work?

2. Identify several descriptive passages in the piece. Why does the author include these passages, and how do they affect the reader?

3. What is Morgan's tone (mood) in this chapter? What specific words indicate this tone?

Writing Suggestions

1. Write an essay explaining the details about one of your favorite holiday celebrations. When and where does the celebration take place? What do you do? Why is this event important to you?

2. Write an essay comparing and contrasting your family's birthday celebration with the Aborigine's "unbirthday" celebration. Does your family recognize birthdays in a special way? Does someone prepare a special meal? Does the birthday boy or girl receive gifts?

Reading and Reflection PROCESS WRITING

[preview] **CHRISTINE NG,** born in Singapore, earned a degree in English with a minor in religious studies from the University of California at Berkeley. She has done technical writing and marketing for several companies, including Sephora, eBay, Omnicell, and Popsugar. In the following essay, Ng offers step-by-step instructions for anyone interested in the art of flirtation. Before reading, think about a time when you have flirted with someone. What did you do? What was the other person's response? Were you sucessful, or did you crash and burn?

Bringing Out the Flirt in You by Christine Ng

Have you ever felt an overpowering urge to make yourself known to another individual? From women's fluttering coy eyelids to men's prowling advances, subtle cues have grown into sexual signals. Why does the desire to use small physical and verbal cues to attract the opposite sex still persist? Simple. People enjoy flirting—the healthy, harmless, usually sexual banter between individuals—and it serves an important, if not necessary, role in socializing. As such, people strive to become experts at the art of flirtation, a process rooted in physical appearance and mannerisms.

Attracting attention and finding a mate in the animal kingdom entails the art of flirtation based largely on physical beauty and strength. The male lion bristles his proud mane, and the lionesses work tirelessly to do his bidding and attract his attention. Similarly, the confident male peacock struts about, with his beautiful tail of blue-green feathers spread out, hoping to attract the plain brown female. Unlike other animals, however, humans are much more discerning about their appearance prior to flirtatious acts. Though the animal mating ritual requires only one mate to preen excessively during a limited time period, humans—both male and female—often spend hundreds of dollars a year making sure they always look attractive. One of the best-selling products on **Sephora.com** is *Lip Fusion,* a lip-gloss that contains marine collagen microspheres that are absorbed into lips and create a beautiful pout, all without the aid of surgery. At thirty-six dollars, this best-selling wonder product costs much more than conventional lip-gloss, yet stores can't seem to keep it in stock! Similarly, with their obsession for designer jeans and expensive hair treatments, men also find themselves drawn to artifice and activities that might help enhance their appearance. Unquestionably, the dawn of the metrosexual has arrived. As a male co-worker jokingly told me while discussing diets and his Lucky Brand jeans, "Hey, it takes a lot of work to look this good!" With all these men and women trying their best to look good, it is clear that in this society, starting to enhance one's finer physical qualities before attempting to flirt is vital.

In addition to physical appearance, physical manner- 3
isms also become important, effective tools—or potential liabilities—during the flirting process. Snorting while laughing, burping the national anthem, and spewing beer out of noses are turn-offs, and few want their other halves (well, at least people who enjoy social etiquette) to practice these behaviors when eating dinner with their families. People need to realize that the skills and behavior they would expect to view on *Jackass,* a crude television show, are not necessary in order to become the center of attention. Flirting between couples should consist of lighthearted, civil interaction with one another that may give the impression of sexual interest, not a locker-room gross-out contest. Once you realize what is or isn't a flirtatious act, using physical appearance and mannerisms to your best advantage, you will be ready to study and implement the rules of flirtation.

First, when flirting, remember to establish eye con- 4
tact rather than looking at the ground. However, do not overdo eye contact while talking. I've seen people stare so intensely they look like crazed stalkers, so tone down if you know your eyes can blaze holes into concrete. Sometimes looking into another's eyes and then turning away will be enough! You have to make the person know you are interested—but certainly not desperate. Also, remember to listen to the object of your flirtation. If you allow your mind to wander, you may miss significant verbal cues requesting a response. Flirting involves a lot of friendly smiles, giggles, and gestures that a person does not share with just anyone. According to Catherine Yumul, a college student, "You can begin flirting by fluttering eyelids, flipping hair, laughing politely, and winking. The inattentive flirt may remain oblivious to the dynamic potential of a situation. That being said, if someone laughs out loud at your jokes, establishes eye contact and comes within the three foot circle of personal space, success is probably close at hand."

Second, allow flirtation to flourish by knowing how to 5
reciprocate flirting cues, whether at an intimate dinner for two, or in a large social setting. First impressions can make or break a successful flirt. This brings to mind a chat I had with my cousin. He asked me for my opinion about a girl he liked, and we began by analyzing her behavior and body language. Time after time, she had laughed at his jokes, established eye contact with him, and hit him on the knee, and she often told him he was funny. Based on her flirtatious overtures, and assuming he would respond mutually—given a chance—I told him to go ahead and ask her out to dinner, confident that the date would go well. I could not have been more wrong. The next day, he revealed to me that he had been half an hour late, showed up dressed in disheveled athletic gear, and even let his female friend tag along! At this point, I slapped myself on the forehead, and called him stupid. It was bad enough to be late and look unconcerned about his appearance, but bringing a female friend was the worst thing he could have done on a date with another woman. Overnight, he seemed to have forgotten that flirting requires "give and take" to thrive. Instead, his looks and actions displayed apparent lack of interest in his date. Successful flirtation, therefore, requires the essential ability to interpret cues and act accordingly

Third, besides avoiding inappropriate behavior, refrain 6
from embracing advice gleaned from superficial flirtation guides. Though they might raise self-esteem or build self-confidence temporarily, magazines like *Cosmopolitan* often fall short of bringing out the true flirt in you, opting instead for sensational headlines that scream, "How to Get Your Man" and telling women that wearing a short skirt with a matching plunging neckline and heels will do the trick. Magazines for men are no better either. In *FHM,* famous for its "100 Sexiest Women" countdown, there is an abundance of articles about "beer, babes and fast facts" that teach men how to get a woman to do a variety of things. These sexist magazines can't teach people anything they don't already know about flirting. An extremely unattractive trait, desperation, can be smelled a mile away. Desperate times do not call for desperate measures in this case, for such tactics will only make one feel cheap.

Fourth, since no best place to flirt exists, select a 7
location that's right for you. Social situations may cause anxiety for many people, but technology has remedied that situation with the introduction of cyber flirting. With the meteoric rise of social networks in the last several years and the increasing acceptance of online dating sites like **Match.com** and OK Cupid, you may even find a friend of a friend you find attractive and ask her or him out. My aforementioned cousin who "struck out" in a conventional flirting situation even has asked a girl out based on seeing her profile on Facebook, and through a series of messages, managed to find his way into a successful dating situation. By testing the waters by looking at profiles and pictures, we now have various avenues and means to initiate flirting on the Internet.

These days, many lonely, insecure people venture into an Internet chat room, flirt, and establish relationships without having ever seen the other person. This increasingly popular method of flirtation liberates people from the confines of conformity and a physical ideal—at least, until they exchange photos. Now, with all the upgrades on instant messenger software, dozens of ways to express flirtatious thoughts and actions exist through icons. A representative list includes:

;-) represents "a wink"	LOL means
# requests "don't tell anyone"	"laughing out loud"
:) or :-) symbolizes "the smile"	XOXO expresses
:-$ indicates "embarrassed"	"love & kisses"
(YN) reveals "fingers crossed"	*g* stands for "giggle"
:-0 projects "surprise"	;-(denotes "sadness"
:\ conveys "the worried face"	:P suggests "joking face"

Clearly, the Internet has answered dreams for want-to-be flirts afraid of social situations. 9

Fifth, whenever and wherever you flirt, remember to behave within social bounds. This applies to all occasions, although when you are in a bar or club, the loud music may never let you exchange eloquent banter. In that case, the combination of desperate intoxicated people and cheesy pickup lines (a very lousy attempt at flirting) might go unnoticed or actually work. Otherwise, remember to stick to being polite and engaging, and let your natural effervescence shine through. Whether face-to-face or online, focus on common interests during conversation, and be enthusiastic when the other half begins to open up. Though some people are not conversationalists, focusing on the other individual and his/her interests is always helpful. 10

Finally, no matter what forum you chose for playful repartee, keep in mind that flirting is natural and should not be forced. When taken to extremes, "over the top" flirting undermines any healthy intent. Indeed, sometimes a fine line exists between innocent flirtation 11

and aggressive behavior that could be considered pornographic. Paris Hilton's infamous Carl's Jr. Spicy BBQ Burger commercial offers a perfect example of this. Considered by many as "too hot for television," Hilton spent only *seven* seconds out of a *sixty* second commercial holding a Spicy BBQ Burger. The rest of the time she sensuously washed a car, taking time to suggestively soap down her own body, tracing her considerable assets with suds. Did she connect with her target audience? No doubt. Did her "over the top" mannerisms befitting a wet t-shirt contest tastefully promote Spicy BBQ Burgers? Probably not.

Thus, although the media attempt to turn flirting into women wearing garments that leave little to the imagination or ogling men with pickup lines penned by clueless minds, we need to ignore such superficial, demeaning stereotypes and trite—possibly offensive—behavior. Instead, focus on self-improvement. Makeover shows that don't rely on plastic surgery such as *What Not to Wear* on TLC constantly demonstrate how a bit of blush on the cheeks or a new outfit can transform one's appearance and improve self-confidence instantly. So go ahead and do the same. Improve your posture, shave your *Unabomber* beard, and let the transformation begin. 12

As concluded by novelist Victor Hugo, "God created the flirt, as soon as he made the fool." Though we are oftentimes fools, flirts or even both, we can try to avoid compromising situations where playful intentions send conflicting messages. Reject the desire to wear that smutty top so you can get a free drink, and resist wearisome pickup lines such as inquiring whether a person's tired because he or she has been running through your mind all night. Be yourself; enjoy the natural pleasures of flirting, and more than anything else, allow your natural confidence and personality to shine through. That way, flirting will make you nobody's fool. 13

Source: C. Ng, "Brining out the flirt in you." In C. Ng, *Visions Across the Americas* (Canada: Cengage Learning, 2007).

[QUESTIONS FOR REFLECTION]

Considering Ideas

1. What are some of the best suggestions for flirting in Ng's essay? What do people need to do to be good at flirting? How does culture play a part in the flirting process? Explain your answers.

2. In addition to telling readers what to do, Ng also tells them what not to do. Why does she do this? What effect does it have on the reader? Include specific examples from the essay to explain your answers.

3. The author discusses using Internet sites, such as **Match.com** and Facebook, to help with the flirting process. Have you ever participated in online flirting or dating, or do you know someone who has? What were the results?

Considering the Rhetorical Star

1. What is the *subject* of Ng's essay? Is this an appealing subject? Why or why not?

2. Who is the intended *audience* for the article? How do you know?

3. What is Ng's primary *purpose* in the essay? Does she effectively achieve her purpose? Why or why not? Is there a secondary purpose as well? If so, what is it?

4. In addition to process analysis, what other writing *strategies* does the author employ? Identify specific passages from the essay to illustrate your point.

5. As part of her *design*, Ng begins with an attention-getter that is separate from the introduction. How does this approach affect the reader?

Considering Writing Strategies

1. Ng uses process writing as her primary writing strategy. Identify several sentences that clearly indicate that this is a process analysis essay. Is process analysis the most effective strategy for her topic? Why or why not?

2. What examples does the author give to support her main points? Are they effective? Why or why not?

3. Ng saves her most important point for last. What is it? What effect does that placement have on the reader?

Writing Suggestions

1. Choose a particular scenario for flirting, such as on campus, online, at a bar, or in another country. Write an essay explaining how to be successful with flirting in that particular environment. You might include specific tips for success and cautions for the readers to consider when flirting.

2. Think about a task that you are particularly adept at performing related to school, a hobby, or your job. Write an essay explaining how to perform the process. Be sure to include specific tips and/or warnings as needed to help the reader to succeed at performing the process.

Reading and Reflection PROCESS WRITING

[preview] **JACK NORWORTH** wrote the famous song "Take Me Out to the Ball Game" on a piece of scrap paper when he was riding a train to Manhattan, New York, in 1908. He gave the lyrics to Albert Von Tilzer, who composed the music to accompany the song. The New York Music Company published the song, which became an instant hit before the year ended. Today baseball fans still sing this classic song, which took Norworth only fifteen minutes to write, during the seventh inning stretch at nearly every baseball game in the United States. You can listen to the song at **www.youtube.com/watch?v=RXvmNesu3Mo**. Before reading, think about sporting events you like to attend with friends or family. What do you find to be exciting about those events?

"Take Me Out to the Ball Game" Lyrics by Jack Norworth, Music by Albert Von Tilzer

Katie Casey was base ball mad.
Had the fever and had it bad;
Just to root for the home town crew,
Ev'ry sou Katie blew.
On a Saturday, her young beau
Called to see if she'd like to go,
To see a show but Miss Kate said,
"No, I'll tell you what you can do."

"Take me out to the ball game,
Take me out with the crowd.
Buy me some peanuts and cracker jack,

I don't care if I never get back,
Let me root, root, root for the home team,
If they don't win it's a shame.
For it's one, two, three strikes, you're out,
At the old ball game."

Katie Casey saw all the games,
Knew the players by their first names;
Told the umpire he was wrong,
All along good and strong.
When the score was just two to two,
Katie Casey knew what to do,

Just to cheer up the boys she knew,
She made the gang sing this song:

"Take me out to the ball game,
Take me out with the crowd.
Buy me some peanuts and cracker jack,

I don't care if I never get back,
Let me root, root, root for the home team,
If they don't win it's a shame.
For it's one, two, three strikes, you're out,
At the old ball game."

[QUESTIONS FOR REFLECTION]

Considering Ideas

1. Have you ever known a baseball fan, or are you one? To what extreme might fans go to see their favorite players?

2. What traditions does Norworth emphasize through his lyrics?

3. What other traditions might be considered American?

Considering the Rhetorical Star

1. What is the main *subject* of the song?

2. Who is the intended *audience*? Is there also a secondary audience? Who else might the song reach besides the primary audience?

3. What is the Norworth's main *purpose* for the song? Does he achieve his purpose? Explain.

4. The author uses process analysis as the primary writing *strategy* for the song. What other strategies does he use?

5. Is the *design* of the song effective? Why or why not?

Considering Writing Strategies

1. Where does Norworth explain a process in the song? How effective is his explanation?

2. What is the tone (mood) of the song? Identify several words that influence the tone.

3. Find several examples of rhyming words in the song. How does Norworth's use of rhyme affect the song?

Writing Suggestions

1. Write an essay explaining a family tradition that a parent or other family member has passed along to you. You might explain what this tradition entails and why it holds special meaning for you, or you may give the reader how-to instructions for following your family's tradition.

2. Write an explanation related to your favorite sport or hobby. One option is to write a step-by-step explanation of how to perform a process, such as the steps for effectively swinging a golf club or blocking a goal in a soccer game. Another option is to explain the process so that your readers will have an understanding of what is involved in the activity, such as what it is like to go skiing or skydiving.

ESOL Tip >

Write about a tradition followed at sports events in your native country. Why is this tradition important to you and the people of your country? When did it begin?

STUDENT WRITING

Cooking Oxtails, Jamaican Style!
by Karen Ebanks

Jamaica is a beautiful island located in the Caribbean Sea, south of Cuba and west of the Dominican Republic. It is known for its beautiful beaches, reggae music and slow, relaxed pace and has long been a favorite tourist destination. Jamaica's population is made up of many different races, resulting in a multifaceted culture that is as diverse as its people. Food is one of the most important aspects of Jamaican culture.

Jamaicans love to cook, and many of the island's popular dishes contain meat that is not traditionally eaten in the United States. Some of those meats include goat, cow's feet, tripe, and oxtails. All of these dishes are standard fare in a Jamaican home and are also served at various traditional events, such as wedding receptions, celebrations, funeral repast services, and the like. Serving a Jamaican dish is a great way to add something different to one's traditional weeknight dinner, and by following the instructions listed below for Jamaican oxtails, it should not be too difficult. Jamaican oxtails are especially tasty as many seasonings are used to create this dish, and although a few hours are required, it is well worth the time.

The following ingredients are necessary to cook this dish: 3

- ❑ 3 lbs. beef oxtail
- ❑ 2 green onion stalks, chopped
- ❑ 1 cup vinegar
- ❑ 4 cloves garlic, chopped
- ❑ 3 tsp. salt
- ❑ 3 pcs. fresh thyme, chopped
- ❑ ¼ tsp. cayenne pepper
- ❑ ½ green pepper
- ❑ 1 tbsp. onion powder
- ❑ 6 pimento berries (also called allspice)
- ❑ 1 tbsp. garlic powder
- ❑ 2 tbsp. vegetable oil
- ❑ 1 tsp. paprika
- ❑ 1 can butter beans, drained
- ❑ 1 tbsp. browning sauce (optional)
- ❑ 2 carrots sliced thinly
- ❑ 1 onion, chopped
- ❑ water

First, trim the fat from the meat and then wash the 4 pieces in a solution of water and vinegar. Next, season the meat with the dry seasonings (salt, pepper, onion powder, garlic powder, and paprika) followed by the browning sauce. If you can, let the meat sit for a few hours or possibly overnight in the refrigerator, which will allow it to season more thoroughly. After that, heat the vegetable oil in a large frying pan and transfer the meat to the pan in order to "brown" it, which means to cook the meat for a short time over medium heat to give it a brown color.

When the meat has browned, transfer the pieces of 5 meat into a pressure cooker pot, along with the remaining seasonings, such as the onions, garlic, thyme, green pepper, and pimento berries. Cooking the meat in a pressure

cooker will allow it to cook much faster, as oxtail meat can be somewhat tough and take a long time to become tender. Next, pour 4½ cups of water into the pot and cook at high pressure for 20 minutes. High pressure is considered the period in which the pressure regulator on the top of the pressure cooker begins to jiggle gently. Remove the pot from the heat and then allow it to cool completely. Running cold water over the pot lid will help it to cool faster. Only when it is fully cooled should you remove the lid from the pressure cooker.

At this point, taste the oxtails to determine if more 6 seasonings are required. If so, add salt, pepper, or other seasonings accordingly. Next, add the carrots and cook for an additional 15 minutes over medium heat, stirring occasionally. Finally, add the butter beans, and after cooking for 5 more minutes, your oxtail dish will be done. This recipe takes about 2½ hours to prepare and serves four people.

Jamaican oxtails make a wonderful, tasty meal that is 7 best served over another popular Jamaican dish called rice and peas. (Of course, it never hurts to serve it with a bit of Jamaican rum as well.) You can find oxtails at any typical Jamaican restaurant here in the U.S., or you can choose to be adventurous and attempt to cook your own. Either way, you will enjoy a delicious Jamaican dish that might make you consider taking a trip to the island itself. Yah Mon!

[QUESTIONS FOR REFLECTION]

1. What does Ebanks accomplish in the first paragraph? She delays the thesis until the second paragraph. Is this approach effective in this essay? Why or why not?

2. The author provides the reader with a list of ingredients. Would the essay be stronger or weaker if the ingredients were in paragraph form? Why?

3. Based on these instructions, would you be able to cook Jamaican oxtails if you had all of the necessary ingredients? Why or why not?

4. What transitions does the author use to help guide the reader? Which ones are the most useful? Why?

5. Which parts of the concluding paragraph leave you with a lasting impression? Why?

STUDENT WRITING

How to Make a Traditional Hawaiian Lei
by Alexander Gehring

Lei making is a very rich and time-honored tradition of Hawaii. Leis were first introduced to the islands from early Polynesian settlers traveling across the Pacific from Tahiti. Traditional leis can be made from just about anything you can find in nature. Flowers, leaves, shells, feathers, and even bone and teeth of various animals can be used. Early Hawaiians constructed and wore leis as a way to beautify and to distinguish themselves from others.

The most significant of all leis is the Maile lei. The Maile lei is known as the "lei of royalty" and is given as a sign of respect and honor. In the past they were used as an offering during times of war. The two opposing chiefs would intertwine the Maile vine, officially establishing peace between the tribes. Today, they are reserved for special and memorable occasions such as weddings, birthdays, graduations, and elections. In a traditional Hawaiian wedding the Kahuna (Hawaiian priest) will use the Maile lei and tie the hands of the bride and groom together signifying their commitment to one another. When students in Hawaii graduate from school, they receive so many leis that sometimes it is hard to see their faces.

The fringed ti leaf lei is one of the oldest and simplest leis to make. To make one, all you need are two large ti leaves. If you are lucky enough to live in an area where ti plants are native, then all you need to do is pick your leaves and wash them. If not, you can order them on the Internet. Ti leaves come in two colors: green and red. Traditionally, green leaves are used when making leis, but the choice is yours.

Before making the lei, you need to remove the stiff center vein of the leaf. To do this, make a shallow cut on the backside of the leaf along the vein, being careful not to cut all the way through the leaf. After you have made your cut, strip off the vein with your fingers. Next, tie the two leaves together at the stems using a square knot. Finally, fringe the leaves by making small strips in them. You now have an authentic Hawaiian lei that you can wear or give to a friend.

There are, however, a few unspoken rules to keep in mind when receiving a lei from someone. The giving of a lei is a friendly celebration and should never be refused. Also, it is considered disrespectful to remove a lei when in the presence of the person who gave it to you. To wear a lei, gently drape it over your shoulders, allowing it to hang down in both the front and back.

Hawaiian leis are a fun part of any celebration. Most people appreciate them and greet them with a smile. Leis are universal and can be given at almost any event. The next time you want to make someone feel special, make him or her an authentic Hawaiian lei.

[QUESTIONS FOR REFLECTION]

1. Look back through the essay and identify some of the different writing strategies that Gehring uses to explain how to make a Hawaiian lei. Why does this combination approach work well for this topic?

2. Does the author use any words that are new to you? Do you think he defines them sufficiently? Why or why not?

3. Do you have enough information to actually make a lei? Explain.

4. Could any parts of the essay be illustrated with a graphic? Which parts would benefit most? What would you include?

5. Which part of the essay is most interesting or memorable? Why?

Cultural Exchange Activity:
Answers will vary.

▶ *Activity*   Cultural Exchange

In pairs or small groups, brainstorm to create a list of family traditions and cultural traditions the members in your group have experienced. Next, each participant will explain one of his or her cultural traditions in detail so the other students have a good idea of its significance. A representative from each group will then share a few ideas with the class. This activity may provide you with ideas for a writing assignment.

In pairs or small groups, write an explanation of a short, easy process that can be performed in a classroom setting. Give your instructions to another student or group to see if they can perform the process. Likewise, you or your group will attempt to perform the instructions from another group. Discuss any steps or details that were lacking in either set of directions. How could the instructions be improved? Share your results with the class.

OPTIONS FOR WRITING A PROCESS ESSAY

Now that you have read one or more examples of process analysis, it's time to write your own. You may choose to write about one of the writing options that follow, the advertisement, the image, or one of the media suggestions. Consider your rhetorical star and the qualities of an effective process paper as you begin to compose your assignment.

Writing Assignment Options

Use one of the following topics to write an informative or instructional essay. Remember to consider your rhetorical star as well as the steps for writing about a process as you compose.

1. How to manage time or stress
2. How to study for an exam or how to pass a class, such as English composition
3. How to achieve success (or failure) in college, on the job, or in life
4. How to perform a process on the job
5. How to make the most of a vacation to a particular location
6. How to construct or assemble a small item
7. How a piece of machinery or equipment works
8. How to plan the perfect wedding or other celebration
9. How to eat right or get in shape
10. How an important event occurred

Source: **http://carryabigsticker.com/**.

Interpreting an Advertisement

While most advertisements appear in magazines or newspapers or on billboards, sometimes people use their cars to advertise their views. What do you think about the "Coexist" bumper sticker on page 162? What message does the artist convey and why? Write a response to this bumper sticker or another one. For example, you might write an essay suggesting ways that people can get along (coexist) better with others.

Writing about an Image

Look at the images throughout this chapter and consider these questions: What cultural tradition does the image represent? What process is being performed? What tone does the image portray? How do the artist's techniques affect the image? What ideas about your own culture and traditions does the image conjure? Choose one of the images in the chapter, such as the NASCAR photo above, that depicts a process you are familiar with, and write an essay relating to it. You might respond to the image, tell what is happening in the image, or explain how to perform a process that relates to the image in some way. For example, you might choose to write an essay giving instructions for how to perform a particular soccer kick or move, or you may decide to explain how to play a musical instrument.

Media Connection for Explaining Processes

You might watch, read, and/or listen to one or more of the media products or outlets listed below to discover additional examples of process analysis. Exploring various media may help you to better understand methods for explaining processes. You may also choose to write about one or more of the media suggestions. For example, you might watch an episode of *No Reservations* with Anthony Bourdain or *Great Weekends with Samantha Brown* on the Travel Channel and then write an essay explaining the best way to experience the culture and take in the sights in a particular city, such as Paris. Be sure to give credit to the source you use in your essay.

Television	*Hell's Kitchen*	Home and Garden (HGTV)	Travel Channel	Do It Yourself Network
Film	*How to Train Your Dragon* (2014)	*How to Lose a Guy in Ten Days* (2003)	*How Stella Got Her Groove Back* (1998)	*How to Survive a Plague* (2012)
Print/ E-Reading	*The World of Chinese*	*Bon Appétit*	*Hispanic Lifestyle*	*Ebony*
Internet	**essortment.com**	**guitarvision.com**	**howstuffworks.com**	**origami-instructions.com**
Music	"50 Ways to Say Goodbye" by Train	"How to Save a Life" by The Fray	"Goodbye Earl" by the Dixie Chicks	"How to Be a Heartbreaker" by Maria and The Diamonds

7.4 ANALYZING THE RHETORICAL STAR FOR EXPLAINING A PROCESS IN WRITING

Teaching Tip

Provide students with a set of instructions and ask them to analyze the author's rhetorical star.

As you prepare to write your process paper, consider the five points of the rhetorical star (Figure 7.1). You might use some of the questions in the chart as you conduct your rhetorical star analysis.

FIGURE 7.1
The Rhetorical Star

Subject	Choose a topic appropriate for a college-level audience. It should be a process you are very familiar with but your readers may not understand or know how to do. Make sure that the process isn't too simple or too complicated.
Audience	Who are your readers? What do they need to know about the process? Do you want your readers to be able to perform the process? Or do you just want them to have an understanding of how something was done or how something works? How much detail do you need to include based on the characteristics and needs of the audience? You are better off giving too much detail than not enough detail if you are not sure how familiar your audience is with the process.
Purpose	Is your main purpose to instruct or inform? An instructional process tells the readers how to make or do something. An informative process tells the readers how something works, how a process was done, or how something was made. What additional goals do you have? Is your explanation meant to entertain the reader? Are you trying to convince your readers that a particular method works better than another? Are you combining purposes? Keep your purpose in mind as you begin writing.
Strategy	Will you include other writing strategies in addition to explaining the process? For example, do you want to use definition, description, or narration to enhance your explanation?
Design	Do you want to explain the process in paragraph form? Or would numbered steps be more effective? How long should your explanation be? What other design elements, such as headings, pictures, or diagrams would help your reader to better understand the process? See Figure 7.2 for an example of process writing with numbered steps and photographs.

FIGURE 7.2 Sample Design for Instructions

Below is an explanation for the process of transferring a patient from a bed to a stretcher using the "draw sheet transfer" method. What features are especially helpful to the design? Do you think you could be successful doing a draw sheet transfer using these instructions? Why or why not?

Draw Sheet Transfer

STEP 1

❏ Loosen the draw sheet on the bed, and form a long roll to grasp.

❏ Prepare the stretcher by unbuckling the straps, adjusting the height of the stretcher so that it is even with the bed, and lowering the side rails.

❏ Set the brakes on the stretcher (if so equipped) to the ON position.

❏ Position the stretcher next to and touching the patient's bed.

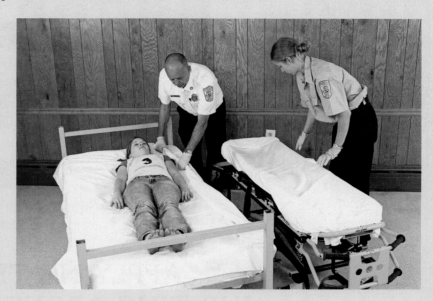

STEP 2

❏ Both rescuers should stand on the same side of the stretcher and then reach across it to grasp the draw sheet firmly at the patient's head and hips.

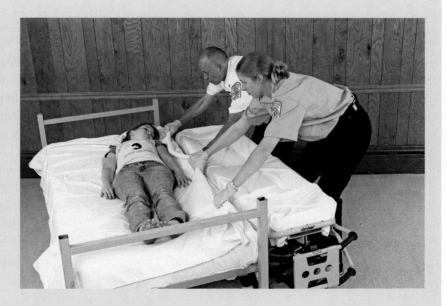

—continued from page 165

STEP 3

❑ On a signal from the rescuer at the patient's head, both rescuers gently slide the patient from the bed to the stretcher.

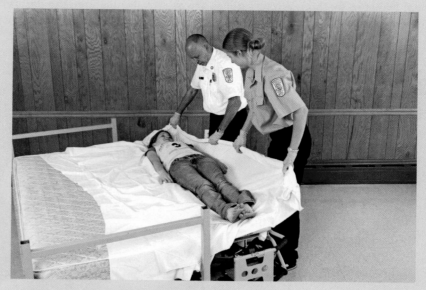

Source: Aehlert, *Emergency Medical Responder,* McGraw-Hill, 2011.

7.5 APPLYING THE STEPS FOR WRITING ABOUT A PROCESS

FIGURE 7.3 The Seven Steps of the Writing Process

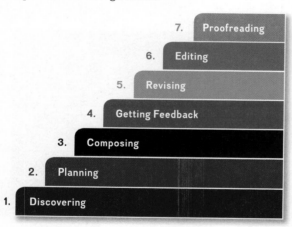

FIGURE 7.4 Explaining a Process

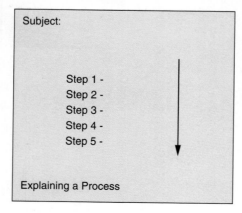

After you have completed your rhetorical star analysis, follow the steps of the writing process (Figure 7.3) to compose your process paper.

1. **Discovering:** When you have chosen a topic, you may want to make a rough sketch of the process or procedure to help aid your writing process. Next, you might brainstorm to determine what materials are needed to complete the process. Additionally, you may want to develop a rough list of the steps you think will be important to include and then put the steps into chronological order by numbering them. Using the Explaining a Process graphic organizer (Figure 7.4) may help you with this.

2. **Planning:** Try creating a list or an outline (informal or formal) to help you organize your ideas. Remember to follow a chronological sequence for your process. Go through the process step-by-step in your mind to make sure that the way you have ordered ideas is clear and logical.

3. **Composing:** Write a first draft of your process analysis. Don't worry too much about grammar and punctuation at this time. Focus on

retelling the details related to the process. Be sure to keep your overall point in mind as you write.

Use the seven qualities of effective process writing you learned earlier in this chapter. These characteristics are a key part of the writing process:

1. Begin with a clear introduction.
2. Include a list of materials as needed.
3. Explain the steps in chronological order.
4. Define special terms as needed.
5. Give helpful tips and warnings as needed.
6. Include visual aids as needed.
7. End with a decisive conclusion.

4. **Getting Feedback:** Have at least one classmate, or other person, read your rough draft and answer the peer review questions that appear below. If you have access to a writing tutor or center, get another opinion about your paper as well. If possible, ask your reviewer to explain which parts are most clear and which steps, if any, need more explanation.

5. Revising: Using all of the feedback available to you, revise your process analysis. Make sure that the steps of your process are clear and follow a chronological order. Additionally, check to see that you have kept your audience's needs in mind throughout your explanation of the process. Try going though the process in your head using your explanation to make sure that you haven't left out any important steps or warnings.

6. **Editing:** Read your process analysis again, this time looking for errors in grammar, punctuation, and mechanics. Pay particular attention to your use of transitions and action verbs because these areas are especially important for writing about processes.

7. Proofreading: After you have carefully edited your essay, read it one last time to look for typographical errors and any other issues that might interfere with the readers' understanding of your explanation.

PEER REVIEW QUESTIONS FOR EXPLAINING A PROCESS

Trade rough drafts with a classmate and answer the following questions about his or her paper. Then, in person or online, discuss your papers and suggestions with your peer. Finally, make the changes you feel would most benefit your paper.

1. Identify the thesis statement. Does it effectively let you know what process will be explained? Why or why not?
2. Are there any additional materials that need to be included or terms that need to be defined? What are they?
3. Do the steps flow logically and smoothly? Why or why not?
4. Which part do you think is explained best? Why?
5. Do you feel that you fully understand the process the author is explaining? If not, which parts could use more details or clarification?
6. Does the author provide the reader with a sense of completion at the end? If so, how?
7. What kinds of grammatical errors, if any, are evident in the explanation?
8. What final suggestions do you have for the author?

WRITER'S CHECKLIST FOR EXPLAINING A PROCESS

Use the checklist below to evaluate your own writing and help ensure that your explanation of the process is complete. If you have any "no" answers, continue working on those areas.

❏ 1. Is my title suitable?

❏ 2. Does my thesis statement clearly identify the process I am explaining?

❏ 3. Does my introduction give the reader an indication of the points I make in the body of my essay or instructions?

❏ 4. If they are necessary, have I identified the materials and quantities effectively?

❏ 5. Have I included all of the necessary steps for the reader to understand or perform the process?

❏ 6. Are all of my steps in chronological order?

❏ 7. Have I used transitions to increase readability?

❏ 8. Have I used active verbs to emphasize each step?

❏ 9. Have I clearly defined terms that my reader may not understand?

❏ 10. Have I indicated when the process is complete?

❏ 11. Have I proofread thoroughly?

[CHAPTER SUMMARY]

1. Use the process writing strategy to explain how to do something or describe how something works or was done.

2. Process writing is an important part of your education, daily life, and career.

3. Every culture in the world has traditions and procedures that it follows. Being sensitive to the processes associated with various cultures will help you to be more successful in the workplace.

4. Interpreting readings and images that relate to processes can help you to prepare to write a process analysis essay.

5. Carefully analyze the rhetorical star before explaining a process in writing: subject, audience, purpose, strategy, and design.

6. Follow these steps when writing about a process: Begin with a clear introduction; include a list of materials as needed; explain the steps in chronological order; define special terms as needed; give helpful tips and warnings as needed; include visual aids as needed; end with a decisive conclusion.

[WHAT I KNOW NOW]

Use this checklist to determine what you need to work on to feel comfortable with your understanding of the material in this chapter. Check off each item as you master it. Review the material for any unchecked items.

❑ 1. I know what **process writing** is.

❑ 2. I can identify several **real-world applications** for process writing.

❑ 3. I can evaluate **readings and images** that explain a process.

❑ 4. I can **analyze** the rhetorical star for writing about a process.

❑ 5. I understand the writing process for **explaining** a process.

❑ 6. I can apply the **seven** qualities of writing about a process.

SmartBook Tip

During the "Recharge" phase, students can return to Chapter 7 and practice concepts that they need to work on.

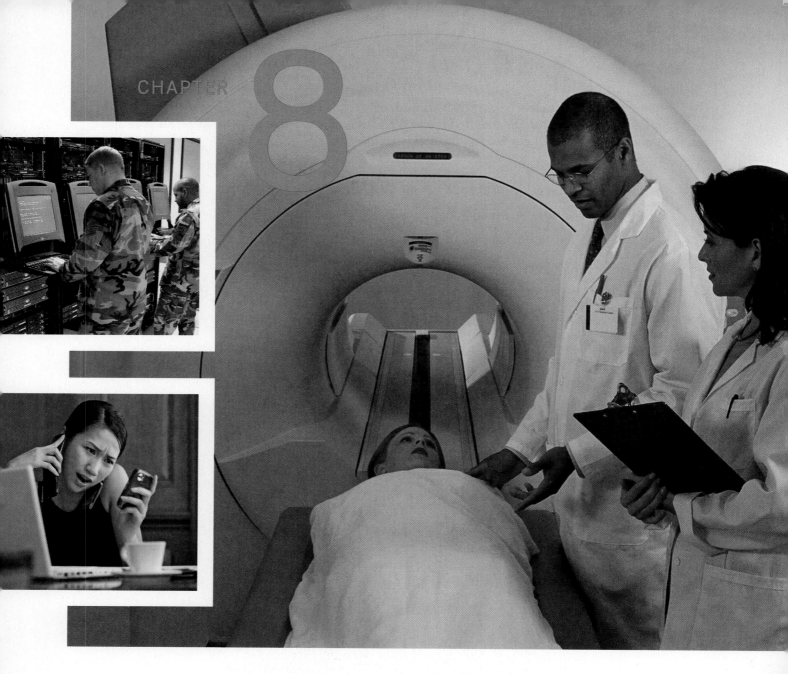

COMPARING AND CONTRASTING: COMPUTERS AND TECHNOLOGY

learning outcomes

In this chapter you will learn techniques for achieving these learning outcomes:

8.1 IDENTIFY REAL-WORLD APPLICATIONS FOR COMPARING AND CONTRASTING.

8.2 UNDERSTAND THE QUALITIES OF COMPARISON AND CONTRAST WRITING.

8.3 INTERPRET IMAGES AND READINGS ABOUT COMPUTERS AND TECHNOLOGY.

8.4 ANALYZE THE RHETORICAL STAR FOR COMPARING AND CONTRASTING.

8.5 APPLY THE QUALITIES OF COMPARISON AND CONTRAST WRITING.

WRITING STRATEGY FOCUS: COMPARING AND CONTRASTING

When you compare and contrast subjects, you are looking at similarities and differences between them. People often use comparison and contrast to better understand one subject in terms of another. Furthermore, the comparison and contrast strategy is useful for making decisions. For example, when you decided to enroll in your current college or university, you probably compared it to one or more other schools to determine which one would best fulfill your needs as a student.

When you compare and contrast subjects, you must use specific points, or criteria, for your comparison. When you were comparing schools, you probably considered some of the following criteria to help make your decision: location, programs offered, class size, facilities, accreditation, and so on. Weighing the relevant criteria is essential to the comparison and contrast process. Being able to write an effective comparison and contrast paper will be useful in school, in your daily life, and in your career.

SmartBook Tip

Students receive an overview of the learning outcomes and topics in Chapter 8 in the "Preview" phase of SmartBook.

8.1 REAL-WORLD APPLICATIONS FOR COMPARING AND CONTRASTING

Writing to Compare and Contrast in College

You will often be asked to identify similarities and differences between two or more subjects in college courses. You might need to compare and contrast characters in a literature class. Your psychology instructor may ask to you compare and contrast two theories or learning styles. In a history class, you may need to compare and contrast significant events, people, or places. Similarly, an instructor in your major course of study may require that you compare and contrast two or more methods for accomplishing a task or performing a skill.

Writing to Compare and Contrast in Your Daily Life

You make comparisons on a daily basis: Deciding what to wear, what to eat, where to go, and what to do all require comparisons. When you decide to make a major purchase, such as an entertainment system, a car, or a home, you'll need to compare the options to see which item best suits your needs and fits within your budget. Additionally, if you need someone to fix your car, babysit your child, or repair your home, then you'll need to compare and contrast your options to make the best possible decision.

Writing to Compare and Contrast in Your Career

Teaching Tip
Ask students to tell how they anticipate using the compare and contrast writing strategy in their future careers.

Being able to write an effective comparison is also extremely useful in the workplace. When you look for a job you will need to compare the offers you get based on a number of factors, such as salary, location, benefits, and work environment. You might need to compare and contrast two software packages or pieces of equipment to decide which one would be more effective to use at your place of employment. Or you may need to compare candidates for a position within your organization to decide which one is most qualified for the job. Here are a few specific applications for comparison and contrast writing in your career:

SmartBook Tip
Key concepts in Chapter 8 are highlighted for students during the "Read" phase. As students demonstrate understanding of these concepts during the "Practice" phase by responding to probes, the highlighting adapts to the individual student's learning by changing color.

Health care: symptoms, treatments, office procedures, or record-keeping methods.

Law: case studies, witnesses' testimonies, or legal procedures.

Education: teaching and learning methods, models, and styles.

Computers: hardware, software, applications, or designs.

Massage therapy: massage techniques, equipment, and lubricants.

Culinary arts: ingredients, cooking styles, menu designs, knives, or cleaning methods.

Business: business models, lending sources, locations, products, and services.

Graduate SPOTLIGHT

Carlos Felix, Software Engineer

Carlos Felix has a degree in computer engineering. He is currently a software engineer for Harris Corporation, which is an information technology and communications company that serves government and commercial markets internationally. Here's what Felix has to say about the importance of written communication in his career:

❝ Writing is a big part of what I do as a software engineer. Before I start on a development project, I have to make sure that there isn't already a product on the market that accomplishes what we need. I compare and contrast existing hardware and software with what I intend to create and write a report documenting my findings and justifying my plan to upper level management. Then I present a tech memo depicting exactly what I am going to do for the project. I have to assume that the reader may not fully understand the material, so I make sure that my paragraphs are clear and that my writing style isn't too technical. I can't skip anything, or it will cause confusion. ❞

On your own, in pairs, or in small groups, brainstorm uses for writing comparisons at school, in your daily life, and on the job. You may want to choose your career field or the prospective career field(s) of the participants in your group. Be prepared to share your results with your instructor or class.

Real-World Comparison and Contrast Writing Activity:

Answers will vary.

8.2 QUALITIES OF COMPARISON AND CONTRAST WRITING

1. Begin by Identifying the Elements You Are Comparing

Somewhere in the first paragraph, mention the items you are comparing. Depending on your subject, you may decide to emphasize similarities, differences, or both. You will want to make your approach clear in your thesis and introduction. For example, if you are comparing two printers, you might focus on differences and write a thesis like this: Printer X is a better choice for college students than Printer Y because of its superior scanning, copying, and printing capabilities.

2. Use a Block or Point-by-Point Approach

There are two basic patterns for organizing a comparison and contrast essay. When you use the *block pattern,* you explain your points of comparison for one item, and then you explain your main points about the second one. If you use the *point-by-point pattern,* you focus on each point you are making and tell about both items as they relate to that point.

Choose the method that seems to work best for your topic. For example, if you are writing an essay comparing two video game systems, the point-by-point method might work best because you can easily highlight the features of each system. However, if you are writing about how technology has changed the way you spend your leisure time, you might use the block pattern to write about the past first and then the present. Here are two sample outlines to help you see the difference between the block and point-by-point organizational patterns:

Thesis: Printer X is a better choice for college students than Printer Y because of its superior scanning, copying, and printing capabilities.

Block Pattern
    I. Printer X
      A. Scanning
      B. Copying
      C. Printing
    II. Printer Y
      A. Scanning
      B. Copying
      C. Printing

Point-by-Point Pattern
    I. Scanning
      A. Printer X
      B. Printer Y

Teaching Tip

Lead a class discussion comparing and contrasting two fast-food restaurants. Develop a list of points for comparison and demonstrate how to organize them in outline form using the block and point-by-point patterns.

LearnSmart Achieve Tip

The Writing Process unit of LearnSmart Achieve determines what students do and do not know about the writing process. Learning outcomes within the Writing Process unit cover planning, organizing, drafting, and revising an informative text. Learning resources and questions automatically adapt to each student's individual needs and help students thoroughly master this content. See the Instructor's Manual for *Write Now* for a list of learning outcomes as well as additional information on how to use LearnSmart Achieve with your students.

        II. Copying
           A. Printer X
           B. Printer Y
        III. Printing
           A. Printer X
           B. Printer Y

3. Describe Your Subjects Fairly and Accurately

Use vivid descriptions so that your reader can imagine the subjects you are comparing and contrasting. Choose the details that your readers will most need to understand. Also, you will want to balance your coverage of the subjects you are comparing and contrasting. If you focus mostly on just one of the items, you may have difficulty convincing the readers that your points are valid.

Furthermore, you will need to ensure that your comparisons are ethical. You don't want to unfairly skew the details and examples you provide about one subject so that you undermine the other. For example, if you are comparing cable and satellite television services, it would be unethical to point out that satellite reception is sometimes interrupted by stormy weather, but neglect to mention that cable reception is also interrupted on occasion for various reasons.

Teaching Tip

Give students additional examples of analogies to ensure a fuller understanding of their usefulness.

4. Consider Using an Analogy

Often you can enhance your comparisons by using some sort of analogy. Typically, an analogy compares something unfamiliar to something familiar. For example, if you are comparing your experience playing two new video games, you might say that one is as exciting as leaping out of an airplane at 30,000 feet, while the other is about as stimulating as reading all of the ingredients on a cereal box. If you do use an analogy, be careful to avoid clichés. Comparing your life to a ride on a roller coaster isn't exactly going to "wow" your readers. You are better off coming up with a fresh, original analogy.

ESOL Tip >
Analogies are especially helpful if your topic is unfamiliar to readers who are unacquainted with your culture.

5. Use Transitions to Help Your Writing Flow Smoothly

If you choose the right transitions, your comparison and contrast essay will be more coherent for your audience. When you are emphasizing similarities, transitions such as *also, similarly,* and *both* can be useful. When you focus on differences, you might try transitional devices such as *however, unlike,* and *on the other hand.* Using transitional expressions can also help you to keep your essay from sounding like a tennis match, where you awkwardly bounce back and forth between the two subjects. Varying your word choice and sentence structure will also help you to avoid the monotony of the tennis ball effect.

6. Conclude Logically

Typically, the conclusion is a good place to restate your main idea and summarize your main points. When writing a comparison, you might come to a logical conclusion that wasn't obvious from the thesis. For example, if you are comparing two video games or movies, you might determine which one you would recommend. If you include your recommendation in the introduction, your readers might not bother reading your complete comparison.

Analogies are useful when writing to compare something unfamiliar to something familiar.

EXAMPLE

In the movie *Forrest Gump,* the title character says, "Life is like a box of chocolates. You never know what you're gonna get."

In pairs, groups, or on your own, come up with an analogy for each of the following subjects. Be careful to avoid clichés. Instead, create original comparisons.

1. Life or happiness
2. A computer, a camera, or another electronic device
3. A joyous occasion, such as a wedding, the birth of a child, or a school graduation
4. A specific messy situation, such as a breakup, job loss, or property foreclosure
5. A specific person or animal from a television show or movie

8.3 COMPARING AND CONTRASTING IN THE CONTEXT OF COMPUTERS AND TECHNOLOGY

Making Analogies Activity: Answers will vary.

We are relying more and more on technological devices for work, school, and entertainment. Most of us use computers, smartphones, and a variety of other gadgets on a daily basis. When we get a break from our hectic schedules, many of us enjoy surfing the Net, watching movies or television, listening to digital music, or playing video games. Additionally, technology has revolutionized the way we communicate with one another. Through e-mail, text messaging, and smartphones, we are able to be in virtually constant contact with our co-workers, classmates, friends, and families. We feel lost when the computer network goes down or our smartphone service is interrupted.

With all of the high-tech products available on the market, we have to make careful decisions about which ones we want to purchase. To make those choices, we need to compare and contrast the items we are considering to determine which ones have the best design, features, and price to meet our needs most effectively. As you analyze the readings and images in this chapter, consider the following questions: How is the technology portrayed? How does it impact people? Has technology simplified or complicated our lives? What does the future of technology have in store for us? Additionally, seeing how other writers have structured their comparison and contrast essays will help you to organize your own essays.

> ## Grammar Window
> ### ADVERBS
>
> You will need to choose precise words when you describe items you are comparing or contrasting. In doing so, you may find adverbs to be quite useful. Adverbs modify (or explain) verbs, adjectives, or other adverbs and typically tell how, when, where, or why. Writers commonly use adverbs incorrectly, so you will want to be careful when writing them. The adverbs are highlighted in the following sentences:
>
> **Incorrect example:** Drive careful when traveling during treacherous weather.
>
> **Correct example:** Drive carefully when traveling during treacherous weather.
>
> **Activity:** Choose a paragraph in a magazine, online article, or this textbook. Add at least three adverbs to the paragraph.

Adverbs Grammar Window: Answers will vary.

[preview] **PETER CARDON** is an associate professor of clinical management communication for the school of business at the University of Southern California Marshall. He has an MBA and a PhD from Utah State University. He has published numerous articles on the topics of intercultural communication and social networking. The two readings that follow are excerpts from Cardon's book titled *Business Communication: Developing Leaders for a Networked World* (2014). Although Cardon uses neither the APA nor the MLA format, he has documented his sources with raised numbers and endnotes. This style of citing sources is common in textbooks. The first reading illustrates the block pattern of comparison; the second reading reflects the point-by-point pattern of comparison. Read both comparisons before answering the questions for reflection that follow the second one.

Block Pattern The Evolving Workplace by Peter Cardon

Industrial Age	Information Age	Social Age
Command-and-control (Little communication between teams and units)	Mass two-way communication (Extensive communication between teams and units)	Networked communication (Extensive communication between individuals with shared interests)
Respect for position	Respect for expertise and position	Respect for expertise and contributions to the network
Holding authority is power	Holding knowledge is power	Sharing knowledge is power
Efficiency, competitiveness, and authority are key values	Autonomy, innovation, and achievement are key values	Transparency, honesty, and camaraderie are key values

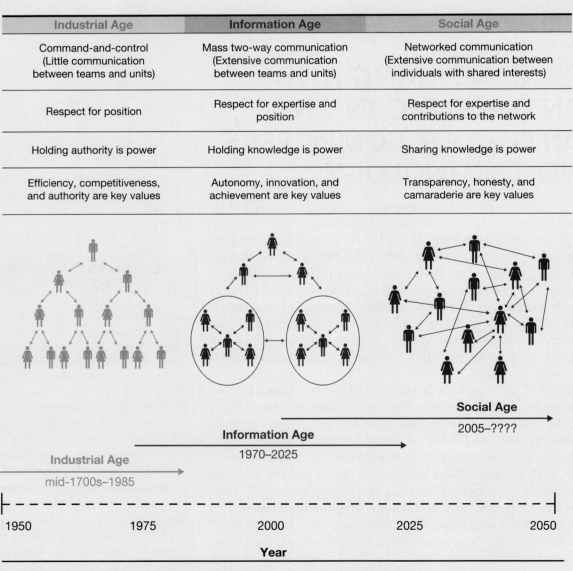

Source: Cardon, *Business Communication: Developing Leaders for a Networked World,* McGraw-Hill, 2014.

Point-by-Point Pattern Characteristics of the Social Age by Peter Cardon

The evolution of the Internet during the past 15 years from Web 1.0 to Web 2.0 platforms is the primary driver of the Social Age. In the original Internet, referred to as **Web 1.0,** most web pages were read-only and static. As the Internet evolved, referred to as **Web 2.0,** what emerged was the read-write web, where users interact extensively with web pages—authoring content, expressing opinions, and customizing and editing web content among other things. Web 2.0 communication tools, often referred to as **social media,** include social networks, blogs, wikis, gaming, podcasts, and information tagging. In simple terms, Web 1.0 communication tools are primarily passive and static. By contrast, Web 2.0 communication tools are interactive, customizable, and *social.*[1] **User 1.0** refers to an individual who primarily uses and prefers Web 1.0 tools, whereas **User 2.0** refers to an individual who primarily uses and prefers Web 2.0 tools (see Table 1).[2] The emerging Social Age is adopting many workplace norms and values from users of Web 2.0 tools.

Increasingly, companies are adopting social networking platforms that contain Web 2.0 communication tools (also called *enterprise social software* and *Enterprise 2.0*) in the workplace. These platforms contain many of the features available on social networking websites: user profiles, microblogs, blogs, wikis, and file uploading. They often include a variety of other communication and collaboration tools as well, including online audio and video calls, shared work spaces, calendars, and private messaging (or e-mail) systems. Thus, most companies—especially medium- to large-sized businesses—are increasingly moving toward corporate intranets that contain both Web 1.0 and Web 2.0 tools. One of the earliest organization-wide adopters of social media was Lockheed Martin, an employer of more than 140,000 worldwide. Lockheed Martin created an internal social networking platform called Unity over a decade ago to meet the challenges of its complex collaborations. Unity includes blogs, wikis, file sharing, tags, discussion forums, social bookmarking, and updates through RSS. Rather than using e-mails, managers use blogs to provide project updates and due dates.[3]

The emerging work culture associated with the Social Age presents many benefits to companies and business professionals in the context of team and networked communication (see Table 2).[4] When social media are used for professional purposes, teams can communicate more efficiently; companies can interface more responsively to customers, clients, and suppliers; customers and other interested individuals can be directly involved in the development of products and services; and anyone with shared professional interests can communicate easily, not needing to travel to see one another.

1. Michael Chui, Andy Miller, and Roger P. Roberts, "Six Ways to Make Web 2.0 Work," *McKinsey Quarterly* [online version] no. 1 (2010).
2. Simon Wright and Juraj Zdinak, *New Communication Behaviors in a Web 2.0 World—Changes, Challenges and Opportunities in the Era of the Information Revolution* (Paris: Alcatel-Lucent, 2008): 10.
3. Todd Henneman, "At Lockheed Martin, Social Networking Fills Key Workforce Needs While Improving Efficiency and Lowering Costs," *Workforce Management* online (March 2010), retrieved November 20, 2010, from www.workforce.com/section/software-technology/feature-lockheed-martin-social-networking-fills-key-workforce/index.html.

TABLE 1

Comparisons between User 1.0 and User 2.0	
User 1.0	**User 2.0**
Passively reading and searching for content	Actively creating and sharing content online
Depends on content creator; does not express own opinion	Can express opinions and even change the content presented
Getting the web as is	Customizing web pages and content
Email is the main communication tool	Peer-to-peer programs are the main communication tools
The computer is the main access point	Connects from various devices
Connected online for time-limited sessions	Connected online all the time

TABLE 2

Benefits and Challenges of Social Media in the Workplace	
Benefits of Social Media	**Challenges and Risks of Social Media**
To Companies: • Team communication and collaboration • Succession planning • Recruitment and on-boarding • Idea sharing/knowledge management • Skills development and training • Interfacing with customers, suppliers, and partners • Decreased time to market for new products and services • More innovative, creative, effective, and profitable approaches to work problems • Less time and fewer resources needed for business travel	*To Companies:* • Lack of adoption and penetration • Lack of permanence • Confusion over which communication channels to use • Distraction from work, too much socializing • Lack of control of information provided externally and internally • Lack of systems for rewarding networked and team communication and collaboration
To Business Professionals: • Build professional networks internally and externally • Access business expertise and knowledge more rapidly • Enhance camaraderie with peers	*To Business Professionals:* • Lack of boundaries between professional and private lives • Lower productivity due to multitasking • Excessive opportunism and self-promotion • Mistakes and incompetence broadcast to larger audiences

4. Wright and Zdinak, *New Communication Behaviors in a Web 2.0 World;* Andreas M. Kaplan and Michael Haenlein, "Users of the World, Unite! The Challenges and Opportunities of Social Media," *Business Horizons* 53, no. 1 (2010): 59–68; AON Consulting, *Web 2.0 and Employee Communications: Summary of Survey Findings* (Chicago: AON Consulting, March 2009); Jacques Bughin, Michael Chui, and Andy Miller, "How Companies Are Benefiting from Web 2.0," *McKinsey Quarterly* 17, no. 9 (2009); Andrew McAfee, *Enterprise 2.0: New Collaborative Tools for Your Organization's Toughest Challenges* (Boston: Harvard Business Press, 2009); Avanade, *CRM and Social Media: Maximizing Deeper Customer Relationships* (Seattle, WA: Avanade, 2008); Jennifer Taylor Arnold, "Twittering and Facebooking While They Work," *HR Magazine* 54, no. 12 (December 1, 2009); Soumitra Dutta, "What's Your Personal Social Media Strategy?" *Harvard Business Review* (November 2010): 127–130.

Source: Peter Cardon, "Business Communication: Developing Leaders for a Networked World 1e, ISBN 0073403199, pg. 190, 191–192. Copyright © 2014 McGraw-Hill Companies.

[QUESTIONS FOR REFLECTION]

1. In the first reading, how effectively do the visuals illustrate the lists above them? Explain.

2. What points does Cardon make in the second reading?

3. Should the second reading include more visual images to support the written text? Why or why not?

4. Which comparison do you find to be more useful? Why?

5. Based on both of these readings, how do you feel about the Social Age? Which aspects of the Social Age and social media do you identify with most and/or least? Explain.

[preview] **DAVID BROOKS,** a graduate of the University of Chicago, is a columnist for the *New York Times,* where the following article originally appeared. He is also a commentator on NPR and *PBS NewsHour.* He has been an editor for a variety of publications, such as the *Wall Street Journal* and *Newsweek,* and has authored several books, including *The Social Animal: The Hidden Sources of Love, Character, and Achievement* (2011). In the essay that follows, Brooks compares and contrasts dating in the past to dating in today's technological era. Before reading the article, consider the following questions: Have you (or has someone you know) ever used an online dating site? What happened? What are the advantages and disadvantages of online dating?

Love, Internet Style by David Brooks

The Internet slows things down. 1

If you're dating in the Age of the Hook-Up, sex is this 2 looming possibility from the first moment you meet a prospective partner. But couples who meet through online dating services tend to exchange e-mail for weeks or months. Then they'll progress to phone conversations for a few more weeks. Only then will there be a face-to-face meeting, almost always at some public place early in the evening, and the first date will often be tentative and Dutch.

Online dating puts structure back into courtship. For 3 generations Americans had certain courtship rituals. The boy would call the girl and ask her to the movies. He might come in and meet the father. After a few dates he might ask her to go steady. Sex would progress gradually from kissing to petting and beyond.

But over the past few decades that structure dis- 4 solved. And human beings, who are really good at adapting, found that the Internet, of all places, imposes the restraints they need to let relationships develop gradually. So now 40 million Americans look at online dating sites each month, and we are seeing a revolution in the way people meet and court one another.

The new restraints are not like the old restraints. The 5 online dating scene is like a real estate market where people go to fulfill their most sensitive needs. It is at once ruthlessly transactional and strangely tender.

It begins with sorting. Online daters can scan through 6 millions of possible partners in an evening and select for age, education, height, politics, religion, and ethnic background. JDate is a popular site for Jews. EHarmony insists that members fill out a long, introspective questionnaire, and thus is one of the few sites where most members are women. Vanity Date is for the South Beach

crowd. "At Vanity Date," the website declares, "we have a vision of creating the largest database of the world's most good-looking, rich, and superficial people."

Most of the sites have programs that link you up with 7 people like yourself. One of the side effects of online dating is that it is bound to accelerate social stratification, as highly educated people become more efficient at finding and marrying one another.

Each member at a dating site creates his or her own 8 Web page. The most important feature on the page is the photo; studies show that looks are twice as powerful as income in attracting mates.

But there are also autobiographical essays. If you 9 judged by these essays, skinny-dipping with intellectuals is the most popular activity in America. All the writers try to show they are sensual yet smart.

The women on these sites are, or project themselves 10 as being, incredibly self-confident. "I am a vivacious, intelligent, warm-hearted, attractive, cool chick, with a sharp, witty, and effervescent personality," writes one on Match.com. Another says: "I am a slender, radiantly beautiful woman on fire with passion and enthusiasm for life. I am articulate, intelligent, and routinely given the accolade of being brilliant."

Still, men almost always make the first contact. Pro- 11 spective partners begin a long series of e-mail interviews. Internet exchanges encourage both extreme honesty (the strangers-on-a-train phenomenon) and extreme dishonesty, as people lie about their ages, their jobs, whether they have kids and, most often, whether they are married. (About a fifth of online daters are married men.)

Considering Ideas

1. What are the similarities and differences between dating in the past and online dating in the present? Which method is better? Why?

2. According to Brooks, what are some of the advantages and disadvantages of online dating? Do you agree or disagree with his ideas. Why?

3. What aspects of online dating still follow the traditional dating model as it was decades ago? Why has that part not changed much over the years?

Considering the Rhetorical Star

1. What is the main *subject* of Brooks's comparison and contrast article? Is the specific topic engaging? Why or why not?

2. Who is the intended *audience* for the article? How do you know?

3. What is the author's main *purpose* (to inform, to interpret, to persuade, to entertain, to express feelings) for the article? Does he use a combination of purposes? How effective is his approach? Explain.

4. The author uses comparison and contrast as the primary *strategy* for the article. Does he employ any other writing strategies? What are they, and how do they affect the piece?

5. What is the *design* of the article? Is it effective? Why or why not?

Considering Writing Strategies

1. What is Brooks's main point in the article? Which sentence or sentences get that point across best? Does he effectively support that point in the body of the essay? Explain.

2. Consider Brooks's diction (word choice) throughout the article. Which words have the strongest impact on the reader? Why?

3. Brooks's article was originally published as a newspaper column. How does this style of writing differ from a formal academic essay? Why do the writing styles need to be different for these two writing occasions?

Writing Suggestions

1. Research two different online dating sites and write a comparison and contrast essay explaining the two sites. Consider whether the block or point-by-point method will work best for your essay.

2. Write a comparison and contrast essay explaining how technology has changed something other than dating. What are the advantages and disadvantages of the old and new ways? What might the future hold?

ESOL Tip >

Compare and contrast the American technology-driven culture (regarding dating or other customs) with another culture with which you are familiar.

Reading and Reflection COMPARING AND CONTRASTING

[preview] **DEBORAH TANNEN,** born in Brooklyn, New York, has published more than 20 books and 100 articles. Her best-selling book, *You Just Don't Understand* (1990), has been translated into 31 languages. Another book of hers, *You Were Always Mom's Favorite!* (2009), is a *New York Times* best seller and winner of a Books for a Better Life Award. She has made appearances on numerous radio and television shows, and she has given lectures around the world. She is a university professor in the linguistics department at Georgetown University. You can read more about her and watch some of her interview clips at **www.deborahtannen.com**. Before reading, think about your communication style. Do you prefer to pick up the phone and call a friend? Or would you rather send an e-mail or a text message?

I was a computer pioneer, but I'm still something of a novice. That paradox is telling.

I was the second person on my block to get a computer. The first was my colleague Ralph. It was 1980. Ralph got a Radio Shack TRS-80; I got a used Apple II+. He helped me get started and went on to become a maven, reading computer magazines, hungering for the new technology he read about, and buying and mastering it as quickly as he could afford. I hung on to old equipment far too long because I dislike giving up what I'm used to, fear making the wrong decision about what to buy, and resent the time it takes to install and learn a new system.

My first Apple came with videogames; I gave them away. Playing games on the computer didn't interest me. If I had free time I'd spend it talking on the telephone to friends.

Ralph got hooked. His wife was often annoyed by the hours he spent at his computer and the money he spent upgrading it. My marriage had no such strains—until I discovered e-mail. Then I got hooked. E-mail draws me the same way the phone does: it's a souped-up conversation.

E-mail deepened my friendship with Ralph. Though his office was next to mine, we rarely had extended conversations because he is shy. Face to face he mumbled, so I could barely tell he was speaking. But when we both got on e-mail, I started receiving long, self-revealing messages: we poured our hearts out to each other. A friend discovered that e-mail opened up that kind of communication with her father. He would never talk much on the phone (as her mother would), but they have become close since they both got online.

Why, I wondered, would some men find it easier to open up on e-mail? It's a combination of the technology (which they enjoy) and the obliqueness of the written word, just as many men will reveal feelings in dribs and drabs while riding in the car or doing something, which they'd never talk about sitting face to face. It's too intense, too bearing-down on them, and once you start you have to keep going. With a computer in between, it's safer.

It was on e-mail, in fact, that I described to Ralph how boys in groups often struggle to get the upper hand whereas girls tend to maintain an appearance of cooperation. And he pointed out that this explained why boys are more likely to be captivated by computers than girls are. Boys are typically motivated by a social structure that says if you don't dominate you will be dominated. Computers, by their nature, balk: you type a perfectly appropriate command and it refuses to do what it should. Many boys and men are incited by their defiance: "I'm going to whip this into line and teach it who's boss! I'll get it to do what I say!" (and if they work hard enough, they always can). Girls and women are more likely to respond, "This thing won't cooperate. Get it away from me!"

Although no one wants to think of herself as "typical"—how much nicer to be *sui generis*[1]—my relationship to my computer is—gulp—fairly typical for a woman. Most women (with plenty of exceptions) aren't excited by tinkering with the technology, grappling with the challenge of eliminating bugs, or getting the biggest and best computer. These dynamics appeal to many men's interest in making sure they're on the top side of the inevitable who's-up-who's-down struggle that life is for them. E-mail appeals to my view of life as a contest for connections to others. When I see that I have 15 messages I feel loved.

I once posted a technical question on a computer network for linguists and was flooded with long dispositions, some pages long. I was staggered by the generosity and the expertise, but wondered where these guys found the time—and why all the answers I got were from men.

Like coed classrooms and meetings, discussions on e-mail networks tend to be dominated by male voices, unless they're specifically women-only, like single-sex schools. Online, women don't have to worry about getting the floor (you just send a message when you feel like it), but, according to linguists Susan Herring and Laurel Sutton, who have studied this, they have the usual problems of having their messages ignored or attacked. The anonymity of public networks frees a small number of men to send long, vituperative,[2] sarcastic messages that so many other men either can tolerate or actually enjoy, but turn most women off.

The anonymity of networks leads to another sad part of the e-mail story: there are men who deluge women with questions about their appearance and invitations to sex. On college campuses, as soon as women students log on, they are bombarded by references to sex, like going to work and finding pornographic posters adorning the walls.

Taking Time

Most women want one thing from a computer—to work. This is significant counterevidence to the claim that men want to focus on information while women are interested in rapport. That claim I found was often true in casual conversation, in which there is no particular information to be conveyed. But with computers, it is often women who are more focused on information, because they don't respond to the challenge of getting equipment to submit.

Once I had learned the basics, my interest in computers waned. I use it to write books (though I never mastered having it do bibliographies or tables of contents) and write checks (but not balance my checkbook). Much as I'd like to use it to do more, I begrudge the time it would take to learn.

Ralph's computer expertise costs him a lot of time. Chivalry requires that he rescues novices in need, and he is called upon by damsel novices far more often than knaves. More men would rather study the instruction

----

[1]*sui generis* Unique.

[2]*vituperative* Harsh and disapproving.

booklet than ask directions, as it were, from another person. "When I do help men," Ralph wrote (on e-mail, of course), "they want to be more involved. I once installed a hard drive for a guy, and he wanted to be there with me, wielding the screwdriver and giving his own advice where he could." Women, he finds, usually are not interested in what he's doing: they just want him to get the computer to the point where they can do what they want.

Which pretty much explains how I managed to be a pioneer without becoming an expert. 15

Source: Deborah Tannen, "Gender Gap in Cyberspace," *Newsweek*, May 16, 1994. Copyright © Deborah Tannen. Reprinted with permission.

[QUESTIONS FOR REFLECTION]

Considering Ideas

1. What similarities and differences do the author and Ralph have when it comes to computers?

2. According to Tannen, how are men and women different in their communication styles? Do you agree or disagree with her assertions?

3. Tannen wrote this essay in 1994. Do you think the gender gap in cyberspace is as big today as it was then? Why or why not?

Considering the Rhetorical Star

1. What is the main *subject* of Tannen's comparison and contrast essay? Is the specific topic engaging? Why or why not?

2. Who is the intended *audience* for the article? How do you know?

3. What is the author's main *purpose* (to inform, to interpret, to persuade, to entertain, to express feelings) for the essay? Does she use a combination of purposes? How effective is her approach? Explain.

4. The author uses comparison and contrast as the primary *strategy* for the story. Does she employ any other writing strategies? What are they, and how do they affect the piece?

5. What is the *design* of the essay? Is it effective? Why or why not?

Considering Writing Strategies

1. Does Tannen use the block or point-by-point method for organizing her comparison? Would her essay have been as effective if she had used the other approach? Why or why not?

2. In addition to comparing and contrasting men and women, Tannen uses the cause-and-effect writing strategy to suggest why they are different. Explain the differences that she perceives between men and women as well as some of the causes for these differences.

3. Instead of ending with a fully developed conclusion, Tannen ends with one simple sentence fragment. Why do you think she does this? What effect does this have on the reader?

Writing Suggestions

1. How would you describe yourself as a computer user? Are you an expert or a novice? Do you go online every opportunity you get, or do you just use the computer enough to get by? Write an essay comparing yourself to someone you know in terms of computer usage. Or you might compare how you use a computer now that you're a college student with how you used a computer before you enrolled in school.

2. Do you ever participate in chat rooms or Weblogs (blogs)? Go online to some of your favorite places and observe the comments written by men and women. How do they differ? Do the comments coincide with Tannen's observations about men and women, or are they different? Write an essay comparing and contrasting your observations with Tannen's.

Reading and Reflection COMPARING AND CONTRASTING

[preview] **MARTY WHIDDON** is a traditional country singer from Headland, Alabama. By the time he was 12 years old he was singing, writing songs, and playing guitar. As teenagers, he and his twin brother, John, joined a radio jamboree in Dothan, Alabama. Although Marty continued with his career in the music business, his brother moved on to become a professional baseball player and signed with the Cleveland Indians. You can learn more about Marty Whiddon by going to **www.soundclick.com/bands/default.cfm?bandID=458081**. In the song that follows, Whiddon pokes fun at the impact that computers have had on his home life. You can find the song on iTunes if you want to listen to it.

Before reading, think about how computers have affected you. Has a family member or significant other ever seemed more interested in a computer than in you? How did you feel? Is it hard to compete with a computer for someone's attention?

Computers, Computers by Marty Whiddon

Computers, computers.
They're taking over my life.
My car and my home,
Television, and phone.
My job and now even my wife.
She plays with her computer
All day and all night.
It's something I don't understand.
A woman who'd rather
Enjoy a computer
Than the company of a good-looking man.
Just thinking about it
Blows a fuse in my mind.
Just listen and understand why.
I stammer and stutter
While she's talking to mother
Through Windows, an electronic vice.
She tries to impress me
With the latest technology
And jibberish I ain't never read.
While just being online
Takes up all her time.
She even takes that blamed old computer to bed.
Computers, computers.
They're taking over my life.
I said, "Honey, that's a sin"
The day that she walked in
Carrying a laptop by her side.
Now it's akin to adultery
Carrying on with that Net.

When she ought to be loving me some instead.
I know she ain't lazy.
She's gone computer crazy.
But I'm the one that's going out of my head.
Just thinking about it
Blows a fuse in my mind.
Just listen; I'll tell you why.
Online in the morning.
Internet in the evening.
A CD ROM a blasting all night.
Instead of playing house,
She plays with a mouse.
It beats all I've ever seen in my life.
Shucks, our life ain't the same
Since she bought that blooming thing.
That computer is ruining my life.
Now listen here honey.
If you want to play with some new way out technology,
I can suggest something right off the top of my head.
Turn off that computer and throw it right out the window,
And let's you and me spend more time together instead.
Computers, computers.
They're driving me crazy.
They're taking over my life.
Uh oh, it's too late.
She's done gone off into cyberspace or outer space . . .

Source: Marty Whiddon, CD, *The Best of Marty Whiddon*. Copyright © by Marty Whiddon, 2002. Marc Dean Music.

[QUESTIONS FOR REFLECTION]

Considering Ideas

1. Compare and contrast Whiddon's view of computers with his wife's. Why do you think their views are so different?

2. What do you imagine Whiddon's life was like before computers? How does that life compare with what he claims his life is like now?

3. Whiddon compares surfing the Net to adultery. Do you think this is a fair comparison? Why or why not?

Considering the Rhetorical Star

1. What is the main *subject* of Whiddon's song? Is the specific topic engaging? Why or why not?

2. Who is the intended *audience* for the song? How do you know?

3. What is the author's main *purpose* (to inform, to interpret, to persuade, to entertain, to express feelings) for the song? Does he use a combination of purposes? How effective is his approach? Explain.

4. The author uses comparison and contrast as the primary *strategy* for the song. Does he employ any other writing strategies? What are they, and how do they affect the piece?

5. What is the *design* of the song? Is it effective? Why or why not?

Considering Writing Strategies

1. Although there is no set pattern, Whiddon uses a fair amount of rhyme in his lyrics. How does the rhyme affect the song?

2. Whiddon switches back and forth between the first and second person points of view. What does he accomplish by doing this?

Writing Suggestions

1. Has someone in your life ever gotten a new gadget, hobby, or other interest that caused you to have to compete for his or her attention? Write an essay comparing how things were before and after the new interest.

2. Think about a new electronic device that you purchased, such as a laptop, iPod, iPad, smartphone, or GPS system. Has the technology been more of a positive or negative influence on your life? Write an essay explaining how this device has affected you. You might compare what your life was like before you got the new gadget with what it was like afterward.

Reading and Reflection COMPARING AND CONTRASTING

[preview] **GEORGE SAUNDERS,** who was born in Amarillo, Texas, is a professor at Syracuse University, where he earned his MFA degree in creative writing. He is an award-winning author of fiction and nonfiction. *Tenth of December: Stories* (2013) and *Congratulations, by the Way: Some Thoughts on Kindness* (2014), two of his more recent works, have been well received along with his numerous prior publications. Go to **www.newyorker.com/online/blogs/books/2013/12/video-office-hours-with-georgesaunders.html** to see a video of Saunders discussing his writing process, kindness, and other thought-provoking topics. In the futuristic short story that follows, Saunders explores the role of advertising in consumerism as a grandfather attempts to take his grandson to see a Broadway show in New York City. Before reading, consider the effect that today's advertising has on you. What influences your purchasing decisions? Do you ever feel overwhelmed by the advertisements you encounter?

My Flamboyant Grandson by George Saunders

I had brought my grandson to New York to see a show. Because what is he always doing, up here in Oneonta? Singing and dancing, sometimes to my old show-tune records, but more often than not to his favorite CD, "Babar Sings," sometimes even making up his own steps, which I do not mind, or rather I try not to mind it. Although I admit that once, coming into his room and finding him wearing a pink boa while singing, in the voice of the Old Lady, "I Have Never Met a Man Like That Elephant," I had to walk out and give it some deep thought and prayer, as was also the case when he lumbered into the parlor during a recent church couples dinner, singing "Big and Slow, Yet So Very Regal," wearing a tablecloth spray-painted gray, so as to more closely resemble Babar.

Being a man who knows something about grandfatherly disapproval, having had a grandfather who constantly taunted me for having enlarged calves—to the extent that even today, when bathing, I find myself thinking unkind thoughts about Grandfather—what I prayed on both occasions was: Dear Lord, he is what he is, let me love him no matter what. If he is a gay child, God bless him; if he is a non-gay child who simply very much enjoys wearing his grandmother's wig while singing "Edelweiss" to the dog, so be it, and in either case let me communicate my love and acceptance in everything I do.

Because where is a child to go for unconditional love, if not to his grandfather? He has had it tough, in my view, with his mother in Nevada and a father unknown, raised by his grandmother and me in an otherwise childless neighborhood, playing alone in a tiny yard that ends in a graveyard wall. The boys in his school are hard on him, as are the girls, as are the teachers, and recently we found his book bag in the Susquehanna, and recently also found, taped to the back of his jacket, a derogatory note, and the writing on it was not all that childish-looking, and there were rumors that his bus driver had written it.

Then one day I had a revelation. If the lad likes to sing and dance, I thought, why not expose him to the finest singing and dancing there is? So I called 1-800-culture, got our Promissory Voucher in the mail, and on Teddy's birthday we took the train down to New York.

As we entered the magnificent lobby of the Eisner Theatre, I was in good spirits, saying to Teddy, The size of this stage will make that little stage I built you behind the garage look pathetic, when suddenly we were stopped by a stern young fellow (a Mr. Ernesti, I believe) who said, We are sorry, sir, but you cannot be admitted on merely a Promissory Voucher, are you kidding us, you must take your Voucher and your Proof of Purchases from at least six of our Major Artistic Sponsors, such as AOL, such as Coke, and go at once to the Redemption Center, on Forty-fourth and Broadway, to get your real actual tickets, and please do not be late, as latecomers cannot be admitted, due to special effects which occur early, and which require total darkness in order to simulate the African jungle at night.

Well, this was news to me, but I was not about to disappoint the boy.

We left the Eisner and started up Broadway, the Everly Readers in the sidewalk reading the Everly Strips in our shoes, the building-mounted miniscreens at eye level showing images reflective of the Personal Preferences we'd stated on our monthly Everly Preference Worksheets, the numerous Cybec Sudden Emergent Screens outthrusting or down-thrusting inches from our faces, and in addition I could very clearly hear the sound-only messages being beamed to me and me alone via various Kakio Aural Focussers, such as one that shouted out to me between Forty-second and Forty-third, "Mr. Petrillo, you chose Burger King eight times last fiscal year but only two times thus far this fiscal year, please do not forsake us now, there is a store one block north!," in the voice of Broadway star Elaine Weston, while at Forty-third a light-pole-mounted Focusser shouted, "Golly, Leonard, remember your childhood on the farm in Oneonta? Why not reclaim those roots with a Starbucks Country Roast?," in a celebrity rural voice I could not identify, possibly Buck Owens, and then, best of all, in the doorway of PLC Electronics, a life-size Gene Kelly hologram suddenly appeared, tap-dancing, saying, "Leonard, my data indicates you're a bit of an old-timer like myself! Gosh, in our day life was simpler, wasn't it, Leonard? Why not come in and let Frankie Z. explain the latest gizmos!" And he looked so real I called out to Teddy, "Teddy, look there, Gene Kelly, do you remember I mentioned him to you as one of the all-time great dancers?" But Teddy of course did not see Gene Kelly, Gene Kelly not being one of his Preferences, but instead saw his hero Babar, swinging a small monkey on his trunk while saying that his data indicated that Teddy did not yet own a Nintendo.

So that was fun, that was very New York, but what was not so fun was, by the time we got through the line at the Redemption Center, it was ten minutes until show-time, and my feet had swollen up the way they do shortly before they begin spontaneously bleeding, which they have done ever since a winter spent in the freezing muck

of Cho-Bai, Korea. It is something I have learned to live with. If I can sit, that is helpful. If I can lean against something, also good. Best of all, if I can take my shoes off. Which I did, leaning against a wall.

All around and above us were those towering walls of light, curving across building fronts, embedded in the sidewalks, custom-fitted to light poles: a cartoon lion eating a man in a suit; a rain of gold coins falling into the canoe of a naked rain-forest family; a woman in lingerie running a bottle of Pepsi between her breasts; the Merrill Lynch talking fist asking, "Are you kicking ass or kissing it?"; a perfect human rear, dancing; a fake flock of geese turning into a field of Bebe logos; a dying grandmother's room filled with roses by a FedEx man who then holds up a card saying "No Charge."

And standing beneath all that bounty was our little Teddy, tiny and sad, whose grandfather could not even manage to get him into one crummy show.

So I said to myself, Get off the wall, old man, blood or no blood, just keep the legs moving and soon enough you'll be there. And off we went, me hobbling, Teddy holding my arm, making decent time, and I think we would have made the curtain. Except suddenly there appeared a Citizen Helper, who asked were we from out of town, and was that why, via removing my shoes, I had caused my Everly Strips to be rendered Inoperative?

I should say here that I am no stranger to innovative approaches to advertising, having pioneered the use of towable signboards in Oneonta back in the Nixon years, when I moved a fleet of thirty around town with a Dodge Dart, wearing a suit that today would be found comic. By which I mean I have no problem with the concept of the Everly Strip. That is not why I had my shoes off. I am as patriotic as the next guy. Rather, as I have said, it was due to my bleeding feet.

I told all this to the Citizen Helper, who asked if I was aware that, by rendering my Strips Inoperative, I was sacrificing a terrific opportunity to Celebrate My Preferences?

And I said yes, yes, I regretted this very much.

He said he was sorry about my feet, he himself having a trick elbow, and that he would be happy to forget this unfortunate incident if I would only put my shoes back on and complete the rest of my walk extremely slowly, looking energetically to both left and right, so that the higher density of Messages thus received would compensate for those I had missed.

And I admit, I was a little short with that Helper, and said, Young man, these dark patches here on my socks are blood, do you or do you not see them?

Which was when his face changed and he said, Please do not snap at me, sir, I hope you are aware of the fact that I can write you up?

And then I made a mistake.

Because as I looked at that Citizen Helper—his round face, his pale sideburns, the way his feet turned in—it seemed to me that I knew him. Or rather, it seemed that he could not be so very different from me when I was a young man, not so different from the friends of my youth—from Jeffie DeSoto, say, who once fought a Lithuanian gang that had stuck an M-80 in the ass of a cat, or from Ken Larmer, who had such a sweet tenor voice and died stifling a laugh in the hills above Koi-Jeng.

I brought out a twenty and, leaning over, said, Look, [20] please, the kid just really wants to see this show.

Which is when he pulled out his pad and began to [21] write!

Now, even being from Oneonta, I knew that being written up does not take one or two minutes, we would be standing there at least half an hour, after which we would have to go to an Active Complaints Center, where they would check our Strips for Operability and make us watch that corrective video called "Robust Economy, Super Moral Climate!," which I had already been made to watch three times last winter, when I was out of work and we could not afford cable. And we would totally miss "Babar Sings"! [22]

Please, I said, please, we have seen plenty of person- [23] alized messages, via both the building-mounted mini-screens at eye level and those suddenly outthrusting Cybec Emergent Screens, we have learned plenty for one day, honest to God we have—

And he said, Sir, since when do you make the call as [24] far as when you have received enough useful information from our Artistic Partners? And just kept writing me up.

Well, there I was, in my socks, there was Teddy, with a [25] scared look in his eyes I hadn't seen since his toddler days, when he had such a fear of chickens that we could never buy Rosemont eggs, due to the cartoon chicken on the carton, or, if we did, had to first cut the chicken off, with scissors we kept in the car for that purpose. So I made a quick decision, and seized that Citizen Helper's ticket pad and flung it into the street, shouting at Teddy, Run! Run!

And run he did. And run I did. And while that Citizen [26] Helper floundered in the street, torn between chasing us and retrieving his pad, we raced down Broadway, and glancing back over my shoulder I saw a hulking young man stick out his foot, and down that Helper went, and soon I was handing our tickets to the same stern Mr. Ernesti, who was now less stern, and in we went, and took our seats, as the stars appeared overhead and the Eisner was transformed into a nighttime jungle.

And suddenly there was Babar, looking with longing [27] toward Paris, where the Old Lady was saying that she had dreamed of someone named Babar, and did any of us know who this Babar was, and where he might be found? And Teddy knew the answer, from the Original Cast CD, which was Babar is within us, in all of our hearts, and he shouted it out with all the other children, as the Old Lady began singing "The King Inside of You."

And let me tell you, from that moment everything changed [28] for Teddy. I am happy to report he has joined the play at school. He wears a scarf everywhere he goes, throwing it over his shoulder with what can only be described as bravado, and says, whenever asked, that he has decided to become an actor. This from a boy too timid to trick-or-treat! This from the boy we once found walking home from school in tears, padlocked to his own bike! There are no more late-night crying episodes, he no longer writes on his arms with permanent marker, he leaps out of bed in the morning, anxious to get to school, and dons his scarf, and is already sitting at the table eating breakfast when we come down.

The other day as he got off the bus I heard him say, to [29] his bus driver, cool as a cucumber, See you at the Oscars.

When an Everly Reader is reading, then suddenly [30] stops, it is not hard to trace, and within a week I received a certified letter setting my fine at one thousand dollars, and stating that, in lieu of the fine, I could elect to return to the originating location of my infraction (they included a map) and, under the supervision of that Citizen Helper, retrace my steps, shoes on, thus reclaiming a significant opportunity to Celebrate My Preferences.

This, to me, is not America. [31]

What America is, to me, is a guy doesn't want to buy, [32] you let him not buy, you respect his not buying. A guy has a crazy notion different from your crazy notion, you pat him on the back and say hey pal, nice crazy notion, let's go have a beer. America to me should be shouting all the time, a bunch of shouting voices, most of them wrong, some of them nuts, but, please, not just one droning glamorous reasonable voice.

But do the math: a day's pay, plus train ticket, plus [33] meals, plus taxis to avoid the bleeding feet, still that is less than one thousand.

So down I went. [34]

That Citizen Helper, whose name was Rob, said he [35] was glad about my change of heart. Every time a voice shot into my ear, telling me things about myself I already knew, every time a celebrity hologram walked up like an old friend, Rob checked a box on my Infraction Correction Form and said, isn't that amazing, Mr. Petrillo, that we can do that, that we can know you so well that we can help you identify the things you want and need?

And I would say, Yes, Rob, that is amazing, sick in the [36] gut but trying to keep my mind on the five hundred bucks I was saving and on all the dance classes that would buy.

As for Teddy, as I write this it is nearly midnight and [37] he is tapping in the room above. He looks like a bird, our boy, he watches the same musical fifteen times in a row. Walking through the mall he suddenly emits a random line of dialogue and lunges off to the side, doing a dance step that resembles a stumble, spilling his drink, plowing into a group of incredulous, snickering Oneontans. He looks like no one else, acts like no one else, his clothes are increasingly like plumage, late at night he choreographs using plastic Army men, he fits no mold and has no friends, but I believe in my heart that someday something beautiful may come from him.

[QUESTIONS FOR REFLECTION]

Considering Ideas

1. How does the grandfather feel about his grandson, Teddy, in Saunders's story? Give specific details from the story to illustrate your point.

2. What are some of the obstacles that the grandfather and his grandson face as they make their way toward the Broadway show? How do the characters overcome these obstacles?

3. Compare and contrast Saunders's futuristic view of society with today's reality. Give several specific examples from the story as points for your comparison. Also, do you feel Saunders's view of the future is possible? Why or why not?

Considering the Rhetorical Star

1. What is the main *subject* of Saunders's short story? Is the specific topic engaging? Why or why not?

2. Who is the intended *audience* for the story? How do you know?

3. What is the author's main *purpose* (to inform, to interpret, to persuade, to entertain, to express feelings) for the story? Does he use a combination of purposes? How effective is his approach? Explain.

4. What is Saunders's primary writing *strategy*? What other strategies does he use? Give specific examples to illustrate your point.

5. What is the *design* of the story? Is it effective? Why or why not?

Considering Writing Strategies

1. Identify several passages in which the grandfather compares and contrasts his current situation to that of his past. What role do these passages play in the story? Explain.

2. The author includes several references to people in the story who presumably work for the government. Identify these characters and explain what purpose they serve in the story. What might Saunders be saying about the government by including them?

3. Many of Saunders's paragraphs begin with the word "and." Why do you suppose the author uses this technique? What effect does this technique have on the reader?

Writing Suggestions

1. In Saunders's story, the grandfather decides to rebel and run away from the Citizen Helper with Teddy because he probably feels that the interrogation and treatment of being written up was unjust. Write an essay comparing and contrasting the grandfather with another literary figure or with someone real, such as a politician or an activist. What do they believe in? What challenges do they face? What do they do to try to accomplish their goals?

2. What do you think the world will be like in fifty years? Will we go back to a simpler lifestyle? Will robots do everything for us? Write an essay comparing and contrasting today's world with what you imagine for the future. You might consider how you believe technology will affect transportation, lifestyle, education, work, and entertainment.

> ### ESOL Tip >
> You may want to compare advertising in the United States to advertising in your home country.

STUDENT WRITING

Kindle vs. iPad
by James Ingram, Amanda Laudato, and Daniel Volpe

If you are looking for an electronic book (e-book) reader, two of the choices available to you are the Amazon Kindle Paperwhite and the Apple iPad Mini. Both devices have a similarly sized screen (6.7" and 7.9", respectively), allow users to surf the Internet, and, most importantly, provide access to literally millions of books and periodicals. Both the iPad and Kindle offer a reasonably pleasant digital reading experience; however, they vary substantially in terms of their overall capabilities.

First, let's look at the reading capabilities of the Amazon Kindle Paperwhite. When you pick it up, it feels very light (at 7.6 ounces) and comfortable in your hands. The Kindle offers consumers the ability to download a book from virtually anywhere using its free 3G service. Once you have downloaded a book, which takes about one minute, you can read the pages in black and white or listen to the book using the text-to-speech feature. The pages look very similar to those in a paperback book, and turning the pages requires only the swipe of a finger. If you need to look up a word, the built-in dictionary is right there at your fingertips. Because the lighting is adjustable, you are able to read the Kindle outside in direct sunlight, and reading the pages for long periods of time will not strain your eyes any more than reading an actual paperback book. Even so, you might decide to move on to another activity.

If you get tired of reading the book or want to further 3 investigate a concept in the book you are reading, you might want to sample some of the other features on your Kindle. For example, you can conduct a Google search to get the information you need. Even though scrolling through the dull, black and white Web pages on the Kindle is a bit awkward, it is functional. You may also decide to shop for more books at the Amazon store. Furthermore, you can download documents from your computer and read and store up to 2 GB of books and data on the Kindle. If you run out of storage, you have the option to archive books and periodicals and retrieve them later to make room for more downloads. Finally, the battery life on the Kindle will last up to 28 hours of constant use.

Similar to the Kindle Paperwhite, the Apple iPad Mini 4 is quite nice to hold, although at 12 ounces it feels slightly heavier than the Kindle. Downloading a book from the iBooks application takes less than a minute, like the Kindle. To download a book, you need to have Wi-Fi access or a 4G data plan. When you read a book on the iPad, the full color palette really comes to life, especially in a magazine or children's book. However, the backlit screen can strain your eyes after a while, and you can barely see the screen in direct sunlight—so much for reading by the pool or on the beach. The methods for turning pages and looking up words are just as easy on the iPad as they are on the Kindle. Furthermore, like the Kindle, the iPad also has a text-to-speech feature so you can listen instead if you like. If you need to take a break from reading, the iPad, unlike the Kindle, offers a number of options.

The major differences between the Kindle and the iPad 5 are most evident when it comes to the other capabilities of the devices besides book reading. On the iPad you can search the Internet in full color using Safari. The touch screen makes navigating Web pages and shopping much easier on the iPad than on the Kindle. On the iPad you have the full range of the Internet, just as you would on a computer. But there's more! An iPad provides you access to hundreds of thousands of Web applications (apps) that are fun and functional. You can read and send e-mail, create and export documents, watch movies and television shows, play games, and listen to music. The apps give the iPad virtually limitless capabilities. Furthermore, you have 16 GB of storage (or significantly more on higher-end models) and can archive books and store documents on the Internet to save space on your iPad. While the battery lasts only about 10 hours during constant use, that is enough to get most people through an entire day before needing to plug in.

The final verdict comes down to how you want to use 6 your device. If your main goal is to have a reader that most resembles a book, then the Amazon Kindle Paperwhite is for you. The free 3G service, easy-on-the-eyes features, and ability to read outside make the Amazon Kindle the clear winner as simply an e-book reader. However, if you are looking for an all around, full-color device that is aesthetically pleasing and more versatile than just an electronic reader, then the Apple iPad is the best choice. The expanded capabilities of the iPad are virtually limitless.

[QUESTIONS FOR REFLECTION]

1. Is the essay organized using the block or point-by-point pattern? Would the essay be more or less effective if the authors had used the other approach? Explain.

2. Which parts of the essay are the most useful? Why?

3. What are some of the similarities and differences between the Kindle and the iPad?

4. Which features are better on the Kindle? Which features are better on the iPad?

5. Based on this comparison, which device would you purchase? Why?

Media Perspectives Activity:
Answers will vary.

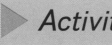 *Activity* **Media Perspectives**

In pairs or small groups, compare two magazine, newspaper, or Web-based articles from different sources that cover the same story or topic. (Another option is to use two online videos on the same topic.) Find similarities in the message, organization, intended audience, and so on between the articles or videos. A representative from each group will share a few of the highlights from the comparison with the class. This activity may give you ideas for writing a comparison and contrast essay.

Now that you have read one or more examples of comparison and contrast writing, it's time to write your own comparison and contrast. You may choose to write about one of the writing options that follow, the advertisement, the image, or one of the media suggestions. Consider your rhetorical star and the qualities of an effective comparison and contrast as you begin to compose your assignment.

Writing Assignment Options

Use one of the following topics to write a comparison and contrast essay.

1. Two musicians, actors, comedians, or sports figures
2. Two paintings, photographs, posters, or sculptures
3. Two essays, short stories, songs, poems, plays, movies, or television shows
4. Two pieces of technology, such as computers, smartphones, or MP3 players
5. Two advertisements, commercials, or infomercials
6. Two people, such as parents, siblings, friends, teachers, employers, or health care workers
7. Two buildings, monuments, or other landmarks
8. A Mac vs. a PC
9. A "then and now" comparison of an opinion, attitude, or belief that has changed
10. A "now and then" comparison of a person, place, or thing that has changed over time

Interpreting an Advertisement

As you can see from the Apple advertisement above, iPad users can open up to nine windows at a time. How might this feature be useful for making comparisons? What kinds of comparisons would you make if you were using an iPad? Does the advertisement compel you to want to purchase an iPad? Why or why not? Write an essay comparing and contrasting two tablets, smartphones, computers, or other pieces of technology. You might make a recommendation for the reader regarding which one is more useful or a better value.

Writing about an Image

Write a comparison and contrast essay that relates to one of the pictures or advertisements in this chapter. You may write about the image itself, or you may choose to write about something the image reminds you of. For example, if you write about the advertisement on page 189, you might compare and contrast two iPad applications.

Media Connection for Comparing and Contrasting

You might watch, read, and/or listen to one or more of the suggested media outlets or products to discover additional examples of comparison and contrast and/or the theme of computers and technology. Exploring various media may help you to better understand methods for comparing and contrasting. You may also choose to write about one or more of the media suggestions. For example, you might watch the news coverage of a specific topic or event on both FOX and CNN and then compare and contrast the coverage given. Or you may decide to listen to Zapp's song "Computer Love" and write an essay that compares and contrasts traditional and online dating techniques. Be sure to give credit to any sources you use in your essay.

Television	The Blacklist	The Bachelor	FOX vs. CNN	The Big Bang Theory
Film	WALL-E (2008)	Her (2013)	The Social Network (2010)	Robot & Frank (2012)
Print/E-Reading	Mother Jones	Consumer Reports	Wired	PC Magazine
Internet	amazon.com	shopper.cnet.com	gizmodo.com	pcworld.com
Music	"Nothing Compares 2 U" by Sinead O'Connor	"According to You" by Nicki Bliss	"Online" by Brad Paisley	"Computer Love" by Zapp

8.4 ANALYZING THE RHETORICAL STAR FOR WRITING A COMPARISON AND CONTRAST ESSAY

FIGURE 8.1
The Rhetorical Star

As you prepare to write your comparison and contrast paper, consider the five points of the rhetorical star (Figure 8.1). You might use some of the questions and suggestions in the chart as you conduct your rhetorical star analysis.

Subject	Although you could compare several items, it is usually best to begin with just two items for a comparison and contrast essay as you are developing your skills with this writing strategy. You may choose two items that seem similar but are different, or you may choose two items that seem drastically different but have something in common.
	Be sure that you can make a worthwhile point through your comparison. While you could compare apples and oranges, think about what the reader will gain from the comparison. If you are analyzing the nutritional value of each fruit and making a recommendation about which one provides the most health benefits, then you might be able to make it work. However, there is no need to simply point out the similarities and differences between apples and oranges without having a specific purpose in mind.
Audience	Who will read your comparison? What will interest your readers about your subject? Do they already know something about the items you are comparing? Are they reading to make a decision, such as whether to buy a PC or a Mac? Or are they just curious about your topic? Think about what kinds of details would be most appropriate for your readers.
Purpose	Think about what you are trying to accomplish through your comparison. You need to have a clear reason for making a comparison. Maybe you want to purchase a new laptop for school, and you've narrowed it down to two brands or models. Or possibly you want to determine which organization would provide you with the best career opportunities. Keep focused on your purpose as you write your comparison.
Strategy	Your main goal may be simply to explore the similarities and/or differences between two people, places, or things. However, you may decide to combine strategies. For example, you might be comparing two smartphones and evaluating which one is the better value or has the most useful features.
Design	How many points do you need to include about each item to make your comparison and contrast clear to the reader? What other design elements, such as photographs or illustrations, might enable your readers to better understand the items you are comparing? Although it wouldn't necessarily be appropriate for a school assignment, if you were creating a brochure for a product you were selling, you might use a chart or bullets to emphasize the similarities and differences between your product and the competition. That way the audience could easily discern why your product is better.

▶ Activity   Comparing and Contrasting Jobs

Research two specific jobs in your career field. Compare and contrast them according to several points and determine which one would better suit you. You might use a list or chart to help organize your thoughts. This comparison could be the basis for an essay.

8.5 APPLYING THE QUALITIES OF COMPARISON AND CONTRAST WRITING

FIGURE 8.2 The Seven Steps of the Writing Process

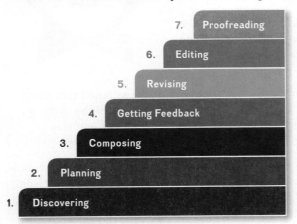

7. Proofreading
6. Editing
5. Revising
4. Getting Feedback
3. Composing
2. Planning
1. Discovering

After you have completed your rhetorical star analysis, follow the steps of the writing process (Figure 8.2) to compose your paper.

1. **Discovering:** After you have chosen your specific topic and two suitable items to compare and contrast, you might brainstorm ideas that relate to each item. You might also make a list of possible points for comparing and contrasting and then complete a freewriting exercise about the items.

2. **Planning:** Once you have decided which subjects to compare, list the similarities and/or differences between the items. Go through the list and determine which ideas would be most interesting and beneficial to your audience. You might also try making a Venn diagram to help you organize your thoughts (Figure 8.3). Draw one large circle for each main point, making sure the circles overlap in the middle. The similarities go in the center part that overlaps, and the differences go on the outside areas.

Once you have your main points worked out, you will need to create your thesis. Make sure the thesis states a significant point. Next, decide whether the block or point-by-point pattern will work best for your essay. Then create an outline using the block or point-by-point method. If you change your mind later, you can easily reorganize your essay to follow the other method.

3. **Composing:** Write a first draft of your comparison and contrast essay using the qualities outlined earlier in the chapter.

    1. Identify the elements being compared.

    2. Use the block or point-by-point method.

    3. Describe the subjects fairly and accurately.

    4. Consider using an analogy.

    5. Include transitions.

    6. End with a logical conclusion.

    As usual, don't focus on grammar and punctuation at the composing step. Instead, work on fully developing the details related to each subject you are comparing or contrasting.

4. **Getting feedback:** Have at least one classmate or other person read your rough draft and answer the peer review questions on page 194. If you have access to a writing tutor or center, get another opinion about your paper as well. If possible, ask your reviewer(s) if your overall approach (block or point-by-point) works well.

5. **Revising:** Using all of the feedback available to you, revise your comparison and contrast essay. Make sure that you have given fairly

FIGURE 8.3   Student Example of a Venn Diagram

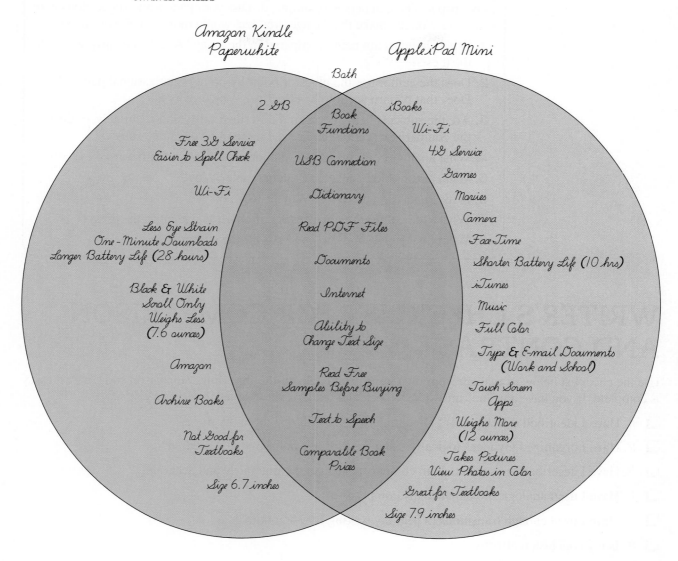

Daniel Volpe
James Ingram
Amanda Laudato

COMPARE & CONTRAST

Amazon Kindle Paperwhite

Apple iPad Mini

Both

Amazon Kindle Paperwhite:
2 GB
Free 3G Service
Easier to Spell Check
Wi-Fi
Less Eye Strain
One-Minute Downloads
Longer Battery Life (28 hours)
Black & White
Scroll Only
Weighs Less (7.6 ounces)
Amazon
Archive Books
Not Good for Textbooks
Size 6.7 inches

Both:
Book Functions
USB Connection
Dictionary
Read PDF Files
Documents
Internet
Ability to Change Text Size
Read Free Samples Before Buying
Text to Speech
Comparable Book Prices

Apple iPad Mini:
iBooks
Wi-Fi
4G Service
Games
Movies
Camera
Face Time
Shorter Battery Life (10 hrs)
iTunes
Music
Full Color
Type & E-mail Documents (Work and School)
Touch Screen
Apps
Weighs More (12 ounces)
Takes Pictures
View Photos in Color
Great for Textbooks
Size 7.9 inches

equal attention to each subject in your paper and that your points flow smoothly. Add, delete, and rearrange ideas as needed. Additionally, if you have used the block method, and encountered problems with it, you might rearrange it to see if the point-by-point method will work better for your topic. Likewise, if you have used the point-by-point method, and have noticed problems, you might reorganize it to see if the block method would work better.

6. **Editing:** Read your essay again, this time looking for errors in grammar, punctuation, and mechanics. Pay particular attention to precise diction (word choice) because the way you describe each subject as you compare and/or contrast will help to give your audience a clear picture of the similarities and differences between them.

7. **Proofreading:** After you have carefully edited your essay, read it one last time. Look for typographical errors and any other issues that might interfere with the readers' understanding of your essay.

WRITER'S CHECKLIST FOR COMPARISON AND CONTRAST

Use the checklist below to evaluate your own writing and help ensure that your comparison and contrast essay
is complete. If you have any "no" answers, go back and work on those areas if necessary.

❏ 1. Have I identified the elements I am comparing and contrasting in my thesis?

❏ 2. Have I organized my ideas logically using the block or point-by-point method?

❏ 3. Have I described the subjects I am comparing and contrasting fairly and accurately?

❏ 4. Have I used analogies to enhance my comparison?

❏ 5. Have I used enough transitions to help my writing flow smoothly?

❏ 6. Is my conclusion effective?

❏ 7. Have I proofread thoroughly?

[CHAPTER SUMMARY]

1. The comparison and contrast writing strategy focuses on the similarities and differences between subjects.

2. Comparison and contrast writing is an important part of your education, daily life, and career.

3. Interpreting readings and images that include comparisons and contrasts can help you to prepare to write
your own comparison and contrast essay.

4. Carefully analyze the rhetorical star before writing a comparison and contrast essay: subject, audience,
purpose, strategy, and design.

5. Use these qualities when writing a comparison and contrast essay: identify the elements being compared; use the block or point-by-point method; describe the subjects fairly and accurately; consider using
an analogy; include transitions; end with a logical conclusion.

[WHAT I KNOW NOW]

Use this checklist to determine what you need to work on in order to feel comfortable with your understanding of the material in this chapter. Check off each item as you master it. Review the material for any unchecked items.

❑ 1. I know what **comparison and contrast** writing is.

❑ 2. I can identify several **real-world applications** for comparison and contrast writing.

❑ 3. I can evaluate **readings and images** that reflect comparisons and contrasts.

❑ 4. I can analyze the **rhetorical star** for comparison and contrast writing.

❑ 5. I understand the **writing process** for comparison and contrast writing.

❑ 6. I can apply the **six qualities** of writing about comparisons and contrasts.

SmartBook Tip

During the "Recharge" phase, students can return to Chapter 8 and practice concepts that they need to work on.

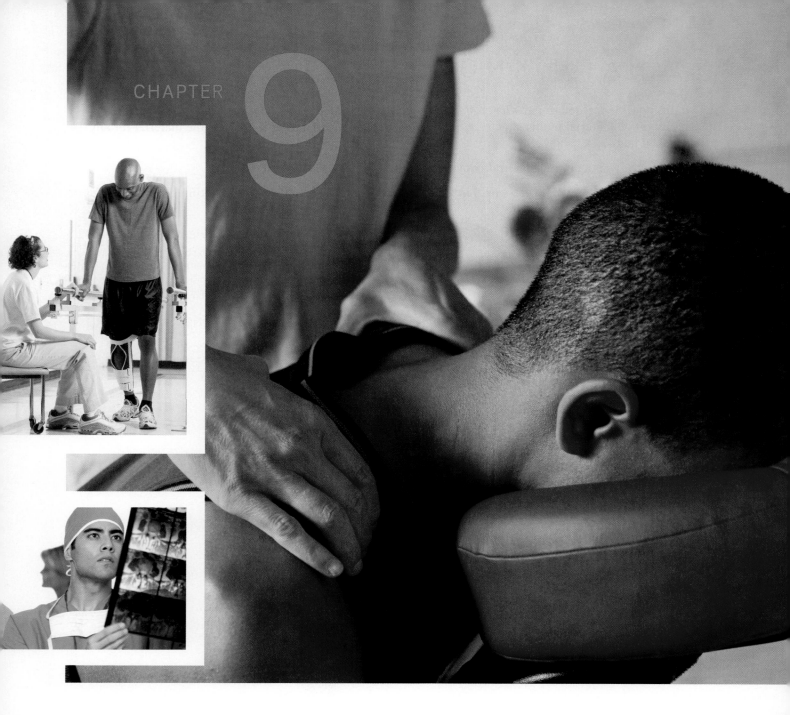

CHAPTER **9**

ANALYZING CAUSES AND EFFECTS: HEALTH AND MEDICINE

learning outcomes

In this chapter you will learn techniques for achieving these learning outcomes:

9.1 IDENTIFY REAL-WORLD APPLICATIONS FOR EXPLAINING CAUSES AND EFFECTS.

9.2 UNDERSTAND THE QUALITIES OF EFFECTIVE WRITING ABOUT CAUSES AND EFFECTS.

9.3 INTERPRET IMAGES AND READINGS ABOUT HEALTH AND MEDICINE.

9.4 ANALYZE THE RHETORICAL STAR FOR EXPLAINING CAUSES AND EFFECTS.

9.5 APPLY THE QUALITIES OF CAUSE-AND-EFFECT WRITING.

WRITING STRATEGY FOCUS: EXPLAINING CAUSES AND EFFECTS

Because human beings are so curious, we often wonder why something has occurred. Why do I feel better today than yesterday? Why is my back sore? Why did I lose (or gain) five pounds last month? Why haven't I been sleeping well? Why don't I have the complete health coverage I need? When we ask "why," we are looking for reasons (causes) that have led to a particular result (effect).

Other times we might wonder about the effects of a particular situation or event. What are the effects of that medication, massage, or physical therapy that I received? What will happen if I discontinue my treatment or try something new? Analyzing causes and effects (known as **causal analysis**) has many applications in your education, personal life, and career.

SmartBook Tip

Students receive an overview of the learning outcomes and topics in Chapter 9 in the "Preview" phase of SmartBook.

Causal analysis Analyzing reasons and results

9.1 REAL-WORLD APPLICATIONS FOR EXPLAINING CAUSES AND EFFECTS

Writing about Causes and Effects in College

You will often be asked to identify causes and effects in college courses. Your biology instructor may ask you on a test to discuss the effects of crossbreeding two species of animals. In a history course you might need to write an essay explaining the major causes for a war. A psychology teacher could ask you to research and report on causes for a particular psychological disorder or condition. In a course in your major, your instructor may require you to write a paper analyzing the cause-and-effect relationship of a particular condition, theory, or technique.

Writing about Causes and Effects in Your Daily Life

You probably face cause-and-effect situations regularly in your personal life. For example, you might wonder why you do not have as much time to study as you feel you need, why your paycheck doesn't stretch as far as it used to, or why your relationship doesn't seem to be working out right now. You can search for the causes of these problems so that you can implement changes to achieve your desired results.

Writing about Causes and Effects in Your Career

Teaching Tip

Ask students to tell how they anticipate using the cause-and-effect writing strategy in their future careers.

Being able to write about causes and effects is essential to your career. Your boss might ask you to write a feasibility study to determine if a new product, service, or procedure is going to meet your needs. You may need to write a report analyzing the possible causes for a work-related problem regarding patients, clients, or customers. Perhaps you will need to investigate the causes for decreased profits or inefficient methods. Here are some additional cause-and-effect relationships you may need to write about on the job:

Health care: causes of symptoms or conditions, effects of medications and other treatments.

Law: causes for an accident or dissolution of a marriage, effects of negligence or a violent act.

Education: causes for student achievement or failure, effects of trying a new teaching method or learning tool.

Computers: causes for computer crashes or software freezes, effects of implementing a new software program or network.

Business: causes for business growth or decline, effects of streamlined office procedures or a new marketing strategy.

Culinary arts: causes of kitchen accidents or food-borne illness, effects of using high-quality ingredients and cookware.

Massage therapy: causes for creating a peaceful ambience, effects of applying too much or too little pressure.

Graduate SPOTLIGHT

Jamie Wheeler, RN

Jamie Wheeler is a registered nurse (RN) with an **AS** degree in nursing. She currently manages patient care at a subacute rehabilitation center. Here's what Wheeler has to say about the importance of written communication in her career:

" Effective communication is often the most important link in patient care. In my job as a care plan coordinator, speaking and writing properly are essential to the patients' daily care. I am expected to devise a written plan of care for over 100 patients and keep them current on a daily basis. I must also be able to explain these plans of care in lay terms to both patients and their families. They must understand the reasons for the plans and the effects of not following them exactly. I would not be able to complete any of these tasks without a proper grasp of the English language. Another facet of my job is communicating patient status to doctors, as well as writing and carrying out orders for the patients. Something as simple as a misspelled word or improper grammar could cause a gross error in patient care and medication. In my case, writing clearly and effectively could truly help save someone's life. **"**

On your own, in pairs, or in small groups, brainstorm uses for analyzing causes and effects at school, in your daily life, and on the job. You may want to choose the prospective career field(s) of the participants in your group. Be prepared to share your results.

9.2 QUALITIES OF EFFECTIVE CAUSE-AND-EFFECT WRITING

Real-World Cause-and-Effect Writing:
Answers will vary.

1. Begin by Identifying the Cause or Effect You Are Analyzing

Start with an attention-getter that relates to your main topic. For instance, if you are writing an essay about the effects of diet and exercise, you might begin by citing statistics, telling a brief story, or asking a question such as this: "Have you ever wished that you had more energy to accomplish all of the tasks you face on a daily basis?"

Next, your thesis statement should give the readers a clear indication of the focus of your essay. For example, a thesis focused on effects might go like this: "Improving your diet and exercise habits can drastically enhance your life." Make sure that you will be able to adequately support your thesis statement in the body of your essay. For instance, you might support the previous thesis statement about health and exercise with details about feeling, performing, and looking better.

SmartBook Tip

Key concepts in Chapter 9 are highlighted for students during the "Read" phase. As students demonstrate understanding of these concepts during the "Practice" phase by responding to probes, the highlighting adapts to the individual student's learning by changing color.

2. Explain the Cause-and-Effect Relationship Convincingly

Don't assume that your readers will automatically accept the cause-and-effect relationship you suggest in your essay. You have to illustrate that the connection exists by presenting your ideas logically and fully supporting your thesis. For instance, you might describe a specific example, provide a testimonial from a credible source, explain a similar or hypothetical situation, or use documented research to back up your ideas. Also, your essay will be more convincing if you focus on major causes and effects rather than shifting to remote or minor causes and effects.

Teaching Tip

Lead a class discussion about causes and effects of a social issue that will interest students (such as the teens dropping out of high school). Emphasize that they can explore causes and effects before deciding whether to write primarily the effects of a major cause or the causes for a major effect.

3. Organize the Causes and/or Effects Effectively

There are three main patterns for organizing a cause-and-effect essay. You might focus on the effects of a major cause, the causes for a major effect, or a chain of events that illustrate the cause(s) or effect(s). When you use the major cause pattern, you begin with the cause and then focus on the effects of the cause. Conversely, when you apply the major effect pattern, you start with a major effect, and then examine the causes that led to that effect. At times you may find it appropriate to write a narrative essay to illustrate the chain of events that led to a particular effect. Use the approach that seems to best fit with your rhetorical star.

On the pages that follow are sample outlines illustrating the three different organizational patterns for a causal analysis essay.

Outline Showing the Effects of a Major Cause

Thesis: Improving your diet and exercise habits can drastically enhance your life.

  I. Feel better
   A. More restful sleep
   B. More energy
 II. Perform better
   A. Physically
   B. Mentally
III. Look better
   A. Healthier skin
   B. Less body fat
   C. Toned muscles

Outline Showing the Causes for a Major Effect

Thesis: Thousands of people regularly suffer from sleepless nights, not realizing that they might be able to minimize their problem if they identify and address some of the factors that lead to insomnia.

  I. Environmental factors
   A. Loud noises
   B. Bright lights
   C. Uncomfortable temperature
 II. Physical factors
   A. Illness
   B. Pain
   C. Drug or alcohol use
III. Psychological factors
   A. Stress
   B. Anxiety
   C. Depression
 IV. Dietary factors
   A. Too much caffeine
   B. Too many carbohydrates

Causal Chain of Events

Thesis: My mother's breast cancer was the major reason I decided to become an oncology nurse.

I. Mom diagnosed with breast cancer
   A. Bad news on November 11, 2013
   B. Family felt scared and helpless
II. Attended doctor's appointments with Mom
   A. Observed the medical staff in action
   B. Impressed with medical equipment
III. Mom survived and lives life to the fullest
   A. Mom grateful to medical staff
   B. Inspiration for joining the medical profession

4. Use Sound Logic

Be sure to avoid using logical fallacies in your causal analysis. You don't want to jump to an erroneous conclusion about a cause-and-effect relationship. For example, if someone works out every day for one week without losing weight, that doesn't mean exercise isn't an effective method for weight loss. Other factors could be present, such as diet and the intensity level of the workout.

Additionally, the fact that one event precedes another doesn't mean the first event caused the second one. For instance, if a student always drinks a diet cola and eats a candy bar before passing an exam, that doesn't mean the cola and candy were the cause of the success. A more likely cause would be that the student read the textbook, paid attention in class, and studied the material to achieve a passing test score. Double-check the claims that you make to ensure that you present a cogent cause-and-effect relationship. (See Chapter 4 for more details about logical fallacies.)

5. Conclude Effectively

As usual, it's a good idea to restate your main idea and summarize your main points in your final paragraph. When writing causal analysis, you will need to be careful not to overgeneralize in your conclusion. You are probably better off saying that a particular cause *may* lead to several effects than claiming that it *will* absolutely lead to those results. Your thesis will be more plausible if you temper your language in anticipation of potential objections to your claim. Finally, end with a memorable statement that will linger in the minds of the readers.

[preview] **ALTHOUGH MOST EMPLOYEES** try to be careful on the job, sometimes accidents occur. When that happens, companies usually require that someone write a report detailing the events surrounding the accident and the causes for the accident. The following is a real accident report filed by the Occupational Safety and Health Administration (OSHA) division of the United States Department of Labor. Have you ever experienced or witnessed an accident on the job? What were the causes? What were the effects?

Accident Report

ACCIDENT SUMMARY No. 69

Accident Type: Death due to burns
Weather Conditions: Unknown
Type of Operation: Excavating for building a road
Size of Work Crew: 2
Competent Safety Monitor on Site: No
Safety and Health Program in Effect: No
Was the Worksite Inspected Regularly: No
Training and Education Provided: No
Employee Job Title: Bulldozer Operator
Age & Sex: 44-Male
Experience at this Type of Work: 15 years
Time on Project: 2 days

BRIEF DESCRIPTION OF ACCIDENT

A bulldozer operator was preparing a road bed by using [1] the machine to lift trees out of the way. A hydraulic line to the right front hydraulic cylinder ruptured, spraying hydraulic fluid onto the engine manifold and into the operator's compartment. Upon contact with the hot manifold, the hydraulic fluid ignited, engulfing the operator in flames. The operator died from the burns he received.

INSPECTION RESULTS

Following an inspection, OSHA issued citations for two [2] serious violations of OSHA standards:

1. Frequent and regular inspections of equipment were not made by competent persons designated by the employer in accordance with 29 Code of Federal Regulations (CFR) 1926.20(b)(2). It was determined that the hydraulic hose had been installed backward so that a bend in the fitting connection made contact with the body of the bulldozer, resulting in wear and abrasion of the hose at the connection. This was not discovered during inspection of the machine.

2. The employees doing inspections were not instructed to examine the hoses for signs of wear and abrasion as required by 29 CFR 1926.21(b)(2).

ACCIDENT PREVENTION RECOMMENDATIONS

- Train maintenance and operating personnel to recognize potential problems with the operation of the machinery.

- Have competent persons perform periodic inspections of all operating equipment.
- Ensure that the employer initiates and maintains a safety and health program, in accordance with 29 CFR 1926.20(b)(1).

SOURCES OF HELP

OSHA Construction Standards [29 CFR Part 1926], which [3] include all OSHA job safety and health rules and regulations covering construction, may be purchased from the Government Printing Office, phone (202) 512-1800, fax (202) 512-2250, order number 869022-00114-1, $33.

OSHA-funded free consultation services are listed in [4] telephone directories under U.S. Labor Department or under the state government section where states administer their own OSHA programs.

OSHA Safety and Health Training Guidelines for [5] Construction, Volume III (available from the National Technical Information Service, 5285 Port Royal Road, Springfield, VA 22161; phone (703) 487-4650; Order No. PB-239-312/AS, $25) can help construction employers establish a training program.

Courses in construction safety are offered by the [6] OSHA Training Institute, 1555 Times Drive, Des Plaines, IL 60018, 847/297-4810.

OSHA regulations, documents and technical infor- [7] mation also are available on CD-ROM, which may be purchased from the Government Printing Office, phone (202) 512-1800 or fax (202) 5122250, order number 729-13-00000-5; cost $79 annually; $28 quarterly. That information also is on the Internet World Wide Web at **www.osha.gov/**.

NOTE: The case here described was selected as being [8] representative of fatalities caused by improper work practices. No special emphasis or priority is implied nor is the case necessarily a recent occurrence. The legal aspects of the incident have been resolved, and the case is now closed.

Source: United States Department of Labor (Occupational Safety and Health Administration), www.osha.gov/OshDoc/data_FatalFacts/f-facts69.html.

1. Discuss the cause-and-effect relationship in the accident report.

2. Review the design of the report, such as the list of details at the beginning and the headings throughout. Is the design effective for this type of report? Why or why not?

3. What could have been done to prevent the accident?

4. Although the details of the settlement are not included in the report, what kind of compensation do you feel the family of the victim should receive? Why?

5. Are you currently employed, or have you ever been? What precautions does your current or former company take to ensure the safety of its employees? What additional measures could the company take to be even more careful?

9.3 ANALYZING CAUSES AND EFFECTS IN THE CONTEXT OF HEALTH AND MEDICINE

Although cause-and-effect analysis has applications in virtually every career field, in this chapter you will have an opportunity to examine a few of the cause-and-effect relationships that occur in health and medicine. This theme is useful to explore whether you are going into a health-related field or not. Every human being has to deal with health-related issues at one time or another. Reading and interpreting what others have written can help you see the structure and style of a cause-and-effect analysis and to write your own causal analysis for school, work, and your daily life.

Reading and Reflection CAUSE-AND-EFFECT WRITING

[preview] **SHIRLEY VANDERBILT** is a staff writer for *Body Sense* and *Massage & Bodywork* magazines. She has written numerous articles on massage therapy, reflexology, nutrition, and other health-related issues. In the following essay, Vanderbilt examines the critical role that food plays in our overall health and explains some of the effects of an alternative medicine technique called nutritional cellular cleansing. In her article, Vanderbilt highlights a few of the main points from a book called *The 28-Day Cleansing Program: The Proven Recipe System for Skin and Digestive Repair* by Scott Ohlgren, a holistic health practitioner, and Joann Tomasulo, a whole foods expert. Before reading, consider your own eating habits. How does what you eat affect how you feel?

Food: Your Body's Natural Healer by Shirley Vanderbilt

Your body can heal itself from skin and digestive disorders, as well as a host of other maladies,[1] if you just give it a chance. What does it take?

According to Scott Ohlgren, holistic health practitioner and proponent of nutritional cellular cleansing, it's as easy as changing what goes from hand to mouth.

What's difficult, he says, is living with the diseased state your diet has created and the rounds of pharmaceuticals that never quite cure what ails you.

If you're filling your body's fuel tank with processed,[2] or even fake foods, the machinery will eventually clog up

---

[1]**Maladies** Diseases of the body.

[2]**Processed foods** Foods that have been altered from their natural states.

and break down. The symptoms that result, whether a mildly annoying acne or more life-threatening colon condition, are a reaction to this toxic overload and dysfunction. Ohlgren says the first thing you need to look at is your diet. Change to a clean, nutritional intake and you can eliminate the symptoms.

To get started on that path, Ohlgren has published, 4 along with coauthor and whole foods expert Joann Tomasulo, a user-friendly guide for nutritional cellular cleansing—*The 28-Day Cleansing Program* (Genetic Press, 2006).

At the heart of this approach is the principle of cel- 5 lular regeneration,[3] a process our bodies go through on a continual basis. Cells are constantly renewing themselves, sloughing off used-up matter and regenerating with fresh matter. The materials they use for replacement are derived directly from what you ingest. What have you been giving them to work with lately?

Unwrapping Our Habits

The evolution of our eating habits from a nutrient-rich 6 diet to processed grocery foods has led to a genetic breakdown, Ohlgren says, with each generation influencing the next. It's not likely your body will have the same fortitude and disease resistance as that of your great grandparents, or even your next-door neighbor who comes from different stock. But rather than pointing a finger at someone in the past, he says, we need to focus on personal responsibility in the present. "I am in trouble. I have these conditions. Now what are the steps I need to take in order to strengthen my genetics, my well-being, my immune system?"

Ohlgren suggests we start with "unwrapping our hab- 7 its of eating." The cleansing foods he recommends are basically what our ancestors ate—foods in a more natural state. Each has an important role in allowing the body to regenerate as nature designed and, in turn, support its innate healing power.

Get With the Program

Ohlgren's first rule of thumb for cellular cleansing is 8 to stop the body's toxic load by eliminating processed food items and replacing them with a variety of grains, beans, vegetables, nuts, and fruits, along with healthy oils, soy products, and, of course, lots of water. To maintain hydration, divide your body weight in half and drink that amount of ounces of pure water every day. Eliminating animal protein is a personal issue, depending on your level of physical activity, but dairy products are out because of their mucus-forming properties.

Next come the three Rs—remineralize, rebacterial- 9 ize, and reenzymize. Organic vegetables and sea algae grown in mineral-rich environments can provide these essential nutrients. Maintaining a healthy level of friendly bacteria is important to proper digestion and impacts other functions such as immunity and detoxification of harmful substances. Restock your gut-friendly bacteria with fermented cultured foods such as kimchi, sauerkraut, tempeh, and miso, but make sure the products are not pasteurized (a process that kills the bacteria and enzymes you need). Ohlgren's guidebook offers two hundred recipes, but as he points out, if you don't have time to cook you can still find much of what is needed at your local whole foods deli. Flexibility is the key, and he'll be the first to tell you there's no dogma in this approach.

To complement the diet, Ohlgren encourages including 10 what he calls "physical transformers" such as skin brushing, saunas, alkalinizing baths, and colon hydrotherapy. He also recommends getting a few sessions of cleansing bodywork—deep tissue, Thai massage, and acupuncture, for example—and adding a cardiovascular workout three times a week. These active supplements will support the internal and external cleansing process, aid in lymph system circulation, and revitalize your energy level.

After completing the four-week program, you can 11 go back to eating as you did before, Ohlgren says, but chances are you won't want to. The results of the cleansing program will give you cause to pause and consider the direct relationship between your food choices and your health. "It really comes down to self-empowerment," Ohlgren says. "I want to get people to pay attention to an incredibly powerful action that we do every day and have done since the first day of our life."

---

[3]**Cellular regeneration** The body's ability to restore or replace cells.

Source: S. Vanderbilt, "Food: Your Body's Natural Healer," *Body Sense,* Spring/Summer 2007, pp. 36–37.

[QUESTIONS FOR REFLECTION]

Considering Ideas

1. What health issues does the author address in her essay?

2. What suggestions does Vanderbilt offer for helping to resolve those health issues?

3. Have you ever paid attention to how you feel when you vary your diet? What effects have you noticed?

Considering the Rhetorical Star

1. What is the *subject* of the article?

2. Who is Vanderbilt's intended *audience?* How do you know?

3. What is the author's *purpose* for writing the article? Does she achieve her purpose? Why or why not?

4. In addition to cause-and-effect analysis, what other writing *strategies* does Vanderbilt use? Give specific examples from the article to illustrate your point.

5. What specific *design* features does the author use to make her writing appealing to the audience?

Considering Writing Strategies

1. Does Vanderbilt focus more on causes or effects? Which organizational pattern has she employed?

2. What techniques does the author use to try to convince the reader that the cause-and-effect relationship is valid? Is her approach effective? Why or why not?

3. Why does Vanderbilt include headings in her essay? Are they useful? Why or why not?

Writing Suggestions

1. Identify a health issue with which you are familiar. Write an essay explaining the causes or effects that relate to that issue. You might also make suggestions for the reader to follow, as Vanderbilt does in her essay.

2. Have you ever tried a trendy diet, such as South Beach or Atkins? Write an essay explaining why you tried it and/or the effects of doing so.

Reading and Reflection CAUSE-AND-EFFECT WRITING

[preview] **SUSAN BORDO** was born in Newark, New Jersey, and is a professor of philosophy and the Otis A. Singletary Chair in the Humanities at the University of Kentucky. She has written a number of works, including *The Creation of Anne Boleyn* (2014) and her best-known book, *Unbearable Weight: Feminism, Western Culture, and the Body* (2004), which was named a Notable Book by the *New York Times,* was nominated for a Pulitzer Prize, and received a Distinguished Publication Award from the Association for Women in Psychology. To learn more about Susan Bordo and see a complete list of her works go to **www.cddc.vt.edu/feminism/bordo.html**. In the following essay, Bordo looks at how the Western media portray women and how this is affecting various cultures across the globe. Before reading, think about how you feel about your own body image. How does the media affect your self-concept about your appearance?

The Globalization of Eating Disorders **by Susan Bordo**

The young girl stands in front of the mirror. Never fat 1 to begin with, she's been on a no-fat diet for a couple of weeks and has reached her goal weight: 115 lb., at 5'4— exactly what she should weigh, according to her doctor's chart. But in her eyes she still looks dumpy. She can't shake her mind free of the "Lady Marmelade" video from *Moulin Rouge.* Christina Aguilera, Pink, L'il Kim, and Mya, each one perfect in her own way: every curve smooth and sleek, lean-sexy, nothing to spare. Self-hatred and shame start to burn in the girl, and envy tears at her stomach, enough to make her sick. She'll never look like them, no matter how much weight she loses. Look at that stomach of hers, see how it sticks out? Those thighs— they actually jiggle. Her butt is monstrous. She's fat, gross, a dough girl.

As you read the imaginary scenario above, whom did 2 you picture standing in front of the mirror? If your images of girls with eating and body image problems have been shaped by *People* magazine and Lifetime movies, she's probably white, North American, and economically secure. A child whose parents have never had to worry about putting food on the family table. A girl with money to spare for fashion magazines and trendy clothing, probably college-bound. If you're familiar with the classic psychological literature on eating disorders, you may also have read that she's an extreme "perfectionist" with a hyper-demanding mother, and that she suffers from "body-image distortion syndrome" and other severe perceptual and cognitive problems that "normal" girls don't share. You probably don't picture her as Black, Asian, or Latina.

Read the description again, but this time imagine 3 twenty-something Tenisha Williamson standing in front of the mirror. Tenisha is black, suffers from anorexia, and feels like a traitor to her race. "From an African-American standpoint," she writes, "we as a people are encouraged to embrace our big, voluptuous bodies. This makes me feel terrible because I don't want a big, voluptuous body! I don't ever want to be fat–ever, and I don't ever want to gain weight. I would rather die from starvation than gain a single pound."[1] Tenisha is no longer an anomaly. Eating and body image problems are now not only crossing racial and class lines, but gender lines. They have also become a global phenomenon.

Fiji is a striking example. Because of their remote location, the Fiji islands did not have access to television until 1995, when a single station was introduced. It broadcasts programs from the United States, Great Britain, and Australia. Until that time, Fiji had no reported cases of eating disorders, and a study conducted by anthropologist Anne Becker showed that most Fijian girls and women, no matter how large, were comfortable with their bodies. In 1998, just three years after the station began broadcasting, 11 percent of girls reported vomiting to control weight, and 62 percent of the girls surveyed reported dieting during the previous months.[2]

Becker was surprised by the change; she had thought that Fijian cultural traditions, which celebrate eating and favor voluptuous bodies, would "withstand" the influence of media images. Becker hadn't yet understood that we live in an empire of images, and that there are no protective borders.

In Central Africa, for example, traditional cultures still celebrate voluptuous women. In some regions, brides are sent to fattening farms, to be plumped and massaged into shape for their wedding night. In a country plagued by AIDS, the skinny body has meant–as it used to among Italian, Jewish, and Black Americans–poverty, sickness, death. "An African girl must have hips," says dress designer Frank Osodi. "We have hips. We have bums. We like flesh in Africa." For years, Nigeria sent its local version of beautiful to the Miss World Competition. The contestants did very poorly. Then a savvy entrepreneur went against local ideals and entered Agbani Darego, a light-skinned, hyper-skinny beauty. (He got his inspiration from M-Net, the South African network seen across Africa on satellite television, which broadcasts mostly American movies and television shows.) Agbani Darego won the Miss World Pageant, the first Black African to do so. Now, Nigerian teenagers fast and exercise, trying to become "lepa"–a popular slang phrase for the thin "it" girls that are all the rage. Said one: "People have realized that slim is beautiful."[3]

How can mere images be so powerful? For one thing, they are never "just pictures," as the fashion magazines continually maintain (disingenuously) in their own defense. They speak to young people not just about how to be beautiful but also about how to become what the dominant culture admires, values, rewards. They tell them how to be cool, "get it together," overcome their shame. To girls who have been abused they may offer a fantasy of control and invulnerability, immunity from pain and hurt. For racial and ethnic groups whose bodies have been deemed "foreign," earthy, and primitive, and considered unattractive by Anglo-Saxon norms, they may cast the lure of being accepted as "normal" by the dominant culture.

In today's world, it is through images–much more than parents, teachers, or clergy–that we are taught how to be. And it is images, too, that teach us how to see, that educate our vision in what's a defect and what is normal, that give us the models against which our own bodies and the bodies of others are measured. Perceptual pedagogy: "How To Interpret Your Body 101." It's become a global requirement.

I was intrigued, for example, when my articles on eating disorders began to be translated, over the past few years, into Japanese and Chinese. Among the members of audiences at my talks, Asian women had been among the most insistent that eating and body image weren't problems for their people, and indeed, my initial research showed that eating disorders were virtually unknown in Asia. But when, this year, a Korean translation of *Unbearable Weight* was published, I felt I needed to revisit the situation. I discovered multiple reports on dramatic increases in eating disorders in China, South Korea, and Japan. "As many Asian countries become Westernized and infused with the Western aesthetic of a tall, thin, lean body, a virtual tsunami of eating disorders has swamped Asian countries," writes Eunice Park in *Asian Week* magazine. Older people can still remember when it was very different. In China, for example, where revolutionary ideals once condemned any focus on appearance and there have been several disastrous famines, "little fatty" was a term of endearment for children. Now, with fast food on every corner, childhood obesity is on the rise, and the cultural meaning of fat and thin has changed. "When I was young," says Li Xiaojing, who manages a fitness center in Beijing, "people admired and were even jealous of fat people since they thought they had a better life. . . . But now, most of us see a fat person and think 'He looks awful.'"[4]

Clearly, body insecurity can be exported, imported, and marketed–just like any other profitable commodity. In this respect, what's happened with men and boys is illustrative. Ten years ago men tended, if anything, to see themselves as better looking than they (perhaps) actually

[1] From the Colours of Ana website (http://coloursofana.com/ss8.asp). [This and subsequent notes in the selection are the author's.]

[2] Reported in Nancy Snyderman, *The Girl in the Mirror* (New York: Hyperion, 2002), p. 84.

[3] Norimitsu Onishi, "Globalization of Beauty Makes Slimness Trendy," *The New York Times*, Oct. 3, 2002.

[4] Reported in Elizabeth Rosenthal, "Beijing Journal: China's Chic Waistline: Convex to Concave," *The New York Times*, Dec. 9, 1999.

were. And then (as I chronicle in detail in my book *The Male Body*) the menswear manufacturers, the diet industries, and the plastic surgeons "discovered" the male body. And now, young guys are looking in their mirrors, finding themselves soft and ill defined, no matter how muscular they are. Now they are developing the eating and body image disorders that we once thought only girls had. Now they are abusing steroids, measuring their own muscularity against the oiled and perfected images of professional athletes, body-builders, and *Men's Health* models. Now the industries in body-enhancement—cosmetic surgeons, manufacturers of anti-aging creams, spas and salons—are making huge bucks off men, too.

What is to be done? I have no easy answers. But I do know that we need to acknowledge, finally and decisively, that we are dealing here with a cultural problem. If eating disorders were biochemical, as some claim, how can we account for their gradual "spread" across race, gender, and nationality? And with mass media culture increasingly providing the dominant "public education" in our children's lives—and those of children around the globe—how can we blame families? Families matter, of course, and so do racial and ethnic traditions. But families exist in cultural time and space—and so do racial groups. In the empire of images, no one lives in a bubble of self-generated "dysfunction" or permanent immunity. The sooner we recognize that—and start paying attention to the culture around us and what it is teaching our children—the sooner we can begin developing some strategies for change.

11

Source: Susan Bordo, "The Globalization of Eating Disorders." Copyright © Susan Bordo, Otis A. Singletary Professor of the Humanities, University of Kentucky. Reprinted by permission of the author.

[QUESTIONS FOR REFLECTION]

Considering Ideas

1. According to Bordo, what factors contribute to the body image problem that some people, especially young women, face? Are these reasons feasible? Why or why not?

2. What comparison does the author make in paragraph 10? Is this a valid comparison? Why or why not?

3. In the concluding paragraph, the writer suggests that eating disorders are a cultural problem. Do you agree or disagree with her claim? Explain your answer.

Considering the Rhetorical Star

1. What is the *subject* of Bordo's essay?

2. Is the intended *audience* limited to people with eating disorders, or would others be interested as well? Explain.

3. What is the author's *purpose* for writing the essay? Does she achieve her purpose? Why or why not?

4. In addition to cause-and-effect analysis, what other writing *strategies* does Bordo use? Give specific examples from the essay to illustrate your point.

5. Does the *design* of the essay seem better suited to academic writing or magazine writing? Explain.

Considering Writing Strategies

1. What type of attention-getter does Bordo use? What purpose does it serve? How effective is the introductory paragraph of the essay?

2. Does the author focus more on the causes or effects of eating disorders? What specific examples does she use to support her position?

3. Although most of the essay is written from the third person point of view, the author occasionally shifts to the first and second person points of view. Identify passages where these shifts occur. Why does she change points of view in those areas? What effect do the shifts have on the reader?

Writing Suggestions

1. Write an essay focusing on the effects of young Americans' obsession with their appearance. You might consider how having a distorted body image will affect them at school, on the job, and in their personal lives.

2. Have you ever known someone with an eating disorder or other psychological condition, such as panic attacks, schizophrenia, or obsessive compulsive disorder? Write an essay explaining the causes or effects of the disorder. Include details about the person you know to provide support for your main points. You may want to use a different name to protect the person's identity. Be sure to cite any resources you use in your paper.

ESOL Tip >

Instead of focusing on American culture, write about how people from your culture perceive body image.

[preview] **ROB SHEFFIELD** is a journalist and a contributing editor at *Rolling Stone* magazine. In the following essay, Sheffield explores some of the causes and effects related to the use of Ambien, a common sleeping pill. Many people take sleeping pills without suffering any consequences, other than feeling a little groggy in the morning. However, some people are not so fortunate. For them, the drug becomes a habit or an addiction. To learn more about the causes and effects of sleeping pill addictions, go to www.wrongdiagnosis.com/s/ **sleeping_pill_addiction/intro.htm#whatis**. Before reading, think about your own sleeping habits. Have you used sleep aids to help you get a restful night of sleep? What were the results?

Welcome to the United States of Ambien by Rob Sheffield

Ambien has been around since 1993, but only now has it reached its cultural saturation point. Like Ecstasy in 1989 or LSD in 1969, it's the drug that unlocks the fantasy of the moment, which for the owners of 27 million prescriptions means pulling a pillow over their heads. Eminem just did an album about getting hooked on it. Coldplay write their songs on it. It has inspired untold hours of binge-eating and Halo-playing, not to mention years of U.S. foreign policy. ("Everybody here uses Ambien," Colin Powell told a reporter in 2003.) If you stay awake past the 15-minute window when it's supposed to zonk you out, you will end up writing nightmarishly bad poetry and sexting your roommate's exes.

Every night, you can practically smell the Ambien fog settling over a nation of Zolpidem[1] zombies. You can see it in your friends, when they start Twittering in those dangerous late-night hours, when the Ambien has gone down but they haven't fallen asleep yet. You can read it in the after-midnight Facebook status updates along the lines of "Speak to cheese arm steak of united face." It inspires sleep-eating, sleep-driving, sleep-shopping, sleep-blogging. Ambien gives you the hallucinatory urge to indulge your most moronic whims—in other words, it turns you into the pitiful jerk you already are. That's the danger of this drug: The side effect is you.

Insomniacs used to get prescribed sedatives like Tuinal, Valium, Seconal, even Thorazine or lithium, just for their meagerly soporific side effects, which is like sticking your head in the microwave for an earache. But Ambien takes a sharpshooter approach, targeting brain receptors to promote gamma-aminobutyric acid—if other sleep aids were Keith Moon,[2] Ambien was Charlie Watts,[3] getting the job done with ruthless efficiency. So it appeals to casual users who have no idea how to handle its heavy hypnotic effect, which means deep sleep for insomniacs, and cheap laughs for the rest of us.

The Ambien alibi, like Ambien amnesia, is part of the lure. There's something about this moment people are eager not to remember, and the empty Doritos Collisions bags on the floor can always be blamed on the drugs, if not forgotten entirely. No wonder it's become America's drug. It's the drug that turns America into America. So what's in the fridge?

Source: R. Sheffield, "Welcome to the United States of Ambien," *Rolling Stone,* June 11, 2009, p. 91.

---

[1]**Zolpidem** A brand name of the Ambien drug.
[2]**Keith Moon** An English drummer for the rock group The Who.
[3]**Charlie Watts** An English drummer for the rock group The Rolling Stones.

[QUESTIONS FOR REFLECTION]

Considering Ideas

1. The author suggests that sleeping pill use is a widespread practice. Do you agree or disagree with this suggestion?

2. What message about sleeping pills is the writer trying to convey to the reader? Is he successful? Why or why not?

3. Have you (or has someone you know) ever tried sleeping pills? Were they helpful? Why or why not?

Considering the Rhetorical Star

1. What is the *subject* of Sheffield's essay?

2. Is the intended *audience* limited to people who have taken sleeping pills, or would others be interested as well? Explain.

3. What is the author's *purpose* for writing the article? Does he achieve his purpose? Why or why not?

4. In addition to cause-and-effect analysis, what other writing *strategies* does Sheffield use? Give specific examples from the article to illustrate your point.

5. Does the *design* of the article seem better suited to academic writing or magazine writing? Explain.

Considering Writing Strategies

1. Does the essay focus more on causes or effects? Explain.

2. Are the ideas organized clearly? Why or why not?

3. Read the conclusion. Is it an effective way to end the essay? Why or why not?

Writing Suggestions

1. Have you ever written a late night e-mail message or social networking post that you regretted? What prompted (caused) you to write it? What were the consequences (effects)? Write an essay about the experience.

2. Have you (or has someone you know) ever had a bad experience with drugs or alcohol? Write an essay focusing on the effects of the event. You may decide to use the causal chain organizational pattern.

Reading and Reflection CAUSE-AND-EFFECT WRITING

[preview] **CHARLES "CHUCK" CORBIN** is a professor in the Department of Exercise Science and Physical Education at Arizona State University and holds a PhD from the University of New Mexico. Corbin has co-authored more than thirty books, published hundreds of papers, and developed dozens of physical activity videos and computer software packages. The excerpt that follows is from a textbook titled *Concepts in Fitness and Wellness: A Comprehensive Lifestyle Approach,* which Chuck Corbin co-authored with Gregory J. Welk, William R. Corbin, and Karen A. Welk. To learn more about the U.S. government's dietary guidelines, visit **www.health.gov/dietaryguidelines/**. Before reading, consider your own views about carbohydrates. Are carbs a big part of your diet, or do you try to limit your intake of them?

Dietary Recommendations for Carbohydrates by Charles B. Corbin

Complex carbohydrates should be the principal source [1] **of calories in the diet.** Carbohydrates have gotten a bad rap in recent years due to the hype associated with low-carbohydrate diets. Carbohydrates have been unfairly implicated as a cause of obesity. The suggestion that they cause insulin to be released and that insulin, in turn, causes the body to take up and store excess energy as fat is overly simplistic and doesn't take into account differences in types of carbohydrates. Simple sugars (such as sucrose, glucose, and fructose) found in candy and soda lead to quick increases in blood sugar and tend to promote fat deposition. Complex carbohydrates (e.g., bread, pasta, rice), on the other hand, are broken down more slowly and do not cause the same effect on blood sugar. They contribute valuable nutrients and fiber in the diet and should constitute the bulk of a person's diet. Lumping simple and complex carbohydrates together is not appropriate, since they are processed differently and have different nutrient values.

A number of low-carb diet books have used an [2] index known as the glycemic index (GI) as the basis for determining if foods are appropriate in the diet. Foods with a high GI value produce rapid increases in blood sugar, while foods with a low GI value produce slower increases. While this seems to be a logical way to categorize carbohydrates, it is misleading, since it doesn't account for the amount of carbohydrates in different servings of a food. A more appropriate indicator of the effect of foods on blood sugar levels is called the glycemic load. Carrots, for example, are known to have a very high GI value, but the overall glycemic load is quite low. The carbohydrates from most fruits and vegetables exhibit similar properties.

Despite the intuitive and logical appeal of this classi- [3] fication system, neither the glycemic index nor glycemic load has been consistently associated with body weight. Evidence also indicates no difference on weight loss between high glycemic index and low glycemic index diets.

There is some evidence linking glycemic load to a higher risk for diabetes but no associations with cancer risk.

Additional research is needed, but excess sugar consumption appears to be problematic only if caloric intake is larger than caloric expenditure. Carbohydrates are the body's preferred form of energy for physical activity, and the body is well equipped for processing extra carbohydrates. Athletes and other active individuals typically have no difficulty burning off extra energy from carbohydrates. Sugar consumption, among people with an adequate diet, is also not associated with major chronic diseases.

Reducing dietary sugar can help reduce risk of obesity and heart disease. Although sugar consumption has not been viewed as harmful, people who consume high amounts of sugar also tend to consume excess calories. The new dietary guidelines clearly recommend decreasing consumption of added sugars to reduce risk of excess calorie consumption and weight gain. The American Heart Association also endorsed this position in a scientific statement entitled "Dietary Sugars Intake and Cardiovascular Health."

The document notes that excessive consumption of sugars (sugars added to foods and drinks) contributes to overconsumption of discretionary calories. Among Americans, the current average daily sugars consumption is 355 calories per day (22.2 teaspoons) as opposed to 279 calories in 1970. Soft drinks and sugar-sweetened beverages are the primary sources of added sugars in the American diet. The AHA's scientific statement recommends no more than 100 calories of added sugars for most women and not more than 150 calories for most men. A typical 12-ounce sweetened soft drink contains 150 calories, mostly sugar. Reducing consumption of sugar-sweetened beverages is a simple, but important, diet modification.

Increasing consumption of dietary fiber is important for overall good nutrition and health. Diets high in complex carbohydrates and fiber are associated with a low incidence of coronary heart disease, stroke, and some forms of cancer. Long-term studies indicate that high-fiber diets may also be associated with a lower risk for diabetes mellitus, diverticulosis, hypertension, and gallstone formation. It is not known whether these health benefits are directly attributable to high dietary fiber or other effects associated with the ingestion of vegetables, fruits, and cereals.

A position statement from the American Dietetics Association summarizes the health benefits and importance of fiber in a healthy diet. It indicates that high-fiber diets provide bulk, are more satiating, and are linked to lower body weights. It also points out that a fiber-rich diet often has a lower fat content, is larger in volume, and is richer in micronutrients, all of which have beneficial health effects. Evidence for health benefits has become strong enough that the FDA has stated that specific beneficial health claims can be made for specific dietary fibers. The National Cholesterol Education Program also recommends dietary fiber as part of overall strategies for treating high cholesterol in adults.

In the past, clear distinctions were made between soluble fiber and insoluble fiber because they appeared to provide separate effects. Soluble fiber (typically found in fruits and oat bran) was more frequently associated with improving blood lipid profiles, while insoluble fiber (typically found in grains) was mainly thought to help speed up digestion and reduce risks for colon and rectal cancer. Difficulties in measuring these compounds in typical mixed diets led a National Academy of Sciences panel to recommend eliminating distinctions between soluble and insoluble fibers and instead to use a broader definition of fiber.

Currently, few Americans consume the recommended amounts of dietary fiber. The average intake of dietary fiber is about 15 g/day, which is much lower than the recommended 25 to 35 g/day. Foods in the typical American

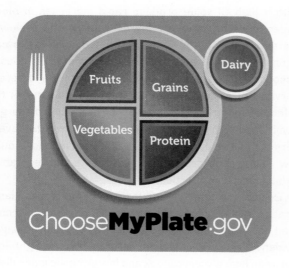

diet contain little, if any, dietary fiber, and servings of commonly consumed grains, fruits, and vegetables contain only 1 to 3 g of dietary fiber. Therefore, individuals have to look for ways to ensure that they get sufficient fiber in their diet. Manufacturers are allowed to declare a food as a "good source of fiber" if it contains 10 percent of the recommended amount (2.5 g/serving) and an "excellent source of fiber" if it contains 20 percent of the recommended amount (5 g/serving). Because fiber has known health benefits, the new dietary guidelines encourage consumers to select foods high in dietary fiber, such as whole-grain breads and cereals, legumes, vegetables, and fruit, whenever possible.

Fruits and vegetables are essential for good health. 11 Fruits and vegetables are a valuable source of dietary fiber, are packed with vitamins and minerals, and contain many additional phytochemicals, which may have beneficial effects on health. The International Agency of Research on Cancer (IARC), an affiliate of the World Health Organization, did a comprehensive review on the links between dietary intake of fruits and vegetables and cancer. It concluded that both human studies and animal experimental studies "indicate that a higher intake of fruits and vegetables is associated with a lower risk of various types of cancer." The clearest evidence of a cancer-protective effect from eating more fruits is for stomach, lung, and esophageal cancers. A higher intake of vegetables is also associated with reduced risks for cancers of the esophagus and colon-rectum. This evidence—plus the evidence of the beneficial effects of fruits and vegetables on other major diseases, such as heart disease—indicates that individuals should strive to increase their intake of these foods. Reports from the 2010 Dietary Guidelines Advisory Committee indicate that beneficial effects on health appear to be linked to a minimum of five servings of fruits and vegetables per day. Additional benefits were noted at even higher consumption levels. These findings contributed to the increased emphasis being placed on a plant-based diet in the new dietary guidelines.

Dietary Recommendations for Carbohydrates" by Charles B. Corbin from Concepts of Fitness and Wellness: A Comprehensive Lifestyle Approach, 10e pp. 327–328, published by McGraw-Hill.

[QUESTIONS FOR REFLECTION]

Considering Ideas

1. What is Corbin's view about carbohydrates? Is his view consistent with other recent literature on the subject? Explain.

2. What are the effects of reducing added dietary sugar? Explain.

3. According to Corbin, what are some of the benefits of eating fruits and vegetables? Give several specific examples.

Considering the Rhetorical Star

1. What is the *subject* of Corbin's text and why is it relevant?

2. Who is the intended primary *audience* for the piece? How do you know? Who might be a secondary audience for the work?

3. What is the *purpose* of the excerpt? Does the author achieve his purpose? Why or why not?

4. In addition to analyzing causes and effects, what other writing *strategies* does Corbin use? Give several specific examples.

5. What is the *design* of the work? Is it effective? Why or why not?

Considering Writing Strategies

1. How would you characterize the tone of the excerpt? Is it more formal or informal? Explain.

2. How are Corbin's ideas organized? Is this organizational strategy effective? Why or why not?

3. Corbin cites numerous sources to support his views on carbohydrates. What effect does this technique have on the reader?

Writing Suggestions

1. What are some of the reasons people change their eating habits? Write an essay focusing on several different causes for modifying one's diet. If you use outside research, be sure to cite your sources.

2. Have you tried modifying your diet for health reasons? Were you successful? If so, were the results lasting? Were you unsuccessful? If so, why didn't the diet work for you? Write a cause-and-effect essay about your experience with dieting.

[preview] **WILLIAM SHAKESPEARE** (1564–1616) was born in Stratford-upon-Avon, England. Known as "the bard" (storyteller), Shakespeare is considered by many to be the greatest writer in the English language or possibly even the world. His works, which consist of 38 plays, 154 sonnets, and several other poems, have been translated into every major living language. In addition to being a writer, Shakespeare was an actor, producer, and part owner in the Lord Chamberlain's Men playing company. Many of his plays, such as *Romeo and Juliet, Hamlet, Othello,* and *Macbeth,* were presented in the famous Globe Theatre in Southwark, England. Visit **www.shakespeare.org.uk/home.html** to learn more about Shakespeare's life and works. In the sonnet that follows, the speaker in the poem tells how he feels about his love. Before reading, consider these questions: Have you ever been in love? How did it make you feel? Did the feelings last, or did something cause a change of heart?

Sonnet 147: My Love Is As a Fever Longing Still by William Shakespeare

My love is as a fever longing still,
For that which longer nurseth the disease;
Feeding on that which doth preserve the ill,
The uncertain sickly appetite to please.
My reason, the physician to my love,
Angry that his prescriptions are not kept,
Hath left me, and I desperate now approve

Desire is death, which physic did except.
Past cure I am, now Reason is past care,
And frantic-mad with evermore unrest;
My thoughts and my discourse as madmen's are,
At random from the truth vainly express'd;
For I have sworn thee fair, and thought thee bright,
Who art as black as hell, as dark as night.

[QUESTIONS FOR REFLECTION]

Considering Ideas

1. Which words in the poem does Shakespeare borrow from the medical field? Why do you think he has chosen those words? What effect do they have on the reader?

2. How does the speaker in the sonnet feel about his love? What causes him to feel that way?

3. What message is Shakespeare trying to convey to the reader? Explain.

Considering the Rhetorical Star

1. What is the *subject* of the sonnet?

2. What kind of *audience* might Shakespeare have had in mind as he wrote the poem?

3. What is the author's *purpose* for writing the poem? Does he achieve his purpose? Why or why not?

4. In addition to cause-and-effect analysis, which other writing *strategies* does Shakespeare use? Give specific examples from the poem.

5. What specific *design* features does Shakespeare use to add interest to his poem?

Considering Writing Strategies

1. Which lines create the most vivid images for the reader? What do you envision?

2. Notice Shakespeare's use of rhythm and rhyme in the sonnet. What effect do these elements of poetry have on the reader?

3. What is the tone or mood of the sonnet? Which specific words emphasize this tone?

Writing Suggestions

1. Have you ever been in love? What effect did that feeling have on you? Write an essay explaining your reasons for falling in love with someone or the effects that falling in love had on you.

2. Have you ever had a romantic relationship not work out? Write an essay explaining what led to the demise of your relationship or how the break-up has affected you (positively or negatively).

STUDENT WRITING

Get Fit with Wii
by Olivia Covey

For busy students, parents, and professionals, trying to fit in a workout in the middle of a hectic day can be difficult. Luckily, Nintendo Wii has come up with a great way for people to get fit and lose inches off their waistlines in the comfort of their own homes. *Wii Fit* is an interactive game designed to help people of all ages and skill levels target specific areas they need to improve by following an individual fitness routine. Exercising with *Wii Fit* will provide gamers with a fun, convenient, and personalized regimen for getting in shape and losing weight.

Wii Fit has become popular in the health and fitness world because it has turned the traditional boring fitness routine into a fun and relaxing game for people of all ages. The game is broken down into various stimulating activities that are geared toward different experience levels. One example is an activity called the "hula hoop," which requires the user to balance on the balance board included with the game, while virtually hula hooping. This simple but stimulating activity provides a great aerobic workout. During a workout, the human body releases a hormone called endorphins. Endorphins are neurotransmitters found in the brain that have been linked to psychological feelings of pleasure. The combination of the natural release of these endorphins and the assortment of fun and challenging activities give the user the ultimate workout experience.

With the vast amount of technology available today, some people may find the idea of having a video game help them with fitness to be too difficult. On the contrary, not only is *Wii Fit* easy to use, it is extremely convenient. *Wii Fit* gives flexible options for the intensity of each session. It also provides interactive feedback and step-by-step instructions on how to do each activity, making it simple for anyone to pick up a controller and get moving. With this technology, people can exercise in their own living rooms anytime they need to without having to make a trip to the gym. The convenience of the *Wii Fit* increases the probability of commitment to a fitness regimen, resulting in a healthier, happier person.

Finally, owning a *Wii Fit* system is like having a personal trainer at home. The system has great features including a program that allows gamers to input information about specific foods they consume through the day to get an estimated calorie intake number. The *Wii Fit* program then takes this number and matches it with an activity with a corresponding MET level. An MET level simply represents the intensity of an activity. For example, if someone is planning to attend a birthday party later in the day, he or she can add a piece of birthday cake to the calorie calculator. The program then comes up with an estimated calorie number for that cake and matches it with activities to burn those calories right off. *Wii Fit* is also great for targeting specific areas of the body. For instance, if someone is particularly concerned with toning mostly the buns and thighs, the *Wii Fit* program can design a series of activities to focus on those specific areas. The *Wii Fit* program then combines and tracks this information on a progress calendar that helps the individual to see goals that have been accomplished and areas in need of improvement. After working out with the *Wii Fit* system for just a few weeks, participants will start to see results.

In closing, exercising with a *Wii Fit* is one of the 5 most innovative ways to get in shape and lose unwanted pounds. It is fun and has a variety of activities to choose from, so players will never get bored doing the same routine over and over again. Furthermore, it is convenient and flexible, providing a variety of activities and instant feedback for everyone from beginners to people who work out regularly. Most importantly, *Wii Fit* is ideal because it is completely personalized. It utilizes a variety of programs to help participants set and achieve specific fitness and weight loss goals. With strong willpower and the help of *Wii Fit*, many gamers can achieve their desired workout results.

[QUESTIONS FOR REFLECTION]

1. Identify Covey's thesis statement. Is it effective? Why or why not?

2. According to the author, what are the effects of using *Wii Fit*? What do you suppose are the causes for someone wanting to use *Wii Fit*?

3. What three reasons does the author give for using a *Wii Fit* program?

4. Are the author's reasons convincing? Why or why not?

5. Have you ever tried using the *Wii Fit* program? How does your experience compare to the ideas in Covey's essay?

▶ *Activity*   **Cause-and-Effect Chart**

Sometimes you may find it challenging to decide whether to write about the causes or effects for a particular subject. If that's the case, creating a chart can help you to make a choice.

Make a chart of causes and effects for one of the following topics (or the topic about which you are going to write an essay). Draw a line down the center of the page and list causes on the left side and effects on the right side.

Dropping out of school	Enrolling in college
Choosing the right career	Beginning a new job
Good or poor self-concept	Exercising more or less
Peer pressure	Gaining or losing weight
Drug use	Alcohol use or abuse

Be prepared to share a few of the highlights with the class. This activity may give you ideas for writing a cause-and-effect essay.

Cause-and-Effect Chart Activity:

Answers will vary.

Now that you have read one or more examples of cause-and-effect writing, it's time to write your own causal analysis. You may choose to write about one of the writing options that follow, the advertisement, the image, or one of the media suggestions. Consider your rhetorical star and the qualities of an effective narrative as you begin to compose your assignment.

Writing Assignment Options

Use one of the following topics to write an essay that emphasizes causes, effects, or both.

1. A decision that has changed the direction of someone's life
2. A person, place, object, or experience that is special
3. A contest, sporting event, or hobby
4. Being on a team or in a club or other organization
5. A mistake that someone you know has made
6. The responsibilities of a new job
7. Gaining or losing a family member or friend
8. A law, policy, or ruling that affects people positively or negatively
9. A fortunate (or an unfortunate) experience, event, or diagnosis
10. Peer pressure to do something bad (or good)

Interpreting an Advertisement

Who is the audience for the advertisement? The image and words in the ad suggest that one's fitness depends on purchasing a *Wii Fit* game and balance board. Is the cause-and-effect relationship logical? Why or why not? Is the advertisement persuasive? Why or why not? Write a cause-and-effect essay related to the *Wii Fit* game or another exercise video game. For this assignment, focus primarily on the effects of the game on its users.

Writing about an Image

Write a cause-and-effect essay that relates to one of the images in this chapter. You may write about the image itself, or you may choose to write about something the image reminds you of. For example, you might write a creative essay about the scenes from *Grey's Anatomy* or *The Doctors* shown above. Or you might write about the photograph of the man on the motorcycle on page 217 using the causal chain pattern to explain the events that led to his broken arm and leg.

Media Connection for Explaining Causes and Effects

You might watch, read, and/or listen to one or more of the suggested media to discover additional examples of cause/effect analysis. Exploring various media may help you to better understand methods for explaining causes and effects. You may also choose to write about one or more of the media suggestions. For example, you might watch an episode of *Grey's Anatomy* and write an essay explaining the causes or effects for a situation that occurs on the show. Be sure to give credit to any sources you use in your essay.

Television	*The Human Body* on Discovery	*Grey's Anatomy*	*The Mindy Project*	*The Doctors*
Film	*Sicko* (2007)	*Supersize Me* (2004)	*Nova: Dying to Be Thin* (2000) (view at **www.pbs.org/wgbh/nova/thin**)	*Side Effects* (2013)
Print/ E-Reading	*Fitness*	*Women's Health*	*Men's Health*	*Natural Health*
Internet	**webmd.com**	**howhealthworks.com**	**goddessofgreens .blogspot.com**	**everydayhealth.com**
Music	"A Bad Cold" by Hal Shows	"Panic on the Streets of Health Care City" by Thursday	"Alcohol" by Brad Paisley	"The A-Team" by Ed Sheeran

9.4 ANALYZING THE RHETORICAL STAR FOR WRITING A CAUSE-AND-EFFECT ESSAY

As you prepare to write your cause-and-effect essay, consider the five points of the rhetorical star (Figure 9.1). You might use some of the questions in the chart as you conduct your rhetorical star analysis.

FIGURE 9.1
The Rhetorical Star

Subject	Be sure to select a topic that is narrow enough to adequately cover within the parameters of your assignment. If you are writing a longer essay or research paper, then you may be able to cover both causes and effects. However, you will probably want to focus on causes or effects (not both) for a shorter paper. For instance, while you could reasonably focus on the causes or effects of staying fit, you probably wouldn't be able to cover the entire history of fitness in America effectively in a brief paper.
Audience	Who will read your essay? Are you aiming at a particular audience, such as college students, parents, or health care workers? Once you have a specific audience in mind, focus on the details that will be most useful to your readers. Is your audience reading just for information, or do the readers need to be able to do something as a result of your essay?
Purpose	Think about what you are trying to accomplish as you write your cause-and-effect essay. Do you want to simply inform the readers about a specific cause-and-effect relationship? Are you writing mainly to persuade your readers that a cause-and-effect relationship exists? Maybe your primary goal is to express your feelings about the serious consequences of a tragic illness or accident that someone you know suffered with a secondary goal of helping others to prevent it from happening to them.
Strategy	Even if your main approach is to explore the causes and/or effects of a particular topic, you may find it useful to combine strategies as well. For example, if you are writing about the effects of your friend's drug use, you might include a description of the behaviors your friend exhibits, compare and contrast your friend's life before and after the drug use began, or offer instructions for someone seeking help to escape a drug addiction.
Design	How should your essay look when you are finished? Do you need to include any photos, illustrations, or graphic organizers to help your reader fully comprehend your ideas? Will other design strategies help your readers to better understand the causes and/or effects you are explaining?

9.5 APPLYING THE WRITING PROCESS FOR EXPLAINING CAUSES AND EFFECTS

FIGURE 9.2
The Seven Steps of the Writing Process

After you have completed your rhetorical star analysis, follow the steps of the writing process (Figure 9.2) to compose your cause-and-effect paper.

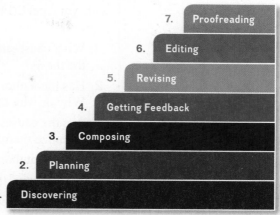

1. **Discovering:** Once you have chosen a topic, you might try making a chart of causes and effects to help you determine which you want to cover in your essay (see Figure 9.3). Next, you may want to complete two freewriting exercises, writing first about causes and then about effects to see which side you can more effectively develop. If you are basing your paper on research, you might want to find some reliable sources on the topic to see which approach will work best for your assignment.

2. **Planning:** Create a cluster or an outline (informal or formal) to help you organize your ideas. Remember to follow one of the cause-and-effect organizational strategies for your essay: the effects of a major cause, the causes for a major effect, or a chain of events that illustrate the cause(s) or effect(s). (See pages 199–201 for more details about these organization patterns.)

3. **Composing:** Write a first draft of your cause-and-effect analysis using the qualities outlined earlier in the chapter. Don't worry too much about grammar and punctuation at this time. Keep focused on the causes or effects you are explaining.

   1. Identify the cause or effect being analyzed.
   2. Explain the cause-and-effect relationship convincingly.
   3. Organize the causes and/or effects effectively.
   4. Use sound logic.
   5. Conclude effectively.

4. **Getting feedback:** Have at least one classmate or other person read your rough draft and answer the peer review questions on page 220. If you have access to a writing tutor or center, get another opinion about your paper as well. You will need to decide which suggestions to accept, reject, or modify.

5. **Revising:** Using all of the feedback available to you, revise your cause-and-effect essay. Make sure that your causal analysis is logical and that you have fully supported your main points. Add, delete, and rearrange ideas as necessary.

6. **Editing:** Read your cause-and-effect essay again, this time looking for errors in grammar, punctuation, and mechanics. You might try reading your essay aloud to "listen" to your word choice and sentence structure.

7. **Proofreading:** After you have carefully edited your essay, read it one last time and look for typographical errors and any other issues that might interfere with the readers' understanding of your essay.

FIGURE 9.3 Explaining Causes and Effects

Trade rough drafts with a classmate and answer the following questions about his or her paper. Then, in person or online, discuss your papers and suggestions with your peer. Finally, make the changes you feel would most benefit your paper.

1. What cause-and-effect relationship is being analyzed? Is it clearly stated in the thesis?

2. Has the author convincingly explained the cause-and-effect relationship? Why or why not?

3. Are the causes and/or effects organized logically? Is there a better way to organize them? Explain.

4. Has the author included any logical fallacies? Explain.

5. What part of the essay is most memorable? Why?

6. Is the conclusion effective? Why or why not?

7. What kinds of grammatical errors, if any, are evident in the cause-and-effect essay?

8. What final suggestions do you have for the author?

WRITER'S CHECKLIST FOR CAUSES AND EFFECTS

Use the checklist below to evaluate your own writing and help ensure that your explanation of the causes and/or effects is complete. If you have any "no" answers, go back and work on those areas if necessary.

❏ 1. Have I identified the cause or effect I am analyzing in my thesis?

❏ 2. Have I explained the cause-and-effect relationship convincingly?

❏ 3. Have I organized my causes and/or effects effectively?

❏ 4. Have I used sound logic?

❏ 5. Have I concluded my essay effectively?

❏ 6. Have I proofread thoroughly?

[CHAPTER SUMMARY]

1. The cause-and-effect writing strategy focuses on reasons and results.

2. Cause-and-effect writing is an important part of your education, daily life, and career.

3. Interpreting readings and images that reflect causes and effects can help you to prepare to write a cause-and-effect essay.

4. Carefully analyze the rhetorical star before writing a cause-and-effect essay: subject, audience, purpose, strategy, and design.

5. Use these qualities when writing a cause-and-effect essay: identify the cause or effect being analyzed; explain the cause-and-effect relationship convincingly; organize the causes and/or effects effectively; use sound logic; conclude effectively.

[WHAT I KNOW NOW]

Use this checklist to determine what you need to work on in order to feel comfortable with your understanding of the material in this chapter. Check off each item as you master it. Review the material for any unchecked items.

SmartBook Tip

During the "Recharge" phase, students can return to Chapter 9 and practice concepts that they need to work on.

❏ 1. I know what **cause-and-effect writing** is.

❏ 2. I can identify several **real-world applications** for cause-and-effect writing.

❏ 3. I can evaluate **readings and images** that reflect causes and effects.

❏ 4. I can analyze the **rhetorical star** for cause-and-effect writing.

❏ 5. I understand the **writing process** for cause-and-effect writing.

❏ 6. I can apply the **five qualities** for writing about causes and effects.

10

PERSUADING:
RELATIONSHIPS

learning outcomes

In this chapter you will learn techniques for achieving these learning outcomes:

10.1 IDENTIFY REAL-WORLD APPLICATIONS FOR PERSUADING.

10.2 UNDERSTAND THE QUALITIES OF EFFECTIVE PERSUASIVE WRITING.

10.3 INTERPRET IMAGES AND PERSUASIVE READINGS ABOUT RELATIONSHIPS.

10.4 ANALYZE THE RHETORICAL STAR FOR PERSUASIVE WRITING.

10.5 APPLY THE QUALITIES OF PERSUASIVE WRITING.

WRITING STRATEGY FOCUS: PERSUASION

Persuasion is all about swaying your audience to see things your way. To encourage others to see your point of view about an opinion or belief requires you to be convincing. When you write for the purpose of persuading your audience, you may present a position, defend a belief, attack a point of view, or encourage someone to take action. To convince readers to agree with you, you will need to support your argument with sound, logical reasons. You may also appeal to your audience's emotions or ethics. The art of persuasion is an important skill to have in college, in your personal life, and in your career.

SmartBook Tip

Students receive an overview of the learning outcomes and topics in Chapter 10 in the "Preview" phase of SmartBook.

10.1 REAL-WORLD APPLICATIONS FOR PERSUADING

Writing Persuasively in College

You will often be asked to write persuasively in your college courses. For example, your political science instructor might ask you to write an argument for or against changing election laws in your city or state. Your literature instructor may require you to write a persuasive essay about a character in one of Shakespeare's plays or Hemingway's novels. You might decide to e-mail an instructor requesting an extension for an assignment because of a personal situation you are experiencing. An instructor in your major may ask you to write a report arguing why one theory or procedure works best for a particular situation.

Writing Persuasively in Your Daily Life

You use persuasion often in your personal life. You might write a persuasive letter to your property manager requesting that repairs be made in a timely manner. You may decide to write a letter to the editor of a newspaper or magazine disagreeing with an article you read. Or maybe you'll design a flyer convincing people in your community to donate money or volunteer to help clean up a park or build a playground.

Graduate SPOTLIGHT

Dat Nguyen, Information Technology Administrator

Dat Nguyen earned his associate's degree in information technology. He currently works in the IT department for a large company. Here's what Nguyen has to say about the types of writing he uses in his career:

" Taking an English composition class helped prepare me for the kinds of writing I do on the job. One of my main tasks is to make sure that we have the most up-to-date firewall in place to keep intruders out of our system. My company handles highly classified information, so it is essential that my research is thorough. I test and evaluate firewall software to make sure that it is secure. Sometimes I write e-mails to software companies to learn more about the weak points of various firewalls. When I make a final decision, I write a report for my boss persuading him which software provides the best protection. New software comes out just about every month, so I have to stay current with the latest technology and keep convincing my boss that we are using the best system for our network. **"**

Teaching Tip

Ask students to tell how they anticipate using the persuasive writing strategy in their future careers.

Writing Persuasively in Your Career

Being able to write persuasively is also extremely useful in the workplace. To get the job you desire, you will need to write a persuasive cover letter and résumé. You might want to persuade your boss to give you a promotion and a raise or some time off for an important out-of-town event you want to attend. You'll also need to convince your clients, patients, or customers that your organization offers the best product or service in your community. Here are some additional ways to use persuasive strategies in the workplace.

Health care: persuading patients to come in for preventive treatments, to follow prescribed treatments, and to take better care of their bodies.

Law: persuading potential clients that you can help them, presenting opening and closing arguments for a trial, arguing for or against a proposed law or amendment.

Education: persuading the administration to provide more materials, equipment, or books; persuading parents to become more involved in their children's education.

Computers: persuading customers that you can meet their needs so they will purchase hardware, software, or services.

Business administration: persuading clients that your company is reliable and convincing them to purchase products or services.

Massage therapy: persuading clients to use exercise techniques at home and to get more massages to improve their health.

Culinary arts: persuading customers to purchase menu items or catering services and to visit your establishment more often.

Activity Real-World Persuasive Writing

In pairs or small groups, brainstorm uses for writing persuasively at school, in your daily life, and on the job. You may want to choose the prospective career field(s) of the participants in your group. Each group may share its results with the class.

10.2 QUALITIES OF EFFECTIVE PERSUASIVE WRITING

1. Introduce the Issue You Are Debating

When you are arguing for your perspective on an issue, hold off a bit before stating your thesis so that readers who disagree with your opinion are more likely to keep an open mind and read further to see what you have to say. Instead of jumping right in with a claim, begin with an explanation of the situation. Provide your readers with enough information to get a basic understanding of the subject. For example, if you are attempting to persuade the reader that younger siblings are sometimes less responsible than older siblings, you might begin by discussing the psychology of birth order. You may need to do some research to adequately explain the issue if you are not completely familiar with the subject from first-hand experience. As always, cite any outside sources you use in your paper.

After you have introduced the subject, then you may want to pose a question to get your reader to think about the issue. However, keep in mind that a question is not a thesis. A question might hint at where you intend to go with your thesis, but it should not replace your thesis. Here are a few examples of thought-provoking questions:

- Should an employee always outwardly agree with his or her boss?
- Should motorists be allowed to talk on cell phones while driving?
- Should a boy be allowed to join the girls' volleyball team if there is no comparable boys' team?
- Do school uniforms help promote a positive learning environment for students?

2. Make a Claim about Your Subject

A **claim** is a debatable assertion. In persuasive writing, the claim serves as the thesis statement. In a persuasive essay, you should state your claim either near the end of the introduction or at the beginning of the conclusion. Whether you are making an assertion about an issue or demanding that something be done, your claim should definitely state your opinion about the issue. You want to make sure your reader knows exactly where you stand.

Avoid using phrases such as "I think, "I believe," and "I feel" because that will make you sound tentative and weaken your argument. Keep a third person point of view and make a strong claim. For example, in a paper about stay-at-home fathers, your thesis might be, "Men who serve as the primary caregivers for their children deserve to be treated with the same respect as women who choose that role."

Real-World Persuasive Writing Activity:
Answers will vary.

SmartBook Tip
Key concepts in Chapter 10 are highlighted for students during the "Read" phase. As students demonstrate understanding of these concepts during the "Practice" phase by responding to probes, the highlighting adapts to the individual student's learning by changing color.

Claim A debatable assertion.

Teaching Tip
Have students write claims individually or in groups. Next, have students share their claims so the class can discuss which ones are strong or weak.

3. Support Your Claim with Evidence That Appeals to Your Audience

Appeals Persuasive strategies used to support claims.

Teaching Tip
Have students work individually or in groups to develop examples of the three types of appeals to share with the class and spark a discussion.

To persuade your audience that your claim is valid, you will need to support it fully. Whether you relate a personal experience, create your own primary source information, or introduce research based on the findings of others, you can use appeals to convince your audience that your argument is credible. **Appeals** are persuasive strategies used to support claims. Three types of appeals are used in argument: ethical (from the Greek word *ethos*), emotional (from the Greek word *pathos*), and logical (from the Greek word *logos*). These appeals can be used individually or in combination. See Table 10.1 for more on these three appeals.

TABLE 10.1

Persuasive Appeals		
Type of Appeal	**Definition**	**Example**
Ethical appeal (*ethos*)	Persuade readers by establishing that you are a trustworthy and credible writer. This is sometimes called *character appeal* because you are demonstrating that you are fair in your approach to the issue. Show that you understand the issue, that you are sensitive to it, and that you have considered all sides of it. If you are an expert on the subject, you can mention your profession, experience, or knowledge. Bringing in the opinion of an authority can help you to establish your credibility if you are writing about a topic with which you have little or no firsthand experience. Use an appropriate tone and correct grammar to help demonstrate your good character.	Now, more than ever before, dual-income families are struggling with how to balance jobs, children, and household tasks. Parents need to work out a fair system for handling these responsibilities. As a counselor, I have helped hundreds of families to deal with these pressures using three simple techniques.
Emotional appeal (*pathos*)	Persuade readers by appealing to their emotions. You can use emotionally charged words to stir the reader's feelings as long as you use them ethically. You might try to gain the sympathy or empathy of the audience about a particular cause for which you are arguing. Using vivid descriptions and narratives of emotional events can help you to appeal to your readers' emotions.	Juanita, age 17, is 5 feet tall, weighs just 88 pounds, and suffers from anorexia. She feels fat in comparison to the women on the covers of fashion magazines. The media need to be more responsible with the wafer-thin images of women they display, or more girls are going to fall prey to serious eating disorders.
Logical appeal (*logos*)	Persuade readers by appealing to their sense of logic with reasons, facts, statistics, and examples. Citing sources from experts on your subject can help you to convince your audience that your evidence is sound. You can also use inductive and deductive reasoning to support your premise logically. (See Figure 10.1 and Table 10.3 for more information about induction and deduction.)	While you and your colleagues may not always agree on important issues, both parties may benefit from working together to resolve conflicts that arise. According to psychologist Joy Peters, learning how to compromise on important issues can lead to better communication, a more productive work environment, and greater job satisfaction.

▶ *Activity* Persuasive Appeals

On your own, in pairs, or in small groups, choose one (or more) of the claims listed below. Make a list of ethical, emotional, and logical appeals that a writer might use to support and/or refute the claim.

- The lottery and other forms of gambling should be illegal in every state.
- Actors and professional athletes are paid too much.
- Beauty pageants are exploitive.
- People who talk on cell phones while driving, or even walking, are a danger to others.
- People are too dependent on computers.
- The election process is unfair.
- Everyone should be concerned about global warming.

A representative from each group may share a few of the highlights with the class.

4. Use Your Supporting Evidence Logically and Ethically

While you do want your argument to be convincing, you don't want to win over your readers by deceiving them. Furthermore, you don't want to mislead them by using logical fallacies or leaving out pertinent information that would shed a different light on your subject. For example, if you are attempting to persuade your readers that the company that employs you is sexist because it doesn't have any women in upper management, then it would be unfair to leave out the fact that one of the key executives is a woman who happens to be temporarily out on maternity leave. See Table 10.2 for more on logical fallacies.

Basically, your audience will be more likely to agree with your claim if your argument seems reasonable. To do that, you will need to maintain an appropriate tone and give fair treatment to other positions on the issue. To give fair treatment to your subject, you need to acknowledge that an opposing point of view exists. You may bring up a counterargument, find the common ground between the two points of view, and then refute the counterargument. For example, your claim might be that participating in extracurricular activities helps build leadership skills. A valid counterargument is that extracurricular activities take time away from study and sleep, both of which are necessary to succeed in college. You may acknowledge the counterargument, yet refute it by stating that if students manage their time wisely, they will have time for schoolwork, sleep, and extracurricular activities. Furthermore, you may add more credibility to your argument by citing reliable statistics or an expert to support your position that extracurricular activities do help students develop leadership skills that are necessary for success in college and beyond.

When you accommodate a counterargument, your argument becomes stronger. However, your readers need to understand *your* position in the debate. While you do need to deal with significant information that may cast doubt on your perspective, most of your comments need to support the opinion in your thesis. Otherwise, you will confuse your readers or, even worse, defeat your own argument.

Note: If you use outside sources, you must cite them. See Chapters 13 and 14 for specific details about finding and documenting sources using the MLA and APA formats.

Persuasive Appeals Activity:
Answers will vary.

LearnSmart Achieve Tip

The Reasoning and Argument Unit of LearnSmart Achieve determines what students do and do not know about persuasion. Learning outcomes within the Reasoning and Argument Unit cover developing claims, defending claims, and using ethical, logical, and emotional appeals to persuade readers. Also, the Writing Process Unit determines what students do and do not know about the writing process. Learning outcomes within the Writing Process unit cover planning, organizing, drafting, and revising an informative text. Learning resources and questions automatically adapt to each student's individual needs and help students thoroughly master this content. See the Instructor's Manual for *Write Now* for a list of learning outcomes as well as additional information on how to use LearnSmart Achieve with your students.

Logical Fallacies Activity (p. 229): Answers

1. Hasty generalization, non sequitur
2. Slippery slope
3. False authority or testimonial
4. Either/or reasoning
5. False analogy

TABLE 10.2

Logical Fallacies			
Logical Fallacies	**Definitions**	**Examples**	**Explanations**
Bandwagon	Implying that an idea must be true if it is popular. Join the crowd.	Everyone knows that holistic medicine is better than traditional medicine.	Even if many people believe it, that doesn't provide scientific proof for the argument.
Card stacking	Providing evidence for only one side of a case, deliberately omitting essential information that would change the reader's opinion.	Sunni should get a promotion because she has never missed a day at work and she completes all of her tasks in a timely manner.	Supervisors consider many factors when deciding whom to promote. Maybe Sunni often arrives late or does poor work.
Character attack or *ad hominem* attack	Attacking a person rather than an issue.	Candidate X should not become the next company president because he divorced his wife and married his assistant.	His private life has nothing to do with whether or not he would make a good company president.
Circular reasoning or begging the question	Attempting to support a position by simply restating it in a different way.	Dr. Brilliant is a good instructor because he teaches his students well.	The idea is merely being repeated without offering any specific evidence as to what makes Dr. Brilliant an effective instructor.
Either/or reasoning	Suggesting there are only two possible solutions to a problem (one right and one wrong) when, in reality, there could be many potential options for resolving the issue.	Either the government needs to subsidize gas costs or our economy is going to collapse.	First of all, does the entire economy depend on the price of gas? Also, there are several ways to cut down on fuel costs other than having the government help to offset the price.
False analogy	Comparing things that are not similar in the most important respects.	The governor hit the jackpot with the new property tax increase proposal.	The governor is not gambling, so the analogy doesn't make sense.
False authority or testimonial	Mentioning an authority figure or celebrity as support for arguing a point.	Eric Zane, who plays Dr. Mark Gnome on *Haye's Anatomy*, recommends taking "Cure It All" pills, so they must be effective.	Eric Zane is an actor playing a role, not a real doctor, so he is not qualified to recommend a specific type of treatment.
False cause or *post hoc*	Suggesting that because one thing happened after another, the first event caused the second one.	I ate chocolate and my sore throat disappeared.	The sore throat could have gone away for another reason unrelated to the chocolate.
Glittering generality	Using emotionally charged words, such as *love, truth, honor, democracy,* and *justice,* to gain the audience's approval.	If you are truly patriotic, you need to do the honorable thing and vote to increase your property taxes.	The implication is that voting a particular way will determine if someone is (or is not) patriotic and honorable.
Hasty generalization	Drawing a conclusion without having sufficient evidence.	A child comes home two days in a row without homework, so the parent assumes that the teacher has stopped assigning homework.	The child may have forgotten to bring home the work or may be intentionally misleading the parent.

Non sequitur	The conclusion does not logically follow from the evidence that is provided.	Fast-food chains are very popular in the United States. No wonder obesity is so common.	Many factors contribute to the high obesity rate in the United States. One can't assume that there is only one cause or that fast-food chains are the cause of obesity.
Red herring	Diverting the reader's attention from the main issue by introducing something irrelevant. It comes from the practice of dragging a stinky fish across the ground to distract tracking dogs away from a scent.	The idea of gay marriages is an important issue, but do gay people really want to deal with all of the pressures associated with marriage?	The second part is irrelevant because it has nothing to do with whether gay marriages should be legal or not.
Slippery slope	Suggesting that if one change occurs, then other, unwanted changes will inevitably occur as well. The analogy is that once someone starts sliding down a "slippery slope," he or she won't be able to stop.	If we allow dogs on the beach, then the next thing you know dogs will be sitting at tables in fine restaurants.	The two events are unrelated, so there's no reason to assume that one event will lead to the other.
Stereotyping	Attaching a trait to people who belong to a particular religious, ethnic, racial, age, or other group.	Old people make terrible drivers, so they shouldn't be allowed to drive.	This is an unfair claim because many senior citizens are fine drivers.
Tradition	If something has always been done a certain way, then it must be the correct way.	Our company has always bought cigars and champagne for our clients during the holidays. We don't need to change to something else.	Just because the tradition is long standing doesn't mean that it's a good one. Some clients may not like cigars, and some might not be able to tolerate alcohol. Another gift might be more appropriate.

▶ *Activity*   **Logical Fallacies**

Label the fallacies in the following sentences. Some sentences contain more than one fallacy.

1. Tristan didn't get the job, so the company must not really be hiring.
2. If we allow employees to dress down on Fridays, then soon they will look sloppy every day.
3. Taylor Swift wears that perfume, so it must smell really good.
4. That new movie is going to be a big hit or a complete flop.
5. If people have to wear helmets when they ride bicycles, then they should have to wear helmets when they ride motorcycles.

FIGURE 10.1 Deductive and Inductive Reasoning Patterns

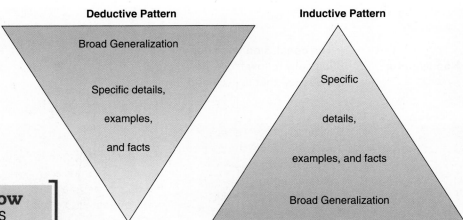

Deductive Pattern

Broad Generalization

Specific details,

examples,

and facts

Inductive Pattern

Specific

details,

examples, and facts

Broad Generalization

Grammar Window
RUN-ON SENTENCES

When you write to persuade, you may have a lot to say to your readers. If you are not careful, this can lead to run-on sentences. A run-on sentence, also known as a fused sentence, occurs when two complete sentences (independent clauses) run together without a proper punctuation mark or coordinating conjunction.

Run-on sentence: My friend Leslie loves watching football on Sunday however, her husband, Steve, isn't interested in sports.

Corrected sentence: My friend Leslie loves watching football on Sunday; however, her husband, Steve, isn't interested in sports.

Discussion: A semicolon needs to be placed before the conjunctive adverb *however* to avoid the run-on.

Activity: Correct the following run-on sentences by adding a comma and a coordinating conjunction *(for, and, nor, but, or, yet, so)*. In some cases, you can correct a run-on sentence by inserting a period or a semicolon between two complete sentences or adding a subordinating conjunction *(because, so that)*.

1. Some parents and students feel that school uniforms are beneficial others find them to be too restrictive.

2. The school is having a meeting tonight parents can weigh the pros and cons of school uniforms.

3. Raul likes not having to argue with his daughter about what is appropriate to wear to school he also likes not having to buy a lot of expensive clothes for her.

4. Ai-shi doesn't like wearing a school uniform she feels they are unflattering.

5. Gabriel prefers to wear a uniform to school he never has to worry about getting picked on for wearing something out of style.

See the Editing Guide for more information on run-on sentences.

5. Organize Your Supporting Evidence Effectively

You can organize the evidence in a persuasive essay in a number of ways. For example, you might begin with your second strongest point, then move to your weaker points, and then end with your strongest point. You may also use *deductive* or *inductive* reasoning in persuasive writing. College writers often organize their essays deductively. They introduce a thesis early in the paper and then support it with specific details, examples, and facts in the body paragraphs. The purpose of deductive reasoning is to apply what you already know to a new situation. However, you may want to try inductive reasoning, where you give specific details, examples, and facts to lead your readers to a conclusion, which is your main point. The purpose of inductive reasoning is to discover something new. Figure 10.1 illustrates both types of reasoning. Table 10.3 provides a definition and example for each one.

6. End Your Essay Effectively

There are several ways to conclude a persuasive essay. One method is to use the traditional approach of restating your thesis and summarizing your main points. Other strategies are to suggest the implications of the issue or to encourage your readers to take some sort of action. Whatever you do, be sure to leave your reader feeling satisfied with your conclusion.

TABLE 10.3

Deductive and Inductive Reasoning		
Organizational Strategy	**Definition**	**Example**
Deduction	To organize an argument deductively, begin with a generalization of the most important idea, which is your *major premise,* or claim. Then provide more specific details and examples of that major premise, which is your *minor premise.* You can move from a major premise to a minor premise and then draw a plausible conclusion. A classic deductive argument has a conclusion that follows with certainty. No other conclusion is possible based on the evidence.	**Topic:** Polygamy **Major premise (claim):** In 1878, the U.S. Supreme Court ruled that polygamy violates criminal law and is not protected by the notion of religious freedom. This ruling has not been overturned. **Minor premise:** While he was living in the United States, Fred married his second wife without divorcing his first wife or nullifying his marriage to her. **Conclusion:** Fred has broken the law.
Induction	To organize an argument inductively, start with specific details, examples, or observations and then progress to a more general idea that the evidence supports. When you use this strategy, you should examine the evidence carefully before drawing a conclusion. An inductive argument has a conclusion that follows with some degree of probability, but not certainty. Other conclusions are possible.	**Topic:** Class discussions **Observed evidence:** During my last eight classes at Genius University, the male students have contributed more to class discussions than female students. **Generalization (claim):** Male college students are more talkative than female students.

Run-On Sentences Grammar Window: Possible Responses

1. Some parents and students feel that school uniforms are beneficial, but others find them to be too restrictive. 2. The school is having a meeting tonight so that parents can weigh the pros and cons of school uniforms. 3. Raul likes not having to argue with his daughter about what is appropriate to wear to school. He also likes not having to buy a lot of expensive clothes for her. 4. Aishi doesn't like wearing a school uniform because she feels they are unflattering. 5. Gabriel prefers to wear a uniform to school, so he never has to worry about getting picked on for wearing something out of style.

Career-Based PERSUASIVE WRITING

[preview] **AFTER YOU GRADUATE** from college, your résumé is one of the most important documents you will ever write. The main goal of your résumé is to persuade a potential employer to invite you to a face-to-face or phone interview. If your résumé doesn't catch the interviewer's eye, then you may never get the chance to explain how great you are in person. Your résumé needs to clearly and concisely convey the message that you are qualified for the job and that you will be a valuable asset to the organization. When you write your résumé, emphasize your best qualifications, organize your strengths logically, and avoid errors in spelling, grammar, punctuation, and mechanics. With the right qualifications and a well-written résumé, you are likely to land the job you desire. The following fictitious résumé illustrates the properties of persuasive writing.

Résumé of Kristin Starr

Kristin Starr

123 Beach View Street
Ft. Lauderdale, FL 33309

954-555-5555 (cell)
kstarr@e-mail.net

Objective: Position as a medical assistant in a fast-paced physician's office

Education: Associate of Science in Medical Assisting, June 2014, GPA 3.5
Keiser University, Ft. Lauderdale, Florida

Key Strengths:
- Proficient with EKG, phlebotomy, and radiology
- Familiar with electronic health records
- Quick to learn office procedures
- Adept at multitasking
- People oriented/team player
- Excellent oral and written communication skills

Certifications: Registered Medical Assistant, 2014 CPR, 2013

Experience: Receptionist, Harmony Medical Center

Teaching Tip
Point out to students that the verbs used to describe current job responsibilities are in the present tense, and that the verbs used to describe previous job responsibilities are in the past tense.

Ft. Lauderdale, Florida, August 2012 to present
- Manage multiple phone lines
- Handle insurance claims
- Schedule appointments for multiple physicians
- Write office newsletter

Intern, Healing Hands Medical Associates

Hollywood, Florida, January–May 2012
- Administered injections
- Conducted EKGs efficiently
- Obtained patients' vital signs
- Maintained and filed medical records
- Handled multiple phone lines
- Scheduled patient appointments

Honors and Activities: Phi Theta Kappa Honor Society, Secretary 2014
Dean's List, Three Semesters
Leadership Distinction Award 2014

Volunteer Work: Serenity Rehabilitation Center
Community Animal Shelter

References: Available upon request

[QUESTIONS FOR REFLECTION]

1. What are some of Starr's key strengths?
2. What part of speech is the word that begins each bullet under "experience"? Why?
3. Why did Starr list her volunteer work on her résumé?
4. Why did she list her education first?
5. If you were an employer with a job opening in this field, would you hire Starr? Why or why not?

[preview] **BRYAN DIK** is a professor, researcher, and writer who works in the psychology department at Colorado State University. He is interested in the significance of how and why people choose their careers. In addition to numerous other publications, Dik co-authored a book with Ryan Duffy titled *Make Your Job a Calling: How the Psychology of Vocation Can Change Your Life at Work* (2012). The following article, which was originally published in the Vocation, Vocation, Vocation section of *Psychology Today*, addresses the challenges people face when deciding on a career path. Before reading, consider what factors you considered in choosing a career.

Career Choice: Easy for Superheroes, Hard for Us: Spider-Man and the Power of Person-Environment Fit by Bryan Dik

The proliferation of Superhero flicks, popularity of Comic-Con, and the expanding reach of Marvel and DC Comics all testify to the obvious: People love superheroes. There are many reasons for this, but one of them has to be envy. Seriously, who among us hasn't imagined how great it would be to wake up one morning with superpowers? One accidental chemical bath and you're stretching your body into any imaginable form. One newly activated mutant gene and you're able to manipulate the weather. One brief exposure to cosmic radiation and you find yourself with superhuman strength, stamina, and a very helpful resistance to physical injury. This would make choosing a career path easy. Many people spin their wheels for years trying to figure out the right line of work for them. But find yourself with a useful superpower, and it isn't a stretch to see that a lifetime of fighting crime is a career choice that just makes good sense.

Psychologists point out that one of the most critical factors in making a wise career choice is "person-environment fit." People have unique patterns of interests, abilities, personality, values, etc., and jobs are unique too, in terms of what needs to get done, what skills are required, what kinds of rewards are offered, etc. The challenge is figuring out what career path is the best fit for the kind of person you are. This is not a complicated concept, but the task is much easier for superheroes than for the rest of us.

To illustrate, take Peter Parker. A fateful spider bite spawned his transformation from skinny, clumsy teen one day to web-shooting, wall-climbing Spider-Man the next. Once he understood that "with great power comes great responsibility," it wasn't a leap for Peter to conclude that fighting New York's evil villains was a vocation that fit his strengths extremely well. Now imagine that Peter had squashed the offending spider before its bite, never to enjoy the benefits (or endure the drawbacks) of life as Spider-Man. Peter may have wondered, as most of the rest of us did (or do), what kind of career path he ought to pursue. Given what we know about Peter, he likely would have scored high on trait measures of abilities having to do with science. He also might have scored high on Investigative and Artistic interests, given his enjoyment of science and photography. A personality test might have shown Peter to be reasonably conscientious and open to experience. This pattern of characteristics may have led Peter to choose a career as a reporter, a research scientist, an engineer, or perhaps a college professor. *Daily Bugle* photographer probably was a good fit, but we can assume that Peter would have worked a lot harder to capture Spider-Man shots for page 1 without his double-identity in place.

Career counselors generally assume that work-related traits can be measured using psychological tests, and that scores on these tests predict real-life outcomes like happiness on the job. Research has generally supported these assumptions, but because there are so many human traits relevant for choosing a best-fitting career, because we are still learning about how all these traits interact, and because multiple occupations (not just one) usually are available to satisfy any one person's unique combination of traits, choosing a career remains as much an art as it is a science—at least for us non-superheroes.

Source: Bryan Dik, "Career Choice: Easy for Superheroes, Hard for Us," Psychology Today, **http://www.psychologytoday.com/blog/vocation-vocation-vocation/201211/career-choice-easy-superheroes-hard-us**. Reprinted by permission of the author.

[QUESTIONS FOR REFLECTION]

1. Who is the primary audience for Dik's article? How do you know?

2. What is the author's claim? Does he state it clearly? Explain.

3. How does Dik support his claim? Is the support convincing? Why or why not?

4. How important is the "person-environment fit" when determining a career? Explain.

5. What are some important factors that people should consider when choosing a career according to Dik? Do you agree or disagree with the author's assertions? Explain.

10.3 PERSUADING IN THE CONTEXT OF RELATIONSHIPS

Relationships can be challenging. Disputes between friends, roommates, neighbors, siblings, parents, spouses, partners, and co-workers are quite common. To say that human beings don't always understand each other would be an understatement. People tend to disagree about everything from politics, laws, and finances to values, morality, and religion. A number of factors can contribute to these disagreements, including gender, cultural differences, and experience.

Too often these disputes lead to arguments at home, at school, in the community, or in the workplace. However, instead of arguing over who's right and who's wrong, we can study the issues to gain acceptance, or at least tolerance, of a different perspective. In the following readings, you'll explore a variety of issues. Some are presented as formal arguments while others are designed to give you something to gently debate with classmates and in writing. Reading what others have written can help you write persuasively for school, your personal life, or the workplace.

Paired Readings

The first two readings in this section reveal opposing viewpoints on the use of social networking sites, such as Facebook. Read both articles before answering the questions for reflection that follow the second one. Consider the following questions before you read the articles: Do you regularly participate on Facebook or another social networking website? If so, what positive or negative experiences have you had with it? If you don't use an online social network, have you ever considered joining one? What has kept you from joining?

Reading and Reflection PERSUASIVE WRITING

[preview] **KATHERINE BINDLEY** has a bachelor's degree in English from Georgetown University and a master's degree in journalism from the Columbia University School of Journalism. She has served as a freelance reporter for the *New York Times* and the *Wall Street Journal.* She is currently a reporter for the *Huffington Post.* Many of her articles are about culture and style. To read other articles by Bindley, got to **www.huffingtonpost.com**. In the following article, which originally appeared in the *Huffington Post,* Bindley argues that the use of Facebook can be detrimental to relationships.

Facebook Relationship Problems: How Social Networking and Jealousy Affect Your Love Life by Katherine Bindley

Lots of us use Facebook as a convenient way of receiving 1 information about the people in our lives we don't call every day—and people we don't know that well whose lives we enjoy watching from afar. Your college friend got engaged, yay! Your favorite cousin is moving across the country, boo. A girl you met once at a party who's baring her midriff in her profile picture wrote on your fiancée's wall—hold on, where'd she come from?

Enter the green-eyed (or in this case, blue and white 2 logo'ed) monster known as Facebook jealousy. Messaging someone you hooked up with before you met your current love interest, analyzing a wall post on your significant other's page, stewing over a suspicious picture but not actually asking about it—all of these have been known to tank relationships.

If you're prone to thinking, "It's just Facebook—can it really 3 cause that many problems in an adult relationship?" consider this: A 2009 study suggested Facebook makes "unique contributions to the experience of jealousy in romantic relationships." Divorce attorneys say Facebook flirtations are frequently cited in their cases. And this poor guy had an asthma attack supposedly prompted by seeing how many men his ex-girlfriend had friended since their breakup. There's even a Facebook page called "I wonder how many relationships Facebook ruins every year" with over 100,000 "Likes."

"It's a very common topic," says Jennine Estes, a 4 couples' therapist from San Diego who reports that she sometimes hears about Facebook issues on a daily basis in her office. Couples come into conflict over everything from one party reconnecting with an ex to one not mentioning the relationship on Facebook at all.

And these problems aren't limited to relationships with 5 pre-existing problems. Facebook presents so many challenges to committed relationships that Jason and Kelli Krafsky wrote a book called, *Facebook and Your Marriage.*

To be clear, Facebook itself isn't to blame for the demise 6 of domestic bliss. Instead, it's an avenue by which threats can develop if you fail to communicate about them, and one that can exacerbate problems that already exist.

According to Estes and the Krafskys, here are the 7 scenarios that cause the most relationship strife, and how to address them:

Over- (or Under-)sharing

Before addressing what you may hide from your partner on 8 Facebook—and the jealousy that behavior may provoke—it's a good idea to first talk about what you're both comfortable sharing. Just because one of you likes to do the Internet equivalent of shouting from the rooftops how in love you are doesn't mean the other one should have to suffer through it. On the other hand, if one of you never references the relationship on your page, the other may begin to wonder why.

"Have a face-to-face conversation about Facebook," says 9 Jason. "You want to have open communication about how much about 'us' is going to be spilled." The same goes for changing your status or friending your significant other's family members: It's best to talk about it first.

Tagged Photos of You With Your Ex

You're not alone (or irrational) if you get a little nauseous 10 every time you see evidence of your significant other's weekend in Cabo with his ex. In the same vein, you shouldn't be surprised if your boyfriend isn't interested in having a reminder of the guy you dated right before him.

"It is hard to see those," says Estes. "For your partner 11 to see you cuddling on the beach on a date? That's going to sting for any human. . . . Other people might have a tougher skin, but I say [err on the side] of caution. Do some preventative work. Better to be safe than sorry."

Having a hard time untagging yourself in those pho- 12 tos? Estes suggests asking yourself why that is.

"Do you need to have it up? That's the big question: 13 What's the purpose of it?"

Jason and Kelli liken the tagging issue to going home 14 to your parent's house and them still having pictures on the wall of you and your old boyfriend.

"There's a creep factor," says Kelli. "It's almost like 15 time has stood still and your life hasn't gone on."

When deciding what to untag (or not), the best 16 approach is for both partners to agree to untag themselves from photos that make the other uncomfortable.

You Just Got a Friend Request From an Ex

Jason and Kelli's suggestion? Deny, deny, deny. 17

"We've heard horror story after horror story," says Kelli. 18 "The moment you open the door, you could be two to three clicks away from making a really poor decision. You could be in a vulnerable state. You could have had a couple glasses of wine. It could open temptation to revisit the past."

But what if you're 100 percent not tempted by an ex? Is 19 there any harm in accepting the request? Yes, says Jason, because you don't know what the person on the other end of that friend request is thinking. They might have been pining for you all of these years, waiting for the day you reconnect.

Estes suggests addressing these requests on a case- 20 by-case basis: It's how you handle it that matters to your current relationship.

"Make your partner part of the decision," she says. 21 "The more included they feel, the safer it is."

Someone You're Already Friends With Gets Friendlier

In some cases, existing friends you have a past with 22 are harmless and can remain that way—though Kelli suggests hiding them on Facebook to avoid trips down memory lane.

Then, there are the people the experts refer to as "red 23 flag" friends. These could be people you've never dated who've started to show an interest or actual exes.

"Facebook allows people to be bolder. They utilize it as 24 a way to say, 'Hey I'm interested,'" says Kelli.

These problem friends can be exes, though they don't 25 have to be, and they're a common enough issue that Estes mentions them on her website:

"Sometimes people may cross a line by posting inap- 26 propriate messages or flirty comments. If this person is a red flag for either you or your partner, it may be time to delete them from your friends list, or you may need to confront the issue straight on."

Either way, the couple needs to agree about these 27 friends. It's a fact that there's an unspoken awkwardness to defriending—won't it show your ex that he or she still has a hold on you?—but in some cases, it's necessary. And it's prob- ably time to stop caring about what your ex thinks, anyway.

You See Something Worrisome on Your Significant Other's Page

When couples see a post on their partner's page that 28 makes them uncomfortable, they shouldn't just let it go. Not asking can lead to mistrust and assuming the worst based on two random sentences whose context you don't know.

"Our minds automatically try to guess what the full story 29 is. Most of the time, [they] go to a worst-case scenario and try to predict something that's not necessarily the case," says Estes.

By not asking about the posts, "They're attempting to pro- 30 tect the relationship, or they don't want to risk being seen as stupid or crazy, but then the problem never gets resolved. They don't get the reassurance that they're needing."

If you follow all the above, you'll avoid the biggest pit- 31 fall of all:

Facebook Secrets

The problem isn't that secrets are no fun; it's that they 32 make otherwise normal people lose trust in each other and morph into amateur private investigators.

"They'll do research, they'll run into interactions that 33 have been going on," Estes warns.

It's not cool for your partner to snoop, but if you're not 34 up-front about your Facebook habits, he or she will prob- ably find that one person who hasn't checked the privacy settings since Facebook changed them for the billionth time, and see evidence of you being inappropriate.

That all said, our experts agree that the golden rule of 35 Facebooking while committed is that on FB, as in life, you shouldn't be doing anything that you wouldn't want your partner to see.

"Facebook isn't usually the problem," says Estes. "It's 36 the behaviors that are the problem."

Source: Katherine Bindley, "Facebook Relationshiop Problems: How Social Network- ing and Jealousy Affect Your Love Life," the *Huffington Post*, www.huffingtonpost .com, October 20, 2011.

Reading and Reflection PERSUASIVE WRITING

[preview] **AL RODRICKS,** who is from Enfield, Connecticut, is a staff writer for the website **ImagineWeMeet.com**, an online dating site that allows people to post free personal ads. Although Rodricks's work covers a vari- ety of topics, some of his most interesting articles relate to the online dating scene. For example, in "How to Make Online Dating Successful," he offers useful tips for anyone looking for love on the Internet. The following article originally appeared on the Imagine We Meet site, and presents an opposing viewpoint to the previous article, "Facebook Relationship Problems: How Social Networking and Jealousy Affect Your Love Life." Where do you stand on the issue? Are social networking sites helpful or harmful to your relationships? Will you agree with Bindley or Rodricks by the time you finish the next article?

The Benefits of Social Networking on YOUR Social Life **by Al Rodricks**

I remember when the Internet was just starting to get 1 really popular. Many folks feared it would be the end of social interaction. They pictured everyone huddled away in their rooms, typing anonymously to strangers, and giv- ing up any form of human contact whatsoever. Well, as we have seen, this is not the case. In fact, thanks to the advent of social networking, people have been more active than ever before meeting new people, re-connecting with old friends, and learning about different cultures from all over the world. One thing that social networking sites have done is give folks a new and perhaps safer method of online dating.

Social networks, unlike traditional methods of meeting someone, allow you a pretty in-depth method of "checking people out" before actually meeting them. Most social network profiles contain information about the person's interests, work life, family life, and much more. You can even see whom a person is connected to as well, and oftentimes this is how folks meet.

Let's imagine that you just re-connected to an old high school friend. You may not have talked to him or her in years, but thanks to social networking sites, here you are, messaging away to your old buddy! Then let's imagine you start scrolling through the pictures of the people they are connected to online. You see someone who is cute, and you would like to know a little more about him or her. Your friend can give you the scoop, and perhaps even do an online introduction. This process can be much simpler than trying to arrange an in-person date, and MUCH less nerve wracking. Spending a few minutes chatting online with someone is far less intimidating than showing up face to face for a blind date, wouldn't you agree?

In addition, meeting someone through a social network can be a lot like meeting someone through a personal ad, only with a few more "quality checkpoints" installed. Online dating personal ads have been around pretty much since the first power-up of the Internet years ago. The problem is, on a dating profile, it seems that people tend to exaggerate just a bit. I know you are shocked, but it's true. They assume that the only people who will see their ad are others who are "looking for love" as well, and they want to seem as desirable as possible. The same can be true of social networks, of course, but while folks may try to put their best foot forward, the fact that all of their friends will see their profile tends to discourage outright lying.

As far as communicating with those you meet on social networks, the methods are plenty. You can message them right through the platform, chat with them in real time, upload video or audio clips, or perhaps even talk to them live using an interface like Skype, for instance.

It is important to keep in mind that many folks who are members of social networks are not on there exclusively for the purpose of dating. But, if you are looking for true love, spending some time on your favorite social network may just help get you there . . .

Source: Al Rodricks, "The Benefits of Social Networking on YOUR Social Life," ImagineWeMeet.com.

[QUESTIONS FOR REFLECTION]

Compare and contrast the articles by Bindley and Rodricks.

Considering Ideas

1. What is each author's claim?
2. Which article presents a more convincing argument? Why?
3. Based on these articles, as well as your own experiences, what effects, if any, do Facebook and other social networking sites have on relationships? Why?

Considering the Rhetorical Star

1. What is the specific *subject* of each article?
2. What is the *purpose* of each article? Does each author achieve his or her goal? Explain.
3. Who is the intended audience for the articles? How do you know?
4. What primary writing *strategy* do Bindley and Rodricks use for their articles? Do they use any other strategies? Explain.
5. Describe the *design* of each article. Which design is more appealing to you? Why?

Considering Writing Strategies

1. Describe the writing styles of each author. Which author do you connect with more? Why?
2. Which types of appeals (logical, emotional, and/or ethical) does each author use? Give specific examples from the articles.
3. Describe the tone (mood) of each article? Which one has a stronger tone? Identify several words from each article to illustrate your point.

Writing Suggestions

1. Has a social networking site, such as Facebook, ever enhanced or harmed one of your relationships? Write an essay persuading readers that the website is beneficial or detrimental to relationships. Use your own experience (and possibly other research as well) to support your position. Be sure to cite any sources you use. See Chapters 13 and 14 for more details about citing sources.
2. If you have never used a social networking site, would you consider using one now? Why or why not? Write an essay persuading readers that using a social networking website has positive or negative effects on relationships. Use one of the previous articles (and possibly other research as well) to support your point of view. Be sure to cite any source you use. See Chapters 13 and 14 for more details about citing sources.

[preview] **DEBORAH TANNEN**, born in Brooklyn, New York, has published more than 20 books and 100 articles. Her best-selling book, *You Just Don't Understand* (1990), has been translated into 31 languages. Another book of hers, *You Were Always Mom's Favorite!* (2009), has also been quite successful. She has appeared on numerous radio and television shows, and she has given lectures around the world. She is a university professor in the linguistics department at Georgetown University. You can read more about her and watch some of her interview clips at **www.deborahtannen.com**. Before reading, think about a friendship or romantic relationship you have had with someone of the opposite sex. What difficulties, if any, did you experience when trying to communicate with one another?

Sex, Lies and Conversation: Why Is It So Hard for Men and Women to Talk to Each Other?
by Deborah Tannen

I was addressing a small gathering in a suburban Virginia living room—a women's group that had invited men to join them. Throughout the evening, one man had been particularly talkative, frequently offering ideas and anecdotes, while his wife sat silently beside him on the couch. Toward the end of the evening, I commented that women frequently complain that their husbands don't talk to them. This man quickly concurred. He gestured toward his wife and said, "She's the talker in our family." The room burst into laughter; the man looked puzzled and hurt. "It's true," he explained. "When I come home from work I have nothing to say. If she didn't keep the conversation going, we'd spend the whole evening in silence." 1

This episode crystallizes the irony that although American men tend to talk more than women in public situations, they often talk less at home. And this pattern is wreaking havoc with marriage. 2

The pattern was observed by political scientist Andrew Hacker in the late '70s. Sociologist Catherine Kohler Riessman reports in her new book *Divorce Talk* that most of the women she interviewed—but only a few of the men—gave lack of communication as the reason for their divorces. Given the current divorce rate of nearly 50 percent, that amounts to millions of cases in the United States every year—a virtual epidemic of failed conversation. 3

In my own research, complaints from women about their husbands most often focused not on tangible inequities such as having given up the chance for a career to accompany a husband to his, or doing far more than their share of daily life-support work like cleaning, cooking, social arrangements and errands. Instead, they focused 4

on communication: "He doesn't listen to me," "He doesn't talk to me." I found, as Hacker observed years before, that most wives want their husbands to be, first and foremost, conversational partners, but few husbands share this expectation of their wives.

In short, the image that best represents the current crisis is the stereotypical cartoon scene of a man sitting at the breakfast table with a newspaper held up in front of his face, while a woman glares at the back of it, wanting to talk. 5

Linguistic Battle of the Sexes

How can women and men have such different impressions of communication in marriage? Why the widespread imbalance in their interests and expectations? 6

In the April [1990] issue of *American Psychologist*, Stanford University's Eleanor Maccoby reports the results of her own and others' research showing that children's development is most influenced by the social structure of peer interactions. Boys and girls tend to play with children of their own gender, and their sex-separate groups have different organizational structures and interactive norms. 7

I believe these systematic differences in childhood socialization make talk between women and men like cross-cultural communication, heir to all the attraction and pitfalls of that enticing but difficult enterprise. My research on men's and women's conversations uncovered patterns similar to those described for children's groups. 8

For women, as for girls, intimacy is the fabric of relationships, and talk is the thread from which it is woven. Little girls create and maintain friendships by exchanging secrets; similarly, women regard conversation as the cornerstone of friendship. So a woman expects her husband 9 to be a new and improved version of a best friend. What is important is not the individual subjects that are discussed but the sense of closeness, of a life shared, that emerges when people tell their thoughts, feelings, and impressions.

Bonds between boys can be as intense as girls', but 10 they are based less on talking, more on doing things together. Since they don't assume talk is the cement that binds a relationship, men don't know what kind of talk women want, and they don't miss it when it isn't there.

Boys' groups are larger, more inclusive, and more 11 hierarchical, so boys must struggle to avoid the sub-ordinate position in the group. This may play a role in women's complaints that men don't listen to them. Some men really don't like to listen, because being the listener makes them feel one-down, like a child listening to adults or an employee to a boss.

But often, when women tell men, "You aren't listen- 12 ing," and the men protest, "I am," the men are right. The impression of not listening results from misalignments in the mechanics of conversation. The misalignment begins as soon as a man and a woman take physical positions. This became clear when I studied videotapes made by psychologist Bruce Dorval of children and adults talk-ing to their same-sex best friends. I found that at every age, the girls and women faced each other directly, their eyes anchored on each other's faces. At every age, the boys and men sat at angles to each other and looked elsewhere in the room, periodically glancing at each other. They were obviously attuned to each other, often mirroring each other's movements. But the tendency of men to face away can give women the impression they aren't listening even when they are. A young woman in college was frustrated: Whenever she told her boyfriend she wanted to talk to him, he would lie down on the floor, close his eyes, and put his arm over his face. This sig-naled to her, "He's taking a nap." But he insisted he was listening extra hard. Normally, he looks around the room, so he is easily distracted. Lying down and covering his eyes helped him concentrate on what she was saying.

Analogous to the physical alignment that women 13 and men take in conversation is their topical alignment. The girls in my study tended to talk at length about one topic, but the boys tended to jump from topic to topic. The second-grade girls exchanged stories about people they knew. The second-grade boys teased, told jokes, noticed things in the room and talked about finding games to play. The sixth-grade girls talked about problems with a mutual friend. The sixth-grade boys talked about 55 different top-ics, none of which extended over more than a few turns.

Listening to Body Language

Switching topics is another habit that gives women 14 the impression men aren't listening, especially if they switch to a topic about themselves. But the evidence of the 10th-grade boys in my study indicates otherwise.

The 10th-grade boys sprawled across their chairs with bodies parallel and eyes straight ahead, rarely looking at each other. They looked as if they were riding in a car, staring out the windshield. But they were talking about their feelings. One boy was upset because a girl had told him he had a drinking problem, and the other was feeling alienated from all his friends.

Now, when a girl told a friend about a problem, the 15 friend responded by asking probing questions and expressing agreement and understanding. But the boys dismissed each other's problems. Todd assured Richard that his drinking was "no big problem" because "some-times you're funny when you're off your butt." And when Todd said he felt left out, Richard responded, "Why should you? You know more people than me."

Women perceived such responses as belittling and 16 unsupportive. But the boys seemed satisfied with them. Whereas women reassure each other by implying, "You shouldn't feel bad because I've had similar experiences," men do so by implying, "You shouldn't feel bad because your problems aren't so bad."

There are even simpler reasons for women's impres- 17 sion that men don't listen. Linguist Lynette Hirschman found that women make more listener-noise, such as "mhm," "uhuh," and "yeah," to show "I'm with you." Men, she found, more often give silent attention. Women who expect a stream of listener-noise interpret silent atten-tion as no attention at all.

Women's conversational habits are as frustrating to 18 men as men's are to women. Men who expect silent atten-tion interpret a stream of listener-noise as overreaction or impatience. Also, when women talk to each other in a close, comfortable setting, they often overlap, finish each other's sentences and anticipate what the other is about to say. This practice, which I call "participatory listenership," is often per-ceived by men as interruption, intrusion and lack of attention.

A parallel difference caused a man to complain about 19 his wife, "She just wants to talk about her own point of view. If I show her another view, she gets mad at me." When most women talk to each other, they assume a con-versationalist's job is to express agreement and support. But many men see their conversational duty as pointing out the other side of an argument. This is heard as disloy-alty by women, and refusal to offer the requisite support. It is not that women don't want to see other points of view, but that they prefer them phrased as suggestions and inquiries rather than as direct challenges.

In his book *Fighting for Life,* Walter Ong points out 20 that men use "agonistic" or warlike, oppositional formats to do almost anything; thus discussion becomes debate, and conversation a competitive sport. In contrast, women see conversation as a ritual means of estab-lishing rapport. If Jane tells a problem and June says she has a a similar one, they walk away feeling closer to each other. But this attempt at establishing rapport can backfire when used with men. Men take too literally women's ritual "troubles talk," just as women mistake men's ritual challenges for real attack.

The Sounds of Silence

These differences begin to clarify why women and men 21 have such different expectations about communication in marriage. For women, talk creates intimacy. Marriage is an orgy of closeness: you can tell your feelings and thoughts, and still be loved. Their greatest fear is being pushed away. But men live in a hierarchical world, where talk maintains independence and status. They are on guard to protect themselves from being put down and pushed around.

This explains the paradox of the talkative man who said 22 of his silent wife, "She's the talker." In the public setting of a guest lecture, he felt challenged to show his intelligence and display his understanding of the lecture. But at home, where he has nothing to prove and no one to defend against, he is free to remain silent. For his wife, being home means she is free from the worry that something she says might offend someone, or spark disagreement, or appear to be showing off; at home she is free to talk.

The communication problems that endanger marriage 23 can't be fixed by mechanical engineering. They require a new conceptual framework about the role of talk in human relationships. Many of the psychological explanations that have become second nature may not be helpful, because they tend to blame either women (for not being assertive enough) or men (for not being in touch with their feelings). A sociolinguistic approach by which male-female conversation is seen as cross-cultural communication allows us to understand the problem and forge solutions without blaming either party.

Once the problem is understood, improvement comes 24 naturally, as it did to the young woman and her boyfriend who seemed to go to sleep when she wanted to talk. Previously, she had accused him of not listening, and he had refused to change his behavior, since that would be admitting fault. But then she learned about and explained to him the differences in women's and men's habitual ways of aligning themselves in conversation. The next time she told him she wanted to talk, he began, as usual, by lying down and covering his eyes. When the familiar negative reaction bubbled up, she reassured herself that he really was listening. But then he sat up and looked at her. Thrilled she asked why. He said, "You like me to look at you when we talk, so I'll try to do it." Once he saw their differences as cross-cultural rather than right and wrong, he independently altered his behavior.

Women who feel abandoned and deprived when their 25 husbands won't listen to or report daily news may be happy to discover their husbands trying to adapt once they understand the place of small talk in women's relationships. But if their husbands don't adapt, the women may still be comforted that for men, this is not a failure of intimacy. Accepting the difference, the wives may look to their friends or family for that kind of talk. And husbands who can't provide it shouldn't feel their wives have made unreasonable demands. Some couples will still decide to divorce, but at least their decisions will be based on realistic expectations.

In these times of resurgent ethnic conflicts, the world 26 desperately needs cross-cultural understanding. Like charity, successful cross-cultural communication should begin at home.

Source: Deborah Tannen, "Sex, Lies, and Conversation: Why Is It So Hard for Men and Women to Talk to Each Other?" Copyright © by Deborah Tannen. Permission granted by International Creative Management, Inc.

[QUESTIONS FOR REFLECTION]

Considering Ideas

1. What is Tannen's overall claim? Where does she most clearly state her thesis?

2. According to the author, how do men and women communicate differently? What kinds of problems can arise in a relationship because of these different communication styles?

3. What can men and women do to try to overcome their communication obstacles?

Considering the Rhetorical Star

1. What is the main *subject* of Tannen's article? Is the specific topic engaging? Why or why not?

2. Who is the primary *audience* for the article? Is there a secondary audience? Explain.

3. What is the author's main *purpose* for the article? Does she convey her purpose clearly? Explain.

4. Tannen uses persuasion as the primary *strategy* for the piece. What other writing strategies does she use, and how do they affect the article?

5. What *design* features does the author use? Are they effective? Why or why not?

Considering Writing Strategies

1. How does the author establish herself as an authority figure on the subject? Is her approach convincing? Why or why not?

2. Does Tannen use inductive or deductive reasoning in her essay? What other methods does she use to support her argument? Identify several specific examples. Which ones seem to be the most effective? Why?

3. In the concluding paragraph, the writer compares cross-cultural communication to charity. How effective is this simile?

Writing Suggestions

1. In her essay, Tannen draws several conclusions about the different communication styles of men and women. Write an essay arguing for or against her perceptions of the ways in which men and women communicate. Be sure to back up your claim with specific supporting evidence.

2. Tannen suggests that once couples understand the types of problems they have communicating, they will be able to improve their relationships. Do you agree or disagree with the author's assertion? Write an essay arguing for or against her claim.

ESOL Tip >

How do men and women communicate in your home country? Is it different from the way in which they communicate in the United States? If so, write a persuasive essay about which communication style works better.

Reading and Reflection PERSUASIVE WRITING

[preview] **JON KATZ,** a media critic, journalist, and novelist, began his career as a reporter and editor for the *Philadelphia Inquirer,* the *Boston Globe,* and the *Washington Post.* He also served as an executive producer of the *CBS Morning News.* His media criticism, columns, and reviews have appeared in a variety of publications, including *Rolling Stone, Wired, GQ,* and the *New York Times.* Additionally, Katz has written nearly 20 books, including a series of mystery books about Kit DeLeeuw, a stay-at-home dad and detective, who uncovers a variety of crimes in Rochambeau, New Jersey. Katz is perhaps best known for his 2007 *New York Times* best seller *Dog Days* and a 2013 title, *The Second Chance Dog: A Love Story.* Katz has contributed to several online magazines, including **Slate.com**. In the following essay, Katz explores the difficulties that a young boy faces as he struggles to grow into manhood, especially if he is a misfit. Before reading, think about what it is like to be a child in a society where bullies are prevalent. What challenges occur?

How Boys Become Men by Jon Katz

Two nine-year-old boys, neighbors and friends, were walking home from school. The one in the bright blue windbreaker was laughing and swinging a heavy-looking book bag toward the head of his friend, who kept ducking and stepping back. "What's the matter?" asked the kid with the bag, whooshing it over his head. "You chicken?"

His friend stopped, stood still and braced himself. The bag slammed into the side of his face, the thump audible all the way across the street where I stood watching. The impact knocked him to the ground, where he lay mildly stunned for a second. Then he struggled up, rubbing the side of his head. "See?" he said proudly. "I'm no chicken."

No. A chicken would probably have had the sense to get out of the way. This boy was already well on the road to becoming a man, having learned one of the central ethics of his gender: Experience pain rather than show fear.

Women tend to see men as a giant problem in need of solution. They tell us that we're remote and uncommunicative, that we need to demonstrate less machismo and more commitment, more humanity. But if you don't understand something about boys, you can't understand why men are the way we are, why we find it so difficult to make friends or to acknowledge our fears and problems.

Boys live in a world with its own Code of Conduct, a set of ruthless, unspoken, and unyielding rules: 5

Don't be a goody-goody.
Never rat. If your parents ask about bruises, shrug.
Never admit fear. Ride the roller coaster, join the fistfight, do what you have to do. Asking for help is for sissies.
Empathy is for nerds. You can help your best buddy, under certain circumstances. Everyone else is on his own.
Never discuss anything of substance with anybody. Grunt, shrug, dump on teachers, laugh at wimps, talk about comic books. Anything else is risky.

Boys are rewarded for throwing hard. Most other activities—reading, befriending girls, or just thinking—are considered weird. And if there's one thing boys don't want to be, it's weird. 6

More than anything else, boys are supposed to learn how to handle themselves. I remember the bitter fifth-grade conflict I touched off by elbowing aside a bigger boy named Barry and seizing the cafeteria's last carton of chocolate milk. Teased for getting aced out by a wimp, he had to reclaim his place in the pack. Our fistfight, at recess, ended with my knees buckling and my lip bleeding while my friends, sympathetic but out of range, watched resignedly. 7

When I got home, my mother took one look at my swollen face and screamed. I wouldn't tell her anything, but when my father got home I cracked and confessed, pleading with them to do nothing. Instead, they called Barry's parents, who restricted his television for a week. 8

The following morning, Barry and six of his pals stepped out from behind a stand of trees. "It's the rat," said Barry. 9

I bled a little more. Rat was scrawled in crayon across my desk. They were waiting for me after school for a number of afternoons to follow. I tried varying my routes and avoiding bushes and hedges. It usually didn't work. 10

I was as ashamed for telling as I was frightened. "You did ask for it," said my best friend. Frontier Justice has nothing on Boy Justice. 11

In panic, I appealed to a cousin who was several years older. He followed me home from school, and when Barry's gang surrounded me, he came barreling toward us. "Stay away from my cousin," he shouted, "or I'll kill you." 12

After they were gone, however, my cousin could barely stop laughing. "You were afraid of them?" he howled. "They barely came up to my waist." 13

Men remember receiving little mercy as boys; maybe that's why it's sometimes difficult for them to show any. 14

"I know lots of men who had happy childhoods, but none who have happy memories of the way other boys treated them," says a friend. "It's a macho marathon from third grade up, when you start butting each other in the stomach." 15

"The thing is," adds another friend, "you learn early on to hide what you feel. It's never safe to say, 'I'm scared.' My girlfriend asks me why I don't talk more about what I'm feeling. I've gotten better at it, but it will never come naturally." 16

You don't need to be a shrink to see how the lessons boys learn affect their behavior as men. Men are being asked, more and more, to show sensitivity, but they dread the very word. They struggle to build their increasingly uncertain work lives but will deny they're in trouble. They want love, affection, and support but don't know how to ask for them. They hide their weaknesses and fears from all, even those they care for. They've learned to be wary of intervening when they see others in trouble. They often still balk at being stigmatized as weird. 17

Some men get shocked into sensitivity—when they lose their jobs, their wives, or their lovers. Others learn it through a strong marriage, or through their own children. 18

It may be a long while, however, before male culture evolves to the point that boys can learn more from one another than how to hit curve balls. Last month, walking my dog past the playground near my house, I saw three boys encircling a fourth, laughing and pushing him. He was skinny and rumpled, and he looked frightened. One boy knelt behind him while another pushed him from the front, a trick familiar to any former boy. He fell backward. 19

When the others ran off, he brushed the dirt off his elbows and walked toward the swings. His eyes were moist and he was struggling for control. 20

"Hi," I said through the chain-link fence. "How ya doing?" 21

"Fine," he said quickly, kicking his legs out and beginning his swing. 22

Source: Jon Katz, "How Boys Become Men." From *The Compact Reader.* Originally appeared in *Glamour* in January 1993.

[QUESTIONS FOR REFLECTION]

Considering Ideas

1. According to Katz, what kinds of challenges do boys face as they are trying to grow up and become men? Do you agree or disagree with the notion that boys often mistreat each other?

2. The writer claims, "Women tend to see men as a giant problem in need of solution." Do you agree or disagree with this assertion? Why?

3. According to the author, what are some ways in which men can learn to become sensitive? Is Katz correct in his analysis? Why or why not?

Considering the Rhetorical Star

1. What is the main *subject* of Katz's article? Is the specific topic engaging? Why or why not?

2. Who is the intended *audience?* How do you know?

3. What is the author's main *purpose* for the article? Does he have any other purposes? Explain.

4. Katz uses persuasion as the primary *strategy* for the piece. What other writing strategies does he use, and how do they affect the article?

5. What is the *design* of the work? Is the design effective? Why or why not?

Considering Writing Strategies

1. Identify examples of logical, emotional, and/or ethical appeals that the author uses to persuade his readers. Which ones seem to be most effective? Why?

2. Why does Katz conclude his essay with an anecdote about a boy who has just been harassed by other boys on the playground? What does this ending suggest to the reader?

3. How persuasive is this essay? Do you agree with the author's notion that boys have to "experience pain rather than show fear" in order to follow the rules of their gender and that understanding this principle will help women to better understand men? Why or why not?

Writing Suggestions

1. What were the rules that governed how boys or girls were expected to behave where you were raised? Write a persuasive essay explaining what these guidelines were.

2. Write a persuasive essay titled "How Girls Become Women." In your essay, identify some of the challenges that girls face and suggest how these obstacles influence them as they grow into adulthood.

ESOL Tip >

How are gender roles viewed in your home country? Write an essay arguing for or against the traditional gender roles in your native country.

Paired Readings

The next two readings discuss androgynous men from the male and female perspectives. Read both articles before answering the questions for reflection that follow the second one. Before reading the articles, think about your own masculinity or femininity. What traits do you have that people might consider to be masculine or feminine?

Reading and Reflection PERSUASIVE WRITING

[preview] **NOEL PERRIN** (1927–2004), born in New York City, was a writer, teacher, and environmentalist. He earned a bachelor's degree from Williams College in Massachusetts and master's degrees from Duke University in North Carolina and Cambridge University in England. After graduation, he became an English instructor at Dartmouth College in New Hampshire and later rose to the position of chair of the English Department. While living on his 85-acre farm in Vermont, Perrin wrote a series of books highlighting some of his experiences with rural life, the last of which is called *Last Person Rural.*

In the following essay, Perrin scrutinizes the traditional definitions of what it means to be masculine or feminine in the American culture.

Androgynous Man **by Noel Perrin**

The summer I was 16, I took a train from New York to Steamboat Springs, Colo., where I was going to be assistant horse wrangler at a camp. The trip took three days, and since I was much too shy to talk to strangers, I had quite a lot of time for reading. I read all of "Gone With the Wind." I read all the interesting articles in a couple of magazines I had, and then I went back and read all the dull stuff. I also took all the quizzes, a thing of which magazines were even fuller then than now.

The one that held my undivided attention was called [2] "How Masculine/Feminine Are You?" It consisted of a large number of inkblots. The reader was supposed to decide which of four objects each blot most resembled. The choices might be a cloud, a steam engine, a caterpillar and a sofa.

When I finished the test, I was shocked to find that [3] I was barely masculine at all. On a scale of 1 to 10, I was about 1.2. Me, the horse wrangler? (And not just wrangler, either. That summer, I had to skin a couple of horses that died—the camp owner wanted the hides.)

The results of that test were so terrifying to me that [4] for the first time in my life I did a piece of original analysis. Having unlimited time on the train, I looked at the "masculine" answers over and over, trying to find what it was that distinguished real men from people like me—and eventually I discovered two very simple patterns. It was "masculine" to think the blots looked like man-made objects, and "feminine" to think they looked like natural objects. It was masculine to think they looked like things capable of causing harm, and feminine to think of innocent things.

Even at 16, I had the sense to see that the compilers [5] of the test were using rather limited criteria—maleness and femaleness are both more complicated than that—and I breathed a huge sigh of relief. I wasn't necessarily a wimp, after all.

That the test did reveal something other than the [6] superficiality of its makers I realized only many years later. What it revealed was that there is a large class of men and women both, to which I belong, who are essentially androgynous. That doesn't mean we're gay, or low in the appropriate hormones, or uncomfortable performing the jobs traditionally assigned our sexes. (A few years after that summer, I was leading troops in combat and, unfashionable as it now is to admit this, having a very good time. War is exciting. What a pity the 20th century went and spoiled it with high-tech weapons.)

What it does mean to be spiritually androgynous is [7] a kind of freedom. Men who are all male, or he-men, or 100 percent red-blooded Americans, have a little biological set that causes them to be attracted to physical power, and probably also to dominance. Maybe even to watching football. I don't say this to criticize them. Completely masculine men are quite often wonderful people: good husbands, good (though sometimes overwhelming) fathers, good members of society. Furthermore, they are often so unself-consciously at ease in the world that other men seek to imitate them. They just aren't as free as us androgynes. They pretty nearly have to be what they are; we have a range of choices open.

The sad part is that many of us never discover that. [8] Men who are not 100 percent red-blooded Americans— say, those who are only 75 percent red-blooded—often fail to notice their freedom. They are too busy trying to copy the he-men ever to realize that men, like women, come in a wide variety of acceptable types. Why this frantic imitation? My answer is mere speculation, but not casual. I have speculated on this for a long time.

Partly they're just envious of the he-man's unconscious ease. Mostly they're terrified of finding that there may be something wrong with them deep down, some weakness at the heart. To avoid discovering that, they spend their lives acting out the role that the he-man naturally lives. Sad. [9]

One thing that men owe to the women's movement is [10] that this kind of failure is less common than it used to be. In releasing themselves from the single ideal of the dependent woman, women have more or less incidentally released a lot of men from the single ideal of the dominant male. The one mistake the feminists have made, I think, is in supposing that all men need this release, or that the world would be a better place if all men achieved it. It wouldn't. It would just be duller.

So far I have been pretty vague about just what the [11] freedom of the androgynous man is. Obviously it varies with the case. In the case I know best, my own, I can be quite specific. It has freed me most as a parent. I am, among other things, a fairly good natural mother. I like the nurturing role. It makes me feel good to see a child eat—and it turns me to mush to see a 4-year-old holding a glass with both small hands, in order to drink. I even enjoyed sewing patches on the knees of my daughter Amy's Dr. Dentons when she was at the crawling stage. All that pleasure I would have lost if I had made myself stick to the notion of the paternal role that I started with.

Or take a smaller and rather ridiculous example. [12] I feel free to kiss cats. Until recently it never occurred to me that I would want to, though my daughters have been doing it all their lives. But my elder daughter is now 22, and in London. Of course, I get to look after her cat while she is gone. He's a big, handsome farm cat named Petrushka, very unsentimental, though used from kittenhood to being kissed on the top of the head by Elizabeth. I've gotten very fond of him (he's the adventurous kind of cat who likes to climb hills with you), and one night I simply felt like kissing him on the top of the head, and did. Why did no one tell me sooner how silky cat fur is?

Then there's my relation to cars. I am completely [13] unembarrassed by my inability to diagnose even minor problems in whatever object I happen to be driving, and don't have to make some insider's remark to mechanics to try to establish that I, too, am a "Man With His Machine."

The same ease extends to household maintenance. [14] I do it, of course. Service people are expensive. But for the last decade my house has functioned better than it used to because I've had the aid of a volume called "Home Repairs Any Woman Can Do," which is pitched just right for people at my technical level. As a youth, I'd as soon have touched such a book as I would have become a transvestite. Even though common sense says there is really nothing sexual whatsoever about fixing sinks.

Or take public emotion. All my life I have easily been 15 moved by certain kinds of voices. The actress Siobhan McKenna's, to take a notable case. Give her an emotional scene in a play, and within 10 words my eyes are full of tears. In boyhood, my great dread was that someone might notice. I struggled manfully, you might say, to suppress this weakness. Now, of course, I don't see it as a weakness at all, but as a kind of fulfillment. I even suspect that the true he-men feel the same way, or one kind of them does, at least, and it's only the poor imitators who have to struggle to repress themselves.

Let me come back to the inkblots, with their assumption 16 that masculine equates with machinery and science, and feminine with art and nature. I have no idea whether the right pronoun for God is He, She or It. But this I'm pretty sure of. If God could somehow be induced to take that test, God would not come out macho, and not feminismo, either, but right in the middle. Fellow androgynes, it's a nice thought.

Source: "Androgynous Man" by Noel Perrin © 1984. Reprinted by permission.

[Preview] **AMY GROSS,** a New Yorker, has worked as a writer or editor of numerous articles that have appeared in various magazines and newspapers, including the *New York Times, Mademoiselle, Elle,* and *Redbook.* After serving as the editor in chief of *O, The Oprah Magazine* for eight years, she has now shifted the focus of her life to the study and teaching of mindful meditation. In the following article, Gross presents a woman's perspective on the androgynous man, as compared to the man's perspective in the previous article by Perrin. As you are reading, consider where the authors agree and disagree. Also, what is your perspective on the androgynous man?

The Appeal of the Androgynous Man by Amy Gross

James Dean was my first androgynous man. I figured 1 I could talk to him. He was anguished and I was 12, so we had a lot in common. With only a few exceptions, all the men I have liked or loved have been a certain kind of man: a kind who doesn't play football or watch the games on Sunday, who doesn't tell dirty jokes featuring broads or chicks, who is not contemptuous of conversations that are philosophically speculative, introspective, or otherwise foolish according to the other kind of man. He is more self-amused, less inflated, more quirky, vulnerable and responsive than the other sort (the other sort, I'm visualizing as the guys on TV who advertise deodorant in the locker room). He is more like me than the other sort. He is what social scientists and feminists would call androgynous: having the characteristics of both male and female.

Now the first thing I want you to know about the 2 androgynous man is that he is neither effeminate nor hermaphroditic. All his primary and secondary sexual characteristics are in order and I would say he's all-man, but that is just what he is not. He is more than all-man.

The merely all-man man, for one thing, never walks 3 to the grocery store unless the little woman is away visiting her mother with the kids, or is in the hospital having a kid, or there is no little woman. All-men men don't know how to shop in a grocery store unless it is to buy a 6-pack and some pretzels. Their ideas of nutrition expand beyond a 6-pack and pretzels only to take in steak, potatoes, scotch or rye whiskey, and maybe a wad of cake or apple pie. All-men men have absolutely no taste in food, art, books, movies, theatre, dance, how to live, what are good questions, what is funny, or anything else I care about. It's not exactly that the all-man's man is an uncouth illiterate. He may be educated, well-mannered, and on a first-name basis with fine wines. One all-man man I knew was a handsome individual who gave the impression of being gentle, affectionate, and sensitive. He sat and ate dinner one night while I was doing something endearingly feminine at the sink. At one point, he mutely held up his glass to indicate in a primitive, even ape-like way, his need for a refill. This was in 1967, before Women's Liberation. Even so, I was disturbed. Not enough to break the glass over his handsome head, not even enough to mutely indicate the whereabouts of the refrigerator, but enough to remember that moment in all its revelatory clarity. No androgynous man would ever brutishly expect to be waited on without even a "please." (With a "please," maybe.)

The brute happened to be a doctor—not a hard hat— 4 and, to all appearances, couth. But he had bought the whole superman package, complete with that fragile beast, the male ego. The androgynous man arrives with a male ego too, but his is not as imperialistic. It doesn't invade every area of his life and person. Most activities and thoughts have nothing to do with masculinity or femininity. The androgynous man knows this. The all-man

man doesn't. He must keep a constant guard against anything even vaguely feminine (*i.e.*, "sissy") rising up in him. It must be a terrible strain.

Male chauvinism is an irritation, but the real problem I have with the all-man man is that it's hard for me to talk to him. He's alien to me, and for this I'm at least half to blame. As his interests have not carried him into the sissy, mine have never taken me very far into the typically masculine terrains of sports, business and finance, politics, cars, boats and machines. But blame or no blame, the reality is that it is almost as difficult for me to connect with him as it would be to link up with an Arab shepherd or Bolivian sandalmaker. There's a similar culture gap.

It seems to me that the most masculine men usually end up with the most feminine women. Maybe they like extreme polarity; I like polarity myself but the poles have to be within earshot. As I've implied, I'm very big on talking. I fall in love for at least three hours with anyone who engages me in a real conversation. I'd rather a man point out a paragraph in a book—wanting to share it with me—than bring me flowers. I'd rather a man ask what I think than tell me I look pretty. (Women who are very pretty and accustomed to hearing that they are pretty may feel differently.) My experience is that all-men men read books I don't want to see paragraphs of, and don't really give a damn what I or any woman would think about most issues so long as she looks pretty. They have a very limited use for women. I suspect they don't really like us. The androgynous man likes women as much or as little as he likes anyone.

Another difference between the all-man man and the androgynous man is that the first is not a star in the creativity department. If your image of the creative male accessorizes him with a beret, smock and artist's palette, you will not believe the all-man man has been seriously short-changed. But if you allow as how creativity is a talent for freedom, associated with imagination, wit, empathy, unpredictability, and receptivity to new impressions and connections, then you will certainly pity the dull, thick-skinned, rigid fellow in whom creativity sets no fires.

Nor is the all-man man so hot when it comes to sensitivity. He may be true-blue in the trenches, but if you are troubled, you'd be wasting your time trying to milk comfort from the all-man man.

This is not blind prejudice. It is enlightened prejudice. My biases were confirmed recently by a psychologist named Sandra Lipsetz Bern, a professor at Stanford University. She brought to attention the fact that high masculinity in males (and high femininity in females) has been "consistently correlated with lower overall intelligence and lower creativity." Another psychologist, Donald W. MacKinnon, director of the

Institute of Personality Assessment and Research at the University of California in Berkeley, found that "creative males give more expression to the feminine side of their nature than do less creative men. . . . [They] score relatively high on femininity, and this despite the fact that, as a group, they do not present an effeminate appearance or give evidence of increased homosexual interests or experiences. Their elevated scores on femininity indicate rather an openness to their feelings and emotions, a sensitive intellect and understanding self-awareness and wide-ranging interests including many which in the American culture are thought of as more feminine. . . ."

Dr. Bern ran a series of experiments on college students who had been categorized as masculine, feminine, or androgynous, In three tests of the degree of nurturance—warmth and caring—the masculine men scored painfully low (painfully for anyone stuck with a masculine man, that is). In one of those experiments, all the students were asked to listen to a "troubled talker"—a person who was not neurotic but simply lonely, supposedly new in town and feeling like an outsider, The masculine men were the least supportive, responsive or humane. "They lacked the ability to express warmth, playfulness and concern," Bern concluded. (She's giving them the benefit of the doubt. It's possible the masculine men didn't express those qualities because they didn't possess them.)

The androgynous man, on the other hand, having been run through the same carnival of tests, "performs spectacularly. He shuns no behavior just because our culture happens to label it as female and his competence crosses both the instrumental [getting the job done, the problem solved] and the expressive [showing a concern for the welfare of others, the harmony of the group] domains. Thus, he stands firm in his opinion, he cuddles kittens and bounces babies and he has a sympathetic ear for someone in distress."

Well, a great mind, a sensitive and warm personality are fine in their place, but you are perhaps skeptical of the gut appeal of the androgynous man. As a friend, maybe, you'd like an adrogynous man. For a sexual partner, though, you'd prefer a jock. There's no arguing chemistry, but consider the jock for a moment, He competes on the field, whatever his field is, and bed is just one more field to him: another opportunity to perform, another fray. Sensuality is for him candy to be doled out as lure. It is a ration whose flow is cut off at the exact point when it has served its purpose— namely, to elicit your willingness to work out on the field with him.

Highly masculine men need to believe their sexual appetite is far greater than a woman's (than a nice woman's). To them, females must be seduced. Seduction is a euphemism for a power play, a con job. It pits man against woman (or woman against man). The jock believes he must win you over, incite your body to rebel against your better judgment: in other words—conquer you.

The androgynous man is not your opponent but your teammate. He does not seduce: he invites. Sensuality is a pleasure for him. He's not quite so goal-oriented. And 14

to conclude, I think I need only remind you here of his greater imagination, his wit and empathy, his unpredictability, and his receptivity to new impressions and connections.

[QUESTIONS FOR REFLECTION]

Compare and contrast the articles by Perrin and Gross.

Considering Ideas

1. How would Perrin and Gross define the term *androgynous?*

2. What kinds of appeals (logical, emotional, and ethical) does each author use to support his or her main point?

3. Do the authors believe that men today have more freedom to display behaviors that were traditionally thought to be feminine? Why or why not? Include specific passages from each article to support your point. How do men and women perceive these behaviors in the 21st century?

Considering the Rhetorical Star

1. What is the main *subject* of each essay? Are the topics engaging? Why or why not?

2. Who is the intended *audience* for the essays? How do you know?

3. What is each author's main *purpose?* Are any other purposes evident? Explain.

4. The authors use persuasion as the primary *strategy* for the essays. Do they employ any other writing strategies? What are they?

5. Describe the *design* of each essay.

Considering Writing Strategies

1. What points are Perrin and Gross arguing for in their essays?

2. What kinds of evidence do the authors provide to support their main points? Is the supporting evidence effective? Why or why not?

3. Which essay is more persuasive? Explain your answer.

Writing Suggestions

1. Write a persuasive essay looking at the subject from the perspective of a woman. What behaviors do some women display that are considered to be more masculine than feminine? How do others perceive these behaviors? Should women feel free to exhibit behaviors that are thought to be traditionally masculine? Why or why not? Emphasize several different examples to support your thesis.

2. Choose a television commercial that stereotypes men or women. Write an essay arguing why the portrayal of men or women in the commercial is unfair.

ESOL Tip >

You might choose a commercial from your home country for writing suggestion 2.

▶ *Activity*   **Interpreting Brad Paisley's Video**

Go to **youtube.com** and watch the official music video for Brad Paisley's song, "I'm Still a Guy." In pairs, groups, or as a class, compare and contrast his view of the androgynous man with that of Perrin and Gross. Note: This activity can serve as a springboard for a writing assignment.

Interpreting Brad Paisley's Video
Activity:
Answers will vary.

Mursing
by Thomas James "TJ" Pinkerton

Not many people are used to seeing a male nurse or "murse" walk into their room in the hospital due to the fact that there are not many males in the nursing profession. However, nursing is a great profession for men to get into, and men can make significant contributions to the nursing field. The physical strength of being a man and the power of male camaraderie are both factors in making nursing a logical career choice for men.

One reason for men to get into the nursing field is the physical requirements of a nursing position. For instance, a nurse might have to move patients who cannot move themselves. One example of this would be if a patient needed to use the restroom but could not find the strength to get out of bed. A male nurse would have the strength to lift most patients off of a bed without needing to call for additional help. Furthermore, during a patient's hospital stay, he or she will often need to be moved from one room to another for testing. In that case a nurse needs to be able to lift the patient out of bed, place him or her into a wheelchair, push the wheelchair to the test site, lift the patient out of the wheelchair, and place him or her on one of the numerous machines used for testing. When the testing is complete, the nurse must repeat this whole process in reverse to return the patient to his or her room. Most men are strong enough to accomplish these tasks on their own, without calling for backup.

Another reason why men may want to consider getting into the nursing field is the rapport they can build with male patients. Of course many of the patients in a hospital are going to be male, and some of them are going to be more comfortable if the nurse attending to them is male also. Some male patients, especially those from an older generation or from a male-dominated culture, are not used to taking orders or advice from women. If that is the case, it is best to assign the patient a male nurse simply as a way to comfort the patient.

Additionally, some male patients may prefer a male nurse because they may be embarrassed about why they are in the hospital, especially if it is for a male-related problem. While the preference for a male nurse may be discriminatory toward women, the hospital is not the place to fix this type of ailment. Getting the patient healthy enough to return to everyday life should always be the first goal of the hospital, and the comfort of the patient while in the care of the hospital should be a close second. No matter how silly the reason for the patient's request for a male nurse is, his or her needs should be met.

Overall, many career fields that have traditionally been reserved mainly for women, including nursing, are opening their doors to men. While in the past it may have seemed a little awkward for a man to pursue a career as a nurse, today the need for men in the nursing field is evident. Men can provide beneficial services for the nursing industry such as physical strength and male companionship for male patients.

[QUESTIONS FOR REFLECTION]

1. Identify Pinkerton's claim (thesis). Is it stated clearly?

2. According to the author, why do some men prefer a male nurse? Do you agree with this point? Why or why not?

3. Which types of appeals (logical, emotional, or ethical) does the author use in his essay to support his claim? Are they effective? Why or why not?

4. Is Pinkerton's argument convincing? Why or why not?

5. Do you think men should be a part of the nursing field? Why or why not?

Activity   The Great Debate

On your own, in pairs, or in small groups, choose one (or more) of the claims listed below. Make a list of arguments for and against the claim. Determine which side seems to have the best support. If possible, share your list with another classmate or other group and discuss your lists. Where do you agree? Where do you disagree? Avoid getting into a heated debate. The point is to discuss different perspectives rather than draw a conclusion about which side is "right."

- The lottery and other forms of gambling should be illegal in every state.
- Actors and professional athletes are paid too much.
- Beauty pageants are exploitive.
- People who talk on cell phones while driving, or even walking, are a danger to others.
- We are too dependent on computers.
- Our election process is unfair.
- Everyone should be concerned about global warming.

A representative from each group may share a few of the highlights with the class. This activity may give you ideas for writing a persuasive essay.

PERSUASION AND MARKETING

One of the most noticeable forms of persuasion is marketing. Virtually every type of organization—whether it sells a product or provides a service—needs to promote itself to increase revenues. As with other types of persuasion, advertisements need to appeal to the audience using logic, emotions, and/or ethics.

Advertising messages are everywhere:

- "Have your surgery at Healthy Hospital, the number one facility in the region."
- "Ace Accounting Associates will provide you with the most accurate audit or tax return."
- "Come to Crazy Carl's Computers for all of your computer networking needs."
- "Dustin's Divine Delicacies is the most exquisite eatery in the East."
- "Support your local friendly fire department or sheriff's office with a donation."
- "Do your part to reduce carbon dioxide emissions; buy a hybrid car from Gregg's Green Garage."

 ## Activity   Appeals Used in Advertising

On your own or in pairs or groups, identify the types of appeals used in the fictitious advertising messages listed above. Now, write six one-sentence ads of your own using a variety of appeals. If possible, have another student or group determine which types of appeals you have used in your ads.

The Great Debate Activity:
Answers will vary.

Teaching Tip
Ask students to bring additional advertisements to analyze in class. One of the ads may spark their interest and lead to a potential topic for a research paper.

Appeals Used in Advertising Activity: Answers to First Part (Appeals Used Above):
1. Logical 2. Logical 3. Logical 4. Emotional 5. Emotional, ethical 6. Emotional, ethical

Answers to Second Part (Student's Ads):
Answers will vary.

Now that you have read one or more examples of persuasive writing, it's time to write your own argument. You may choose to write about one of the writing options that follow, the advertisement, the image, or one of the media suggestions. Additionally, keep your ears open for hot topics at school or work; you may hear a conversation that sparks your interest. You might also read an online newspaper or magazine to find a controversial topic. Remember to keep track of any sources you use in case you need to cite them in your paper. Consider your rhetorical star and the qualities of effective persuasive writing as you begin to compose your assignment.

Writing Assignment Options

Use one of the following topics to write a persuasive essay.

1. Division of labor for household chores, earning an income, and/or raising children
2. Environmental issue, such as going green, recycling, or avoiding pesticides
3. Laws about smoking cigarettes in public places
4. Health care issue, such as benefits, mandatory vaccinations, or alternative medicines
5. Animal testing for research
6. Cell phone usage while driving or walking
7. Helmet laws for bicyclists and/or motorcyclists
8. The legal drinking age
9. Gun control laws
10. The death penalty

Interpreting an Advertisement

Who is the specific audience for this advertisement? How do you know? Do you think the target audience would want to purchase beauty products from Mac? Why or why not? Is the ad persuasive? Why or why not? The Mac cosmetics advertisement uses celebrities in an attempt to sell the product. How effective is this practice? Is it fair or misleading? Write a persuasive essay arguing for or against the use of celebrity testimonials. You may want to combine purposes and incorporate a cause-and-effect writing strategy along with persuasion. Be sure to cite any sources you use to support your argument.

Who is the audience for the Carlsberg advertisement? What effect do the images and text suggest that drinking Carlsberg has on friendships among men and women? Do you agree? Why or why not? Is the ad persuasive? Why or why not? Can drinking beer be a catalyst for bringing people together? Conversely, can drinking too much beer create problems in relationships? Write a persuasive essay related to the Carlsberg advertisement and how drinking beer can affect relationships. Make a positive or negative claim about drinking beer and support your thesis convincingly. If you use outside sources, be sure to cite them.

► *Activity*   **Writing an Advertisement**

Create an advertisement for a fictitious product on your own, in pairs, or in groups. Include text and images to help convince your audience to purchase your product.

Note: You'll find an extended group project called "Sales Pitch" as well as suggestions for preparing and presenting group presentations in Chapter 15.

Writing about an Image

Write a persuasive essay about one of the images in this chapter. Make a claim about the image itself, or you may choose to write about something that relates to it. For example, you might write an essay about the Carlsberg advertisement, arguing that beer companies glamorize the use of their products. Or you may choose to write about the Mac ad and discuss the ways advertisers use sex appeal to market their products.

Media Connection for Persuading

You might watch, read, and/or listen to one or more of the suggested media to discover additional examples of persuasion in the context of relationships. Exploring various media may help you to better understand methods for persuading. For example, you might watch the 2014 movie *Endless Love* or listen to (or watch the video of) Taylor Swift's song "Love Story" and write an essay arguing for or against parents telling their children whom they can date.

Television	*Dr. Phil*	*Modern Family*	*The Jerry Springer Show*	*Two and a Half Men*
Film	*The Lottery Ticket* (2010)	*The Blind Side* (2009)	*About Last Night* (2014)	*Endless Love* (2014)
Print/ E-Reading	*O* (The Oprah Magazine)	*Super Charm*	*Psychology Today*	*The Constant Heart* (2012) by Craig Nova
Internet	**www.createhealthy relationships.com**	**www.psychologytoday .com/topics/relationships**	**www.savemymarriage .com**	**www.yourtango .com/relationships**
Music	"I Won't Give Up" by Jason Mraz	"Love Story" by Taylor Swift	"All of Me" by John Legend	"Say Something" by A Great Big World and Christina Aguilera

10.4 ANALYZING THE RHETORICAL STAR FOR WRITING PERSUASIVELY

FIGURE 10.2
The Rhetorical Star

As you prepare to write your persuasive paper, consider the five points of the rhetorical star (Figure 10.2). You might use some of the questions in the chart as you conduct your rhetorical star analysis.

Subject	Choose a debatable topic as the focus for your essay. You should have strong feelings about the issue or controversy. You might want to write about a subject that is currently in the news or one that you have experienced on a personal level. For example, you might write about a law or policy that seems unfair or insufficient. Be sure that your topic is neither too narrow nor too broad for the length of your assignment.
Audience	Who will read your persuasive essay? How much does your audience know about the issue you are addressing? What audience characteristics can you appeal to in your argument? Are you aiming at readers who are personally involved with the issue, or are they just interested in learning more about it? How do your readers feel about the issue? Are they likely to be supportive of your position, hostile toward your stance, or unsure of their own perspective on the issue? \n\n Include details that will appeal to your specific audience. For instance, you might write an article for your campus newspaper in an attempt to persuade your readers that more students should take leadership roles in school organizations, such as student government or honorary fraternities, because they will gain leadership skills and strengthen their résumés. In that case your primary audience would be college students.
Purpose	Think about what you are trying to accomplish through your persuasive essay. Are you trying to convince the readers to change their minds about a controversial issue? Do you want the audience to take some sort of action? Maybe you just want the readers to understand your position, even if they have a different stance. Keep your purpose in mind as you carefully craft your argument.
Strategy	Even if your primary goal is to persuade your reader, you may also employ other writing strategies. For example, if you are writing an essay persuading the readers that depression should be taken more seriously, then you might define what depression is, describe the symptoms that occur, give a brief narrative or anecdote of someone who suffers from it, and then argue why people need to pay more attention to it and suggest where to go for help.
Design	How many points do you need to make about your subject to fully support your argument? Also, what other design details, such as a photographs or charts, might enhance your persuasive document? Do you want to include headings to help your reader clearly identify your main points? Will including a list of bulleted examples add credibility to your claim? Design your document to be as persuasive as possible.

10.5 APPLYING THE WRITING PROCESS FOR PERSUADING

After you have completed your rhetorical star analysis, follow the steps of the writing process (see Figure 10.3) to compose your paper.

FIGURE 10.3 The Seven Steps of the Writing Process

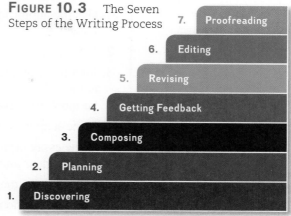

1. **Discovering:** Once you have decided on a topic, make a list of ideas that support your argument as well as a list of ideas from the opposing point of view (see Figure 10.4). You may also try completing a freewriting exercise to help get the ideas flowing. You may also want to talk with classmates, friends, or family members to learn about opposing viewpoints related to your topic.

2. **Planning:** As you plan your draft, list the main points you would like to use to support your persuasive essay. Number your supporting points from most to least persuasive. Then reorder the ideas by putting the second most important supporting point first and the most persuasive supporting point last. Ending with your most persuasive point will usually make the strongest impression on your reader. To help you visualize your organization, create a cluster, an outline (informal or formal), or a graphic organizer (see Figure 10.4).

FIGURE 10.4 Persuading Graphic Organizer

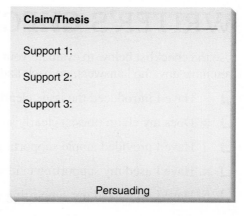

3. **Composing:** Write a first draft of your persuasive essay. Don't worry too much about grammar and punctuation at this time. Be sure to keep in mind the qualities of persuasive writing outlined earlier in the chapter:

    1. Introduce the subject you are debating.

    2. State a claim about your subject. (This is your thesis.)

    3. Support your claim with evidence that appeals to your audience.

    4. Use supporting evidence ethically and logically.

    5. Organize supporting evidence effectively.

    6. End with a logical conclusion.

4. **Getting feedback:** Have at least one classmate or other person read your rough draft and answer the peer review questions on page 254. If you have access to a writing tutor or center, get another opinion about your paper as well.

5. **Revising:** Using all of the feedback available to you, revise your persuasive essay. Make sure that your main supporting point is the strongest evidence for your claim or thesis. Add, delete, and rearrange ideas as necessary.

6. **Editing:** Read your persuasive essay again, this time looking for errors in grammar, punctuation, and mechanics. Make sure you are using transitions effectively to help your reader follow your logic as you work to persuade your audience.

7. **Proofreading:** After you have carefully edited your essay, read it one last time, looking for typographical errors and any other issues that might interfere with the readers' understanding of your essay.

WRITER'S CHECKLIST FOR PERSUADING

Use the checklist below to evaluate your own writing and help ensure that your persuasive essay is effective. If you have any "no" answers, go back and work on those areas if necessary.

❑ 1. Have I introduced the issue clearly and effectively?

❑ 2. Does my claim (thesis) clearly state my opinion about the issue?

❑ 3. Have I provided ample supporting evidence to persuade the reader that my perspective is valid?

❑ 4. Have I used my supporting evidence ethically and logically?

❑ 5. Have I organized my supporting evidence effectively?

❑ 6. Is my conclusion sufficient?

❑ 7. Have I proofread thoroughly?

[CHAPTER SUMMARY]

1. Use the persuasive writing strategy to prove a point.

2. Persuasive writing is an important part of your education, daily life, and career.

3. Carefully analyze the rhetorical star before writing a persuasive essay: subject, audience, purpose, strategy, and design.

4. Interpreting persuasive readings and images can help you to prepare to write a persuasive essay.

5. Use these qualities when writing a persuasive essay: introduce the subject; state a claim; give supporting evidence; include ethical, emotional, and/or logical appeals; use supporting evidence ethically and logically; organize supporting evidence effectively; end with a logical conclusion.

[WHAT I KNOW NOW]

Use this checklist to determine what you need to work on in order to feel comfortable with your understanding of the material in this chapter. Check off each item as you master it. Review the material for any unchecked items.

❑ 1. I know what **persuasive writing** is.

❑ 2. I can identify several **real-world applications** for persuasive writing.

❑ 3. I can **evaluate** persuasive readings and images.

❑ 4. I can analyze the **rhetorical star** for persuasive writing.

❑ 5. I understand the **writing process** for persuasive writing.

❑ 6. I can apply the **six qualities** of persuasive writing.

SmartBook Tip

During the "Recharge" phase, students can return to Chapter 10 and practice concepts that they need to work on.

CHAPTER 11

EVALUATING: FILM AND THE ARTS

In this chapter you will learn techniques for achieving these learning outcomes:

11.1 IDENTIFY REAL-WORLD APPLICATIONS FOR EVALUATING.

11.2 UNDERSTAND THE QUALITIES OF AN EFFECTIVE EVALUATION.

11.3 INTERPRET IMAGES AND EVALUATIVE WRITING ABOUT FILM AND THE ARTS.

11.4 ANALYZE THE RHETORICAL STAR FOR EVALUATIVE WRITING.

11.5 APPLY THE QUALITIES OF EVALUATIVE WRITING.

WRITING STRATEGY FOCUS: EVALUATING

When you evaluate a subject, you make an overall judgment about it. An effective evaluation needs to be based on several specific criteria or standards for judging the subject. To make an evaluation convincing, you need to support it with specific details and examples. You probably make informal evaluations quite often. For example, if you turn on the television and catch the beginning of a new situation comedy, you will probably decide within a few minutes whether you like the show or not. Your evaluative criteria might include the premise of the story line, the quality of the acting, and the use of humor. Knowing how to structure a formal written evaluation is useful to you at school, in your daily life, and in your career.

SmartBook Tip

Students receive an overview of the learning outcomes and topics in Chapter 11 in the "Preview" phase of SmartBook.

11.1 REAL-WORLD APPLICATIONS FOR EVALUATING

Evaluative Writing for College

You will often be asked to evaluate subjects in your college courses. If you work in collaborative groups, you may be asked to evaluate the experience or your teammates. You might need to evaluate two different programs of study to determine which one will provide you with the most satisfying career in the long run. In a course in your major, you may need to evaluate a method or procedure for accuracy or effectiveness. Near the end of the term you will likely evaluate the course, your textbook, and your instructor.

Evaluative Writing in Your Daily Life

You evaluate various subjects on a daily basis. If you eat at a restaurant, you are likely to evaluate the meal, service, and overall dining experience. When you see a movie, you probably judge whether it was worth your time and money or if you were satisfied with the characters, plot, or ending. As a consumer you make judgments every time you purchase something. Was it worth the price? Did you receive the service or product that you were promised? In elections, you evaluate each candidate and decide who you feel will do the best job in the position.

Evaluative Writing in Your Career

Having strong evaluation skills is extremely useful in the workplace. You may need to write a self-evaluation to get a raise or a promotion. When you are offered several positions, you will need to evaluate which one is the best fit for your needs. Once you are on the job, you will likely need to use your evaluation skills regularly. Which vendor can provide you with the best products and services? What plan will have the most positive results? What is the most efficient and cost-effective way for you to reach your goals?

Teaching Tip
Ask students to tell how they anticipate using the evaluative writing strategy in their future careers.

Health care: evaluations of patients, equipment, and procedures.

Occupational therapy: evaluations of a patient's mobility, life skills, and needs.

Law: evaluations of cases, clients, crime scenes, and who is at fault in an accident.

Education: evaluations of students, faculty, classrooms, lessons, and programs.

Computers: evaluations of hardware, software, personnel, and procedures.

Culinary arts: evaluations of cooking techniques, meals, and ingredients.

Business: evaluations of business plans, facilities, employees, products, and services.

Graduate SPOTLIGHT

Tawana Campbell, Occupational Therapy Assistant

Tawana Campbell earned a degree in occupational therapy assisting. She currently works as an occupational therapy assistant for a pediatric outpatient facility. Here's what Tawana has to say about the importance of writing in her career:

❝ I take careful notes about each session I have with a patient and write a case study. I document everything that happens because the philosophy where I work is, 'If it isn't written down, it didn't happen.' When I meet with a patient, I write out an evaluation of his or her condition and needs, and I determine ways to get effective treatment. Written proof of my evaluation is necessary to persuade the insurance company that special adaptive equipment, such as a wheelchair, splint, or orthotic insert, is necessary.

Because I work with children, I have to be very creative with how I go about treatment. For example, one child had a deficiency in communication skills, so I showed him a movie and asked him to retell the plot. Another child was having problems with sensorimotor skills, so I taught her to dance using her favorite songs from *High School Musical.* Also, I frequently use arts and crafts with children because something as simple as gluing a bead on a piece of construction paper is a useful task. These techniques work great for helping me to establish a good rapport with the children and evaluate their progress. They think we are just playing, but they are really working to overcome the challenges that they face. ❞

Activity Real-World Evaluative Writing

In pairs or small groups, brainstorm uses for writing evaluations at school, in your daily life, and on the job. You may want to choose the prospective career field(s) of the participants in your group. Each group may share its results with the class.

Real-World Evaluative Writing Activity:

Answers will vary.

11.2 QUALITIES OF EFFECTIVE EVALUATIVE WRITING

1. Describe the Subject You Are Evaluating

You will need to provide your readers with enough information to understand your subject. For example, if you are evaluating a movie, you might want to explain the premise of the film. That description might include what type of film it is (documentary, comedy, action adventure, and so on) as well as where and when the events in the film take place. You may also decide to introduce the main characters and actors briefly. Be careful to avoid merely summarizing the plot of the movie. In fact, if you include too much summary, then your readers probably won't want to see the movie you are evaluating. If you are evaluating a work of art, you may want to include a picture of the work along with your review. Include just enough details for your readers to be able to grasp your meaning.

2. Make a Claim about the Subject You Are Evaluating

Your thesis should state your overall opinion of the subject you are evaluating. Is the movie a great piece of cinema or a ridiculous waste of time? Does the painting leave you awed and inspired or unmoved? Keep in mind that an evaluation must do more than simply express your overall like or dislike for your subject. You will need to be able to support your claim in the body of your essay. Your reader should have a strong sense of your attitude toward the subject right from the beginning of your essay.

3. Choose Several Criteria for Your Evaluation

For your evaluation to seem valid to your readers, you will need to base your overall opinion on several specific **criteria.** Criteria are principles or standards writers use to judge or evaluate something. If you are evaluating a movie, you might consider criteria that fit with the type of movie you are reviewing. For example, for an action adventure film, you might consider the special effects, sound track, and intensity level. If you're evaluating a play, you might judge the actors, costumes, dialogue, and stage props.

4. Make a Judgment about Each Criterion

Most of your essay should focus on your evaluative criteria, and your topic sentences should each make a claim about one criterion. For example, if you are evaluating a film, one of your topic sentences might be something like this: Another reason the Imax film *The Hobbit: An Unexpected Journey 3D* (2012) is

LearnSmart Achieve Tip

The Writing Process unit of LearnSmart Achieve determines what students do and do not know about the writing process. Learning outcomes within the Writing Process unit cover planning, organizing, drafting, and revising an informative text. Learning resources and questions automatically adapt to each student's individual needs and help students thoroughly master this content. See the Instructor's Manual for *Write Now* for a list of learning outcomes as well as additional information on how to use LearnSmart Achieve with your students.

Criteria Principles or standards used to evaluate something.

Teaching Tip

Show students pictures of paintings or other works of art and ask them to make judgments about them based on specific evaluative criteria.

1. Michael Jackson's video *Thriller*
is the most popular video of all
time. 2. *ET, Transformers,* and
Indiana Jones are all Steven
Spielberg movies with corresponding amusement park
attractions in Orlando, Florida.
3. Viewers can look at Leonardo
da Vinci's famous painting *Mona
Lisa* for hours, wondering why
she has that expression on her
face. 4. William Faulkner's novel
As I Lay Dying is much more
humorous than the title implies.
5. The 2008 movie version of the
musical *Mamma Mia!* is absolutely
hilarious.

worth seeing is that the actors Ian McKellen and Martin Freeman give stunning performances as Gandalf and Bilbo Baggins.

5. Support Your Judgments with Specific Evidence

Once you have determined how successfully your subject fulfills each criterion, you will need to support your judgments with specific details. These details should help you back up the overall claim in your introduction. For example, if you are recommending *The Hobbit* to your readers, then your supporting material will come from the movie. If one of your judgments is that the acting is superb, you might support it with specific details about what Ian McKellan and Martin Freeman do to bring their characters vividly to life.

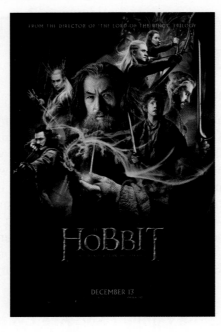

Grammar Window
PRESENT TENSE VERBS

Use present tense verbs when writing about a creative work, even if the author, musician, filmmaker, or artist who created it is deceased. The work lives on even if the creator does not.

Incorrect past tense verbs: Through his song "Imagine," John Lennon *inspired* his fans to envision a peaceful world where everyone *shared*.

Corrected present tense verbs: Through his song "Imagine," John Lennon *inspires* his fans to envision a peaceful world where everyone *shares*.

Discussion: Lennon's song still inspires his fans, even though he was assassinated in 1980. Therefore, present tense verbs are more appropriate than past tense verbs.

Activity: Revise the following sentences, changing the past tense verbs to present tense verbs.

1. Michael Jackson's video *Thriller* was the most popular video of all time.

2. *ET, Transformers,* and *Indiana Jones* were all Steven Spielberg movies with corresponding amusement park attractions in Orlando, Florida.

3. Viewers could look at Leonardo da Vinci's famous painting *Mona Lisa* for hours, wondering why she had that expression on her face.

4. William Faulkner's novel *As I Lay Dying* was much more humorous than the title implied.

5. The 2008 movie version of the musical *Mamma Mia!* was absolutely hilarious.

SmartBook Tip

Key concepts in Chapter 11 are highlighted for students during the "Read" phase. As students demonstrate understanding of these concepts during the "Practice" phase by responding to probes, the highlighting adapts to the individual student's learning by changing color.

6. Be Fair with Your Judgments

You want your evaluation to seem reasonable to your audience. For example, if you dislike a television show that you are review-ing, you might acknowledge that it has one redeeming quality. If your overall claim about the television show *My Big Fat Redneck Wedding* is that it is condescending to the viewers, you might show that you are open-minded by mentioning that there are some funny lines in the show. However, you don't want to provide your reader with a completely balanced view of your subject. If you merely tell what you liked and didn't like about the subject, then your reader might be confused about your overall opinion. The majority of your comments need to support the judgment in your thesis.

7. End with a Final Claim about Your Subject

In addition to restating your thesis and summarizing your main points, you might also make a broader judgment that wasn't stated in the thesis. For example, you might end your movie review with a star rating or other general comment so your readers will know for sure your judgment about the movie. If you give the movie four and a half out of five stars, then your readers will know for sure how strong your recommendation is.

Career-Based EVALUATIVE WRITING

[preview] **PERFORMANCE EVALUATIONS** are common in the workplace. Employers often use employee evaluations to determine raises and promotions. Your employer may ask you to complete a self-evaluation in addition to the one your supervisor completes. Furthermore, as you advance in your career, you may need to evaluate employees you supervise. When writing an employee evaluation, be sure to include specific details to support the judgments you make. Also, be objective and accurate when writing an evaluation.

Sample Employee Evaluation Form

Name: *John Smith*
Date of Hire: *January 5, 2013*
Supervisor: *Jill Johnson*

Deptartment: *Customer Service*
Date of Review: *September 1, 2014*
Date of Last Review: *April 6, 2013*

Rating System	
1 = Unsatisfactory	2 = Needs Improvement
3 = Satisfactory	4 = Exceeds Expectations
5 = Significantly Exceeds Expectations	

1. Quality of employee's work — 4

Comments *John does very good work for the company. His attention to detail and ability to provide quality support for his projects and co-workers meet expectations.*

2. Exercise of good judgment — 5

Comments *John has shown exceptional judgment, particularly in regard to prioritizing key accounts and customers.*

3. Attendance — 3

Comments *While John has not missed an excessive number of days, his absences and shorter days are higher than we would normally like to see. John needs to plan ahead a bit better so that his absences can be anticipated and kept to a minimum.*

4. Employee involvement/participation in team effort — 5

Comments *John is an exceptional team player. He strives to work collaboratively with co-workers, and his projects often utilize input from multiple departments. He spearheaded an initiative to better utilize company-wide resources.*

5. Attention to company policies and procedures — 4

Comments *John always maintains strict adherence to company guidelines and is quick to verify any new idea or procedure. He does occasionally require a reminder when procedures change, but he is quick to learn new workflows.*

6. Interpersonal relationships and communication with co-workers — 5

Comments *One of John's key strengths is his ability to work well with others. He is a natural leader and communicates clearly with others.*

7. Taking initiative to achieve goals and complete assignments — 4

Comments *John has good ideas and innovations, but they tend to be at the direction of others. Some of his biggest successes were the implementation of others' ideas. I would like to see John suggest more projects. I know from meetings that he has excellent vision, but he is often hesitant to share it with others.*

8. Responsiveness to changing work requirement — 4

Comments *There were two instances this year in which John used outdated forms and, in one case, an outdated workflow. He was quick to rectify the situation, but he should pay closer attention to interoffice memos and trainings.*

9. Work ethic   5

Comments *John has an excellent work ethic. He is attentive to project details and dead-lines. His ability to meet or exceed date expectations has helped his projects run successfully.*

10. Overall performance rating   4.3

Comments *John has expressed an interest in continued career growth within the company and he is on track for promotion and greater responsibility. I encourage him to double-check details and be a bit more consistent in minor areas of performance. Overall, John's performance has exceeded expectations for the year.*

Areas of Strength:
John works very well with others and strives for the best possible outcomes for everything he takes on. His professionalism and willingness to work toward innovation are excellent. He communicates effectively and collaborates with others.

Areas of Improvement:
I would like to see John take on more responsibility this year. He has natural leadership skills and tends to bring the best out in others. I would encourage him to continue doing this in a more strategic way. By his next review I would like to see him initiate and complete a project on his own.

Employee's Comments:
I think the assessment of my performance is a good reflection of my skills and areas of improvement. During my review I discussed strategies for taking on leadership roles and being a more consistent presence in the overall process. I am committed to my continued communication with all members of my team. I also discussed plans to launch monthly employee information-sharing sessions that will help with consistency.

Date: *September 1, 2014*

_____
Employee's Signature

[QUESTIONS FOR REFLECTION]

1. What are John's strengths?
2. What are his weaknesses?
3. Which comments need more explanation? What is missing?

4. What specific criteria does the supervisor use to evaluate John? Which ones are most important? Why?
5. Using this same form, how would you rate yourself as an employee? How would you rate your boss?

11.3 EVALUATING IN THE CONTEXT OF FILM AND THE ARTS

What would the world be like without film and the arts? Today we have easy access to more types of fine arts than ever before. Through film, television, the Internet, and other media, we can watch a Broadway play, visit the Louvre museum in Paris, take in a hip-hop concert, or listen to an author read her own poetry aloud without ever leaving the comfort of our own homes. We can use the arts to explore ourselves and our beliefs, learn about the world and other cultures, and escape from reality. With so many options available, how do we decide what is worth our precious time? How do we evaluate the arts when personal preference plays a big part in our perceptions of artistic expressions?

We have to base our judgments on clear criteria and specific supporting evidence. The skills you use to evaluate film and the arts will translate to a variety of other areas in your life. Read and discuss one or more of the following evaluations. Doing so will help you to write your own evaluations.

Reading and Reflection EVALUATIVE WRITING

[preview] **SIMON BENLOW** is a fan of *The Simpsons,* a show that has been entertaining audiences for more than 25 years. The topics and themes are as relevant to today's viewers as they were a quarter of a century ago. In the following review, Benlow accomplishes more than merely suggesting what he likes about the cartoon. He also comments on what *The Simpsons* reveals about American entertainment and society as a whole. Visit **www.thesimpsons.com** to view full episodes and to learn more about the characters, the show, and specific episodes. You can also check out the star rating for each episode and participate in a variety of interactive activities and discussions. Before reading the following essay, think about cartoons you have watched or read over the years. Do they just provide entertainment, or is there some truth to them? What do they say about society?

Revealing the Ugly Cartoonish Truth: *The Simpsons* by Simon Benlow

1 It's not often that a television sitcom does more than tickle our most simplistic pleasures. The vast majority of sitcoms, past and present, fill twenty-two minutes (or is it nineteen?) with cliché moralism, empty characters, and adolescent dialog. Every fall we can look forward to a new parade of bad jokes and simpleton plots—created primarily to allow American viewers to gawk at the latest celebrity hairstyles and tight shirts.

2 However, amidst an exhausting list of here-and-then-gone "real-life" sitcoms, *The Simpsons* has managed to create a new class of television. It has stretched what can (and should) be expected in prime-time entertainment. It goes where most sitcoms, most American entertainment, will not. It satirizes everything (and nearly anything) mainstream America cherishes. From SUVs to friendly fast-food chains, the familiar elements of everyday life are revealed as ridiculous creations of a culture blind to its own vices. Certainly, it takes shots at big targets: nuclear power, organized labor, corporate fraud, slick politicians, organized religion, hyper-consumerism, hyper-consumption, and even television programming (often slamming its own network, FOX). But these are more than easy targets; these are the entities that seem to run amuck consistently, the institutions that maintain their status despite repeated failings, the bullies of our culture that always seem in need of a punch to their maniacal eye sockets.

3 In "Homer's Odyssey," an episode from the first season, the show does its usual deconstruction of everyday life. The episode reveals some ugly truth: Beneath the daily façade, there lurks an entire set of systems barely working, hardly accomplishing anything beyond their own survival. In the first scene, in front of Springfield Elementary, the children wait for the tardy, pot-smoking bus driver, Otto (who loves to "get blotto"). Once they get settled, they drive in circles through town. They pass by the toxic waste dump where happy workers casually pour mysterious fluid into the river; they pass the prison where they are greeted by hosts of prisoners (who were set free during the children's last field trip). They pass the Springfield tire yard (which becomes the Springfield tire fire in later episodes), and finally arrive at the nuclear power plant. At the gate, several signs announce "employees only," but the guard is sucking on a beverage and watching Krusty the Clown on television, so the children pass through unnoticed.

4 In the power plant, we see the gross fumblings and even grosser cover-ups of an unchecked system. While Joe Fission, a cartoon icon, feeds the children pro-nuclear propaganda, Homer flummoxes[1] his job and wreaks havoc in the plant. Homer is the poster boy of

_____
[1]**Flummoxes** Confuses.

incompetence—yet he's granted a typical place in the ill-defined bureaucracy of power: Is he the "supervising technician" or the "technical supervisor"? No one knows. Through the episode, Homer is fired and then, for no good reason, hired back. The status quo prevails; three-eyed fish swim happily in the lake and the town continues to live on the brink of nuclear disaster.

In the animated town of Springfield, nothing is worthy 5 of the praise it wants. Schools are not great institutions of learning; they are poorly funded bureaucracies run by flawed and desperate individuals. Government is not "of the people"; it is a mob of self-perpetuating boozers and womanizers. Business is not ethical or productive; it is a race to monopolize and swindle everyone in sight. These are the hard truths that *The Simpsons* offers us. Of course, we get these truths thrown at us in sanctimonious movies and bad morning talk shows, but *The Simpsons* manages to reveal these ideas without romanticizing its own characters or actors.

The Simpsons throws at us what we all might be think- 6 ing had we not been programmed to dismiss it. We all might briefly consider the lies the nuclear power industry feeds us, the laziness and self-righteousness of city governments, or the emptiness and humiliation of most jobs, but we've been trained out of being appalled. We've become distracted by our own lives, and the constant barrage of material goodness, so we allow our own institutions to bully us, to humiliate us, to dismiss our general welfare entirely. But *The Simpsons* reminds us of the slip-shod work and flagrant thievery going on just outside our own television sets.

Some may argue that *The Simpsons* is just a show; 7 it can't possibly have that much meaning. However, one thing we've learned in America is that our entertainment has more significance than history, literature, philosophy, and politics. Mainstream society gets its values, its slogans, its hairstyles, even its dialects from entertainment. We are, as the world knows, an over-entertained nation. The average American citizen reads very little (maybe a few books per year), but fills thousands of hours being massaged by the television. As the last thirty years proves undoubtedly, Americans can change their minds at the drop of a hat (about almost anything) if the television set prompts us to do so. When television maintains such influence, it is significant and meaningful when the television itself plays with, pokes at, and parodies that influence.

In a swirling array of giddy and capricious entertain- 8 ment, *The Simpsons* is far more real than any "real-life" sitcom hopes to be (or wants to be). In its relentless pursuit to overturn our romantic notions of ourselves and our lovely creations, it is probably more real than the audience it attracts (and certainly more real than those whom it doesn't). In fact, if we take the show as seriously as it deserves, we might even see the broad strokes of its irony: that *we* are the cartoons, drawn and colored by the ridiculous institutions that constitute our society. However, as soon as we go that far, Homer belches, Bart moons a head of state, and Grandpa soils himself; *The Simpsons* won't allow anything, including itself, to be taken too seriously.

Source: Simon Benlow, "Revealing the Ugly Cartoonish Truth: *The Simpsons*" from J. Mauk and J. Metz, *The Composition of Everyday Life: A Guide to Writing* (Boston: Thomson Wadsworth, 2004), pp. 376–77.

[QUESTIONS FOR REFLECTION]

Considering Ideas

1. What does Benlow suggest by the title of the essay? What is the "truth" about *The Simpsons* as he sees it? Do you agree or disagree with his notion?

2. *The Simpsons* pokes fun at a lot of things that are wrong with Springfield. Think about the community where you grew up. How similar or dissimilar is your hometown to Springfield? Based on the examples in the essay, what situations seem to be exaggerated on the show?

3. Benlow asserts that "*we* are the cartoons, drawn and colored by the ridiculous institutions that constitute our society." What does he mean by this claim? Do you agree or disagree with him? Why?

Considering the Rhetorical Star

1. What is the main *subject* of the evaluation? Is the topic engaging? Why or why not?

2. Who is the intended *audience* for the essay? Explain.

3. What is Benlow's main *purpose* for writing the essay? Does he achieve his purpose? Why or why not?

4. The author uses evaluation as the primary *strategy* for the essay. What other writing strategies are evident in the work?

5. Describe the *design* of the essay. Is it effective? Why or why not?

Considering Writing Strategies

1. What does Benlow accomplish with the introductory paragraph? Why does he delay his thesis until the second paragraph? What effect does this strategy have on the readers?

2. Which supporting details from the essay stand out most? How do those details help to support his main idea?

3. Benlow uses many examples from episodes of *The Simpsons* in his essay. What purpose do these examples serve? How do these examples affect the reader?

Writing Suggestions

1. Watch an episode of *The Simpsons* or another animated situation comedy. Write an essay evaluating the show. Be sure to base your evaluation on several specific criteria and to support your ideas with specific examples from the show. You might argue a point about the significance of the show (or lack thereof) in your review.

2. Watch a full-length animated movie. Write an essay evaluating the movie. You might consider some of the following questions: What is the point (theme) of the movie? Is it merely a form of entertainment, or does it reveal something more serious about society? Is the film strictly for children, or does it reach adults on another level? Be sure to back up your judgments with specific details and examples from the film.

Reading and Reflection EVALUATIVE WRITING

[preview] **KENNETH TURAN,** who has an MS degree from Columbia University, is the film critic for the *Los Angeles Times* and NPR's *Morning Edition.* He has written several books, including *Free for All: Joe Papp, the Public, and the Greatest Theater Story Ever Told* (2009). In the following article, Turan evaluates the final film based on the hugely successful series of Harry Potter books written by J. K. Rowling. You may want to check out **www.jkrowling.com** to learn more about Rowling's books and characters.

Before reading the article, consider the qualities that make a good movie. What elements are required for a movie to earn a high rating from you?

Movie Review: *Harry Potter and the Deathly Hallows—Part 2* by Kenneth Turan

After seven previous films over a 10-year span, $2 billion in domestic box office and still more treasure overseas, Warner Bros. has unwrapped the Harry Potter advertising line it hoped it would never have to use: "It all ends."

In a classic storybook finish, however, *Harry Potter and the Deathly Hallows—Part 2* turns out to be more than the last of its kind. Almost magically, it ends up being one of the best of the series as well.

The Harry Potter films, like the boy wizard himself, have had their creative ups and downs, so it's especially satisfying that this final film, ungainly title and all, has been worth the wait. Though no expense has been spared in its production, it succeeds because it brings us back to the combination of magic, adventure and emotion that created the books' popularity in the first place.

It also succeeds because the franchise has stuck to its conservative creative guns and seen them pay off. With occasional exceptions like Alfonso Cuarón's *Prisoner of Azkaban* adventure, the Potter films have rarely been daring, valuing superb craftsmanship and care over cutting-edge audacity. Now that we've come to the much-anticipated finale, that expert husbanding of a once-in-a-lifetime franchise has had a cumulative effect that is not to be denied.

Not only did the series' three leads—Daniel Radcliffe, Rupert Grint and Emma Watson—turn out to be expertly cast, the production has been able to retain their services through all eight films. And they've been supported by such a deep bench of top-flight British acting talent (Ciarán Hinds is the latest to be added, playing Dumbledore's brother) that when Bill Nighy joined the cast for *Deathly Hallows—Part 1,* he said he'd feared he'd be the only English actor of a certain age who wasn't in a Harry Potter film.

All that talent couldn't have come cheap, and the other consistent factor in the Potter universe is the production's refusal to skimp or pinch pennies. That willingness to do whatever it took to bring Stuart Craig's exceptional production designs to life no matter how painstaking the task is central to the new film's success as well.

To give just two examples, more than 200,000 golden coins and thousands of other pieces were created to convincingly fill a vault at Gringotts bank, and so much furniture and objects were bought to make Hogwarts' enormous Room of Requirement look more crowded than Charles Foster Kane's storehouse that the set dressing department was busy for months buying up bric-a-brac. Nothing's too good for our Harry. 7

Deathly Hallows—Part 2 also benefits from sticking with experienced and capable people at the top. Screenwriter Steve Kloves has scripted seven of the eight Potter films, and David Yates has directed four of them. All this practice has allowed the creative team, 8 including returning cinematographer Eduardo Serra, to relax into its best self without having to learn the territory all over again.

Splitting the final Potter volume into two films was also to the advantage of Part 2, as was the fact that this film deals only with roughly the final third of the book. This enables it to avoid the tiresome teen angst that hampered Part 1 and devote almost all its time to action and confrontation, starting with the film's initial image of the dread Voldemort (Ralph Fiennes) pointing the all-powerful Elder Wand to the sky and creating . . . the Warner Bros. logo. 9

Source: Kenneth Turan, "Movie Review: *Harry Potter and the Deathly Hallows—Part 2*," *Los Angeles Times*, July 13, 2011. Reprinted by permission.

[QUESTIONS FOR REFLECTION]

Considering Ideas

1. What is Turan's overall opinion of *Harry Potter and the Deathly Hallows—Part 2?* If you have seen the movie, do you agree or disagree with his judgment? Why?

2. According to the author, what are some of the best features of the film? Are his reasons compelling? Why or why not?

3. Which details in the essay are most convincing for you as the reader? If you haven't seen the film, would you see it based on Turan's review? Why or why not?

Considering the Rhetorical Star

1. What is the *subject* of the essay? Is it an engaging subject? Why or why not?

2. What is Turan's *purpose* for writing the essay? Does he effectively achieve his purpose? Why or why not?

3. Who is the intended *audience* for the piece? Explain.

4. What is Turan's primary writing *strategy?* Does he use any other writing strategies? Which ones? Give examples to illustrate your point.

5. What is the *design* of the essay? Is the design effective? Why or why not?

Considering Writing Strategies

1. What evaluative criteria does Turan use in his review? Does he fully support the judgments he makes? Explain your answer with examples from the essay.

2. As part of his evaluation, Turan compares this movie to other Harry Potter films, such as *The Prisoner of Azkaban* and *Deathly Hallows—Part 1.* Why does he use this technique? Is it effective? Why or why not?

3. Rather than summarizing his main points in a traditional manner, the author concludes by mentioning the image of Voldemort "pointing the all-powerful Elder Wand to the sky and creating . . . the Warner Bros. logo." Is this an effective conclusion for the article? Why or why not?

Writing Suggestions

1. Write a review of one of the Harry Potter movies. Select several criteria for your evaluation, such as the characters, acting, setting, musical score, special effects, and dialogue. Use specific details and examples from the movie to support the judgments you make about each criterion.

2. For a longer project, read one of the Harry Potter books and write an evaluative essay comparing it to the movie based on the book. You might consider some of the following questions as you write your essay: Which medium is more captivating for the audience? Which version is more satisfying? Would you recommend either one to your readers? Why or why not?

ESOL Tip >

As an alternative writing suggestion, write a review of a movie or book that is famous in your native country. Be sure to translate the title to English for your instructor.

[preview] **PETER TRAVERS,** who has been a movie buff since childhood, is a *Rolling Stone* movie critic who also hosts "Popcorn," a celebrity interview segment on *ABC News*. He authored the book *Top 10 Hits: A Pop Cultural Novel* (2008) and co-authored several other books as well. In the following article, which originally appeared in *Rolling Stone,* Travers evaluates the first of *The Hunger Games* movies. *The Hunger Games* trilogy, written for young adults by Suzanne Collins, has been a smash hit with readers of all ages. Additionally, this science fiction series has brought about a resurgence of postapocalyptic fiction. The movie version has also been widely popular, as is evident in Travers's review. Before reading, consider what is important for a science fiction film to be successful. What standards do viewers use to pass judgment on a movie? What criteria are necessary for you to give your stamp of approval?

Movie Review: *The Hunger Games* by Peter Travers

Relax, you legions of Hunger Gamers. We have a winner. Hollywood didn't screw up the film version of Suzanne Collins' young-adult best seller about a survival-of-the-fittest reality show that sends home all its teen contestants, save the victor, in body bags. The screen *Hunger Games* radiates a hot, jumpy energy that's irresistible. It has epic spectacle, yearning romance, suspense that won't quit and a shining star in Jennifer Lawrence, who gives us a female warrior worth cheering. 1

That's more than you can say for the castration job that the suits did on Stephenie Meyer's *Twilight* franchise. I'll admit that *Games* isn't the scary, eruptive firecracker of my dark, Tarantino-fueled imagination. And if you're among the 26 million who devoured the Collins trilogy—*The Hunger Games* followed by *Catching Fire* and *Mockingjay*—you know it could have been. But even wearing a PG-13 harness to ensure profitability, *The Hunger Games* gets your pulse racing. It's about something pertinent, the mission to define yourself in a world that's spinning off its moral axis. 2

As 16-year-old Katniss Everdeen, the renegade hunter who kills with a bow and arrow and stands up to take the place of her younger sister in the deadly Games, Lawrence reveals a physical and emotional grace that's astonishing. Give her the deed, because she owns this movie. It's not just that Katniss makes *Twilight*'s Bella Swan look like the wimp she is, it's that Lawrence, 21, is an acting dynamo with the skills to let us into Katniss' searching mind. Last year, Lawrence won an Oscar nomination for playing an Ozark girl in *Winter's Bone*. She's just as affecting this time, lending primal force to this dystopian[1] fable of a society out of sync with human values. 3

At 142 minutes, *The Hunger Games* can go from rushed to draggy. But director Gary Ross (*Pleasantville, Seabiscuit*) hits the high spots, using action to define character instead of obliterate it. He wisely brought in Collins to collaborate on the script he wrote with Billy Ray (*Shattered Glass*). That way, even when the book's events are condensed or characters eliminated, the feeling stays true. 4

The Games are a punishment invented by the Capitol of Panem (read: North America) for the 12 districts whose rebellion against Capitol rule was crushed more than 74 years ago. The attitude of President Snow (Donald Sutherland, wily in his evil) is "You screwed us, so we'll screw you." Every year on Reaping Day, a boy and a girl (ages 12 to 18) from each district are chosen by lottery to fight to the death in a televised gladiator event devised by head Games-maker Seneca Crane (Wes Bentley). Ratings are not a problem. Even in downtrodden District 12, where Katniss hunts for scraps to feed her sister and her widowed mother, viewing the Games is mandatory. You won't need your arm twisted to see the movie, artfully shot by Tom Stern (*Mystic River*) as the scene shifts from the perverse lushness of the Capitol to the stark landscape of the battle zone. And did I mention makeovers? All the Tributes (that's what contenders are called) get them. Katniss has fashion genius Cinna (Lenny Kravitz doing a fun spin on Tom Ford) to create a wow dress that bursts into flame at the hem. Nice one. 5

Like Bella before her, Katniss is pursued by two laddies-in-waiting, in this case Gale Hawthorne (Liam Hemsworth), the strapping District 12 hunk and fellow illegal hunter she leaves behind, and Peeta Mellark (Josh Hutcherson), the baker's son who joins Katniss in the Games and secretly pines for her. Are you Team Gale or Team Peeta? You might not care as much, since neither has the exotic allure of a vampire or a wolf. But 6

---

[1]**Dystopian** An undesirable or frightening society. The opposite of *utopian*.

Hemsworth (*The Last Song*, with girlfriend Miley Cyrus) quickly establishes a strong, appealing presence. And Hutcherson (*The Kids Are All Right*) brings humor and a bruised heart to a boy who needs to mature fast.

Dynamite actors dot the film. Stanley Tucci is a brilliant blend of mirth and malice as Caesar Flickerman, a TV host who reps the dark side of Ryan Seacrest in this lethal version of *American Idol*. Elizabeth Banks brings malicious wit to the bewigged and powdered PR guru Effie Trinket. "May the odds be ever in your favor," announces Effie with inane sincerity. And the reliably stellar Woody Harrelson cuts deep as the perpetually shit-faced Haymitch Abernathy, a former victor in the Games now acting as mentor to both Katniss and Peeta. When he's not falling-down drunk, Haymitch instructs his protégés on how to suck up to sponsors who send supplies into the arena when a Tribute wins audience favor. So-called reality TV is given a sharp, satirical kick as Tributes learn to play and pander to hidden cameras. Is Katniss really falling for Peeta as she nurses his wounds, or is she faking it to save her ass and his? Discuss.

Sadly, the erotic heat that Collins generates between Katniss and Peeta in a hidden cave never rises above room temperature onscreen. Hand-to-hand combat does fuel the intensity as Katniss fights career Tributes trained to go medieval on enemy ass. Check out machete-wielding Cato (Alexander Ludwig) and knife-throwing Clove (Isabelle Fuhrman), not to mention a swarm of deadly, genetically engineered wasps called Tracker Jackers. The caring bond Katniss forms with Rue (Amandla Stenberg), the youngest Tribute, is just a brief break from the assaults aimed to make Katniss trade her soul for survival.

For all its compromises, *The Hunger Games* is a zeitgeist movie that captures the spirit of a soul-sucking age in which ego easily trumps common cause. Ironically, the kill-to-win ethos that dominates movies from 1987's prophetic *The Running Man* to the undiluted brutality of Japan's *Battle Royale* in 2000, may find its largest viewership in *The Hunger Games*. But will mainstream audiences respond to the moral challenge churning under the pop-culture razzle-dazzle? It's anybody's guess. My advice is to keep your eyes on Lawrence, who turns the movie into a victory by presenting a heroine propelled by principle instead of hooking up with the cutest boy. That's what makes Katniss revolutionary. May the odds be ever in her favor.

Source: Peter Travers, "The Hunger Games," *Rolling Stone*, March 21, 2012.

[QUESTIONS FOR REFLECTION]

Considering Ideas

1. What is Travers's claim (thesis) in his review of *The Hunger Games?* If you have seen the movie, do you agree or disagree with him? Why?

2. Which ideas from the review have the greatest impact on you as the reader? Why? Quote specific passages to explain your point.

3. Whether you have seen the movie or not, after reading Travers's review, would you want to see it? Why or why not?

Considering the Rhetorical Star

1. What is the *subject* of the essay? Is it an engaging subject? Why or why not?

2. What is Travers's *purpose* for writing the essay? Does he effectively achieve his purpose? Why or why not?

3. Who is the intended *audience* for the piece? Explain.

4. What is Travers's primary writing *strategy?* Does he use any other writing strategies? Which ones? Give examples to illustrate your point.

5. What is the *design* of the article? Is the design effective? Why or why not?

Considering Writing Strategies

1. What specific criteria does Travers use to evaluate this movie? Are they logical criteria? Does he support his judgments with enough evidence to be convincing? Explain your answer using examples from the essay.

2. While the author gives the movie a positive review, he also makes a few negative comments about the movie. Why does he do that? How do those comments add credibility to the review? Include specific passages from the essay to explain your answer.

3. On more than one occasion, Travers compares *The Hunger Games* to the *Twilight* series. Why does he do that? What effect does this technique have on the reader?

Writing Suggestions

1. Write a review of one of *The Hunger Games* movies or another movie based on a book that you feel has merit. What is significant about the movie? Why is it so popular? Do you feel it will be popular for many years to come, or is it just a passing trend?

2. Find a current example of popular art, such as a CD cover, video game cover, or movie poster that you find appealing (or unappealing). Write an essay evaluating why it is appropriate (or inappropriate). Judge the image using several criteria. You might consider how well it fits with the media it is intended to support. Does it make consumers want to buy the product or see the movie? Or is it a turn-off? You will need to include a copy of the image with your essay so your readers can judge it for themselves.

Reading and Reflection EVALUATIVE WRITING

[preview] **ANN POWERS**, who was born in Seattle, is a critic and correspondent for NPR Music. Before joining NPR in 2011, she was the chief pop music critic for the *Los Angeles Times*. She has also been a rock music critic for the *New York Times*, the *Village Voice*, and *Blender* magazine. Additionally, she wrote the book *Weird Like Us: My Bohemian America* and co-authored *Tori Amos: Piece by Piece* with Amos. In the following essay, Powers evaluates the Black Eyed Peas' album, *The E.N.D.*, which stands for "energy never dies." Will.i.am, Apl.de.ap, Taboo, and Fergie make up the Black Eyed Peas, a band that has gained international fame. Go to **www.blackeyedpeas.com** to learn more about the group. If possible, watch the video for "I Gotta Feeling" or "Boom Boom Pow" on YouTube before reading the following review. Also, think of some of your favorite albums. What criteria do you use to evaluate music?

Album Review: Black Eyed Peas' *"The E.N.D."* by Ann Powers

The Los Angeles–based quartet Black Eyed Peas is possibly the greatest bubble gum group of the Extreme Ice Fruit Explosion era. Following in the path forged by the Monkees, the Archies, and the Spice Girls, the Peas present themselves as a cast of zany characters whose music is, on one level, like a child's game, and on another, as calculatedly smart and seductive as test-marketed pop gets. 1

The titles of the Peas' biggest hits tell the story: the giggle-inducing pun of "Don't Phunk With My Heart," the cheerily crude anatomical gesture of "My Humps," and now the Imax-ready sound effects burst of the chart-topping "Boom Boom Pow." Crass, good-hearted, funny, unfailingly loud scavengers of every shiny thing lying on pop's cross-cultural dance floor, the Peas present themselves as juvenile, but there's a lot going on behind the mugging. 2

The E.N.D., the group's fifth studio album and the third since the singer Stacy Ferguson (better known as Fergie) joined and took it from the earnest hip-hop underground to the glamorous, necessarily compromised pop mainstream, is more accomplished and more confounding than any of the foursome's previous efforts. It's likely to dominate radio and the Internet this summer, its sharp flavors simultaneously driving listeners nuts and drawing them back. 3

Will.i.am., the Peas' lead rapper and main idea man, has said that he doesn't envision *The E.N.D.* (The acronym is for "The Energy Never Dies," a nod to quantum physics that's further explained by a robotically voiced introduction to the opening track) as a regular album. Instead, it's a template, designed to be constantly reworked through remixes, both in the recording studio and by DJs on the dance floor. Indeed, this collection has none of the attributes that make listeners love albums: no narrative arc, no ebb and flow, no break from the in-your-face beats and high-fructose hooks. 4

As a plunge into the users' manual of post-disco dance pop, *The E.N.D.* is quite charming, if predictably goofy. Working with club-savvy collaborators including MSTRKRFT, David Guetta, and Keith Harris, Will takes on electro, deep house, dancehall, and dance-punk, to name just a few trends. 5

Ever true to their defining characteristic, the Peas have no shame. Fergie puts on ill-fitting dreadlocks for the faux-Jamaican "Electric City" and goes hilariously punk in "Now Generation," a rant about social media that sounds something like Bob Dylan's "Subterranean Homesick Blues" rewritten on a Sidekick. "Ring-a-Ling" is a strangely innocent celebration of drunken booty-calling; "One Tribe" follows a bouncing-ball beat as Will suggests that world peace might come from an amnesia epidemic. 6

As always, Fergie's performances provide the most interest throughout the album. More than the rappers Taboo and Apl.de.ap, whose spotlight turns are always competent but downplayed, or Will, who clings to an Everyman persona that belies his role as the group's Wizard of Oz, Fergie embraces the essential cartoonishness of being a Pea. 7

Whether she's being weepy in "Meet Me Halfway" or superbad in "Imma Be," she takes her part to its logical end. Her obviousness once seemed to reflect a lack of skill, but by now it's clear that it's a strategy. As a means of grabbing attention from a hopelessly distracted audience, it works. 8

Most of *The E.N.D.* doesn't ask too much from those fans. Its more substantive musical and thematic statements are interrupted by many others showing the Peas' deep, deep commitment to a good party. There's "Rock That Body," "Party All the Time," "Rockin' to the Beat," and "Out of My Head," and those are just the ones with telegraphic titles. 9

This filler, still waiting to be magically morphed by remixes, doesn't add a lot to the experience of listening to *The E.N.D.* all the way through. Yet a strange kind of bliss does arise after being pummeled by nearly 70 minutes' worth of booms, baps, and pows. 10

And sometimes in the midst of it, the Peas do let in some human sweetness and light. Consider "I Gotta Feeling," whose recently leaked video features brazen images of leggy women kissing, partygoers guzzling booze, and Fergie in a thong and a bra. 11

And yet the song itself works on a less blatant level. Produced by French house music veteran Guetta with Frederic Riesterer, it's reminiscent of the Five Stairsteps' soul classic "Ooh Child," emulating that song's use of a repetitive, warm vocal line to signify a good mood coming on. That sunlight-colored hook is interrupted by silly raps; by the time Will and his mates are shouting "Mazel Tov!" it's impossible to begrudge the high. 12

Yes, the song says, this is a sloppy party. But it's one where you're welcome. So come on in. 13

Source: Ann Powers, "Album Review: Black Eyed Peas' *The E.N.D.*" *Los Angeles Times*, June 2, 2009. http://latimesblogs.latimes.com/music_blog/2009/06/album-review-black-eyed-peas-the-end.html.

[QUESTIONS FOR REFLECTION]

Considering Ideas

1. Powers compares the Black Eyed Peas to a number of other artists. Does this help the reader to understand her assessment of the Peas? Why or why not?

2. She includes several lines from the lyrics in her essay. How does this affect you as the reader? Are you familiar with any of them? Could you hear the music in your head as you read them?

3. What is Powers's overall evaluation of the Black Eyed Peas album? Is her claim convincing? Why or why not?

Considering the Rhetorical Star

1. What is the *subject* of Powers's review? How thoroughly does she cover the subject?

2. Who is the intended *audience* for the review?

3. What is Powers's *purpose* for the review? Does she achieve her purpose? Why or why not?

4. In addition to evaluation, what other writing *strategies* does Powers use? Give specific examples from the article to illustrate your point.

5. The original article featured a photograph of the Black Eyed Peas in concert. What effect does including photographs have on the reader?

Considering Writing Strategies

1. How effective is Powers' initial description of the group? Which words in her description catch your attention most? Why?

2. What does she use to evaluate the album? Are these criteria appropriate for the subject? Why or why not?

3. Does she include enough supporting details for the reader to have a good concept of what the album is? Why or why not?

Writing Suggestions

1. Write a review of a new album by one of your favorite music artists or groups. You may want to compare it with a previous album by the same group to give your audience a clearer understanding of the new one. Be sure to base your album on clear criteria and include specific supporting examples from the songs on the album to back up your judgments.

2. Find a review of a concert or other performance that you have attended. Write an essay agreeing or disagreeing with the author's evaluation. Support your view with specific details from the performance.

[preview] **HAL SHOWS** was influenced by his viewing of the movie *Lawrence of Arabia* when he wrote the poem "Empire Burlesque," which appears in his book called *Parasol: Poems 1977–2007*. The title of the poem comes from an old Bob Dylan album from the 1980s. Shows grew up in and around the beach towns of North Florida, a fact manifest in many of the poems in *Parasol*. He spent much of the 1970s living in Florence, Italy, where he worked as a waiter, a salesman of gold and silver, a teacher of English, and a translator. These years gave him the chance to explore Europe from Edinburgh to the Peloponnese. A graduate of the writing programs at Florida State University and Goddard College, he has translated the work of Cavalcanti, Leopardi, Rilke, Ungaretti, Pasolini, and other foreign poets, and written extensively on literature and popular culture. Since the early 1980s he has been writing, performing, and recording music that defies genre but is actually only rock and roll. He owns and operates Witching Stick Studio, near Tallahassee, Florida, where he lives with his family. You can listen to Shows's albums, *Lifeboat* and *Native Dancer*, on iTunes. Before reading the poem, think about what it would be like to take a long trip to a foreign country. Have you ever experienced a long journey or seen a movie about one? How was the experience?

Empire Burlesque by Hal Shows

"Every scene must service the plot," and so on.
But I was thinking of a fine, ghostwritten film
subtle as any of the tales my grandmother told.
Maybe it made the papers; here is its gist:
a west-ender heads east, with a vast wardrobe.
After the disastrously comic lateness of the train
he arrives in colonial pomp but is unreceived.
He feels like a lost bag in the empty station.

What makes the movie is the fact he finds a home.
Half-starved, always hauling his half-digested
European baggage around, he shreds himself.
Skins later he's given away his tailored clothes,
has grown sane and lustrous in the long dusk,
and all the explosive natives take him to heart.

Source: H. Shows, "Empire Burlesque," *Parasol: Poems 1977–2007* (Beckington, UK: Luniver Press, 2007), p. 53.

[QUESTIONS FOR REFLECTION]

Considering Ideas

1. In the first line, Shows states, "Every scene must service the plot." Do you agree with this criterion for evaluating movies or other narrative works? Why or why not?

2. A burlesque is a kind of satire or parody, usually presented on stage. In what sense does this poem present a "burlesque" of "empire"?

3. The author suggests that the traveler "has grown sane" after he has "given away his tailored clothes." What do you think he means by this line?

Considering the Rhetorical Star

1. What is the main *subject* of the poem? Is the topic engaging? Why or why not?

2. Who is the intended *audience* for the poem?

3. What is the poet's main *purpose* for writing the poem? How do you know?

4. Shows uses evaluation as the primary *strategy* for the poem. What criteria does he suggest are important for evaluating a movie?

5. Describe the *design* of the poem. Is it effective? Why or why not?

Considering Writing Strategies

1. What effect does the poet achieve by omitting the film's title, or any title, in "Empire Burlesque"?

2. What effect does the simile at the end of the first stanza have on you as the reader? Have you ever felt like a "lost bag" before? What happened?

3. What vivid images does Shows include in his poem? Which parts created a visual image for you as you were reading? What did you envision?

Writing Suggestions

1. Watch the 1962 movie *Lawrence of Arabia* and write a review of it. Base your review on specific criteria, and back up your claims with specific details from the film. You might also compare it to other adventure movies that were produced later.

2. Write a review of a poem that has special meaning to you. You might focus on the ideas in the poem as well as the author's techniques. Be sure to support your opinions with specific examples from the poem.

STUDENT WRITING

Adventures in Crime
by Amanda Archer

The *Incredibles,* a Pixar Animated Studios production, is an action adventure movie filled with excitement. Although *The Incredibles* may be great fun for a family's movie and popcorn Friday night, its PG rating is perhaps not strong enough. The film opens with the local super-heroes revealing their previous thoughts and feelings about their work in candid interviews. As the story progresses the audience learns that these characters have been forced into a protection program that keeps what seemed like good deeds at bay. This introduces the characters to average working class lives where the Parr family has been relocated with middle-class employment; however, underneath their average suburban life they are superheroes, or "supers" as they call themselves. The Parr family members struggle with normal everyday challenges and conceal their above average abilities from the public's eyes. The film portrays many positive values that a mature audience can glean. However, be warned that there are plenty of adult situations and undertones. Furthermore, many good deeds are accomplished with violence that will amuse adults but can negatively influence younger viewers.

The Incredibles can have educational value for the right age group; adults can interpret the characters' comments and understand what messages lie underneath. The Parr family goes through events that help them cope with their skills and find constructive outlets that help them lead as normal a life as possible. Mr. and Mrs. Parr revive their struggling marriage, and family members discover new abilities, which they use to promote teamwork and strengthen their family ties. This movie can remind viewers that it is possible to teach children morals and values through events that the family encounters. Robert Parr, who is Mr. Incredible, tries to keep his gifted wife Helen, known as Elastigirl, and their children in a recreational vehicle to keep them safe while he attempts to destroy an enemy. He tells them that he cannot let them join him because he is afraid of losing them and would not know what to do without them. Helen tells him that she will not let him fight alone and she explains that together as a family they can accomplish more. Through events that arise, each character is able to learn about the special abilities he or she possesses and use these abilities as a cooperative team. This demonstrates the value of providing support for family members.

From the beginning of the movie, the adult content can be overwhelming for younger viewers. The humor and sexual innuendos are definitely created to amuse and entertain an older age group. For example, in one of the opening scenes, Mr. Incredible and Elastigirl are up on a rooftop trying to determine who will receive the credit for defeating a criminal when Elastigirl makes a remark to Mr. Incredible that he needs to be more "flexible." While her comment may seem harmless, her tone of voice has a strong sexual connotation. Additionally, the language and actions of the adult characters are constantly geared toward adults and the ability to see through what is said and read into the stereotyping of each character they meet.

Furthermore, the numerous acts of violence are impossible to miss. The superheroes are seemingly regular people who have taken it upon themselves to intercede for the greater good where they see fit. This involves participating in a large number of violent situations. For example, as Mr. Incredible wraps up his first good deed in the movie, to assist an elderly woman retrieve her cat from a tree, he jumps into his car and is shocked to find a child in his passenger seat. The child exclaims that he is Mr. Incredible's biggest fan and aspires to be his sidekick, Incrediboy. Mr. Parr, who dislikes the annoying boy, ejects the child from the seat, sending him into the air and over the top of the vehicle before crashing onto the ground. This scene reinforces the acceptable use of violence for amusement. Toward the end of the film, Elastigirl tries to sneak into a facility wherein she gets her body stuck in a electronic door and then uses her body as a weapon to knock out several guards and stuff them into a panel in the wall. The continual use of violence toward children as well as "bad guys" is entertaining but not beneficial for young, impressionable viewers. Young children sometimes mimic the superheroes they see on television, but these role models do not set a good example.

Overall, *The Incredibles* portrays several positive family values that audience members sometimes forget. However, the rating of this movie should be PG13 so that people are aware that young children should not view it without parental supervision. The humor is enjoyable for viewers who can understand the adult content and undertones throughout the script. As a result, this would be a great movie to view after young children have gone to bed for the night. So sit back, pop some popcorn, and enjoy the comic stereotyping of characters and the superheroes' zany reactions to the situations that occur.

[QUESTIONS FOR REFLECTION]

1. What is Archer's overall claim about the movie?
2. Is her description of the premise of the film sufficient? Why or why not?
3. What criteria does she use to evaluate the film?
4. Are her judgments fully supported? Explain.
5. What is your reaction to Archer's review? Would you watch the movie? Would you show it to a child under the age of thirteen? Why or why not?

▶ *Activity* Artistic Evaluation

In pairs or small groups, choose a work of art to review. You might consider using a painting, photograph, sculpture, song, poem, comic strip, or other work that you can evaluate in a reasonably short amount of time. Work together to choose criteria for your evaluation, make a judgment about each criterion, and present an overall opinion of your subject. Your group members may share your results with the class. If possible, provide your audience with a visual image or copy of the poem or song as appropriate. This activity may give you ideas for writing an evaluative essay.

Artistic Evaluation Activity:
Answers will vary.

Now that you have read one or more evaluations, it's time to write your own evaluation. You may choose to write about one of the writing options that follow, the advertisement, the image, or one of the media suggestions. Additionally, keep your ears open for hot topics at school or work; you may hear a conversation that sparks your interest. You might also read through an online newspaper or magazine to find a subject to evaluate. Remember to keep track of any sources you use in case you need to cite them in your paper. Consider your rhetorical star and the qualities of effective evaluative writing as you begin to compose your assignment.

Writing Assignment Options

Use one of the following topics to write an evaluative essay.

1. A book, short story, play, poem, or website
2. A movie, documentary, or television show
3. A song, a music video, or an album
4. A performance, such as a concert, a musical, a play, an opera, or a ballet
5. A work of art, such as a painting, sculpture, or photograph
6. A college course or teacher
7. A job, boss, or co-worker
8. A parent, friend, or significant other
9. A weekend trip or vacation
10. The dining experience at a particular restaurant

Interpreting an Advertisement

The advertisement depicts "The Battle for Middle Earth" video game. What effect does the artwork have on you? Is it intriguing or repulsive? What kind of audience might be interested in the game? If you are a gamer, would you consider buying this game based on the advertisement? Why or why not? Write an essay evaluating this advertisement or another video game advertisement. Base your evaluation on several specific criteria. Consider what needs to be included in an effective advertisement to persuade a gamer to purchase the game.

Writing about an Image

Starry Night by Vincent van Gogh

Write an essay evaluating one of the images in this chapter. You might start by describing the photograph or painting. Rather than merely focusing on likes and dislikes, evaluate your subject using several criteria that make sense for it. You might consider whether the subject has value as a work of art and why it is worthy of being called art. For example, you might listen to Josh Groban's version of the song "Vincent," look at Vincent van Gogh's painting *Starry Night,* and write your own evaluation of the painting based on specific criteria, such as use of color, shading, and composition.

Media Connection for Evaluating

You might watch, read, and/or listen to one or more of the suggested media to discover additional examples of evaluation. Exploring various media may help you to better understand methods of evaluating. You may choose to write about one or more of the media suggestions. For example, you might watch an episode of *American Idol* and evaluate one of the contestants for musical ability, showmanship, and rapport with the audience. Be sure to give credit to any sources you use in your essay.

Television	*American Idol*	*Dancing with the Stars*	*The Voice*	*America's Got Talent*
Film	*Rock of Ages* (2012)	*The Simpsons Movie* (2007)	*Divergent* (2014)	*The Hunger Games* trilogy (2012–2015)
Print/E-Reading	*Consumer Reports*	*Entertainment Weekly*	*Rolling Stone*	*The Artist's Magazine*
Internet	**metacritic.com**	**nybooks.com**	**rottentomatoes.com**	**music-critic.com**
Music	"Performance Evaluation" by Cocoa Tea	"Vincent (Starry, Starry Night)" by Josh Groban	"Mona Lisa" by Grant-Lee Phillips	"Skyfall" by Adele

11.4 ANALYZING THE RHETORICAL STAR FOR WRITING AN EVALUATION

FIGURE 11.1
The Rhetorical Star

As you prepare to write your evaluation, consider the five points of the rhetorical star (Figure 11.1). You might use some of the questions in the chart as you conduct your rhetorical star analysis.

Subject	Choose a topic that interests you to evaluate. You might write a review related to film and the arts, such as a review of a movie, television show, book, song, or piece of art. If you choose a movie or television show to evaluate, you will want to record it, if possible, so that you can watch it more than once if necessary. You could also look through an art book or online art museum to find a suitable topic. You may choose to evaluate something school related, such as a class or textbook. Another option is to write an evaluation of a work-related subject, such as your boss or work environment. Be sure to select a topic that you feel qualified to evaluate.
Audience	Who will read your evaluation? What will interest your readers about your subject? Are you offering your readers advice about what to watch, read, or listen to? Do you intend for your audience to do something based on your evaluation, or do you just want your readers to understand your position? Think about what kinds of details would be most appropriate to share with your audience.
Purpose	Determine what you are trying to accomplish through your evaluation. If you saw a movie or show that you loved, you might write a review convincing others to view it. Maybe your goal is to simply inform others about a fantastic website that is educational or entertaining. On the other hand, you might want to persuade your audience to take a particular class or go to a specific concert or play.
Strategy	Even if your primary goal is to evaluate your subject, you may decide to use additional writing strategies as well. For example, if you are evaluating a new movie, you might compare and contrast it with an older version of the movie or with a similar movie. If you are evaluating a problem, you may come up with possible solutions for the problem and argue that a particular solution is the most effective.
Design	How many criteria do you need to use to fully support your evaluation of your subject? Also, what other design details, such as photographs or charts, might enhance your evaluation? Will you use some kind of symbol or rating system to make your evaluative criteria clear for the reader?

11.5 APPLYING THE WRITING PROCESS FOR EVALUATING

After you have completed your rhetorical star analysis, follow the steps of the writing process (Figure 11.2) to compose your evaluation.

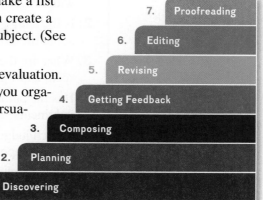

FIGURE 11.2 The Seven Steps of the Writing Process

1. **Discovering:** Once you have chosen a topic, you might make a list of criteria to consider for your evaluation. You could even create a checklist or graphic organizer to help you analyze your subject. (See Figure 11.3.)

2. **Planning:** Decide which criteria you want to use for your evaluation. Create a cluster or an outline (informal or formal) to help you organize your ideas. Because evaluative writing needs to be persuasive, you might save your strongest point for last. Doing so will make your most convincing criterion more memorable for your audience.

3. **Composing:** Write a first draft of your evaluation. Remember to focus each body paragraph on one main criterion that relates to your overall opinion about your subject. Don't worry too much about grammar and punctuation at this time. Use the qualities outlined earlier in the chapter:

    1. Describe the subject being evaluated.
    2. Make a claim about the subject.
    3. Use several specific criteria for the evaluation.
    4. Make a fair judgment about each criterion.
    5. Support each judgment with specific evidence.
    6. End with a final claim about your subject.

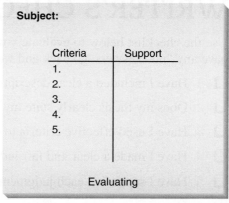

FIGURE 11.3 Evaluating Graphic Organizer

4. **Getting feedback:** Have at least one classmate or other person read your rough draft and answer the peer review questions on page 278. If you have access to a writing tutor or center, get another opinion about your paper as well.

5. **Revising:** Using all of the feedback available to you, revise your evaluation. Make sure that your evaluation is based on specific criteria and that you have fully supported each judgment that you make. Additionally, make sure that your essay is unified. In other words, every judgment you make needs to help support the opinion in your thesis (your claim). Add, delete, and rearrange ideas as necessary.

6. **Editing:** Read your evaluation again, this time looking for errors in grammar, punctuation, and mechanics. Pay particular attention to your consistency with verb tenses. Generally it is best to use the present verb tense when discussing your subject. For example, write that the artist, filmmaker, or author "captivates" the audience rather than "captivated" the audience.

7. **Proofreading:** After you have carefully edited your essay, read it one last time. Look for typographical errors and any other issues that might interfere with the readers' understanding of your evaluation.

Trade rough drafts with a classmate and answer the following questions about his or her paper. Then, in person or online, discuss your papers and suggestions with your peer. Finally, make the changes you feel would most benefit your paper.

1. Has the author described the subject being evaluated clearly and effectively without giving away too much?

2. Is the author's claim (thesis) clear? What is the author's overall opinion about the subject?

3. What are the author's criteria for evaluating the subject? Do these criteria seem appropriate? Why or why not?

4. Has the author stated a clear judgment about each criterion? What are the judgments? Are they fair? Why or why not?

5. Is each judgment supported with specific details and examples? Is there enough support?

6. Is the concluding paragraph effective? Why or why not?

7. What kinds of grammatical errors, if any, are evident in the evaluation?

8. What final suggestions do you have for the author?

WRITER'S CHECKLIST FOR EVALUATING

Use the checklist below to evaluate your own writing and help ensure that your evaluation is effective. If you have any "no" answers, go back and work on those areas if necessary.

❑ 1. Have I included a clear description of the subject I am evaluating?

❑ 2. Does my thesis clearly state my opinion of the subject I am evaluating?

❑ 3. Have I used effective criteria to evaluate my subject?

❑ 4. Have I made a clear and fair judgment about each evaluative criterion?

❑ 5. Have I supported each judgment with specific details and examples?

❑ 6. Have I ended with an effective conclusion?

❑ 7. Have I proofread thoroughly?

[CHAPTER SUMMARY]

1. Use the evaluative writing strategy to make a judgment about one or more subjects.

2. Evaluative writing is an important part of your education, daily life, and career.

3. Carefully analyze the rhetorical star before writing an evaluation: subject, audience, purpose, strategy, and design.

4. Interpreting evaluative readings and images can help you to prepare to write an evaluation.

5. Use these qualities when writing an evaluation essay: describe the subject being evaluated; make a claim about the subject; use several specific criteria for the evaluation; make a fair judgment about each criterion; support each judgment with specific evidence; end with a final claim about the subject you are evaluating.

[W H A T   I   K N O W   N O W]

Use this checklist to determine what you need to work on to feel comfortable with your understanding of the material in this chapter. Check off each item as you master it. Review the material for any unchecked items.

❑ 1. I know what **evaluative** writing is.

❑ 2. I can identify several **real-world applications** for writing evaluations.

❑ 3. I can evaluate **readings and images** about film and the arts.

❑ 4. I can **analyze** the rhetorical star for writing an evaluation.

❑ 5. I understand the **writing process** for writing an evaluation.

❑ 6. I can apply the **six qualities** of an evaluation.

SmartBook Tip

During the "Recharge" phase, students can return to Chapter 11 and practice concepts that they need to work on.

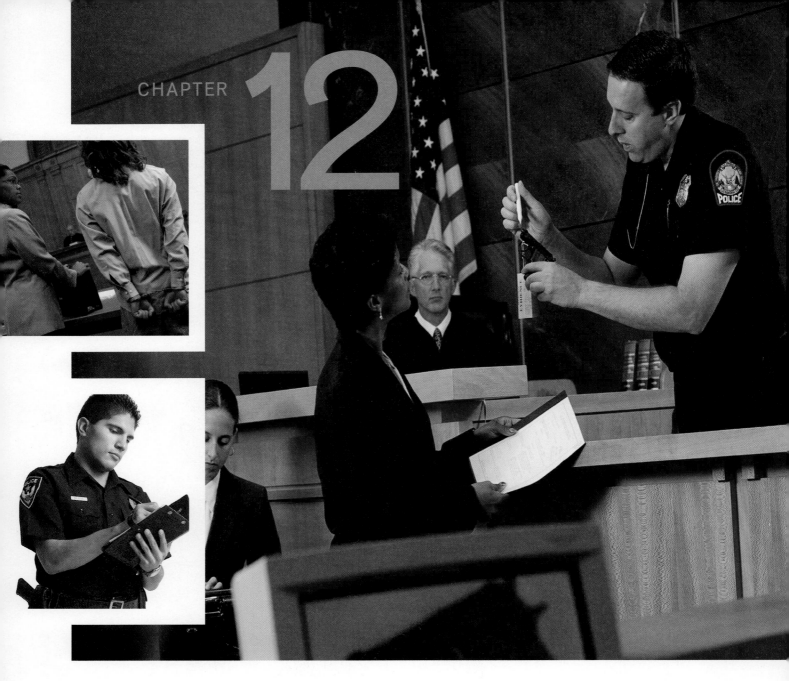

CHAPTER

12

SOLVING A PROBLEM:
CRIME AND JUSTICE

learning outcomes

In this chapter you will learn techniques for achieving these learning outcomes:

12.1 IDENTIFY REAL-WORLD APPLICATIONS FOR SOLVING A PROBLEM.

12.2 UNDERSTAND THE QUALITIES OF AN EFFECTIVE PROPOSAL TO SOLVE A PROBLEM.

12.3 RESPOND TO AND ANALYZE IMAGES AND READINGS ABOUT CRIME AND JUSTICE.

12.4 ANALYZE THE RHETORICAL STAR FOR SOLVING A PROBLEM.

12.5 APPLY THE QUALITIES OF AN EFFECTIVE PROPOSAL TO SOLVE A PROBLEM.

WRITING STRATEGY FOCUS: SOLVING A PROBLEM

You don't have to look far to find problems that need to be solved. Instead of just complaining about a problem, you can attempt to do something about it. What can you do to help mitigate a problem? One way to initiate change is to write about the problem and offer one or more solutions. If you don't know the answer to a problem, then you can investigate to see what you can learn about the situation. You might conduct research to find an answer to the problem. As always, you will need to document any sources that you use for your paper.

SmartBook Tip

Students receive an overview of the learning outcomes and topics in Chapter 12 in the "Preview" phase of SmartBook.

12.1 REAL-WORLD APPLICATIONS FOR SOLVING A PROBLEM

Writing to Solve a Problem in College

You may be asked to write problem-solving papers in your college courses. In an environmental science course, your instructor may ask you to propose solutions for reducing our dependency on gasoline. Your sociology instructor might assign a paper requiring you propose a solution for a social issue, such as juvenile delinquency or domestic violence. In a course in your major, you may need to write about solutions for improving the public's awareness of an important issue, such as breast cancer, computer piracy, or identity theft.

Writing to Solve a Problem in Your Daily Life

Proposing solutions to problems is also important in your personal life. You might need to come up with a solution for managing your time if you are working and going to school full-time. If you and your roommate or significant other have difficulty in deciding who is responsible for certain tasks at home, then you might solve the problem by writing a proposal for an equitable way to divide the chores. If you are having trouble making your finances stretch as far as they need to, then you might solve the problem by drafting a proposed budget for covering all expenses.

LearnSmart Achieve Tip

The Writing Process unit of LearnSmart Achieve determines what students do and do not know about the writing process. Learning outcomes within the Writing Process unit cover planning, organizing, drafting, and revising. Learning outcomes within the Reasoning and Argument Unit cover developing claims, defending claims, and using ethical, logical, and emotional appeals to persuade readers. Learning resources and questions automatically adapt to each student's individual needs and help students thoroughly master this content. See the Instructor's Manual for *Write Now* for a list of learning outcomes as well as additional information on how to use LearnSmart Achieve with your students.

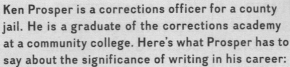

Graduate SPOTLIGHT

Ken Prosper, Corrections Officer

Ken Prosper is a corrections officer for a county jail. He is a graduate of the corrections academy at a community college. Here's what Prosper has to say about the significance of writing in his career:

❝ In my career, I have to write on a daily basis. The most critical reports are incident reports because they are public record and can be used in a court of law. For example, if the state presses charges against an inmate for criminal activity, the report has to be extremely detailed to win the case. Conversely, if an inmate accuses an innocent officer of using undue force, the report can help to prove the officer's innocence. I also write daily logs, witness statements, and other documents. Writing is so important in this field that officers earn extra compensation for completing college level writing courses. Being an effective writer is crucial to my job security and advancement. **❞**

Writing to Solve a Problem in Your Career

Teaching Tip

Ask students to tell how they anticipate using the problem-solving writing strategy in their future careers.

SmartBook Tip

Key concepts in Chapter 12 are highlighted for students during the "Read" phase. As students demonstrate understanding of these concepts during the "Practice" phase by responding to probes, the highlighting adapts to the individual student's learning by changing color.

Real-World Problem-Solving Writing Activity:

Answers will vary.

Being able to write an effective proposal is extremely useful in the workplace. You could suggest solutions to upper-level management that would improve working conditions and morale. Your employer may assign you to write a proposal for solutions that would cut expenses, increase profits, and save jobs. Furthermore, you might need to write a problem-solving report proposing to implement a new program or procedure in your office. Here are some additional ideas for problem-solving writing on the job:

Health care: proposals for purchasing new equipment, implementing a new clinical procedure, or providing better health care coverage.

Law: proposals for reducing crime, improving security, or changing crime scene investigation procedures.

Business: proposals for increasing productivity, personnel, and profits.

Education: proposals for increasing student retention or raising funds for a field trip or a new computer lab.

Computers: proposals for updating software, strengthening network connectivity, or upgrading hardware.

Massage therapy: proposals for gaining more clients, improving the equipment, or creating a more appealing ambience.

Culinary arts: proposals for increasing the customer base, changing the menu, or improving sanitation.

▶ *Activity* **Real-World Problem-Solving Writing**

In pairs or small groups, brainstorm uses for problem-solving writing at school, in your daily life, and on the job. You may want to choose the prospective career field(s) of the participants in your group. Each group may share its results with the class.

12.2 QUALITIES OF EFFECTIVE PROBLEM-SOLVING WRITING

1. Identify a Problem and Demonstrate That It Exists

Because solutions to problems are often intended to be persuasive, you might delay your claim a little bit so that your reader will be more likely to believe that there is a problem that needs to be addressed. First, you will need to explain what the problem is and prove that it is real. Provide details, examples, a brief narrative, or statistics to convince your audience that there really is a problem. For example, if you are writing about the vandalism in your apartment complex, you might begin by describing specific incidents that have occurred. Maybe Mr. Montana in apartment 27B discovered graffiti on his front door last week, and Ms. Lively in apartment 35C found broken beer bottles and rotten eggs on her terrace yesterday.

Teaching Tip

Have students work individually or in groups to develop a list of problems related to crime and justice in their community. Later, students may practice writing claims related to the list they developed and eventually come up with potential solutions to one or more problems they identified.

2. Appeal to Your Audience

Make the problem relevant to the audience so that they will care about the situation. For instance, if your audience is the other tenants in the complex, then you could point out that they could be targeted next if they don't help to solve the problem. If your audience consists of leaders in the community, then you might suggest that if they ignore the vandalism, then the crimes may escalate into something more serious or become more widespread.

3. State Your Claim

Your thesis might claim that a problem exists and assert that something needs to be done about it. Another option is to claim that a particular solution or combination of solutions is the way to solve the problem. For example, your claim might be that your apartment complex needs to implement a better security system because of all the crime that has been occurring lately.

4. Propose One or More Solutions to the Problem

You might focus on one main solution, several potential solutions, or a combination of solutions. By analyzing several potential solutions, you can show the readers that you have thoroughly investigated ways to solve the problem. Even if you settle on one primary solution, you should acknowledge that other possible solutions exist. For example, one way to help prevent vandalism from occurring in your apartment complex is to hire more security. Another possible solution is to organize a neighborhood watch program. A third solution might be to set up surveillance cameras in an attempt to discourage vandals and catch anyone who causes trouble. You can weigh the pros and cons of each solution and then propose the best one(s).

By considering alternative solutions, you can show readers that you have carefully considered a variety of options. You can then refute options except for the solution or combination of solutions you feel would best solve the problem. For instance, although hiring additional security guards might be effective, maybe that solution would be too expensive. Additionally, even though setting up a neighborhood watch system sounds like a good idea, maybe that wouldn't work well for your neighborhood because the vandalism happens during the day when most of the residents are at work or school. Finally, you might argue that setting up surveillance cameras is the best solution because it is fairly cost effective, and visible cameras would deter potential vandals from causing trouble. If an incident occurs, the apartment supervisor could easily review a video recording and provide it to the police.

5. Organize Your Solution(s) Effectively

You have several options for organizing your paper. Table 12.1 outlines two possibilities. Option A takes an inductive approach, where you state your proposal up front and then support it. On the other hand, Option B uses the deductive method, where you explain the problem and possible solutions before proposing a final solution. You may apply these options in various ways.

6. Persuade Your Audience That Your Solution or Combination of Solutions Is Feasible and Worthwhile

Once you have made your claim about the best solution or combination of solutions for the problem, you will need to persuade your

TABLE 12.1

Organizational Patterns for Solving a Problem	
Option A	**Option B**
Introduction and claim (thesis)	Introduction and explanation of problem
Explanation of problem	Solution one—evaluate pros and cons
Proposed solution	Solution two—evaluate pros and cons
Support for proposed solution	Solution three—evaluate pros and cons
Conclusion	Conclusion and final recommendation

reader that your solution is necessary and workable. Illustrate how the proposal will work and/or suggest what could happen if nothing is done about the problem. If it is appropriate for your subject and assignment, you may be able to use personal knowledge and experience to support your essay.

Most proposals to solve problems, however, need to be backed up with evidence that you obtain by conducting research. Citing specific statistics, details, and examples will help to make your proposal more credible for the readers. For example, if one of your solutions is to install security cameras in your apartment building, then you might include statistics about the effectiveness of using security cameras from a reliable source. If you do use outside sources, you will need to document them appropriately. Be sure to avoid logical fallacies (see Chapter 10) in your reasoning.

7. End with a Call to Action

You might conclude your essay by summarizing the problem and solution(s). You may also want to encourage your readers to take action to help solve the problem. Your call to action can take several forms. You might ask the readers to write a letter, get involved, or donate money to help solve the problem.

You might even suggest what the consequences might be if nothing is done to alleviate the problem. However, avoid making idle threats or exaggerating the possible implications of inaction.

Career-Based PROBLEM-SOLVING WRITING

[preview] **HAVE YOU EVER** had trouble finding a parking spot? Have you been tempted to park somewhere that you know you shouldn't? The following article addresses the issue of illegal parking by government employees in New York City. At the time the article was written, in 2006, Michael Bloomberg, who assumed office in 2001 and served three consecutive terms, hoped to correct the problem by reducing the number of parking permits issued. How would you feel if you received a ticket with a hefty fine, but someone with a government parking sticker didn't—even though you both parked illegally?

Above the Law: Government Parking Abuse in NYC

The Problem

Many government agencies and offices issue parking permits to select employees. Typically placed on a vehicle's dashboard, permits allow government employees to park their vehicles in designated areas. The permits are not meant to allow government employees to block fire hydrants, avoid paying parking meters, park on sidewalks or anywhere else they want. Yet, this is exactly what parking permits are used for. Only in the rarest of circumstances does the NYPD enforce against illegally parked government employees.

Thanks to a lack of enforcement and an unchecked proliferation of government-issued parking permits— legitimate and fraudulent—the widespread abuse of parking permits has persisted for decades and has grown significantly worse in recent years. By default, the ability to abuse a parking permit has become a closely held entitlement, a perk of holding certain government jobs.

Though it may not be explicit policy, the NYPD's traffic enforcement division essentially operates under the premise that citywide there is a "no hit" policy on vehicles with permits in the window. Permit abusers talk of the NYPD extending a "courtesy" to agencies to break the law; business owners and Business Improvement Districts relay accounts of local enforcement officers repeatedly refusing to give tickets to permit holders while ticketing non-permit holders parked in their midst.

While Mayor Bloomberg has vowed to reduce the number of permits on the street, the problem persists. Transportation Alternatives estimates that over 150,000 drivers have access to free parking in the form of valid government-issued parking permits (including the more than 30,000 NYPD "Self-Enforcement Zone" permits and 75,000 teacher permits). Thousands more illicitly enjoy the same privileges by photocopying permits, or by minting their own. In part because of this parking privilege, census data clearly show that government workers drive to work twice as much as private-sector workers.

The Price

Unfortunately, when drivers with permits cannot find a legal spot, they often park in illegal spaces at the curbside and important metered spaces, hurting businesses that rely on parking turnover and sharply cutting into city revenues that would be generated by meters. Even more egregiously, many government workers endanger public safety by parking in front of fire hydrants, on sidewalks, in crosswalks, in intersections, and in bus stops.

In addition, illegal permit parking generates unnecessary traffic in several ways:

1. Due to their parking privileges, many commuters who could be taking transit opt to drive instead.
2. Because they super-saturate the curb, illegal parkers cause other vehicles to troll to find ever-elusive curbside space.
3. When drivers cannot find a spot, they double park, compounding traffic problems by blocking lanes and forcing erratic maneuvers.

4. Illegal permit parking degrades the quality of the air that New Yorkers breathe, which contributes to increased risk of health problems like asthma, diabetes, heart disease, and cancer.
5. Illegal permit parking erodes the trust of government and law enforcement in the communities that are overrun by vehicles.

Recommendations

While the recently announced $400,000 Department of Transportation study of parking and permit abuse in downtown Manhattan is a positive step toward better understanding parking patterns, the Mayor need not wait for another study to begin upholding the law and reducing the numbers of permits in circulation. The Mayor and the NYPD should immediately implement the following recommendations that would ameliorate the problem overnight:

- Enforce the law.
- Take inventory of permits and reduce the total.
- Educate government workers to eliminate the "culture of entitlement."
- Update parking signage to reflect the community's needs.

Source: Transportation Alternatives, "UNCIVIL SERVANTS: A Survey of Government Worker Parking Abuse in NYC's Chinatown and Civic Center," April 26, 2006. transalt.org/news/reports.

[QUESTIONS FOR REFLECTION]

1. Who is the primary audience for the report? How do you know? Who else might the author be addressing as well?
2. What is the major problem? Is it explained in a convincing way? Why or why not?
3. What are some of the side effects of the major problem?
4. What solutions does the writer propose? Which solution or solutions do you feel would work best to solve the problem? Why?
5. What additional material might the author include to strengthen the report? Explain.

12.3 SOLVING A PROBLEM IN THE CONTEXT OF CRIME AND JUSTICE

If you pay any attention to the news media, you are constantly reminded of problems related to crime and injustice in our society. When you go online, listen to the radio, watch television, or read a newspaper or magazine, you will often come across stories about criminal activity, such as murders, domestic violence, drug trafficking, and home invasions. You will also be exposed to reports of injustices, such as people being treated unfairly because of their race, gender, beliefs, or values. As you are discussing the readings and images in this chapter, think about what is right or fair as you work toward proposing solutions to problems. In the words of Dr. Martin Luther King Jr., "Injustice anywhere is a threat to justice everywhere."

[preview] **LEE E. BERLIK** is the founder and managing member of his prestigious, award-winning law firm, BerlikLaw, in Virginia. He graduated cum laude with a law degree from the Washington College of Law at American University. In the following article, which originally appeared in the *Virginia Defamation Law Blog*, Berlik discusses a serious problem that occurred for employees at a sheriff's office in Virginia because of what they "liked" on Facebook. After this article was published, the federal court ruled that Facebook "liking" is protected free speech. Before reading the article, consider the following questions: Are you a Facebook user? Do you sometimes hit the "like" button to show your support for a site or cause? Would it seem fair to you to be penalized at work for something you "liked" on Facebook?

Facebook "Likes" Not Protected Speech, Says Virginia Court by Lee E. Berlik

Think twice before clicking that Facebook "like" button. 1 You may think you're expressing a constitutionally protected right to express support for a political candidate, for which you cannot be terminated, but Judge Raymond A. Jackson of the Eastern District of Virginia recently ruled that merely "liking" a candidate on Facebook is not sufficiently substantive to warrant First Amendment protection. Expect this ruling to get appealed.

Sheriff B.J. Roberts of the Hampton sheriff's office 2 was up for re-election when he learned that several of his employees were actively supporting one of his opponents, Jim Adams. The employees alleged that Sheriff Roberts learned of their support of Adams because they "liked" Adams's Facebook page. They also attended a cookout with Adams and told others of their support, but there was no evidence that the sheriff was aware of these activities. One employee sported a pro-Adams bumper sticker on his car and used choice words to describe the sheriff's campaign literature in speaking with a colleague at the election booth.

After winning re-election, Sheriff Roberts did not 3 retain the employees. Sheriff Roberts claimed various benign reasons for the firings, including a reduction in force and unsatisfactory work performance. The employees sued Sheriff Roberts alleging that the firings were in retaliation for exercising their right to free speech and that the sheriff had violated their right to free political association. Sheriff Roberts argued that plaintiffs had not alleged protected speech or political association and that he was entitled to qualified and sovereign immunity[1] even if plaintiffs' speech was protected.

To state a claim under the First Amendment for retal- 4 iatory discharge, public employees must prove that they were terminated on the basis of "speech" on a matter of public concern. Here, the court concluded that merely "liking" a Facebook page is insufficient speech to merit constitutional protection. The court examined holdings in which constitutional speech protection extended to Facebook posts, and it noted that in those cases, actual statements existed within the record. Conversely, it found, simply clicking the "like" button on a Facebook page is not the kind of substantive statement that warrants constitutional protection. Likewise, the court found that the presence of a bumper sticker supporting Adams did not constitute protected speech without any evidence that the sheriff was aware of the bumper sticker. The court also found that statements describing the sheriff's campaign literature, regardless of expletives, did not constitute protected speech because they did not address a matter of public concern but were instead descriptive of personal opinion.

The court also held that even if the plaintiffs' First 5 Amendment arguments had merit, their claims would have failed anyway because the sheriff was entitled to both qualified and sovereign immunity.

As several commentators have already pointed out, 6 this ruling seems contrary to Supreme Court precedent affording First Amendment protection to such acts as saluting a flag, refusing to salute, and wearing an armband. But I disagree with Professor Eugene Volokh, who writes that "the whole point" of the "like" button is to convey "a message of support for the thing you're liking." When you "like" a Facebook page, you get updates from the page you liked in your news feed. Therefore, "liking" a person's Facebook page may be intended as nothing more than a means of monitoring that person's public statements; it doesn't necessarily mean you like or support those statements. It will be interesting to see how the Fourth Circuit deals with this.

[1] **Qualified and sovereign immunity** Legal doctrines that protect government officials from liability and criminal prosecution if they have unknowingly broken a law without malice.

Source: Lee E. Berlik, "Facebook 'Likes' Not Protected Speech, Says Virginia Court," *The Virginia Defamation Law Blog*, May 6, 2012, **www.virginiadefamationlawyer.com**.

Considering Ideas

1. What problem does Berlik identify in his blog? Do you think this is a genuine concern? Why or why not?

2. Should people who post comments or hit the "like" button on Facebook expect their information to be confidential? Why or why not?

3. Should law enforcement, school officials, or employers have the authority to punish someone for what he or she posts online under any circumstances? Explain.

Considering the Rhetorical Star

1. What is the *subject* of Berlik's article?

2. Who is the intended *audience* for the article? Explain.

3. What is Berlik's *purpose* for writing the article? Is it more informative or persuasive? Identify specific passages from the article that indicate the author's purpose.

4. What is the author's primary writing *strategy?* What other strategies does he use?

5. What is the *design* of the article? Is it effective? Why or why not?

Considering Writing Strategies

1. Although much of Berlik's blog focuses on the facts of the case, he does state his position on the issue. What is his position? Where does he most clearly state that position?

2. What is the author's purpose for writing the article? Rather than proposing solutions to the problem, he uses another tactic. What is it? Is it effective? Why or why not?

3. What evidence does Berlik give to support his point in the concluding paragraph? Is his evidence convincing? Explain.

Writing Suggestions

1. Write an essay proposing a solution for the issue that Berlik describes in his article. Is the solution to consider Facebook posts as private and off-limits to employers? Is the solution to hold employees accountable for everything they post online? Is there a compromise between the different points of view? Take a stand on the issue and convince your readers your proposed solution will work. You may want to include additional research in your essay. If you do so, be sure to cite your sources.

2. If you have your own Facebook page, think about what you have posted there. Have you included anything that would embarrass you if your classmates, instructors, or employers read it? Write an essay proposing a way to self-monitor Facebook posts. You might create hypothetical scenarios to support your thesis.

Reading and Reflection PROBLEM-SOLVING WRITING

[preview] **LILIANA SEGURA**, originally from the Washington, DC, area, is a graduate of Barnard College and resides in New York City. Many of her works, which have appeared in numerous publications, focus on topics such as the death penalty, harsh sentencing laws, and the criminal justice system. Segura was an associate editor of *The Nation,* where the following article was originally published. Before reading, consider what types of crimes you feel justify sentencing a criminal to life in prison.

Why Should Thousands of Prisoners Die Behind Bars for Nonviolent Crimes? by Liliana Segura

This past August, the Lafayette-based *IND Monthly* published a story about a 54-year-old man named Bill Winters, incarcerated at a medium-security prison in Epps, Louisiana. Winters, who is black, was arrested in June 2009, after he drunkenly entered an unlocked oncologist's office on a Sunday morning, setting off a security alarm. When police arrived, he had rummaged through a desk drawer, and was in possession of a box of Gobstoppers candy. Winters was convicted of simple burglary a week before Thanksgiving, and given a seven-year prison sentence—hardly a slap on the wrist. But a few days later, the prosecutor in his case, Assistant District Attorney Alan Haney, sought additional punishment for Winters, under the state's habitual offender law. Based on his record of nonviolent offenses, which went back to 1991 and ranged from cocaine possession to burglary, the trial court resentenced Winters to twelve years without any chance of parole. But Haney was still not satisfied. He appealed the ruling, arguing that the court had imposed an "illegally lenient sentence" and that the rightful punishment was life without the possibility of parole.

At a subsequent hearing, Lafayette Police Chief Jim [2] Craft estimated that Winters had been arrested more than twenty times, calling him a "career criminal who victimized a lot of citizens in our city." But it seemed clear that he was more of a thorn in the side of law enforcement than a looming threat to society. His brothers, Dennis and James, testified that Winters had been homeless at the time of his offense and that he had a history of addiction; James had overcome his own drug problems and said that he would be willing to "take [Winters] in and work with him." A former Lafayette police officer who had once worked at a correctional facility where Winters was held, said that although he did not know him well, Winters "didn't cause problems" and had potential for rehabilitation. But this past summer, the Third Circuit Court of Appeals issued its decision: "The state asserts that because of the defendant's particular multiple offender status, the law mandates a minimum sentence of life in prison without benefit of parole, probation, or suspension of sentence. We agree."

Dennis Winters was incredulous when he heard the [3] news about his brother. "What? This makes no sense," he told *IND Monthly*. "I don't understand what these people are trying to do. He's not a violent person. He's fragile. He wouldn't hurt anybody, except maybe himself. I just don't get how they're going to give him life for some Gobstopper candy."

Today, Winters joins hundreds of Louisiana prisoners [4] sent to die in prison after committing similarly nonviolent offenses, from drug possession to property crimes. The national numbers are tallied in a major new study released today by the American Civil Liberties Union, titled "A Living Death: Life without Parole for Nonviolent Offenses," which documents scores of cases with echoes of Winters's story. Across the country, defendants have been given life without parole for such crimes as having a crack pipe, "siphoning gasoline from a truck" and, in another Louisiana case, shoplifting a $159 jacket.

Tales of outsized sentencing for minor crimes may [5] not surprise anyone familiar with the well-documented

excesses of three-strikes sentencing in California, for example. But the ACLU's report is the first to attempt to grasp the national numbers, specifically concerning nonviolent offenders sentenced to die behind bars. The report found 3,278 prisoners serving life without parole in 2012 for nonviolent crimes, of which 79 percent were for drug crimes. This is not the complete picture—Bill Winters himself is not among the prisoners covered—and crucially, only includes formal life-without-parole cases. It does not include life sentences where parole is a possibility—if largely only in theory, given the increasing reluctance of parole boards to free prisoners. It also does not include, say, 100-year sentences, or the kinds of stacked, decades-long sentences that are, in effect, permanent life sentences. "The number of people serving death-in-prison sentences after being convicted of nonviolent crimes is not known," the report concludes, "but it is most certainly higher than the number of prisoners serving formal life-without-parole sentences for nonviolent crimes."

Indeed, a report released earlier this year by the [6] Sentencing Project found that one in nine prisoners in the U.S. is serving a life sentence and that "those with parole-eligible life sentences are increasingly less likely to be released." Including life with parole, the report estimated that "approximately 10,000 lifers have been convicted of nonviolent offenses."

Determining what qualifies as "nonviolent" is similarly [7] complicated. As the ACLU points out, "Although the term 'violent crime' brings to mind very serious offenses such as rape and murder, some jurisdictions define violent crime to include burglary, breaking and entering, manufacture or sale of controlled substances, possession of a firearm by a convicted felon, or extortion." In other words, the number of prisoners serving life without parole who are far from the "worst of the worst" is higher still.

Regardless of the exact numbers, and perhaps not [8] surprisingly for the state known as the prison capital of the world, it is clear that Louisiana is home to a disproportionate number of these sentences. It also provides a dramatic illustration of the explosion of permanent life sentences over the past four decades: "In Louisiana, just 143 people were serving LWOP sentences in 1970," the ACLU notes. "That number had increased to 4,637 by 2012." The report found that Louisiana had the highest number of nonviolent offenders serving life without parole out of all the states: 429. Florida was a distant second, with 270. (Thanks to the drug war, federal prisoners accounted for the largest share at 2,074.)

Among the Louisiana prisoners highlighted in the [9] report are Fate Vincent Winslow, who, while homeless, "acted as a go-between in the sale of two small bags of marijuana, worth $10 in total, to an undercover police officer"; Timothy Jackson, who stole a jacket from a department store in New Orleans; Paul Carter, convicted of "possession of a trace amount of heroin residue that was so minute it could not be weighed"; and Sylvester Mead, a Shreveport man who drunkenly threatened a police officer while seated, handcuffed, in the back of a patrol car.

Mead's case, like Winters's, shows the way in which prosecutors' wishes consistently trump judicial power when it comes to sentencing people for such crimes. Not only did his trial judge oppose the initial charge of public intimidation, he made it repeatedly clear he opposed sending Mead to die in prison. Mead's verbal offense "does not warrant, under any conscionable or constitutional basis, a life sentence," he said. But Mead's prosecutor appealed multiple times seeking a harsher sentence because of his old convictions. After his previous sentences were vacated by a higher court multiple times, Judge Leon L. Emanuel was bound by Louisiana's mandatory sentencing statute to hand down a sentence of life without parole. "No matter how long this Court were to deliberate about this matter, it cannot fashion a legal result to explain that the life sentence without probation or suspension of sentence is unconstitutionally excessive," he concluded.

Such statements from judges are not unusual, it turns out. "In case after case reviewed by the ACLU, the sentencing judge said on the record that he or she opposed the mandatory LWOP sentence as too severe but had no discretion to take individual circumstances into account or override the prosecutor's charging decision," the ACLU found. Mandatory sentencing schemes are certainly to blame—in Louisiana, they account for almost all—97.6 percent—of the surveyed nonviolent LWOP sentences. But while mandatory sentencing ties the hands of judges, such punishments do not impose themselves. Prosecutors have the power to seek or not seek them.

Bill Winters was not the first defendant to find himself in the crosshairs of Lafayette ADA Alan Haney. Indeed, in 2007, Haney created a "career criminal program," as described by the local *Daily Advertiser*, to "identify repeat offenders all over Lafayette Parish."

"We basically had to start this whole project from scratch," he told the City-Parish Council in September 2010, according to the *Advertiser*. Thus far, he boasted, some forty-nine people had been sentenced as habitual offenders with the help of the initiative.

In the fall of 2009, the same year Winters was convicted for stealing Gobstoppers, a 29-year-old black man named Travis Bourda was convicted for possessing 130 grams of marijuana "with intent to distribute." Writing to the ACLU, Bourda insists that no drugs were actually found in his posession and that his court-appointed lawyer "filed no motions, failed to investigate," and "made no objections at trial." His initial sentence of eight years was increased to fourteen after Haney filed habitual offender charges based on Bourda's previous

record, which included "carnal knowledge of a juvenile" when he was 19. Responding to Haney's attempt to seek a sentence of life without parole for Bourda, the trial judge wrote: "I believe a life sentence under the circumstances . . . would be an unconstitutional sentence. I believe that fourteen years is more than enough considering the underlying charge was possession with intent to distribute marijuana, and that the amount of marijuana involved was not significant."

But in 2011 the Court of Appeals for the Third Circuit agreed with Haney, vacating the fourteen-year sentence and imposing life without parole. Today, Bourda is serving his sentence at the Louisiana State Penitentiary, famously known as Angola.

Angola prisoners were not allowed to receive visits or speak on the phone to the ACLU. But in response to the questionnaire sent out by attorney Jennifer Turner, who authored the report and corresponded with more than 600 prisoners, Bourda described himself as "the most miserable person there is." He wrote that he was diagnosed as schizophrenic when he was 13 and that he hears voices that tell him to do things. In a separate, handwritten letter, he wrote to "share my thoughts about the Habitual Offender law," which he describes as "the most unconstitutional law there is."

"We paid our debts to society for the past crimes we committed," Bourda wrote. ". . . There is never any forgiveness once you have a record." In his opinion, he added, "the prosecution is abusing his discretion on a certain race of people which we know to be black individuals."

Whether or not prosecutorial discretion is to blame, Bourda's observation about race is certainly supported by the numbers. The ACLU report shows, and Turner wrote to me in an e-mail, that "the racial disparity in life without parole sentencing for nonviolent crimes in Louisiana is staggering." While the state would not provide figures according to race, the ACLU calculated that black prisoners "comprise 91.4 percent of the nonviolent LWOP prison population in Louisiana," despite the fact that "Blacks make up only about one-third of the general population in the state." Black defendants in Louisiana "were 23 times more likely than whites to be sentenced to LWOP for a nonviolent crime."

There are many factors that could explain this. "The racial disparity can result from disparate treatment at every stage of the criminal justice system, including stops and searches, points of arrest, prosecutions and plea negotiations, trials, and sentencing," Turner explains. She adds, "In Louisiana, it may also have to do with how prosecutors wield their enormous discretion in deciding whether to charge defendants as habitual offenders."

I contacted Alan Haney's office by phone and e-mail to discuss his Habitual Offender Division, but have not received a response. In the meantime, the ACLU report is only the most recent to cast a stark light on Louisiana's sentencing excesses. While some recent reforms in the state have sought to mitigate some of Louisiana's harshest sentencing statutes, they still preserve the power of the prosecutor to decide if and when to trigger mandatory sentences. In a report released by the Reason Foundation last month, which closely examines the state's determinate sentencing laws and makes recommendations for reform, the authors found that a 2012 law signed by Governor Bobby Jindal to allow courts to waive mandatory minimums in some cases put all the power in prosecutors' hands, giving prosecutors "much more power than they previously had."

The ACLU also makes recommendations for reform. It calls on the states and federal government to get rid of laws that mandate or allow life without parole for nonviolent crimes, and exhorts state governors, as well as the Obama administration, to commute such disproportionate punishments. "Life without parole sentences for nonviolent offenses defy common sense," it concludes, and "are grotesquely out of proportion to the conduct they seek to punish." 21

In Bourda's words, "I never committed a capital offense such as murder. . . . I don't deserve to be sentenced like a hard-core criminal." 22

Source: Liliana Segura, "Why Should Thousands of Prisoners Die Behind Bars for Nonviolent Crimes," reprinted from *The Nation,* http://www.thenation.com/blog/177139/why-should-thousands-prisoners-die-behind-bars-nonviolent-crimes.

[QUESTIONS FOR REFLECTION]

Considering Ideas

1. What is your reaction to Winters's sentence for stealing a box of Gobstoppers and Bourda's sentence for possessing 130 grams of marijuana? Do these sentences seem fair? Why or why not?

2. The author suggests that people of different races are not treated equally in the justice system. Do you agree or disagree with this assertion? Why?

3. Do you believe nonviolent criminals should be sentenced to life in prison without the possibility of parole? Why or why not?

Considering the Rhetorical Star

1. What is the *subject* of Segura's proposal? How thoroughly does she cover the subject?

2. Who is the intended *audience* for the proposal? Explain.

3. What is Segura's *purpose* for the article? Does she achieve the purpose? Why or why not?

4. In addition to problem solving, what other writing *strategies* does Segura use? Give specific examples from the article to illustrate your point.

5. Is the *design* of the article effective? Why or why not?

Considering Writing Strategies

1. What is Segura's claim? Where does it appear in the article? Is her placement of the claim effective for a proposal? Why or why not?

2. Segura uses several examples of nonviolent criminals to support her point. Are her examples effective? Explain.

3. Identify several emotionally charged words in the essay. Why does the author include them? What effect do those words words have on the reader?

Writing Suggestions

1. Write a proposal suggesting how to reduce crime in your community.

2. Write a proposal offering one or more methods for rehabilitating prisoners.

Reading and Reflection PROBLEM-SOLVING WRITING

[preview] **CLIVE THOMPSON** is a columnist for *Wired* magazine and a contributor to the *New York Times Magazine* as well as other publications. From 2002 to 2003 Thompson was a Knight Science Journalism Fellow at the Michigan Institute of Technology. He runs his own website, *Collision Detection,* where bloggers comment on issues related to science, technology, and culture. To participate in Thompson's website, go to **www.collisiondetection.net**. In the following essay, which originally appeared in *Wired* magazine, Thompson explains a new technology that is emerging and ponders the legal implications of this technology. Before reading, think about your innermost private thoughts. Would you want someone to have any idea of what you are thinking?

It's All in Your Head: Why the Next Civil Rights Battle Will Be Over the Mind by Clive Thompson

Strolling down the street in Manhattan, I suddenly hear a woman's voice. 1

"Who's there? Who's there?" she whispers. I look around but can't figure out where it's coming from. It seems to emanate from inside my skull. 2

Was I going nuts? Nope. I had simply encountered a new advertising medium: hypersonic sound. It broadcasts audio in a focused beam, so that only a person standing directly in its path hears the message. In this case, the cable channel A&E was using the technology to promote a show about, naturally, the paranormal. 3

I'm a geek, so my first reaction was, "Cool!" But it also felt creepy. 4

We think of our brains as the ultimate private sanctuary, a zone where other people can't intrude without our knowledge or permission. But its boundaries are gradually eroding. Hypersonic sound is just a portent of what's coming, one of a host of emerging technologies aimed at tapping into our heads. These tools raise a fascinating, and queasy, new ethical question: Do we have a right to "mental privacy"? 5

"We're going to be facing this question more and more, and nobody is really ready for it," says Paul Root Wolpe, a bioethicist and board member of the nonprofit Center for Cognitive Liberty and Ethics. "If the skull is not an absolute domain of privacy, there *are* no privacy domains left." He argues that the big personal liberty issues of the 21st century will all be in our heads—the "civil rights of the mind," he calls it. 6

It's true that most of this technology is still gestational. But the early experiments are compelling: Some researchers say that fMJR brain scans can detect surprisingly specific mental acts—like whether you're entertaining racial thoughts, doing arithmetic, reading, or recognizing something. Entrepreneurs are already pushing dubious forms of the tech into the marketplace. You can now hire a firm, No Lie MRI, to conduct a "truth verification" scan if you're trying to prove you're on the level. Give it 10 years, ethicists say, and brain tools will be used regularly—sometimes responsibly, often shoddily. 7

Both situations scare civil libertarians. What happens when the government starts using brain scans in criminal investigations—to figure out if, say, a suspect is lying about a terrorist plot? Will the Fifth Amendment protect you from self-incrimination by your own brain? Think about your workplace, too: Your boss can already demand that you pee in a cup. Should she also be allowed to stick your head in an MRI tube as part of your performance review? 8

But this isn't just about reading minds; it's also about bombarding them with messages or tweaking their chemistry. Transcranial magnetic stimulation—now used to treat epilepsy—has shown that it can artificially generate states of empathy and euphoria. And you've probably heard of propranolol, a drug that can help erase traumatic memories. 9

Let's say you've been assaulted and you want to take propranolol to delete the memory. The state needs that memory to prosecute the assailant. Can it prevent you from taking the drug? "To a certain extent, memories are societal properties," says Adam Kolber, a visiting professor at Princeton. "Society has always made claims on your memory, such as subpoenaing you." Or what if you use transcranial stimulation to increase your empathy. Would you be required to disclose that? Could a judge throw you off a jury? Could the Army turn you away? 10

I'd love to give you answers. But the truth is no one knows. Privacy rights vary from state to state, and it's unclear how, or even if, the protections would apply to mental sanctity. "We really need to articulate a moral code that governs all this," warns Arthur Caplan, a University of Pennsylvania bioethicist. 11

The good news is that scholars are holding conferences to hash out legal positions. But we'll need a broad public debate about it, too. Civil liberties thrive only when the public demands them—and understands they're at risk. The means we need to stop seeing this stuff as science fiction and start thinking about how we'll react to it. Otherwise, we could all lose our minds. 12

Source: Clive Thompson, "It's All in Your Head: Why the Next Civil Rights Battle Will Be Over the Mind," *Wired*, April 2008, p. 60.

[QUESTIONS FOR REFLECTION]

Considering Ideas

1. How do you feel about the development of new technology that could potentially allow others to have an inkling of what you are thinking? Should this technology eventually be used for criminal investigations? Why or why not?

2. How would you respond to Thompson's ethical question: "Do we have a right to 'mental privacy'?" Would you hire a firm, such as No Lie MRI, to conduct a "truth verification" scan to prove your innocence if someone falsely accused you of committing a crime? Why or why not?

3. The author delays his proposal until the second to last paragraph; what is his claim?

Considering the Rhetorical Star

1. What is the *subject* of Thompson's article?

2. Who is the intended *audience* for the article? Explain.

3. What is Thompson's *purpose* for writing the article? Identify specific passages from the article that indicate the author's purpose.

4. What is the author's primary writing *strategy?* What other strategies does he use?

5. What is the *design* of the article? Is it effective? Why or why not?

Considering Writing Strategies

1. What cause-and-effect relationship does Thompson highlight in his proposal? Is this relationship logical? Why or why not?

2. What action is the author asking the readers to take? Is this a reasonable request? Explain your answer.

3. How effective is the last part of the writer's final sentence: ". . . we could all lose our minds"? Is he expecting the reader to take him seriously? Why or why not?

Writing Suggestions

1. Write a proposal suggesting what lawmakers should do if the technology explained in Thompson's article comes into widespread use. To support your proposal, you might focus on potential positive outcomes or possible negative outcomes of the technology. For example, you might predict possible effects of using this new technology for criminal investigations.

2. Do you feel that anyone has a right to know what someone is thinking? Is the right to have one's own private thoughts different for an ordinary citizen on the street than for a potential criminal? Write a proposal suggesting a fair use for the technology described in Thompson's essay. Who, if anyone, should have the right to know what someone else is thinking?

Reading and Reflection PROBLEM-SOLVING WRITING

[preview] **SEKOU SUNDIATA** (1948–2007) was born in Harlem. A poet, playwright, songwriter, performer, educator, and activist, he had compassion for the human experience, particularly for African-Americans. His artistic performances were infused with music that crossed a wide range of genres, including blues, jazz, funk, and Afro-Caribbean rhythms. He performed throughout the United States and abroad, and he was featured on the HBO series *Def Poetry Jam* and the PBS poetry series *The Language of Life.* Before becoming a professor of writing at Eugene Lang College of New School University in New York City, he earned degrees from City College of New York and City University of New York. Tragically, after surviving a kidney transplant and a serious car accident, Sundiata met his untimely death in 2007 at the age of 58 due to heart failure. To learn more about Sundiata and hear some of his music, go to **www.puremusic.com/sekou.html**. You can listen to him read poetry on YouTube as well. In the following poem, Sundiata tells about a situation with "the Law." Before reading, think about your own experience. Have you ever been pulled over by a police officer while you were driving? Did you think you had done anything wrong? How did you feel about the incident?

Blink Your Eyes by Sekou Sundiata

I was on my way to see my woman
but the Law said I was on my way
thru a red light red light red light
and if you saw my woman
you could understand,
I was just being a man.
It wasn't about no light
it was about my ride
and if you saw my ride
you could dig that too, you dig?

Sunroof stereo radio black leather
Bucket seats sit low you know,
the body's cool, but the tires are worn.
Ride when the hard time come, ride
When they're gone, in other words
the light was green.

I could wake up in the morning
without a warning
and my world could change:

blink your eyes.
All depends, all depends on the skin,
all depends on the skin you're living in.

Up to the window comes the Law
With his hand on his gun
what's up? what's happening?
I said I guess
that's when I really broke the law.
He said a routine, step out the car
a routine, assume the position.
Put your hands up in the air
you know the routine, like you just don't care.
License and registration.
Deep was the night and the light
from the North Star on the car door, déjà vu
we've been through this before,
why did you stop me?
Somebody had to stop you.
I watch the news, you always lose.

You're unreliable, that's undeniable.
This is serious, you could be dangerous.

I could wake up in the morning
without a warning
and my world could change:
blink your eyes.
All depends, all depends on the skin,
all depends on the skin you're living in
New York City, they got laws
can't no bruthas drive outdoors,
in certain neighborhoods, on particular streets
near and around certain types of people.
They got laws.
All depends, all depends on the skin,
all depends on the skin you're living in.

Source: Sekou Sundiata, "Blink Your Eyes" (1995) in Wayne Stein, Deborah Israel, and Pam Washington, *Fresh Takes: Explorations in Reading and Writing* (New York: McGraw-Hill, 2008), pp. 375–76.

[QUESTIONS FOR REFLECTION]

Considering Ideas

1. What problem has Sundiata identified in his poem?
2. Do you agree with the poet that the law treats people differently based on the color of their skin? Why or why not?
3. Have you ever felt that you were treated differently (better or worse) than someone else because of your ethnicity? What happened?

Considering the Rhetorical Star

1. What is the *subject* of Sundiata's poem?
2. Who is the intended *audience* for the poem? Explain.
3. What is Sundiata's *purpose* for writing the poem? Does he achieve his purpose? Explain.
4. What is the poet's primary writing *strategy*? What other strategies does he use?
5. What is the *design* of the poem? How does the design affect the readers?

Considering Writing Strategies

1. Which lines does Sundiata repeat in his poem? What is the effect of the repetition?
2. What point is the poet making through the following lines? "I watch the news, you always lose. You're unreliable, that's undeniable. This is serious, you could be dangerous." Is his point convincing? Why or why not?
3. What is the significance of the title of the poem? What might be different in the morning? What is Sundiata's implied proposal?

Writing Suggestions

1. Write a proposal suggesting how to get people, such as law enforcement officers, to treat others fairly, regardless of their race.
2. What can college students do to help people of different ethnicities get along better together? Write a proposal detailing one or more specific suggestions.

Reading and Reflection PROBLEM-SOLVING WRITING

[preview] **SUSAN GLASPELL** (1876–1948) was a Pulitzer Prize–winning playwright and best-selling fiction writer. After graduating from Drake University, in her home state of Iowa, she worked as a journalist for the *Des Moines Daily News,* and her stories appeared in several publications, including *Harper's* and *Ladies' Home Journal.* She was the founder and director of the Provincetown Players on Cape Cod, Massachusetts, for which she wrote 11 plays. She also wrote more than 50 short stories and nine

novels. Many of her works focus on feminist issues. Visit **http://blogs.shu.edu/glaspellsociety/sample-page/** to learn more about the author and her works. In the following play, which is her most popular, Glaspell reveals the details of a murder investigation. The mystery, however, is not one of whodunit, but one of motive. Glaspell later transformed the play into a short story called "A Jury of Her Peers." If possible, read this play aloud with classmates or other people. Before reading, think about whether you feel that there is any situation in which it is OK for someone to cover up a crime. Under what circumstances, if any, would that option be acceptable?

Trifles by Susan Glaspell

CHARACTERS

GEORGE HENDERSON, *County Attorney*

HENRY PETERS, *Sheriff*

LEWIS HALE, *A Neighboring Farmer*

MRS. PETERS

MRS. HALE

Scene: *The kitchen in the now abandoned farmhouse of* JOHN WRIGHT, *a gloomy kitchen, and left without having been put in order—unwashed pans under the sink, a loaf of bread outside the breadbox, a dish towel on the table—other signs of incompleted work. At the rear the outer door opens, and the* SHERIFF *comes in, followed by the* COUNTY ATTORNEY *and* HALE. *The* SHERIFF *and* HALE *are men in middle life, the* COUNTY ATTORNEY *is a young man; all are much bundled up and go at once to the stove. They are followed by the two women—the* SHERIFF's *wife first; she is a slight wiry woman, a thin nervous face.* MRS. HALE *is larger and would ordinarily be called more comfortable looking, but she is disturbed now and looks fearfully about as she enters. The women have come in slowly, and stand close together near the door.*

COUNTY ATTORNEY [*rubbing his hands*]: This feels good. Come up to the fire, ladies.

MRS. PETERS [*after taking a step forward*]: I'm not—cold.

SHERIFF [*unbuttoning his overcoat and stepping away from the stove as if to mark the beginning of official business*]: Now, Mr. Hale, before we move things about, you explain to Mr. Henderson just what you saw when you came here yesterday morning.

COUNTY ATTORNEY: By the way, has anything been moved? Are things just as you left them yesterday?

SHERIFF [*looking about*]: It's just the same. When it dropped below zero last night, I thought I'd better send Frank out this morning to make a fire for us—no use getting pneumonia with a big case on; but I told him not to touch anything except the stove—and you know Frank.

COUNTY ATTORNEY: Somebody should have been left here yesterday.

SHERIFF: Oh—yesterday. When I had to send Frank to Morris Center for that man who went crazy—I want you to know I had my hands full yesterday, I knew you could get back from Omaha by today and as long as I went over everything here myself—

COUNTY ATTORNEY: Well, Mr. Hale, tell just what happened when you came here yesterday morning.

HALE: Harry and I had started to town with a load of potatoes. We came along the road from my place and as I got here I said, "I'm going to see if I can't get John Wright to go in with me on a party telephone." I spoke to Wright about it once before and he put me off, saying folks talked too much anyway, and all he asked was peace and quiet—I guess you know about how much he talked himself; but I thought maybe if I went to the house and talked about it before his wife, though I said to Harry that I didn't know as what his wife wanted made much difference to John—

COUNTY ATTORNEY: Let's talk about that later, Mr. Hale. I do want to talk about that, but tell now just what happened when you got to the house.

HALE: I didn't hear or see anything; I knocked at the door, and still it was all quiet inside. I knew they must be up, it was past eight o'clock. So I knocked again, and I thought I heard somebody say, "Come in." I wasn't sure, I'm not sure yet, but I opened the door—this door [*indicating the door by which the two women are still standing*], and there in that rocker— [*pointing to it*] sat Mrs. Wright.

[*They all look at the rocker.*]

COUNTY ATTORNEY: What—was she doing?

HALE: She was rockin' back and forth. She had her apron in her hand and was kind of—pleating it.

COUNTY ATTORNEY: And how did she—look?

HALE: Well, she looked queer.

COUNTY ATTORNEY: How do you mean—queer?

HALE: Well, as if she didn't know what she was going to do next. And kind of done up.

COUNTY ATTORNEY: How did she seem to feel about your coming?

HALE: Why, I don't think she minded—one way or other. She didn't pay much attention. I said, "How do, Mrs. Wright, it's cold, ain't it?" And she said, "Is it?"—and went on kind of pleating at her apron. Well, I was surprised; she didn't ask me to come up to the stove, or to set down, but just sat there, not even looking at me, so I said, "I want to see John." And then she—laughed. I guess you would call it a laugh. I thought of Harry and the team outside, so I said a little sharp: "Can't I see John?" "No," she says, kind o' dull like. "Ain't he home?" says I. "Yes," says she, "he's home." "Then why can't I see him?" I asked her, out of patience. "'Cause he's dead," says she. *"Dead?"* says I. She just nodded her head, not getting a bit excited, but rockin' back and forth. "Why—where is he?" says I, not knowing what to say. She just pointed upstairs—like that [*Himself pointing to the room above*]. I got up, with the idea of going up there. I walked from there to here—then I says, "Why, what did he die of?" "He died of a rope round his neck," says she, and just went on pleatin' at her apron. Well, I went out and called Harry. I thought I might—need help. We went upstairs, and there he was lyin'—

COUNTY ATTORNEY: I think I'd rather have you go into that upstairs, where you can point it all out. Just go on now with the rest of the story.

HALE: Well, my first thought was to get that rope off. It looked. . . [*Stops, his face twitches.*] . . . but Harry, he went up to him, and he said, "No, he's dead all right, and we'd better not touch anything." So we went back downstairs. She was still sitting that same way. "Has anybody been notified?" I asked. "No," says she, unconcerned. "Who did this, Mrs. Wright?" said Harry. He said it businesslike—and she stopped pleatin' of her apron. "I don't know," she says. "You don't *know?*" says Harry. "No," says she. "Weren't you sleepin' in the bed with him?" says Harry. "Yes," says she, "but I was on the inside." "Somebody slipped a rope round his neck and strangled him and you didn't wake up?" says Harry. "I didn't wake up," she said after him. We must 'a looked as if we didn't see how that could be, for after a minute she said, "I sleep sound." Harry was going to ask her more questions but I said maybe we ought to let her tell her story first to the coroner, or the sheriff, so Harry went fast as he could to Rivers' place, where there's a telephone.

COUNTY ATTORNEY: And what did Mrs. Wright do when she knew that you had gone for the coroner?

HALE: She moved from that chair to this over here [*Pointing to a small chair in the corner*] and just sat there with her hands held together and looking down. I got a feeling that I ought to make some conversation, so I said I had come in to see if John wanted to put in a telephone, and at that she started to laugh, and then she stopped and looked at me—scared. [*The COUNTY ATTORNEY, who has had his notebook out, makes a note.*] I dunno, maybe it wasn't scared. I wouldn't like to say it was. Soon Harry got back, and then Dr. Lloyd came, and you, Mr. Peters, and so I guess that's all I know that you don't.

COUNTY ATTORNEY [*looking around*]: I guess we'll go upstairs first—and then out to the barn and around there. [*To the SHERIFF*] You're convinced that there was nothing important here—nothing that would point to any motive?

SHERIFF: Nothing here but kitchen things.

[*The* COUNTY ATTORNEY, *after again looking around the kitchen, opens the door of a cupboard closet. He gets up on a chair and looks on a shelf. Pulls his hand away, sticky.*]

COUNTY ATTORNEY: Here's a nice mess.

[*The women draw nearer.*]

MRS. PETERS [*to the other woman*]: Oh, her fruit; it did freeze. [*To the* COUNTY ATTORNEY] She worried about that when it turned so cold. She said the fire'd go out and her jars would break.

SHERIFF: Well, can you beat the women! Held for murder and worryin' about her preserves.

COUNTY ATTORNEY: I guess before we're through she may have something more serious than preserves to worry about.

HALE: Well, women are used to worrying over trifles.

[*The two women move a little closer together.*]

COUNTY ATTORNEY [*with the gallantry of a young politician*]: And yet, for all their worries, what would we do without the ladies? [*The women do not unbend. He goes to the sink, takes a dipperful of water from the pail and pouring it into a basin, washes his hands. Starts to wipe them on the roller towel, turns it for a cleaner place.*] Dirty towels! [*Kicks his foot against the pans under the sink.*] Not much of a housekeeper, would you say, ladies?

MRS. HALE [*stiffly*]: There's a great deal of work to be done on a farm.

COUNTY ATTORNEY: To be sure. And yet [*with a little bow to her*] I know there are some Dickson county farmhouses which do not have such roller towels.

[*He gives it a pull to expose its full length again.*]

MRS. HALE: Those towels get dirty awful quick. Men's hands aren't always as clean as they might be.

COUNTY ATTORNEY: Ah, loyal to your sex, I see. But you and Mrs. Wright were neighbors. I suppose you were friends, too.

MRS. HALE [*shaking her head*]: I've not seen much of her of late years. I've not been in this house—it's more than a year.

COUNTY ATTORNEY: And why was that? You didn't like her?

MRS. HALE: I liked her all well enough. Farmers' wives have their hands full, Mr. Henderson. And then—

COUNTY ATTORNEY: Yes—?

MRS. HALE [*looking about*]: It never seemed a very cheerful place.

COUNTY ATTORNEY: No—it's not cheerful. I shouldn't say she had the homemaking instinct.

MRS. HALE: Well, I don't know as Wright had, either.

COUNTY ATTORNEY: You mean that they didn't get on very well?

MRS. HALE: No, I don't mean anything. But I don't think a place'd be any cheerfuller for John Wright's being in it.

COUNTY ATTORNEY: I'd like to talk more of that a little later. I want to get the lay of things upstairs now.

[*He goes to the left, where three steps lead to a stair door.*]

SHERIFF: I suppose anything Mrs. Peters does'll be all right. She was to take in some clothes for her, you know, and a few little things. We left in such a hurry yesterday.

COUNTY ATTORNEY: Yes, but I would like to see what you take, Mrs. Peters, and keep an eye out for anything that might be of use to us.

MRS. PETERS: Yes, Mr. Henderson.

[*The women listen to the men's steps on the stairs, then look about the kitchen.*]

MRS. HALE: I'd hate to have men coming into my kitchen, snooping around and criticizing.

[*She arranges the pans under sink which the* COUNTY ATTORNEY *had shoved out of place.*]

MRS. PETERS: Of course it's no more than their duty.

MRS. HALE: Duty's all right, but I guess that deputy sheriff that came out to make the fire might have got a little of this on. [*Gives the roller towel a pull.*] Wish I'd thought of that sooner. Seems mean to talk about her for not having things slicked up when she had to come away in such a hurry.

MRS. PETERS [*Who has gone to a small table in the left rear corner of the room, and lifted one end of a towel that covers a pan*]: She had bread set.

[*Stands still.*]

MRS. HALE [*eyes fixed on a loaf of bread beside the breadbox, which is on a low shelf at the other side of the room. Moves slowly toward it*]: She was going to put this in there. [*Picks up loaf, then abruptly drops it. In a manner of returning to familiar things.*] It's a shame about her fruit. I wonder if it's all gone. [*Gets up on the chair and looks.*] I think there's some here that's all right, Mrs. Peters. Yes—here. [*Holding it toward the window.*] This is cherries, too. [*Looking again.*] I declare I believe that's the only one. [*Gets down, bottle in her hand. Goes to the sink and wipes it off on the outside.*] She'll feel awful bad after all her hard work in the hot weather. I remember the afternoon I put up my cherries last summer.

[*She puts the bottle on the big kitchen table, center of the room. With a sigh, is about to sit down in the rocking-chair. Before she is seated realizes what chair it is; with a slow look at it, steps back. The chair, which she has touched, rocks back and forth.*]

MRS. PETERS: Well, I must get those things from the front room closet. [*She goes to the door at the right, but after looking into the other room, steps back.*] You coming with me, Mrs. Hale? You could help me carry them.

[*They go in the other room; reappear,* MRS. PETERS *carrying a dress and skirt,* MRS. HALE *following with a pair of shoes.*]

MRS. PETERS: My, it's cold in there.

[*She puts the clothes on the big table, and hurries to the stove.*]

MRS. HALE [*examining the skirt*]: Wright was close. I think maybe that's why she kept so much to herself. She didn't even belong to the Ladies Aid. I suppose she felt she couldn't do her part, and then you don't enjoy things when you feel shabby. She used to wear pretty clothes and be lively, when she was Minnie Foster, one of the town girls singing in the choir. But that—oh, that was thirty years ago. This all you was to take in?

MRS. PETERS: She said she wanted an apron. Funny thing to want, for there isn't much to get you dirty in jail, goodness knows. But I suppose just to make her feel more natural. She said they was in the top drawer in this cupboard. Yes, here. And then her little shawl that always hung behind the door. [*Opens stair door and looks.*] Yes, here it is.

[*Quickly shuts door leading upstairs.*]

MRS. HALE [*abruptly moving toward her*]: Mrs. Peters?

MRS. PETERS: Yes, Mrs. Hale?

MRS. HALE: Do you think she did it?

MRS. PETERS [*in a frightened voice*]: Oh, I don't know.

MRS. HALE: Well, I don't think she did. Asking for an apron and her little shawl. Worrying about her fruit.

MRS. PETERS [*starts to speak, glances up, where footsteps are heard in the room above. In a low voice*]: Mr. Peters says it looks bad for her. Mr. Henderson is awful sarcastic in a speech, and he'll make fun of her sayin' she didn't wake up.

MRS. HALE: Well, I guess John Wright didn't wake when they was slipping that rope under his neck.

MRS. PETERS: No, it's strange. It must have been done awful crafty and still. They say it was such a—funny way to kill a man, rigging it all up like that.

MRS. HALE: That's just what Mr. Hale said. There was a gun in the house. He says that's what he can't understand.

MRS. PETERS: Mr. Henderson said coming out that what was needed for the case was a motive; something to show anger or—sudden feeling.

MRS. HALE [*who is standing by the table*]: Well, I don't see any signs of anger around here. [*She puts her hand on the dish towel which lies on the table, stands looking down at table, one half of which is clean, the other half messy.*] It's wiped to here. [*Makes a move as if to finish work, then turns and looks at loaf of bread outside the breadbox. Drops towel. In that voice of coming back to familiar things.*] Wonder how they are finding things upstairs. I hope she had it a little more red-up[1] up there. You know, it seems kind of *sneaking*. Locking her up in town and then coming out here and trying to get her own house to turn against her!

MRS. PETERS: But Mrs. Hale, the law is the law.

MRS. HALE: I s'pose 'tis. [*Unbuttoning her coat.*] Better loosen up your things, Mrs. Peters. You won't feel them when you go out.

[MRS. PETERS *takes off her fur tippet, goes to hang it on hook at the back of room, stands looking at the under part of the small corner table.*]

MRS. PETERS: She was piecing a quilt.

[*She brings the large sewing basket and they look at the bright pieces.*]

MRS. HALE: It's log cabin pattern. Pretty, isn't it? I wonder if she was goin' to quilt it or just knot it?

[*Footsteps have been heard coming down the stairs. The* SHERIFF *enters, followed by* HALE *and the* COUNTY ATTORNEY.]

SHERIFF: They wonder if she was going to quilt it or just knot it.

[*The men laugh; the women look abashed.*]

COUNTY ATTORNEY [*rubbing his hands over the stove*]: Frank's fire didn't do much up there, did it? Well, let's go out to the barn and get that cleared up.

[*The men go outside.*]

MRS. HALE [*resentfully*]: I don't know as there's anything so strange, our takin' up our time with little things while we're waiting for them to get the evidence. [*She sits down at the big table, smoothing out a block with decision.*] I don't see as it's anything to laugh about.

MRS. PETERS [*apologetically*]: Of course they've got awful important things on their minds.

[*Pulls up a chair and joins* MRS. HALE *at the table.*]

MRS. HALE [*examining another block*]: Mrs. Peters, look at this one. Here, this is the one she was working on, and look at the sewing! All the rest of it has been so nice and even. And look at this! It's all over the place! Why, it looks as if she didn't know what she was about!

---

[1]**Red-up** To clean or tidy up.

[*After she has said this, they look at each other, then start to glance back at the door. After an instant* MRS. HALE *has pulled at a knot and ripped the sewing.*]

MRS. PETERS: Oh, what are you doing, Mrs. Hale?

MRS. HALE [*mildly*]: Just pulling out a stitch or two that's not sewed very good. [*Threading a needle.*] Bad sewing always made me fidgety.

MRS. PETERS [*nervously*]: I don't think we ought to touch things.

MRS. HALE: I'll just finish up this end. [*Suddenly stopping and leaning forward.*] Mrs. Peters?

MRS. PETERS: Yes, Mrs. Hale?

MRS. HALE: What do you suppose she was so nervous about?

MRS. PETERS: Oh—I don't know. I don't know as she was nervous. I sometimes sew awful queer when I'm just tired. [MRS. HALE *starts to say something, looks at* MRS. PETERS, *then goes on sewing.*] Well, I must get these things wrapped up. They may be through sooner than we think. [*Putting apron and other things together.*] I wonder where I can find a piece of paper, and string.

MRS. HALE: In that cupboard, maybe.

MRS. PETERS [*looking in cupboard*]: Why, here's a birdcage. [*Holds it up.*] Did she have a bird, Mrs. Hale?

MRS. HALE: Why, I don't know whether she did or not—I've not been here for so long. There was a man around last year selling canaries cheap, but I don't know as she took one; maybe she did. She used to sing real pretty herself.

MRS. PETERS [*glancing around*]: Seems funny to think of a bird here. But she must have had one, or why should she have a cage? I wonder what happened to it?

MRS. HALE: I s'pose maybe the cat got it.

MRS. PETERS: No, she didn't have a cat. She's got that feeling some people have about cats—being afraid of them. My cat got in her room and she was real upset and asked me to take it out.

MRS. HALE: My sister Bessie was like that. Queer, ain't it?

MRS. PETERS [*examining the cage*]: Why, look at this door. It's broke. One hinge is pulled apart.

MRS. HALE [*looking too*]: Looks as if someone must have been rough with it.

MRS. PETERS: Why, yes.

[*She brings the cage forward and puts it on the table.*]

MRS. HALE: I wish if they're going to find any evidence they'd be about it. I don't like this place.

MRS. PETERS: But I'm awful glad you came with me, Mrs. Hale. It would be lonesome for me sitting here alone.

MRS. HALE: It would, wouldn't it? [*Dropping her sewing.*] But I tell you what I do wish, Mrs. Peters. I wish I had come over sometimes *she* was here. I—[*Looking around the room.*]—wish I had.

MRS. PETERS: But of course you were awful busy, Mrs. Hale—your house and your children.

MRS. HALE: I could've come. I stayed away because it weren't cheerful—and that's why I ought to have come. I—I've never liked this place. Maybe because it's down in a hollow, and you don't see the road. I dunno what it is, but it's a lonesome place and always was. I wish I had come over to see Minnie Foster sometimes. I can see now—

[*Shakes her head.*]

MRS. PETERS: Well, you mustn't reproach yourself, Mrs. Hale. Somehow we just don't see how it is with other folks until—something comes up.

MRS. HALE: Not having children makes less work—but it makes a quiet house, and Wright out to work all day, and no company when he did come in. Did you know John Wright, Mrs. Peters?

MRS. PETERS: Not to know him; I've seen him in town. They say he was a good man.

MRS. HALE: Yes—good; he didn't drink, and kept his word as well as most, I guess, and paid his debts. But he was a hard man, Mrs. Peters. Just to pass the time of day with him— [*Shivers.*] Like a raw wind that gets to the bone. [*Pauses, her eyes falling on the cage.*] I should think she would 'a wanted a bird. But what do you suppose went with it?

MRS. PETERS: I don't know, unless it got sick and died.

[*She reaches over and swings the broken door, swings it again. Both women watch it.*]

MRS. HALE: You weren't raised round here, were you? [MRS. PETERS *shakes her head.*] You didn't know—her?

MRS. PETERS: Not till they brought her yesterday.

MRS. HALE: She—come to think of it, she was kind of like a bird herself—real sweet and pretty, but kind of timid and—fluttery. How—she—did—change. [*Silence; then as if struck by a happy thought and relieved to get back to every day things.*] Tell you what, Mrs. Peters, why don't you take the quilt in with you? It might take up her mind.

MRS. PETERS: Why, I think that's a real nice idea, Mrs. Hale. There couldn't possibly be any objection to it, could there? Now, just what would I take? I wonder if her patches are in here—and her things.

[*They look in the sewing basket.*]

MRS. HALE: Here's some red. I expect this has got sewing things in it. [*Brings out a fancy box.*] What a pretty box. Looks like something somebody would give you. Maybe her scissors are in here. [*Opens box. Suddenly puts her hand to her nose.*] Why—[MRS. PETERS *bends nearer, then turns her face away.*] There's something wrapped up in this piece of silk.

MRS. PETERS: Why, this isn't her scissors.

MRS. HALE [*lifting the silk*]: Oh, Mrs. Peters—It's—

[MRS. PETERS *bends closer.*]

MRS. PETERS: It's the bird.

MRS. HALE [*jumping up*]: But, Mrs. Peters—look at it. Its neck! Look at its neck! It's all—other side *to*.

MRS. PETERS: Somebody—wrung—its neck.

[*Their eyes meet. A look of growing comprehension, of horror. Steps are heard outside.* MRS. HALE *slips box under quilt pieces, and sinks into her chair. Enter* SHERIFF *and* COUNTY ATTORNEY. MRS. PETERS *rises.*]

COUNTY ATTORNEY [*as one turning from serious thing to little pleasantries*]: Well, ladies have you decided whether she was going to quilt it or knot it?

MRS. PETERS: We think she was going to—knot it.

COUNTY ATTORNEY: Well, that's interesting, I'm sure. [*Seeing the birdcage.*] Has the bird flown?

MRS. HALE [*putting more quilt pieces over the box*]: We think the—cat got it.

COUNTY ATTORNEY [*preoccupied*]: Is there a cat?

[MRS. HALE *glances in a quick covert way at* MRS. PETERS.]

MRS. PETERS: Well, not now. They're superstitious, you know. They leave.

COUNTY ATTORNEY [*to* SHERIFF PETERS, *continuing an interrupted conversation*]: No sign at all of anyone having come from the outside. Their own rope. Now let's go up again and go over it piece by piece. [*They start upstairs.*] It would have to have been someone who knew just the—

[MRS. PETERS *sits down. The two women sit there not looking at one another, but as if peering into something and at the same time holding back. When they talk now it is the manner of feeling their way over strange ground, as if afraid of what they are saying, but as if they can not help saying it.*]

MRS. HALE: She liked the bird. She was going to bury it in that pretty box.

MRS. PETERS [*in a whisper*]: When I was a girl—my kitten—there was a boy took a hatchet, and before my eyes—and before I could get there—[*Covers her face an instant.*] If they hadn't held me back, I would have—[*Catches herself, looks upstairs where steps are heard, falters weakly.*]—hurt him.

MRS. HALE [*with a slow look around her*]: I wonder how it would seem never to have had any children around. [*Pause.*] No, Wright wouldn't like the bird—a thing that sang. She used to sing. He killed that, too.

MRS. PETERS [*moving uneasily*]: We don't know who killed the bird.

MRS. HALE: I knew John Wright.

MRS. PETERS: It was an awful thing was done in this house that night, Mrs. Hale. Killing a man while he slept, slipping a rope around his neck that choked the life out of him.

MRS. HALE: His neck. Choked the life out of him.

[*Her hand goes out and rests on the birdcage.*]

MRS. PETERS [*with rising voice*]: We don't know who killed him. We don't know.

MRS. HALE [*her own feeling not interrupted*]: If there'd been years and years of nothing, then a bird to sing to you, it would be awful—still, after the bird was still.

MRS. PETERS [*something within her speaking*]: I know what stillness is. When we homesteaded in Dakota, and my first baby died—after he was two years old, and me with no other then—

MRS. HALE [*moving*]: How soon do you suppose they'll be through, looking for evidence?

MRS. PETERS: I know what stillness is. [*Pulling herself back*]. The law has got to punish crime, Mrs. Hale.

MRS. HALE [*not as if answering that*]: I wish you'd seen Minnie Foster when she wore a white dress with blue ribbons and stood up there in the choir and sang. [*A look around the room.*] Oh, I wish I'd come over here once in a while! That was a crime! That was a crime! Who's going to punish that?

MRS. PETERS [*looking upstairs*]: We mustn't—take on.

MRS. HALE: I might have known she needed help! I know how things can be—for women. I tell you, it's queer, Mrs. Peters. We live close together and we live far apart. We all go through the same things—it's all just a different kind of the same thing. [*Brushes her eyes; noticing the bottle of fruit, reaches out for it.*] If I was you, I wouldn't tell her her fruit was gone. Tell her it ain't. Tell her it's all right. Take this in to prove it to her. She—she may never know whether it was broke or not.

MRS. PETERS [*takes the bottle, looks about for something to wrap it in; takes petticoat from the clothes brought from the other room, very nervously begins winding this around the bottle. In a false voice*]: My, it's a good thing the men couldn't hear us. Wouldn't they just laugh! Getting all stirred up over a little thing like a—dead canary. As if that could have anything to do with—with—wouldn't they laugh!

[*The men are heard coming down stairs.*]

MRS. HALE [*under her breath*]: Maybe they would—maybe they wouldn't.

COUNTY ATTORNEY: No, Peters, it's all perfectly clear except a reason for doing it. But you know juries when it comes to women. If there was some definite thing. Something to show—something to make a story about—a thing that would connect up with this strange way of doing it—

[The women's eyes meet for an instant. Enter HALE from outer door.]

HALE: Well, I've got the team around. Pretty cold out there.

COUNTY ATTORNEY: I'm going to stay here awhile by myself [To the SHERIFF.] You can send Frank out for me, can't you? I want to go over everything. I'm not satisfied that we can't do better.

SHERIFF: Do you want to see what Mrs. Peters is going to take in?

[The COUNTY ATTORNEY goes to the table, picks up the apron, laughs.]

COUNTY ATTORNEY: Oh, I guess they're not very dangerous things the ladies have picked up. [Moves a few things about, disturbing the quilt pieces which cover the box. Steps back.] No, Mrs. Peters doesn't need supervising. For that matter, a sheriff's wife is married to the law. Ever think of it that way, Mrs. Peters?

MRS. PETERS: Not—just that way.

SHERIFF [chuckling]: Married to the law. [Moves toward the other room.] I just want you to come in here a minute, George. We ought to take a look at these windows.

COUNTY ATTORNEY [scoffingly]: Oh, windows!

SHERIFF: We'll be right out, Mr. Hale.

[HALE goes outside. The SHERIFF follows the COUNTY ATTORNEY into the other room. Then MRS. HALE rises, hands tight together, looking intensely at MRS. PETERS, whose eyes make a slow turn, finally meeting MRS. HALE's. A moment MRS. HALE holds her gaze, then her own eyes point the way to where the box is concealed. Suddenly MRS. PETERS throws back quilt pieces and tries to put the box in the bag she is wearing. It is too big. She opens box, starts to take bird out, cannot touch it, goes to pieces, stands there helpless. Sound of a knob turning in the other room. MRS. HALE snatches the box and puts it in the pocket of her big coat. Enter COUNTY ATTORNEY and SHERIFF.]

COUNTY ATTORNEY [facetiously]: Well, Henry, at least we found out that she was not going to quilt it. She was going to—what is it you call it, ladies!

MRS. HALE [her hand against her pocket]: We call it—knot it, Mr. Henderson.

Curtain

Source: Susan Glaspell, *Trifles*, 1916.

[QUESTIONS FOR REFLECTION]

Considering Ideas

1. How do the men and women differ in their separate investigations of Mr. Wright's murder? Why are their approaches so dissimilar?

2. How had Mrs. Wright changed since she was Minnie Foster 30 years ago? What do you suppose led to that change?

3. What problem do Mrs. Peters and Mrs. Hale face as they uncover the details of the investigation? How do they finally decide to resolve that problem at the end

of the play? Do you feel that their resolution is justified? Why or why not?

Considering the Rhetorical Star

1. What is the *subject* of Glaspell's play?

2. Who is the intended *audience* for the play? Explain.

3. What is Glaspell's *purpose* for writing the play? Does she achieve her purpose? Explain.

4. What is the playwright's primary writing *strategy*? What other strategies does she use?

5. What is the *design* of the play? Is it effective? Why or why not?

Considering Writing Strategies

1. What is ironic about the title *Trifles?* Do you prefer this title or "A Jury of Her Peers," the short story version of the play? Why?

2. What analogy does Glaspell draw between the canary and Mrs. Wright? What is the significance of the cage in this analogy?

3. How does the writer appeal to the audience? Has she made you feel compassion for Mrs. Wright? Why or why not?

Writing Suggestions

1. In response to Glaspell's *Trifles,* write a proposal suggesting what Mrs. Peters and Mrs. Hale should do with the evidence they found. You might weigh the pros and cons of several possible solutions before making your final recommendation.

2. Write an essay proposing ways for women, or men, to deal with domestic abuse.

STUDENT WRITING

Drinking and Driving
by Brittney Balogh

Every weekend, countless people go to bars with their friends and have a few too many drinks. Even after drinking too much, many of these individuals get into their cars and drive home without giving any thought to the people who are driving around them. These drunk drivers are a menace on the roadways and frequently cause car crashes that can result in serious injury or even death for innocent drivers and passengers. This common practice needs to change. Bar owners should take responsibility to help prevent their patrons from drinking and driving. Three possible solutions to this potentially deadly practice are for bar owners to offer a breath test, facilitate a designated driver system, or provide a ride home for intoxicated customers.

One solution for solving the dangerous problem of drinking and driving is for bar owners to give their customers an opportunity to take a breath test to determine if they register over the legal blood-alcohol ratio limit for driving. Before leaving the bar, customers could blow into one of these little handheld devices, which can be found on eBay for as little as $5.00, to see if they are safe to drive home. The main benefit of using this device is that it would help to cut down on the number of people who leave bars intoxicated. On the downside, the bar would have to purchase protective covers for the machine to prevent customers from sharing germs and diseases with one another through the mouthpiece that the customers breathe into.

A second solution that would help solve the drinking and driving problem is for bar owners to encourage customers to participate in a designated driver system. Each establishment could allow groups of friends to choose a designated driver for the group. The bars could provide each designee with a hand stamp or wristband so that bartenders would know who is not allowed to purchase alcoholic drinks. Additionally, bartenders could offer free non-alcoholic drinks to the designated drivers. Getting a free cola product, iced tea, or cup of coffee might be a good incentive for the designated drivers to stay sober. This solution would be very cost effective, and it would reduce the number of drunk drivers out on the road. However, it isn't foolproof. The designated drivers could remove their stamps or wristbands, or they could add their own alcohol to their free drinks.

A third solution for helping to reduce drinking and driving is for bar owners to provide rides home for guests who are clearly intoxicated. Bartenders could take notice of patrons who seem to be drinking too much and encourage them to accept a free ride home. Similar to the first two solutions, this procedure would help to ensure that the drunken customers would not get behind the wheel and cause harm to themselves or others. However, it could be costly for bars to pay for drivers, cars, and the insurance to make this operation work. Also, people may refuse to take the free ride home.

Overall, the best solution for reducing the number of drunk drivers endangering the lives of other drivers and passengers is for bar owners to offer breath tests and a designated driver program for all customers. They might reserve calling a taxi or giving a ride home to drunken customers only if the first two methods fail. Even though bar patrons should be responsible for their own actions, when they drink too much, they can lose the ability to make a good decision about how to get home. Therefore, bar owners should step up and help those who are not able to or chose not to take care of themselves. Doing so will make the roads safer for everyone.

[QUESTIONS FOR REFLECTION]

1. Does Balogh's introduction convince the reader that the problem exists? Explain.

2. What three possible solutions does Balogh propose?

3. What are the pros and cons of each possible solution?

4. Is the author's final solution convincing? Why or why not?

5. What other solutions might help to solve the problem?

▶ *Activity* **Proposing Solutions**

On your own or in small groups, identify three problems that you have experienced at home, school, or work. Brainstorm several possible solutions for each problem. Weigh the pros and cons of each possible solution, and determine which solution seems to be the most feasible. Be prepared to share your results with the class. This activity may give you ideas for writing a problem-solving essay.

Proposing Solutions Activity:
Answers will vary.

OPTIONS FOR WRITING A PROBLEM-SOLVING ESSAY

Now that you have read one or more examples of problem-solving writing, it's time to write your own proposal. You may choose to write about one of the writing options that follow, the advertisement, the image, or one of the media suggestions. Additionally, keep your ears open for problems at school or work; you may hear a conversation that sparks your interest. You might also read through an online newspaper or magazine to find a problem that calls for a solution. Remember to keep track of any sources you use in case you need to cite them in your paper. Consider your rhetorical star and the qualities of effective proposal writing as you begin to compose your assignment.

Writing Assignment Options

Write a proposal about a problem related to one of the following topics. You'll need to narrow the topic to something you can reasonably cover within the scope of your assignment.

1. Managing time or money
2. Relationships
3. Teenage pregnancy
4. Drug or alcohol abuse
5. Drinking and driving
6. Divorce
7. Plagiarism or cheating on tests
8. Overcrowded prisons
9. Pollution
10. Poverty or homelessness

ESOL Tip >
You may choose to propose a solution to a problem that exists in your culture or native country.

Interpreting an Advertisement

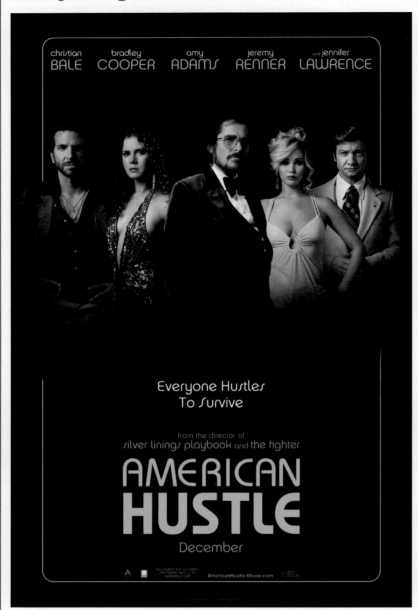

Who might be interested in the *American Hustle* advertisement? How do the images and text interact? What details catch your eye? Does the movie look appealing? Why or why not? Is the advertisement effective? Why or why not? Write a proposal related to the movie poster above or another crime movie you have seen. For example, you might propose a particular law that you believe should be in effect to help prevent people from being conned by scam artists, or you may propose a law that would punish those who have conned others. Remember to identify the problem and then propose one or more solutions to the problem.

Writing about an Image

Write a problem-solving essay related to one of the images in this chapter. What kind of crime has occurred? Could it have been prevented? What should be done about it? You may write about the image itself, or you may choose to write about something that relates to it. For example, you might write an essay about the first image in the chapter, which shows a courtroom and gun. Your essay would propose a solution for dealing with gangs and guns. Or you may choose to write about the image above, which depicts a drug raid, suggesting ways to help reduce the sale and use of illegal drugs in the United States.

Media Connection for Solving a Problem

You might watch, read, and/or listen to one or more of the suggested media to discover additional examples of problem solving. Exploring various media may help you to better understand methods for solving problems. You may also choose to write about one or more of the media suggestions. For example, you might watch the movie *The Wolf of Wall Street* and propose alternate solutions for how the characters dealt with the problems they faced. Be sure to give credit to any sources you use in your essay.

Television	CSI, NCIS	Sons of Anarchy, Criminal Minds	Law and Order	Homeland
Film	Gambit (2013)	American Hustle (2013)	The Wolf of Wall Street (2013)	The Gangster Squad (2013)
Print/ E-Reading	Conflict Resolution Quarterly (magazine)	Criminal Justice (journal)	Crime & Justice (journal)	Homeland Security Today (magazine)
Internet	http://justicejournalism.org	www.rider.edu/~suler/psycyber/conflict.html	www.crimeandjustice.org/	www.trulia.com/crime/
Music	"Please Man" by Big & Rich	"I Fought the Law" by Green Day	"Hurricane" by Bob Dylan	"Criminal" by Fiona Apple

FIGURE 12.1
The Rhetorical Star

12.4 ANALYZING THE RHETORICAL STAR FOR SOLVING A PROBLEM

As you prepare to write your proposal, consider the five points of the rhetorical star (Figure 12.1). You might use some of the questions in the chart as you conduct your rhetorical star analysis.

Subject	Identify a problem that you have observed in your community, at home, or at work. The issue can be one you have witnessed or experienced firsthand or one that you have noticed in the media. For example, maybe you have heard that someone has been vandalizing apartments in your complex and want to urge someone to do something about it. Or perhaps you feel your credit card company is taking unfair advantage of you by charging outrageous interest rates and you want to do something about it.
Audience	Who will read your proposal? What will interest your readers about your subject? What do they already know about the problem? Why will they care about it? Are your readers experiencing the problem or contributing to it? Will the problem affect them in some way? Are they in a position to do something about the problem? Think about what kinds of details would be most appropriate to share with your audience. Appeal to the interests and needs of your specific audience and anticipate their potential responses to your proposal. For example, if you are writing about problems in your apartment complex, then your audience could be the landlord, supervisor, other tenants, surrounding community members, security personnel, and/or the police department.
Purpose	Think about what you are trying to accomplish through your proposal. Do you simply want your readers to have a better understanding of the problem and possible solutions for solving it? Do you intend for your audience to do something based on your proposal? Either way, your main goal is to convince your readers that a problem exists and offer a reasonable solution.
Strategy	Even if your primary goal is to propose a solution to a problem, you may decide to use additional writing strategies as well. For example, you might show the causes of the problem or the effects of allowing it to continue, you may compare and contrast what the situation will be like in the future if your solution is implemented or not, or you could decide to evaluate several possible solutions before persuading your reader that one particular solution is the best.
Design	What is the best format for your proposal? Should you write an essay or a newspaper article? Would a letter or an e-mail be appropriate? Could you post a flyer at work, on campus, or in the community? Also, what other design details might enhance your proposal? Using bullets, headings, photographs, or charts might strengthen your problem-solving essay.

12.5 APPLYING THE WRITING PROCESS FOR SOLVING A PROBLEM

After you have completed your rhetorical star analysis, follow the steps of the writing process (Figure 12.2) to compose your problem-solving paper.

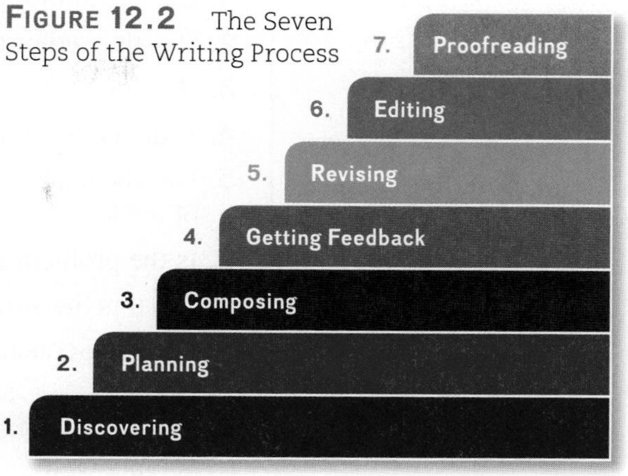

1. **Discovering:** Once you have decided on a problem, you might try discussing the problem with a classmate or friend to get some ideas for solving it.

2. **Planning:** Once you have chosen a topic, you might write out the problem and then make a list of potential solutions. Consider the pros and cons of each solution before choosing which one or ones to include in your essay. Use a graphic organizer (Figure 12.3) or create a cluster or an outline (informal or formal) to help you arrange your ideas.

FIGURE 12.2 The Seven Steps of the Writing Process

3. **Composing:** Using your plan from the previous step, write a first draft of your problem-solving essay. Don't worry too much about grammar and punctuation at this time. Keep focused on explaining the problem and offering viable solutions. Use the qualities of problem-solving writing.

   1. Identify a problem and demonstrate that it exists.
   2. Appeal to your audience.
   3. State your claim (thesis).
   4. Propose a solution or several possible solutions to the problem.
   5. Organize your solution(s) effectively.
   6. Persuade your readers that your proposal is feasible.
   7. End with a call to action.

4. **Getting feedback:** Have at least one classmate or other person read your rough draft and answer the peer review questions on page 310. If you have access to a writing tutor or center, get another opinion about your paper as well.

5. **Revising:** Using all of the feedback available to you, revise your problem-solving essay. Be sure that your overall solution is reasonable and explained clearly. Add, delete, and rearrange ideas as necessary.

6. **Editing:** Read your problem-solving essay again, this time looking for errors in grammar, punctuation, and mechanics. Pay particular attention to your choice of words and tone. Also, keep in mind that there may be other possible solutions that would work, so you don't necessarily want to imply that your solution is the only viable one.

7. **Proofreading:** After you have carefully edited your essay, read it again. This time, look for typographical errors and any other issues that might interfere with the readers' understanding of your problem-solving essay. Make your final corrections.

FIGURE 12.3 Solving a Problem Graphic Organizer

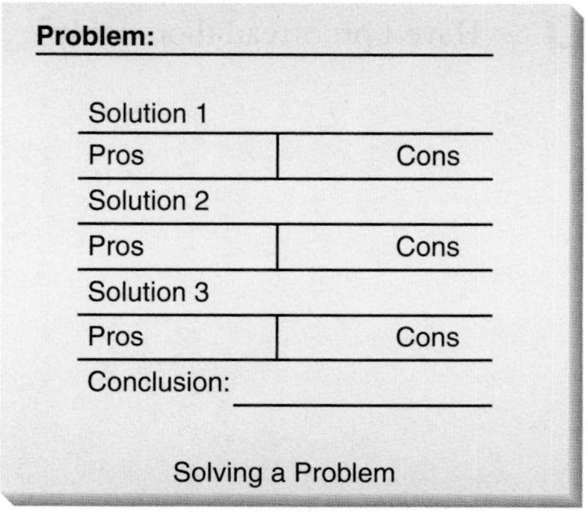

Trade rough drafts with a classmate and answer the following questions about his or her paper. Then, in person or online, discuss your papers and suggestions with your peer. Finally, make the changes you feel would most benefit your paper.

1. Has the author clearly identified a problem? What is it?
2. Has the author demonstrated that a problem exists?
3. How does the author appeal to the audience?
4. What is the author's claim (thesis)? Is it clear?
5. Has the author effectively supported the problem-solving essay? What kind of evidence is included?
6. Is the problem-solving essay organized effectively? Why or why not?
7. What is the strongest part of the essay?
8. Does the conclusion contain a call to action? Is it effective? Why or why not?
9. What kinds of grammatical errors, if any, are evident in the problem-solving essay?
10. What final suggestions do you have for the author?

WRITER'S CHECKLIST FOR PROBLEM SOLVING

Use the checklist below to evaluate your own writing and to help ensure that your problem-solving essay is effective. If you have any "no" answers, go back and work on those areas if necessary.

- ❏ 1. Have I clearly identified the problem?
- ❏ 2. Have I demonstrated that the problem exists?
- ❏ 3. Have I appealed to my audience?
- ❏ 4. Have I stated a clear claim?
- ❏ 5. Have I proposed a reasonable solution or solutions?
- ❏ 6. Have I organized my proposal effectively?
- ❏ 7. Have I supported my solution in a convincing manner?
- ❏ 8. Have I included a call to action in my conclusion?
- ❏ 9. Have I proofread thoroughly?

[C H A P T E R S U M M A R Y]

1. Use the problem-solving strategy to determine a solution to a challenging issue or situation.

2. Problem-solving writing is an important part of your education, daily life, and career.

3. Interpreting readings and images related to problems and solutions can help you to prepare to write a problem-solving essay.

4. Carefully analyze the rhetorical star before writing a problem-solving essay: subject, audience, purpose, strategy, and design.

5. Use these qualities when writing an effective problem-solving essay: identify a problem and demonstrate that it exists; appeal to your audience; state your claim; propose one or more solutions organize your solution(s) effectively; persuade your readers that your proposed solution is feasible; end with a call to action.

[W H A T I K N O W N O W]

Use this checklist to determine what you need to work on in order to feel comfortable with your understanding of the material in this chapter. Check off each item as you master it. Review the material for any unchecked items.

SmartBook Tip

During the "Recharge" phase, students can return to Chapter 12 and practice concepts that they need to work on.

❏ 1. I know what **problem-solving** writing is.

❏ 2. I can identify several **real-world applications** for problem-solving writing.

❏ 3. I can **evaluate** readings and images that reflect problems and solutions.

❏ 4. I can analyze the **rhetorical star** for problem-solving writing.

❏ 5. I understand the **writing process** for writing about problems and solutions.

❏ 6. I can apply the **seven qualities** of problem-solving writing.

PART 3

Research Guide

Why Research Skills Are Essential

The chapters in Part 3 are geared toward helping you plan, write, document, and present a research paper. In the real world, you often conduct research when you want to know the answer to a question, even if you don't realize that is what you are doing. For example, if you want to know where to go to get your computer fixed without spending a fortune, then you might ask a friend who is a computer science major for suggestions. If you are looking for a job, you may go to **monster.com** or look in the classifieds section of your local newspaper for possible employment opportunities. If you want to know who the lead singer is for a new band, you can go online and conduct a Google search to find out whose voice it is that you keep replaying in your head. All of these activities require research of one type or another.

Being able to write an effective research paper is an essential skill for college, the work world, and your personal life. You need to be able to gather pertinent information and put it together in a meaningful way. You also need to avoid plagiarism throughout the research process. That's why documentation methods are so important.

If you panic when you hear the words *research essay*, you are not alone. The good news is that writing a research paper can be a rewarding and worthwhile experience. The keys to success are choosing the right topic, planning your paper effectively, selecting appropriate sources, and budgeting enough time to revise and complete the paper by the due date. You will probably spend more time on this assignment than any other you complete for your composition course. Therefore, you will need to get organized and make the most of your opportunity to learn and write about something new and interesting.

OVERVIEW of Part 3

13

PLANNING AND WRITING A RESEARCH PAPER

In this chapter you will learn techniques for achieving these learning outcomes:

13.1 DISCOVER A MEANINGFUL RESEARCH TOPIC.

13.2 NARROW YOUR RESEARCH TOPIC.

13.3 CREATE A RESEARCHABLE QUESTION.

13.4 WRITE A PRELIMINARY THESIS.

13.5 LOCATE LIBRARY AND INTERNET SOURCES.

13.6 EVALUATE RESEARCH SOURCES.

13.7 TAKE NOTES FROM RESEARCH MATERIALS.

13.8 CONDUCT PRIMARY RESEARCH

THROUGH A SURVEY OR AN INTERVIEW.

13.9 CREATE AN OUTLINE.

13.10 COMPOSE A FIRST DRAFT OF YOUR RESEARCH PAPER.

13.1 DISCOVERING A RESEARCH TOPIC

The first step when you are conducting research is to find a suitable topic. To do that, you must understand the parameters of the assignment. Read the instructions carefully and make sure you know what topics are acceptable and what your instructor expects from you. Ask questions to clarify any uncertainties you have. Your instructor may assign a topic or allow you to choose a topic to explore. If you do have an opportunity to select your own topic, then you will want to make your selection carefully. You will spend a fair amount of time on your research assignment, so you will want to choose a topic that is interesting and meaningful to you.

Perhaps you would like to know more about your major field of study so that you can have a clearer understanding of what types of duties you will be expected to perform on the job. Maybe you have always wondered what it would be like to go into outer space or to go scuba diving. Your topic doesn't have to be stuffy or academic. If you choose a topic you genuinely want to learn more about, you will find the research process can be quite enjoyable. To find an appropriate topic, you can brainstorm ideas, skim through written sources, browse the library, surf the Internet, watch television, listen to the radio, or discuss your assignment with others.

SmartBook Tip

Students receive an overview of the learning outcomes and topics in Chapter 13 in the "Preview" phase of SmartBook.

13.2 NARROWING A RESEARCH TOPIC

After you have selected a topic, you will want to narrow it so that you can adequately cover it within the parameters of your assignment. For example, if you choose space exploration as your broad topic, then you might focus on how space exploration affects life on Earth. You can narrow that topic even further by focusing on how National Aeronautics and Space Administration (NASA) technology designed for space exploration can be used to improve everyday household items.

Teaching Tip

Have students work individually or in groups to brainstorm broad topics and then narrow them.

Similarly, if you decide to write about a hobby you would like to try, such as scuba diving, you might narrow your subject by focusing on what you would need to get started. Understanding the specific requirements for the assignment will also help you decide how to narrow your topic. Consider the length of the assignment, the number and type of sources you need to use, and the due date when determining how to focus your topic.

13.3 CREATING A RESEARCHABLE QUESTION

You can develop a research question to help guide you through the research process. Having a good research question can help you to focus your essay. Also, the answer to your research question can help you to develop a working thesis statement. An effective research question has enough depth to help you develop a thesis, but is narrow enough to fit within the guidelines of your assignment. Think about what you already know about your subject and what you would like to learn. Make sure that you don't already know the answer to the question and that you truly want to know the answer. You can always revise your question after you have begun your preliminary research.

Sample Questions

- **Too broad:** How has NASA affected the average American citizen?
- **Too narrow:** Has NASA affected the average American citizen?
- **Appropriate:** How has NASA's technology designed for space exploration helped to improve everyday household products?
- **Too broad:** What does scuba diving involve?
- **Too narrow:** What is scuba diving?
- **Appropriate:** What is required to begin scuba diving?

13.4 WRITING A PRELIMINARY THESIS STATEMENT

Developing a researchable question can help give you a sense of direction for your research process, but it will not substitute for a clear thesis. As you begin the research process, you will need to draft a preliminary thesis, sometimes called a working thesis. As with any essay, your research paper needs a thesis that includes your subject and an opinion. Having a working thesis will help you as you begin to select sources. You may decide to refine your original thesis later as you come across new ideas in the sources you find.

Sample Thesis Statements

- NASA has developed a number of high-tech devices for space exploration that have practical applications for everyday household products.
- The most essential requirements for becoming a scuba diver are purchasing (or borrowing) equipment, taking lessons, and getting certified.

13.5 LOCATING LIBRARY AND INTERNET SOURCES

Finding the right sources to use is essential for experiencing success with a research project. For most research topics you will benefit from using a variety of sources, including books, periodicals, the Internet, and primary research. Learning how to conduct library and Internet research effectively will save you valuable time. Going to a library on campus or in your community is one of the best ways to gather information about your topic. You can use Internet sources to supplement the traditional sources you will find in the library.

If you are not familiar with the library where you will be conducting your research, then you should check to see if the library offers a workshop or tour that shows you how to find useful sources for your subject. If one of those options is not available, then you can ask if there is a brochure or online tutorial that you can use to learn your way around the library. You can also benefit from talking to a librarian. In addition to providing books, periodicals, and films on your subject, your library probably has a variety of other sources, such as specialized databases and reference materials that

SmartBook Tip

Key concepts in Chapter 13 are highlighted for students during the "Read" phase. As students demonstrate understanding of these concepts during the "Practice" phase by responding to probes, the highlighting adapts to the individual student's learning by changing color.

FIGURE 13.1   Keiser University Library Catalog

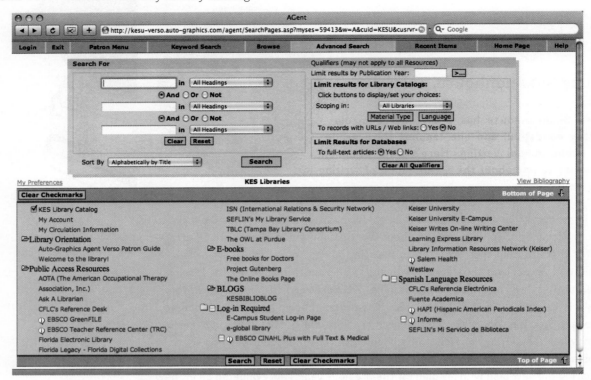

will help you in the search process. As you learn more about the library, look for the following features:

Computerized Library Catalog

Computerized catalog An index of a library's holdings with specific information about each item.

Keywords Significant words or phrases used to narrow a database search.

More than likely, the library you use will have a **computerized catalog,** which is an index of the library's holdings with specific information about each item (see Figure 13.1). You can use the catalog to find library resources, such as books, periodicals, reference materials, and audiovisual materials. You may also be able to determine if an item you need is on the shelf or checked out by another library patron. The library catalog is an excellent place to begin your research. Typically, you can search by title, author, or subject.

Type keywords into the catalog to find what you need. **Keywords** are significant words or phrases used to narrow a database search. Be careful to spell the words correctly, or you may not find anything that matches your topic. Also, you may need to experiment with different keywords until you find exactly what you need. Use the words *and, or,* or *not* (known as Boolean logic) to help narrow your search (see p. 323 for more on Boolean logic). Print out or jot down important information about the sources that are relevant to your topic, such as the author, title, call number, and date of publication. Having that information will help you locate the source on the shelf.

TABLE 13.1

Systems for Organizing a Library's Holdings	
Dewey Decimal System	
000–099	General Knowledge
100–199	Psychology and Philosophy
200–299	Religions and Mythology
300–399	Social Sciences and Folklore
400–499	Languages and Grammar
500–599	Math and Science
600–699	Medicine and Technology
700–799	Arts and Recreation
800–899	Literature
900–999	Geography and History
Library of Congress Classification System	
A	General Works
B	Philosophy, Psychology, Religion
C	Auxiliary Sciences of History
D	World History
E–F	History of the Americas
G	Geography, Anthropology, Recreation
H	Social Sciences
J	Political Sciences
K	Law
L	Education
M	Music
N	Fine Arts
P	Language and Literature
Q	Science
R	Medicine
S	Agriculture
T	Technology
U	Military Science
V	Naval Science
Z	Bibliography, Library Science, Information Resources

LearnSmart Achieve Tip

The Research Process unit of LearnSmart Achieve determines what students do and do not know about writing research papers. Learning outcomes within the Research Process unit cover developing a research plan, evaluating information and sources, integrating source material into a text, and using information ethically and legally. Learning resources and questions automatically adapt to each student's individual needs and help students thoroughly master this content. See the Instructor's Manual for *Write Now* for a list of learning outcomes as well as additional information on how to use LearnSmart Achieve with your students.

Stacks

Take the list of potential sources you found in the library catalog and head to the stacks (shelves of books) to retrieve them. The easiest way to find the sources is to use the call number, located on the spine of the book. Check to see if your library uses the Dewey Decimal System or Library of Congress Classification System to organize materials. Each method organizes the materials in the stacks differently. The Dewey Decimal System divides subjects into 10 numbered categories, and the Library of Congress Classification uses 20 lettered categories. (See Table 13.1.) As you locate the sources you found in the catalog on the shelf, look at nearby books to see if any of them are relevant to your topic as well. If a book you need is not on the shelf or is at another branch of the library, ask a reference librarian to help you locate the book. You may be able to obtain it using interlibrary loan.

Teaching Tip

If possible, arrange a campus library tour for your students or take them to your campus library and show them how to locate appropriate research paper sources.

TABLE 13.2

Online Periodical Sources	
The Internet Public Library	www.ipl.org
Newspapers.com	www.newspapers.com
CNN Interactive	www.cnn.com
CSPAN Online	www.c-span.org
Free Management Library	www.managementhelp.org

Periodicals

In the periodical section of the library, you will find recent issues of magazines, newspapers, and professional journals. Periodicals make good sources for research papers because they contain information that is precise and current. Magazine and newspaper articles tend to be more general than professional journals. They appeal to the average reader whereas journal articles usually go into more depth and are geared toward an audience that is knowledgeable in a particular field.

Current periodicals and newspapers are usually shelved alphabetically by title. Back issues may be bound and stored in the stacks or another area of the library. The online or print version of the *Reader's Guide to Periodical Literature* can help you to find relevant sources. Table 13.2 lists a few of the many websites you can use to locate additional periodical sources that may not be available in your library.

Computerized Databases

Database A comprehensive collection of related data organized and accessible via computer.

Teaching Tip

If possible, use a projector to demonstrate how to use your college's database. Walk students through searching for keywords to see what yields better or worse results.

A **database** is a comprehensive collection of related data organized and accessible via computer. You can use a database to help you find relevant articles related to your chosen research topic.

Most libraries have computers available for you to use to conduct research. Also, your school may subscribe to a specific database network, such as the Library and Information Resources Network (LIRN). If so, a school librarian or administrator can provide you with a password that will allow you to access the databases from the library, your own home, or anywhere you can find Internet access. Databases provide abstracts (summaries) of articles and often make the full text of articles available as well.

To help you locate promising sources for your paper, you can read the abstracts of the articles that look promising. When you find a source that you think will be suitable, you can e-mail yourself the article or print it out. Be sure to use the full text, not just the abstract, for your research paper. Abstracts may be inaccurate and are often not written by the author of the article. Table 13.3 lists a few databases that might provide useful sources on your research topic.

Reference Materials

In the reference area of the library you will find encyclopedias, dictionaries, almanacs, handbooks, periodical indexes, and other sources. Typically, reference materials are not checked out, so they are always available to library patrons. Be careful not to rely too heavily on reference materials, such as dictionaries and

TABLE 13.3

Computer Databases	
Info Trac	eLibrary
ProQuest	eGlobal Library
LexisNexis	

encyclopedias, for your research. You may use these types of references to look up words or find basic information about your topic, but you will need to locate additional sources to find more in-depth information.

Online reference materials are available as well. Wikipedia is not a credible source for a research paper, however. Anyone can add, modify, or delete information that has been posted on a topic; therefore, there is no guarantee that the material is accurate. You may, however, use Wikipedia to find sources by reviewing the references at the end of an entry. Also, you can find a wealth of reputable resources by going to the website of the American Library Association (ALA) **www .guidetoreference.org/homepage.aspx** and signing up for a free trial membership.

Audiovisual Materials

Many libraries have an area where you can locate nonprint media, such as films, music CDs, slides, and other audiovisual materials. You may find a suitable source for your research paper there, such as a documentary about your research topic. These materials are often organized by type and shelved alphabetically. However, there is no standard method for classifying audiovisual materials. Ask your librarian for help if you have trouble locating what you need.

Internet Searches

The Internet is a valuable research tool. You can access a great variety of sources on the World Wide Web by using a Web browser, such as Google Chrome, Microsoft Internet Explorer, Safari, or Mozilla Firefox.

The Internet contains massive amounts of information; consequently, finding exactly what you need can be a challenge. Fortunately, you can use a **search engine** to help you find the websites that pertain to your research topic. A search engine serves the same purpose as a catalog in a library. Using a search engine will help you to sift through the billions of Web pages to find what you need. For example, if you want to find websites that include information about NASA and household products, then you might try a search using Google, the most popular search engine. Figure 13.2 illustrates a Google search for NASA. Table 13.4 lists popular search engines.

Search engine A computer program used to locate information on the Internet.

FIGURE 13.2 Google Search

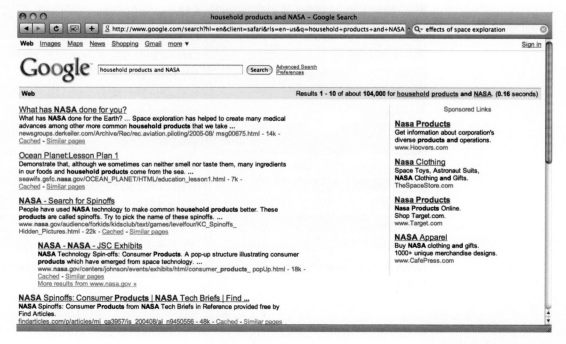

Note: A search engine is not a source. For example, instead of citing Google you should cite an article you find using Google.

Discussion Groups

Discussion group An online forum where individuals can share ideas about a specific topic.

In addition to all of the websites, periodicals, and reference materials available on the Internet, you can use a search engine to participate in discussion groups on your topic. A **discussion group** is an online forum where individuals can share ideas about a specific topic. For example, you can find discussion groups on topics such as recreation, arts and entertainment, science and technology, society, and health at **groups.google.com**. Using a search engine, you can find a discussion group about virtually any topic. You might come across some interesting ideas. Keep in mind, however, that anyone can post comments to discussion groups, so you will need to check the accuracy of any information you gather. Mailing lists, newsgroups, and blogs are three types of discussion groups you might find useful as you research your topic.

Mailing lists: If you sign up for a mailing list on your subject, you will periodically receive updates about your topic via e-mail.

Newsgroups: You can find newsgroups on select subjects by going to **groups.google.com**. These groups are similar to mailing lists except that

TABLE 13.4

Search Engines	
Alltheweb	www.alltheweb.com
Alta Vista	www.altavista.com
Ask	www.ask.com
Excite	www.excite.com
Google	www.google.com
Google Scholar	scholar.google.com
HotBot	www.hotbot.com
Kartoo	www.kartoo.com
Lycos	www.lycos.com
MSN Search	www.msn.com
Open Directory Project	www.dmoz.org
WebCrawler	www.webcrawler.com
Yahoo!	www.yahoo.com
Meta-Search Engines	
Clusty	www.clusty.com
Copernic Agent	www.copernicagent.com
Dogpile	www.dogpile.com
Mamma	www.mamma.com
SurfWax	www.surfwax.com

Note: A meta-search engine is a search engine that searches other search engines.

you will need to find the information online, rather than have it e-mailed to you.

Blogs: Short for Weblog, a blog is a personalized online journal. Businesses, organizations, and individuals can create blogs. Typically, almost anyone interested in the discussion can post a comment to a blog.

FIGURE 13.3 Web Page Navigation Arrows

Tips for Conducting Internet Searches

1. **Spell your keywords correctly.** Otherwise, your search may not yield the results you need.

2. **Use Boolean logic (*and, or, not*) to make your search more precise.**
   - Use the word *and* to tell the search engine to look for sources that contain both terms. Example: "phobias and famous people"
   - Use the word *or* to tell the search engine to look for any of two or more words. Example: "phobias or fears or aversions"
   - Use the word *not* to tell the search engine to exclude one or more words. Example: "phobias not obsessions"

3. **Click on hyperlinks to get more information.** If you see a highlighted word or a special icon, you can usually click on it to learn more information about the term.

4. **Use the back and forward arrows to navigate Web pages.** For example, if you click on a hyperlink and want to return to the previous page, click the back button (see Figure 13.3). If you keep clicking the back button, you can get all the way back to your original search. This will allow to you go to another source without retyping your search.

5. **Bookmark or print out useful sources.** Keeping track of sources you may want to use in the future will save you time later if you decide to use them.

13.6 EVALUATING RESEARCH SOURCES

Using Search Engines Activity:
Answers will vary.

You are likely to come across far more information on your subject than you could ever incorporate into your research paper; therefore, you will need to evaluate the print and Web-based sources you locate before choosing which are the most appropriate to use. The accuracy and credibility of your paper depend on your use of high-quality sources. Here are some tips for evaluating research sources:

1. **Author and publisher:** Is the author an expert in the field with the appropriate credentials? Is the publisher or website reputable? If you have doubts about the reliability of the source, then you may want to investigate by searching for a biography of the author or the history of the publisher or sponsoring organization.

2. **Date:** Check to see when the information was published or posted on the Internet. If you are reporting on a famous study or historical event, then you may find that older sources are appropriate for your research paper. In other cases, you will need to have the most up-to-date information. New discoveries in science and technology are being made every day. If the information seems too old, then find a more current source.

3. **References:** Has the author documented his or her sources? Most reputable sources will include a bibliography to back up the information presented. If there is a list of sources, look to see if they seem appropriate. If no sources are cited, be wary of the information unless the author is an expert with the appropriate credentials.

Evaluating Sources Activity:
Answers will vary.

4. **Bias:** Is the information objective and fair, or does the author seem to have a hidden agenda? For example, a website sponsored by a drug company may not be the most reliable source to use to determine if a particular drug is the best treatment for an illness.

5. **Effectiveness:** How useful is the content? Is it relevant to the specific areas you plan to cover in your research paper? Is it presented clearly and logically? Does the material seem accurate?

13.7 TAKING NOTES FROM RESEARCH MATERIALS

After you have determined which sources will be the most useful for your research paper, then you will need to begin reading them and taking notes from them. Taking effective notes from the sources you find is essential to successfully completing a research paper. You can take notes as summaries, paraphrases, or quotations. Whether you use a computer, a research journal, a legal pad, or index cards to keep track of your notes is your personal choice. You might want to make two columns, one side for your notes and the other side for your thoughts on why those ideas are relevant and where they might fit into your paper. Be sure to note exactly where you found the information by labeling it with the author, title, date, and page number or URL. Doing so will help you later as you draft your paper and document your sources.

Any time you use summarized, paraphrased, or quoted material in your paper, you must give credit to the original source(s) to avoid **plagiarism,** the uncredited use of borrowed material. Your instructor will let you know which system of documentation you need to follow in your final research paper. (See Chapter 14 for information on the MLA and APA systems of documentation.) If you add personal comments to your notes, be sure to include them in brackets [ ] so that you can distinguish your ideas from the concepts presented in your source materials.

> **Plagiarism** The use of another's words or ideas without giving appropriate credit.

Summarizing

When you write a **summary,** you condense ideas from an article, a chapter, or a passage, using your own words. Include the main ideas, but leave out most of the specific details and examples. Summarizing is useful in helping you manage large amounts of information. The following tips will help you to write a summary:

> **Summary** A condensed version of an original document using different wording.

- Read the original work and make sure you understand it.
- Underline the thesis statement.
- Rewrite the thesis in your own words.
- Identify the main point in each paragraph.
- Rewrite main points in your own words.
- Put your rewrites together to create the summary.
- Review the original document to ensure that you have not changed the intended meaning or added anything in your summary.

The following is a summary of the essay "How Urban Myths Reveal Society's Fears," which appears on pages 123–124 in this textbook.

Although urban myths lack merit, they often catch the attention of the public. They represent our modern-day version of folklore because they combine unreal circumstances with everyday occurrences. People tend to believe urban legends because they tap into the fears that they have. Even though urban legends have been found to be completely false, some people will claim to have witnessed the incredible events that are portrayed through them. People may support these legends because the stories explain the unexplainable. Everyone who shares an urban legend has a hand in shaping it and takes ownership of its creation.

Source: From "How Urban Myths Reveal Society's Fears," Neal Gabler, *Los Angeles Times,* November 12, 1995.

Paraphrasing

Paraphrase A reworded version of a sentence or short passage from an original work.

When you **paraphrase,** you restate a sentence or passage from an original work in your own words. Unlike a summary, your goal is not to condense the original. Instead, your aim is to express the idea or ideas in the original sentences in your own way. As you paraphrase, change the sentence structure and word choice so that the new sentences are not too similar to the original, even though they express the same ideas. When you finish, highlight any words in your paraphrase that are the same as in the original document. You should have very few exact words. If you have several, reword them. Although it should be used sparingly, paraphrasing is useful when the original sentence or passage is complex or technical.

illustrate a POINT Paraphrase

>> Original Passage

"Though urban legends frequently originate with college students about to enter the real world, they are different from traditional fairy tales because their terrors are not really obstacles on the road to understanding, and they are different from folklore because they cannot even be interpreted as cautionary. In urban legends, obstacles aren't overcome, perhaps can't be overcome, and there is nothing we can do to avoid the consequences."

Inappropriate Paraphrase

Neal Gabler says that even though urban legends often originate with university students who are about to go into the real world, they are not the same as fairy tales because their terrors are not roadblocks on the way to comprehending, and they are not the same as folklore because they aren't cautionary. In urban legends, roadblocks are not overcome, and we can't avoid the repercussions.

Appropriate Paraphrase

According to Neal Gabler, many urban myths begin with students who are about to graduate from college and join the workforce. However, urban myths should not be confused with fairy tales because they do not provide a warning for the reader, and the results are inevitable.

Discussion

The inappropriate paraphrase follows the original passage too closely and uses exact words from Gabler's essay. The highlighted areas are exactly the same as in Gabler's essay, and the words in between are simply synonyms used to replace exact wording. Occasionally substituting a word with a synonym does not constitute an acceptable paraphrase. On the other hand, the appropriate paraphrase covers the main ideas presented in Gabler's original passage, but the sentence structure and word choice are unique.

Source: From "How Urban Myths Reveal Society's Fears," Neal Gabler, *Los Angeles Times,* November 12, 1995.

Quoting

When you include a **quotation** in your paper, you take someone else's exact words and put quotation marks around them. Like paraphrasing, quoting should be used sparingly. Introduce a quote only when the original is particularly vivid or expressive or when you want to use an authority figure's exact words to add credibility to your paper. Be sure to carefully copy any quotes you use word for word. If you decide to leave out part of a sentence that you are quoting, then use an ellipsis (. . .) to show that you have omitted words. However, do not alter the intended meaning of the author. Also, if you find an error (such as a misspelled word) in the sentence or passage you are quoting, include the Latin word *sic* in brackets right after the error to show that the mistake was the original author's, not yours, and that you copied the quote faithfully. (See Chapter 14 for examples of quoted material in the MLA and APA formats.)

> **Quotation** An author's exact words enclosed in quotation marks.

▶ *illustrate* a POINT   Quotation

According to Gabler, "Though urban legends frequently originate with college students about to enter the real world, they are different from traditional fairy tales because their terrors are not really obstacles on the road to understanding, and they are different from folklore because they cannot even be interpreted as cautionary."

Remember to follow the documentation method that your instructor requires any time you summarize, paraphrase, or quote material from a source. If you don't give appropriate credit to the source, then you are plagiarizing.

Discussion

When you use a quotation in your paper, you will often include a signal phrase to introduce the author's name at the beginning, as the example above illustrates: "According to Gabler. . . ." Another method is to include the author's name after the quote in a parenthetical citation. The MLA and APA formats require additional information to be included in the parenthetical citation as well. (See Chapter 14 for more information on citing sources in your paper.)

Source: From "How Urban Myths Reveal Society's Fears," Neal Gabler, *Los Angeles Times*, November 12, 1995.

Note Taking Activity:
Answers will vary.

▶ *Activity*   Note Taking

Choose a magazine or newspaper article, or use one provided by your instructor.

1. Write a summary of the article. Be sure to include the most important ideas and to put all of the ideas into your own words.

2. Write a paraphrase of two or three sentences in the article. Be sure to include every idea from the original source, but put the ideas into your own words.

3. Write a direct quote from the source. Introduce the author and/or title of the work, and use quotation marks around exact wording.

13.8 CONDUCTING PRIMARY RESEARCH

Primary or field research Information collected firsthand from sources such as surveys, interviews, and experiments.

In addition to using the research of others, you can gather firsthand information about your subject by conducting **primary** or **field research.** Conducting a survey or personal interview is a credible way to supplement the information you find in the library and other sources. One benefit of conducting field research is that you can tailor it to yield the exact results you need. For example, in addition to using books and magazines about scuba diving, you might send out a survey to several divers, asking for their opinions about the most important things to know before beginning to dive. Similarly, if you are writing about a topic related to your major, then you may choose to interview an instructor in that program or a professional in your chosen field who works in your community.

Surveys

A *survey* is a questionnaire geared toward gaining information from people who are familiar with the subject you are researching. Surveys are particularly useful for learning about the habits or opinions of a particular group of people. For example, you might use a questionnaire for a college-related topic, such as study skills, school resources, or extracurricular activities. While surveys can be useful, keep in mind that they can be challenging to create, administer, and interpret. Check with your instructor to see if a survey is appropriate for your subject. Here are some tips for designing and conducting a survey if you decide that one will benefit your research paper.

1. **Clarify your purpose.** Make sure you know exactly what kind of information you hope to gain from the survey, and make your purpose known to the respondents. You might include a cover letter or note at the top of the survey explaining why you are conducting the survey and how you will use the information. For example, if you are writing a persuasive research paper about the benefits of being actively involved in student organizations, such as student government or an honorary fraternity, then you might mention to the respondents that you will share the results with the school administration and that more extracurricular activities might become available as a result of their participation in your survey.

2. **Choose your participants carefully.** Decide who will be able to provide the best answers for your survey. Make sure your target audience is very familiar with the subject you are researching. For instance, if you are writing about student organizations, then you might invite some students who are involved in organizations on campus and some who are not. You might separate the responses according to those two criteria in your analysis. Additionally, you will want to make sure that your audience represents a fair sampling of the student population, so you will need to include males and females as well as people with different majors and ethnicities in your survey group.

3. **Set clear expectations for the respondents.** Be sure to give a reasonable deadline for the recipients to respond. Allowing them a few days to complete the questionnaire should be enough. Also, make it easy for the participants to respond. If you are polling your class, then you might hand out a survey on campus or send out a survey via e-mail.

4. **Design effective questions.** Make sure that your questions or potential answers don't overlap. You may want to test your questions on a few respondents before sending them out to more people so that you can modify the

TABLE 13.5

Sample Survey Questions
• True/False I belong to an extracurricular student organization. _____True _____False
• Rating System Participating in a student organization helps the participants to strengthen their leadership skills. _____ 1. Strongly agree _____ 2. Agree somewhat _____ 3. Neither agree nor disagree _____ 4. Disagree somewhat _____ 5. Strongly disagree
• Checklist Check all that apply. Belonging to student organizations . . . _____ helps students to strengthen their leadership skills. _____ provides students with more scholarship opportunities. _____ impresses potential employers on a résumé. _____ takes away from valuable study time. _____ doesn't have any benefits. _____ isn't worth the effort required.
• Multiple Choice Choose one answer. How much time do you spend with extracurricular student organizations each week? _____ 0 hours _____ 1–2 hours _____ 3–4 hours _____ 5 or more hours
• Open-Ended How has belonging to an extracurricular student organization affected you?

survey as needed. To prevent confusion, avoid using too many different kinds of questions. One or two should be sufficient. Choose the type(s) of question(s) that will give you the best results for your subject (see Table 13.5).

5. **Compile and interpret the results.** Tally the results from the surveys that are returned to you and analyze their significance. Be sure to include information in your report that reflects all of the completed results, not just the ones that support the position you are taking in your paper. Also, you should include the raw data you receive as an appendix to your research paper so that your readers can review the information for themselves. Keep in mind, the results you gather are merely the opinions of the respondents, so you can't necessarily assume that these results will hold true for college students in general, just for the ones you survey.

Personal Interviews

Sometimes, conducting a personal interview can provide you with additional insights that are not available through the library and online sources. You may find an expert on your subject who can answer specific questions that would

Teaching Tip

Ask students to work individually or in groups to develop sample survey questions about a topic of your choice or theirs.

be difficult to answer through your research. Here are some suggestions for planning and conducting a personal interview.

1. **Clarify your purpose.** Make sure you know exactly what kind of information you hope to gain from the personal interview, and make your purpose known to the interviewee. Keep your interview focused on the information that will be useful for your paper.

2. **Choose your interviewee carefully.** You may need to make several phone calls before you discover who would be the best person to provide you with the specific information you need for your paper. You may decide that someone in your community or at your college campus will be able to aid your research process.

3. **Determine how you will conduct the interview.** Whenever possible, a face-to-face interview is ideal. If you are able to schedule a meeting in person, then call ahead to make an appointment. If the interviewee is not available to meet in person, then schedule a phone call or communicate via e-mail.

4. **Prepare your questions.** To ensure that your interview session runs efficiently, have 5 to 10 questions written out. The questions will help guide the interview. If you feel that you will get nervous during the interview, you might test your questions on someone before the real interview. Typically, open-ended questions work best for interviews. For example, if you are researching what it would be like to specialize in pediatric nursing, you might ask a pediatric nurse several questions, including the following:

- What are the most rewarding aspects of being a pediatric nurse?
- What challenges do you face on the job?
- Would you recommend your area of specialty to someone just getting started in the nursing field? Why or why not?

Teaching Tip

Have students practice writing questions, interviewing one another, and taking notes during the interview.

5. **Be courteous to the interviewee.** Show up on time for the interview and dress appropriately. Also, tell the interviewee a little bit about what you are trying to accomplish through the interview. Listen carefully to what the interviewee has to say, and ask additional questions if you need the interviewee to clarify or expand on a point of interest. Be sure to thank the interviewee for taking the time to help you with your research project.

6. **Take thorough notes during the interview.** Even if you have a good memory, you will need to take copious notes during the discussion. Make sure to document the time and date of the interview as well as the interviewee's name and title. Additionally, write the answers to all of the questions you ask. If you would like to record the conversation, ask the interviewee permission first. Some people may be uncomfortable being recorded. If you are able to record the interview session, then you will need to go back and transcribe the answers later. Carefully documenting the entire interview will make it easier for you to include ideas from the interview in your research paper.

ESOL Tip >

You may be more comfortable taking your interview notes in your native language and transcribing them into English later.

Develop and administer a survey and/or conduct a personal interview to gain information about your research subject. Follow the steps on the previous pages. Keep track of your raw data as well as your interpretation of the information you gain through your primary research.

13.9 CREATING AN OUTLINE

Conducting Primary Research
Activity:

Answers will vary.

After you have gathered all of your research notes, you will need to organize them into a logical sequence by drafting a preliminary outline. Determine the major points you want to cover in your paper and make sure that all of the points help to support your thesis statement. The outline will serve as the framework for your entire paper. You might begin with a topic outline and then expand it into complete sentences. Stay flexible as you begin drafting your paper. You may find that you can't get to everything on your outline, or that you need to include additional points to fully substantiate your thesis. If your instructor requires that you submit an outline with your final paper, then you will need to revisit your outline and make any necessary changes to ensure that your final outline reflects the organization of your final research paper.

STUDENT RESEARCH PAPER OUTLINE

How Scared Are You?
by Neil Harris

Thesis: Although some people may think phobias sound silly or trivial, they are a frighteningly real phenomenon for those who suffer from them. Fortunately, with proper treatment, many people are able to live a reasonably normal life despite their phobias.

I. Description of phobias
   A. Categories
      1. Panic disorders
      2. Anxiety disorders
   B. Symptoms
II. Types of phobias
   A. Common phobias
   B. Strange phobias
   C. Ironic phobias
III. Treatment for phobias
   A. Relaxation and exercise
   B. Psychotherapy
      1. Changing view of phobia
      2. Exposure or desensitization
   C. Flooding
   D. Medications

Teaching Tip

Ask students to develop an outline for their research paper in a reasonable period of time before the paper is due. This may help them with time management for completing the research assignment.

13.10 COMPOSING YOUR RESEARCH PAPER

Following the preliminary outline you constructed, write a first draft of your research paper. Remember to consider your rhetorical star (subject, audience, purpose, strategy, and design) and follow the steps of the writing process (discovering, planning, composing, getting feedback, revising, editing, and proofreading).

As you compose your essay, you may combine the ideas in your notes from secondary sources as well as any primary research you may have conducted. Even though most of the ideas in your research paper will come from outside sources, you will want to make sure that your voice is the strongest in the paper. Use the research paper to support your own point on the topic. To do that, you will need to consider how all of the information you have gathered fits together. Keep in mind that a research essay is more than merely a string of quotes or series of facts. Choose your angle on the topic, and shape your paper to make it an original work.

A research paper follows the same basic structure as a traditional essay; however, you may need two or more paragraphs to fully develop each supporting point. Also, you must cite sources throughout your paper to indicate exactly where you have

Synthesize To combine material from two or more works to create something new.

used primary or secondary research in your paper. As you **synthesize** (combine) ideas from your sources, be careful to note the author, work, and page number (or the website address) so that you know exactly where you obtained the information. Later, you can put source information into the specific format that your instructor requires, such as APA or MLA. (See Chapter 14 for documentation methods.)

STUDENT RESEARCH PAPER ROUGH DRAFT

Here is a portion of Harris's rough draft. You will notice that he chose to use numbers to keep track of his sources. Also, he covers his points in a different order in his draft than he does in his outline. He addressed these issues in later drafts.

How Scared Are You?
by Neil Harris

When confronted with a phobia, the individual experiences what is in effect a panic attack. Symptoms include but are not limited to rapid heartbeat, high bloodpressure, dry mouth, nausia, and rapid breathing. "A phobia is a type of anxiety disorder"[4] grouped into two categories, panic disorder and generalized anxiety disorder (GAD). Panic disorders are "Recurrent episodes of unprovoked feelings of terror or impending doom"[2] while generalized anxiety disorder is "exaggerated worry about health, safety, money, and other aspects of daily life that lasts 6 months or more." GAD may be a response to a 24-hour news cycle and the times we live in. But panic disorders are very serious. Life activity condition phobias are grouped into three genres—specific, social, and agoraphobia. Specific phobias entail the individual being paniced by one trigger.[3] This phenomenon will be discussed later in detail. Social phobias or social anxiety disorder (SAD) is the fear of public situations. Individuals suffering from SAD will avoid public places. Some are worried about being embarrassed or calling attention to themselves.[1] Last, agoraphobia is a category in and of itself defined as

"fear of having a panic attack in public,"[5] agorophobia is typically portrayed as fear to leave safe confines. People suffering from this disorder can progress to home confinement but are often observed with lesser degrees.

Many well-known personalities deal with phobias, which vary widely from normal to very strange. Some phobias were much more prominent in the past. Napolean Bonapart, Augustus Caesar, Julius Caesar, and Alexander the Great all suffered from ailurophobia or fear of cats. Others are more recent developments. Germophobia is the fear of germs. Howard Hughes, Howie Mandell, and Donald Trump are "GERMOPHOBES." Madonna shares her phobia with many dogs; brontophobia is the fear of thunder. The phobias can seem strange such as David Beckham's fear of disorder—ataxophobia. Anything out of place will drive him crazy. Billy Bob Thorton is terrified of antique furniture, called panophobia. There is nothing funny about clowns to Johnny Depp and Sean Combs who suffer from coulrophobia, the fear of clowns. Famous former Monday night football anouncers John Madden and Tony Cornheiser will not fly. Their fear of flying is called aerophobia. Marilyn Monroe suffered from agorophobia, the fear of open spaces, while Uma Thurman is claustrophobic, which is the fear of confined spaces.

Some people suffer from phobias that clash with their characters. Roger Moore, who played James Bond 007 for years, is afraid of guns, or hoplophobic. The famous vampire novelist Anne Rice is acarophobic; she is afraid of the dark.[6] Sheryl Crow has one of the more common phobias called acrophobia, or the fear of heights. Odd phobias would include Nicole Kidman's lepidopterophobia or fear of butterflies and Christina Ricci's botanophobia or fear of indoor plants. But maybe phobias are there for a reason. Natalie Wood suffered from hydrophobia or a fear of water, which, sadly she drowned in.[2] By far one of the best phobias is hippopotomonstrosesquipedaliophobia which is the fear of long words. Linguists have their jokes too.[7]

Now you should be ready to get started on the first draft of your research paper. Chapter 14, "Documenting a Research Paper," addresses avoiding plagiarism and documenting your sources.

[CHAPTER SUMMARY]

1. Choose a research topic that is interesting and meaningful to you.
2. Narrow your topic to fit within the parameters of your assignment.
3. Create a researchable question to investigate.
4. Write a preliminary thesis statement to guide your research paper.
5. Locate appropriate library and Internet sources for your paper.
6. Evaluate your research sources carefully.
7. Take notes from your sources by summarizing, paraphrasing, and quoting the ideas presented in them.
8. If the project requires it or would benefit from it, conduct firsthand research through a survey or interview to supplement your library and Internet sources.
9. Create an outline to help you organize the ideas you want to include in your paper.
10. Compose a first draft of your research paper.

[WHAT I KNOW NOW]

Use this checklist to determine what you need to work on in order to feel comfortable with your understanding of the material in this chapter. Check off each item as you master it. Review the material for any unchecked items.

❏ 1. I know how to discover and narrow a meaningful **research topic.**

❏ 2. I understand how to create a **researchable question** and write a preliminary thesis.

❏ 3. I understand how to locate and evaluate library and Internet **sources.**

❏ 4. I know how to take **notes** from research materials by summarizing, paraphrasing, and quoting appropriately.

❏ 5. I know that I need to **document** all sources appropriately in my research paper.

❏ 6. I understand how to conduct **primary research** through a survey or interview.

❏ 7. I know how to create an **outline** for my research paper.

❏ 8. I know how to compose a first **draft** of my research paper.

14

DOCUMENTING A
RESEARCH
PAPER

learning outcomes

In this chapter you will learn techniques for achieving these learning outcomes:

14.1 AVOID PLAGIARISM.

14.2 DETERMINE WHEN TO CITE OR NOT CITE A SOURCE.

14.3 APPLY THE MLA FORMAT FOR IN-TEXT CITATIONS, A WORKS-CITED PAGE, AND A RESEARCH PAPER.

14.4 APPLY THE APA FORMAT FOR IN-TEXT CITATIONS, A REFERENCES PAGE, AND A RESEARCH PAPER.

14.1 AVOIDING PLAGIARISM

Would you walk into a store, take something off the shelf, and shove it into your backpack because you think no one is looking? That is unethical, right? Stealing someone's words or ideas without properly citing them is just as wrong. Many people cringe when they hear the word *plagiarism,* especially college students and English teachers. To understand how to avoid plagiarism, you need to be sure of exactly what it entails. According to the Merriam-Webster Online Dictionary, the four definitions for the verb *plagiarize* are as follows:

1. To steal and pass off (the ideas or words of another) as one's own.

2. To use (another's production) without crediting the source.

3. To commit literary theft.

4. To present as new and original an idea or product derived from an existing source.

All of these definitions represent serious forms of academic dishonesty. Go to **www.plagiarism.org** for additional details about plagiarism. The consequences for committing plagiarism at the college level range anywhere from failure of an assignment or the entire course to permanent dismissal from college. This problem goes beyond college, however. In the workplace, people can be terminated for plagiarism. However, there is no need to panic. If you learn the proper techniques for avoiding plagiarism, then you will have nothing to fear.

Basically, unless you are reporting commonly known facts or your original ideas, you need to document every source that you incorporate into your essay to avoid plagiarism. For example, if you are writing an essay on the effects of television violence on young children, and you want to include some statistics to support your thesis, then you will need to cite your source. Similarly, in a persuasive essay you may want to include a quote from a famous doctor about a new medical treatment for curing the common cold. To cite sources in some types of essays, your instructor may allow you to note the source in your paper with an informal citation, as the following fictitious examples illustrate:

Examples of Informal Citations

- According to psychologist Amy Telly, children who watch television for more than 50 hours per week are more likely to demonstrate violent behaviors at school than children who watch fewer than 25 hours per week.

SmartBook Tip

Students receive an overview of the learning outcomes and topics in Chapter 14 in the "Preview" phase of SmartBook.

LearnSmart Achieve Tip

The Research Process and Writing Process units of LearnSmart Achieve determine what students do and do not know about writing research papers. Learning outcomes within the Research Process unit cover integrating source material into a text, using MLA or APA documentation, and using information ethically and legally. Learning outcomes within the Writing Process unit cover identifying MLA and APA text format. Learning resources and questions automatically adapt to each student's individual needs and help students thoroughly master this content. See the Instructor's Manual for *Write Now* for a list of learning outcomes as well as additional information on how to use LearnSmart Achieve with your students.

Some countries do not emphasize plagiarism in academia as much as the United States. Be sure you know the correct documentation guidelines.

- As Dr. Maverick stated in the introduction to his book *Killing a Cold* (2014), "*Incredicold* is the biggest breakthrough in cold treatment since the invention of the tissue."
- *Incredicold* is a new product that is taken orally, in gel or pill form, and that helps to relieve patients of nearly all of their cold symptoms (**www.incredicold.com**).

Citing sources in the ways shown above is appropriate for some writing situations. Your instructor may ask you to provide a copy of the original source(s) to be sure that you summarized, paraphrased, and/or quoted materials correctly (see Chapter 13 for more on note taking). However, if your primary assignment is to write a formal research paper, then your instructor will probably require that you follow the specific guidelines of the Modern Language Association (MLA) or the American Psychological Association (APA). The rules for each format are extremely precise, so follow the directions very carefully so that you document your papers correctly and avoid plagiarism.

14.2 DETERMINING WHEN TO CITE OR NOT CITE A SOURCE

As you gather information from various sources, you will need to know what needs to be cited in your paper. Using and citing sources accurately will add credibility to your paper.

What Doesn't Need to Be Cited?

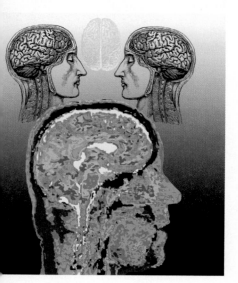

1. **Common knowledge:** Common knowledge includes widely known facts that can be found in multiple sources. No one *owns* these facts. For example, the fact that George Washington was the first president of the United States is commonly known. Likewise, many people know that Betsy Ross sewed the first American flag.

2. **Your original research:** If you conduct your own research, such as through a survey, then you do not need to document a source. However, you might need to include your raw data in an appendix. Check with your instructor about his or her preference.

3. **Personal experience:** If it is relevant, you may decide to incorporate your own personal experience into your paper. For example, if you are writing a paper about autism and want to include your sibling or child as an example, then you would not need to cite a source for that information. Ask your instructor if using a personal example is appropriate for your paper.

Teaching Tip

Remind students that if they are in doubt about whether or not to cite a source, they should cite a source. It is better to over-cite too than to under-cite.

What Does Need to Be Cited?

1. **Direct quotes:** Anytime you use someone else's exact words in your paper, you must enclose the exact wording in quotation marks and give credit to the source.

2. **Facts that aren't common knowledge:** Even if you come across the same idea in several sources, it may not be considered common knowledge. For example, you may find several sources that explain how brain surgery is performed, but your average reader would probably not be familiar with the intricacies of that process. Think about what your audience is likely to know

about your subject. If most people won't know about your subject, then cite your source. If you're not sure, cite it just to be safe.

3. **Opinions:** If you come across an interesting opinion in one of your sources and want to include it in your paper, then you must give credit to the original source. For instance, if you are writing a research paper for an economics course, you might cite an economist whose opinions about the state of the current economy help support your thesis.

4. **Statistics:** Anytime you incorporate statistics into your paper, you must give credit to the originator. For instance, you might decide to include statistics from a reputable source to support your thesis that earning a college degree will lead to a higher-paying job.

5. **Original ideas:** Often writers will create original theories or ideas for their publications. Be sure to give appropriate credit to the author. If you decide to write a paper about the theory of relativity for a science class, then be sure to mention Albert Einstein in addition to citing the sources you used to find the information.

6. **Studies and experiments:** If you are writing a paper for a behavioral science course, you might want to refer to a professional study or experiment. For example, in a psychology paper on sleep deprivation you might cite a landmark study to illustrate your main idea.

Basically, cite a source in your paper every time you present summarized or paraphrased material that isn't common knowledge or your original idea. If you are not sure whether you need to cite an idea in your paper, then you should be cautious and document the source. You are better off over-citing than under-citing. Also, you can check with your instructor if you are in doubt.

SmartBook Tip

Key concepts in Chapter 14 are highlighted for students during the "Read" phase. As students demonstrate understanding of these concepts during the "Practice" phase by responding to probes, the highlighting adapts to the individual student's learning by changing color.

Graduate SPOTLIGHT

Eric Osborn, eTime Administrator

Eric Osborn earned BA degrees in business administration and accounting. He is the system administrator and supervisor for the time and attendance system in the workforce management and planning department of eBay Enterprise. Here's what Osborn has to say about the writing he does in his career:

❝ At eBay Enterprise I am responsible for the overall system functions and setup of the time and attendance system. Communicating in writing is critical to my career. I communicate with over 3,000 employees regarding payroll and policies. Additionally, I write weekly summaries and reports, procedure guides for tasks related to my department, and proposals for changes to policies or procedures. For example, I recently convinced the management to provide additional training to new supervisors on the time and attendance system to better review and approve time cards. In my report, I documented cases where lack of approvals and reviews were causing loss of revenue and inaccurate pay to the employee. I also cited specific statistics to support my proposal. By implementing my proposal, eBay Enterprise will see better labor reporting, a gain in revenue, and happier employees with fewer pay inaccuracies. To make my reports believable, I must be thorough with my research and meticulous with my documentation. My overall goal is to propose written solutions to ensure that my company's operating expenses are cost-effective. ❞

14.3 MLA FORMAT

Many English and humanities courses use the Modern Language Association (MLA) format. The most up-to-date information about the MLA format is included in the 7th edition of *MLA Handbook for Writers of Research Papers* (2009). You can find more information about the MLA format by going to **www.mla.org**. The MLA style of documentation requires that you cite sources in your text as well as on a *works-cited* page at the end of your paper. The following examples will help you to cite sources using the MLA format. You may also want to try using an electronic tool, such as **www.noodletools.com**, to help you correctly document your sources.

MLA In-Text Citations

An *in-text citation,* also known as a *parenthetical citation,* shows the reader exactly where you have borrowed ideas from outside sources in your paper. When using the MLA format, you generally need to include the author's last name and the page number on which the borrowed material appears in the original source. Providing this information allows the readers to locate the correct entry on the works-cited page so they can find additional information about your topic if desired. You may include the author's last name in the text or in parentheses with the page number. If there is no author, use the title of the work. If there is no page number, such as for a website, omit that part. Vary the way in which you introduce sources in your paper to keep your writing fresh and to show how the idea from the source is connected to your point. Be sure to include the correct information and make it clear exactly what material comes from a particular source. The following examples show how to cite various types of sources in your text.

One Author

According to Bernsten, people who have popular first names or last names should make sure that they receive the correct treatment when hospitalized (173).

People who have popular first names or last names should make sure that they receive the correct treatment when hospitalized (Bernsten 173).

Two Authors

Barber and Takemura recommend that sushi eaters use only small amounts of soy sauce to avoid "drowning" the flavor of the sushi or making it come apart (230).

Sushi eaters should use only small amounts of soy sauce to avoid "drowning" the flavor of the sushi or making it come apart (Barber and Takemura 230).

Three Authors

Ma, Mateer, and Blaivas have observed that even though three-dimensional ultrasound technology can provide amazing images, it is currently not the best tool for making a diagnosis (25).

Even though three-dimensional ultrasound technology can provide amazing images, it is currently not the best tool for making a diagnosis (Ma, Mateer, and Blaivas 25).

Four or More Authors

According to Bishop et al., image editors, such as Macromedia Fireworks or Adobe Photoshop, are useful for enhancing images in a document or Web page (C22).

Image editors, such as Macromedia Fireworks or Adobe Photoshop, are useful for enhancing images in a document or Web page (Bishop et al. C22).

Note: Use the Latin term *et al.,* which means "and others," to show that you have omitted all but the first author. Notice there is no period after *et* but there is one after *al.* Also, this book includes section letters and page numbers.

Multiple Works by the Same Author

Morrison begins her novel *Paradise* with a powerful scenario in a small, racist town: "They shoot the white girl first. With the rest they can take their time" (3).

Morrison depicts the racist attitudes of a small town by catching the reader's attention right from the start: "They shoot the white girl first. With the rest they can take their time" (*Paradise* 3).

Some of the most successful writers begin with a shocking statement to immediately engage their readers, as in the following example: "They shoot the white girl first. With the rest they can take their time" (Morrison, *Paradise* 3).

Note: In addition to the author's name and page number, cite a shortened version of the title of the book to distinguish it from another book by the same author that you are citing in your paper. Place a comma after the author's name.

No Author

According to the book *Getting Yours,* public relations is about getting credit for doing a good job (3).

Basically, public relations is about getting credit for doing a good job (*Getting Yours* 3).

Note: Use the first few of the words of the title in place of an author's name. The entry needs to match the beginning of the corresponding entry on the works-cited page.

Corporate Author

Children's Hospital Boston suggests that the parenting process becomes less demanding when a child enters school (277).

The parenting process becomes less demanding when a child enters school (Children's Hospital Boston 277).

Indirect Source

According to Budman et al., studies show that children who have Tourette Syndrome may experience "rage" attacks when they see a specialist at a clinic (qtd. in Chowdhury 61).

Note: Use this example if you want to use a quote or information you find in a source that was cited by a different author. Give credit to the original author of the material in your text and the source where you found the quote or information in your parenthetical citation.

Multiple Works

The most common side effect of having a Botox injection is droopy eyelids (*Botox Cosmetic;* Langdon 75).

Note: Use this example when you find the same information in two sources and want to cite both to add credibility to your paper. Cite each work the same way you normally would, and add a semicolon between the works in parentheses. In the above example, the first work is a website with no author or page number, and the second is a book.

Long Quote

Glave urges his readers to help do their part to save the planet:

> Do something. Do it now. Dream up your own Eco-Shed, Eco-Car, Eco-Boat, Eco-Garden, Eco-Concrete, Eco-Whatever, and start on it today. Sit right up front and take charge of the process. Stop thinking about what you have to give up, or whom you might tick off, and start thinking about what you'll gain. Each of us must earn our own green belt at our own pace. But believe me, once you begin punching and kicking in that direction, you won't ever look back. (248-249)

Note: For quotes that are longer than four lines, set off the entire quote from the text and begin it on a new line. Indent the quote one inch from the left margin (about ten spaces) and double-space it. Omit the quotation marks and place the final period before the citation.

TABLE **14.1**

MLA Directory to Works Cited Examples

MLA List of Works Cited

When using the MLA format, you must include a *works-cited* page at the end of the paper to fully document your sources. Literally, this means that you list any *work* you have *cited* in your paper. You may need to look at several examples of works-cited entries to find the exact format you need to document a research source (see Table 14.1). For example, if you need to cite the fourth edition of a book with three authors, then you would need to look at the sample entries for "Book with Two or Three Authors" and "Book in Edition Other Than the First." Generally, you will alphabetize the works-cited entries according to the authors' last names. If there is no author, begin with the title. Ignore words such as *a* and *the* when alphabetizing an entry by the title in the list of works cited.

Books Here is a list of the basic information you need to include for book sources using the MLA format. List the information in each works-cited entry in order, and follow the punctuation guidelines of the examples. You should be able to find all of the information you need on the title and copyright pages of the book. (See Figures 14.1 and 14.2.)

1. **Author:** List the author's last name, followed by a comma and the author's first name and middle name or initial as it appears on the title page of the book. Do not include degrees or titles, such as "PhD" or "Sister," with the author's name. If the book has more than one author, invert only the first author's name and include a comma between authors. If the author is unknown, begin with the title of the book.

2. **Title:** Italicize the complete title of the book. Use title case capitalization, which means that you capitalize every word except articles (words such as *a* and *the*), conjunctions (words such as *but* and *for*) and prepositions (words such as *to, from, for,* and *with*). If there is a subtitle, add a colon between the title and subtitle and capitalize the first word after the colon, even if it is an article, a conjunction, or a preposition. You may need to include additional information after the title, depending on the type of source you are citing. For example, you may be using an edition other than the first or one volume of a multivolume set. See the corresponding examples that follow.

3. **Place of publication:** List the city followed by a colon. If multiple cities are included in the book, list only the first one.

4. **Publisher:** Include a shortened version of the publisher's name. For example, use McGraw instead of McGraw-Hill, U of California P for University of California Press, and Gale rather than Gale Research, Inc. The point is to give the reader enough information to be able to find the publisher if necessary. Eliminate extraneous words such as *books, house,* and *publisher.* If the publisher is named after a person, use only the last name. For instance, W. W. Norton & Company simply becomes Norton.

FIGURE 14.1
Book Title Page

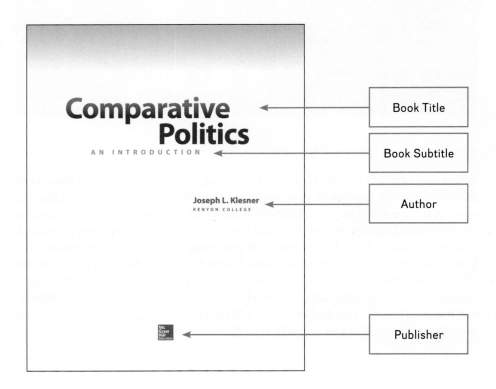

5. **Date of publication:** List the year, followed by a period.

6. **Publication medium:** Include the word *Print* (not italicized) after printed sources. This distinguishes a printed book from an online or electronic book. MLA added this element in the 2009 update to the citation guidelines.

Sample MLA Book Citation

• Author's Last Name, First Name. *Title of Book*. City of Publication: Publisher, Year of Publication. Publication Medium.

Book Example

Klesner, Joseph L. *Comparative Politics: An Introduction*. New York: McGraw, 2014. Print.

Book by One Author

Bernsten, Karin Janine. *The Patient's Guide to Preventing Medical Errors*. Westport: Praeger, 2004. Print.

Chowdhury, Uttom. *Tics and Tourette Syndrome: A Handbook for Parents and Professionals*. New York: Kingsley, 2004. Print.

Langdon, Robert. *Understanding Cosmetic Laser Surgery*. Jackson: UP of Mississippi, 2004. Print.

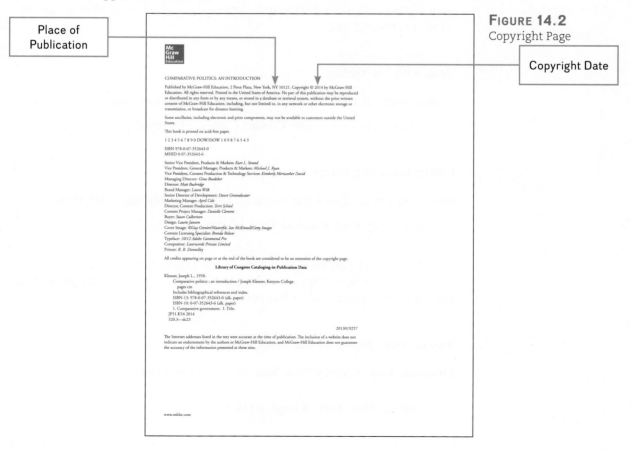

FIGURE **14.2**
Copyright Page

Place of Publication

Copyright Date

Book by Two Authors

Barber, Kimiko, and Hiroki Takemura. *Sushi: Taste and Technique.* New York:

DK, 2002. Print.

Vernberg, F. John, and Winona B. Vernberg. *The Coastal Zone: Past,*

Present, and Future. Columbia: U of South Carolina P, 2001. Print.

Note: Invert only the first author's name. The first author was listed on the book as F. John Vernberg.

Book by Three Authors

Ma, O. John, James R. Mateer, and Michael Blaivas. *Emergency Ultrasound.*

2nd ed. New York: McGraw, 2008. Print.

Book by Four or More Authors

Teaching Tip

Tell students that they may need to look at several examples to determine how to cite a particular source.

Bishop, Sherry, et al. *The Web Collection.* Boston: Course Technology, 2004.

Print.

Wysocki, Anne Frances, et al. *Writing New Media: Theory and Applications for*

Expanding the Teaching of Composition. Logan: Utah State UP, 2004. Print.

Note: Use the Latin term *et al.,* which means "and others," to show that you have omitted all but the first author. Notice there is a period after *al* but not after *et* in the example.

Book with No Author

Getting Yours: A Publicity and Funding Primer for Nonprofit and Voluntary

Organizations. Lincoln: Contact Center, 1991. Print.

Edited Book in a Series

Harris, Nancy, ed. *Space Exploration.* Detroit: Greenhaven, 2005. Print.

Exploring Science and Medical Discoveries.

Note: If there are two editors, use the plural abbreviation for editor, *eds.* The name of the series appears at the end of the entry. If there is an author, begin with the author rather than the editor.

Two or More Books by the Same Author

Morrison, Toni. *A Mercy.* New York: Knopf, 1998. Print.

---. *Paradise.* New York: Knopf, 2008. Print.

Note: Use three hyphens in place of the author's name for the second book (and subsequent books). Alphabetize the books on the works-cited page by the author and title. Ignore words such as *a* and *the* when alphabetizing the titles. Use the second word instead. In the examples above, *Mercy* comes before *Paradise* regardless of the word *a*.

Book in an Edition Other Than the First

Baker, Nancy L., and Nancy Huling. *A Research Guide for Undergraduate Students: English and American Literature.* 6th ed. New York: MLA, 2006. Print.

Book by a Corporate Author

Children's Hospital Boston. *The Children's Hospital Guide to Your Child's Health and Development.* Boston: Children's Hospital Boston, 2001. Print.

Discovery Channel. *North American & Alaskan Cruises.* London: Insight, 2005. Print.

Work in an Anthology

Poe, Edgar Allan. "The Raven." 1845. *The Norton Anthology of American Literature.* Shorter 8th ed. Ed. Nina Baym. New York: Norton, 2013. 688-691. Print.

Note: An anthology is a collection of works selected by one or more editors. Use this example if you are citing an essay, letter, poem, short story, or other work that appears in an edited collection or compilation of works by different authors. "The Raven" was originally published in 1845, and it appears on pages 688–691 in the anthology.

Multivolume Book

LaBlanc, Michael L., ed. *Poetry for Students: Presenting Analysis, Context, and Criticism on Commonly Studied Poetry.* Vol. 10. Detroit: Gale, 2001. Print.

Note: This book has an editor rather than an author.

Dictionary or Encyclopedia Article

"Italy." *The World Book Encyclopedia.* 2014 ed. Print.

Note: Use the word you looked up in the reference book as the title in quotation marks.

Printed Periodicals (Journals, Magazines, Newspapers) Here is a list of the basic information you need to include for periodical sources using the MLA format. List the information in each works-cited entry in order, and follow the punctuation guidelines of the examples. You should be able to find all of the information you need on the cover of the periodical and in the article itself. (See Figures 14.3 and 14.4.)

1. **Author:** Include the author's last name, followed by a comma and the author's first name and middle name or initial as it appears on the article. Do not include titles or degrees (such as "PhD" or "Sister") with the author's name. If the article has more than one author, invert only the first author's name and include a comma between authors. If the author is unknown, begin with the title of the article.

2. **Title:** Put the complete title of the article in quotation marks. Use title case capitalization, which means that you capitalize every word except articles (words such as *a* and *the*), conjunctions (words such as *but* and *for*), and prepositions (words such as *to, from, for,* and *with*). If there is a subtitle, add a colon between the title and subtitle. Capitalize the first word after the colon, even if it is an article, a conjunction, or a preposition.

3. **Publication:** Italicize the title of the periodical and use title case capitalization.

4. **Volume and issue numbers:** If the periodical has volume and issue numbers, use only the numerals to cite them, putting a period between them. For example, you would cite an article that appears in volume 10 of issue 3 this way: 10.3.

5. **Date of publication:** Include as much information about the date as you can find on the journal, magazine, or newspaper. If you find the day, month, and year, list the day first, followed by the month, and the year, like this: 21 Apr. 2015. If you find just the month(s) and year, cite it this way: July-Aug. 2015. Follow the date with a colon.

6. **Page number(s):** List the inclusive page numbers of the article, not just the ones you used. If the pages are consecutive, write them this way: 25-31. If the pages are not consecutive, then use a plus sign. For example, if the article starts on page 13 and then skips to page 26, cite it like this: 13+. For a newspaper, include the section letter before the page number: A4. Follow the page number(s) with a period.

7. **Publication medium:** Include the word *print* after the source for most printed sources. This distinguishes a printed article from an online or a CD version. MLA added this element in the 2009 update to the citation guidelines.

Sample MLA Periodical Citation

- Author's Last Name, First Name. "Title of Article." *Name of Periodical*
  Volume. Issue (Date): Page(s). Medium.

Periodical Example

Barrow, Melissa A. "Even Math Requires Learning Academic Language." *Phi
Delta Kappan* 95.6 (March 2014): 35-38. Print.

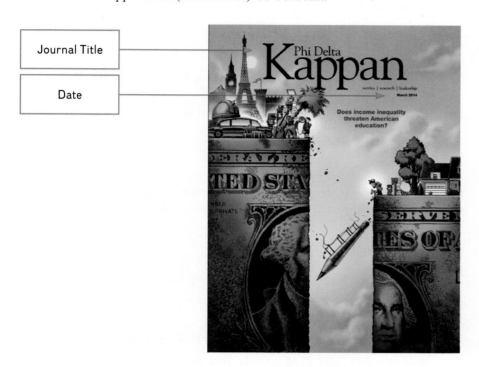

Journal Title

Date

FIGURE 14.3
Journal Cover

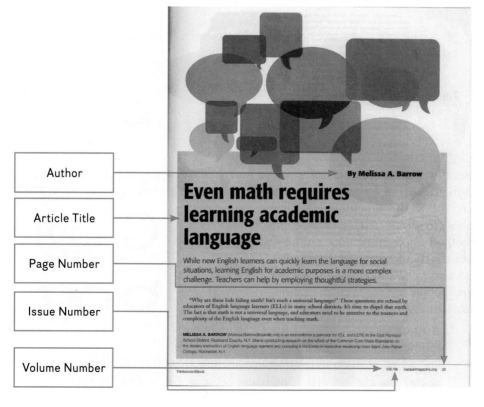

Author

Article Title

Page Number

Issue Number

Volume Number

FIGURE 14.4
Journal Article

Scholarly Journal Article

Teaching Tip
Bring various types of sources to class to have students practice developing works-cited entries.

Black, Anne C., et al. "Advancement via Individual Determination: Method Selection in Conclusions about Program Effectiveness." *Journal of Educational Research* 102.2 (2008): 111-123. Print.

DeVoe, Jennifer E., Carrie Tillotson, and Lorraine S. Wallace. "Uninsured Children and Adolescents with Insured Parents." *JAMA* 30.16 (2008): 1904-1913. Print.

Magazine Article

Flaim, Denise. "Nothin' but a Hound Dog." *Dog Fancy* Dec. 2008: 38-41. Print.

Lashinsky, Adam. "Apple: The Genius Behind Steve." *Fortune* 24 Nov. 2008: 71+. Print.

Note: Use the complete date if it appears on the cover. Also, the "+" sign after the page number indicates that the article started on page 71 and continued later in the magazine with interruptions of advertisements and/or other articles.

Newspaper Article

Tierney, John. "You Won't Stay the Same, Study Finds." *New York Times* 4 Jan. 2013: A15. Print.

Winslow, Ron. "Cholesterol Drug Cuts Heart Risk in Healthy Patients." *Wall Street Journal* 10 Nov. 2008: B1+. Print.

Note: The section number is included before the page number for newspaper articles.

Letter to the Editor

Kramer, Diane. *Wall Street Journal.* 4 Jan. 2013: A12. Print.

Electronic Sources

Here is a list of the basic information you need to include for electronic sources using the MLA format. List the information in each works-cited entry in order, and follow the punctuation guidelines of the examples. In 2009, MLA changed its recommended method for documenting online sources by taking out the requirement for listing the URL or website address. The rationale is that URLs often change, and people are more likely to find the correct website using the author's name and/or the article's title.

1. **Author:** Begin with the author's last name, followed by a comma, the author's first name, and a period. If there is no author, include the editor, compiler, narrator, or director of the work. If no name is listed, begin with the title.

2. **Article title:** Italicize the title if it is an independent work, and put it in quotation marks if it is part of a larger work. Use title case capitalization, which means that you capitalize every word except articles (words such as *a* and *the*), conjunctions (words such as *but* and *for*), and prepositions (words such as *to, from, for,* and *with*). If there is a subtitle, add a colon between the title and subtitle and capitalize the first word after the colon, even if it is an article, a conjunction, or a preposition.

3. **Website title:** Italicize the website name and use title case capitalization. Omit this part if the title of the work and website are the same. Also include the edition or version you accessed if applicable.

4. **Publisher, sponsor, or periodical title:** Include this information even if the publisher or sponsor is the same as the title of the website. If the publisher or sponsor information is not available, use *n.p.* instead to indicate that there is no publisher.

5. **Date of publication:** Include the day, month, and year if they are available, like this: 15 Jan. 2015. Use the month and year or just the year if that is all that is available. If there is no publication date, use *n.d.*

6. **Medium of publication:** Use *Web* to show you found the information on the Internet.

7. **Access date:** Include the day, month, and year you accessed the source. This is important because websites frequently change.

Sample MLA Electronic Citation

- Author's Last Name, First Name. "Title." *Website.* Publisher or Sponsor, Date of Publication. Medium. Access Date.

Electronic Source Example

"Endeavour Crew Returns Home after 'Home Improvement' in Orbit." *NASA.* NASA, n.d. Web. 22 Jan. 2015.

Note: The article has no author, so it begins with the title. Also, the article was not dated, so *n.d.* replaces the publication date.

FIGURE 14.5
Website Article

Website Article

Shute, Nancy. "Apes Have Food, Will Share for a Social Payoff." National Public Radio. 3 Jan. 2013. Web. 11 Nov. 2014.

Online Scholarly Journal Article

Nayar, Pramod K. "New Media, Digitextuality and Public Space." *Postcolonial Text* 4.1 (2008): n. pag. Web. 24 Jan. 2015.

Note: Use *n. pag.* when no page number is available.

Online Magazine Article

Fallows, James. "Be Nice to the Countries That Lend You Money." *TheAtlantic .com*. Atlantic Monthly Group, Dec. 2008. Web. 24 Jan. 2015.

Online Newspaper Article

Phillips, Rich. "Ex-FBI Agent Faces 30 Years to Life for Mob Hit." *CNN.com*. Cable News Network, 4 Dec. 2008. Web. 24 Jan. 2015.

Online Encyclopedia or Dictionary

"Albuquerque." *Encyclopaedia Britannica Online*. Encyclopaedia Britannica, 2014. Web. 23 Jan. 2015.

"Carpaccio." *Merriam-Webster Online Dictionary*. Merriam-Webster, 2013. Web. 1 Feb. 2015.

Periodical Article from an Online Database

Waterman, K. Krasnow, and Matthew T. Henshon. "What's Next for Artificial Intelligence and Robotics?" *Scitech Lawyer* 5.1 (2008): 20-21. *Proquest.* Web. 8 Dec. 2015.

Note: Follow the MLA guidelines for the type of source you are citing, and then add the database information and your access date to the end of the citation.

e-Book

Angelou, Maya. *Mom & Me & Mom*. New York: Random, 2013. Kindle e-Book file.

E-Mail

Record, Michael. "Using SmarThinking." Message to Karin Russell. 20 Oct. 2014. E-mail.

Other Sources You may decide to use other types of sources in your research paper. Each type of source has its own unique format. Be sure to give readers enough information to be able to find the source if they so desire. Many of the MLA rules from previous examples apply to the following sources.

Advertisement

Apple iPod Touch. Advertisement. *Wired* Nov. 2015: 150. Print.

AT&T. Advertisement. CNN. 6 July 2015. Television.

Personal Interview

Blush, Linda. Personal interview. 6 Jan. 2015.

Vining, Ashley. Telephone interview. 12 Dec. 2014.

Broadcast Interview

Sweeney, Alison. Interview by Ellen Degeneres. *The Ellen Degeneres Show.*
    NBC.WESH, Orlando. 3 Jan. 2013. Television.

Note: After the network, include the call letters and city of your local station.

Work of Visual Art

Bonnard, Pierre. *Before Dinner.* 1924. Oil on canvas. Metropolitan Museum
    of Art, New York.

Simmons, Laurie. *Walking House.* 1989. Photograph. Museum of Mod. Art,
    New York.

Note: Include the medium and current location of the artwork after the date
of its creation.

Music Recording

Keys, Alicia. "Brand New Me." *Girl on Fire.* RCA Records, 2012. CD.

Note: Begin with the artist or group as appropriate. If the music recording is
digital, replace *CD* with *MP3* (not italicized).

Spoken-Word Recording

Gore, Al. *The Assault on Reason.* 2007. Narr. Will Patton. Penguin, 2007. CD.

Note: The first date is the publication for the book, and the second is for the
sound recording. They just happen to have the same date in this example.
Also, *Narr.* refers to the narrator (reader).

Television Broadcast

"P!nk." *Behind the Music.* VH1. 3 Jan. 2013. Television.

Film

No Country for Old Men. Dir. Joel Coen and Ethan Coen. Perf. Tommy Lee

　　Jones, Javier Bardem, Josh Brolin, and Kelly MacDonald. 2007.

　　Miramax, 2008. DVD.

Note: Include the original date of release as well as the DVD date.

Brochure or Pamphlet

Abraham Lincoln: A Man of His Time, a Man for All Times. New York: Gilder

　　Lehrman Institute of American History, 2008. Print.

Note: Include an author if there is one.

MLA Research Paper Formatting Guide

1. **Margins:** Use one-inch margins at the top, bottom, and sides of the paper.
2. **Heading:** Place your heading at the upper-left corner of your paper, one inch from the top and one inch from the left edge of your paper. Include the following information, double-spaced: Your name, your instructor's name, the course name and number, and the date in this style: 15 November 2015.
3. **Header:** Include your last name and the page number on every page of your paper in the upper-right corner, one-half inch from the top and one inch from the right edge of your paper.
4. **Title:** Center your title on the page, two spaces down from the date. Your title should be descriptive and, if possible, creative. Avoid italicizing, underlining, or boldfacing your title or putting it in quotation marks. Use title case capitalization.
5. **Text formatting:** Throughout the paper, use a 12-point font with a typeface that is easy to read, such as Times New Roman. Do not justify the right-hand margin of the text; the text should have a ragged (uneven) right margin. Double-space the entire paper, and indent each paragraph one-half inch, about five spaces. Leave one space between sentences. Do not include an extra space between paragraphs. Include in-text citations to indicate where you have borrowed quoted, paraphrased, and summarized ideas from your sources.
6. **Visual elements:** If you decide to include tables or illustrations, such as maps, charts, or works of art, in your paper, place them near the text in which you refer to them. Label the item Table or Fig. (short for figure) and consecutively number each one. In the body of the paper, where you refer to the table or illustration, write the following in parentheses: (see fig. 1). Include the label and complete source information below the table or figure.

FIG. 1. Monet, Claude. *Villas at Bordighera.* 1884. Oil on canvas. The Santa Barbara Museum of Art, California.
Note: Because you will include the complete source information with the table or figure, you will not need to duplicate it on the works-cited page.

From Stigma to Status
by Margaret Rowland

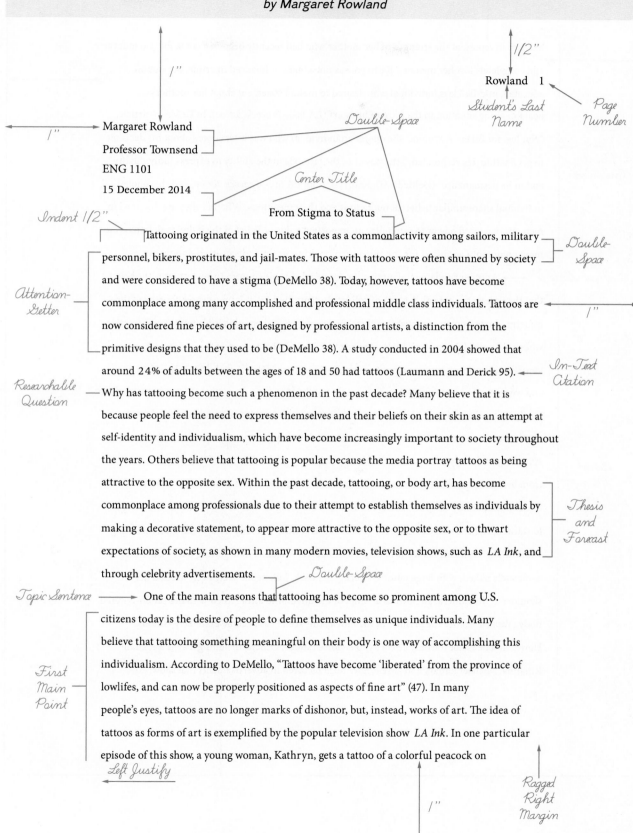

1/2"

Rowland   1

Student's Last Name

Page Number

1"

Margaret Rowland

Double-Space

Professor Townsend

ENG 1101

15 December 2014

Center Title

Indent 1/2"

From Stigma to Status

Tattooing originated in the United States as a common activity among sailors, military

Double-Space

personnel, bikers, prostitutes, and jail-mates. Those with tattoos were often shunned by society

and were considered to have a stigma (DeMello 38). Today, however, tattoos have become

Attention-Getter

commonplace among many accomplished and professional middle class individuals. Tattoos are

1"

now considered fine pieces of art, designed by professional artists, a distinction from the

primitive designs that they used to be (DeMello 38). A study conducted in 2004 showed that

around 24% of adults between the ages of 18 and 50 had tattoos (Laumann and Derick 95).

In-Text Citation

Researchable Question

Why has tattooing become such a phenomenon in the past decade? Many believe that it is

because people feel the need to express themselves and their beliefs on their skin as an attempt at

self-identity and individualism, which have become increasingly important to society throughout

the years. Others believe that tattooing is popular because the media portray tattoos as being

attractive to the opposite sex. Within the past decade, tattooing, or body art, has become

commonplace among professionals due to their attempt to establish themselves as individuals by

Thesis and Forecast

making a decorative statement, to appear more attractive to the opposite sex, or to thwart

expectations of society, as shown in many modern movies, television shows, such as *LA Ink*, and

through celebrity advertisements.

Double-Space

Topic Sentence

One of the main reasons that tattooing has become so prominent among U.S.

citizens today is the desire of people to define themselves as unique individuals. Many

believe that tattooing something meaningful on their body is one way of accomplishing this

First Main Point

individualism. According to DeMello, "Tattoos have become 'liberated' from the province of

lowlifes, and can now be properly positioned as aspects of fine art" (47). In many

people's eyes, tattoos are no longer marks of dishonor, but, instead, works of art. The idea of

tattoos as forms of art is exemplified by the popular television show *LA Ink*. In one particular

episode of this show, a young woman, Kathryn, gets a tattoo of a colorful peacock on

Left Justify

Ragged Right Margin

1"

her arm to represent the strength of her mother who had recently been in a coma for two months

and completely lost her memory. Kathryn was not a biker or involved in crime, but was an

educated, middle-class individual who desired to make a statement about her mother's

heartbreaking situation in the form of body art (*LA Ink—Peacock Tattoo*). In DeMello's article,

"Not Just for Bikers Anymore," she quotes an individual who was interviewed about his decision

to get a tattoo. He responded, "The power of the tattoo is in the ability to express individuality

and in its permanence" (DeMello 41). Kathryn, from *LA Ink—Peacock Tattoo*, and this quoted

individual share similar beliefs about tattoos and their meanings. Whether they are designed in

memory of a loved one or to symbolize an important value or belief of the individual, tattoos are

most commonly acquired for the purpose of making unique, decorative statements.

Another fundamental motivation for people in this country to get tattoos is the belief

that they create sex appeal. A study of college students found that "almost three-fourths of the

undergraduate women reported that they 'sometimes' viewed openly visible tattoos as attractive

when on a man" (Horne et al. 1011). On the other hand, "58.8 percent of the undergraduate men

viewed such visible tattoos as attractive when on a woman" (Horne et al. 1011). Therefore, men

and women may get tattoos if they feel that they will add to their sex appeal. A large portion of this

thinking has derived from the fact that many celebrities have tattoos, and, because celebrities are

often seen as sex icons, common people believe that if they get tattoos then they will be

appealing to the opposite sex as well (Horne et al. 1011). DeMello states, "Tattooing has moved

from being a symbol of the outcast to that of a rock star, model, and postmodern youth, and with

this shift in public perception has come a shift in meaning as well, as tattoo moves from stigma

to status" (49). The idea that tattoos are sexy is exemplified in many modern movies, including

Wanted. The most famous scene of this movie depicts Angelina Jolie getting out of a bathtub,

completely naked, with large tattoos covering her back. Jolie seductively peers around her

shoulder at the camera, an obvious attempt of the director to attract men with her tattoo-covered

body (*Wanted*). Since the premier of the movie, this scene has become extremely famous.

However, Jolie is not the only celebrity to endorse tattoos. Others, including David Beckham,

Rihanna, Michael Jordan, and Gisele, have been pictured in advertisements that show

First Main Point Continued

Topic Sentence

Second Main Point

MLA Format

MLA Format

MLA Format

1/2"

1"

Second Main Point Continued

off, or endorse, tattoos. In his ad for Emporio Armani, Beckham poses in underwear, revealing his muscular body and a large tattoo on his right arm (Emporio Armani Underwear). Advertisements and movies like these, which depict extremely attractive celebrities with revealed tattoos, contribute in a major way to the idea tattoos are sexy. For this reason, many people get tattoos in order to make themselves more attractive to the opposite sex.

Topic Sentence

The final reason for individuals to get tattoos so frequently today is their desire to stray from the norms of society. Often people feel that society dictates what they should look like and how they should act. In response, they feel the need to rebel against the idea of being a perfect, cookie-cutter citizen and believe that getting unique tattoos with help them do so. Another individual quoted in DeMello's article stated that he got a tattoo to "go against what people want you to do. All of your life you're computerized to do what people want you to do" (41). Therefore, some people desire a release from the constrains that they feel society puts on them, and they achieve this release by getting a tattoo. This idea of rebellion as a reason for body art is clearly represented in the television show *One Tree Hill*. In episode nine of season one, "With Arms Outstretched," Lucas gets an impulsive tattoo of a Chinese symbol on his upper arm. At the time, his mother is out of town and he is looking for a way to act out against authority in a rebellious way. As the episode suggests, some people get tattoos as an attempt to resist authority. This reason for getting a tattoo, however, is more common among males than females. Through their studies, Horne et al. found that almost half of the male sample set agreed with the statement "tattoos are symbols of our resistance to culture" (1011). This differs from the 31.5% of women who agree with the statement (Horne et al. 1011). As a result, people often get tattoos as an attempt to rebel against the person that society and authority tells them they should be. However, males are more likely to cite this reason than females, who more often get tattoos to contribute to their attractiveness or to make a decorative statement.

Third Main Point

1"

1"

Reworded Thesis Statement

Tattoos are no longer only for bikers, sailors, convicts, and prostitutes, but have risen in status and are now decorating the bodies of a quarter of the nation. These people include middle-class professionals holding jobs as lawyers, bankers, doctors, and other high-profile career positions (DeMello 40). Individuals get tattoos so often today for three main

1"

1/2"

1"

Reworded Thesis Statement Continued

reasons: to make a statement by defining their individuality, to make themselves more appealing to the opposite sex, or to stray from the norms of society in the United States. These reasons are extremely visible in entertainment and in the media, for they are represented in modern

Summary of Main Points

television shows, movies, and celebrity advertisements. These outlets illustrate that the media and entertainment have a major impact on the way some Americans think and act. If television

1"

shows did not endorse the idea of getting tattoos, would people get them? If celebrities did not have tattoos all over their bodies, would people put tattoos all over bodies? The answer is most likely no. Essentially, tattoos are just another fashion trend. Just as different forms of fashion are depicted in celebrity advertisements and used as costumes in movies and television shows, so are tattoos. The real question is, will the popularity of tattooing eventually die like most other

Memorable Ending

fashion trends, leaving those who have them to regret their tattoos for the rest of their lives? Only time will tell.

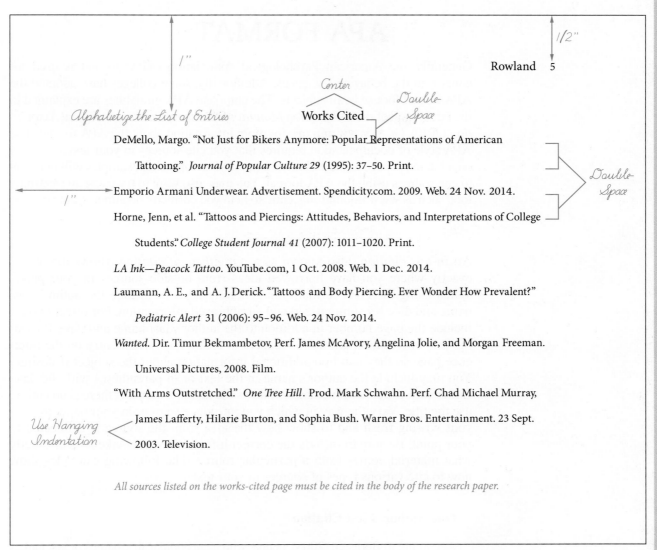

Alphabetize the List of Entries

Center

Works Cited

Double Space

Rowland 5

1"

1/2"

DeMello, Margo. "Not Just for Bikers Anymore: Popular Representations of American Tattooing." *Journal of Popular Culture 29* (1995): 37–50. Print.

Emporio Armani Underwear. Advertisement. Spendicity.com. 2009. Web. 24 Nov. 2014.

Horne, Jenn, et al. "Tattoos and Piercings: Attitudes, Behaviors, and Interpretations of College Students." *College Student Journal 41* (2007): 1011–1020. Print.

LA Ink—Peacock Tattoo. YouTube.com, 1 Oct. 2008. Web. 1 Dec. 2014.

Laumann, A. E., and A. J. Derick. "Tattoos and Body Piercing. Ever Wonder How Prevalent?" *Pediatric Alert* 31 (2006): 95–96. Web. 24 Nov. 2014.

Wanted. Dir. Timur Bekmambetov, Perf. James McAvory, Angelina Jolie, and Morgan Freeman. Universal Pictures, 2008. Film.

"With Arms Outstretched." *One Tree Hill*. Prod. Mark Schwahn. Perf. Chad Michael Murray, James Lafferty, Hilarie Burton, and Sophia Bush. Warner Bros. Entertainment. 23 Sept. 2003. Television.

Use Hanging Indentation

Double Space

All sources listed on the works-cited page must be cited in the body of the research paper.

Source: Rowland, Margaret, From Stigma to Status. Reprinted by permission of the author.

[QUESTIONS FOR REFLECTION]

1. Based on Rowland's introductory paragraph, what three main points does she promise to cover in the body of her paper? Does she follow through with her promise?

2. What supporting details and examples does she offer for her first main point? Are they sufficient? Why or why not?

3. What supporting details does Rowland offer for her second main point? Which details are the most convincing? Why?

4. Which ideas from the author's third body paragraph are most memorable? Why?

5. What is Rowland's thesis? Do you think she fully supports her thesis in the body of the paper? Why or why not?

14.4 APA FORMAT

Generally, the American Psychological Association (APA) format is used for courses in the behavioral sciences. Additionally, some colleges have adopted the APA format for use in all subjects. The complete APA guidelines are explained in the 6th edition of the *Publication Manual of the American Psychological Association* (2010). Go to **www.apa.org** for more information about the APA format. The APA style of documentation requires that you cite sources in your text as well as on a reference page at the end of your paper. The following examples will help you to cite sources using the APA format. You may also want to try using an electronic tool, such as **www.noodletools.com**, to help you correctly document your sources.

APA In-Text Citations

An *in-text citation,* also known as a *parenthetical citation,* shows the reader exactly where you have borrowed ideas from outside sources in your paper. When using the APA format, you generally need to include the author's last name and date for summarized and paraphrased information. For direct quotes, include the page number in addition to the author's last name and date. Providing this information allows the readers to locate the correct entry on the reference page so they can find additional information about the subject if desired. You may include the author's name in the text or in parentheses with the date. Either way, the date immediately follows the author's name. If there is no author, use the title. Vary the way in which you introduce sources in your paper to keep your writing fresh and to show how the idea from the source is connected to your point. Be sure to include the correct information and make it clear exactly what material comes from a particular source. The following examples show how to cite various types of sources in your text.

One Author: First Citation

According to Bernsten (2004), people who have popular first names or last names should make sure that they receive the correct treatment when hospitalized.

People who have popular first names or last names should make sure that they receive the correct treatment when hospitalized (Bernsten, 2004).

One Author: Subsequent Citation within the Same Paragraph

Bernsten (2004) also suggests . . .

Note: If you cite the source again later in the paper, list the author's name and date again.

Two Authors

Barber and Takemura (2002) recommend that sushi eaters use only small amounts of soy sauce to avoid "drowning" the flavor of the sushi or making it come apart (p. 230).

Sushi eaters should use only small amounts of soy sauce to avoid "drowning" the flavor of the sushi or making it come apart (Barber & Takemura, 2002, p. 230).

Note: Include the page number when you quote any words from the original text. Use an ampersand (&) between the authors' names in parentheses.

Three to Five Authors: First Citation

Ma, Mateer, and Blaivas (2008) have observed that even though three-dimensional ultrasound technology can provide amazing images, it is currently not the best tool for making a diagnosis.

Even though three-dimensional ultrasound technology can provide amazing images, it is currently not the best tool for making a diagnosis (Ma, Mateer, & Blaivas, 2008).

Three to Five Authors: Subsequent Citations

Ma et al. (2008) have observed that even though three-dimensional ultrasound technology can provide amazing images, it is currently not the best tool for making a diagnosis.

Even though three-dimensional ultrasound technology can provide amazing images, it is currently not the best tool for making a diagnosis (Ma et al., 2008).

Note: For works with three or more authors, list all of the authors' last names the first time you cite the source. For subsequent citations, use the Latin term *et al.,* which means "and others," to show that you have omitted all but the first author. Notice there is a period after *al* but not after *et.*

Six or More Authors

Wilson et al. (2015) discovered that . . .

Note: Even though you list only the first author's name in the in-text citation, you will need to cite up to seven authors' names on the reference list. For eight or more authors, use *et al.* for the in-text citation, but on the reference list include only the first six authors' names followed by an ellipsis (. . .) and the last author's name.

Multiple Works by Authors with the Same Last Name

J. E. Rivera (2006) and A. M. Rivera (2010) recommend . . .

N. D. Goldstein and Hertz (2011) and S. P. Goldstein and Michaels (2007) found . . .

Note: Include the initials to clearly distinguish the authors with the same last names. Omit the initials for authors with different names.

No Author

According to the book *Getting Yours* (1991), public relations is about getting credit for doing a good job.

Basically, public relations is about getting credit for doing a good job (*Getting Yours,* 1991).

Note: Use the first few words of the title in place of the author's name. The entry needs to match the beginning of the corresponding entry on the reference list.

Anonymous Author

Studies show that . . . (Anonymous, 2015).

Note: Use this only when the source lists its author as "Anonymous."

Corporate or Group Author

Children's Hospital Boston (2001) suggests that the parenting process becomes less demanding when a child enters school.

The parenting process becomes less demanding when a child enters school (Children's Hospital Boston, 2001).

Indirect Source

According to Budman et al. (as cited in Chowdhury, 2004), studies show that children who have Tourette Syndrome may experience "rage" attacks when they see a specialist at a clinic (p. 61).

Note: Use this example if you want to use a quote or information you find in a source by a different author. Give credit to the original author of the material in your text and the source where you found the quote or information in your parenthetical citation.

Multiple Works

The most common side effect of having a Botox injection is droopy eyelids (*Botox Cosmetic,* 2015; Langdon, 2004).

Note: Use this example when you find the same information in two sources and want to cite both to add credibility to your paper. Cite each work the same way you normally would, and add a semicolon between the works in parentheses. In the above example, the first work is a website with no author, and the second is a book.

Personal Communication

According to M. Record (personal communication, October 20, 2014) SmarThinking is a valuable resource for students to receive constructive feedback on their rough drafts.

Note: Use the above format for personal e-mails, personal interviews, telephone conversations, and other forms of personal communication.

Long Quote

Glave (2008) urges his readers to help do their part to save the planet:

> Do something. Do it now. Dream up your own Eco-Shed, Eco-Car, Eco-Boat, Eco-Garden, Eco-Concrete, Eco-Whatever, and start on it today. Sit right up front and take charge of the process. Stop thinking about what you have to give up, or whom you might tick off, and start thinking about what you'll gain. Each of us must earn our own green belt at our own pace. But believe me, once you begin punching and kicking in that direction, you won't ever look back. (pp. 248–249)

Note: For quotes that are longer than forty words, set off the entire quote from the text and begin it on a new line. Indent the quote a half inch (about five to seven spaces) from the left margin and double-space it. Omit the quotation marks and place the final period before the citation.

APA References

When using the APA format, you must include a list of *references* at the end of the paper to fully document your sources. This means that you list any *work* you have *referenced* (cited) in your paper. You may need to look at several examples of reference entries to find the exact format you need to document a research source. (See Table 14.2 on page 362.) For example, if you need to cite the fourth edition of a book with three authors, then you would need to look at the sample entries for "Book with Three or More Authors" and "Book in Edition Other Than the First." Generally, you will alphabetize the list according to the authors' last names. If there is no author, begin with the title. Ignore words such as *a* and *the* when alphabetizing an entry by the title on the list of references.

Books Here is a list of the basic information you need to include for book sources using the APA format. List the information in each reference entry in order, and follow the punctuation guidelines of the examples. You should be able to find all of the information you need on the title and copyright pages of the book. (See Figures 14.6 and 14.7.)

1. **Author:** List the author's last name, followed by a comma and the author's first initial and middle initial (if you have it). Do not include degrees or titles, such as "PhD" or "Sister," with the author's name. If the book has more than one author, list the additional authors in the same manner as the first author, include a comma between authors, and include a comma and an ampersand (&) between the final two authors' names. If the author is unknown, begin with the title of the book.

2. **Date of publication:** List the year in parentheses, followed by a period.

3. **Book title:** Italicize the complete title of the book. Capitalize only the first word of the title and proper nouns. If there is a subtitle, add a colon between the title and subtitle and capitalize the first word after the colon. You may need to include additional information after the title, depending on the type of source you are citing. For example, you may be using an

TABLE **14.2**

Directory to APA References Examples

edition other than the first or one volume of a multivolume set. See the corresponding examples that follow.

4. **Place of publication:** List the city, followed by a comma, and the two-letter state abbreviation used by the United States Postal Service, followed by a colon. (Go to **www.usps.com** for a complete list.) If multiple cities are included in the book, list only the first one. For a country other than the United States, list the city followed by the country: London, England.

5. **Publisher:** List the publisher's name in brief form. Omit terms such as *Publishers, Co.,* and *Inc.* If the author and publisher are exactly the same, list the word *Author* (not italicized), where you would normally list the publisher.

Sample APA Book Citation

• Author's Last Name, First Initial. Middle Initial. (Year of Publication). *Title of book.* Place of Publication: Publisher.

Book Example

Klesner, J. L. (2014). *Comparative politics: An introduction.* New York, NY: McGraw-Hill.

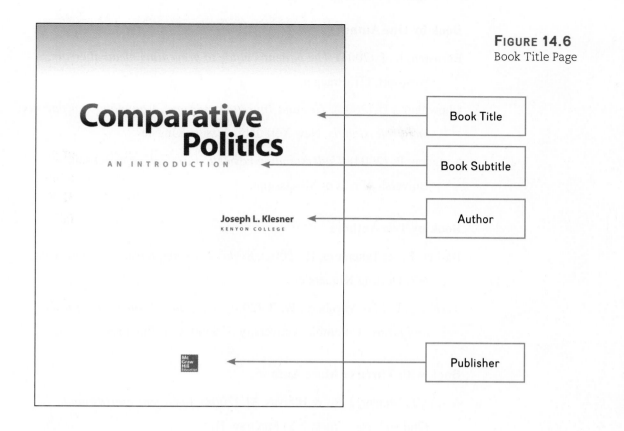

FIGURE 14.6
Book Title Page

Book Title

Book Subtitle

Author

Publisher

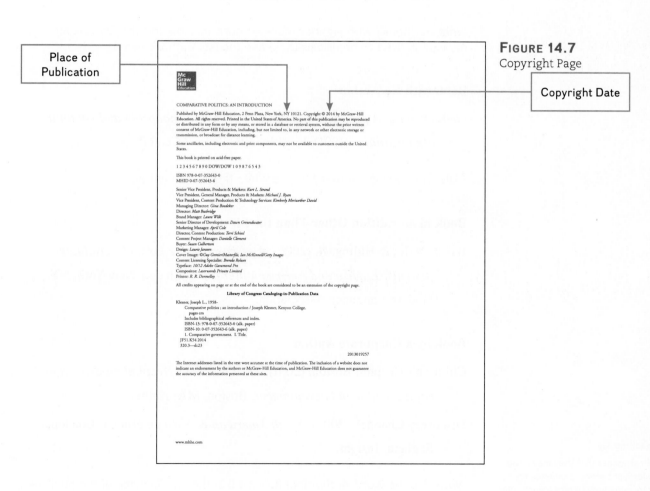

Place of Publication

FIGURE 14.7
Copyright Page

Copyright Date

Book by One Author

Bernsten, K. J. (2004). *The patient's guide to preventing medical errors.* Westport, CT: Praeger.

Chowdhury, U. (2004). *Tics and Tourette syndrome: A handbook for parents and professionals.* New York, NY: Jessica Kingsley.

Langdon, R. (2004). *Understanding cosmetic laser surgery.* Jackson: University Press of Mississippi.

Book by Two Authors

Barber, K., & Takemura, H. (2002). *Sushi: Taste and technique.* New York, NY: Dorling Kindersley.

Vernberg, F. J., & Vernberg, W. B. (2001). *The coastal zone: Past, present, and future.* Columbia: University of South Carolina Press.

Book with Three or More Authors

Ma, O. J., Mateer, J. R., & Blaivas, M. (2008). *Emergency ultrasound* (2nd ed.). New York, NY: McGraw-Hill.

Note: For books with eight or more authors, include only the first six authors' names followed by an ellipsis (. . .) and the last author's name.

Book with No Author

Getting yours: A publicity and funding primer for nonprofit and voluntary organizations. (1991). Lincoln, NE: Contact Center.

Note: The date goes after the title when there is no author.

Book in an Edition Other Than the First

Baker, N. L., & Huling, N. (2006). *A research guide for undergraduate students: English and American literature* (6th ed.). New York, NY: Modern Language Association.

Book by a Corporate Author

Children's Hospital Boston. (2001). *The Children's Hospital guide to your child's health and development.* Boston, MA: Author.

Discovery Channel. (2005). *North American & Alaskan cruises.* London, England: Insight.

Note: Use the word *Author* (not italicized) at the end, in place of the publisher, when the corporate author and publisher have the same name.

Teaching Tip
Tell students that they may need to look at several examples to determine how to cite a particular source.

Work in an Anthology

Poe, E. A. (2013). The raven. In N. Baym (Ed.), *The Norton anthology of*

American literature (Shorter 8th ed., pp. 688–691). New York, NY:

Norton. (Original work published 1845)

Note: An anthology is a collection of works selected by one or more editors. Use this example if you are citing an essay, letter, poem, short story, or other work that appears in an edited collection or compilation of works by different authors. The editor is listed by first initial and last name.

Multivolume Book

LaBlanc, M. L. (Ed.). (2001). *Poetry for students: Presenting analysis,*

context, and criticism on commonly studied poetry (Vol. 10).

Detroit, MI: Gale Group.

Note: This book has an editor rather than an author.

Printed Periodicals (Journals, Magazines, Newspapers) Here is a list of the basic information you need to include for periodical sources using the APA format. List the information for each entry on the reference page in order, and follow the punctuation guidelines of the examples. You should be able to find all of the information you need on the cover of the periodical and the article itself. (See Figures 14.7 and 14.8.)

1. **Author:** List the author's last name, followed by a comma and the author's first initial and middle initial (if you have it). Do not include degrees or titles, such as "PhD" or "Sister," with the author's name. If the source has more than one author, list the additional authors in the same manner as the first author, include a comma between authors, and include a comma and an ampersand (&) between the final two authors' names. If the author is unknown, begin with the title of the article.

2. **Date of publication:** Include as much information about the date as you can find on the journal, magazine, or newspaper. If you find the day, month, and year, list the year first, followed by a comma, the month, and the day, like this: (2015, April 21). If you find just the month(s) and year, list it this way: (2014, July/August). Enclose the date in parentheses, followed by a period.

3. **Article title:** List the complete article title, capitalizing only the first word and proper nouns. If there is a subtitle, add a colon between the title and subtitle. Capitalize the first word after the colon.

4. **Publication:** List the complete title of the periodical in italics. Use title case capitalization, which means that you capitalize every word except articles (words such as *a* and *the*), conjunctions (words such as *for* and

but), and prepositions (words such as *to, from, for,* and *with*). Follow the periodical title with a comma.

5. **Volume and issue numbers:** If the periodical has a volume number, list it in italics. If the periodical has an issue number, and each issue begins on page one, list the issue number in parentheses, but not italicized, immediately after the volume number. For example, cite an article that appears in volume 10 of issue 3 this way: *10*(3). Follow this information with a comma. If the periodical does not have volume and issue numbers, list the year followed by the month or season, like this: (2015, Spring).

6. **Page number(s):** List the inclusive page numbers of the article, not just the ones you used, like this: 25–31. If the page numbers are not continuous, list the specific pages for the article this way for magazines and periodicals, 6, 8, 12–14, and this way for newspaper articles, pp. B1, B4, B6–7. Follow the page number(s) with a period.

Sample APA Periodical Citation

- Author's Last Name, First Initial. Middle Initial. (Date of Publication). Title of article. *Name of Periodical, Volume*(Issue), Page(s).

Periodical Example

Barrow, M. A. (2014, March). Even math requires learning academic language. *Phi Delta Kappan, 95*(6), 35–38.

Journal Article

Lleras, C. (2008, December). Race, racial concentration, and the dynamics of educational inequality across urban and suburban schools. *American Educational Research Journal, 45,* 886–912.

FIGURE 14.8
Journal Cover

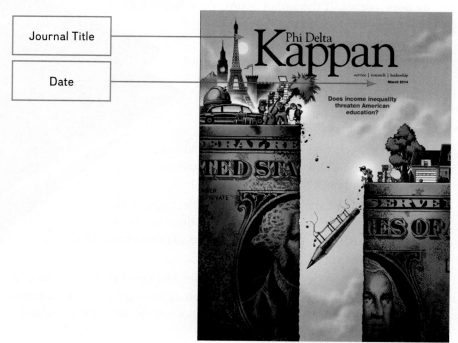

Journal Title

Date

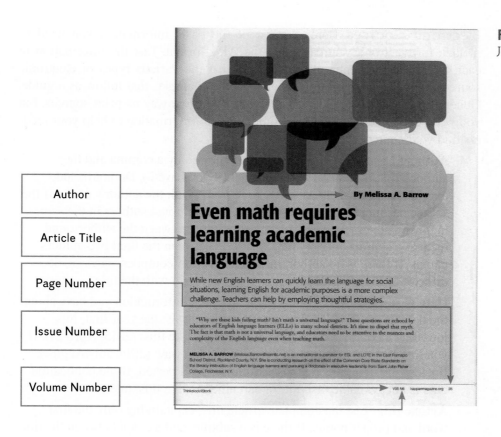

FIGURE 14.9
Journal Article

Author

Article Title

Page Number

Issue Number

Volume Number

By Melissa A. Barrow

Even math requires learning academic language

While new English learners can quickly learn the language for social situations, learning English for academic purposes is a more complex challenge. Teachers can help by employing thoughtful strategies.

"Why are these kids failing math? Isn't math a universal language?" These questions are echoed by educators of English language learners (ELLs) in many school districts. It's time to dispel that myth. The fact is that math is not a universal language, and educators need to be attentive to the nuances and complexity of the English language even when teaching math.

MELISSA A. BARROW (Melissa.Barrow@kornllc.net) is an instructional supervisor for ESL and LOTE in the East Ramapo School District, Rockland County, N.Y. She is conducting research on the effect of the Common Core State Standards on the literacy instruction of English language learners and pursuing a doctorate in executive leadership from Saint John Fisher College, Rochester, N.Y.

Roberts, K. T., Robinson, K. M., Stewart, C., & Wright, J. C. (2008).

Integrated mental health practice in a nurse-managed health center.

The American Journal for Nurse Practicioners, 12(10), 33–34,

37–40, 43–44.

Magazine Article

Flaim, D. (2008, December). Nothin' but a hound dog. *Dog Fancy,* 38–41.

Lemos, R. (2009, January). Use encryption to safeguard your data. *PC World,* 47–48.

Newspaper Article

Tierney, J. (2013, January 4). You won't stay the same, study finds. *The New York Times,* p. A15.

Koppel, N., Scheck, J., & Stecklow, S. (2008, December 19). Fast living, bold ambitions drove lawyer's rise and fall. *The Wall Street Journal,* pp. A1, A14.

Note: The section number is included before the page number for newspaper articles. Also, for newspaper articles, precede the page numbers with *p.* (for one page) and *pp.* (for multiple pages).

Teaching Tip

Bring in various types of sources to class to have students practice developing reference entries.

Electronic Sources Here is a list of the basic information you need to include for electronic sources using the APA format. List the information in each reference page entry in order. Note that the various types of electronic sources require different information. Use the examples that follow as a guide. Generally, you will cite electronic sources the same way as print sources, but you will need to add enough electronic retrieval information to help your readers find your source.

1. **Author:** List the author's last name, followed by a comma and the author's first initial and middle initial (if you have it). Do not include degrees or titles, such as "PhD" or "Sister," with the author's name. If the source has more than one author, list the additional authors in the same manner as the first author, include a comma between the authors, and include a comma and an ampersand (&) between the final two authors' names. If there is no author, include the editor, compiler, narrator, or director of the work. If no name is listed, begin with the title.

2. **Date of publication:** List all of the available information you have about the date. If you find the day, month, and year, list the year first, followed by a comma, the month, and the day, like this: (2015, April 21). If you find just the month(s) and year, list it this way: (2014, July/August). Enclose the date in parentheses, followed by a period. If the publication date is not available, list *n.d.* in parentheses, like this: (n.d).

3. **Article title:** List the complete article title, capitalizing only the first word and proper nouns. If there is a subtitle, add a colon between the title and subtitle. Capitalize the first word after the colon.

4. **Periodical information:** For online periodicals, list the title of the periodical (in italics) followed by volume (in italics) and issue number (in parentheses). Follow the same guidelines as you would for print periodical sources.

5. **DOI:** Some online journals contain a digital object identifier (DOI), which is a set of numbers and letters that is unique to a particular digital source. If the source you wish to document has a DOI, the publisher will display it on the front page of the article. Unlike a URL, which can change, a DOI is a permanent identifier.

6. **URL:** List the URL only if a digital object identifier (DOI) is not available. Include the entire URL for Internet sources. Copy the URL very carefully so that your readers can access the information if desired. Do not include a period after the URL. Remove the blue font and underline.

Sample APA Electronic Citation

- Author's Last Name, First Initial. Middle Initial. (Date of Publication).
  Article title. Periodical information. DOI or URL

Electronic Source Example

Endeavour crew returns home after "home improvement" in orbit. (n.d.).
  Retrieved from http://www.nasa.gov

Note: Include an author if there is one, and list the date immediately after the author. Do not include a period at the end of the entries that end with a URL.

FIGURE **14.10**
Website Article

APA Format

Website Article

Shute, N. (2013, January 3). Apes have food, will share for a social payoff.
Retrieved from http://www.npr.org/blogs/thesalt/2013/01/03/
168527985/apes-have-food-will-share-for-a-social-payoff

Online Journal Article with a DOI

Anderson, C. B., Hughes, S. O., & Fuemmeler, B. F. (2009). Parent-child
attitude congruence on type and intensity of physical activity: Testing
multiple mediators of sedentary behavior in older children. *Health
Psychology, 28,* 428–438. doi: 10.1037/a0014522

Online Journal Article without a DOI

Nayar, P. K. (2008). New media, digitextuality and public space.
Postcolonial Text, 4(1). Retrieved from http://journals.sfu.ca/
pocol/index.php/pct/article/view/786/521

Note: The URL is included because there is no DOI.

Online Magazine Article

Fallows, J. (2008, December). Be nice to the countries that lend you money.
The Atlantic. Retrieved from http://www.theatlantic.com/magazine/
archive/2008/12/be-nice-to-the-countries-that-lend-you-money/307148/

Online Newspaper Article

Chopra, D. (2013, January 4). Secrets to a better brain. *CNN.* Retrieved
from http://www.cnn.com/2013/01/04/health/chopra-better-brain/index
.html?hpt=hp_abar

Online Encyclopedia Article

Robotics. (2013). In *Encyclopaedia britannica.* Retrieved from

http://www.britannica.com/search?query=robotics

e-Book

Angelou, M. (2013). *Mom & me & mom* [Kindle version]. Retrieved from

Amazon.com

Other Sources You may decide to use other types of sources in your research paper. Each type of source has its own unique format. Be sure to give your readers enough information to be able to find the source if they so desire. Many of the APA rules from previous examples apply to the following sources.

Brochure or Pamphlet by a Corporate Author

Gilder Lehrman Institute of American History. (2008). *Abraham Lincoln:*

A man of his time, a man for all times [Brochure]. New York, NY: Author.

Note: List *Author* in place of the publisher if they are the same.

Motion Picture

Curling, C., & Meurer, J. (Producers), & Hoffman, M. (Director). (2010).

The last station [Motion picture]. United States: Sony Picture Classics.

Music Recording

Pearson, D., & Holden, G. (2012). Home [Recorded by P. Phillips]. On *The world*

from the side of the moon [MP3 file]. Santa Monica, CA: Interscope Records.

Swift, T. (2008). Love story. On *Fearless* [CD]. Nashville, TN: Big Machine Records.

Note: The in-text citation for this source would look like this: "Love Story" (Swift, 2008, track 3).

Painting

van Gogh, V. (1889). *Starry night* [Painting]. New York, NY: Museum

of Modern Art.

van Gogh, V. (1889). *Starry night* [Painting]. Retrieved from

http://www.vangoghgallery.com/painting/starryindex.html

Note: If you viewed the painting online instead of in the museum, use the second example to enable your readers to view it as well.

Personal Communications (E-Mail, Personal Interview, Phone Conversation)

Cite personal communications in the body of your paper, but not on your reference page. For example, A. Vining (personal communication, December 12, 2014) suggests that . . .

Television Episode in a Series

Meyer, G., et al. (Writers). (2012). Gone Abie gone [Television series episode].

In M. Groening & J. L. Brooks (Executive producers), *The Simpsons*.

Beverly Hills, CA: Fox Broadcasting.

APA Research Paper Formatting Guide

1. **Title Page:** Include the following information on your title page.

   a. **Running head:** This is a shortened version of your title (50 or fewer characters, including spaces), in all capital letters, at the upper-left corner of the page, about a half inch from the top edge and one inch from the left edge of the paper. The running head will appear on every page of your paper. The words *Running head* followed by a colon will appear on the first page of your paper but not on subsequent pages.

   b. **Page number:** Put this at the upper-right corner of the title page, about one half inch from the top and an inch from the right edge of the paper. The page number will appear on every page of your paper.

   c. **Title:** Center the full title of your paper about six lines below the running head. Your title should be descriptive and, if possible, creative. Avoid italicizing, underlining, or boldfacing your title or putting it in quotation marks. Use title case capitalization.

   d. **Your name:** Place your name, and any co-authors' names, double-spaced and centered below the title.

   e. **School:** Write your school name, double-spaced and centered below your name.

Note: Although not an official part of the APA format, your instructor may prefer for you to include his or her name and the due date as well. If so, include those on separate lines below the school name, double-spaced and centered on the page.

2. **Abstract:** The abstract is a brief (150- to 250-word) summary of your paper that will enable your readers to have an idea of what to expect in your paper. Center the word *Abstract* one inch down from the top of your paper. Avoid italicizing, underlining, or boldfacing the word or putting the word *Abstract* in quotation marks. Begin your abstract at the left one-inch margin, without indenting it. Your abstract should not be a copy of your introduction or conclusion.

3. **Text formatting:** Throughout the paper, use a 12-point font with a typeface that is easy to read (Times New Roman is preferred). Do not justify the right-hand margin of the text; the text should have a ragged (uneven) right margin. Center the title of your paper one inch from the top of the first page, but not on subsequent pages. Double-space the entire paper, and indent each paragraph one tab space, about five to seven spaces. Do not include an extra space between paragraphs. Include in-text citations to indicate where you have quoted, paraphrased, or summarized ideas from your sources. The APA format allows for headings. Ask your instructor if headings are preferred or not.

4. **Figures:** If you decide to include graphs, tables, charts, maps, drawings, or photographs with your paper, place them at the end of your paper, after the references page. Label them consecutively, beginning with Figure 1.

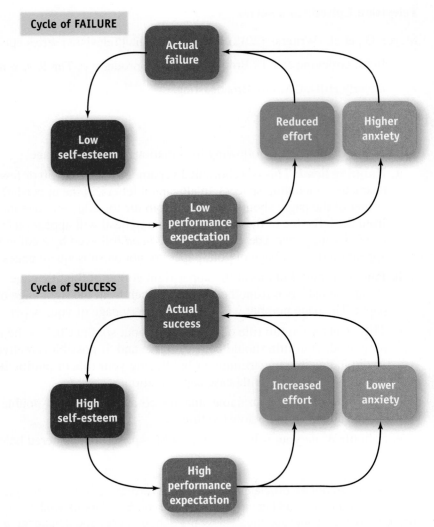

FIGURE 1. Chart comparing the cycle of failure to the cycle of success. Adapted from *Power learning* by R. S. Feldman, 2011, p. 75. Copyright 2011 by McGraw-Hill.

In the body of the paper, where you refer to the figure, write the following in parentheses: (see Figure 1). Include the label, a brief description, and the complete source information below the figure.

5. **References:** Your references page gives credit to your sources and provides your readers with a way to locate your sources. Continue with the running head and page number at the top of the page. Next, center and capitalize the word *References* about an inch from the top of the page. Avoid italicizing, underlining, or boldfacing the word *References* or putting it quotation marks. Alphabetize the list of references according to the author's last name or the word that begins the entry, not including words such as *a* or *the*. Use hanging indentation, which means that the first line of each entry begins at the left margin and the second and subsequent lines are indented one-half inch, about five to seven spaces. Double-space the entire page, without including extra spaces between each entry. Follow the precise APA guidelines for each entry.

6. **Appendixes:** If your instructor asks you to include any additional material, place it after the references page. This may include interview notes, visual aids, or survey data you collected that would be awkward or distracting to include in the body of your paper.

From Stigma to Status
by Margaret Rowland

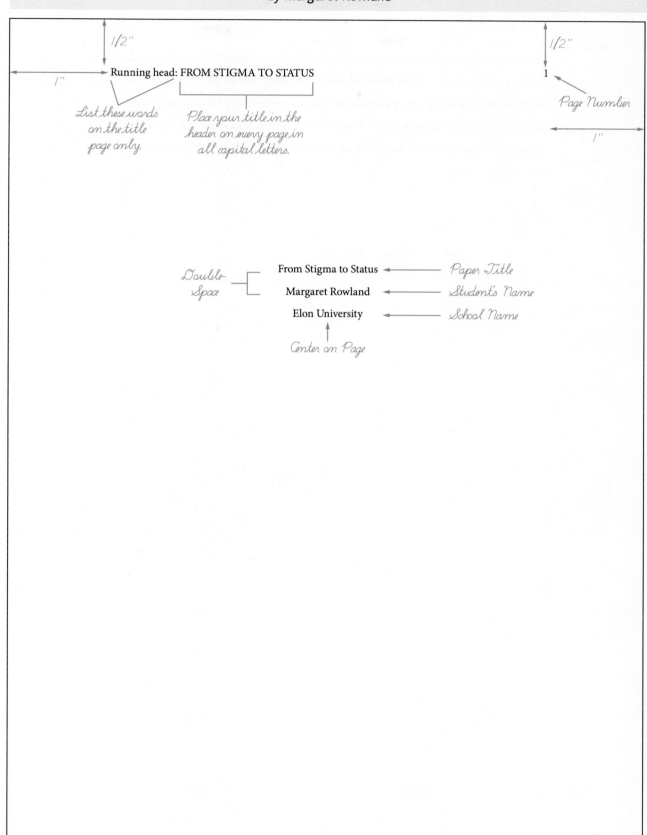

1/2"

Running head: FROM STIGMA TO STATUS

List these words on the title page only.

Place your title in the header on every page in all capital letters.

1/2"

1

Page Number

1"

1"

Double Space

From Stigma to Status ⟵ *Paper Title*

Margaret Rowland ⟵ *Student's Name*

Elon University ⟵ *School Name*

Center on Page

APA Format

APA Format
APA Format

1/2"

FROM STIGMA TO STATUS 2

1" Page Number

Center

Abstract

Double-Space

1"

Tattoos have become a popular form of expression in the United States. Originally, tattoos were common among sailors, military personnel, bikers, prostitutes, and jail-mates. Now, however, the use of tattoos is increasing among professionals and other people. Why has tattooing become such a phenomenon in the past decade? Many people feel that it is because people who get tattoos want to express their individuality, appeal to the opposite sex, or rebel against the expectations of society.

Double-Space

Ragged Right Margin

Left Justify

The abstract is a short overview of the paper.

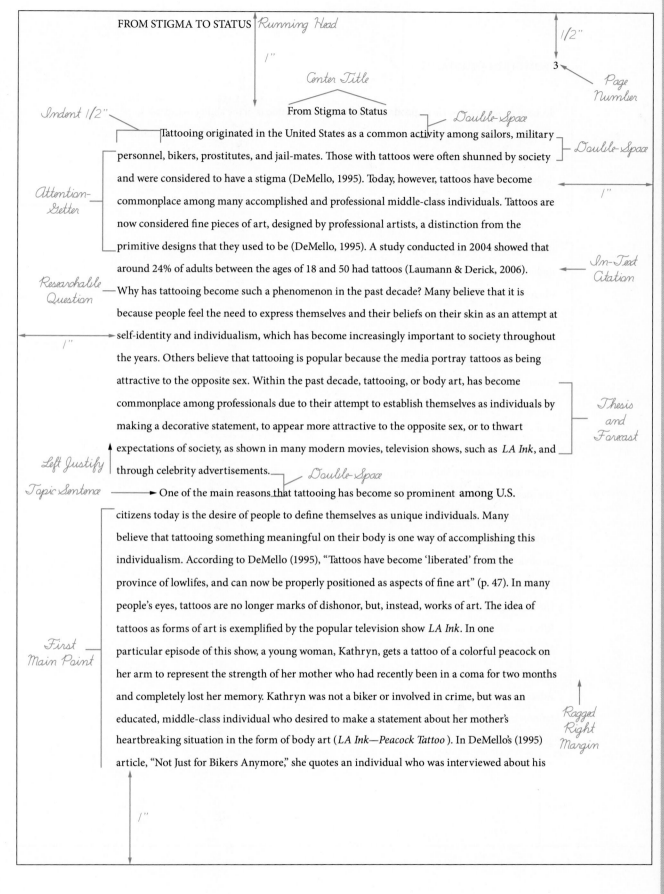

FROM STIGMA TO STATUS *Running Head*

1"

Center Title

1/2"

3 → *Page Number*

From Stigma to Status

Indent 1/2" — *Double-Space*

Tattooing originated in the United States as a common activity among sailors, military

personnel, bikers, prostitutes, and jail-mates. Those with tattoos were often shunned by society — *Double-Space*

1"

and were considered to have a stigma (DeMello, 1995). Today, however, tattoos have become

Attention-Getter

commonplace among many accomplished and professional middle-class individuals. Tattoos are

now considered fine pieces of art, designed by professional artists, a distinction from the

primitive designs that they used to be (DeMello, 1995). A study conducted in 2004 showed that

← *In-Text Citation*

around 24% of adults between the ages of 18 and 50 had tattoos (Laumann & Derick, 2006).

Researchable Question

Why has tattooing become such a phenomenon in the past decade? Many believe that it is

because people feel the need to express themselves and their beliefs on their skin as an attempt at

1" →

self-identity and individualism, which has become increasingly important to society throughout

the years. Others believe that tattooing is popular because the media portray tattoos as being

attractive to the opposite sex. Within the past decade, tattooing, or body art, has become

commonplace among professionals due to their attempt to establish themselves as individuals by

Thesis and Forecast

making a decorative statement, to appear more attractive to the opposite sex, or to thwart

expectations of society, as shown in many modern movies, television shows, such as *LA Ink*, and

Left Justify

through celebrity advertisements. — *Double-Space*

Topic Sentence →

One of the main reasons that tattooing has become so prominent among U.S.

citizens today is the desire of people to define themselves as unique individuals. Many

believe that tattooing something meaningful on their body is one way of accomplishing this

individualism. According to DeMello (1995), "Tattoos have become 'liberated' from the

province of lowlifes, and can now be properly positioned as aspects of fine art" (p. 47). In many

people's eyes, tattoos are no longer marks of dishonor, but, instead, works of art. The idea of

tattoos as forms of art is exemplified by the popular television show *LA Ink*. In one

particular episode of this show, a young woman, Kathryn, gets a tattoo of a colorful peacock on

First Main Point

her arm to represent the strength of her mother who had recently been in a coma for two months

and completely lost her memory. Kathryn was not a biker or involved in crime, but was an

Ragged Right Margin

educated, middle-class individual who desired to make a statement about her mother's

heartbreaking situation in the form of body art (*LA Ink—Peacock Tattoo*). In DeMello's (1995)

article, "Not Just for Bikers Anymore," she quotes an individual who was interviewed about his

1"

First Main Point Continued

decision to get a tattoo. He responded, "The power of the tattoo is in the ability to express individuality and in its permanence" (p. 41). Kathryn, from *LA Ink—Peacock Tattoo*, and this quoted individual share similar beliefs about tattoos and their meanings. Whether they are designed in memory of a loved one or to symbolize an important value or belief of the individual, tattoos are most commonly acquired for the purpose of making unique, decorative statements.

Second Main Point

Another fundamental motivation for people in this country to get tattoos is the belief that they create sex appeal. A study of college students found that "almost three-fourths of the undergraduate women reported that they 'sometimes' viewed openly visible tattoos as attractive when on a man" (Horne, Knox, Zusman, & Zusman, 2007, p. 1011). On the other hand, "58.8 percent of the undergraduate men viewed such visible tattoos as attractive when on a woman" (Horne et al., 2007, p. 1011). Therefore, men and women may get tattoos if they feel that it will add to their sex appeal. A large portion of this thinking has derived from the fact that many celebrities have tattoos, and, because celebrities are often seen as sex icons, common people believe that if they get tattoos then they will be appealing to the opposite sex as well (Horne et al., 2007, p. 1011). DeMello (1995) states, "Tattooing has moved from being a symbol of the outcast to that of a rock star, model, and postmodern youth, and with this shift in public perception has come a shift in meaning as well, as tattoo moves from stigma to status" (p. 49). The idea that tattoos are sexy is exemplified in many modern movies, including *Wanted*. The most famous scene of this movie depicts Angelina Jolie getting out of a bathtub, completely naked, with large tattoos covering her back. Jolie seductively peers around her shoulder at the camera, an obvious attempt of the director to attract men with her tattoo-covered body (Silvestri & Bekmambetov, 2008). Since the premier of the movie, this scene has become extremely famous. However, Jolie is not the only celebrity to endorse tattoos. Others, including David Beckham, Rihanna, Michael Jordan, and Gisele, have been pictured in advertisements that show off or or endorse tattoos. In his ad for Emporio Armani, Beckham poses in underwear, revealing his muscular body and a large tattoo on his right arm (Emporio Armani Underwear, 2009). Advertisements and movies like these, which depict extremely attractive celebrities with revealed tattoos, contribute in a major way to the idea that tattoos are sexy. For this reason, many people get tattoos in order to make themselves more attractive to the opposite sex.

Topic Sentence → The final reason for individuals to get tattoos so frequently today is their desire to stray from the norms of society. Often people feel that society dictates what they should look like and how they should act. In response, they feel the need to rebel against idea of being a perfect, cookie-cutter citizen and believe that getting unique tattoos will help them do so. Another individual quoted in DeMello's (1995) article stated that he got a tattoo to "go against what people want you to do. All of your life you're computerized to do what people want you to do" (p. 41). Therefore, some people desire a release from the constraints that they feel society puts on them, and they achieve this release by getting a tattoo. This idea of rebellion as a reason for body art is clearly represented in the televison show *One Tree Hill*. In episode nine of season one, "With Arms Outstretched," Lucas gets an impulsive tattoo of a Chinese symbol on his upper arm. At the time, his mother is out of town, and he is looking for a way to act out against authority in a rebellious way (Schwan & Prange, 2003). As the episode suggests, some people get tattoos as an attempt to resist authority. This reason for getting a tattoo, however, is more common among males than females. Horne et al. (2007) found that almost half of the male sample set agreed with the statement "tattoos are symbols of our resistance to culture" (p. 1011). This differs from the 31.5% of women who agree with the statement (Horne et al., 2007). As a result, people often get tattoos as an attempt to rebel against the person that society and authority tells them they should be. However, males are more likely to cite this reason than females, who more often get tattoos to contribute to their attractiveness or to make a decorative statement.

Tattoos are no longer only for bikers, sailors, convicts, and prostitutes, but have risen in status and are now decorating the bodies of a quarter of the nation. These people include middle-class professionals holding jobs as lawyers, bankers, doctors, and other high-profile career positions (DeMello, 1995, p. 40). Individuals get tattoos so often today for three main reasons: to make a statement by defining their individuality, to make themselves more appealing to the opposite sex, or to stray from the norms of society in the United States. These reasons are extremely visible in entertainment and in the media, for they are represented in modern television shows, movies, and celebrity advertisements. These outlets illustrate that the media and entertainment have a major impact on the way some Americans think and act. If television shows did not endorse the idea of getting tattoos, would people get them? If celebrities

Summary of Main Points Continued did not have tattoos all over their bodies, would people put tattoos all over their bodies? The answer is most likely no. Essentially, tattoos are just another fashion trend. Just as different forms of fashion are depicted in celebrity advertisements and used as costumes in movies and television shows, so are tattoos. The real question is, will the popularity of tattooing eventually *Memorable Ending* die like most other fashion trends, leaving those who have them to regret their tattoos for the rest of their lives? Only time will tell.

$1"$

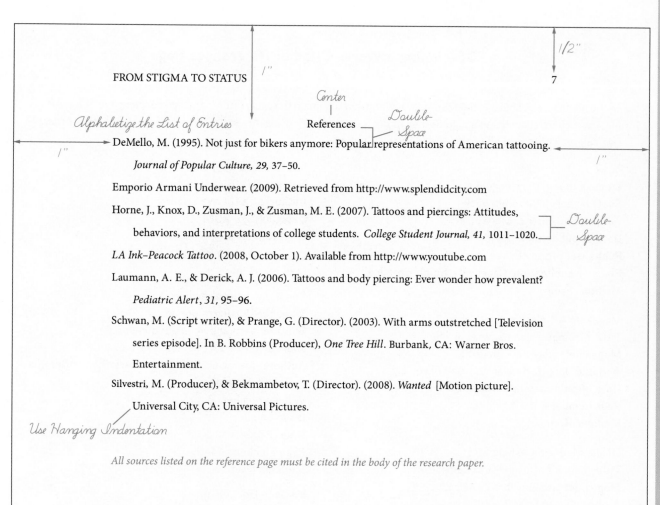

FROM STIGMA TO STATUS   1"

1/2"
7

Alphabetize the List of Entries   Center
|
References   *Double-*
Space

DeMello, M. (1995). Not just for bikers anymore: Popular representations of American tattooing.

Journal of Popular Culture, 29, 37–50.

Emporio Armani Underwear. (2009). Retrieved from http://www.splendidcity.com

Horne, J., Knox, D., Zusman, J., & Zusman, M. E. (2007). Tattoos and piercings: Attitudes,   *Double-*
                                                                                                Space
behaviors, and interpretations of college students. College Student Journal, 41, 1011–1020.

LA Ink–Peacock Tattoo. (2008, October 1). Available from http://www.youtube.com

Laumann, A. E., & Derick, A. J. (2006). Tattoos and body piercing: Ever wonder how prevalent?

Pediatric Alert, 31, 95–96.

Schwan, M. (Script writer), & Prange, G. (Director). (2003). With arms outstretched [Television

series episode]. In B. Robbins (Producer), One Tree Hill. Burbank, CA: Warner Bros.

Entertainment.

Silvestri, M. (Producer), & Bekmambetov, T. (Director). (2008). Wanted [Motion picture].

Universal City, CA: Universal Pictures.

Use Hanging Indentation

All sources listed on the reference page must be cited in the body of the research paper.

[QUESTIONS FOR REFLECTION]

1. Based on the introductory paragraph, what three main points does Rowland promise to cover in the body of her paper? Does she follow through with her promise?

2. What supporting details and examples does she offer for her first main point? Are they sufficient? Why or why not?

3. What supporting details does Rowland offer for her second main point? Which details are the most convincing? Why?

4. Which ideas from the author's third body paragraph are most memorable? Why?

5. What is Rowland's thesis? Do you think she fully supports her thesis in the body of the paper? Why or why not?

Using the six fictitious sources below, create a works-cited page in the MLA format or a references page in the APA format. Be sure to follow the exact guidelines of the format you are using. Arrange your entries in alphabetical order.

Tip: You may not need all of the information provided.

Book
Title: all that glitters is gold
Subtitle: earning the big bucks
Author: Showmei Z. Money
Date of publication: 2015
Publisher: Greedy Green Publishing Company, Inc.
Place of publication: Greenville, South Carolina
Medium: Print

Magazine Article
Title: a computer can save your life
Magazine: today's computers
Authors: Joey T. Hacker and Betty Lynn Byte
Date of publication: October 2010
Page numbers: 10, 11, and 16
Medium: Print

Online Magazine Article
Title: justice for juveniles in Jamestown
Magazine: crimesolversareus.com
Author: Jamal J. Jolly
Date of publication: August 19, 2014
Page numbers: None
URL: www.crimesolversareus.com/juvenilesingreenville
DOI: 10.1234/0011-2233.45.6.789
Retrieval Date: January 14, 2015
Medium: Internet

Newspaper Article
Title: stray alligator terrorizes shopping mall
Subtitle: two shoppers injured
Newspaper: trivia tribune
Author: Liza L. Love-Lizzard
Date: July 27, 2014
Page Numbers: 4, 5, and 8
Section number: B
Medium: Print

Scholarly Journal Article
Title: best business practices
Subtitle: earn and keep good customers
Journal: universal business journal
Authors: Kiefer G. Consumer, Mario López Servicio, Fahad Al-Safar
Volume number: 6
Issue number: 3
Date: 2013
Page numbers: 14–15
Medium: Print

Website Document
Title: a healthier you
Subtitle: living life to the fullest
Author: Elsie B. Eatwell
Website: Living Well
Date of publication: April 23, 2013
Retrieval Date: March 25, 2015
Page number: none
URL: www.livingwell.org/ebeatwell/livinglife
Medium: Internet

PEER REVIEW QUESTIONS FOR A RESEARCH PAPER

1. Identify the thesis statement in the introduction. Is it clear and effective? Why or why not?
2. What are the author's main points? Are they fully developed? Explain.
3. What is your favorite part of the research paper?
4. Are any areas confusing? Explain.
5. Does the paper flow well? Which parts, if any, could be smoother?
6. Is the concluding paragraph effective? Why or why not?
7. What kinds of grammatical errors, if any, are evident in the research paper?
8. Are all sources clearly and properly documented in the text and on the works-cited or references page? Identify any areas that need attention.
9. What final suggestions do you have for the author?

SmartBook Tip

During the "Recharge" phase, students can return to Chapter 14 and practice concepts that they need to work on.

WRITER'S CHECKLIST FOR A RESEARCH PAPER

Use the checklist below to evaluate your own writing and help ensure that your research paper is effective. If you have any "no" answers, continue work on those areas as needed.

❑ 1. Does my introduction clearly state my thesis and give the reader an indication of the direction my essay will take?

❑ 2. Are my topic sentences and body paragraphs clear and well developed?

❑ 3. Have I fully supported my thesis with ample supporting details and examples?

❑ 4. Have I used a sufficient number and variety of sources in my paper?

❑ 5. Are all of my sources properly cited in the body of my paper according to the MLA or APA format?

❑ 6. Does my conclusion effectively summarize my main points and restate my thesis in different words?

❑ 7. Have I carefully proofread and revised my paper for sentence variety, word choice, grammar, and punctuation?

❑ 8. Does my works-cited or references page include every source I cited in the text, and is it in the correct format?

❑ 9. Have I used the correct margins, line spacing, and other format issues required by my instructor and the MLA or APA guidelines?

[CHAPTER SUMMARY]

1. Avoid plagiarism by clearly citing sources you use in a research paper.

2. Follow the specific guidelines of the format your instructor requires you to use, such as MLA or APA.

3. Cite sources within your text and on a works-cited page (MLA format) or on a references page (APA format).

4. Use the correct MLA or APA format for your entire research paper.

[WHAT I KNOW NOW]

Use this checklist to determine what you need to work on in order to feel comfortable with your understanding of the material in this chapter. Check off each item as you master it. Review the material for any unchecked items.

❑ 1. I know what **plagiarism** is and understand how to avoid it.

❑ 2. I understand what **sources** I need to cite in a research paper.

❑ 3. I know that I need to cite sources in the body of my paper as well as on a **works-cited** or **references page.**

❑ 4. I know how to use this textbook to cite sources using the **MLA** or **APA** format.

❑ 5. I know how to **format a paper** using the MLA or APA guidelines.

CHAPTER 15

GIVING AN ORAL PRESENTATION

15.1 PLANNING AN ORAL PRESENTATION

Does the idea of giving an oral presentation make you nervous? You're not alone! Some people fear public speaking more than spiders, snakes, or even death. Fortunately, with careful planning and practice, you can become more confident and effective at giving oral presentations. This chapter is not designed to be a complete guide to public speaking. Your school may require that you take a separate speech communications course and read an entire textbook devoted to delivering speeches. This chapter, however, will give you a brief introduction to giving a research paper presentation in your writing class (or another class) in case you haven't taken a speech class yet. If you have already taken a public speaking class, this chapter will serve as a quick refresher.

You will have many opportunities to give presentations at school, on the job, and in your personal life. Many instructors require students to give presentations based on course material or papers they have written. At work you may need to give a presentation to supervisors, colleagues, clients, customers, or patients. Or you may need to say a few words to friends or family members at a special occasion or event, such as a wedding or a reunion. Regardless of what type of speaking engagement you may face, you will benefit from preparing what to say and do ahead of time. Planning a speech is very similar to writing an essay. For both you will need to have an introduction, a body, and a conclusion.

SmartBook Tip

Students receive an overview of the learning outcomes and topics in Chapter 15 in the "Preview" phase of SmartBook.

Developing the Introduction

Similar to your research essay, the introduction of your speech should do three things: capture your audience's attention, state the thesis, and give a forecast of your main points.

1. **Gain the audience's attention.** The fact that you have an audience assembled in front of you doesn't guarantee that they will actually listen to you. Try beginning with a thought-provoking question, a relevant quote, a brief story or description, a shocking statistic, a surprising statement, or a comparison to help hook your listeners. For example, you might begin a presentation explaining how to budget money with the

Teaching Tip

Have students work in pairs or small groups to practice delivering attention-getters.

question, "Have you ever wished you had more money to spend?" Your goal is to entice your listeners to want to hear what you have to say.

2. **State the thesis.** For a presentation based on your research paper, you may choose to use the exact thesis from your paper. Be sure your thesis covers the topic you are addressing as well as your overall opinion about it and that it isn't too wordy for your audience to remember. For example, the thesis might be, "If you effectively plan for your financial future now, you will reap the benefits for a lifetime." Memorize your thesis statement so that you can look right at your audience when you state it.

3. **Give a forecast of the main points.** Provide your listeners with a preview of what they should get from your presentation. For instance, you might say, "There are three steps you can take to reduce your debt and improve your financial prospects. These three steps are . . ." Being clear about the main points will also help your audience members to take notes if they need to. If you are using a research paper as the basis for your presentation, you can go through your paper and determine which points will be most interesting and relevant to the group. You may choose not to include every main point from your paper.

Developing the Body

In the body of your presentation, you want to give the audience what you promised in your forecast. Although you probably will not want to write out your main points word for word, you will need to decide exactly what you will cover in your presentation. Use an outline or note cards to help you keep track of ideas you want to emphasize in your speech.

1. **Emphasize the main points.** Cover your points in a logical order. Give relevant details and examples to help you support your main ideas. If your presentation is based on a research paper, you do not need to include every example from your paper. Choose the ones your audience will find most interesting and useful. You can use the same strategies you learned about in Chapters 5–12 to organize your speech (see Table 15.1). Depending on your subject, you may focus on one particular strategy or combine two or more strategies to get your point across to your audience.

2. **Make transitions smoothly.** Determine your transitions ahead of time so that you don't forget to use them during your presentation. As you move from one point to another, use a transition to signal the change to the listeners. For example, you might use the transitions *first, second, third,* and *last* to help your audience keep track of your main points.

Suze Orman

3. **Cite sources.** If you use words or ideas from an outside source, you need to mention the source to give appropriate credit to the originator of the material. For example, you might say, "According to Suze Orman, a financial expert who has her own television show, people need to spend below their means to get ahead financially." Omitting citations in a speech is just as unethical as leaving them out of a research paper. Work on incorporating your citations smoothly so that they don't interfere with the flow of your presentation.

Developing the Conclusion

The conclusion of your speech serves the same purpose as the conclusion to an essay. You want to restate your main points and leave your audience with a lasting impression. Keep the conclusion short and interesting.

TABLE 15.1

Organizational Strategies	
Narrating	Tell a story about something that happened. Usually you will present the details of the event in chronological order, but occasionally a flashback can be useful. Be sure to cover who, what, where, when, why, and how.
Describing	Use words to paint a picture of an object, scene, or event for your audience, appealing to as many senses as are appropriate for your subject: sight, sound, taste, smell. Include many colorful adjectives to give your listeners a clear impression of your subject.
Explaining a Process	Tell how something works or what something does. You may give step-by-step instructions so your listeners can perform the task or write an explanation so that your listeners are able to understand your subject.
Comparing and Contrasting	Show how two people, places, or objects are similar and/or different. Be sure to make a worthwhile point while doing this.
Explaining Causes and Effects	Examine how one event or situation caused another to occur, or determine the effects of an event or situation. Be careful to apply sound logic as you analyze causes and effects.
Persuading	Take a stand about an important or controversial issue, and convince your audience that your position is valid. Use research to support your main idea.
Evaluating	Make a judgment about your subject by determining how well it meets specific criteria that you feel are important for that subject.
Solving a Problem	Explain a problem to your audience and offer several solutions. You may evaluate each possible solution before persuading your listeners that one specific solution is best.

1. **Restate the thesis.** Remind your listeners of your thesis by restating it using slightly different words than the ones you used in the introduction.

2. **Summarize the main points.** Mention your main points again, but do not restate your specific details and examples. You might say something like, "Remember, the three steps for becoming more financially secure are . . ."

3. **End with a memorable statement.** Leave your audience with a final vivid thought. You might tell a brief story that relates to your topic or suggest a call to action. Another option is to end with a quote that fits with your overall purpose.

4. **Say thank you.** Saying "thank you" at the end of your presentation is courteous, and it provides a definite signal to your audience that your speech is over. Your listeners will know when it is time to clap and ask questions, if appropriate.

5. **Answer questions.** If you are in a situation where the audience will have an opportunity to ask you questions after your presentation, then you will need to be prepared. Try to anticipate the types of questions your listeners might have. Have your notes handy in case they might be helpful. It's

all right if you don't know every answer. Be honest and say, "I'm not sure. I didn't research that particular area." Or you might answer, "That's a good question; I'll have to get back to you on that." Don't fake it.

Graduate SPOTLIGHT

Frank Ragozino, Medical Assistant

Frank Ragozino has an AS degree in medical assisting and is the lead medical assistant for a family practice medical center. Here's what Ragozino has to say about the importance of communication in his career:

At the medical center where I work, having good oral and written communication skills is second only to patient care. Every day I talk to patients to learn about their conditions, symptoms, allergens, and so on. I have to listen very carefully to what they say so that I can communicate the information to the doctors and meet the patients' needs. I also have to be able to explain to a patient how to use an inhaler or glucometer or how to give an insulin injection. Additionally, as the lead medical assistant I am responsible for training new employees and student interns and explaining all of the aspects of becoming a medical assistant. Writing is another important skill I use while on the job. I have to carefully document everything that takes place when I see a patient. I have to use a lot of detail when writing on a patient's chart. This is important not only for the patient's health but also for the liability of the medical center. In my career, being able to communicate effectively orally and in writing is critical to the well-being of the patients.

15.2 CHOOSING VISUAL AIDS

Visual aids can be a true asset to any presentation. Choose your visual aids carefully. Make sure that each one enhances your speech without overshadowing it. Keep your audience in mind as you decide which visual aids are most appropriate for your presentation.

Objects or Models

Sometimes a three-dimensional object or model can be an effective visual aid. Make sure it is large enough for the audience to see, but not so large that it would be difficult to bring to your presentation. For example, if you were giving a presentation about techniques used in sailing, a sailboat would obviously be too large for the room; however, a 1/18-scale model would be appropriate.

Posters

You may find a poster board to be a useful visual aid for your presentation. You can use it to display photographs, drawings, maps, charts, graphs, timelines, or fairly small three-dimensional items. You may hold up the poster for your audience to see, hang it on the wall, or place it on an easel. Make sure your poster looks neat and professional and that your audience will be able to see it.

Flip Charts or Whiteboards

Writing words or drawing simple figures on a whiteboard or flip chart can be useful during your presentation, especially if you are soliciting responses from your audience. Be sure to write large enough so that everyone can see it. This method is appropriate only for small amounts of information. If the room is equipped with a smart board, use that instead of a whiteboard because the images projected on the wall will be larger and easier to see than what you put on a whiteboard or chalkboard. Face your listeners as much as possible as you are writing or drawing.

Media Presentations

Developing a media presentation using PowerPoint, Keynote, Lotus, Adobe, or another software application can help you to give a smooth speech if you use it correctly. Be careful to include a reasonable number of words on each slide. Write short sentences or phrases on each slide, and elaborate on them during your speech. Avoid making your slides too busy. Combining too many colors and styles may be distracting for your audience. (See Figures 15.1 and 15.2.)

You may want to incorporate artwork into some of your slides. Choose images that relate to your topic and enhance your presentation. Also, choose transitions that are interesting but not overdone. You don't want to make your audience dizzy with too many spinning or bouncing objects and words. Sound clips, movie clips, and other features can add a little pizzazz to your presentation as well. If you are creating a media presentation for an online class, you will probably want to design it to play automatically, so that your viewers don't have to click from slide to slide. Follow your instructor's guidelines for media presentations.

Teaching Tip

Have students do a peer review of each other's slides using the criteria in Figures 15.1 and 15.2 before the presentation is due.

Too Much for One Slide

This slide has too many details. Because too many ideas have been included, the words are so small that some of the audience members will have trouble seeing them, especially if they are near the back of the room. **Another problem with this slide is that it uses too many different colors and styles.** AVOID MAKING EVERY SENTENCE A DIFFERENT COLOR. USING ONE COLOR OR ALTERNATING BETWEEN TWO WORKS MUCH BETTER. Furthermore, the main points all run together without any bullets or spaces between ideas. This slide would work better if just key ideas were included rather than a complete paragraph. See the next slide for a better example.

FIGURE 15.1
Inappropriate Slide

Teaching Tip

Show the students an example of a good media presentation developed by a student in a previous class (with the student's permission, of course).

FIGURE 15.2
Appropriate Slide

Video Clips

Depending on the type of presentation you are giving, you might find it useful to show a short video clip that relates to your topic. For instance, if your presentation is on scuba diving, you might show a one- or two-minute clip of an underwater coral reef with divers and interesting marine life moving about. Similarly, if the point of your presentation is to give a review of a book you have read, you might show a brief YouTube or movie clip of a critical scene from the book that relates to one of your key points. Be sure to have the clip ready so that you can show the right scene on demand. If you are using a videotape or DVD, then pause the scene so that you can just hit the play button when you are ready to show the clip.

Handouts

A handout may serve as an appropriate visual aid for your presentation, especially as a backup in case you have a technical problem with a media presentation. If you decide to create a handout for your audience, consider giving it out after rather than during your presentation. You don't want to unintentionally lose your listeners by diverting their attention elsewhere. Handouts should look professional and be visually appealing. Be sure to proofread them carefully for content and grammar.

15.3 DELIVERING AN ORAL PRESENTATION

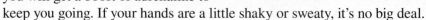

1. **Get psyched.** Pump yourself up on the day of the presentation. Focus on positive thoughts. Visualize yourself giving a great presentation. Being a little nervous is fine and even desired because you will get a boost of adrenaline to keep you going. If your hands are a little shaky or sweaty, it's no big deal.

You are probably the only person who will notice. Just before you get up before the audience, take a deep breath and try to relax. Look out at your audience and smile. Look at someone who smiles back as you begin your presentation.

2. **Use an outline or note cards.** You will probably be able to use an outline or 3-by-5-inch note cards to help guide you through the presentation. Avoid writing out your entire speech word for word. Instead, use an outline or note cards to help you keep track of the main points you want to cover. Include any quotes, statistics, and sources you want to mention so that you will give the correct information to your audience. Be careful not to rely on these tools too heavily. Spend more time looking at your listeners than at your notes.

STUDENT OUTLINE

Texting While Driving
by Anita Jitta

Speech Goal: To inform my audience about the dangers of texting while driving.

Introduction

Hook: On November 2, 2009, my husband, Anthony, was driving home when a teenaged girl slammed into him with her car. What was she doing? She was texting while driving. Luckily enough, another driver saw what this girl was doing and decided to wait at the scene of the accident to be a witness when the police arrived. The teenager ended up receiving a citation for reckless driving, but the results could have been much worse, even deadly.

  Thesis: Texting while driving is extremely dangerous and can lead to devastating consequences.

  Preview: First, you will learn what happens when you text while driving. Second, you will learn how people feel about texting while driving. Finally, you will learn about what some famous people are doing to try to prevent drivers from texting while driving.

Body

  I. What can happen when someone text messages and drives? According to the Text Free Driving Organization, "57% of American drivers admit to texting behind the wheel."

  II. How do people feel about texting and driving? The 2009 AAA survey brought about some interesting responses.

  III. Who is against texting and driving, and what do they plan to do about it? President Obama and Oprah Winfrey are trying to change the legislation to help tackle this problem.

Sources

Bruno, Laura. (June 12, 2007). "Stop Text Messaging, Drivers Urged." *USA Today.* Retrieved from **www.usatoday.com**.

Cooney, Michael. (November 4, 2009). "FCC and DOT Team-Up, Want High-Tech Cure for Distracted Driving." *Networkworld.* Retrieved from **www.infoworld.com**.

Jaimungal, Anthony. (February 10, 2010). Personal interview.

Richtell, Matt. (October 2, 2009). "Texting While Driving Banned for Federal Staff." *The New York Times,* B3.

Schulte, Bret. (February 11, 2008). "Outlawing Text Messaging While Driving: Legislatures in Several States Respond to Safety Concerns." *US News and World Report.* Retrieved from **www.usnews.com**.

Text Free Driving Organization. (No date). Retrieved from **http://textfreedriving.org**.

Traffic Safety Culture. (September 25, 2009). "Disctracted Driving—Time to Start Addressing the Problem." Retrieved from **http://trafficsafetyculture.blogspot.com**.

Note: The sources listed in the above outline are not listed in a particular format. Your instructor may request that you list your sources in the MLA or APA format. If so, please see Chapter 14 for the exact guidelines.

3. **Speak clearly and enthusiastically.** If you are excited about your topic, your audience will be too. Vary your pitch and tone to emphasize important words and keep your listeners interested. Enunciate your words carefully so that your audience can hear each word. Also, make sure your pace is appropriate. Speaking too slowly will give your audience too much time to think about other things. However, if you speak too rapidly, your listeners might not catch everything and get frustrated.

4. **Communicate nonverbally.** In addition to listening to what you have to say, your audience will be paying attention to the nonverbal cues you display. Your clothing, poise, posture, movements, hand gestures, facial expressions, and eye contact all affect the message you are attempting to convey to your audience. You want to communicate an attitude of professionalism and confidence as you give your presentation. If you make a mistake or forget something, don't apologize or stop. Just pick up where you left off and keep going.

5. **Incorporate visual aids.** Decide ahead of time exactly when and how you will show your visual aids to enhance your presentation. Generally, you should display each visual aid only when you are talking about it. As you show each item, hold it up and away from your body so that everyone in your audience can see it. Avoid passing visual aids around the room. You might even walk around the room so everyone can get a closer look. If you are using a PowerPoint or Keynote presentation, talk about each slide as you show it to your audience. Don't read your presentation from the slides. Instead, use the keywords on the slide to help you remember what to say.

6. **Have a backup plan.** As you are well aware, things don't always go as they are planned. What happens if the projector doesn't work the day of your presentation? What will you do if the computer freezes? Have a secondary plan. Bring additional materials with you to ensure that you are able to give an effective presentation even if you experience a technological glitch. For example, write out some note cards in case your PowerPoint or Keynote presentation won't work.

7. **Practice your presentation.** Before the big day, practice delivering your presentation several times. If you can, assemble a small audience to simulate the experience as closely as possible. If no one is around, stand in front of a mirror. Explore different methods for using your visual aids, note cards, hand gestures, and so on to see what feels most comfortable and seems to work best. You may even want to videotape or digitally record your presentation so that you can watch and critique yourself. Make adjustments as needed to smooth out your presentation. Also, time yourself to ensure that your presentation falls within the time requirements.

ESOL Tip >

Practice your speech for a native English speaker to ensure that your listeners will understand everything you say. For example, some non-native speakers pronounce *i*'s as *e*'s.

PRESENTER'S CHECKLIST

Use this checklist before you give your presentation to make sure that you are ready. Keep working on any items that don't yet earn a "yes."

- ❏ 1. Are my outline and note cards ready?
- ❏ 2. Are my thesis and main points clear and well organized?
- ❏ 3. Do I have the right number of details and examples to support my main points fully?
- ❏ 4. Have I planned how to make transitions from one point to the next?
- ❏ 5. Are my visual aids useful and appropriate for the audience?
- ❏ 6. Do I have a backup plan in case something goes wrong?
- ❏ 7. Am I ready to give an enthusiastic presentation?
- ❏ 8. Have I practiced my presentation several times?

Comments:

OBSERVER'S CHECKLIST

Use this checklist to evaluate someone else's oral presentation.

- ❏ 1. Were the thesis and main points clear?
- ❏ 2. Was the organization of the presentation effective?
- ❏ 3. Did the presentation flow well?
- ❏ 4. Was the speaker enthusiastic?
- ❏ 5. Were the visual aids useful and handled well?
- ❏ 6. Did the presenter speak clearly and effectively?
- ❏ 7. Did the speaker look at the audience?
- ❏ 8. Were the presenter's posture and movements effective?
- ❏ 9. What suggestions do I have for the speaker?
- ❏ 10. What was the best part of the presentation?

Evaluating a Presentation
Activity:

Answers will vary.

Comments:

▶ *Activity*   **Evaluating a Presentation**

Go to **YouTube.com** and find Dr. Martin Luther King's "I Have a Dream" speech. Watch King's speech and evaluate it according to the observer's checklist. Write at least one paragraph explaining what was most memorable or inspiring about his famous speech. You may be asked to share your reaction in groups or with the class.

Note: Another famous speech could be used as an alternative. Additionally, **YouTube.com** has numerous student speeches to evaluate.

Using the ideas from a research paper you have written, plan and deliver an oral presentation.

1. Use your paper to develop an outline or note cards for your presentation.
2. Organize the introduction, body, and conclusion of your presentation.
3. Keep track of your sources so you can cite them as needed.
4. Prepare appropriate visual aids for your presentation.
5. Be ready to answer questions from your listeners.
6. Pay attention to your nonverbal communication and time constraints as you practice delivering your presentation.
7. Relax—this is not a life-or-death situation!
8. Deliver your presentation.

15.4 GROUP PRESENTATIONS

Oral Research Presentation
Activity

Answers will vary.

You will have many opportunities to participate in group presentations in school and at work. One of the benefits of working with others is that you gain the perspective of all of the participants. Follow these steps to ensure that your group presentation goes smoothly.

1. **Establish goals.** Everyone in the group needs to understand what the goals are and be willing to help achieve those goals. Keep your overall purpose in mind as well as the effect you want to have on the audience. The goals you develop need to be reasonable. You may want to set benchmarks for accomplishing specific tasks to ensure that you prepare an effective presentation and meet your deadline.

2. **Assign roles.** Each member of the group needs to have a particular role. For example, if your group has five members, then each person might take one of the following roles: leader, note taker, researcher, encourager, and harmonizer. The roles of the group members will vary based on the parameters of the assignment. The group members will also need to determine who is responsible for each task that needs to be completed before the presentation. While many details can be worked out together, each member may need to work on certain parts of the presentation away from the group.

3. **Participate in group meetings.** If you do not have an opportunity to meet with your group members during class, then you will need to establish meeting times. Find a time that works best for everyone in the group. If face-to-face meetings are impossible or inconvenient, then have virtual meetings via e-mail, teleconferencing, videoconferencing, or online threaded discussions. Everyone needs to cooperate in the meetings and contribute ideas for the presentation.

4. **Organize the group presentation.** Work as a team to organize the introduction, body, and conclusion of the presentation. Decide what each person will say and/or do during the presentation. Listen to everyone's ideas and be open to suggestions.

If the group has trouble agreeing on a particular issue, then the group members can go with majority rule or work to come to a consensus. Be willing to compromise for the sake of helping the group to accomplish its goals.

5. **Practice the group presentation.** Practice your presentation before giving it. Have a dress rehearsal complete with visual aids to make sure that everyone and everything is ready. Make sure your presentation flows smoothly and that everyone knows his or her part.

6. **Deliver the group presentation.** On the day of the presentation, everyone should show up prepared to do his or her part. If someone doesn't make it, then the other members need to step in and fulfill that person's duties. The group members need to show enthusiasm, communicate nonverbally, and incorporate visual aids smoothly during the presentation. If someone makes a mistake or forgets something, keep going as if everything is fine.

Group Presentation Activity:
Answers will vary.

▶ *Activity*   Group Presentation: Sales Pitch

In groups of three to six, invent a realistic or futuristic product or service that you would love to see on the market. For example, maybe you would like to offer a vacation package to Pluto. How will your customers get there? What will they do for fun and relaxation once they arrive? Why is this vacation worth taking? Or maybe you would prefer to present a new product that will wow your audience, such as a robot that will clean your home from top to bottom while you are away or a chocolate bar that helps you to remember important concepts on test day.

Work cooperatively to develop a mini-infomercial to present to your live class or a magazine advertisement to present to your online class. Every member in the group needs to participate in the preparation and presentation of your sales pitch. For this one assignment only, you may invent the supporting details. Use the following guidelines for your sales pitch:

1. Grab your audience's attention with a catchy opening.

2. Describe the product or service and emphasize the benefits it will have to the consumer. You want audience members to be interested in your product or service so that they want to buy it.

3. Create testimonials, statistics, or other data to promote your product or service and convince your audience that your product or service is worth buying.

4. Display appropriate visual aids to enhance your presentation.

5. Let your audience members know how much your product or service costs and what they need to do to get it. Do they need to call a 1-800 number, visit your store, or go online?

6. You might mention any disclaimers or side effects that the product or service may cause the consumer.

Note: Making up the data is appropriate only as an exercise. You should never invent support for a product or service that you are really selling because it is unethical.

[CHAPTER SUMMARY]

1. If you plan carefully, you can become more confident and effective at giving oral presentations.

2. Organize your presentation with a clear introduction, body, and conclusion.

3. Carefully design your visual aids, such as objects, models, posters, flip charts, whiteboards, media presentations, video clips, and handouts, to enhance your presentation.

4. When you deliver an oral presentation, think positive thoughts, use an outline or notes, speak clearly and enthusiastically, communicate nonverbally, and incorporate visual aids smoothly.

5. Always have a backup plan in case your equipment fails during your presentation.

6. Practice, practice, practice your presentation before delivering it.

7. When planning to deliver a group presentation, establish goals, assign roles, work cooperatively, and organize the presentation effectively.

[WHAT I KNOW NOW]

Use this checklist to determine what you need to work on to feel comfortable with your understanding of the material in this chapter. Check off each item as you master it. Review the material for any unchecked items.

❏ 1. I know how to plan and develop the **introduction, body, and conclusion** of an oral presentation.

❏ 2. I can choose and **prepare visual aids** for an oral presentation.

❏ 3. I understand how to deliver an oral presentation using an **outline or note cards.**

❏ 4. I can plan and deliver an effective **group presentation.**

SmartBook Tip

During the "Recharge" phase, students can return to Chapter 15 and practice concepts that they need to work on.

PART 4

Editing Guide

While you may not need to worry about style, grammar, punctuation, and mechanics when you send a text message to a friend or write a note to yourself or a loved one, most academic and career-related writing occasions require that you follow the conventions of standard American English. When you write a report for your instructor or boss, a letter to a client or patient, or an e-mail to a co-worker, you need to take a few minutes to edit it carefully before you submit or send it.

Others will judge you on how well you write. If your document is filled with errors, the recipients will question your credibility and the content of your message. As you edit your documents, pay particular attention to your sentence structure, word choice, grammar, punctuation, mechanics, and spelling. Being adept at following the conventions of the English language will help you to communicate your message clearly to your audience and achieve success in your personal, academic, and professional life.

This guide is designed to make it easy for you to find answers to questions you may have about proper sentence structure and diction. It will help you edit your writings for grammar, punctuation, mechanics, and spelling. Activities are included throughout to help with comprehension.

OVERVIEW of Part 4

A. EDITING SENTENCES

Fragments

Most academic and professional writing situations require that you write in complete sentences. A complete sentence must contain a subject and a verb and express a complete thought. A **sentence fragment** is a group of words that cannot stand on its own because it is lacking one or more of the elements of a complete sentence. Often you can correct a sentence fragment by adding a subject or verb or by connecting it to another sentence.

FRAGMENT:	Is fun and relaxing.
REVISED:	Camping is fun and relaxing.
DISCUSSION:	The fragment lacks a subject.

FRAGMENT:	Especially on a hot day.
REVISED:	Going to a lake is refreshing, especially on a hot day.
DISCUSSION:	The fragment lacks a subject and a verb.

FRAGMENT:	While I was driving to school today.
REVISED:	While I was driving to school today, I saw a red car with yellow flames painted on it.
DISCUSSION:	The fragment has a subject and verb, but it does not express a complete thought.

 Activity **Editing for Sentence Fragments**

Revise the following sentences to eliminate sentence fragments.

EXAMPLE

Fragment: Many students have strengths and weaknesses in different areas. Especially in subjects such as math and English.

Revised: Many students have strengths and weaknesses in different areas, especially in subjects such as math and English.

1. Many colleges offer tutoring services. For students who need to strengthen their skills in math or English.

2. Because he has good math skills. Hector tutors other college students.

3. He enjoys helping others. And feels good about himself after each tutoring session.

4. Even though Hector is very strong in math. He sometimes needs help with his writing.

5. Hector is grateful that he benefits from the tutoring services. Offered at his college.

Run-Ons and Comma Splices

A **run-on sentence,** also known as a *fused* sentence, occurs when two complete sentences (*independent clauses*) run together without a proper punctuation mark or a comma and coordinating conjunction. A **comma-spliced sentence** occurs when two complete sentences are joined improperly with just a comma.

RUN-ON SENTENCE: Sara likes to exercise before going to work Enrique prefers to exercise after work.

COMMA-SPLICED SENTENCE: Sara likes to exercise before going to work, Enrique prefers to exercise after work.

To revise a run-on or comma-spliced sentence, try one of these five methods:

1. Separate the sentences.

    REVISED: Sara likes to exercise before going to work. Enrique prefers to exercise after work.

2. Combine the sentences using a comma and a coordinating conjunction. A **coordinating conjunction** is a word that joins words or independent clauses that are equal and shows how they are related. Figure 1 provides the seven coordinating conjunctions and an easy way to remember them.

    REVISED: Sara likes to exercise before going to work, but Enrique prefers to exercise after work.

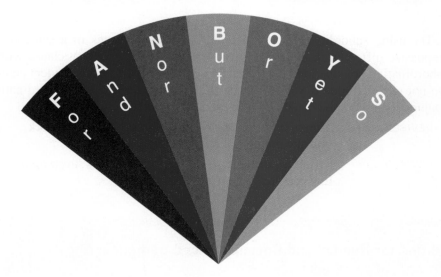

FIGURE 1 The Seven Coordinating Conjunctions (FANBOYS)

3. Combine the sentences using a semicolon. Use this method only if the sentences are fairly short and are similar in content and structure.

    REVISED: Sara likes to exercise before going to work; Enrique prefers to exercise after work.

4. Combine the sentences using a semicolon and a conjunctive adverb. A **conjunctive adverb** is an adverb that serves as a transition between two independent clauses.

Common Conjunctive Adverbs			
accordingly	furthermore	meanwhile	similarly
also	hence	moreover	still
anyway	however	namely	then
besides	incidentally	nevertheless	thereafter
certainly	indeed	next	therefore
consequently	instead	nonetheless	thus
finally	likewise	otherwise	undoubtedly

| REVISED: | Sara likes to exercise before going to work; however, Enrique prefers to exercise after work. |

5. Combine the sentences by using a subordinating conjunction. A **subordinating conjunction** is a dependent word that helps to show the relationship between the ideas in two independent clauses.

Editing for Run-On and Comma-Spliced Sentences Activity: Possible Answers

1. Watching movies is a popular way for people to unwind because movies provide an escape from reality.
2. Some prefer action adventure movies; others prefer comedies.
3. Action adventure movies are exciting, and they keep the audience riveted to their seats.
4. Good comedies are hilarious; furthermore, they can keep the audience laughing from start to finish.
5. It's fun to watch movies in the theater. Watching them at home can be entertaining too.

Common Subordinating Conjunctions			
after	as though	if only	until
although	because	now that	what(ever)
as	before	provided (that)	when(ever)
as if	even if	since	where(ever)
as long as	even though	so that	whether
as much as	how	though	which(ever)
as soon as	if	unless	while

Try using subordinating conjunctions in different places in a sentence to emphasize different ideas. If you introduce the first independent clause with a subordinating conjunction, add a comma before the second independent clause. Do not use a comma if you introduce the second clause with a subordinating conjunction unless the conjunction introduces a contrast.

| REVISED: | *Although* Sara likes to exercise before going to work, Enrique prefers to exercise after work. |
| REVISED: | Sara likes to exercise before going to work, *even though* Enrique prefers to exercise after work. |

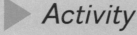 *Activity*   **Editing for Run-On and Comma-Spliced Sentences**

Revise the following sentences to eliminate run-ons and comma splices. Try different methods to see which one works the best to correct each run-on or comma splice.

1. Watching movies is a popular way for people to unwind movies provide an escape from reality.
2. Some people prefer action adventure movies, others prefer comedies.
3. Action adventure movies are exciting they keep the audience riveted to their seats.
4. Good comedies are hilarious, they can keep the audience laughing from start to finish.
5. It's fun to watch movies in the theater watching them at home can be entertaining too.

Mixed Constructions

If the first part (subject) of a sentence doesn't fit logically with the second part (predicate), the sentence has a **mixed construction.** Using mixed constructions can confuse readers.

MIXED:	The best career field for me is becoming a nurse.
REVISED:	Nursing is the best career field for me.
DISCUSSION:	A nurse isn't a career field, but nursing is.

MIXED:	The reason I want to be a Web designer is because I am good with computers.
REVISED:	I want to become a Web designer because I am good with computers.
DISCUSSION:	Avoid using the construction *the reason . . . is because.*

MIXED:	The fact that I got a new computer is why I'm so excited.
REVISED:	I'm so excited because I got a new computer.
DISCUSSION:	Avoid using the construction *the fact . . . is why.*

MIXED:	The chefs, although they created delicious dishes, but were not awarded a prize by the committee.
REVISED:	Although the chefs created delicious dishes, the committee did not award them a prize.
DISCUSSION:	Avoid using the construction *although . . . but.*

 Activity   **Editing for Mixed Constructions**

Revise the following sentences to eliminate mixed constructions.

1. The best car I could ever hope for is driving a BMW.
2. The reason I like BMWs is because they are luxurious cars.
3. The fact that my friend Kenny loves his BMW is why I am so interested in getting one.
4. Because BMWs are fast is what makes them fun to drive.
5. The reason I want to get a used BMW is because new ones are too expensive.

Faulty Parallelism

Parallelism occurs when similar ideas in a sentence are expressed in a similar grammatical manner.

Ideas in a sentence that have the same level of importance are parallel and, therefore, should be expressed in parallel grammatical constructions. When sentence elements such as nouns, verbs, and phrases are parallel, sentences flow more smoothly.

> **Parallelism** Occurs when similar ideas in a sentence are expressed in a similar grammatical manner.

PARALLEL NOUNS:	Laura bought a <u>hotdog,</u> a <u>pretzel,</u> and a <u>soft drink</u> at the concession stand.
PARALLEL VERBS:	On the weekends I enjoy <u>bicycling,</u> <u>hiking,</u> and <u>fishing.</u>
PARALLEL PHRASES:	He drove the car <u>around the tree,</u> <u>across the sidewalk,</u> and <u>into the lake.</u>
NOT PARALLEL:	Whether she is with a patient, drawing blood, or administering a shot, Kathie is always a professional.
REVISED:	Whether she is helping a patient, drawing blood, or administering a shot, Kathie is always a professional.
NOT PARALLEL:	Marcello needs to write his résumé, fill out an application, and he should apply for a job.
REVISED:	Marcello needs to write his résumé, fill out an application, and apply for a job.

Activity — Editing for Faulty Parallelism

Revise the following sentences to give them parallel structure.

1. The local hospital offers employees good salaries, flexible hours, and it offers meals that are inexpensive.
2. Employees who work on the top floor go down a hallway, through a lobby, and then they ride an elevator up to get to their station.
3. Employees spend much of their time helping patients, writing charts, and they also develop procedures.
4. Patients are very satisfied with the personnel, treatment, and they are also pleased with the facilities at the hospital.
5. The hospital is raising funds to update the cardiac and pediatric facilities, and it is also raising funds for updating the oncology facilities.

Active and Passive Voice

Active voice Occurs when the subject performs the action in the sentence.

Passive voice Occurs when the subject receives the action in the sentence.

Many instructors prefer that you use the active voice when writing essays. When you write in the **active voice,** the subject performs the action in the sentence. When you write in the **passive voice,** the subject receives the action in the sentence.

PASSIVE VOICE:	The award <u>was won</u> by the best writer in the class.
ACTIVE VOICE:	The best writer in the class <u>won</u> the award.
DISCUSSION:	Placing the subject up front emphasizes the subject of the sentence.

Writing in the active voice is more direct and less wordy. However, occasionally you may want to use the passive voice, especially if you need to emphasize the recipient of the action, don't know who performed the action, or prefer not to say who performed the action.

ACTIVE VOICE:	James <u>broke</u> the copy machine.
PASSIVE VOICE:	The copy machine <u>is broken.</u>
DISCUSSION:	Is it necessary for everyone to know who broke the machine? If not, the passive voice has a friendlier tone and is more tactful.

ACTIVE VOICE:	Someone <u>hired</u> Veronda immediately after her interview.
PASSIVE VOICE:	Veronda <u>was hired</u> immediately after her interview.
DISCUSSION:	If you do not know who hired Veronda, then using the passive voice is appropriate.

Revising for Active or Passive Voice Activity: Possible Answers

1. Star University hosted the job fair.
2. The career placement director invited the graduates to attend the job fair.
3. Well-known employers in the area recruited most of the graduates.
4. Their new employers gave some of the recruits signing bonuses.
5. Unfortunately, some of the completed job applications were lost.

Activity — Revising for Active or Passive Voice

Revise the following sentences by changing the passive sentences to the active voice and the active sentence to the passive voice.

1. The job fair was hosted by Star University.
2. The graduates were invited to attend the job fair by the career placement director.
3. Most of the graduates were recruited by well-known employers in the area.
4. Some of the recruits were given signing bonuses by their new employers.
5. Unfortunately, Susan lost some of the completed job applications.

B. EDITING WORDS (DICTION)

As you edit your documents, pay attention to your choice of words, also known as **diction.** You want to select words that create the most precise and accurate image in the minds of your readers. You also want to choose words that will not offend your readers. Using good diction will help you to communicate your message more clearly to your audience.

[**Diction** A writer's or speaker's choice of words.

Denotation and Connotation

Denotation refers to the dictionary definition of a word; **connotation** refers to all of the meanings of a word, including the attitudes and feelings people associate with it. For example, a surgery and a procedure have similar denotative meanings; however, the term *surgery* has more negative connotations than the term *procedure.* Similarly, while *residence* and *home* have similar definitions, *home* has warmer connotative feelings. Keep in mind that not all readers will have the same connotative meanings for words.

[**Denotation** The dictionary definition of a word.

[**Connotation** The meaning of a word, including the attitudes and feelings people associate with the word.

As a writer, you want to be sure to choose words that will suggest the right connotative meaning to your readers. This doesn't mean that emotionally charged words are inappropriate or ineffective. You just want to be sure that you evoke the desired emotions from your readers. For instance, the terms *childish* and *childlike* have similar denotations. However, saying someone is *childish* has more negative connotations than saying someone is *childlike.* If your goal is to illustrate how immature a particular adult is, then *childish* might be the correct term to use.

Interpreting Connotations
Activity: Possible Answers

1. The word "*employee*" has fairly positive connotations, while "*worker*" is more neutral, and "*grunt*" has negative connotations.

2. The words "*intelligent*" and "*smart*" have more positive connotations than "*brainy.*"

3. While all three words can have somewhat negative connotations, "*artificial*" has slightly more positive connotations than "*fake*" or "*counterfeit.*"

4. The word "*educate*" has fairly positive connotations, while "*train*" is more neutral, and "*drill*" is more negative.

5. The word "*sip*" has positive connotations, while "*guzzle*" and "*slurp*" are negative.

> ▶ *Activity* **Interpreting Connotations**

Explain the connotative differences for each set of words.

1. worker, grunt, employee
2. smart, brainy, intelligent
3. artificial, fake, counterfeit
4. educate, train, drill
5. sip, guzzle, slurp

Jargon and Slang

Jargon is the specialized vocabulary that people connected to a particular career field, group, or interest use. **Slang** is similar to jargon, except that jargon tends to be formal, and slang tends to be informal and nonstandard. Professionals in the legal, medical, computer, education, and business fields use vocabulary that is specific to those areas. Likewise, athletes, musicians, surfers, and video gamers use terms that are specific to their interests.

[**Jargon** Specialized vocabulary that people connected to a particular career field, group, or interest use.

Jargon and slang can be acceptable when writing for an audience whose members share the vocabulary of the field. For example, a professional in the health care field may use medical jargon in an e-mail to a co-worker. As long as the writer and recipient of the message understand the terminology, effective communication can take place.

[**Slang** Informal, nonstandard vocabulary that people connected to a particular career field, group, or interest use.

However, if your audience might not understand the vocabulary of a particular field, then you are better off using terms that are more generic or standard.

For instance, if you write a flyer for patients with instructions for practicing a stretching technique at home, then you will need to explain the key terms or replace the jargon with more common terms.

JARGON:	When Deveney bought a new PC, she nuked her old one.
REVISED:	When Deveney bought a new personal computer, she deleted her directories without saving her individual files.
SLANG:	The dude was totally barnwalling on the gnarly wave.
REVISED:	The surfer was exhibiting poor technique on the treacherous wave.

▶ *Activity*   **Revising for Jargon and Slang**

Replace the italicized words with standard terminology.

1. I *totally blew off my* history assignment.
2. Adam *Christmas treed* his psychology test because he didn't bother to study.
3. The new math instructor is a *nut case*.
4. I need to *catch some Z's* before the *monster* test tomorrow.
5. The student who sits next to me in biology class is *da bomb*.

Clichés

Cliché A worn-out expression.

A **cliché** is a worn-out expression. While it may have once been original and fresh, by now it has been used so many times that it has lost its impact. Avoid using clichés because they make your writing sound dull and uninspired. Instead, take the time to find a more interesting way to express your ideas.

CLICHÉD:	Employees who *stab their co-workers in the back* rarely find success on the job.
REVISED:	Employees who *betray their co-workers* rarely find success on the job.

Clichés to Avoid	
above and beyond the call of duty	easy as cake (or pie)
add insult to injury	dry as a bone
back stabber	few and far between
black as night	first and foremost
bright-eyed and bushy-tailed	free as a bird
busy as a bee (or a beaver)	green with envy
cold as ice	hard as nails (or as a rock)
come hell or high water	in my wildest dreams
cool as a cucumber	last but not least
cream of the crop	last straw
cried like a baby	Life is like a box of chocolates.
crystal clear	like taking candy from a baby
Don't burn your bridges.	not the sharpest tool in the shed
dumber than a box of rocks	older than dirt (or the hills)

on top of the world	stick out like a sore thumb
over the hill	sweet as syrup (or honey)
skating on thin ice	That's the way the cookie crumbles.
skeleton in the closet	too little too late
slower than molasses	tried and true

 Activity **Editing for Clichés**

Write five complete sentences, each including a different cliché. Revise each sentence by replacing the cliché with fresh, original language. Keep the intended meaning of the cliché as you revise.

EXAMPLE
Clichéd: The executive was as *cool as a cucumber* when she delivered her presentation.
Revised: The executive was *calm and poised* when she delivered her presentation.
Note: Pairs or small groups of students may trade sentences to revise.

Biased Language

As you revise your writing, look for biased language that you may have inadvertently used. **Biased language** reflects an unfair assumption or prejudice about someone. Be sensitive to gender, culture, and age as you choose your words. You don't want to stereotype people or be condescending toward them.

> **Biased language** Reflects an unfair assumption or prejudice without cause.

Gender Bias

One way to eliminate bias in your writing is to avoid words that unnecessarily refer to gender, also known as **sexist language.** Sometimes you can avoid or correct sexist language by making the subject of the sentence plural.

> **Sexist language** Words that unnecessarily refer to gender.

SEXIST:	A nurse should treat *her* patients with kindness and respect.
REVISED:	Nurses should treat their patients with kindness and respect.
DISCUSSION:	Men and women can be nurses. Unless you are referring to a particular nurse, leave the sentence gender neutral.

Sexist Language	Gender Neutral Language
chairman	chair/chairperson
chicks/girls	women
male nurse	nurse
fireman	firefighter
mankind	humankind/people
mailman	mail carrier
policeman/lady cop	police officer
stewardess/steward	flight attendant
waitress/waiter	server

Cultural Bias

Culturally biased language stereotypes people positively or negatively. Assuming someone has a particular attribute because of his or her culture is unfair and can be offensive. Consequently, you'll want to avoid using culturally stereotypical language in your writing.

STEREOTYPICAL:	Natsumi is very hardworking because she is Japanese.
REVISED:	Natsumi is very hardworking.

Age Bias

Identifying someone's relative age can be useful, but you should do it in a dignified way. Avoid using language that is insulting or condescending toward people.

INSULTING: The old geezer who lives next door invited me to watch the big game with him.

REVISED: The retired firefighter who lives next door invited me to watch the big game with him.

▶ *Activity* **Revising Biased Language**

Identify and revise the biased language in the following sentences.

1. A member of the armed forces should be commended for serving his country.
2. The chick who was hired to replace my boss is intelligent.
3. Because she is Italian, Nancy is a great cook.
4. Like most black people, Rick is a terrific basketball player.
5. The punk who lives across the street won an award for his science project.
6. The old hag would like a refund for the defective merchandise.

Revising Biased Language
Activity: Possible Answers

1. Replace "*his*" with "*his or her.*"
2. Replace "*chick*" with "*woman.*"
3. Delete "*Because she is Italian.*"
4. Delete "*Like most black people.*"
5. Replace "*punk*" with "*student*" or "*boy.*"
6. Replace "*old hag*" with "*woman*" or "*lady.*"

Wordiness

Including unnecessary words is tiresome for the reader and can make a text hard to understand. Often you can tighten a wordy passage by substituting a single word for a long phrase or by taking out words that are repetitive or don't add meaning to a sentence. You want to be as clear and concise as possible.

WORDY: It seems to be true that much of humankind enjoys having pets, such as felines or canines, around to help alleviate feelings of emptiness or loneliness.

CONCISE: Many people enjoy having cats and dogs around to keep them company.

Wordy	Concise
at this point in time	now
arrive at a conclusion	conclude
at a later point in time	later
bear a resemblance to	resemble
purple in color	purple
due to the fact that	because
in many cases	often
in the near future	soon
in this day and age	now
on a weekly basis	weekly
persons of the male gender	men
provide aid for	help
small in size	small
without a doubt	certainly

Revise the following paragraph to make it clearer and more concise. You may eliminate words and phrases and combine sentences as you revise.

There is little doubt that technology has changed the way that people can communicate with other people who are male or female, young or old. Because computers used to be so large in size that they took up an entire room, very few people had access to computers. Additionally, computers used to be extremely expensive; therefore, very few people could afford to own them. Due to the fact that computers have become smaller in size and less expensive, computers are readily available to a wide range of people. Desktop computers and laptop computers are quite common these days. People use them to make phone calls, send text messages, and e-mail other people with whom they want to communicate. Also, in today's day and age, many adults, teenagers, and children have smartphones that they carry around with them in their pockets, purses, backpacks, or briefcases. They can use these phones to call, text message, and e-mail their friends, family members, and co-workers. One can only imagine how computers will continue to affect communication in the near or distant future.

C. EDITING GRAMMAR

Pronouns

Pronoun-Antecedent Agreement

Pronouns (words that replace nouns) need to agree with their **antecedents** (the nouns they refer to) in number and gender.

Use singular pronouns to refer to singular nouns; use plural pronouns to refer to plural nouns.

SINGULAR:	The stethoscope was on the floor because *it* fell off the table.
SINGULAR:	Each of the patients received *his or her* lunch at noon.
SINGULAR:	Everybody in the lobby was waiting to see *his or her* loved one.
PLURAL:	The hazardous materials containers were removed because *they* were full.

Note: Some indefinite pronouns, such as *everybody, anybody, each,* and *everyone,* seem plural, but they are really singular. Therefore, you will need to use a singular pronoun to refer back to those words.

Nouns and pronouns can be feminine, masculine, or neutral.

FEMININE:	Carmen was thrilled because *she* got an extra shift at the hospital.
MASCULINE:	John was happy because *he* passed the RN exam.
NEUTRAL:	That building is older than *its* neighbors.

Collective nouns can be singular or plural, depending on how you use them. Therefore, you may use a singular or plural pronoun with a collective noun. (See pp. 408–409 for more on collective nouns.)

SINGULAR:	The band received an award for *its* performance.
DISCUSSION:	The band is used singularly as one unit that won one award.
PLURAL:	The band are tuning *their* instruments.
DISCUSSION:	The band members are acting individually rather than as one unit.

Note: You can say *band members* to clarify that you are using the collective noun in a plural manner.

Pronouns Words that replace nouns.

Antecedents Nouns that pronouns refer to.

Revising for Wordiness Activity: Answers will vary.

LearnSmart Achieve Tip

LearnSmart Achieve determines what students do and do not know about grammar, common sentence problems, punctuation, mechanics, style, and word choice. Learning outcomes cover all of these topics. Learning resources and questions automatically adapt to each student's individual needs and help students thoroughly master this content. See the Instructor's Manual for *Write Now* for a list of learning outcomes as well as additional information on how to use LearnSmart Achieve with your students.

Pronoun Reference

A pronoun needs to clearly refer back to a noun (*an antecedent*). Typically, a pronoun will refer back to a preceding noun that matches it in number and gender, if applicable. Sentences need to clearly identify who is doing what to whom.

UNCLEAR:	The patient received a call from his brother, but he wasn't happy about it.
REVISED:	The patient wasn't happy about the call he received from his brother.
DISCUSSION:	The first sentence does not clarify who is not happy. Is it the patient or the brother?
UNCLEAR:	Lucinda had facial plastic surgery six weeks ago, and it already looks better.
REVISED:	Lucinda had facial plastic surgery six weeks ago, and her face already looks better.
DISCUSSION:	The first sentence implies that Lucinda's face looks better, but the pronoun actually refers back to the facial surgery. Saying that the facial plastic surgery looks better does not make sense.
UNCLEAR:	It is a nice facility.
REVISED:	The facility is nice.
DISCUSSION:	The word *it* does not refer to anything. Sometimes a sentence can start with the pronoun *it* if the word *it* refers to a noun in a previous sentence.
EXAMPLE:	The new outpatient clinic opened yesterday. It is a nice facility.

Pronoun Case

Pronouns can be subjects, objects, or possessives.

Pronoun Types			
	Subjective	**Objective**	**Possessive**
First person singular	I	me	my, mine
First person plural	we	us	our, ours
Second person singular	you	you	your, yours
Second person plural	you	you	your, yours
Third person singular	he, she, it, who	him, her, it, whom	his, her, hers, its, whose
Third person plural	they, who	them, whom	their, theirs, whose

Subjective pronouns perform the action in a sentence.

SUBJECTIVE PRONOUN:	*She* is going to see a nutritionist.

Objective pronouns receive the action in the sentence or are part of a prepositional phrase.

OBJECTIVE PRONOUN:	The nutritionist gave *her* a diet plan.
OBJECTIVE PRONOUN:	Between you and *me,* I am having trouble with my diet.

Possessive pronouns show ownership.

POSSESSIVE PRONOUN: The diet plan from the nutritionist is *hers.*

Using the correct type can be tricky at times, especially when a sentence has a compound subject or object, makes a comparison, includes an appositive, or uses *who* or *whom.*

Compound Subjects and Objects When the subject is compound, eliminate the double subject to figure out which pronoun to use.

SINGLE SUBJECT:	*I* donated blood.
COMPOUND SUBJECT:	My mother and *I* donated blood.
SINGLE OBJECT:	Dr. D'Alessandro gave a list of exercises to *me.*
COMPOUND OBJECT:	Dr. D'Alessandro gave a list of exercises to Todd and *me.*

Comparisons Using the correct pronoun when making a comparison is essential to getting the correct message across to your audience. Choosing the correct type can be difficult because sometimes words are implied rather than stated. To find the correct pronoun, mentally add the missing words.

COMPARISON:	Kristin likes Denny more than *I* [like Denny].
DISCUSSION:	The sentence means that Kristin likes Denny more than I like Denny.
COMPARISON:	Kristin likes Denny more than [she likes] *me.*
DISCUSSION:	The sentence means that Kristin likes Denny more than she likes me.

Appositives An **appositive** is a word or phrase that renames a noun or pronoun. Eliminate the appositive to determine which pronoun to use.

APPOSITIVE:	We *Floridians* like not having to wear a coat in the winter.
DISCUSSION:	*Floridians* renames *we. We* like not having to wear a coat in winter.

Appositive A word or phrase that renames a noun or pronoun.

Who and Whom Use *who* as the subject of a sentence. Use *whom* as the object of a sentence.

SUBJECTIVE PRONOUN:	Dennis wants to know *who* is going to the party.
OBJECTIVE PRONOUN:	For *whom* did Michelle buy that gift?
TIP:	The word *whom* often appears in a prepositional phrase: to whom, for whom, with whom.

Problems with Pronouns
Activity: Answers
1. his or her
2. I
3. me
4. We
5. Who

▶ *Activity*   **Problems with Pronouns**

Choose the correct pronouns for the following sentences.

1. Each of the participants received (his or her/their) certificate.
2. Patti and (I/me) will ride together to the show.
3. Melissa gave the box of chocolates to Liza and (I/me).
4. (Us/We) college students need to stick together.
5. (Who/Whom) is going to donate money for the charity?

Verbs

Subject-Verb Agreement

Singular and Plural Subjects The subject and verb in a sentence need to match (agree). A singular subject needs to have a singular verb; a plural subject needs to have a plural verb.

SINGULAR SUBJECT AND VERB:	The *guitar player is* amazing.
SINGULAR SUBJECT AND VERB:	The *sound* from the speakers *is shaking* the entire arena.
DISCUSSION:	The subject in the sentence above is *sound,* so the verb is singular. The word *speakers* is in a prepositional phrase, so it does not affect subject-verb agreement.
PLURAL SUBJECT AND VERB:	The *speakers are* shaking the entire arena.
DISCUSSION:	In the sentence above, *speakers* is the plural subject of the sentence, so the verb is plural.

Compound Subjects When two or more subjects are combined, the subject is compound. Compound subjects joined by the word *and* are usually plural, so the verb needs to be plural.

COMPOUND SUBJECT:	*Ashley* and *Jenny are* hosting the event.
DISCUSSION:	Ashley and Jenny are separate subjects, so the verb is plural.

Sometimes, however, the word *and* appears as part of a singular subject, so the verb needs to be singular.

SINGULAR SUBJECT:	*Rock and roll is* one of my favorite types of music.
DISCUSSION:	Rock and roll is one subject, so the verb is singular.

Compound subjects joined by *or, nor, either . . . or,* or *neither . . . nor* are singular. Therefore, the verb needs to be singular.

SINGULAR SUBJECT:	*Mark* or *Gregg is* going to advance to the next race.
SINGULAR SUBJECT:	*Briana is* not going to give up, nor *is Natalie.*
SINGULAR SUBJECT:	Either *Ellen* or *Margaret is* going to win the contest.
SINGULAR SUBJECT:	Neither *Edward* nor *Jorge* displays bad sportsmanship.
DISCUSSION:	The sentences above refer to each person individually, not collectively, so the subjects and verbs are singular.

Collective Nouns Collective nouns have a singular form. However, the verbs that go with them can be singular or plural depending on how writers use them. Below are some examples of collective nouns.

Collective Nouns		
audience	faculty	majority
band	family	pack
class	group	swarm
choir	herd	team
committee	jury	tribe

When you use a collective noun, consistently treat it as singular or plural in a passage. If you are referring to the collective noun as a single unit, use a singular verb.

SINGULAR COLLECTIVE NOUN:	The *jury is* undecided.
DISCUSSION:	The jury, as a whole, is not ready to make a decision.

If you are referring to the collective noun as a group of individuals, use a plural verb.

PLURAL COLLECTIVE NOUN:	The *faculty have* moved into their new offices.
DISCUSSION:	Here, the sentence refers to all of the members of the faculty as individuals with separate offices.

Sometimes you are better off clarifying the collective noun to avoid sounding awkward.

AWKWARD:	The committee were excited about completing the proposal.
REVISED:	The committee members were excited about completing the proposal.

Indefinite Pronouns *Indefinite pronouns* refer to an unspecific number of subjects. Indefinite pronouns can be singular, plural, or varied (singular or plural depending on the context). You need to determine whether the indefinite pronoun is singular or plural in a particular sentence to make sure that the verb agrees with the subject.

SINGULAR INDEFINITE PRONOUN:	*Everyone is* thrilled about the new policy.
VARIABLE INDEFINITE PRONOUN (SINGULAR):	*Most* of the lasagna *is* very cheesy.
VARIABLE INDEFINITE PRONOUN (PLURAL):	*Most* of the employees *are* hardworking.
PLURAL INDEFINITE PRONOUN:	*Many* of the cupcakes *have* been eaten.

Indefinite Pronouns		
Singular	**Variable (Singular or Plural)**	**Plural**
anybody	all	both
anyone	any	few
anything	more	many
each	most	others
either	none	several
everybody	some	
everything		
neither		
nobody		
no one		
nothing		
somebody		
someone		
something		

Inverted Subject and Verb Determining subject-verb agreement can be tricky if the verb is inverted (comes before the subject). Make sure that the verb agrees with the subject of the sentence, rather than another word that is closer to the verb.

INVERTED SUBJECT AND VERB:	Sitting in the courtroom *were two suspects.*
DISCUSSION:	The subject (*two suspects*) is plural, so the verb (*were*) needs to be plural as well.

Separated Subject and Verb Determining subject-verb agreement can be tricky if the verb is separated from the subject.

SEPARATED SUBJECT AND VERB:	The *lawyers,* waiting for the judge to arrive, *are* exhausted from the lengthy trial.
DISCUSSION:	The plural subject (*lawyers*) needs a plural verb (*are*).

► *Activity*   **Subject-Verb Agreement**

Identify the subject of each sentence. Choose the verb that agrees with the subject.

1. The music coming from the instruments (is/are) melodic.
2. Lori and Megan (was/were) hoping to attend the concert.
3. Frank, who is one of the guitar players, (is/are) the lead singer.
4. Waiting patiently backstage (is/are) Vicki and Jill.
5. Everyone attending the concert tonight (is/are) going to get a free CD.

Regular Verbs

With regular verbs, you can simply add -*d* or -*ed* to the infinitive (base) form of the verb to change the tense. See the examples below.

Regular Verbs		
Infinitive	**Past Tense**	**Past Participle**
arrive	arrived	arrived
earn	earned	earned
graduate	graduated	graduated
receive	received	received
walk	walked	walked

Irregular Verbs

Many verbs in the English language are irregular. The chart that follows includes some of the most common irregular verbs.

Irregular Verbs

Infinitive	Past Tense	Past Participle
arise	arose	arisen
be	was, were	been
become	became	become
begin	began	begun
bind	bound	bound
bite	bit	bitten
buy	bought	bought
catch	caught	caught
choose	chose	chosen
come	came	come
dig	dug	dug
drink	drank	drunk
drive	drove	driven
eat	ate	eaten
forbid	forbade	forbidden
freeze	froze	frozen
get	got	gotten
give	gave	given
go	went	gone
grind	ground	ground
grow	grew	grown
have	had	had
hide	hid	hidden
hold	held	held
lay (to put or place)	laid	laid
lay (to recline)	lay	lain
mistake	mistook	mistaken
pay	paid	paid
proofread	proofread	proofread
ride	rode	ridden
ring	rang	rung
rise	rose	risen
sing	sang	sung
see	saw	seen
seek	sought	sought
set	set	set
speak	spoke	spoken
swear	swore	sworn
think	thought	thought
throw	threw	thrown
wring	wrung	wrung
write	wrote	written

Linking Verbs

Linking verbs show existence and explain what something is, was, or will become. Linking verbs connect the subject of a sentence to a *complement* (a word that renames or describes the subject).

LINKING VERB: Laura *is* a media specialist.

LINKING VERB: Ryan *seems* distracted.

Linking Verbs			
Forms of the Verb *Be*		**Verbs That Can Function as Linking Verbs**	
am	is	appear	remain
are	was	become	seem
were	be	feel	smell
being	been	grow	sound
		look	taste

Adjectives and Adverbs

Adjectives and Adverbs

Adjectives and adverbs are modifiers, words that describe or *modify* other words. **Adjectives** are words that modify nouns or pronouns.

Adjectives Words that modify nouns or pronouns.

ADJECTIVE: Scott is *intelligent.*

DISCUSSION: The adjective *intelligent* modifies the noun *Scott.*

ADJECTIVE: She is *pretty.*

DISCUSSION: The adjective *pretty* modifies the pronoun *she.*

Adverbs Words that modify adjectives, verbs, and other adverbs.

Adverbs are words that modify adjectives, verbs, and other adverbs. Adverbs often end in *-ly* and tell *how.*

ADVERB: The chili is *especially* good tonight.

DISCUSSION: The adverb *especially* modifies the adjective *good.*

ADVERB: The chef worked *diligently* on the new recipe.

DISCUSSION: The adverb *diligently* modifies the verb *worked.*

ADVERB: Julie smiled *very* sweetly.

DISCUSSION: The adverb *very* modifies the adverb *sweetly.*

The following adjectives and adverbs often cause problems for writers: good/well; bad/badly; real/really. Remember, adverbs often tell *how.*

Good and Well

Good and *well* are commonly confused words. *Good* is an adjective (or sometimes a noun) and *well* is an adjective or adverb, depending on the context.

ADJECTIVE: The sushi is *good.*

ADVERB: The chef prepared the sushi *well.*

ADJECTIVE:	Gina feels *good* about the exam.
ADVERB:	Gina performed *well* on the exam.
DISCUSSION:	Use *good* when you use a linking verb (see p. 412) and *well* when you use an active verb.

Bad and Badly

| ADJECTIVE: | The bananas have gone *bad.* |
| ADVERB: | Marge used the *badly* bruised bananas for banana bread. |

| ADJECTIVE: | The *bad* dog went to obedience school. |
| ADVERB: | The dog behaved *badly* in class. |

Real and Really

| ADJECTIVE: | These pearls are *real.* |
| ADVERB: | Rhonda worked *really* hard to make the necklace. |

| ADJECTIVE: | The *real* problem is that we have too many choices. |
| ADVERB: | We are *really* confused about all of the choices we have. |

Note: Real = genuine

Comparatives and Superlatives

Comparatives are adjectives and adverbs that compare two items. *Superlatives* are adjectives and adverbs that compare three or more items. Usually you can make comparative and superlative forms be adding *-er* and *-est, more* and *most,* or *less* and *least.*

BASE ADJECTIVE FORM:	Toby is a *cute* puppy.
COMPARATIVE FORM:	Toby is *cuter* than Roofus.
SUPERLATIVE FORM:	Toby is the *cutest* puppy in the litter.

Avoid doubling comparatives and superlatives.

| INCORRECT: | Jack is the *most sweetest* boy I know. |
| REVISED: | Jack is the *sweetest* boy I know. |

Comparatives and Superlatives

Adjective or Adverb	Comparative Form	Superlative Form
big	bigger	biggest
pretty	prettier	prettiest
good	better	best
expensive	more expensive	most expensive
unusual	more unusual	most unusual
wonderful	more wonderful	most wonderful
desirable	less desirable	least desirable
fascinating	less fascinating	least fascinating
rapidly	less rapidly	least rapidly

Choose the correct word or words for each sentence.

1. Tamika works (good/well) with her group mates.
2. Marco wanted to fire the (bad/badly) employee.
3. William tried (real/really) hard to finish the report on time.
4. John is the (more/most) gifted of the two students.
5. Ava is the (better/more better/best/bestest) swimmer on the team.

Adjectives and Adverbs Activity:
Answers

1. well
2. bad
3. really
4. more
5. best

Dangling and Misplaced Modifiers

Dangling Modifiers

As you write, you need to make sure that your modifiers clearly describe something specific that is stated in the sentence. Otherwise, you might create a *dangling modifier* and confuse your readers.

DANGLING MODIFIER:	While driving south on I-95, an iguana ran in front of his car.
QUESTION:	Was an iguana really driving the car?
REVISED:	While Pat was driving south on I-95, an iguana ran in front of his car.
DISCUSSION:	The revised sentence clearly explains that Pat was driving the car.
DANGLING MODIFIER:	While talking on a cell phone, Pat's car swerved and missed the iguana.
QUESTION:	Was the car talking on the cell phone?
REVISED:	While talking on a cell phone, Pat swerved his car and missed the iguana.
DISCUSSION:	The revised sentence clearly explains that Pat was talking on his cell phone.

Misplaced Modifiers

Misplaced modifiers occur when they appear too far away from the words they describe.

MISPLACED MODIFIER:	The reckless driver almost angered every other driver on the road.
REVISED:	The reckless driver angered almost every other driver on the road.
DISCUSSION:	The first sentence suggests that the driver may not have angered any of the drivers.
MISPLACED MODIFIER:	Tammy threw the Frisbee for the dog still dressed in her nightgown.
REVISED:	Still dressed in her nightgown, Tammy threw the Frisbee for the dog.
DISCUSSION:	The first sentence suggests that the dog was wearing a nightgown.

Revise the following sentences to eliminate dangling and misplaced modifiers.

1. The exquisite food was prepared by chefs ranging from lobster bisque to tuna tartar.
2. The jury took a lunch break still undecided about the guilt of the suspect.
3. Worried about spreading germs, an antibacterial soap dispenser was installed near every entrance to the hospital.
4. Susan bought a cell phone for her daughter with broken buttons.
5. Getting ready for Sullivan's grand opening, the jewelry was displayed in glass cases.

D. EDITING PUNCTUATION

Commas (,)

Some writers place commas wherever they might pause as they are speaking; however, that approach doesn't always work. Learning the following comma rules will help prevent you from confusing your readers.

Introductory Phrase or Clause
Use a comma to set off introductory material in a sentence.

EXAMPLE:	*After she got to the grocery store,* Diane realized that she had forgotten her purse.
EXAMPLE:	*According to her son,* Diane often forgets things.
EXAMPLE:	*For instance,* one time Diane forgot to bring her running shoes to a marathon in which she was competing.

Nonessential Phrase or Clause
If you can omit a phrase or clause in a sentence without changing the meaning, the phrase or clause is nonessential and should be enclosed in commas. Essential phrases and clauses should not be enclosed in commas.

NONESSENTIAL:	Juanita, *who is my friend's cousin,* loves listening to music.
DISCUSSION:	The main point of the sentence is that Juanita loves listening to music. The italicized clause doesn't change that.
ESSENTIAL:	The song *now playing on the radio* is one of Juanita's favorites.
DISCUSSION:	The reader wouldn't know which song is Juanita's favorite without the italicized phrase.

Interrupters
Use commas to set off words that interrupt the flow of a sentence. Interrupters can occur at the beginning, middle, or end of a sentence.

EXAMPLE:	*Of course,* Steve may want to choose his own pizza toppings.
EXAMPLE:	We are having tilapia, *one of my favorite foods,* for dinner tonight.
EXAMPLE:	The mayor had a snack attack on Saturday, *according to the local newspaper.*

Items in a Series

Use commas to separate three or more words, phrases, or clauses in a series.

EXAMPLE:	Jamal loaded many items into his backpack, such as *clothes, food,* and *water.*
EXAMPLE:	The dog chased the squirrel *around the tree, over the log,* and *into the house.*

Before Coordinating Conjunctions

Use a comma before a coordinating conjunction (*for, and, nor, but, or, yet, so*) that separates two independent clauses. (See FANBOYS on p. 397.)

EXAMPLE:	I was hoping to bring Bryan to the concert, *but* he wasn't feeling well.
EXAMPLE:	Emma got elected president of the Student Government Association, *so* she is likely to develop some new leadership skills.

Note: Do not use a comma to separate words or phrases joined by a coordinating conjunction.

EXAMPLE:	Elaine's clothing is simple *but* stylish.

Conjunctive Adverbs

Use commas to set off conjunctive adverbs, such as *however, furthermore,* and *therefore.*

EXAMPLE:	Dave was, *however,* more experienced than James.
EXAMPLE:	*Therefore,* Dave got a promotion.

Adjectives

Use commas to separate adjectives if they modify (describe) the same noun and have equal emphasis.

EXAMPLE:	It is a *hot, sticky* day.
EXAMPLE:	The *cool, refreshing* ocean waves are the perfect remedy for the heat.
TIP:	If you can replace the comma with the word *and,* then you need a comma. If not, leave the comma out.
EXAMPLE:	Brad was sitting in the *red lifeguard* booth.
DISCUSSION:	You would not say it was a *red and lifeguard* booth, so leave out the comma.

Dialogue

Use commas to separate dialogue from the speaker. You do not need commas to separate indirect quotations.

EXAMPLE:	Ann Marie exclaimed, "I see a shark in the water!"
EXAMPLE:	"It's just a dolphin," replied Brad, "so you have nothing to fear."
EXAMPLE:	Brad told Ann Marie that she had nothing to fear.

Direct Address

Use commas to set off a direct address.

EXAMPLE:	Children, please be quiet.
EXAMPLE:	Please, Randall, I need your advice.
EXAMPLE:	Here, kitty, I have a treat for you.

Titles or Degrees
Use commas to set off a title or degree that comes after a name.

EXAMPLE:	Curtis Counter, CPA, does my taxes each year.
EXAMPLE:	Neil Healer, MD, is a great physician.
EXAMPLE:	One of my favorite teachers was Eric Illuminator, PhD.

Addresses and Dates
Use commas to separate items in addresses and dates.

EXAMPLE:	I enjoyed visiting the French Quarter in New Orleans, Louisiana.
EXAMPLE:	He was born on November 30, 2002.

 Activity **Correcting Comma Errors**

Add commas as needed to the following sentences.

1. After Nessa finished her salad she wanted a piece of dark chocolate.
2. Carlos who lives next door bought a new boat last week.
3. Susan stocked her medicine cabinet with aspirin cough drops and cold medicine.
4. Heather was looking for a bargain so she shopped at a discount store.
5. Stewart is however a talented singer.
6. Geoff dreaded entering the damp musty cave.
7. Debbie shouted "You're the best friend ever!"
8. Ladies please be seated.
9. I have an appointment with Glen Martin DDS to get my teeth whitened.
10. Lisa visited San Francisco California on August 25 2014.

Semicolons (;) and Colons (:)

Semicolons (;)

Independent Clauses Use a semicolon between two main clauses if the conjunction is left out and if the clauses are closely related in content and style.

EXAMPLE:	Sally likes vanilla caramel ice cream; Gale prefers chocolate ice cream.

Conjunctive Adverbs Use a semicolon before and a comma after a conjunctive adverb that joins two independent clauses. (See p. 397 for a list of common conjunctive adverbs.)

EXAMPLE:	Sally likes vanilla caramel ice cream; however, Gale prefers chocolate ice cream.

Items in a Series with Commas Use semicolons to separate items in a series when commas are present within one or more of the items.

EXAMPLE:	Some of the most exciting cities to visit are London, England; Paris, France; Rome, Italy; and Athens, Greece.

Colons (:)

List of Items Use a colon after a main clause (complete sentence) to introduce a list of items.

CORRECT:	When going on a Caribbean cruise, always pack the following items: a bathing suit, a bottle of suntan lotion, and a book to read.
INCORRECT:	When going on a Caribbean cruise, always pack: a bathing suit, suntan lotion, and a book to read.
CORRECT:	When going on a Caribbean cruise, always pack a bathing suit, suntan lotion, and a book to read.
DISCUSSION:	If what precedes the list is not a complete sentence, then a colon is not needed.

Explanation or Emphasis Use a colon after a main clause when what follows it explains or emphasizes the subject in the main clause.

EXAMPLE:	Maggie is going to school for one reason: to get a better job.

Quotations Use a colon to introduce a quotation after a main clause.

EXAMPLE:	Oscar Wilde, a Victorian playwright, had an interesting view of himself: "I am so clever that sometimes I don't understand a single word of what I am saying."

Salutations Use a colon to follow the salutation of a business letter or formal correspondence.

EXAMPLE:	Dear Ms. Snider:

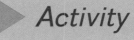

Activity — Editing for Colons and Semicolons

Add colons and semicolons to the following sentences as necessary. Note, not every sentence needs a semicolon or colon added.

1. Fred is going hiking Julie is going shopping.
2. Tina wants to get a new job furthermore, she expects higher pay.
3. Pete and Barb have one expectation of their vacation relaxation.
4. For the cookout, Rose is going to buy chips, potato salad, and soft drinks.
5. My father always gave me this advice "Never give up on your dreams."

Quotation Marks (" ") and (' ')

Double Quotation Marks

Exact Words Use a set of double quotation marks to enclose the exact words that someone spoke or wrote.

EXAMPLE:	Malcolm X once stated, "Education is our passport to the future, for tomorrow belongs to the people who prepare for it today."

Titles of Short Published Works Use quotation marks to enclose the title of essays, articles, book chapters, poems, and short stories.

EXAMPLE: "Annabel Lee" is a powerful poem by Edgar Allan Poe.

Note: Do not place quotation marks around your own title in your essay. If you refer to your essay in another document, such as in the cover letter for a portfolio, then use quotation marks.

Emphasis Use double quotation marks around a word or phrase that introduces a concept that might be unfamiliar to readers or when a word or phrase is used ironically, satirically, or as unfamiliar slang. Do this sparingly. You may use italics for this purpose as well. Be consistent with how you emphasize words in a particular document.

EXAMPLE: The word "textese" refers to the informal language favored by those who send text messages.

Single Quotation Marks

Use a set of single quotation marks to enclose a quote within a quote.

EXAMPLE: Carol recalled, "I once heard an instructor say, 'A prepared student is a passing student.'"

Note: The single quotation mark at the end of the quote within a quote goes inside of the double quotation marks.

 Activity   **Editing for Quotation Marks**

Add quotation marks to the following sentences as needed.

1. Michael's mother once exclaimed, I brought you into this world, and I can take you out of it!
2. For an extra thirty dollars, explained the dental hygienist, you can have a flavored fluoride treatment.
3. In class we read a student essay called Adrenaline Rush.
4. People assign different meanings to the word love.
5. My friend said, I thought I had received a bad grade on my paper until my instructor exclaimed, Yours was the best in the class!

Ellipses (. . .)

Omission from a Quote

An *ellipsis* is a series of three dots (periods) used to show that something has been intentionally omitted from a quotation. An ellipsis may occur at the middle or end of a sentence, but not at the beginning. Be careful to not change the intended meaning of the original sentence or passage.

ORIGINAL SENTENCE: The future graduates lined up at the ceremony, eagerly anticipating the walk across the stage, the handshake with the school president, and the roar of the crowd when the degrees are conferred.

EXAMPLE: "The future graduates lined up at the ceremony, eagerly anticipating . . . the roar of the crowd when the degrees are conferred."

Editing for Quotation Marks
Activity: Answers

1. Michael's mother once exclaimed, "I brought you into this world, and I can take you out of it!"

2. "For an extra thirty dollars," explained the dental hygienist, "you can have a flavored fluoride treatment."

3. In class we read a student essay called "Adrenaline Rush."

4. People assign different meanings to the word "love."

5. My friend said, "I thought I had received a bad grade on my paper until my instructor exclaimed, 'Yours was the best in the class!'"

EXAMPLE: "The future graduates lined up at the ceremony, eagerly anticipating the walk across the stage, the handshake with the school president, and the roar of the crowd. . . ."

Note: Use four dots instead of three if the ellipsis ends the sentence.

Incomplete Thought

Use an ellipsis to indicate an incomplete thought.

EXAMPLE: This year we are working to pay off the car and the boat. Next year we hope to . . . well, we will worry about that later.

Apostrophes (')

Possessives

Use an apostrophe to show possession (ownership) for nouns and some indefinite pronouns. (See p. 409 for a list of indefinite pronouns.)

To show possession, add an apostrophe and an -*s* to singular nouns or indefinite pronouns that do not end in -*s*.

EXAMPLE: The teddy *bear's* eyes are green.

EXAMPLE: My *sister-in-law's* recipes are delicious.

EXAMPLE: *Everyone's* paychecks have grown a little this year.

EXAMPLE: Nicholas received an extra *week's* pay for his unused vacation.

To show possession, add an apostrophe and an -*s* to a singular noun that ends in -*s*.

EXAMPLE: The *bus's* passengers are all looking out of the windows.

EXAMPLE: *Carlos's* motorcycle is parked in the garage.

To show possession, add just an apostrophe (but no -*s*) to a plural noun that ends in -*s*.

EXAMPLE: The *protesters'* signs are insulting to the spectators.

Note: Do not use an apostrophe with a possessive pronoun, such as *its, his, hers, whose,* or *theirs*.

Contractions

Use an apostrophe to indicate where letters are missing in a contraction.

EXAMPLE: *I've* never seen a sunset that beautiful before.

Common Contractions	
are not	aren't
do not	don't
has not	hasn't
have not	haven't
he will	he'll
I will	I'll
is not	isn't
it is or it has	it's
she will	she'll
should not	shouldn't

that is or that has	that's
we are	we're
we have	we've
we will	we'll
who is or who has	who's
you are	you're

Missing Letters or Numbers

Use an apostrophe to indicate where numbers or letters are missing.

EXAMPLE: Gurmeet graduated in the class of *'12.*

EXAMPLE: The polite country boy said, *"Ma'am,* I am going *fishin'* today."

Note: Apostrophes can be used in a quote to reflect a speaker's dialect.

▶ *Activity*   **Editing for Apostrophes**

Add or delete apostrophes as needed in the following sentences.

1. The kicker said to the reporter, "Ive been playin football my whole life."
2. The coaches hearts were racing as the football soared toward the goal post.
3. The quarterback couldnt believe he had thrown the pass so far.
4. The fans cheered when the team won it's final game of the season.
5. Bobby Bowden, the Florida State University coach, retired in 09.

Hyphens (-) and Dashes (—)

Hyphens (-)

Adjectives   Use a *hyphen* to combine two or more words that serve as a single adjective preceding (but not following) a noun.

EXAMPLE: Shakespeare is a *well-known* playwright.

EXAMPLE: The playwright Shakespeare is *well known.*

EXAMPLE: Simon loves *chocolate-covered* pretzels.

EXAMPLE: Simon loves pretzels that are *chocolate covered.*

Note: Do not use a hyphen with *-ly* adverbs: quickly eaten dessert.

Compound Numbers   Use a *hyphen* with compound numbers.

EXAMPLE: Judy is *thirty-three* years old.

EXAMPLE: The *two-year-old* boy was returned safely to his parents.

EXAMPLE: Trent ate *three-fourths* of the pizza.

Prefixes   Use hyphens with the following prefixes: *all-, ex-,* and *self-.*

EXAMPLE: The spa treatment package is *all-inclusive.*

EXAMPLE: He and his *ex-wife* get along remarkably well.

EXAMPLE: The business owner was a real *self-starter.*

Editing for Apostrophes Activity: Answers

1. The kicker said to the reporter, "I've been playin' football my whole life."
2. The coaches' hearts were racing as the football soared toward the goal post.
3. The quarterback couldn't believe he had thrown the pass so far.
4. The fans cheered when the team won its final game of the season.
5. Bobby Bowden, the Florida State University coach, retired in '09.

Dashes (—)

Create a *dash* with two hyphens, or use the dash character if your word processing program has one. Use a dash to create emphasis; to illustrate a change in direction; or to replace parentheses, semicolons, colons, or commas. Use dashes sparingly, so they do not lose their intended effect of creating interest for your readers.

EXAMPLE:	The storm is drawing near—where are the children?
EXAMPLE:	Jennifer told me—much to my dismay—she is not going to attend Joey's recital.
EXAMPLE:	I know why Salvatore did not show up to work today—although I wish I didn't.

> ▶ *Activity* **Editing for Hyphens and Dashes**
>
> Add hyphens and dashes to the following sentences as needed.
> 1. My father in law is going to help us repair our stone covered walkway.
> 2. Kevin's exroommate is getting a well deserved letter in the mail.
> 3. The triplet six year olds each ate one third of the birthday cake.
> 4. Joy won the lottery how amazing!
> 5. Holly's landlord that rat has given her only two weeks to move out!

Editing for Hyphens and Dashes Activity: Answers

1. My father-in-law is going to help us repair our stone-covered walkway.
2. Kevin's ex-roommate is getting a well-deserved letter in the mail.
3. The triplet six-year-olds each ate one-third of the birthday cake.
4. Joy won the lottery—how amazing!
5. Holly's landlord—that rat—has given her only two weeks to move out.

Parentheses ( ) and Brackets [ ]

Parentheses ( )

Use *parentheses* to set off a comment you want to include in or after a sentence when the comment may be relevant to the main point but is not essential to the reader's understanding of it.

EXAMPLE:	My favorite actor (who happens to be from my hometown) is starring in a Broadway play.
EXAMPLE:	I'm going to see a Broadway play starring my favorite actor (who happens to be from my hometown).
EXAMPLE:	My favorite actor is starring in a Broadway play. (He happens to be from my hometown.)

Note: If the parentheses enclose a complete sentence, the period goes inside the parentheses. If the sentence appears in parentheses within another sentence, however, it does not begin with a capital letter or end in a period.

Use parentheses to set off numbers or letters in a list of items.

EXAMPLE:	Follow these three rules if you are on fire: (1) stop moving, (2) drop to the floor, and (3) roll around to extinguish the flames.

Use parentheses for in-text citations in research papers that follow the guidelines of the Modern Language Association or the American Psychological Association.

MLA EXAMPLE:	"Eating dark chocolate makes us feel better" (Rich 65).
APA EXAMPLE:	"Eating dark chocolate makes us feel better" (Rich, 2011, p. 65).

Brackets [ ]

Use *brackets* to indicate that you have modified or added a letter, word, or group of words to a direct quote.

ORIGINAL:	Eating dark chocolate makes us feel better.
MLA EXAMPLE:	According to Rich, "[Consuming] dark chocolate makes us feel better" (65).
APA EXAMPLE:	According to Rich (2011), "[Consuming] dark chocolate makes us feel better" (p. 65).

Use the word *sic* enclosed in brackets immediately after an error in a direct quote. This lets your readers know you are aware of the error and that you quoted it exactly as it appeared in the original.

EXAMPLE:	According to Dr. Smock, "An elegant black dress is flatering [*sic*] on most women."
DISCUSSION:	The writer used [*sic*] to acknowledge that Dr. Smock misspelled the word *flattering*.

E. EDITING MECHANICS

Capitalization

Titles

Capitalize the titles of articles, books, poems, plays, songs, brochures, and so on. Capitalize all main words, but not articles (*a, an, the*), prepositions (*to, from, in*), or conjunctions (*and, but, or*). Always capitalize the first word of a title as well as the first word after a colon, even if it is an article, a preposition, or a conjunction.

POEM:	"Because I Could Not Stop for Death"
SONG:	"If I Had a Million Dollars"
BOOK:	*The Travel Book: A Journey through Every Country in the World*

Names

Capitalize the names of specific people, characters, and animals:

Dr. Wigelsworth	Professor Davis	Pastor Calhoun
Judge Crawford	Aunt Mary	Grandpa Chuck
Batman	Snow White	Miss Piggy
Fido	Nellie	Fuzzball

Note: Do not capitalize words that are not part of a proper noun, such as the professor, the judge, and my mom.

Capitalize name brands.

Coca-Cola	Doritos	Godiva

Regions, Locations, Buildings, and Monuments

Capitalize specific regions, but not directions.

Mitch is from the Midwest.	Drive north on I-95.

Capitalize geographical locations, buildings, and monuments.

Austin, Texas	Paris, France	Ocala National Forrest
Pacific Ocean	Lake James	Jetty Park
World Trade Center	Eiffel Tower	Statue of Liberty

Seasons and Events

Capitalize events but not seasons.

The Spring Fling is next week.

My favorite season is summer.

Capitalize historical events, documents, and movements.

Civil War   Declaration of Independence   Renaissance

Language, Ethnic, and Religious References

Capitalize nationalities, languages, and ethnicities.

American   Spanish   Asian
Greek architecture   Hispanic culture   Japanese cuisine

Capitalize religions, religious books, religious followers, religious holidays, and words referring to God.

Christian   Jewish   Muslim
Methodists   Holy Bible   Torah
Easter   Yom Kippur   Buddha
Allah   Jehovah   the Trinity

Courses

Capitalize language courses and complete course names.

French   English 1101   General Biology II

Note: Do not capitalize general subjects: psychology, math, and biology.

▶ *Activity* Editing for Capitalization

Edit the following sentences for capitalization errors.

1. Terrence loves to visit mount dora every Spring.
2. My sister-in-law amy is looking forward to taking psychology II and calculus.
3. My friend shalerie, who is from france, loves to eat yoplait yogurt.
4. The famous dr. oz wrote a book called *you: the owner's manual: an insider's guide to the body that will make you healthier and younger.*
5. One of professor tiffany's favorite songs is called "single ladies."

Editing for Capitalization
Activity: Answers

1. Mount Dora, spring
2. Amy, Psychology II
3. Shalerie, France, Yoplait
4. Dr. Oz, *You: The Owner's Manual: An Insider's Guide to the Body That Will Make You Healthier and Younger*
5. Professor Tiffany's, Single Ladies

Abbreviations

Abbreviations in School Papers

Do not use these abbreviations in your papers for school:

&   b/c   co.   dept.   Eng.
Fri.   gov't.   Prof.   thru   w/o

Titles and Degrees

Abbreviate titles that appear before names:

Dr. Goldstein   Ms. Gibson   St. Thomas

Abbreviate titles and degrees that appear after names:

Frieda Walker, PhD (or Ph.D.)   Charles Rowland, Jr.   Ed Ellis, DDS (or D.D.S.)

Acronyms

Generally, spell out a name before using an abbreviation:

EXAMPLE: The Children's Home Society (CHS) is a good organization.

Some familiar acronyms are nearly always abbreviated:

EXAMPLE: The FBI is working with NASA and IBM.

Times and Dates

For exact times, use uppercase or lowercase abbreviations for A.M. (a.m.) and P.M. (p.m.).

EXAMPLE: The space shuttle is scheduled to launch at 6:51 A.M.

EXAMPLE: The fundraiser lasts from 7:30 p.m. until 1:00 a.m.

Do not abbreviate days or months in formal writing.

EXAMPLE: You are invited to attend the Rose Gala on Saturday, August 20.

Place Names

Spell out names of places except in addresses.

EXAMPLE: Laurie visited Rochester, New York, during her vacation.

EXAMPLE: Mail the payment to 555 Generic Street, Rochester, NY 55555.

Numbers

Spell out numbers for the following situations:

- One- or two-word numbers, such as four, thirty-three, six million.
- Numbers beginning a sentence.

  EXAMPLE: *Two hundred and ten* people participated in the self-defense workshop.

  EXAMPLE: The self-defense workshop drew *210* participants.

- Numbers forming compound words.

  EXAMPLE: The *seven-year-old* boy gave *one-half* of his toys to charity.

- Times using *o'clock*.

  EXAMPLE: I was up writing a paper until *three o'clock* this morning.

Use numerals for these situations:

- Exact times and dates.

  EXAMPLE: The show starts at 6:30 p.m.

  EXAMPLE: Graduation will take place on May 23, 2019.

- Numbers with three or more words.

  EXAMPLE: Nico and Leslie invited 425 guests to their wedding.

  EXAMPLE: The meeting room will hold 1,250 attendees.

- Addresses.

  EXAMPLE: Marsden lives at 444 Apple Lane.

- Money and percentages.

  EXAMPLE: The bake sale raised $695.50.

  EXAMPLE: According to the survey, 78% of the students voted for the new policy.

- Numbers in a series or list.

  EXAMPLE: Melony still needs to work on problems 2, 5, 7, and 11.

▶ *Activity*   Editing for Abbreviations and Numbers

Edit the following sentences for errors with abbreviations and numbers.

1. The science dept. just received funding for three hundred and twenty new microscopes.
2. Doctor Snow is hosting a seminar on Thurs., Feb. tenth at 2 o'clock.
3. Sandra is looking forward to her trip to San Francisco, CA on May fifth.
4. Prof. Smith, Doctor of Philosophy is hosting a field trip for 20 students.
5. Jared & Josie are going to the visit the gov't building in Tallahassee, FL at three p.m.

Italics and <u>Underlining</u>

Italics and underlining are equivalent. Use italics when typing on a computer, and use underlining when handwriting.

Emphasis

Italicize or underline words you want to emphasize in your writing.

> **EXAMPLE:** The word *hate* can be so destructive.

Note: You may use quotation marks for this as well. Be consistent with how you emphasize words in a particular document.

Titles of Longer Works

Italicize or underline titles of books, plays, newspapers, magazines, works of art, CDs, movies, television shows, and websites.

> **EXAMPLE:** I read a book called *The History of Art* that featured van Gogh's painting *Starry Night*.

Foreign Words

Italicize or underline foreign words that have not become common in the English language.

> **EXAMPLE:** When Paul spilled his cup of coffee, he said, "*C'est la vie.*"
>
> **EXAMPLE:** Marcella is going to eat a burrito with salsa for lunch.
>
> **DISCUSSION:** The words *burrito* and *salsa* have become common in the English language.

▶ *Activity*   Editing for Italics and Underlining

Identify words in the following sentences that need to be italicized or underlined.

1. The show The Voice has attracted a lot of attention during the last several years.
2. The word plagiarism scares many novice writers.
3. Brett graduated magna cum laude.
4. I'm hoping to see the Mona Lisa when I'm in France.
5. I read an article about a serial killer in USA Today.

F. EDITING SPELLING

Commonly Misspelled Words

While the spell checker on your computer may help you to identify some misspelled words, you still need to proofread all of your papers before submitting them. Otherwise, you may end up with some spelling errors that could cause your readers to think you are careless.

You may remember a couple of spelling rules from your younger days, such as "use *-i* before *-e* except after *-c*" or "drop the *-y* and add *-ies*." You will find an extensive list of spelling rules at The Purdue Online Writing Lab: **http://owl .english/purdue.edu/owl**.

Knowing the rules can be useful; however, you have probably already realized that the rules have many exceptions. If you are not sure how to spell a word, look it up in a dictionary or go to **http://dictionary.reference.com**.

You also can study a list of commonly misspelled words, such as the following. Many of the words are irregular or are spelled differently than they sound. Watch out for these words as you edit your writing.

Commonly Misspelled Words			
absence	conscience	harass	occasionally
acceptable	conscientious	height	occurrence
accessible	conscious	hierarchy	pastime
accidentally	consensus	humorous	prejudice
accommodate	convenience	hypocrisy	privilege
accuracy	criticism	ignorance	probably
achievement	criticize	immediately	questionnaire
acquaintance	deceive	incredible	receive
acquire	definitely	intelligence	recommend
a lot	disappoint	interest	reference
amateur	disastrous	jewelry	relevant
analyze	discipline	judgment	restaurant
apparent	efficient	knowledge	rhyme
appearance	eligible	leisure	rhythm
argument	embarrass	license	ridiculous
believe	environment	loneliness	schedule
boundary	exaggerate	maintenance	separate
business	exhilarate	maneuver	sergeant
calendar	existence	medieval	successful
category	experience	memento	tendency
cemetery	familiar	millennium	thorough
changeable	fascinate	miniature	through
collectible	foreign	minuscule	truly
characteristic	gauge	mischievous	vacuum
column	grammar	misspell	villain
committed	grateful	necessary	weird
conceive	guarantee	noticeable	writing

Identify and revise the misspelled words in the following sentences. Each sentence has two misspelled words.

1. Writers should proofread for grammer and mispelled words.
2. Dave is eligable for a garanteed student loan.
3. Cindy is an amature guitarist who plays with great acuracy.
4. The employee tried to acomodate the customer who had alot of complaints.
5. Raul was greatful for the raise he recieved.

Editing for Misspelled Words Activity: Answers

1. grammar, misspelled
2. eligible, guaranteed
3. amateur, accuracy
4. accommodate, a lot
5. grateful, received

Homonyms

Homonyms are words that sound the same but are spelled differently. Watch out for these homonyms as you edit your writing. If you use the wrong word, you will likely confuse your readers.

Homonyms	Examples
accept—to receive or approve **except**—to take out or exclude	Many local hospitals *accept* interns. Everyone has voted *except* Trisha.
affect—to change or influence **effect**—the result or outcome	His decision *affected* everyone in his family. The counselor had a positive *effect* on her.
allowed—permitted **aloud**—spoken	Monica *allowed* Shannon to borrow her car. Troy read the example *aloud* for the class.
allusion—an indirect reference to **illusion**—a fantasy or deceptive appearance	The rap song makes an *allusion* to a Greek play. Jim created the *illusion* of always studying when he was really reading a magazine.
already—by now **all ready**—fully prepared	Minh has *already* studied for the test. Jessica was *all ready* to give the presentation.
all together—all in one place or time **altogether**—completely	Let's go for a ride *all together*. Susan is *altogether* responsible for her bills.
appraise—to determine the value **apprise**—to tell or notify	The ring was *appraised* for $2,000. She was *apprised* of the status of her request.
cite—to refer to, to give an example **sight**—vision, something to see **site**—a location	John *cited* Benjamin Franklin in his paper. The Statue of Liberty is an amazing *sight*. The *site* for the new student lounge is perfect.
coarse—rough **course**—path of travel	The exterior paint was very *coarse*. He is on the right *course* to success.
complement—to complete, a counterpart **compliment**—to praise	The curtains *complement* the window. Anna received a *compliment* on her new outfit.
confidant—someone to confide in **confident**—self-assured	Jordan was Edward's best friend and *confidant*. Sue was *confident* she would pass the exam.
conscience—moral right or wrong **conscious**—aware of one's feelings	Bob followed his *conscience* and told the truth. Susan was not *conscious* of her depression.
discreet—confidential or tactful **discrete**—distinct or separate	They were *discreet* about their relationship. They kept their finances *discrete*.
elicit—to bring out **illicit**—illegal	The essay *elicits* feelings of compassion. He was arrested for selling *illicit* drugs.

every day—happening daily everyday—ordinary	I ride my scooter to class *every day*. Riding my scooter to class is an *everyday* event.
fair—impartial, evenhanded fare—payment	The instructor's policies are *fair*. Trent paid his cab *fare*.
faze—to stun phase—part of a sequence	Vicki was *fazed* by the news of her award. Jill started a new *phase* in her life.
its—possessive of *it* it's—contraction of *it is*	The dog wagged *its* tail. *It's* time for the show to start.
lead—a heavy metal led—past tense of *to lead*	Sidney suffered from *lead* poisoning. The millionaire *led* a good life.
loose—not securely attached lose—to fail to win or keep	The door handle was *loose*. Shaquanda didn't want to *lose* her scholarship.
principal—head of school, main principle—a general rule or truth	The administration's *principal* goal is student success. You can't go wrong if you follow this *principle*.
stationary—not moving, fixed stationery—writing paper	Kevin rode a *stationary* bike in the winter. Tanisha loves to send letters on pretty *stationery*.
than—comparison then—at that time or after that	Francesca is taller *than* Maria. First we'll work, and *then* we'll play.
their—possessive form of *them* there—in or at that place they're—contraction of *they are*	It is *their* decision to make. Please put the book over *there* on the shelf. I hope *they're* not late for the meeting.
to—toward too—excessively or also two—the number 2, a couple	I'm going *to* the library. Sasha is *too* hungry to think straight. Amy has *two* papers to write next week.
who's—contraction of *who is* whose—possessive of *who*	*Who's* attending the conference in Arizona? *Whose* presentation did you like best?
your—possessive of *you* you're—contraction of *you are*	*Your* positive attitude will take you far. *You're* likely to get a great job after graduation.

SmartBook Tip

During the "Recharge" phase, students can return to the Editing Guide and practice concepts that they need to work on.

 Activity **Editing for Homonyms**

Identify and revise the incorrectly used homonyms in the following sentences.

1. Angelica blushed when her boyfriend paid her a complement.
2. Your not going to be able to attend the seminar next week.
3. Terry is more skilled at designing Web pages then Jake is.
4. Bruce was confidant that he would get a promotion soon.
5. Misty was careful to sight her sources in her paper.

Editing for Homonyms Activity: Answers

1. compliment
2. You're
3. than
4. confident
5. cite

A

Active voice Occurs when the subject performs the action in the sentence. 400

Adjectives Words that modify nouns or pronouns. 412

Adverbs Words that modify adjectives, verbs, and other adverbs. 412

Antecedents Nouns that pronouns refer to. 405

Appeals Persuasive strategies used to support claims. 226

Appositive A word or phrase that renames a noun or pronoun. 407

Audience People who will read or hear the message. 5

B

Biased language Reflects an unfair assumption or prejudice without cause. 403

Brainstorming Writing whatever comes to mind about a topic. 18

C

Causal analysis Analyzing reasons and results. 197

Claim A debatable assertion. 225

Cliché A worn-out expression. 402

Comma-spliced sentence Two independent clauses that are joined improperly with just a comma. 397

Computerized catalog An index of a library's holdings with specific information about each item. 318

Conjunctive adverb An adverb that serves as a transition between two independent clauses. 397

Connotation The meaning of a word, including the attitudes and feelings people associate with the word. 401

Coordinating conjunction A word that joins words or independent clauses that are equal and shows how they are related. 397

Criteria Principles or standards used to evaluate something. 259

Critical thinking Interpreting ideas and reflecting on them. 67

D

Database A comprehensive collection of related data that is organized and accessible via computer. 320

Denotation The dictionary definition of a word. 401

Design The genre, format, length, and appearance of a message. 9

Diction A writer's or speaker's choice of words. 401

Discussion group An online forum where individuals can share ideas about a specific topic. 322

E

Essay A group of paragraphs related to a particular subject. 56

F

Forecast Helps the reader predict the main points. 57

Freewriting Unstructured writing for a set amount of time. 19

J

Jargon Specialized vocabulary that people related to a particular career field, group, or interest use. 401

Journal A place to keep track of thoughts and feelings. 19

K

Keywords Significant words or phrases used to narrow a database search. 318

L

Listing Making a list about ideas related to a specific topic. 18

Logical fallacies Occur when someone draws a conclusion not based on sound reasoning. 79

M

Mixed construction Occurs when the subject of a sentence does not fit logically with the predicate of the sentence. 398

O

Outline A blueprint of the divisions and subdivisions in a paper. 25

P

Paragraph A group of sentences related to one idea. 52

Parallelism Occurs when similar ideas in a sentence are expressed in a similar grammatical manner. 399

Paraphrase A reworded version of a sentence or short passage from an original work. 326

Passive voice Occurs when the subject receives the action in the sentence. 400

Plagiarism The use of another's words or ideas without giving appropriate credit. 325

Primary or field research Information collected first-hand from sources, such as surveys, interviews, and experiments. 328

Pronouns Words that replace nouns. 405

Purpose Reason for writing. 7

Q

Quotation An author's exact words enclosed in quotation marks. 327

R

Run-on sentence Two independent clauses that run together without a proper punctuation mark or a comma and a coordinating conjunction. 396

S

Search engine A computer program used to locate information on the Internet. 321

Sentence fragment A group of words that cannot stand on its own because it lacks one or more elements of a complete sentence. 396

Sexist language Words that unnecessarily refer to gender. 403

Slang Informal, nonstandard vocabulary that people related to a particular career field, group, or interest use.   401

Strategy Approach to writing that best serves your purpose and audience.   9

Subject A general concept, such as health, technology, or crime.   5

Subordinating conjunction A dependent word that helps to show the relationship between the ideas in two independent clauses.   398

Summary A shortened version of an original work including only the main ideas and using different wording.   69, 325

Synthesis A combination of ideas from different sources to form a new whole.   69, 332

T

Thesis Identifies the main idea of an essay.   22, 56

Topic Narrower focus than the subject.   5

Topic sentence States the main idea of a paragraph.   50

U

Unity Ensures every idea relates to the overall thesis of the essay.   58

V

Visual literacy The ability to read and interpret a variety of visual texts.   72

Table of Contents   Page vi: © Andersen Ross/ Getty Images; p. ix: © image 100 Ltd.; p. x: © Don Hammond/Design Pics/Corbis RF; p. xi: © Photos 12/Alamy; xii: © Rubberball Productions.

Preface   Page xiv: © Karin L. Russell; p. xv (top): © Ingram Publishing; p. xv (bottom): © Jupiterimages/Imagesource.

About the Author   Page xxii (top): © Rhonda Wetherington; p. xxii (center): © Rose Farhat-Goodson; p. xxii (bottom): © Rose Farhat-Goodson.

Chapter 1   Page 2: © ML Harris/Getty Images; p. 2 (top inset): © David Fischer/Getty Images; p. 2 (bottom inset): © Corbis/PunchStock; p. 4: © Radius Images/Alamy; p. 6: © Tracy Wetrich; p. 7: © Hero/Corbis/Glow Images; p. 12: © Artville/ Getty Images RF; p. 15: © image 100 Ltd.

Chapter 2   Page 16: © Barry Rosenthal/Getty Images; p. 16 (top inset): © Keith Brofsky/Getty Images; p. 16 (bottom inset): © Image Source/ Getty Images RF; p. 20 (top): © Andersen Ross/Blend Images/Corbis RF; p. 20 (bottom): © Royalty-Free/Corbis; p. 21: © Karin L. Russell; p. 26 (top): © Glow Images/SuperStock; p. 26 (bottom): © Glow Images/SuperStock; p. 28: © Medioimages/Photodisc/Getty Images RF; p. 31: © Andersen Ross/Getty Images; p. 32: © Digital Vision; p. 43: © Karin L. Russell.

Chapter 3   Page 48: © Mike Powell/Getty Images; p. 48 (top inset): © Image Source; p. 48 (bottom inset): © Jupiterimages/Creatas/Alamy; p. 49: © Comstock Images/Jupiterimages; p. 51: © John Miller/Getty Images; p. 52: © Stockbyte/ PunchStock; p. 54: © Corbis. All rights reserved; p. 55 (top): © Patrick Lane/Somos Images/Corbis RF; p. 55 (bottom): © Karin L. Russell; p. 56: © Laurence Mouton/Getty Images; p. 59: © John Lund/Drew Kelly/Blend Images/Corbis RF; p. 64: © Design Pics/PunchStock.

Chapter 4   Page 66: © Photodisc Collection/ Getty Images; p. 66 (top inset): © Comstock/ PunchStock; p. 66 (bottom inset): © Dave Thompson/Life File/Getty Images; p. 67: © Goodshoot/PunchStock RF; p. 69: © The McGraw-Hill Companies, Inc./Christopher Kerrigan, photographer; p. 71: © Digital Vision/ Getty Images; p. 72: © John David Harris; p. 73: © Lars A. Niki; p. 74: © Larry Downing/Reuters/ Corbis; p. 74 (inset): © Larry Downing/Reuters/ Corbis; p. 76: Image Courtesy of The Advertising Archives; p. 78: © Kristian Dowling/Getty Images; p. 79: Image Courtesy of The Advertising Archives; p. 81: © PRNewsFoto/Kia Motors America; p. 82: © AP Photo/Marion Curtis/StarPix.

Chapter 5   Page 86: © Ariel Skelley/Getty Images; p. 86 (top inset): © Ariel Skelley/Getty Images; p. 86 (bottom inset): © Royalty-Free/ Corbis; p. 88 (left): © iStock RF; p. 88 (right): © Karin L. Russell; p. 89: © U.S. Air Force photo by Master Sgt. Efrain Gonzalez; p. 91: © Daniel J. Cox/Getty Images; p. 92 (top): © bilderlounge/ Masterfile; p. 92 (bottom): © Jose Luis Pelaez Inc./Blend Images; p. 95: © David R. Frazier Photolibrary, Inc.; p. 96 (top): © Getty Images/ Comstock Images; p. 96 (bottom): © Getty Images for AFI; p. 100: © ZUMA Press, Inc./Alamy; p. 103: © Ingram Publishing; p. 105: © Matt Gray/ Getty Images RF; p. 106: © Digital Vision/Getty Images; p. 109: © St Augustine, Ponte Vedra &

The Beaches Visitors & Convention Bureau; p. 110: © Chris Robbins/Getty Images.

Chapter 6   Page 116: Photo by FOX via Getty Images; p. 116 (top inset): © B. O'Kane/Alamy; p. 116 (bottom inset): © AFP/Getty Images; p. 118: © Karin L. Russell; p. 119: © Image Source/ Getty Images; p. 120 (left): © Creatas/PunchStock; p. 120 (right): © Royalty-Free/Corbis; p. 121: © Ingram Publishing; p. 123: © Brand X Pictures/ PunchStock; p. 125: © Image 100/PunchStock; p. 128: © James Leynse/Corbis; p. 130: © Hulton Archive/Getty Images; p. 133: © AP Photo/Alvin Ailey American Dance Theater, Paul Kolnik; p. 134: © Katherine Andriotis/Alamy; p. 135: © Karin L. Russell; p. 137: Image Courtesy of The Advertising Archives; p. 138: © Sunset Boulevard/ Corbis.

Chapter 7   Page 144: © Stewart Cohen/Blend Images/Corbis RF; p. 144 (top inset): © Jose Luis Paelez/Blend Images LLC; p. 144 (bottom inset): © Piecework Productions/Getty Images; p. 146: © Karin L. Russell; p. 147 (top): © Jonnie Miles/ Getty Images; p. 147 (bottom): © Stockbyte/Getty Images; p. 148 (top): © Digital Vision/PunchStock; p. 148 (bottom): © Peggy Greb/USDA; p. 149: © image 100/PunchStock; p. 153: © Penny Tweedie/Getty Images; p. 155: © Jasmine Tan; p. 158: © imac/Alamy; p. 161: © Royalty-Free/ Corbis; p. 162: "Coexist" design by Peacemonger— www.peacemonger.org; p. 163: © George Tiedemann/GT Images/Corbis; p. 165 (top): © The McGraw-Hill Companies, Inc./Rick Brady, photographer; p. 165 (bottom): © The McGraw-Hill Companies, Inc./Rick Brady, photographer; p. 166: © The McGraw-Hill Companies, Inc./Rick Brady, photographer.

Chapter 8   Page 170: © Royalty-Free/Corbis; p. 170 (top inset): © U.S. Air Force photo by Mr. Gerald Sonnenberg; p. 170 (bottom inset): © Ken Seet/Corbis RF; p. 172: © Karin L. Russell; p. 179: © Design Pics/Kelly Redinger; p. 180: © moodboard/Corbis RF; p. 182: © Ryan McVay/ Getty Images; p. 184: © Steve Hamblin/Alamy; p. 189: Image Courtesy of The Advertising Archives; p. 190: © AF archive/Alamy.

Chapter 9   Page 196: © Duncan Smith/Getty Images; p. 196 (top inset): © Ingram Publishing/ AGE Fotostock; p. 196 (bottom inset): © Tetra Images/Corbis RF; p. 198: © Karin L. Russell; p. 200 (top): © Whisson/Jordan/Corbis RF; p. 200 (bottom): © Stockbyte/PunchStock; p. 201: © Chris Hondros/Getty Images; p. 203: © Nancy R. Cohen/Getty Images; p. 205: © Duncan Smith/Getty Images; p. 209: © Image Source/ Glow Images; p. 210 (left): US Department of Agriculture/Public Domain; p. 210 (right): © David Buffington/Getty Images; p. 212: © GL Archive/Alamy; p. 215: Image Courtesy of The Advertising Archives; p. 216: © Mathew Imaging/Getty Images; p. 217 (top): Photo: Vivan Zink/© ABC/Courtesy Everett Collection; p. 217 bottom: © Catherine Cabrol/Kipa/Corbis.

Chapter 10   Page 222: © Sean Justice/Corbis RF; p. 222 (top inset): © Monalyn Gracia/Corbis RF; p. 222 (bottom inset): © BananaStock/ PunchStock; p. 224: © Karin L. Russell; p. 225: © McGraw-Hill Companies, Inc./Gary He, photographer; p. 227: © Ryan McVay/Getty Images; p. 233: © AF archive/Alamy; p. 234: © Image Source/Getty Images RF; p. 236: © Ron Levine/Getty Images RF; p. 238: © Tom Grill/

Corbis; p. 241: © Laurence Mouton/Photoalto/ PictureQuest; p. 243: © Chase Swift/Corbis RF; p. 248: © Jupiterimages/Imagesource; p. 250 (left): Image Courtesy of The Advertising Archives; p. 250 (right): Image Courtesy of The Advertising Archives; p. 251: © Everett Collection/Alamy.

Chapter 11   Page 256: © Buena Vista Pictures/ Courtesy Everett Collection; p. 256 (top inset): © Comstock Images/Alamy; p. 256 (bottom inset): © Lance Manion/Retna Ltd./Corbis; p. 258: © Karin L. Russell; p. 259: © Blend Images/Getty Images; p. 260: © Photos 12/Alamy; p. 263: © 20th Century Fox/Courtesy Everett Collection; p. 265: © AP Photo/Warner Bros. Pictures, Jaap Buitendijk; p. 267: © B. O'Kane/Alamy; p. 269: © Kiyoshi Ota/ Getty Images; p. 271: © John Springer Collection/ Corbis; p. 272: © Walt Disney Pictures/Pixar Animation; courtesy Mary Evans/Everett Collection; p. 274: Image Courtesy of The Advertising Archives; p. 275: © Antiquarian Images/Alamy.

Chapter 12   Page 280: © Guy Cali/Corbis RF; p. 280 (top inset): © Brand X Pictures; p. 280 (bottom inset): © Rubberball Productions; p. 282: © Ken Prosper; p. 283: © Tim Graham/Getty Images; p. 284: © Comstock/Jupiterimages; p. 287: © Jacek Lasa/Alamy RF; p. 288: © Brand X. Pictures; p. 291: © Royalty-Free/Corbis; p. 293: © Brand X Pictures; p. 294: © Photodisc/ Getty Images; p. 306: © Photos 12/Alamy; p. 307: © Mikael Karlsson.

Chapter 13   Page 314: © moodboard/Corbis RF; p. 314 (top inset): © BananaStock/Jupiterimages; p. 314 (bottom inset): © Tetra Images/Getty Images; p. 316: © Jack Hollingsworth/Corbis RF; p. 317: © Karin L. Russell; p. 318: © BananaStock/Jupiterimages; p. 321: © Google; p. 323: © Blend Images/Getty Images; p. 324: © Ryan McVay/Getty Images; p. 327: © UpperCut Images/SuperStock; p. 330: © MBI/Alamy; p. 333: © Stockdisc/Stockbyte/Getty Images.

Chapter 14   Page 334: © Indexstock/Photolibrary; p. 334 (top inset): © BananaStock/Alamy; p. 334 (bottom inset): © Purestock/SuperStock; p. 336 (top): Library of Congress, Prints and Photographs Division [LC-USZ62-7265]; p. 336 (bottom): © Brand X Pictures/PunchStock; p. 337 (top): © Royalty-Free/Corbis; p. 337 (bottom): © Karin L. Russell; p. 346: © The McGraw-Hill Companies, Inc./John Flournoy, photographer; p. 347: Cover image © Phi Delta Kappan/Cover illustration © Mario Noche; p. 352: © Peter Horree/Alamy; p. 365: © The McGraw-Hill Companies, Inc./Ken Cavanagh photographer; p. 366: Cover image © Phi Delta Kappan/Cover illustration © Mario Noche; p. 372: Lineart: Adapted from *Power Learning* by R.S. Feldman, 2011, p. 75. Copyright 2011 by McGraw-Hill.

Chapter 15   Page 382: © epa european pressphoto agency b.v./Alamy; p. 382 (top inset): © Lucas Jackson/Reuters/Corbis; p. 382 (bottom inset): © Daily Mail/Rex/Alamy; p. 383: © David P. Hall/Corbis; p. 384: © Axel Koester/Corbis; p. 385: © PunchStock/Image Source; p. 386 (top): © Karin L. Russell; p. 386 (bottom): © Ingram Publishing/SuperStock; p. 387: © PhotoSpin, Inc/ Alamy; p. 388 (top): © Comstock Images/Alamy; p. 388 (bottom): © Comstock Images/Jupiterimages; p. 390 (top): © PictureNet/Corbis RF; p. 390 (bottom): © Digital Vision/Getty Images; p. 391: © Image100/Corbis; p. 392: © amana productions/ Getty Images; p. 393: © Eyewire/Getty Images.

topic, 52
  variety in using, 50–51
  writing complete, 49
Series, items in, 416, 417
"Sex, Lies, and Conversation" (Tannen), 238–240
Sexist language, 403
Shakespeare, William, 212
Shannonhouse, Ashley, 317
Sheffield, Rob, 208
Shows, Hal, 271
Sic, use of, 423
Similes, 120
Single quotation marks, 419
Singular subjects, 408
Sketching ideas, 20
Slang, 401–402
Slippery slope fallacy, 81, 229
Solutions to problems, 283–284
  See also Problem-solving writing
Sources
  citing in research papers, 336–337
  of website information, 77
Spelling, 427–429
  checking for errors in, 33
  commonly misspelled words, 427
  homonyms, 428–429
Spoken-word recordings, 351
Stacks, library, 319
Star approach. *See* Rhetorical star analysis
Starry Night (van Gogh), 275
Statistics, citing, 337
"Steps in Venipuncture" (Farhat-Goodson), 151
Stereotyping, 81, 229
Strategy, writing, 9
Subject
  determining for projects, 5
  of research papers, 315–316
  of visual texts, 73
Subjective descriptions, 119, 120
Subjective pronouns, 406
Subject-verb agreement, 408–410
Subordinating conjunctions, 398
Summarizing
  readings, 69
  research materials, 325–326
Sun, Calvin, 149
Sundiata, Sekou, 293
Superlatives, 413
Supporting sentences, 52–53
Surveys
  primary research, 328–329
  writing attitude, 62–64
Synthesizing ideas, 69, 332

T

"Take Me Out to the Ball Game" (Norworth and Von Tilzer), 158–159
Talking to others, 20
Tannen, Deborah, 180, 181, 238
Technological context, 175–188
Television shows
  evaluative writing about, 263–264
  formats for citing, 351, 371
  See also Media examples
"10 Ways to Improve Your Office Etiquette" (Sun), 149–150
Text formatting, 352, 371
Thesaurus, online, 4
Thesis statements
  concluding paragraph, 59
  examples of, 58
  introductory paragraph, 56–57
  narrative writing and, 89
  oral presentation, 384
  writing preliminary, 22, 316
Thinking critically, 67
Thompson, Clive, 291, 292
Time
  abbreviations for, 425
  establishing in narratives, 90
  planning for your writing, 3
Titles
  capitalizing, 423
  italicizing or underlining, 426
  narrative writing, 89
  process writing, 147
  quotation marks around, 419
Tolliver, Doug, 88
Tone, 7
Topic outline, 27
Topic sentences, 52
Traditional/cultural context, 153–163
Tradition fallacy, 81, 229
Transitions, 53–54
  activity on using, 54
  comparison and contrast, 174
  oral presentation, 384
  types of, 53
Travers, Peter, 267
"Trifles" (Glaspell), 295–303
Turan, Kenneth, 265
Tutors, writing, 30

U

Underlining, 426
Unity in essays, 58–59

V

Vanderbilt, Shirley, 203
Van Gogh, Vincent, 275
Venn diagram, 25, 192, 193
Verbs, 50, 408–412
  editing guide for, 408–412
  irregular, 410–411
  linking, 412
  regular, 410
  subject-verb agreement, 408–410
  tenses of, 90–91, 260
Video clips, 388
Viewing process, 20
Visual aids, 11
  narrative writing, 92
  oral presentation, 386–388, 390
  process writing, 148, 165–166
  research paper, 352, 371–372
Visual literacy, 72
Visual representations, 69
Visual texts, 72–77
  advertisements, 76
  graphs, 75
  photographs, 74
Volpe, Daniel, 187
Von Tilzer, Albert, 158

W

Weber, Joseph, 13
Web resources
  on critical thinking, 83
  on documenting sources, 338, 358
  on essay writing, 15, 65
  on writing process, 15, 47
Websites
  citing sources from, 348–350, 368–370
  reading and interpreting, 77–79
  See also Internet research
"Welcome to the United States of Ambien" (Sheffield), 208
Wetrich, Tracy, 6
Wheeler, Jamie, 198
Whiddon, Marty, 182, 183
White, Elwyn Brooks, 99
Whiteboards, 387
Who/whom usage, 407
"Why Should Thousands of Prisoners Die Behind Bars for Nonviolent Crimes?" (Segura), 288–291
Wilson, Sally, 107
Wine, Bill, 125, 126
Word choice (diction), 32, 401–405
  biased language and, 403–404

clichés and, 402–403
denotation and connotation, 401
jargon and slang, 401–402
wordiness and, 404–405
Workplace. *See* Careers
Works-cited list, 340–352
  activity on developing, 380
  book sources on, 341–345
  electronic sources on, 348–350
  miscellaneous sources on, 350–352
  printed periodicals on, 346–348
  See also MLA format
Writer's checklists. *See* Checklists
Writing
  attitude about, 62–64
  environment for, 3–5
  formal vs. informal, 7
  importance of, 1
  planning time for, 3
  purpose for, 7, 9
  visual texts and, 73
Writing attitude survey, 62–64
Writing centers, 30
Writing process, 17–47
  cause-and-effect, 219
  checklist for, 47
  comparison and contrast, 192–193
  composing in, 28, 36–37
  descriptive, 140–141
  discovery in, 17–21, 34
  editing in, 32–33, 42–43
  evaluative, 277
  example of following, 33–46
  explaining a process, 166–167
  getting feedback in, 28–31, 32, 37–40
  narrative, 112–113
  overview of steps in, 17, 33
  persuasive, 253
  planning in, 22–28, 35–36
  problem solving, 309
  proofreading in, 33, 43–45
  revising in, 31, 40–42
  summary points about, 47
  Web resources on, 47
Writing strategies, 9, 10
  cause and effect, 197–221
  comparison and contrast, 171–195
  descriptive, 117–143
  evaluative, 257–279
  narrative, 87–115
  persuasive, 223–255
  problem solving, 281–311
  process-related, 145–169
Writing tutors, 30

Editing and Proofreading Marks

Use these editing marks to help you as you edit and proofread documents. Also, your instructor may use them when grading your papers.

Mark	Meaning	Mark	Meaning
ab	abbreviation	logic	not logical
ad	adjective problem	mm	misplaced modifier
adv	adverb problem	nc	not clear
agr	agreement problem	nonst	nonstandard language
ambig	ambiguous wording	num	numbers error
⌄	insert apostrophe	⌗	new paragraph
appr	inappropriate language	//	not parallel
awk	awkward expression	omit	omitted word
cap ≡	capitalize	pass	passive voice
case	case error	⊙	insert period
⌐⌐	center horizontally	pro ref	pronoun reference
⊟	center vertically	" " ∧ ∧	insert quotation marks
◯	check this	rep	too repetitive
choppy	choppy style	;	insert semicolon
⌃	insert comma	ro	run-on sentence
:	insert colon	shift	shift in tense or person
coord	faulty coordination	⌒	close space
cs	comma splice	# ∧	insert space
✔	delete	ⓢⓟ	spelling
d	diction	ss	sentence structure
dev	develop idea more	stet	let it stand
dm	dangling modifier	sub	faulty subordination
d neg	double negative	support	add more evidence
ds	double space	t	wrong verb tense
doc	documentation problem	thesis	thesis
frag	sentence fragment	ts	topic sentence
gen	be more specific	trans	weak transition
gram	grammatical error	tr ⌐⌐	transpose
inf	too informal	vary	add variety
irr	irregular verb error	voice	inconsistent voice
∧	insert	w	wordy
ital ___	italicize or underline	wc	word choice
lc	use lowercase	wo	word order